Politics of Culture in Liberal Italy

From Unification to Fascism

Axel Körner

Routledge
Taylor & Francis Group
New York   London

First published 2009
by Routledge
270 Madison Ave, New York, NY 10016

Simultaneously published in the UK
by Routledge
2 Park Square, Milton Park, Abingdon, Oxon OX14 4RN

Routledge is an imprint of the Taylor & Francis Group, an informa business

Typeset in Sabon by IBT Global.
Printed and bound in the United States of America on acid-free paper by IBT Global.

Library of Congress Cataloging in Publication Data
Körner, Axel, 1967-
    Politics of culture in liberal Italy : from unification to fascism / by Axel Körner.
        p. cm.—(Routledge studies in modern European history ; 12)
    Includes bibliographical references and index.
    ISBN 978-0-415-96291-9
    1. Federal-city relations—Italy.   2. Italy—Cultural policy.   3. Italy—Politics and government—1870–1914.   I. Title.
    JS5735.K67 2008
    306.0945'09034—dc22
    2007050576

ISBN 10: 0-415-96291-9 (hbk)
ISBN 10: 0-203-89528-2 (ebk)

ISBN 13: 978-0-415-96291-9 (hbk)
ISBN 13: 978-0-203-89528-3 (ebk)

For Elsa

Contents

List of Illustrations   ix
List of Tables   xi
List of Biographical Boxes   xiii
Abbreviations   xv
Acknowledgments   xix

Introduction   1

PART I
Political and Social Conflict

1   *Notabili*: The Local Persistence of the Old Régime   21

2   The Theatre of Social Change: The Opera Industry and the End of Social Privilege   47

3   Money and Culture   66

PART II
Writing the Past

4   The Middle Class and the Historicising of the Present   87

5   Medieval Revival   103

6   Etruscans, Romans and Italians   128

PART III
The City, the Nation and European Culture

7   Urban Space and Civic Culture: Representing City and Nation   163

8   *Margherita*: Umbertian Italy and its Monarchy   197

9   *"Viva Rossini—Morte a Wagner"*? From *Campanilismo* to the Future   221

10 Conclusions and Epilogue: Modernity, the Political Power of Culture and the Collapse of Liberal Democracy   263

Notes   285
Bibliography   359
Index   405

Illustrations

I.1 The Unification of Italy 1815–1870. (Map based on William R. Shepherd, *Historical Atlas*. New York: H. Holt and Company, 1911)   4

2.1 One of the First Photographs of the Interior of Bologna's Teatro Comunale, ca. 1870. (Reproduction by Kind Permission of Pàtron editore.)   48

3.1 Camillo Casarini. (Reproduction by Kind Permission of the Biblioteca dell'Archiginnasio, Bologna, Italy.)   76

4.1 Zannoni's Excavations at the Certosa. (Antonio Zannoni, *Gli scavi della certosa di Bologna*. Bologna: Regia tipografia, 1876)   93

5.1 Palazzo del Podestà. (Reproduction by Kind Permission of the Collezioni d'Arte e di Storia della Fondazione Cassa di Risparmio, Bologna.)   114

5.2 Portico della Morte. (Reproduction by Kind Permission of the Biblioteca dell'Archiginnasio, Bologna, Italy.)   119

6.1 Sepolcreto Nord di Marzabotto. (*Congrès international d'anthropologie préhistorique. Compte rendu de la cinquième session de 1871*. Bologne: Fava & Garagnani, 1873)   132

6.2 Excavations at the Certosa di Bologna. (Antonio Zannoni, *Gli scavi della certosa di Bologna*. Bologna: Regia tipografia, 1876)   141

6.3 Anacleto Guadagnini, *Sfilata del carnevale 1874*. (Reproduction by Kind Permission of the Biblioteca dell'Archiginnasio, Bologna, Italy.)   144

6.4   Chariot of the Commander. (Emilio Roncaglia,
      *Balanzoneide: descrizione dell'ingresso degli Etruschi
      in Bologna nel carnevale dell'anno 1874.* Bologna:
      Zanichelli, 1874)   146

7.1   Teatro Rossini, Lugo. (Reproduction by Kind Permission
      of the Fondazione Teatro Rossini and the Comune
      di Lugo.)   187

8.1   King Umberto and Queen Margherita Visiting Bologna
      in 1878. (Author's Collection.)   206

8.2   Attempted Assassination of King Umberto in Naples.
      (Author's Collection.)   208

9.1   Angelo Mariani. (Author's Collection.)   232

9.2   Stefano Gobatti, 1873. (Reproduction by Kind
      Permission of Pàtron editore.)   244

(The author wishes to thank Maria Tuya and Carla Sofia Ramos in Princeton for their generous help with the preparation of the illustrations.)

Tables

3.1   Growth of Population and Municipal Revenue in the
       Commune of Bologna during the Years 1867 to 1897.   81

3.2   Income and Expenditure of the Communes in the
       Province of Bologna for the Years 1876, 1886, 1891,
       1895 (in Million Lire).   82

3.3   Income and Expenditure of the Commune of Bologna
       for the Years 1877, 1887, 1892, 1897 (in Million Lire).   83

3.4   Expenditure for Public Education in the Commune of
       Bologna for the Years 1882 and 1892 (in Lire).   83

Biographical Boxes

1.1   Count Carlo Pepoli and Marquis Gioacchino Pepoli   25

1.2   Marco Minghetti   29

1.3   Alberto Dallolio   31

5.1   Alfonso Rubbiani   110

Abbreviations

ACC	*Atti del Consiglio Comunale*
AFGF	*Annali Fondazione Giangiacomo Feltrinelli*
AFLET	*Annali della Fondazione Luigi Einaudi Torino*
AfM	*Archiv für Musikwissenschaft*
AHR	*American Historical Review*
AISIG	*Annali dell'Istituto storico italo-germanico in Trento*
AJPH	*Australian Journal of Politics and History*
AJS	*American Journal of Semiotics*
AM	*Archeologia medievale*
AMDSPR	*Atti e Memorie della Deputazione di storia patria per le province di Romagna*
Arch.	*L'Archiginnasio. Bullettino della Biblioteca Comunale di Bologna*
ASB	*Archivio di Stato di Bologna*
ASCB	*Archivio Storico Comunale Bologna*
ASI	*Archivio Storico Italiano*
BeM	*Bijdragen en Medelingen betreffende de geschiedenis der Nederlanden*
BJS	*The British Journal of Sociology*
BMR	*Bollettino del Museo del Risorgimento*
CA	*Carteggio Amministrativo*
Car.	*Il Carrobbio*
CdE	*Corriere dell'Emilia*
CEH	*Central European History*

COJ	*Cambridge Opera Journal*
CW	*Cronaca Wagneriana*
DNP	*Der Neue Pauly*
DSPR	*Deputazione di Storia Patria per le province di Romagna.*
EF	*Ethnologie française*
EHQ	*European History Quarterly*
GdE	*Gazzetta dell'Emilia*
GdR	*Gazzetta delle Romagne*
GG	*Geschichte und Gesellschaft*
GH	*German History*
GHILB	*German Historical Institute London Bulletin*
HaT	*History and Theory*
HU	*Histoire Urbaine*
HZ	*Historische Zeitschrift*
Ill.Ital.	*Illustrazione Italiana*
IRASM	*International Review of the Aesthetics and Sociology of Music*
ISAP	*Istituto per la scienza dell'amministrazione pubblica*
JCH	*Journal of Contemporary History*
JHI	*Journal of the History of Ideas*
JIH	*Journal of Interdisciplinary History*
JMEH	*Journal of Modern European History*
JMH	*Journal of Modern History*
JMIS	*Journal of Modern Italian Studies*
JoM	*The Journal of Musicology*
MD	*Le Monde Diplomatique*
MdB	*Il Monitore di Bologna*
MEFRIM	*Mélanges de l'Ecole Française de Rome. Italie et Méditerranée*
MeR	*Memoria e Ricerca*
MEW	*Marx Engels Werke*

MI	*Modern Italy*
MOS	*Movimento operaio e socialista*
MRSSS	*Meridiana. Rivista di Storia e Scienze Sociali*
NA	*Nuova Antologia di lettere arti e scienze*
NCM	*Nineteenth-Century Music*
NFP	*Neue Freie Presse*
NGC	*New German Critique*
PAM	*Perspectives in American History*
PeP	*Passato e Presente*
PSI	*Partito Socialista Italiano*
QdS	*Quaderni di Storia*
QFIAB	*Quellen und Forschungen aus italienischen Archiven und Bibliotheken*
QS	*Quaderni Storici*
RB	*Rivista Bolognese*
RdC	*Il Resto del Carlino*
RHMC	*Revue d'histoire moderne et contemporaine*
Ris.	*Il Risorgimento*
RSI	*Rivista Storica Italiana*
SAC	*Storia Amministrazione Costituzione*
SeS	*Società e Storia*
SH	*Social History*
Soc.Int.	*Sociologia Internationalis*
Soc.Anth.	*Social Anthropology*
SSB	*Strenna Storica Bolognese*
SU	*Storia Urbana*
SV	*Studi Verdiani*
TPV	*Terrorism and Political Violence*
Vita Citt.	*La Vita Cittadina. Rivista mensile di cronaca amministrativa e di statistica del Comune di Bologna*
Vita Civ.	*La Vita Civica*

Acknowledgments

My interest in the politics of culture in Liberal Italy started while working on a comparative research project on municipal culture in Bologna, Leipzig, Linz and Ljubljana. The project was based at the universities of Linz and Graz in Austria and directed by Reinhard Kannonier and Helmut Konrad. Both have been a great source of support for my work. Reinhard's role in my intellectual development has been incomparably greater than I can express in these acknowledgments. Most of the research for this book was undertaken while I was teaching in the History Department of University College London, whose wonderful colleagues and students continue to offer me a stimulating environment for my work. Successive heads of department were generous enough to accept further delays in the completion of this book. During all these years Nicola Miller was an important source of inspiration and encouragement. Most chapters of this book benefited from critical discussions with her. Patrick Chorley read most of the manuscript and I am immensely grateful for his criticism, his help with linguistic improvements and the translation of quotes, and for his patience regarding my obsession with social theory. Martin Thom helped to edit several of my chapters and made valuable suggestions regarding my use of concepts and their translation from the Italian. During the final stages of my work, in Princeton, Herman Bennett and I competed in finishing our books and, surprisingly, it was he who knew what I had to say in my conclusions. Nearly everything that happened in my life while writing this book I also discussed with Antonio Sennis and I feel privileged to have him as a friend and colleague, sharing many of my academic passions.

I am grateful to many colleagues and friends for their support during the years of work on this book. In Italy these were Silvia Evangelisti, Luisa Passerini, Rolf Petri, Ilaria Porciani, Daniele Serafini, Simonetta Soldani, Carlotta Sorba, Bo Stråth and Stuart Woolf. Further, I want to thank Christopher Abel, Valentina Arena, Ruth Ben-Ghiat, Catherine Brice, Laurence Cole, Martin Daunton, Kate Ferris, John Foot, David French, Catherine Hall, Heinz Gerhard Haupt, Maurizio Isabella, Daniel Laqua, Antonis Liakos, John Lindon, Bob Lumley, Italo Marconi, David Morgan, Karen Radner and Donald Sassoon. A special thanks should go to my

PhD students. Glen Bowersock, Tim Cornell, Michael Crawford, Arianna Esposito, Amélie Kuhrt, John North and Renate Schlesier advised me on the history of archaeology. Sebastian and Agnes Prüfer shared my interest in Busoni and supported me with their friendship in Berlin. Kathy Burk, David D'Avray and Roger Parker each read chapters and helped with their expertise in the respective fields. John A. Davis, Nikki Miller and Adam Smith commented on my book proposal and I am grateful to Gilles Pécout, Adrian Lyttelton, Lucy Riall and Carlotta Sorba for their reports and to my Routledge editors for accepting the manuscript. Finally I should thank Rachel Aucott, Helen Matthews, Nazneen Razwi and Simon Renton for their administrative and technical support. Reinhart Koselleck continues to have a great influence on my work, but he did not live to see this book completed. Mikael af Malmborg died long before I completed the manuscript and I still find it painful to think about my research without being able to share the results with him.

I had the opportunity to discuss my work at the Modern Italian History seminar of the IHR in London; the Cultural History Group of my department and the Mellon Project at UCL; the Cambridge Modern European History Seminar; the Cultural Construction of Community Project in Malmo and Berlin; the European History Seminars in Halle and in Durham; the Politics of Opera conference at the European University Institute in Florence and the Modern Europe seminar at the Institute for Advanced Study in Princeton. The Archivio Storico Comunale di Bologna was, over many years, the most important resource for my research. I have to thank in particular William Baietti and Maria Cristina Scagliarini for their assistance and friendship during the summers spent in their reading room. I am grateful to the Biblioteca dell'Archiginnasio and in particular to Giacomo Nerozzi, who helped to shed light on my confusions regarding the names of Bologna's old families. I also received valuable assistance at the Museo del Risorgimento, the Archivio di Stato di Bologna and the Gabinetto Vieusseux in Florence. While the *Direttrice* of the Sala Musica at the Biblioteca Nazionale in Florence tried to make my research as difficult as possible, I am grateful for the help I received from the librarians at the EUI, at UCL, and in particular at the British Library, a remarkable resource for research on Modern Italy. The initial funding for the project came from the Österreichische Forschungsfond. Twice I received funding from the British Academy. The Dean's and the Departmental Travel Funds of UCL supported my archival work in Italy. During the final stages of my work I was elected a member of the Institute for Advanced Study in Princeton. Thanks to the financial support of the Friends of the Institute, I benefited from a most intense period of learning, which helped me immensely in finishing this project. During this period I enjoyed discussions with Annette Becker, Robert Darnton, Nicola di Cosmo, Chris Hailey, Jonathan Israel, Irving and Marilyn Lavin, Carl Levy, Arno Mayer, Francesca Rochberg, Heinrich von Staden, and others mentioned above. Karen

Downing, Gabriella Hoskin, Marcia Tucker and in particular Maria Tuya were unfailingly competent and often too generous in helping me to collect materials for my book and in preparing the illustrations.

My family probably does not know what I have been writing all these years, but they supported me when I needed them. Lenka Nahodilova contributed to the completion of the book in rather unexpected ways. The greatest joy of my life is my daughter Elsa. What her love and her company mean to me I cannot express in words, but I dedicate this book to her.

Obviously, none of the friends and colleagues mentioned here bears any responsibility for what follows.

Introduction

WAGNER CONTRA VERDI

During the summer of 1913 the North-Italian town Parma celebrated the centenary of its most famous son, the greatest composer of nineteenth-century Italy and an icon of Italian nationalism: Giuseppe Verdi. The anniversary was staged in connection with a three-month agricultural exhibition in the gardens of the former Ducal Palace, a reference to Verdi's supposedly "rough peasant origins," turning him into a man of the people and of the soil. During the opening night of the celebrations fireworks illuminated the scenery and brass bands from all over Italy entertained visitors with medleys of Verdi's most popular tunes, especially the famous choruses from *Nabucco* and *Aida*. Over the following weeks seven Verdi operas were performed at the Teatro Regio. Films about Verdi and his birthplace were screened. A new, grandiose monument to Verdi was begun, although it was not completed until 1920. Parma presented itself to its citizens and to visitors from all over Europe as a combination of music and the soil, of Verdi and agriculture, a mixture of local traditions and national pride. The emphasis on Verdi's agrarian roots created an explicitly anti-modern image, based on ideas which Verdi himself had carefully crafted and which were reproduced in numerous biographical accounts, in the composer's widely circulated photographs, and in poetic elegies such as the hymn *In Morte di Giuseppe Verdi* by the proto-Fascist Gabriele D'Annunzio.[1]

It is not surprising that music and opera loomed so large in the image Parma had created of itself, since the theatre was a site of great symbolic importance in every Italian city and the focus of a complex web of local sociability.[2] Opera was considered the nation's principal art form, synonymous with being Italian. But was Parma's stress on the soil and tradition typical of the way Italian cities represented themselves in the wake of World War I? Apart from Verdi, there is another name which immediately comes to mind when thinking about nineteenth-century opera: Richard Wagner. Both men were born in 1813. In 1913, Bologna decided against Verdi and in favour of Wagner, the fear being that the city would remain in Parma's shadow if it celebrated Verdi's anniversary. Unlike Parma, Bologna had no direct relationship to Verdi; and Parma had already secured the king's patronage for the events and the prime minister Giovanni Giolitti served as honorary president. All over Italy Verdi was honoured with busts and commemorative medals, making it difficult for any city to stand out.[3] Instead of Verdi, Bologna chose to focus on "the music of the future," celebrating the centenary of Richard Wagner. Wagner's name was synonymous with the vanguard of European music-theatre, and represented an engagement with the experience of modernity through symbolist aesthetics. To honour the German composer was to vaunt Bologna's cosmopolitan ambitions. Moreover, the political meaning of Wagner in Italy was very different from our contemporary associations and from the political contextualisation of Wagner in Germany. The Italian Wagner stood not for aggressive *völkisch* nationalism, but for the barricades of the 1848 Revolution in Dresden. He was known as a friend of the Russian anarchist Bakunin, supposedly the model for Siegfried. The composer's reform of the theatre was understood as a response to the ideas of the Republican leader of Italy's national movement, Giuseppe Mazzini. Since Bologna's *Lohengrin* of 1871, the first Wagner opera ever staged in Italy, the city had become the capital of Italian Wagnerism, as befitted a modern, progressive and cosmopolitan centre of European culture. Most Italian versions of Wagner's operas had been premiered at Bologna's Teatro Comunale, and the city opened the 1913 centenary-season with its tenth staging of *Lohengrin,* followed on 1 January 1914 by the Italian premiere of *Parsifal,* considered by many Wagner's most mythical-medieval, but also his most sublime and modern work.[4]

The modernist-cosmopolitan image Bologna created with the help of its Wagner centenary contrasts dramatically with Parma's emphasis on Verdi and the soil. Cultural policy on the municipal level entails representing the urban self through images such as these, images used by the municipal administration to communicate an idea of the city to its citizens, to the nation, and beyond. Spectacular exhibitions and opera performances which attract international visitors serve precisely this purpose. As the examples of Parma and Bologna illustrate, policies of cultural self-representation offer choice, in this case the choice between traditional and modern images, between national pride and cosmopolitan ambition. In opting for one policy rather than another, municipal administrators and political representatives make a statement about the city, but they also relate the city to the nation and the wider world. Thus, the cities' cultural representation speaks a local language as well as a national and transnational language. This last point is particularly important when referring to Italy, a country often associated with the combination of an underdeveloped political culture and the aggressive nationalism which paved the way for Fascism. However, when examining Italian identity, not only do we have to take account of regional diversity and strong municipal traditions, but also we should appreciate that Italian culture engages closely with wider European experiences. Challenging the stereotypical idea of a nation obsessed with its own traditions and absorbed in its music, its culinary culture and organised crime, I see Italy's political, intellectual and cultural transformation during the nineteenth century as closely linked to the European experience of modernity, reflected in philosophical attempts at making modern change meaningful, in aesthetic debates and in particular in Italy's cosmopolitan approach to music and opera, an art form which had played a crucial role in the Italians' cultural self-representation since the eighteenth century. The Italy which emerges from my research is a profoundly European and cosmopolitan country. In this view the long crisis of the liberal system, and its ultimate collapse, were closely connected to the European experience of modernity. Another stereotype dominating much of the historiography on liberal Italy is its narrow focus on the country's cultural pessimism, malaise and decline after Unification, often presented as an explanation for the collapse of the liberal regime after World War I.[5] In this perspective liberal Italy was "the antechamber of Fascism."[6] While a consciousness of crisis played an important role in the country's intellectual discourse during the *fine secolo*, Italy's opening towards European modernism also stands for attempts to find solutions to this crisis, for a new beginning and a positive attitude towards the future.

FROM RESURGENCE TO COLLAPSE

This book is concerned with the relationship between cities and the nation, and the attitudes of those cities towards modernity, as articulated through municipal cultural policy. It covers Italy from its Unification as a nation-state at the end of the 1850s to the crisis of the liberal system and its collapse under Fascism during the early 1920s. Italy's Unification as a nation-state was the result of the *Risorgimento*. The term means resurgence and refers to the mythical idea that Italy had once existed as a nation; but due to foreign dominion and internal divisions, often associated with the "barbarian invasions" and the medieval conflict between Papacy and Empire, Italy was politically divided and had lost its sense of nationhood. Since the late eighteenth century the idea of an Italian nation had re-emerged and given rise to a political movement, which had as its protagonists, among many others, Mazzini, Garibaldi, Gioberti, the Piedmontese kings Carlo Alberto and Vittorio Emanuele II as well as two political groupings, the Moderate *Destra Storica* (Historic Right) around Count Cavour and the Democratic *Sinistra Storica* (Historic Left), which originally included Republicans and later also men and women who associated themselves with the Internationalists of the early Labour Movement. The process of Unification took several decades. For a short period the Napoleonic wars had led to a rudimentary form of Unification, but after 1815 Italy was again divided into several kingdoms and duchies, with important regions in the North and the centre under Austrian rule. Arguably the most important ruler of the Italian peninsula was the pope, the sovereign of the so-called Papal States, which extended from coast to coast and from the North to the centre of the peninsula.[7] The Northern part of the Papal States formed the Papal Legations, with Bologna as their capital, and the residence of the *Cardinale legato*. Despite the important role of the Papal

States in the diplomatic history of Europe, the majority of contemporary observers considered the Papal States to be among the least developed regions of the peninsula, governed by an autocratic ruler who could retain his power only thanks to the Austrian troops which occupied most of his territory. After several revolutions during the first half of the nineteenth century and the military campaigns led by Piedmont and Garibaldi's volunteers against Austria and Italy's ancient states, the nation was eventually united under the crown of Piedmont-Sardinia, forming in 1861 the Kingdom of Italy.

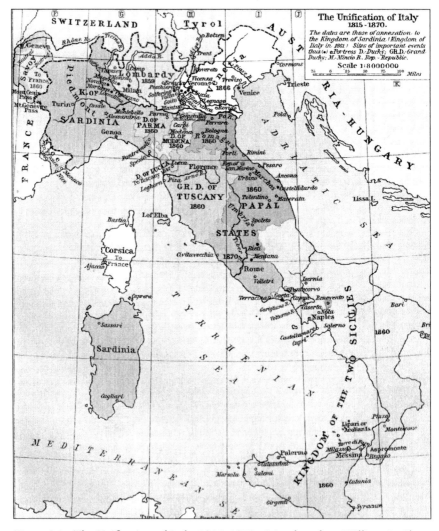

Figure I.1   The Unification of Italy 1815–1870. (Map based on William R. Shepherd, *Historical Atlas*. New York: H. Holt and Company, 1911)

My book starts from the results of this process, the liberation of the Papal Legations in 1859 and their annexation by Piedmont. Based on a case study of Bologna, the book takes us through the so-called liberal period of Italian history starting with Unification, up to its collapse under Fascism. It demonstrates the connections between political developments, social change and culture. Culture helped in the process of constructing urban and national identities after Unification; but in the case of Bologna the city's politics of culture also became a political target for those fighting against the liberal institutions and democracy, explaining why Bologna was the first city in which the Fascists ended democratic rule, two years before their March on Rome. Thus, in addition to explaining the transformation of Italy during the liberal period, my book also offers a new perspective on the origins of Fascism in Italy.

CITIES, IDENTITIES AND CULTURAL POLICY

An important concept in thinking about the Italian nation is *l'Italia delle cento città,* the "nation of the hundred cities," an image that stands for the idea that Italy was constituted as an ensemble of countless, centuries-old municipalities. Due to the peninsula's internal divisions the cities have always played a vital role in Italian history, politically as well as culturally. Many of them once constituted sovereign city states; others had been the capital cities of ancient states. With reference to this concept and its history my book understands the cultural policy of the Italian cities as a major instrument through which Italians related local identity to the experience of the nation and of being European. While Gramsci criticized the persistence of Italy's "municipal particularism" after Unification and understood cosmopolitism to be a legacy of Catholicism,[8] my analysis of the cities' politics of culture reveals how municipal identity became the key to engaging with the nation as well as with European culture. Thus, municipal policy becomes a vehicle for understanding the cultural ramifications of attitudes towards societal change, the nation-state and the European experience of modernity. Through cultural policy the urban elites constructed a link between their cities and the nation-state. However, using opera, architecture and town planning as their idiom, they also engaged with transnational responses to the challenges of modernity, presenting an important intellectual and aesthetic bridge between Italy and wider European experiences.

Within this conceptual framework the former Papal Legations and their capital Bologna serve as a case study, which, through references to other Italian cities, is integrated into a general survey of Italy's social, cultural and political transformation since Unification. While research on identity and culture during the age of nationalism often concentrates on capital cities, my book contributes to recent debates on the role of "second cities" during the making of nation-states.[9] The contrast between the region's relative socioeconomic backwardness and Bologna's rich cultural infrastructure is instructive, illuminating the contradictions which marked the Italian experience of modernity and allowing us to illustrate the role of culture in the attempts made to come to terms with continuity and change during the decades around the turn of the century. The Papal States played a crucial role in the struggle for Unification; the Romagna became a breeding ground for Italy's revolutionary Left; and it was in Bologna where the Fascist squads first ousted a democratic administration. Nevertheless, we know relatively little about the city and the region during the period between Unification and Fascism. Most of the Anglo-American literature on modern Italy builds upon the examples of Piedmont, Tuscany, Venetia and Lombardy, or analyses the specific circumstances of Unification in the South. Moreover, historians concerned with the political and intellectual history of the Risorgimento and the liberal period have tended to neglect the specificity of local attitudes towards the formation of the nation-state, and often underestimate the rivalry between the cities regarding their individual role in the new kingdom.

Understanding the transformation of social and political realities as an aspect of modernity which affected Europe as a whole, Italians compared their experiences with transnational intellectual debate and aesthetic forms of expression, a process in which municipal cultural policy became a crucial mode of communication. The municipalities played a similar role in communicating ideas of the nation. Contrary to the official and centrally staged celebrations of the kingdom, the cities' politics of cultural self-representation were often marked by enthusiasm for what was understood to be the local dimension of a national revolution.[10] Directed from the centre, state formation challenged these local practices, leading to what Antonio Gramsci saw as the Risorgimento's lack of a popular dimension and the "people's indifference towards the battles for national independence", which, he argued, persisted after 1859 and 1870.[11] On the basis of this assumption, historians study the attempts made to craft a national community, the ritualistic social function of invented traditions and the *"religione della patria"*. Through the symbolism of the Church these ceremonial and cultural practices were often familiar to Italians, but they were not always embraced.[12] The imposition of national celebrations and the official role assigned to Piedmont in representations of the nation left little space for local or regional diversity or for a concept of the nation founded on the people's own consciousness and will. As a consequence, municipal forms of cultural representation gained in importance. Ideas about cultural self-representation created conflicts between Moderates and Democrats, Monarchists and Republicans, Catholics and Liberals, men and women, young and old. To differing degrees these groups conceived of themselves in terms of a national and a municipal self, but their ideas of what constituted the city and the nation did not necessarily coincide.

Study of the celebrations for the centenaries of Verdi and Wagner may serve to illustrate the spectrum of semantic diversity evident in Italy's municipal cultural policies during the period. Cultural policy refers here to the ways in which cities represent themselves through culture, although the term is an analytical concept which did not exist in the contemporary vocabulary of nineteenth-century Italy.[13] The analytical emphasis of my work is less on the economic ramifications and socio-political objectives of the cities' cultural policies, than on aesthetic forms of expression as the focus of cultural administrators. Instead of concentrating my research on the cities' attempts to sustain their citizens' leisure activities through the provision of cultural infrastructures, my aim here is to analyse the ways in which political and cultural actors offered their citizens abstract keys to the experience of past, present and future. The relative proximity between political actors, cultural actors and citizenry on the municipal level presents us with a dimension of communication which we rarely find on the national level. Nations are "imagined communities" whose members do not know each other in person and their politics of cultural representation are not based on direct communication with citizens.[14] By contrast, on the municipal level cultural actors, political actors and citizens communicate directly with each other and within a common sphere. Despite internal hierarchies and conflicts, municipal cultural policy is the direct result of this level of communication.

THE CASE STUDY

The geographical location of Bologna, the dichotomy of progress and backwardness in its economic, political and cultural development, and the city's key role in the events between Unification and Fascism make of it an ideal case for the study of the transformation of liberal Italy and its politics of culture at the municipal level. The Papal States bordered the Empire in the North and the Kingdom of the Two Sicilies in the South, forming one of the largest states of the peninsula. Almost half of the subjects of the pope lived in the territories which, after Unification, became part of the region Emilia Romagna, with 2,284,000 inhabitants smaller in population than Lombardy and Piedmont, but more populated than Tuscany and Venetia, and counting more than twice as many inhabitants as the region of Lazio.[15] Bologna, the capital of the Legations, was the second city of the Papal States after Rome, located on the road from the Adriatic coast to Milan and at the head of Italy's most important pass over the Apennines. Seat of Europe's most ancient university, famous for its school of painting and a leading centre of Italy's musical life, renowned across the continent, Bologna occupied a major place in the cultural and political history of the Italian peninsula. The city was the home of the glossators of Roman law, its Accademia filarmonica awarded Mozart his diploma as composer, through experiments conducted at the Archiginnasio Galvani discovered electricity, and Rossini revived the famous Liceo musicale after his retirement as an active opera composer from Paris. It was in Bologna that Pope Julius II celebrated the consolidation of his temporal power and that Charles V received the imperial crown. Napoleon made the city capital of the Cispadanian Republic and considered it to become the capital of a unified Italy.[16] With its revolutions in 1831 and 1848 Bologna played a key part in the Risorgimento and many of its protagonists became influential politicians after 1861. While Turin struggled with decline after it lost its status as the kingdom's capital city and Naples became increasingly regarded as "ingovernabile," Bologna recovered from decades of stagnation under the later Papal regime. Soon after Unification the city enjoyed international recognition as one of Italy's leading centres of cultural and academic life. Crispi assigned the city an important strategic role in the country's military defence. Neither Modena, its old regional rival, nor Parma, once the splendid capital of a duchy, was allowed to represent Italy on the relief for the national monument to the nation's founder Vittorio Emanuele II in Rome, whereas Bologna figured proudly—along with Milan, Florence and Turin—as one of the great cities which had made the modern Italian nation.[17]

Meanwhile, however, the region around Bologna, the Romagna, was among the least developed parts of the country, in many respects a "South" in the North of Italy.[18] While Piedmont and Lombardy could boast 1374 kilometers of railways at the moment of Unification, the entire territory of the Papal States and the Kingdom of the Two Sicilies had only 200 kilometers. After centuries of deforestation, about a quarter of the Romagna's territory consisted of barren hills and mountains, offering little prospect for modern agricultural exploitation. The division of Emilia-Romagna between three different states before 1859 had hindered the development of a unified market and at the beginning of the twentieth century even the Campania and Sicily were still industrially more developed than Emilia-Romagna.[19] Compared to most of Western Europe, Italy had an exceptionally high rate of infant mortality, with Emilia-Romagna leading the nation's woeful record.[20] In 1870 70% of Italians were illiterate, compared to only 31% of the French and 12% of the Prussian population. The Romagna exceeded the national average, attaining 82% of illiteracy, with 90% in some centres and among the female population, comparable only to the provinces of Naples and Grosseto. In Bologna itself illiteracy reached 78% in 1861 and was still as high as 56% twenty years later.[21] In 1860 Bologna's university suffered the lowest number of student enrolments in its entire history. With 454 students, it could nevertheless claim to have four times as many students as nearby Ferrara, while the remaining universities of the Papal States—Camerino, Urbino, Marcerata and Perugia—together had a tally of no more than 358 students.[22] Given such a situation, it is not surprising to discover that the administration of the

Papal States was marked by a lack of regulations for the recruitment of its civil servants. Procedures suffered due to corruption, arbitrary public services and the disastrous state of the archives.[23]

As a consequence of this general picture, Bologna's political and cultural elites had to fight hard to improve the city's image after the fall of the Papal regime. Unable to rival the economic development of cities like Milan or Genoa, they competed with Florence and Naples, their ambition being to establish Bologna as one of the cultural centres of the new Kingdom of Italy. Some of Italy's most ancient noble families were from Bologna—the Bentivoglio, Bevilacqua, Malvezzi, Pepoli—and many of them played an important role in local or national politics. Leading figures in the Risorgimento and in Italy's cultural and political life after Unification came from or lived and worked in Bologna—the Moderate prime minister Marco Minghetti; the Republican Aurelio Saffi; the poet and politician Giosuè Carducci, Nobel laureate for literature in 1907; the publisher Zanichelli; musicians and writers such as Enrico Panzacchi, Giuseppe Martucci, Arrigo Boito, to name but a few.

Music and opera played a prominent role in the cities' cultural self-representation. With seventy-three theatres built between the eighteenth century and the Fascist period, Emilia-Romagna was an important centre for the performing arts.[24] Nevertheless, at the end of the Papal regime Bologna hardly knew the works of French *Grand Opéra* and had difficulties appreciating Verdi. The city's aristocracy, which occupied the old family-boxes in Bologna's beautiful Bibiena theatre, preferred the *bel canto* of an earlier period—Bellini, Donizetti, and, above and beyond all, Rossini, despite his rapprochement with the Austrian occupying forces after the revolution of 1831. It is more than a little startling, then, to discover that, just a few years after Unification, the repertoire contained everything that was considered progressive in Europe's major theatres, including Gounod's *Faust* and the Italian premieres of Meyerbeer's *L'Africaine* and Verdi's *Don Carlos*. Thus, in 1871, Bologna was the first Italian city to stage Wagner's "musica del futuro", *Lohengrin*, followed shortly after by *Tannhäuser* and *Rienzi*. Within months of Wagner's death Bologna saw the entire *Ring* cycle. On the occasion of its Great Exhibition in 1888 the city staged the first Italian performance of *Tristan und Isolde,* and likewise in 1914, at the Teatro Comunale, that of *Parsifal*. Bologna had become the capital of Italian Wagnerism, and the scene of controversial debates on the future of European opera and on the part to be played by Italy. Bologna rescued Boito's *Mefistofele* after its fiasco at La Scala, and experimented with the French avant-garde. The Comunale, in particular, was one of the first opera houses to welcome works from Russia. For decades it was associated with celebrated conductors such as Angelo Mariani, Franco Faccio and Arturo Toscanini, at a time when the local theatres staged new dramas by D'Annunzio, with Sarah Bernhardt and Eleonora Duse in starring roles. Shortly before World War I Ferruccio Busoni, one of the principal representatives of Europe's musical avant-garde, became director of the Liceo musicale.

The city attracted international attention not only for its theatres and its musical life. The archaeological museum became a model for the ways in which to engage with the pre-historic past, admired by visitors and scientists from all over the world. After Carducci's death in 1907 his chair at the university was held by Giovanni Pascoli, then Italy's most important living poet. During the Jacobin years, Bologna produced eighteen different newspapers and periodicals, which disappeared along with the Republican regime and the arrival of the Austro-Russian armies.[25] As a consequence, at the moment of Unification Bologna was less acquainted with a free press than were most other Italian cities.[26] A generation later Bologna was publishing some of Italy's most influential newspapers and journals and, long before the title passed to Florence, the city was considered the centre of Italy's literary vanguard. This cultural and intellectual context provided Bologna with the means to articulate its national and municipal identity and to relate to the wider European experience of modernity.

However, Bologna's progressive role as a cultural centre did not go hand-in-hand with the city's political development after Unification. The relationship between political developments and cultural representation constitutes one of the book's main concerns. Italy's "parliamentary revolution" of 1876 ended the Moderate governments of the Historic Right, which had been close to the original ideas of Italy's first prime minister, Count Cavour. Italy turned first to the Democratic Left and then towards *trasformismo,* a political practice whereby the government was based on ever-changing majorities in parliament, and therefore on a blurring of the ideological distinction between the main political groups. However, in Bologna, even after this shift in national politics, the municipal council continued to be dominated by conservative alliances of Moderates (later including the Catholics), supported principally by the city's old landed aristocracy. Only twice, in 1868 and again in 1903, the Moderate hegemony in the local council was challenged by majorities of the Left, representing the Democratic middle class and the Republican and Socialist movements. They used their brief spells in power to advance their ideas regarding the city's cultural self-representation, thus challenging the city's image in the eyes of the nation.[27] According to Gramsci's theory of "passive revolution," Italian nationalism and the Risorgimento had lacked mass participation and revolutionary leadership. In his view this was largely the fault of the bourgeoisie, while the Moderate aristocracy for its part had been unwilling to involve the masses in the project and to create a positive national identity, a *"cultura nazionale."*[28] However, even if the Risorgimento had not been a "bourgeois revolution," the Democratic middle class had at least recognised the political power of culture and its role in crafting a sense of national identity. The municipalities became for them a stage, upon which to give a meaning to liberal institutions and citizenship. As John Davis has argued, "everywhere local administration now offered the critical interface around which bourgeois Italy took shape, partly because local government was an important new source of jobs but above all because it was now a primary focus of economic and political activity."[29] Local administration was also a primary focus of cultural activity. While the nation struggled to convey a cultural and political identity to its citizens, Italians learned to identify with the liberal institutions and the nation through their municipalities. The politics of culture gave the Democratic middle class power, a power based on close collaboration between political actors, cultural actors and professional experts in the administration. Due to the particular configuration of local politics in Bologna, which was still dominated by the Moderate elites, the city exemplifies the complexities of the relationship between politics and culture: cultural representation does not necessarily mirror political majorities; instead, it reflects the role of educated elites, cultural experts and intellectuals in their specific social and political contexts. In 1914, as a consequence of the widened suffrage and the region's socioeconomic development, Bologna was suddenly among the first Italian cities in which the Socialist party obtained an absolute majority. The Socialists carried Bologna's sense of identity into a new era. During World War I the city became a symbol of anti-interventionism, the campaign against Italy's participation in the war, and of *socialismo municipale*. It also became a target for all those political forces intent upon challenging the interpretation of the liberal and democratic institutions which Bologna's politics of culture had conveyed. As a consequence, although Fascism was at least partly rooted in rural Labour conflicts, Bologna became the first Italian city in which the Fascist squads curtailed democratic rule.

Bologna's political and cultural history constitutes in many ways a special case, which differs from the experience of Milan, Florence, or the cities of the South, referred to in most histories of nineteenth-century Italy. At the same time, the cultural policy of Bologna's local administration and the discussions within the city's intellectual elite reflected and anticipated social and economic developments which were representative of Italian society as a whole. Local conflicts regarding the role of the theatre's private box owners in determining the repertoire of the opera help us to understand the social and political tensions in the former capital of the Papal Legations. These same conflicts also shed light upon Italy's transition after the *ancien régime*, when the recently unified nation-state had to cope with dramatic challenges to social conventions and cultural traditions. Claiming access to the city's cultural institutions, the rising middle class questioned the social and political position of Bologna's landed aristocracy, which for centuries had served the Papal regime. Most of the former Italian states had to deal with similar issues after Unification. Related to this is the question of how Italians identified with the new Kingdom of Italy. Bologna had to negotiate the complex relationship between local and national identities, to replace ancient loyalty to the Papal States with modern nationalism, and to compete with cities such as Florence, Modena and Milan in defining its place within the young nation-state. As a consequence, municipal policies never simply reflected developments within the city walls. Moreover, for Bologna being modern was a cosmopolitan ambition and a way to distinguish itself in the context of the new nation-state. Thus, Europe became a major point of reference in the formation of urban selves. The cities' self-representation after Unification contributed to the creation of a new civic culture, which profoundly marked Italian society as a whole.

THE METHODOLOGICAL APPROACH

The book deals with the role of Italian cities in shaping the nation's social, political and cultural realities, placing the emphasis on the cities' discourse about their cultural self-representation through theatres, architecture, exhibitions, commemorations, archaeological excavations and museums. The aesthetics of reception, and the meaning political actors ascribed to this same culture, are at the heart of my analysis. Thus, the book differs in its approach and its use of sources from traditional forms of urban history, which concentrate on the history of administration and town planning.[30] There are many aspects of cultural life, however, which do not form part of this stratum of cultural representation.[31] Many facets of popular entertainment, the events in the Arena del Sole, the programmes of the commercial theatres and the "aerostatic performances" with captive balloons, although much loved by the Bolognesi, are only indirectly relevant to this book. The book does not narrate the rough and ready tales of Bacchelli's, Guerrini's, Beltramelli's or Panzini's popular Romagna. Instead, it is concerned with the municipality's cultural policy and self-representation, a culture which constituted politics, and which thus illustrates the political power of culture.

Theatre and music, art and architecture, as well as public debate on cultural self-representation reflect in a complex way on power, social change and conflict. As Raymond Williams argued, "an essential hypothesis in the development of the idea of culture is that the art of a period is closely and necessarily related to the generally prevalent 'way of life,' and further that, in consequence, aesthetic, moral, and social judgements are closely interrelated."[32] However, Williams did not speak about art in terms of cultural policy, for his interest was less in the reception and the public use of art than in the impact of politics and social change on the artist and his work. By contrast, my work investigates how the arts are used to do politics. Despite the connection between culture and its socio-political context, culture does not simply "confirm the present form of domination," as Tibor Kneif suggests in his sociology of music,[33] since it can also be used to undermine and destabilise dominion, or to anticipate societal change. Stylistic developments in Bologna's theatres, the city's town planning, and

its historical commemorations reflected political decisions as well as aesthetic perceptions of a changing milieu. They generated public debate and
marked the city's and the nation's political life. These debates, rather than
the works of art themselves, constitute the social and political realities with
which this book is concerned.

Political meanings associated with works of art, the repertoire at the
opera, or styles in architecture are always specific to the social and political
context of their reception.[34] Many of Bologna's artistic developments during
the *fine secolo*, the decades around the turn of the century, followed transnational patterns. However, the medieval revival in nineteenth-century
Bologna differed in its specific political connotations from the meaning
of the Gothic revival in Germany or Victorian Britain, or indeed in other
Italian cities. The widespread interest in the peninsula's pre-Roman civilisations contributed to national foundation myths; in Bologna, however,
popular *Etruscomania* also helped to foster local pride and anti-Roman
sentiment. While Bismarckian Germany celebrated the victory over France
in 1870 with Wagner's *Kaisermarsch*, the first performance of *Lohengrin*
in Bologna, a year later, stood for cosmopolitan and democratic values.
In order to assess these very specific meanings of culture, the historian's
source should consist not of the work of art itself but of the discursive
structures informing its use and its reception.

My research is therefore largely based on the analysis of political language relating to cultural representation. My book reconstructs the discursive relationship between cultural elites, political elites and the public, with
the help of sources from Bologna's municipal administration, the records of
council meetings, private correspondence, political speeches and memoirs
of politicians and intellectuals, including the proceedings of the Deputazione di Storia Patria, the local press, the records of Bologna's Great Exhibition of 1888. On the basis of these sources my research proposes a new
approach to cultural history and the history of the middle classes, aiming
to reconcile trends in cultural studies and the history of cultural practices
with more traditional approaches in intellectual history and the history of
ideas. In my view an interest in the cultural practices of social groups should
not preclude work on society's more abstract forms of cultural expression,
on the aesthetic content of the arts and its reception. Therefore I take into
account Bourdieu's work on culture and social distinction, but also de Certeau's concept of reception as a creative process and Pomian's approach
to the deconstruction of semiophores. On this basis my research aims to
understand perceptions of change; the dichotomy of late socio-economic
modernisation and the early embrace of aesthetic modernism; the relationship between cultural challenge and political reaction. Koselleck's approach
to the semantics of historical time helps me to refine the frequently rather
schematic accounts of the relationship between modernisation, modernity
and modernism. My book makes reference to current debates on Italy's
fine secolo crisis, but avoids explaining departures from historiographical

"models of modernisation" by means of stereotyping references to Italy's exceptionalism and eternal backwardness. Recent research on the European middle classes and their concepts of nationality are crucial to these debates. Banti's critique of Chabod's classification of European nationalism shows that Italy stands between an ethnic-cultural form of nationalism and the politically motivated "plebiscite" of the French tradition. The book illustrates this idea through the analysis of the negotiation between local, regional and national identities, which were made meaningful through a wider European and cosmopolitan contextualisation.

CULTURE, INTELLECTUALS AND THE MIDDLE CLASSES

The cultural self-representation of the Italian cities after Unification and the fostering of a historically informed civic identity was largely the project of the middle classes. Their role in this process questions certain positions of Gramscian historiography. Bearing in mind the dominant position of Bologna's Moderate elites in local politics it might seem surprising that the Democratic middle class was able to assume this role. As John Davis has argued, "the ideology of Moderate liberalism, at once progressive in material terms and conservative in social terms, dominated Italian culture, and won over the professional and bureaucratic classes."[35] However, as this case study suggests, the Moderates laid the ideological and institutional foundations of the Italian State, but with limited effects on the public sphere, civic culture and the domain of cultural representation, leaving behind a vacuum which the Democratic middle class was able to fill. Rather than "dominating Italian culture," the Moderates largely ignored the nation's and the cities' cultural representation. The educated middle class took advantage of this situation. Instead of becoming passive receivers of culture, they imposed their own cultural values and their aesthetic reflection upon the experience of modernity. The battles over the private boxes and the repertoire of Bologna's Teatro Comunale, analysed in Chapter 2, or the role of the middle class in debates on the city's conservation projects serve as examples of this process. The Democratic middle class was able to impose its views on the basis of its "structural advantage" as professional experts and members of the intellectual elite. Kocka defines the educated middle class through "anerkannte Bildung," by which he means a broadly recognised and certified education that determined its social position as well as its influence in society.[36] The Moderates had little to pit against this.

The process of academic specialisation and intellectualisation assigns the professional middle class a special role in the disenchanted modern world. Professionalisation allowed important sections of the middle classes "to exploit their positions within the state to enhance their prestige."[37] What Bourdieu describes as *"les principes de divisions pratiques, symboliques*" no longer corresponded to the political and social realities of Italian society after Unification, opening the door to new professional elites from a middle class background.[38] For the Moderates after Unification liberty meant "the spontaneous authority of knowledge, of rectitude, of capacity," which for too long had been hindered by the spirit of the *ancien régime*.[39] Urban and administrative historians of nineteenth-century Italy have stressed the growing influence of technical experts in networks of local power. Mariapia Bigaran defines these experts as "frontier groups," which had limited economic and political power and yet played a strategic role in the process of institutional and political modernization.[40] On this basis they enjoyed privileged access to cultural institutions, exemplified in Bologna by people like Carducci, Panzacchi and Zannoni. The occupation of ideological territory by Italy's professional middle class corresponds to the bureaucratisation of culture described by Janik and Toulmin in *Wittgenstein's Vienna*. This process transformed the educated middle class into experts, in Bourdieu's words *"professionnels de la manipulation des biens symboliques."*[41] While in Vienna changes in the social organization of culture followed the crumbling of the dynastic system, in Italy this happened as a consequence of the cultural vacuum created by the Moderate elites.[42]

This constellation invites us to reassess the practical implications of Gramsci's interpretation of hegemony. For Carl Schmitt elites are empowered by the consent of the *demos* or its agencies; one should add that this consent is often passive or based on coercion.[43] Nevertheless, in the case of liberal Italy the political elites empowered cultural elites. Certain groups within the *società civile* were granted prestige as long as they did not directly and explicitly undermine the dominant ideology. The Moderates recognised that the national and cosmopolitan values of the middle classes did less harm to their own project than did the forces which opposed the liberal nation state outright. Consequently, they granted the middle class political rights and a certain degree of freedom in fashioning cultural representation, which found its sphere of expression at the municipal level in particular. They were allowed to communicate their ideas within the ambiguous framework of artistic abstraction and aesthetic communication. It is an inherent part of this strategy to maintain that the arts are not political and do not serve as ideological propaganda.[44] Their political and ideological strategies were indeed complex. As a matter of fact, the middle class occupied its position not simply as educated professionals, but as intellectuals. Confronted with a situation Christophe Charle has described as "the isolation of the intellectuals," Pier Paolo Pasolini accounted for the indirect power of intellectuals in the political sphere in terms of their "codified mode of intervention," which characterises the difference between the merely educated and the "intellectual."[45] According to Ernesto Ragionieri the intellectual had emerged as a protagonist and mediator of conflict in Italy around World War I, when Croce became the most prominent advocate of the Liberal State.[46] However, as the case of Bologna suggests, this process had in fact started with the Unification of Italy, when Carducci became one of the protagonists of Italy's intellectual life. This constellation profoundly marked the civic identity of the Italian cities and the culture of Italy's *fine secolo*.

THE BOOK'S STRUCTURE

The book is divided into three main parts, containing three chapters each, framed by this introduction and a conclusion. The chapters are conceived thematically while providing a chronological outline of cultural and political developments from Unification to the collapse of the liberal institutions after World War I. The first chapter sets the scene for the case study, analysing the socio-economic and political transition from the Papal regime to the constitution of the Kingdom of Italy. With reference to Arno Mayer's argument about the Persistence of the Old Regime,[47] the chapter addresses the continuities among the city's social and political elites after the departure of the cardinals and challenges the idea of a radical transformation of power structures after Unification. This particular configuration accounts for the long-lasting political hegemony of the Moderates in the local political institutions. Chapter 2, on Bologna's Teatro Comunale and the Italian opera industry, illustrates conflicts between the city's ancient aristocratic elites and the modern administration over cultural representation, with the theatre a battleground as regards social status and political influence. "Money and Culture," the third chapter, compares municipal finance under Moderate and Democratic administrations, showing in particular how the implementation of Italy's national legislation affected local administration with regard to their spending on culture.

Part II of the book looks at the ways in which Italy's nineteenth-century cities used narratives of its ancient and medieval past to endow the present with historical meaning. Historicising discourse in nineteenth-century Italy did not invariably contribute to national foundation myths. Indeed local histories often undermined national narratives. "The Middle Class and the Historicising of the Present" explains how Bologna claimed legitimacy as one of the historical and intellectual centres of the young nation-state through institutions such as its archaeological museum, its historical archives and its ancient university. "Medieval Revival" then explores how nineteenth-century references to the "communal age of freedom" during the early Middle Ages were pitted against the later period of "Papal enslavement," so as to justify symbolically the "patricide" of 1859, the city's liberation from the Papal regime. "Etruscans, Romans and Italians" analyses the widespread enthusiasm for the region's early, and newly rediscovered, Italic civilisations. Differences in material culture, which the Antiquarians had largely ignored, were now interpreted in terms of an ethnic framework, and the distinction between Ancient Rome and Bologna's own Villanovan and Etruscan past was used to negotiate the difficult relationship between local, regional and national identities.

Part III of the book looks at the ways in which the city related to the nation and to European culture. "Urban Space and Civic Culture," examines the local commemorations of the Risorgimento, subscriptions for monuments, the naming of streets and squares, and the "competition" between Bologna and her "sister towns," Modena, Florence, Milan and others. Chapter 8 examines the Italians' changing relationship to nation and monarchy during the Umbertian period. The cult surrounding the young queen Margherita led to a "gendering" of the language used in the construction of collective identities, and thus rendered the crown more accessible to the nation. "'*Viva Rossini—Morte a Wagner*'? From Campanilismo to the Future" analyses the symbolic-political meaning behind changes in the theatre's repertoire and the city's musical life. For the Democratic middle class the opening-up of the repertoire, first towards Verdi and Meyerbeer, and then towards Wagner's *musica del futuro*, was a statement in favour of a modern, cosmopolitan conception of urban selves. Initially, Bologna's traditional audiences rejected the trend towards the modern European repertoire in the theatre as un-Italian and as cultural propaganda for the Democratic administration. However, when Bologna's theatre suddenly appeared on the front pages of the international press, even the conservative elites were proud of the Teatro Comunale's renewed fame. Bologna became the capital of modern music-theatre, in a country where opera was still regarded as the principal art form. The experience of modernity was articulated through the transnational language of aesthetic modernism in music.

LIBERALISM, SOCIALISM AND FASCISM

In the autumn of 1920 Bologna elected for the second time a Socialist mayor. Within minutes of the election, the Fascist squads launched an armed assault on the town hall, killed nine of those assembled to hear the mayor's address in Piazza Maggiore and left more than fifty injured. For the first time the Fascists had removed a democratically elected administration, handing power over to the prefecture. Why did they choose Bologna? Why did the seizure of power start on the municipal level, considering that the local labour conflicts took place in the countryside? Why did it oust the Socialist administration and yet not replace it with the Fascist *ras*? Although my work on the municipal politics of culture deals mostly with the liberal period, it also offers a new perspective on the origins of Fascism. In 1942, the Socialist historian Gaetano Salvemini denied that the Italians' political backwardness could account for the collapse of liberal democracy.[48] Rather than its citizens, he held the institutions of the liberal state, the liberal party, the Church and the economic and military elites responsible for not backing democratic rule against the Fascist assault. In line with Salvemini's account, one may note that Bologna's highly developed sense of citizenship was betrayed by the institutions which backed the Fascist coup. However, this does not explain why Bologna became the first victim of Fascism. The municipal government played only a tangential role in the region's rural Labour conflicts which had given rise to agrarian Fascism. The assault on the town hall had not been economically motivated, and had no direct impact on the coercive powers which determined the conflicts in the countryside. Instead, the Fascists' target was Bologna's civic identity. The city's politics of culture had created a sense of identity, which connected its citizens to the democratic institutions of the liberal state, at any rate at the municipal level. If there was one concept of the nation that had proved successful after Unification it was *l'Italia delle cento città*, that is, municipal Italy. Bologna's civic identity allowed its citizens to confront the experience of modernity in a positive fashion, an approach diametrically opposed to the brutally destructive answer that Fascism had to offer. Bologna's "municipal socialism" built on earlier experiences of municipal cultural policy, representing a synthesis between the city's modern ambitions and the attempt to resolve the dramatic social question. The Fascists wanted to undermine and destroy the democratic institutions; the ideas represented by Bologna's administration stood in their way. The politics of culture at the municipal level during the liberal period help us to explain why the Fascist seizure of power started from the cities, where a sense of the intrinsic worth of the institutions was more widespread than on the national level.[49] The fall of Bologna was followed by the collapse of all the major democratically elected administrations in the region—well before the March on Rome, which represented the final step in the seizure of power, the Fascist assault on the state itself, and which marked the end of liberal democracy in Italy.

Part I
Political and Social Conflict

1 *Notabili*
The Local Persistence of
the Old Régime

. . . relics of past regimes which refuse to die out

(Antonio Gramsci)[1]

ANCIENT NAMES

On 18 October 1859 the Marquis Gioacchino Napoleone Pepoli and his family arrived at the commune of San Giorgio in the province of Bologna. With fireworks, music and cheers to "our king Vittorio Emanuele" the local population celebrated their annexation to Piedmont. As soon as the people noticed the arrival of the noble family they formed a procession and presented the Marquis the royal coat of arms.[2] This enthusiasm for the liberation from the Papal regime and the unification of Italy would not prevent the same local population from staging uprisings against the imposition of new taxes and conscription to the Piedmontese army. Occasionally, cheers for Vittorio Emanuele were replaced by cheers for the ancient ruler, the pope. However, whatever their attitudes towards the Italian State, the majority remained loyal to the local nobility.

A study on politics of culture at a municipal level has to examine the social composition of the local political elites and their economic background. Italian historians have largely rejected Arno Mayer's now classical study on *The Persistence of the Old Régime*.[3] Although Mayer's thesis is not unproblematic if applied across Europe, an analysis of social and political elites in the former Papal Legations presents convincing evidence for the persistence of the Old Regime, despite the watershed of Italian Unification. According to James Sheehan, Mayer fails to demonstrate "that aristocratic élites were relatively more important than other élites." However, the case of the former Papal States seems to show exactly that: the aristocratic elites continued to occupy a predominant role on all levels of social and political representation, well after Unification.[4] Only where a specific professional expertise was required was their position eventually challenged by a new professional elite of middle class origin. It is for this reason that municipal cultural policy deserves special attention, and it is here that one aspect of

Mayer's argument seems less convincing: Mayer suggests that the hege-monic role of the ancient elites is directly reflected at the level of cultural representation, in the arts and architecture of the period.[5] However, decod-ing aesthetic debates about the theatre's repertoire or urban planning, a more complex relationship between power, administration and cultural representation emerges. At the level of the cities' cultural self-representa-tion the ancient elites, which constituted the Moderates' local power base, were increasingly superseded by cultural and technical experts of profes-sional and middle class origin, who were often Democratic in their political orientation. Although the educated middle class suffered from a "struc-tural disadvantage" with respect to their socio-economic position and their political role in the local administration, they were supported by Italy's changing political climate after the parliamentary revolution of 1876, when the Democratic Left came to power. They were able to exploit their profes-sional expertise to impose their aesthetic values and, in more general terms, they discovered the political power of culture as the means of breaking into the existing hegemonies.

Piero Aimo differentiates between a period of "*amministrazione dei 'notabili'*" until 1865 and a period of "*amministrazione dei 'borghesi'*" dating from 1865 to 1900.[6] As a description of the social background of the local elites these categories seem not unproblematic. In Reggio Emilia, for instance, Moderate landowners dominated local politics until the electoral reforms of the 1880s. While these *notabili*, rooted in the Risorgimento tra-dition, were in their majority of middle class background, part of the *bor-ghesia terriera*, the case of Bologna seems more complex.[7] Here, *la fin des notables* was postponed until well into the twentieth century. For several decades after Unification local politics remained dominated by patrician families, aristocratic landowners resident in the Legations' capital.

In his *History of Italy*, Croce explained the role of Italy's nobility in the municipal administrations after 1860 in terms of "the people's general and spontaneous trust in the patricians, the gentry, the princes, dukes, and marquises".[8] In most parts of Italy people voted primarily according to the personal prestige of local candidates, if they voted at all. As late as 1886 the prefect of Modena declared that "the predominant aspect of the election was [the voters'] complete political indifference." Not political programmes, but the candidates' social status determined the vote.[9] After Unification the prestige of the ancient names lived on, in spite of the fact that the kingdom did not grant their bearers any significant privileges. Since the eighteenth century monarchical powers had challenged noble privileges in the Ital-ian states and feudal rights of jurisdiction had been abolished.[10] With the exception of the hereditary princes of the royal family, the Piedmontese constitution did not even grant the aristocracy seats in the upper house.[11] Numerous noble titles or names, still in use after 1860, were not recognized in the heraldic hand-books. Nevertheless, before the parliamentary revolu-tion of 1876 43.3% of the members of the upper chamber belonged to the aristocracy, including four out of the five *senatori* from Bologna nominated in 1860.[12] Likewise 29.4 % of the members of the lower chamber and 43% of the members of the government were of noble origin.[13] "As the closest advisors and favourites of a powerful monarchy," the Piedmontese nobility in particular was able to assert its leadership. Anthony Cardoza has challenged scholarship which stressed the fusion of new and old elites and the nobility's marginalisation after 1861.[14] The role of the nobility in the political institutions of the kingdom might appear less important than in Britain or Prussia during the same period, but considering the nobility did not fulfil a constitutional role, its position seems remarkable. According to Croce it was owing to the

> prestige of their names, the custom of seeing them since centuries in these positions, the fact that unlike the *gente nuova* they seemed to offer major guarantees of disinvolvement, of rectitude, of love towards the public well-being and the glory of their city.[15]

In 1860 the *Corriere dell'Emilia,* which was owned by Bologna's later mayor the Marquis G. N. Pepoli, justified the strong presence of the nobility in the city's elected representation:

> The council has to represent our illustrious city. The reason why so many of the famous names of our nobility are represented here is because there are no important differences keeping them apart from us. For the mere sake of declaring war against the aristocracy we do not want to fall into a primitive democracy. Rather than appearing generous, such a reaction would express a lack of enlightenment, distinction and education. An industrialist might figure rather well [among the members of the council], but we do not understand why the musician, the painter, the stone-mason, the teacher, the doctor, the surgeon, the pharmacist and so on is needed to constitute the town council. This would mean that any trade, any profession, including the mimes of the theatre and the beggars of the street should have the right to represent their commune.[16]

For decades after Unification local politics in Bologna remained dominated by the Moderate *Destra.* In the Piemontese parliament the *Destra,* the Historic Right, was referred to as the "*partito aristocratico,*" while the *Sinistra,* the Historic Left, was the "*partito borghese.*"[17] Characterising the *Destra*'s approach to politics, Cammarano speaks of an "*aristocratic concept of politics,*" conceived as "*arte di governo,*" which was based on exclusive upbringing and excellent education.[18] As late as 1884, Minghetti's successor as chairman of Bologna's *Associazione Costituzionale* and long time deputy for Imola, Count Giovanni Codronchi, invoked this ideal in a letter to Count Nerio Malvezzi, urging him to stand for election:

It seems to me that the upper classes have the duty of involving themselves in public life in order to prevent society from falling into the
hands of the worst elements. . . . You have an illustrious name and I
must invoke *noblesse oblige* to induce you to accept an office that will
acquire authority and decorum through your name.[19]

A Socialist councillor from Bologna could still in 1896 oppose "democratic
councillors" to "aristocratic councillors." While the Democrats, he averred,
shared at least some of the Socialists' concerns, the Moderates were only
interested in serving the interests of the local notables.[20]

In particular the local and provincial administrations and the office
of the mayor played an important role in the political careers of the local
aristocracy. While Dennis Mack Smith insists on the decline of the Italian
aristocracy during the nineteenth century, he describes local government
as "their perquisite."[21] As a young mayor of the small town Grinzane,
near Alba in Piedmont, Count Camillo Benso di Cavour provided the most
prominent example of a Moderate aristocrat, who from a position in the
local administration went into national and international politics.[22] From
the fourteenth century his family had belonged to the local ruling class.
Likewise in Bologna the prestige of ancient names and the ownership of
land determined membership in the local administration. Under the Papal
regime the cardinal nominated the *magistrati* or *conservatori* who formed
the local government. After Unification, with Rattazzi's law on communal
administration, the council elected a *giunta* to lead the administration,
while the king nominated the mayor. However, in Bologna the names of
the men in charge hardly changed from one political regime to the next.[23]
During the transition the administration was first led by Count Giovanni
Malvezzi, whose family had occupied important positions in the Papal
administration since the sixteenth century. In November 1859 the Marquis Luigi Pizzardi, the last *conservatore* of the Papal government, was
elected *Senatore* (mayor). Even though the first *giunta* included a few representatives of the middle classes, they had been elected on the list of the
"aristocratic" *Destra Storica*. All the important positions of the *giunta*
were occupied by the landed aristocracy—Count Carlo Marsili, Count
Giovanni Massei, Count Agostino Salina and Count Achille Sassoli.[24] In
January 1862 the king nominated Count Carlo Pepoli mayor, succeeded
in 1866 by the Marquis Gioacchino Pepoli. Between November 1868 and
February 1872 the Democrat Camillo Casarini led for a short period the
local administration, the first representative of the middle classes in this
office. After a short interregnum Gaetano Tacconi became mayor of Bologna (1875–1889), a landowner of middle class origin, governing with a
Moderate majority. The first mayor elected directly by the council was
again a representative of landed aristocracy, Marquis Luigi Tanari, who
declined the nomination.[25] After more than a decade under Alberto Dallolio, a Moderate landowner of middle class origin, the Marquis Giuseppe

Tanari, became mayor from 1905 to 1911. A comparison with Milan presents a rather different picture during the same period, even if all mayors still belonged to the *Destra*. While the first mayor after Unification was a landowner (Antonio Beretta, 1860–1867), the second mayor of Milan was a banker (Giulio Belinzaghi, 1868–1884), the third a philosopher and man of letters (Gaetano Negri, 1884–1889).[26]

Box 1.1   Count Carlo Pepoli and Marquis Gioacchino Pepoli

The political career of the Pepoli exemplifies the role of Bologna's ancient nobility in the administration after the city's liberation. Two Pepoli, Count Carlo Pepoli and the Marquis Gioacchino Napoleone Pepoli succeeded each other as mayors, the first in office from 1862 to 1866, the second from 1866 to 1868. Descendents of the famous Taddeo Pepoli, who held Bologna's *signoria* in the fourteenth century, they belonged to one of Italy's most ancient noble families. "How much history in these two names!," as Giovanni Spadolini remarked.[27] In addition to their political careers, they were patrons of the arts and themselves pursued artistic ambitions.

Carlo, born in 1796, wrote prose and drama, including the libretto for Bellini's opera *I Puritani* (1835). He also produced a popular translation of St. Mathew's Gospel in Bolognese dialect.[28] Part of the Legations' provisional government in 1831, he was imprisoned for nine months after the revolution and then forced into exile. After Marseille, Paris and Genoa he went to London, where he married the wealthy Elizabeth Fergus of Kirkaldy, with whom he settled in a house named Felsina Cottage, a reference to Bologna's Etruscan origins. Supported by John Stuart Mill and Mazzini, he succeeded Antonio Panizzi as professor of Italian literature at University College, where he is remembered as an "undistinguished scholar".[29] The revolution of 1848 brought him for a short period back to Bologna to become deputy and senator for the electoral college in Rome and inspector general of the Papal State. Sent back on a secret mission to London, it was a further decade before he was able to return to Bologna on a permanent basis.

The Marquis Gioacchino Pepoli wrote a patriotic tragedy, *Crescenzio–Odio contro i tedeschi ed il giogo de' preti*, and a drama on the female Bolognese painter *Elisabetta Sirani*, a success in Bologna in 1851; less acclaimed was his *Gabriella*, presented in Modena in 1874.[30] Marco Minghetti attributed Gioacchino's "unbalanced vanity" to his earlier success as a playwright.[31] From a young age he also followed a career as a diplomat. Born in 1825 to Guido Taddeo Pepoli and the Princess Letizia Murat, he was a cousin of the later Emperor Napoleon III. In 1844 Gioacchino married his cousin Princess Friederika von Hohenzollern-Sigmaringen, a daughter of Antonietta Murat. The family was at the time one of the biggest landowners of the German federation.[32] Commander of the city's Civic Guards

(continued)

Box 1.1 Count Carlo Pepoli and Marquis Gioacchino Pepoli *(continued)*

in 1848, Gioacchino was referred to as "the king of Canaglia". During his exile in Paris he developed close links with his imperial cousin and with Cavour.[33] He became minister of finance in the provisional government of the Romagna, then foreign minister, governor of Umbria, and later was elected to parliament. He was among the founders of Bologna's artistic periodical *L'Arpa* and owned the newspaper *Corriere dell'Emilia*, which positioned itself in the centre of the political spectrum.[34] Rattazzi made him minister of agriculture and industry, and put him in charge of the legislation on the monetary unification of Italy. He was appointed ambassador in St.Petersburg and—after his term as mayor of Bologna—he became ambassador in Vienna.[35] Due to his family connections he was often suspected of being *Murattiano* rather than a follower of Vittorio Emanuele, favouring the Bonaparte as future kings of Italy. Spokesman of the French emperor during the war of 1859 and one of the architects of the 1864 September convention, in the eyes of many Italian patriots he seemed to serve French rather than Italian interests, in the words of the Democratic leader Camillo Casarini "un miserabile".[36] Only the events of Mentana in 1867—the use of the French Chassepots against Garibaldi's troops—made him distance himself from the policies of Napoleon III.[37] In parliament Gioacchino Pepoli voted occasionally with the Centre-Left—mostly on issues concerning the relationship between state and church. He frequently criticized the financial policies of the Moderates, and from the 1870s until his death in 1881, he dedicated most of his political activities to Bologna's Workingmen's Society and the workers' pension fund.[38] Nevertheless, his career exemplifies the role which Bologna's ancient elites continued to play after the unification of Italy.

Of seventy-five councillors elected in 1859 and 1860 thirty-three belonged to the group of *possidenti* or landowners, who paid a high land-tax and belonged in large part to the aristocracy. This category did not include owners of medium-sized or small properties who at the same time pursued another professional activity. Sixteen councillors were active in the commercial or industrial sector; another sixteen belonged to the liberal professions or were university teachers. Nevertheless, property often constituted the major source of income for the group of academics and professionals, and they represented similar economic and political interests as the group of *possidenti*.[39] The local and provincial councils counted among their members famous names such as Bevilacqua, Codronchi, Grabinsky, Hercolani, Isolani, Malvezzi, Tacconi, Zucchini, all of them important landowners and most of them members of the nobility.[40] Bologna's prefects also belonged predominantly to the aristocracy, facilitating the relationship with the local elites. The first prefect after the liberation was Count Ercole Oldofredi Tadini. Marquis Massimo Cordero di Montezemolo occupied the office from 1862 to 1865 and Cesare Bardesono Count of Rigras from 1868 until 1873, followed by Count Guglielmo Capitelli. After 1876 he was succeeded by a member of the Sicilian nobility, Marquis Luigi Gravina, before the office went for nine months to Nicola Petra Duke of Vastogirardi and Marquis of Caccavone.[41] For about twenty years all prefects of Bologna belonged to the nobility. A leading Moderate from Bologna's aristocracy, Count Codronchi, became prefect of Naples in 1889.

Some of the region's large landowners were not even resident in Italy—like the Bonaparte, whose enormous property in Budrio was leased to Annibale Certani, who later became a protagonist of the region's modernisation in farming methods.[42] Analysing the wealthy elites in Florence after 1862, Raffaele Romanelli speaks about a "Renaissance Paradigm, in which forms of rural and urban seigniorial power were combined."[43] In many respects Bologna's nobility still lived according to the ancient model of the Mediterranean cities, representing a "landed aristocracy . . . , propertied in the country but domiciled in the town . . . , and controlling by urban residence the government, economy, and culture of both." Unlike anywhere else in Europe, the Italian nobility was essentially urban and had remained so over centuries.[44]

ANCIENT LOYALTIES

Croce emphasised the extent to which the leading figures of the liberal era had lived "part of their best years under the old Italian states, full of memories of past times, in love with their region, lenient to see their legitimate interests, their dear and respectable feelings offended."[45] Even if they adhered to the idea of an Italian nation-state, they often were afraid of losing their social status and political influence under the liberal régime. Bologna's press after 1860 demonstrates a strong "*antipiemontismo*," opposition to a system that "subordinates Italy under Piedmont, the nation under the interests of a province and a dynasty."[46] This complicated the nobility's integration into the new nation-state. During the Risorgimento, liberalism and identification with the Italian nation had progressed among the social and political elites of the Papal Legations; but this involved an often painful break with ancient loyalties. As Alberto Banti has shown, the concept of *patria* originally referred to small units such as the birth-place, city-state or province, without reference to a form of government. Before Unification Bologna called its archaeological collections *Museo di Memorie Patrie*, referring to a *patria* within the borders of the Papal Legations; and the painter Pelagio Palagi referred in his will to the city of Bologna as his "*diletta patria*."[47] Only recently had this concept acquired a new meaning, referring also to the emerging nation-state.[48] From the eighteenth century the concept *nazione* was used with reference to an Italian cultural community, but it also continued to describe entities such as the province or city.[49] Even protagonists of the Risorgimento continued to refer to the ancient states of Italy as *nazione* or *patria*: Carlo Botta spoke of *nazione lombarda*, Ugo Foscolo called Venice his *patria*, and Manzoni, in the 1827 edition of his *Promessi Sposi*, used the term *patria* exclusively with reference to the State of Milan or the Republic of Venice.[50] Still in 1903, referring to the relation between Bologna and the nation, the mayor of Bologna spoke about a big and a small *patria*.[51] Paolo Macry has described the coolness of the Neapolitan nobility towards the institutions of the new State.[52] For Bologna's noble families, who over generations had served the Papal administration, the *patria* was the Romagna in the lands of Saint Peter. The revolution of 1831 stood for liberal reforms and the autonomy of the administration rather than national Unification and still in 1848 the primary aim was the "restoration of the papacy" in a modernised form—made explicit in the title of one of Minghetti's political pamphlets—not the abolition of Papal rule.[53] If at all, traditional patriotism could be combined with the idea of an Italian federation, but not with a central government.[54] After 1849 this option had ceased to exist, but Minghetti's later plans for a regionalisation and decentralisation of the unitary state still reflected the same current of thought.[55] Although legitimism played a less important role than in France after 1830, during the first decades after Unification the national governments remained concerned about the nostalgia for the former rulers.[56] Taking the Papal State as their point of reference, the clerical opposition, particularly in the former Legations, and after 1870 in Rome, hoped for a restoration of the Papal regime. In December 1862 the prefect of Bologna, Marquis Massimo Cordero di Montezemolo, complained to the minister of the interior about the nobility's widespread indifference towards the new nation-state and their complete lack of collaboration with the local administration. Although the propertied classes constituted an important part of the electorate and dominated the political system on the local and the national level, only a small minority showed an interest in public affairs.[57] In 1869 the prefect of Bologna complained that the country was deeply divided between those who still believed in the restoration of the former states and those who set their hopes on a Democratic revolution.[58] Only parts of Bologna's ancient elites supported the new nation-state; others were loyal to the Papal regime. Even organisations such as the *Società Agraria* were divided along these lines.[59] In the long term passive opposition against the nation-state dominated the picture rather than political activism. The Bolognese architect Alfonso Rubbiani later described the legitimism of his early years as a juvenile "chivalry" encouraged by his personal affinity with local aristocratic circles. "I was guided by my heart, a crude enough poetry perhaps . . . . Once I started to reason coolly . . . I ceased to be a standard-bearer of the legitimist army."[60] However, despite the loss of its territories, the Vatican consolidated its political influence and in particular its control over the Italian Church.[61] In the former capital of the Papal Legations the participation in elections remained below the nation's average: between 1866 and 1887 only between 29% and 38% of those having the right to vote participated in elections.[62] The Catholic opposition defined this "*astensionismo*" as "*la politica del papa.*"[63] After the liberation of Rome national participation in elections was at 45.5%, indicating the widespread opposition towards this important patriotic achievement, despite the public euphoria reported in Bologna's newspapers.[64] Suspicion against the new state was also reflected in the choice of education. In 1868 the Liceo of the Padri Barnabiti was still more popular among Bologna's better families than the new secondary school.[65]

POLITICS AND PROPERTY

Despite the widespread loyalties towards the old regime, the Moderates of the *Destra Storica* were able to fill the relevant political positions with local noblemen who were close to their liberal views. Members of the local *classe dirigente* usually occupied more than just one political mandate, holding simultaneously positions in government, in parliament, the provincial and local councils. The Deputazione provinciale, a small committee of between four and eight men chaired by the prefect, authorised the communes' "facultative spending," municipal loans and taxes, making it a highly influential institution of municipal politics.[66] Count Agostino Salina, a local patron of the arts, served as municipal and provincial councillor, mayor of the commune of Malalbergo and president of both the Cassa di Risparmio and the Monte di Pietà. Count Francesco Isolani was also a local and provincial councillor, mayor of Ozzano and president of the Banca Popolare. Marquis Luigi Tanari was a member of the town council, the second chamber and later of the Senate. He became prefect of Pesaro, Pisa and Perugia, and succeeded the Marquis Giambattista Ercolani as president of the *Società Agraria*, opening its doors to the Catholic reaction.[67] Berti, Bevilacqua, Codronchi, Lugli, Malvezzi, Marescalchi, Mazzacorati and Pizzardi all played leading roles in local politics, while representing Bologna in parliament or holding positions

---

Box 1.2   Marco Minghetti

As a former minister in the Papal government in Rome, Minghetti's own political *début* predated the liberation of the Legations. After Unification he determined political decisions in the Bolognese as local councillor and leader of the Moderates in parliament. From 1860 to 1861 he was minister of interior and therefore in a position to control Bologna's prefects. From 1861 to 1863 he presided over the provincial council, before twice becoming prime minister, from 1863 to 1864 and from 1873 to 1876, the longest serving prime minister during the years of the Right. From 1877 to his death in 1886 he presided again over the provincial council. Throughout his political career he represented the agrarian interests of the Right.[69]

in government. Most members of the local elite were associated with the "*consorteria Minghettiana*," an example of personal networking that characterized Moderate politics in many Italian cities.[68]

Research on the history of the European middle classes has emphasised the appeal of the aristocratic mores to the rising bourgeoisie.[70] Through lifestyle, marriage or office Italy's land-owning middle-class, wealthy families like the Minghetti, sought to assimilate themselves into the nobility. Although Napoleon wanted to create a new landed middle class in Italy, a broad group of wealthy landowners destined to become Italy's socio-political elite, after 1815 the aristocracy still controlled half of the land in the province. Lacking other opportunities of investment, by 1860 the middle class owned 54% of the land in the province.[71] This development brought them closer to the nobility and deepened the gap between them and the less wealthy parts of the middle class. The overall number of large estates increased rather than the number of small and medium-sized properties.[72] At the time more than 130,000 hectares were in the hands of 603 large landowners. About half of this wealthiest group of landowners belonged to the nobility. There were remarkable differences in the size of properties: between 200 and 300 landowners held about 66% of the land, the biggest estate being the property of Prince Carlo Torlonia with 2954 hectares. In the next category 5800 medium-sized landowners together owned 140,000 hectares. The remaining 73,000 hectares were owned by 58,000 smallholders.[73]

Although the "non-noble landowners" were usually more open to modern forms of commercial farming, they shared the economic and political interests of the nobility, represented by the *Destra Storica*. Minghetti's family possessed a total of 1598 hectares spread over various communes of the province. In his memoirs Minghetti expressed his admiration for William Gladstone, exemplifying a certain model of social mobility: like Gladstone, Minghetti came from the propertied middle class and made his way into national and international politics.[74] Over the decades the key positions within the ranks of Bologna's Moderates were increasingly occupied by landowners of middle class origin.

Both Minghetti's and Dallolio's careers are characteristic of the propertied upper middle class among Bologna's Moderates. They joined the liberal aristocracy in their efforts to build the nation-state, and their social and cultural background made them well suited to merge with the ancient aristocracy in a perfect symbiosis of shared economic, social and political interests.[79] They spent long periods in the countryside, "*in villa*," assuming the lifestyle of the nobility and demonstrating their social distinction.[80] In some cases this *nobilitazione* included marriages into the nobility: Marco Minghetti married Laura Acton, princess and widow of Camporeale. Through his wife's daughter, Maria di Camporeale, Minghetti was linked to the von Dönhoffs and later the von Bülows in Germany, which gave him direct access to the Imperial court.[81] Change in *habitus* went

---

Box 1.3   Alberto Dallolio

The career of Alberto Dallolio, a leading Moderate and mayor of Bologna between 1891 and 1902, is representative of this socio-political milieu.[75] Like Minghetti or Pini, he did not belong to the local nobility, but to the rich, land-owning strata of the upper middle class. Alberto's father Cesare had been a close collaborator of Minghetti, town mayor of Pianora (province of Bologna), member of the 1859 Regional Assembly and later local and provincial councillor. His mother was closely connected to Carlo Berti Pichat, another leading Liberal and nobleman of the Risorgimento period. Alberto studied law in Bologna, a common preparation for the class of urban-dwelling landowners and an entrance ticket into the *classe dirigente*. He suceeded his father as mayor of Pianora, before being elected to Bologna's town council, a position he occupied for more than a quarter of a century, from 1875 to 1902. From 1876 to 1891 he was part of the local government as *assessore* for education. Like his father before him, he was elected to the provincial council (1884), a position he maintained for nearly thirty years. He occupied leading positions in the local Moderate organisation, the *Associazione Costituzionale delle Romagne*, the *Comitato Liberale permanente* and the *Unione Monarchico Liberale*. Mayor of Bologna from 1891, he resigned in 1902 in response to protests against his tax policies.[76] The "popular" government which succeeded Dallolio's administration in December 1902 survived only until the end of 1904. The city's new administration was headed again by a representative of the local aristocracy. Dallolio remained an influential figure in local and national politics. In 1905 he became president of the provincial council, a position he held until 1913. In 1908 he constituted a committee for the history of the Risorgimento and was appointed to the Senate, where he took nationalist and later interventionist positions.[77] He enthusiastically supported the rise of Mussolini. His brother Alfredo pursued a career in the army and was appointed to the Senate. During World War I he became minister for armament and munitions, exemplifying the rise of the middle class in the military at a time when the number of aristocrats among officers fell to 3%.[78]

---

along with social mobility. In 1869 the entire city of Bologna was excited about the duel fought between the young Marquises Pizzardi and Mazzacorati, which took place on Minghetti's estate. It was understood as affirmation of aristocratic status. While he was prime minister Minghetti himself wounded his predecessor Rattazzi in a duel, after a confrontation in parliament.[82] (A few months earlier Luigi Carlo Farini, at the time prime minister, confronted the king with a knife, trying to force a declaration of war on Russia. Considered mentally deranged, he was persuaded to resign but still granted a state pension.)[83] However, noble rank was not exclusively symbolised through violence. Minghetti became the preferred *cavalliere* of Queen Margherita and a central figure of her *salotto* in Rome. Hence, as Alberto Banti and Marco Meriggi remarked, "during the 19th century it is possible to become privileged, one does not any longer need to be born privileged." The only condition was that "social borders are re-drawn, that the languages of stratification are rewritten."[84] In the Bolognese, most large landowners of middle class origin lived this symbiosis better than Don Calogero in Giuseppe Tomasi di Lampedusa's novel *The Leopard*, who despite his proximity in terms of wealth, continued to represent a cultural world quite different from that of Prince Fabrizio Salina di Donnafugata. What mattered was, in Bourdieu's words, the *habitus*, "à la fois principe générateur des pratiques objectivement classables et système de classement (principium divisionis) de ces pratiques."[85]

As regards their social profile, Bologna's ruling elite mirrors in accentuated form the general trend of Italy's political class after Unification. Although 45% of the ministers in the governments of the Right before 1876 came from the liberal professions, including 15% lawyers, this seemingly high percentage is related to the fact that Italy had one of the highest university attendance rates in Europe. Earlier than elsewhere the professions were well regulated and a university degree was required to achieve professional recognition, at a time when in other parts of Europe self-made lawyers without academic background were still allowed to become judges.[86] The categories used in the parliamentary handbooks are not unproblematic. Many lawyers were "*avvocati solo di nome*," spending most of their time on the administration of their estates.[87] Often landowners of aristocratic background held degrees in law, like Bologna's Count Massei, who played a major role in the local organisation of the rural economy, but represented the legal profession in parliament. In Reggio Emilia, in 1875, the electoral committee of the Moderates was constituted by four lawyers; all but one, a Jewish merchant, were landowners.[88] Rather than on his studies or his professional experience, a lawyer's prestige depended on his family's social status. As a matter of fact, 97% of the lawyers in the governments of the Right belonged to the nobility.[89] In contrast to the often unemployed lawyers from the South, who were proud of their intellectual background and closely linked to the Democrats, there is little reason to count the wealthy, landowning lawyers from North and Central Italy as belonging to the liberal professions.[90] Moreover, some members of the legal profession without property were closely linked to aristocratic families, whom they served as estate administrators. At the meetings of the theatre's box owners many of Bologna's noble families were represented through lawyers, who were frequently employed on a permanent basis by just one family.[91] While law had the reputation of being a noble profession in Italy, we even find a veterinarian among Bologna's Moderate establishment. Marquis Giambattista Ercolani held a chair at the university, corresponded with Darwin on parasitology and was the founding editor of the first international journal in veterinary science, later becoming rector of the university. However, he also was an important landowner and succeeded Minghetti as president of Bologna's *Società Agraria*. As a result of their erudition, their interest in local history and their knowledge of the local collections of arts and antiquities, the nobility frequently occupied positions in public libraries, archives and museums.[92] Hence, academic titles and membership in professional organisations did not undermine noble status, with the result that academia and the professions were not exclusively the domain of the middle classes.

THE MIDDLE CLASS AND POLITICS

As Francesco Saverio Nitti remarked, the Italian *borghesia* consisted to a large degree in landed property owners, particularly in the North and the Centre. Until the early twentieth century real estate accounted for over 50% of aggregate wealth in Italy. Compared to elsewhere in Europe the structure of assets shifted only slowly to financial and business investments, bank deposits, government funds or shares. In most cities that part of the professional middle class, which did not have direct interests in the agrarian sector, remained relatively small. Milan, with its relatively large group of professionals and white collar employees, remained an exception.[93]

Vittorio Emanuele II had voiced his hostility towards the rise of the *"uomini nuovi*, the avôcatass," among the political elites; and Cavour used to describe the representatives of the liberal professions in parliament as *"dottoruzzi di villaggio."* To a large extent these were elected in the South, on the lists of the Left. They benefited from the fact that a large portion of the Southern aristocracy remained hostile towards the Italian nation-state and therefore did not use their active and passive rights of suffrage.[94]

Until the late 1880s Bologna hardly had an industrial or commercial middle class to occupy positions in politics. Owners of medium-sized businesses like the publisher Zanichelli were exceptional among Bologna's Moderates, the party of the local *classe dirigente*.[95] Meanwhile, despite the prestige of Bologna's university, the role of academics and intellectuals in local politics came nowhere near that of the agricultural elite. In 1869 Carducci was elected councillor in Bologna, but the seat he won in the parliamentary elections of 1876 was for Lugo rather than Bologna and for procedural reasons he was not allowed to take it up.[96] When he received his nomination as senator, in 1891, he had long become a supporter of the monarchy.

The hegemony of Italy's Moderate *classe dirigente* during the early years after Unification was consolidated through control over the administration, the universities and the civil service, leaving little space for the Democratic middle class and oppositional politics. Moreover, the law granted the prefects wide ranging freedom to incriminate political opposition. "Get rid of Mazzini and his crowd . . . And why do we need a free press? I think a bit of soldiery is the right medicine for these people": this was the method by which Minghetti imagined integrating the former Italian states into the new structures of government.[97] Count Codronchi was known for his hard line on social unrest in the region, writing in June 1874 to Minghetti about "considerable unrest in the cities," convinced that "we need to crush it; to crush it soon, all at the same time destroying the organisational network which grows bigger every day. . . ."[98] This unrest was associated with the broad spectrum of the political Left, which included Radicals and Republicans, but also Democrats of the Historic Left. Therefore, civil servants had to be loyal to the party of government, making public support for the Democrats almost impossible. Important positions in the local administration depended not so much on professional qualifications as on proofs of loyalty towards the *classe dirigente*. A local example of this is the appointment of Bologna's first *segretario comunale*, the head of the municipal administration. Ottavio Tubertini had a degree in law and from 1845 he had served as secretary of the *Congregazione del canale del Reno e della chiusa di Casalecchio*, a consortium of agricultural entrepreneurs for the exploitation of the river Reno, which was an organisational base of the political elite which guided Bologna through the transition from the Papal to the liberal regime.[99] Tubertini won the job against fourteen competitors, several of whom had previous experience as secretaries of smaller towns. Appointing Tubertini, Bologna's elite did not have to fear political conflicts with the head of the local administration. The *Sinistra Storica* and the followers of Garibaldi were perceived as a threat to the political system established by Cavour. Frequent references to the Moderati as *partito di governo* or *partito ministeriale* were in themselves significant. Those parts of the middle class which identified with Garibaldi's or Mazzini's ideas were seen as *antiministeriale*. Before 1876 they could hardly hope for careers in the administration,[100] even though the Democratic spectrum was often dominated by respectable academics. Carducci was suspended from teaching for Republican propaganda and his open support for Garibaldi.[101] Likewise Giuseppe Ceneri and the well-known professor of chemistry Pietro Piazza were suspended for commemorating the twentieth anniversary of the Roman Republic.[102] An exemplary figure of the Republican academic in local politics is Quirico Filopanti, a name translating as "Citizen, Lover of the People." He was the secretary of the Roman Republic under Mazzini before spending long periods of exile in London. He became chairman of the local Labour association, represented the radical Left in the town council and became mayor of Budrio in the vicinity of Bologna. Teaching civil engineering at the university, he was denied a chair due to his political convictions. He was a central figure among the local freemasons and dedicated a number of publications to a pantheist neo-Christian religion.[103] In addition to these theological writings he published historical works and regularly wrote for the local press.

As most of the *borghesia umanistica* identified with the Historic Left, its influence during the years of the Right remained limited. Even in its traditional domain of expertise—education, preservation of monuments, museums, and so on—*"titres de noblesse culturelle"* (Bourdieu) counted initially rather little.[104] Before 1876, a third of the ministers responsible for education and culture belonged to the aristocracy. In Bologna it took until the second half of the 1880s for university professors, the representatives of the commercial middle class and of the liberal professions to occupy about 50% of the seats in the town council.[105] The other half of the *Consiglieri* still came from the aristocracy or the agrarian bourgeoisie. Gaetano Tacconi was Bologna's first Moderate mayor of middle class origin. In office from 1875 to 1889, he was still surrounded by a Giunta representing Bologna's traditional elite, barons and counts like the Malvezzi, Mazzacorati, Zucchini and Massei.

The middle class in liberal Italy included a growing number of lower employees and civil servants, even if their income hardly allowed them to maintain a decent standard of living. Together with school teachers, university professors and intellectuals they joined the political associations of the Left.[106] The expectations of the *borghesia media* and *bassa* towards the nation-state differed dramatically from those of the landowning middle class, the conservative *clientela* of the *Destra Storica*. Reflecting upon these stratifications within the Italian middle class, Meriggi and Banti, like Croce half a century earlier, have questioned the usefulness of the concept *borghesia* altogether. Already during the nineteenth century the *letterati* underlined the heterogeneity of this social category: While the educated middle class pursued civic ideals and was concerned about the well-being of society as a whole, the propertied bourgeoisie for the most part followed its own economic interests. Throughout the nineteenth century these contrasting attitudes were perceived as a real threat to the project of a unified nation.[107] During its later decades the social position of the *borghesia umanistica* gained in importance, mostly through careers in the civil service, as a consequence of the country's expanding administration. The rise of the *borghesia umanistica* in the civil service went in tandem with complaints about the state's bureaucratisation and increased the political fragmentation.[108] While in Germany the educated middle class and the industrial bourgeoisie joined together within the ranks of the National Liberals, Italy showed a sharp, politically defined demarcation between *borghesia umanistica* and the propertied middle class. The educated middle class saw itself represented by *Sinistra Storica*, Radicals and Republicans; the landed middle class associated itself with the liberal aristocracy among the *Moderati*.

Before the electoral reform of 1882, the law granted the vote to men over the age of twenty-five, who were literate and paid at least forty Lire of direct tax, which limited the number of voters to less than 2% of the total population. In 1861 only 1.7% of Italians were allowed to vote, compared to over 26% in France, almost 10% in Prussia and 5% in England.[109] In local elections the suffrage was granted to men over the age of twenty-one, paying between five and tenty-five Lire taxes (depending on the size of the communes); and to the so-called "capacities": public employees, teachers and professors, fellows of the academies, holders of decorations, stockbrokers and middlemen, and members of certain professions like notaries, accredited accountants, liquidators, surveyors, doctors, pharmacists or veterinarians. Widows or separated women who entered into the census quota could delegate their vote to a son or son-in-law.[110] Despite the inclusion of the "capacities" in the suffrage, property owners and entrepreneurs made twice as many voters as those exercising the liberal professions.[111] In Bologna about 5% of the population had the right to vote.[112] The *borghesia umanistica* represented 37.5% of the electorate in Naples and 44.8% of the electorate in Palermo, but only 18.5% nationwide.[113] As late as 1881 Bologna's liberal professions counted only 1154 members in total. Medical doctors, lawyers and engineers together made up no more than 0.48% of the population, a proportion that increased negligibly to 0.53% in 1901, but fell again to 0.42% in 1911.[114] These figures were only slightly above the national percentages of about 0.3%, which include the entire rural and illiterate population. Because the city's industrial and commercial bourgeoisie was also negligible, election results were determined to a large extent by landowners paying sufficient tax to be included in the electorate. This socio-political structure of the electorate largely corresponded to the views of Italy's Moderate *classe dirigente* after Unification. Nevertheless, in 1869 some prefects suggested reducing the vote for "capacity" to give even more weight to the propertied classes, who were more likely to sustain the Moderates. Moreover, because of the aristocracy's widespread "indifference" towards the nation-state, members of parliament were often elected with less than 150 votes.[115] The electoral reform of 1882 extended the right to vote to all literate men above the age of twenty-one, which increased the electorate to 6.9% of the total population, still far from Mazzini's concept of "equal citizenship," based on universal (male and female) suffrage.[116]

Hence, for fifty out of fifty-five years between Unification and the First World War, Bologna was governed by Moderate or Conservative alliances. Exceptions were Camillo Casarini's government, between November 1868 and February 1872, as well as the administrations of the Democrat Carlo Carli in 1890, the Republican Enrico Golinelli (1902–1904) and, from 1914, the Socialist Francesco Zanardi.[117] In the context of Depretis' *trasformismo* and the growing strength of the Radicals, Minghetti tried to overcome the social and political exclusiveness of the Moderates through an opening of the party towards the Historic Left.[118] In Bologna, Cesare Lugli and Enrico Panzacchi presented themselves as "dissidents" on the electoral lists of the Moderates. As a result the Democrats became closer to Republicans and Internationalists.[119] However, the local elections of 1880 demonstrated again the Left's inability to challenge the Moderates' structural majority in Bologna: only four candidates of the Left were elected, against ten candidates of the Right.[120] From the 1880s the former capital of the Papal Legations became the centre of political Catholicism in Italy.[121] Under the mayors Tacconi (1875–1889) and Dallolio (1891–1902) the *Moderati* fostered their political hegemony in local politics through alliances with this new political current. Many of Bologna's Catholic leaders came from a similar social background. Together with the Moderate elite the so-called "black aristocracy," the Marsigli, Grabinski, Ranuzzi and Sassoli Tomba, formed a new "party of order."

A comparison with Pisa illustrates the alternatives to the formation of a conservative hegemony based on the city's ancient elites. Unlike Bologna, Pisa witnessed a remarkable turnover in its *classe dirigente* during the first two decades after Unification. While in 1860 and 1865 the *possidenti* still occupied the majority of the seats in the council, resulting in solid Moderate majorities, their weight diminished considerably in subsequent years. Generational turnover coincided with a change in the councillors' social background. As early as 1869 twenty-five of the original members of the local council were replaced, among them fourteen owners of large estates and several other agrarians. The new members of the council were lawyers, professors of the university, civil servants and engineers politically close to the Democrats. The propertied classes now held less than a quarter of the council seats.[122] Only one landowner, Count Mastiani-Brunacci joined the local government. From 1873 onwards Pisa's *giunta* was formed exclusively from members of the liberal professions and the *borghesia umanistica,* representing the *Sinistra Storica.* The contrast with the developments in Bologna could not be more striking and can be explained with the different socio-economic structures as well as the city's different political history. Similarly, in Ravenna, Modena and Parma a social change of the political class became evident from the 1870s, with the Democrats dominating local governments, occasionally in coalitions with Republicans or Socialists. In the 1880s Ravenna, Faenza, Imola and several towns in the Modenese had administrations supported by Democratic-Socialist-Republican alliances.[123] In Turin the municipal administration remained dominated by the aristocracy, but they were not in a position "to exercise a true hegemony in the town council." Journalists, the academic and the administrative elite enjoyed influential positions too. The aristocracy's economic and political interests coincided largely with those of the wealthy bourgeoisie. Subsequently, Turin fully subscribed to the *trasformismo* of Depretis' and Crispi's politics on the national level, making any distinction between Left and Right impossible.[124] In Sicily, for instance, in Syracuse, the municipal elites were dominated by the middle classes, which included *possidenti,* but also merchants, intellectual elites, professionals and civil servants.[125]

HONORATIOREN AND *NOTABILI*

The persistence of the old nobility as the constitutive part of Bologna's social and political elite is inconsistent with the thesis of the aristocracy's decline during the nineteenth century. The situation in the former Papal States seems rather to confirm the opposite thesis put forward by historians such as Arno Mayer, Anthony Cardoza and Yves Lequin: *"Partout, l'aristocratie terrienne a de bien beaux restes!"*[126] Of course, Bologna's political elite was not exclusively constituted from members of the aristocracy and its socio-economic composition requires a wider category of analysis. In France, since the eighteenth century, the term *notable* was frequently applied to a social elite which included the aristocracy as well as the wealthy middle class.[127] Although some historians describe the *"société de notables"* as a French *"Sonderweg,"* the concept seems applicable to Italy, and in particular to Bologna after 1860.[128] According to Jean Tudesq's definition a notable is one who owns property, is educated, maintains an influential network of social relations and exercises power through public functions or offices. The title, the name and the father's role in society are crucial in defining this elite. In the former Legations the defining criterion was primarily aristocratic origin, but the role of the landed middle class within this social category increased. Unlike in France, financial and industrial groups did not occupy an important place among the elite. Hence, in social and in economic terms Bologna's *notabili* were more narrowly defined than their French counterpart. The term "notable" also refers to a socio-political function in society. They acted as *Honoratioren,* to use Max Weber's concept, rather than professional politicians; they were of independent means, and used their social-economic background to pursue a political career.[129] In order to retain their privileges and to conquer new positions of power they took control over the new state, preventing the middle class from adopting "an organic and national political programme."[130] Although the Romagna was a stronghold of Republican and later Socialist *associazionismo,*[131] its impact on the middle class and on national politics remained for a long time negligible.

Due to their social position Bologna's notables were able to impose candidates in elections, but in the long term the narrow definition of this political class led to an alienation from the rest of civil society.[132] Because the political groupings rarely extended beyond the men who occupied the seats in the elected assemblies, a differentiation between the political elite and a wider political class, or between *classe dirigente* and *classe politica,* seems impossible.[133] As late as 1896 Domenico Zanichelli maintained that the local Moderates did not constitute "a true and proper party, but a gathering of men who shared a relatively clear idea of what had to be done in order to accomplish the national programme."[134] In his 1884 critique of the parliamentary system Gaetano Mosca pointed out that in Italy a member of parliament is not chosen by the voter, but by his friends "who get him elected [*che lo fanno eleggere*]." Presenting a candidate is always the work of "an organised minority," which imposes the candidate upon the "unorganised majorities."[135]

The picture that emerges allows us to question the functioning of liberal-democratic principles in Italy after Unification. To use two further concepts of political theory, Bologna's *notabili* constituted a *Positionselite*, occupying leading positions in government and elected assemblies, as well as a *Funktionselite*, with a leading role in the local banking sector, the *Società Agraria* and occasionally in the city's cultural institutions.[136] In the former Legations it is not the bourgeoisie which formed the State into the guardian of its economic interests, following a Marxist definition, but the much smaller social group of the local notables, representing a specific stage of socioeconomic development.[137]

The Rural Economy

The elite's basis in landed property delayed Italy's industrialisation. Romanelli describes the men of the Right as "*ruralistici per nulla progressivi.*"[138] Italy's small manufacturing sector in the late nineteenth century concentrated on consumer rather than producer goods. Between 1874 and 1901 the role of agriculture in national income was reduced from 57.6% to 50.2%, but the percentage of the population working in the agricultural sector increased during the same period from 57.6 to 59.1%.[139] Despite the growing role of the landed middle class in the rural economy, agriculture remained behind modern developments in other parts of Europe, especially in the Romagna. Moreover, the region around Bologna witnessed a process of dis-industrialisation during the nineteenth century, largely due to the decline of the local textile industry, a consequence of the competition with the mechanized industry in England. The relatively small amount of employment in the textile industry was largely occupied by women. In 1860 about a third of the population of Bologna was without a permanent source of income.[140] In other regions of Italy, for instance in Piedmont, income from agriculture was to a larger extent invested in commercial activity and industrialisation increased more quickly. In the 1870s Leone Carpi, an economist from Ferrara and political correspondent of the *Rivista Bolognese di Scienze, Lettere, Arti e Scuole* condemned the widely flourishing "*dolce far niente*" among the middle classes. Similarly the *Gazzetta dell'Emilia* lamented in 1871 that "the Bolognesi love the *dolce far niente*: Walk along the streets and I wager that if you see one man working you will see three watching him with their hands in their pockets."[141] Romanelli described the lower middle class as "*inoperosa*"; as a consequence they hardly paid any taxes, which was used as an argument for excluding it from the electorate.[142]

The pre-industrial society in the Bolognese mirrored the economic attitudes of the local elites, which contrasted with the changing economic orientation of the nobility in other regions of Italy.[143] After several journeys to a number of highly industrialised regions in Northern and Western Europe, Marco Minghetti thought that Italy, due to its "extremely fertile soil," should concentrate its economic activities on agriculture.[144] Having studied Adam Smith and Jeremy Bentham, Minghetti was convinced that the division of labour turned the worker into "nothing different than a machine."

Machines and free competition . . . are damaging; given the present
economic, moral and political conditions of society . . . the benefits of
mechanisation seem to me out of proportion to their disadvantages, because every new invention, every improvement further aggravates the
situation . . . . In my view it is time to tell the Italians: "Take care of your
agriculture, because heaven provided you with a fertile soil and a climate
which is sweeter than any other in Europe. Remember that this is the
most noble of all arts, which keeps the body in healthy condition, which
trains the intellect and creates sweet affection in the soul . . . ."[145]

The source of man's alienation, the division of labour, was at the origin
of all the evils of the industrialised societies. Italy should be proud of its
position as the "garden of the world." The *Giornale Agrario Italiano*, published in Forlì, also argued that "big industry will certainly lead to misery,
disorder and social decline." Similarly, Paolo Predieri, in a speech to the
Societa' Agraria, warned of the social cost of industrialisation.[146] For Minghetti and the social elite which met in Bologna's *Società Agraria*, Italy's
future had to be a commitment to its past as an agrarian country.

Bologna was famous for teaching modern agronomy—generations of
students read the volumes of Carlo Berti Pichat's *Corso teorico e pratico di
agricoltura*.[147] Nevertheless, until the 1880s the Bolognesi largely ignored
modern commercial principles and technological developments.[148] Despite
some very large, noble estates in the Bolognese, the majority of agricultural
units remained small. Sharecropping diminished during the nineteenth century, but still prevailed over wage labour.[149] Cattle were mostly used for
field-work rather than meat production. Until the 1870s, even a city like
Bologna did not provide modern infrastructure for large-scale slaughter-
ing. Mechanization in agriculture was limited to a minimum; the use of
fertilizers and the rotation of crops remained rare. The only change which
had occurred after Unification was a higher degree of specialisation in production and the introduction of potatoes. The traditional class of landowners lacked the necessary capital to invest on a large scale in the drainage of
marshland; the success of later initiatives remained limited.[150] The region
had played a certain role in the production of raw silk, but during the second half of the nineteenth century China and Japan largely replaced Italy
in the supply of silk for the famous "fabrique lyonnaise."[151] While the silk
industry in Piedmont still managed to progress and to export, in the province of Bologna, by 1860, the trade employed no more than 500 people. In
the three decades since 1851 the regional production of cereals had doubled, but unlike in Piedmont this process had been helped by drainage of
land rather than mechanization and the use of fertilizers. Apart from small
quantities of rice and hemp produced for the national market, agricultural
product was used for subsistence or sold at local markets.[152] Until the crisis
of the 1880s local production increased by about 1.5% annually. This was
above the national average, but due to the region's backwardness under

the Papal regime this development started from a very low level; and the increase in agricultural production was not complemented by the growth of the industrial sector. Economic historian Vera Zamagni characterises the majority of Bologna's landholders during the decades following Unification as conservative in their methods and attitudes, unable to implement the necessary steps to bring about a modern agriculture. The majority of the agrarian middle class developed a *Rentiers-Mentalität*, which was not conducive to commercial modernization.[153]

As in other regions of Italy, the local elite pursued its economic interests through numerous associations, consortia and financial institutions.[154] Marco Minghetti and Count Carlo Bevilacqua, his successor as president of the *Società Agraria*, Count Gaetano Zucchini and Count Carlo Marsili founded in 1855 the *Banca pontificia delle quattro Legazioni*. Cesare Zucchini was director of the *Cassa di risparmio*, president of the local *Camera di commercio*, and president of the *Loggia dei Agricoltori*, while maintaining family links to the *Banca delle Legazioni*. The counts Pizzardi and Bevilacqua, whose families were represented in the administration of the *Cassa di Risparmio*, were among the founders of Bologna's mining company.[155] The *Consorzio di Scolo*, a society for the drainage of land in the region, included among its members Count Bentivoglio, Count Grabinsky, Count Isolani, Count Malvezzi, the Prince Antonio d'Orléans, Marquis Luigi Pizzardi, Marquis Tanari, Count Zucchini and many others. In 1900 the *Consiglio Amministrativo* of *Aemilia Ars,* a co-operative for the promotion of traditional crafts, counted among its members Countess Lina Cavazza Bianconi, Count Francesco Cavazza, Count Giovanni Enrico Sturani, Marquis Giuseppe Tanari, and Countess Carmelita Zucchini-Solimei Cagnola. The *Loggia dei agricoltori*, the *Società Agraria* and the *Consorzio Agrario* were structured in a similar way. The few representatives of middle class origin in these associations were usually administrators of noble estates. Most of these institutions survived without changes in their social structures, well into the twentieth century. In 1924 the *Società Agraria* nominated Mussolini "*socio onorario . . . ob pacem agris restitutam.*"[156]

The *Banca delle quattro legazioni* promoted the region's industrialisation, without significant results. Most of the financial institutions concentrated their activities on the rural economy, but for small and medium-sized landholders access to credit or capital investment remained difficult. Forty per cent of credits provided by the *Banca delle quattro legazioni* went into agriculture, but nearly exclusively to the region's thirty biggest landowners. Not even the development of the railway network received much support locally.[157] In 1883 the Moderate Cesare Orsini deplored the advance of the railway in the Romagna, because it destroyed the market function of the smaller towns:

Once the railway arrived, the state of affairs naturally began to change . . . . When travelling in the Romagna you will be surprised

to find fair-sized towns, which were once flourishing, but which have
now fallen into a fatal decline. In the streets and in the inns a melan-
choly solitude reigns . . . , while far away, there on the railway you
hear the whistling of the passing steam train, which takes with it all
that activity and commerce on which the wealth of these places had
been based.[158]

While this is probably an accurate analysis of the situation in places where
the modern infrastructure did not arrive, it is a surprising statement for a
leading politician of the railway age. Investments in the development of modern industry remained rare, as the example of the local *Cassa di risparmio*
shows. Apart from providing credit for agriculture, it mostly financed the
local building sector, which occupied about 3% of Bologna's active population. Between 1897 and 1906 its biggest financial operations consisted of a
one million Lire credit to the municipality; 1,300,000 Lire (together with
the *Banca popolare*) went into university extensions; 800,000 Lire into the
new postal building in Piazza Minghetti; six million (together with several smaller banks) were used to finance public works of the municipality.
Local politicians financed public building works largely through financial
institutions which they themselves controlled. When towards the end of
the century industrialisation took off, the region was among the country's
least developed areas. At the time only 4% of the population were occupied
in the industrial sector. Even the Campania and Sicily were more industrialised than Emilia Romagna.[159]

From the end of the nineteenth century a small group of agronomists—
often of middle class origin—began the modernization of local farming.
An important role in this process was played by the *Federconsorzi*.[160] In
the Bolognese, Alfredo Benni, Ignazio Benelli, Vittorio Venturi, Agostino
Ramponi and Antonio Bonora pioneered modernisation in rice, tobacco
and sugar beet production. Enrico Pini introduced and started producing chemical fertilizers. Radical changes in local crops were linked to new
agricultural tariffs imposed in 1887.[161] National and foreign capital was
invested in mechanization and the development of modern food processing,
allowing Bologna to reach national and international markets. Nevertheless, an important group of traditional landowners continued to use the
local agrarian associations to voice their opposition to the idea of commercial farming and the capitalist exploitation of land. Regarding the growing
tension between agrarians and the rural labour force, Count Francesco
Massei reminded the Agrarian Society in December 1901 that the farmers had "firm rights to safeguard" their interests, but also duties to review
the contracts with their peasants. Landowners should sacrifice some of
their profits for the sake of social peace.[162] Before World War I, agricultural production grew about 5% annually, twice the national average. The
region's social question was aggravated by these modern developments:
mechanization reduced the need for manpower and the concentration of

capital-investment on food-processing failed to create enough employment to absorb the mass of rural workers who increasingly migrated to Bologna and the surrounding towns.[163] Hence, the rural economy was marked by continuities in the economic and political elites as well as by a delayed modernisation, with dramatic effects for the social question.

THE REPRESENTATION OF STATUS

The social divisions within the citizenry were reflected in the organisation of urban space. For Naples Paolo Macry has demonstrated how the wealthy families of the *grande bourgeoisie,* aiming at an aristocratic lifestyle, moved into specific residential areas of the city and rented the expensive but prestigious *Seicento palazzi* of the local nobility.[164] In Bologna the medieval centre had a similar function. The best families, including the aristocracy and increasingly the propertied middle class, lived along an axis which went from Piazza Maggiore eastwards along Via Rizzoli. Occupying this space in the city centre, Bologna's social elite was able to set limits to the expansion of certain economic functions (banking, insurance sector, commerce), which usually mark the structural transformation of modern city centres during the second half of the nineteenth century.[165] The less wealthy strata of the middle class, liberal professions and university professors, occupied the areas outside the historical centre. Cities like Turin and Florence likewise witnessed a reorganisation of space during the nineteenth century, which abolished the spatial demarcation between the upper middle class and the nobility while accentuating the internal divisions within the middle classes.[166]

Bologna's notables were keen to create symbols and signals in the urban landscape to reflect their social and political position after Unification, especially in the cultural centre of the eastern parts of the medieval city, where the theatres, museums, the clubs and the university were located.[167] Much debate was provoked when in 1871 the palace of the *Cassa di Risparmio* in Via Farini was inaugurated, "*quella principessa residenza,*" which cost the bank 1,200,000 Lire.[168] Fabulously decorated by Luigi Samoggia, Giuseppe Pacchioni, Stefano Galletti, Arturo Colombarini and other famous artists of nineteenth century Italy, it was here that Bologna's agrarian elite held their meetings and here that they founded the *Scuola Superiore di Agraria.* The building itself was designed by Giuseppe Mengoni, one of the most prestigious architects of the new Italy, known for the Palazzo Cavour in Turin, the "Vittorio Emanuele" arcades in Milan, the covered market of San Lorenzo in Florence and, in Bologna, the design of Palazzo Cavazza near the new seat of the *Cassa di Risparmio.* Modesty was not one of Mengoni's qualities and his declared aim was to "exceed every living artist, to be one day recognised as reigning next to Raffaello and Michelangelo."[169] He was a major adversary of Coriolano Monti, the city's chief civil engineer, who supervised the city's architectural preservation and urban planning after Unification. One of the first major building projects completed in Bologna after the departure of the cardinals, the monumental design of the Cassa di Risparmio was criticized even by commentators close to the local Moderates, as offending aesthetic principles and the city's medieval setting through its uncoordinated mishmash of different historical styles.[170] The neighbouring palace of the *Banca Nazionale*, built by the Neapolitan architect Antonio Cipolla in the classical style of *Roma Imperiale,* was considered a symbol of the economic integration of the nation. The *Cassa di Risparmio,* on the contrary, was seen as a disproportionate symbol of the local elite's power—of the Pizzardi, Zucchini and Bevilacqua. *Il Monitore di Bologna* described the building as "*un monumento faraonico, sardanapalico, degno del piu' fastoso degli imperatori romani.*"[171] According to Bottrigari, the Marquis Bevilacqua had used the savings of Bologna's small artisans to finance his palace, rather than employing them for the benefit of all.[172] With this criticism Bottrigari pointed to a problem which reflected the political and financial concentration of power in the hands of the agrarian elites. Rather than helping the region's industrial development through credits for artisans and small entrepreneurs, the financial activities of the *Cassa di Risparmio* largely served the interests of Bologna's conservative landowners, who until the late 1880s did not even support modern concepts of commercial farming.[173] What the debate also shows is that within a decade after Unification critical opinion made itself heard in Bologna, distancing itself from the local elites and engaging in a debate about the symbolic representation of urban space.

Not only through public buildings but also in private Bologna's elite was keen to distinguish itself from other strata of society. Minghetti knew very well how his propertied family differed in *habitus* from the wider middle class. In his memoirs, he remembered an invitation to a grand ball in the Tuileries in 1844. For the young Italian traveller "there were too many *borghesi:* as our old Florentines would have said, fat *popolani,* officers of the national guard and so forth. Such festivities are neither pleasant nor entertaining if the guests lack education and manners."[174] Bologna's notables were used to more exclusive entertainment than what the court of Louis-Philippe had to offer. Bottrigari describes in his *Cronaca* the balls in the house of the Marquis Pepoli after the liberation of Bologna and the ball offered by the Governor Farini in the former Palazzo Ducale in Modena—"splendid occasions, bringing together all the Ministers and other high personalities."[175] Bologna's better families also organised *salotti* and *circoli*. While the aristocracy usually had access by right of their name, the rare visitors of middle class origin had to be invited.[176] D'Attore describes the *Societa' Agraria* as an "alternative to the *salotto* or the aristocratic circle," but it was not less exclusive.[177] Membership was limited to forty, in contrast to the professional organisations of book-keepers or engineers, which tried to include all the representatives working in the profession. In these polite circles even political rank could not make up for the lack of *etiquette:* In a letter to Cavour, Minghetti complained about the inappropriateness of Bologna's first prefect after the Liberation:

Mayr is an intelligent, able and hard-working man; he is efficient and speeds up administrative matters. But his manners are hardly urbane. He lives like a peasant. His wife is ugly and dubious; all this makes him unacceptable to the aristocracy. . . . I think he is out of place in Bologna, and he is aware of this.[178]

He was made to leave Bologna shortly after, in July 1861. Rather than politics, literature, science and music were the main subject of conversation in the "*salotto di cultura*." Count Carlo Pepoli was introduced to artists and writers at the house of Berni Degli Antoni. Academic and scientific circles met in the homes of Count Gozzadini and Count Malvezzi. Teresa Gozzadini sponsored Giovanni Capellini's first geological field work in the United States. Later Carducci also belonged to her circle and Schliemann was among her famous visitors.[179] But the encounters between the aristocracy and the middle class were not always without tension. Already a famous poet of international renown, Carducci was invited to Casa Lovatelli in Rome, and there was mockery about his middle class manners.[180]

Dating back to the second half of the eighteenth century, the *Società del Casino* organised musical events and public readings. An entire generation of Bologna's Moderates, the circle around Marco Minghetti in particular, had been marked by it. Also referred to as *Casino dei Nobili*, membership was until 1796 exclusively reserved for the aristocracy.[181] During the early nineteenth century its statutes were liberalised. Partly for economic reasons, the association had to open its doors to the upper middle class, usually families who during the Napoleonic years had acquired large estates in the province. The club became a base for the aristocratic liberalism which promoted political reform during the Risorgimento. An important aspect of the Casino's activity was centred on the *cabinet de lecture,* which in 1832 offered forty-one periodicals. Minghetti was for a while the *direttore* of the collection. The Papal administration tolerated the club's political debates to prevent its transformation into a secret society. When after 1848 the *Casino* refused to invite Austrian officers, the occupiers shut its doors. Under the liberal regime the associational culture of Bologna's elite changed only slowly. The *Casino* was succeeded by the *Domino Club*, which met in Palazzo Salina Armorini, but whose membership never possessed the social diversity of, for instance, the *Società del Casino* in Reggio Emilia.[182] While in Venice the *Gabinetti di lettura* attracted the wider middle class, in Bologna the use of libraries and reading rooms remained a privilege of the city's better families or of academics: even if Bologna had a number of public libraries, the opening hours were inconvenient for the working population, and, as the council still noted in 1916, "there is no place to consult newspaper and modern journals."[183]

During the nineteenth century many European cities witnessed the development of a flourishing concert life for the middle classes.[184] Performances were usually public and organized by voluntary associations. The

Società del Quartetto in Florence dated back to 1861 and from the very beginning it appealed to a wider audience, organising concerts in the afternoon and in public theatres. The *Società del Quartetto* in Turin, established in 1854, followed the example of similar associations in Vienna, Leipzig and Berlin, organising popular symphonic concerts, for which the cheapest ticket was only about half the cost of the cheapest ticket for the opera.[185] However, Bologna's musical life remained for a long time confined to the *palazzi* of the local nobility.[186] The *Società del Quartetto*, founded in 1877, organized concerts in the palace of Count Camillo Pizzardi.[187] Taking Bologna's traditional Gentlemen's clubs as a model, even women were initially excluded from attending concerts, as was Bologna's middle class. At the end of 1879 the concerts of the *Società del Quartetto* became public, but even in the 1880s the charity concerts organised at the Liceo Musicale were conceived as events for the local nobility. Before even mentioning the concert programme, reviews in the local newspapers presented lists of the "signore della *high life* bolognese" seen on the occasion: Princess Simonetti-Fava, Countess Caimi, Countess Malvezzi Trotti, Countess Solimei Zucchini, Countess Martuzzi, Lady Bingham, Countess Bianconcini "with her elegant daughter," and Count Zucchini with the mayor.[188] While the performance of serious chamber music in the *Società del Quartetto* was considered a privilege for learned noblemen, charity concerts with mixed programmes were principally aimed at noble women.

Not the exclusive *Società del Quartetto*, but the directors of the Teatro Comunale and the Liceo Musicale, Mancinelli and Martucci, started organising concerts of symphonic music for wider audiences, with a focus on musical education rather than elite entertainment. These "popular concerts" usually took place in the Teatro Brunetti, a commercial theatre, which was big enough to offer cheap seats. The prestige of the famous conductors was such that even Bologna's better families attended these events, bringing together "*tutta la buona borghesia,* in short, the audience for the great occasions."[189] Slowly, Bologna's middle class started occupying public space. The city's ancient elites contested these challenges to their traditional status in society. Bologna's theatre, the Teatro Comunale, represents the most dramatic example of these conflicts about the use of public space and its administration through modern liberal institutions.

2 The Theatre of Social Change
The Opera Industry and the End of Social Privilege

The Athenian: *Hence the theatregoers became noisy instead of silent, as though they knew the difference between good and bad music, and in place of an aristocracy in music there sprang up a kind of base theatrocracy. For if in music, and music only, there had arisen a democracy of free men, such a result would not have been so very alarming; but as it was, the universal conceit of universal wisdom and the contempt for law originated in the music, and on the heels of these came liberty. For, thinking themselves knowing, men became fearless; and audacity begat effrontery. For to be fearless of the opinion of a better man, owing to self-confidence, is nothing else than base effrontery; and it is brought about by a liberty that is audacious to excess.*

Megillus: *Most true.*

Plato, *Laws* III[1]

PAPAL LEGACIES

In October 1859 Count Giovanni Bentivoglio was elected to the town council of Bologna.[2] The Count's ancestors had dominated the city during most of the fifteenth century. The city's famous Teatro Comunale, once among Europe's finest opera houses, was built on the site of the Bentivoglio family's former palace, with its three hundred lavishly decorated rooms at the time considered to be the most expensive city palace ever built in Italy, according to Bologna's most influential architect of the *fine secolo*, Alfonso Rubbiani, "more beautiful than the Medici palace in Florence."[3] The Bentivoglio palace was destroyed in 1507, after the defeat of the family by Pope Julius II, leaving behind the so-called "*Guasto*," symbolising the victory of the Papal regime over Bentivoglio's *signoria* and the surrender of the most rebellious city of the Papal States. During his time as Bishop of Bologna, from 1483, Julius' influence on the city had remained limited, due to the outstanding position of the Bentivoglio family as the city's rulers. When he conquered the city as pope, the event was staged as the return of the Roman *imperator*, later described by the Bolognesi as the beginning of their Papal enslavement. Julius was accompanied by his entire court, including twenty-six cardinals with their private households. To commemorate the expedition Julius issued a medal bearing the inscription IULIUS CAESAR PONT.II.[4] With the consolidation of the pope's rule in the Papal States during the early sixteenth century, the court of Rome was "transformed into one of the great monarchical courts of Europe" and the new *Tempelstaat* increasingly invested in its self-representation through culture.[5] Julius II, governing during the time of Michelangelo, Raphael, Bramante and del Sarto, belongs to the greatest patrons of the arts in history. Unlike other Italian *signoria*-courts at the time, and despite their political power and the *grandeur* of their palace, the Bentivoglio family had never exercised cultural leadership in Bologna.[6] From the sixteenth century the cardinal-legate assumed this role and invested in the cultural infrastructure of Bologna. Culture was supposed to "civilise" the bellicose nobility—*Affekt-dämpfung* in the sense of Norbert Elias.[7] During the Counterreformation of the sixteenth century Bologna's theatres were unable to compete with those of the courts of the Este or Farnese. But from the seventeenth century opera became a major art form at the Papal court in Rome; and Bologna was keen to follow this example—first in private theatres, in particular the *Malvezzi* in Borgo San Sigismondo, and, after this had been destroyed by fire in 1743, in the new Teatro Comunale, built on the site of the Bentivoglio family's palace, as a publicly owned opera house. The building was financed by the Papal government, which subsequently sold the theatre's private boxes to Bologna's nobility.[8] Thus, the nobility shared the ownership of the theatre; and the term "Comunale" stood for a "community" of noble owners rather than for a "public" institution in the modern sense of the word. In this respect Bologna's

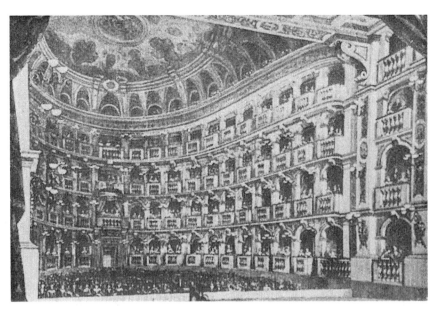

Figure 2.1   One of the First Photographs of the Interior of Bologna's Teatro Comunale, ca. 1870. (Reproduction by Kind Permission of Pàtron Editore.)

Comunale differs from theatres such as the San Carlo in Naples, which was largely "an extension of the court" and a "critical point of contact between the court and the capital."[9] The work of Italy's most famous theatre-architect, Antonio Galli, known as il Bibiena, the Comunale was inaugurated on 14 May 1763 with the first presentation of Gluck's *Trionfo di Clelia,* on a libretto by Metastasio. A preferred composer of the Roman court, Christoph Willibald Gluck had been knighted by the pope shortly before the opening of Bologna's new theatre.[10]

Most of the noble councillors who owned boxes in the theatre after Unification supported the theatre's municipal grant, despite the fact that due to their economic principles the Moderates had an aversion to public expenditure. While they wished to maintain the theatre's social exclusivity and keep it out of the hands of the new political institutions, they needed a municipal grant in order to stage a season which was able to compete with the theatres in Milan, Venice or Naples.

THE *IMPRESARIO* AND L'ANNO TEATRALE

The Teatro Comunale had usually at least two opera seasons, in autumn and during the carnival. The autumn season started early in October and ended on 25 December after about thirty-five performances. The carnival season, with about twenty-five performances, started at the end of December and lasted until Shrovetide. At times the theatre opened for about fifteen performances at Lent (Quaresima) and another twenty in spring (Easter to the end of May). When the theatre stayed open for all four seasons a total of about one hundred performances were staged.[11] From 1820 the city provided a grant, *la dote,* for the opera, put at the disposal of a commercial agent, the *impresario* or *appaltatore.*[12] In addition to the municipal grant the owners of the theatre's private boxes paid an annual fee to the *impresario*. With the help of the grant and the box owners' fees, the *impresario* was expected to stage during the main or autumn season a *spettacolo grandioso* or *regio,* that is, important works of *opera seria* and ballet, "*di genere eroico e grandioso.*"[13] Under the Papal regime the Comunale was often the only theatre in Bologna which was granted the right to present operas and to organise balls during the carnival season—an economic and social privilege of the municipality's theatre and the owners of its prestigious boxes.[14] During the smaller seasons, Lent and spring, the *impresari* usually presented *opere buffe* or *semiserie.*[15] These were less expensive, being performed by a smaller orchestra and less famous artists, and so the council did not necessarily approve a municipal grant.[16] Beyond the grant and the fees, the *impresario* received the income of the box-office, of the theatre's café and restaurant, and he had the right to organise a certain number of lucrative lotteries and masked balls. The *impresario's* expenditure included the honorarium for the orchestra and chorus (numbers were determined by the contract with the local administration), and a staff of about thirty (cloak room, mechanics, usherettes, firemen, and so on), all paid per evening. He had to cover the lighting and heating of the theatre, the emptying of toilets. Even more essential, he had to pay for the rights of performance, usually contracted with the publishers of the scores, if operas were not commissioned directly from the composer (which was less often the case). The *impresario* also provided the *compagnia di canto*, the cast of soloists, increasingly an international business and "at all times by far the greatest single cost of an opera season in a leading theatre."[17] Often the *impresari* used commercial agents to take singers under contract.[18] On occasions composers intervened in the negotiations, hoping to ensure that their works were performed by appropriate singers.[19] From the mid-1860s up to 15% of the theatre's income per evening went toward the composer's royalties. After 1868 the State took 10% tax on the total of the theatres' revenue.[20] Particularly during the autumn season, when the most prestigious and expensive works were presented, the *impresario* often operated at a loss, trying to recover financially during the smaller seasons and through the organisation of masked balls, lotteries and other entertainment.[21] Every detail of the contract was negotiated between *impresario* and municipality, including the number of candles in the theatre (on Bologna's main chandelier alone a total of 180), or the quality of the olive-oil for the other lamps. The contract also fixed the names of the tailors, painters and mechanics working behind the stage, through which the municipality hoped to "provide the bread for the city's respectable and numerous labourforce."[22] Bologna's Academy of Fine Arts had a school for scenery painting with an international reputation; and it was not unusual for the contract to oblige the *impresario* to employ its professors.[23] Only at a later stage, once rehearsals had started, did the conductors intervene in questions of staging and sets, reflecting their new role and growing prestige in Italian theatres from the 1860s. In this respect Angelo Mariani, Bologna's most famous conductor during the 1860s and 70s, became a model for future generations of Italian conductors.[24]

Usually in May the mayor advertised an invitation to present projects for the exercise of the coming *anno teatrale;*[25] occasionally, or when no applications were received, the local administration contacted specific *impresari* directly. Beyond the cast of singers and the total number of performances, the project fixed one new opera by an acclaimed composer; the rest of the repertoire remained "to be announced." The season had to include at least one opera by an Italian composer. The works the *impresario* proposed to the municipal administration often depended on the singers he had under contract for the season (who had the opportunity to impose changes to the score).[26] If the negotiations between the municipality and the agent went on for too long both sides risked finding that the artists in question had already signed contracts with other *impresari,* so that a new cast had to be chosen. Likewise, a publisher could decide to sell the rights for a specific opera to a different *impresario,* and the programme for the season had to be planned anew.[27] Occasionally, contracts between the *impresario* and the municipality were fixed for up to six years, but not infrequently they were broken before completion. From the later decades of the nineteenth century, rather than providing a global grant for the *impresario*, the municipality covered certain of his expenses—*spese serali*—including the payment of orchestra and chorus, dancers, mutes, stage mechanics, lighting, cloakroom attendants and usherettes.[28] The quality of individual performances did not only depend on the artistic and political instincts of the *impresario*. His capacity to place famous composers or their publishers under contract, to attract celebrated divas, or to employ able tailors and scene painters, helped to fill the box-office till, thus generating the necessary revenue for a respectable performance. Beyond this, the quality and success of a season largely depended on subsidies—the grant provided by a monarch, a private businessman, the State, or the municipality. It was possible to lease Bologna's Comunale to an *impresario* without providing a formal *dote* or without covering for the theatre's daily expenditure (*spese serali*); but without a public subsidy, the *impresario* could hardly obtain "*artisti di fama europea*" and compete with the theatres of more generous cities.[29]

The programmes for the theatre's season and the projects of the *impresari* were discussed by the *Deputazione dei pubblici spettacoli*, the municipal committee in charge of most of the city's cultural institutions, public celebrations and popular entertainment.[30] The *Deputazione* took a vote on the projects presented by the different *impresarios*, to be ratified by the *giunta*, the local government, before the mayor signed a contract with the *impresario*.[31] During the transition from the Papal regime to the annexation by Piedmont-Sardinia the mayor received several anonymous letters urging him to introduce new people into the Deputazione, less "incompetent and unsuitable" than those who had dominated the theatre's administration since the 1840s.[32] While under the Papal administration the members of the Deputazione remained in office for up to forty years, under the liberal regime they were appointed for three years only and a third of the members was re-elected every year. For some of Bologna's dignitaries these reforms meant a loss of status and influence. For instance, the secretary of the Academy of Fine Arts, Cesare Masini, known mostly for his religious paintings, had been a member of the Deputazione from 1827 to 1867; after that he had hoped to remain at least an honorary member. Members who had served the Deputazione for such long periods protested against their sudden exclusion from the prestigious committee.[33] But the mayor was determined to modernise the institution. Until 1847 the Deputazione had been presided over by the head of the Papal police, who was viewed by reformers and patriots with suspicion.[34] Under Pius IX the *senatore* (mayor) chaired the Deputazione and after Unification either the mayor or the council's *assessore* in charge of education assumed the presidency. Though nominated by local government, membership did not depend exclusively on—or change with—the council's political majorities. The Democrat Casarini remained part of the Deputazione after his resignation as mayor in 1872; and the Radical Golinelli was a member of the Deputazione together with the Conservative Enrico Pini and the former Moderate mayor Alberto Dallolio; the latter remained the Deputazione's vice president after 1914 when it was chaired by the Socialist mayor Francesco Zanardi.[35] A number of members were politically distinguished—former mayors or members of the Senate. Due to the particular role of the Teatro Comunale in Bologna's cultural self-representation, most members were appointed on the basis of their expertise in music, which favoured the presence of the educated middle classes and of academics, at a time when the majority of Bologna's Moderates still belonged to the city's ancient nobility. In 1867, of the Deputazione's fourteen members six possessed an academic title (*dottore* or *professore*).[36] Despite the Liberals' economizing financial policy, there were a number of opera lovers among the local Moderates who were eager to develop Bologna into an internationally recognised centre of Italy's new musical life. Their artistic priorities did not necessarily differ from the views of the Democratic middle class with an academic or professional background. Prince Hercolani and Count Salina, active both as private patrons and members of the Deputazione, belonged to this group, and so did the Marquis Bevilacqua, honorary president of the Istituzione Rossiniana, the theatre's orchestra. As president of the Deputazione the Moderate Count Salina was in favour of financial support for the theatre even though the Moderate council majority was to limit public expenditure. Correspondingly, a man of the Left like Camillo Casarini was respected by politicians of the Right, due to his competence in music; and when his emphasis on the Comunale's new repertoire brought Bologna into the headlines of the international press, the Moderates too were proud of their ancient theatre's new fame. Decisions of the Deputazione, for example on the projects presented by the *impresari,* were usually taken by secret vote, making it difficult for political observers to analyse preferences in relation to party programme.[37] Moreover, because the Deputazione always comprised a certain number of people who did not support the current political majority in the local council, the mayor was often able to base his decisions on majorities which went beyond his own political affiliation.[38]

Nevertheless, the regular renewal of the Deputazione after 1860 politicised artistic decisions, because it provoked internal debate and impelled members to justify their ideas in front of the mayor, the council and the public. An ancient institution was transformed from an instrument of continuity into an agent of change. Bologna was able to attract the avant-garde of Italy's conductors, men like Angelo Mariani, Franco Faccio, Marino and Luigi Mancinelli and later Arturo Toscanini. The repertoire was transformed from the old *bel canto* tradition to a new emphasis on *grand opéra,* and, later, from Verdi to Wagner. From the time of Luigi Mancinelli, popular symphonic concerts were organized, with tickets that a wider audience could afford. Views on continuity versus change, on *campanilismo* versus *cosmopolitismo,* or musical heritage versus musical futurism were constitutive of public debate in Bologna. The debates transcended political party majorities, but were nevertheless political in content, because they stood for conflicting ideas about the city's self-representation and Bologna's profile as a major centre in the young nation-state.

BOLOGNA'S THEATRES DURING THE POLITICAL AND SOCIAL TRANSITION

Unlike the revolution in Brussels in 1830 the liberation of the Papal Legations in 1859 did not start with an opera; but for Bologna's theatres an important page of history was turned. The privileges of the Teatro Comunale, originally granted by the cardinals, were abolished. These included the exclusive right to present operas during certain periods of the year, when other theatres had to remain closed, or the monopoly on particular balls during the carnival.[39] While early in May 1860 the prefect reminded the provincial police that censorship was still to be applied, a week later it was officially abolished and then replaced with the new Piedmontese legislation.[40] When the theatre's contracts for the next season had to be fixed, the constitution of the new nation-state was far from being completed. An atmosphere of uncertainty reigned in the former Papal Legations and in Italy as a whole. While Bologna wanted to be entertained, wanted to go to the opera and to dance at the theatre's masked balls—its cultural life to go on as usual—the atmosphere in the theatres, and even the contracts between *impresari* and the municipality reflected the political turmoil of the past months:

> In the interest of an honest contract, with a considerable expenditure at risk, the illustrious municipality will agree that it has in some way to insure the smallest possible damage in case of certain eventualities; and it is for this reason that the management proposes for the unexpected case (God forbid!) that political disorders return, war or any other, the contractor has the possibility of suspending performances.[41]

Citing "the practice in other Italian cities" or using as a pretext "the regulations and habits of Piedmont, to which we now legitimately belong," the *impresari* tried to introduce all kinds of changes into their contracts with the municipality. Bologna's Deputazione was not impressed by such arguments and affirmed its own municipal traditions.

The transition from the Papal to the liberal regime was more important for the private theatres than for the Comunale. While the municipal theatre remained under the control of the local administration, the authorities were now deprived of much of their influence over the private theatres.[42] As early as June 1859, illustrating the dynamic of the political change and its symbolic meaning, the owners of the private theatres asked the authorities to relinquish the boxes which under the past regime had to be kept available to them; and they did not hesitate to go to court with their requests if the authorities refused to move.[43] This trend was partly reversed in the mid-1860s, with the increase of central control over the periphery under the 1865 bill on public security. Theatres were again obliged to reserve a box for the prefect and the officers in charge of public security, a decision very much contested by the owners of the theatres.[44] The authorities had the right to attend rehearsals and to inspect the backstage. However, public control of private theatres was now restricted to issues of security. Aware of the rather picturesque customs of some of Bologna's popular theatres, the *questore* of the provincial police forbade access to dogs and other animals, or to people suffering "mental alterations."[45] It was prohibited to offend public morality or the institutions of the family and religion, the institutions of the State and other countries, or to instigate legal disobedience. But on the content of the theatres' programmes the authorities had to remain silent. As Rosmini's compendium on the legislation of theatres sets out: "The freedom of opinion and of the press cannot be violated and any government having this in mind should be aware of this! The times of immobility are passed: this is unmistakably the world of reason, freedom and progress."[46]

Private theatres were not necessarily commercial. During the seventeenth century the majority of Bologna's theatres were private, but most of them were located in the palaces and villas of the nobility.[47] Instead of buying a ticket at the box-office or renting a box, one usually had to be invited to the performances. This practice was the same for most of the nobility's "mundane" entertainment—balls, concerts, intellectual circles—allowing for social exclusiveness and the maintenance of a certain style. Since the times of the Cisalpine Republic numerous commercial theatres, of different size and for different audiences, had opened their doors. Some of these new theatres were built in former convents, like Antonio Contavalli's theatre in the former convent of S. Martino, an important stage for dramatic art, but occasionally also for *opera buffa:* the local premiere of Rossini's *Barbiere* took place there.[48] Until its restoration in the 1860s the Teatro Brunetti was among the less expensive theatres, attracting mostly the middle classes, but also students and workers. From the 1880s it became Bologna's preferred stage for operettas; and later it presented international stars like Eleonora Duse and Sara Bernhardt, who were able to enthuse the entire city: "Run, fat citizens of Bologna, run noble ladies; run to hear Mademoiselle Bernhardt tonight!" the poet Carducci ridiculed the phenomenon.[49] By that time Italy had a total of more than one thousand theatres in eight hundred communes.

Bologna became a major centre in Italy's theatre industry, hosting in 1905 the first "Congresso dei Proprietari e Dirigenti di Teatro."[50] Under the liberal regime the attempts of the private theatres to obtain public subsidies or regular grants, similar to those of the Teatro Comunale, were regularly rejected by the local administration.[51] Privately owned by individual businessmen, they did not belong to those institutions of the municipality which were used by the administration to shape the city's cultural profile. Nevertheless, they were part of a nascent public sphere and their performances enlivened intellectual and political debate in Bologna. Some theatres presented the dramatic works of younger authors, containing social or political criticism; others did not go beyond popular entertainment in local dialect, or vaudevilles presented by amateur players.[52] In this respect the private theatres were very different from the public Teatro Comunale. The local administration, "tutor of the people's civil and moral education," was severely criticised in council when, during the carnival season, they opened the Teatro Comunale for comedies, or for popular sixteenth-century plebeian scenes in dialect. A Moderate administrator like Alberto Dallolio considered "a certain freedom in the use of language" a characteristic of Italian literature, and not out of place at Bologna's most important stage, harmless comedy compared to "the nudism of certain choreographic exhibitions of the modern theatre." But according to the independent councillor Giuseppe Ceri the presentation of such "dirty" and "obscene" comedies "offends morality and civilisation."[53] The Teatro Comunale was supposed to concentrate on opera and ballet. In this, the private companies of the smaller theatres were unable to compete with the Comunale. The Teatro del Corso, Bologna's second theatre after the Comunale, owned by Giuseppe Badini, also rented out private boxes, held by Bologna's wealthy families for contracts of three, six or nine years. In particular foreign visitors admired the Corso. They usually stayed next door to the theatre, in Bologna's most expensive hotel, also owned by Badini. The theatre had been opened in the presence of Emperor Napoleon on 19 May 1805 with the premiere of Ferdinando Paër's *Sofonisba,* starring the young soprano Gioachino Rossini.[54] Mostly during the smaller seasons, Badini was occasionally able to present a *prima* by Rossini (*L'equivoco stravagante*) and he was also responsible for Bologna's first "modern" staging of Mozart's *Don Giovanni* (1818); but only the Comunale, with its permanent orchestra and chorus, was able to compete with Italy's most famous opera houses, La Scala, La Fenice and San Carlo. Only the Comunale was regularly able to attract *impresari* such as Alessandro Lanari, (called by contemporaries "the Napoleon of the *impresari*"); or Gaetano Rambaldi, who presented the legendary sopranos Maria Malibran and Giuseppina Strepponi, later Verdi's wife.[55] Unlike the Comunale, the Teatro del Corso often staged "curiosities." Its performances included "an entertainment with African animals and many dogs of different breeds," Scottish bagpipes, and tableaux vivants.[56] The Corso was also an important stage for spoken drama; but opera, in particular *opera seria,* still enjoyed a higher status in Italy. Despite its role in the municipality's cultural self-representation after Unification, the Comunale's prestigious autumn season of opera and ballet, financed to a large extent through the annual fees of the noble box owners, gave the house the reputation of being Bologna's "aristocratic theatre," a reputation lasting well into the twentieth century.[57]

The Comunale's artistic quality during the nineteenth century was largely based on Bologna's musical infrastructure, notably the Accademia Filarmonica, an institution of great international prestige founded in the seventeenth century, part of which was the conservatory, the Liceo Musicale.[58] The Liceo's professors, chosen by the Accademia and appointed by the town council, constituted the Comunale's orchestra, which was bigger than those in Florence, Venice or Rome. It could be further increased by members of the academy, students of the Liceo and by the municipal band, providing the Teatro Comunale with an excellent structural framework;[59] and not infrequently other famous theatres in Italy, like the Regio in Parma or the Pergola in Florence, asked Bologna for help when they themselves lacked enough trained musicians.[60]

SOCIAL PRIVILEGE, TASTE AND MODERNISATION

For the Papal nobility in Rome the opening of the carnival season at the Teatro Apollo was the most important social event of the year, starting a sequence of six performances per week, with at least one prestigious premiere every season.[61] In Bologna, the second city of the Papal States, the theatre had a similar function. The Comunale's monopoly on certain balls during the carnival season was not only an economic privilege. It also meant that attendance at a ball during carnival remained an exclusive privilege of a few of Bologna's better families, those able to afford a ticket or owners of a private box. Carnival in the Papal Legations was famous: unlike in other parts of Italy, wearing masks was allowed during the entire period of the carnival. Many families spent five or six evenings per week at the theatre, where opera and ballet alternated with balls, gambling or banquets, providing the Papal regime with an useful source of revenue.[62] Hence, participation in the carnival balls was a sign of social distinction—as long as no other theatre was allowed to organise similar events. When after Unification the Comunale lost its ancient privileges the administration and the private box owners sought to maintain at least an idea of the theatre's exclusiveness. Contracts between the municipality and the *impresari* established that the visitors attending the balls had to be decently dressed, and no tobacco, boots, spurs or overcoats were permitted.[63]

Not only the balls but also the musical events at the theatre still reflected the customs and the expectations of Bologna's nobility. Some councillors complained that the theatre remained closed until October, only because the nobility spent the summer "at their villas, returning to town on the first of the month," when the theatre had to be ready.[64] However, the social composition of audiences changed. A growing number of foreign tourists was keen to visit Bibiena's famous theatre during the late summer and the increasingly internationalised opera business made it difficult for the *impresari* to sign contracts with the best artists if the season was too short. The council discussed on many occasions the possibility of moving the opening date of the theatre a month earlier or changing the traditional pattern of autumn and carnival seasons altogether, but against the resistance of the box owners these attempts remained unsuccessful. For Bologna's nobility the Teatro Comunale was the preferred backdrop for staging their social status, even if that status had been challenged since the beginning of the nineteenth century.[65] Going to the opera was the most important leisure activity for the better families, the occupation for most evenings of the *stagione*. After Unification the theatre offered the welcome illusion that the social exclusiveness of their position could be maintained a little longer. Its enactment was renewed during every autumn season; but it depended on the boxes remaining in the nobility's possession—boxes which were more or less prestigious, boxes of first, second or third tier, and more or less exposed to view from the stalls. Used as "miniature drawing rooms," occasionally with an adjacent mini kitchen, most of the boxes were kept by the same families for many generations, decorated individually, often with the family's coat of arms in the centre of the ceiling.[66] Count Carlo Pepoli remembered people "reading, dreaming or sleeping" during the performance, while another contemporary observer maintained that one also went there "*per far l'amore.*"[67] As the municipality's original advertisement of 1762 explains, the boxes were sold for the "*comodo maggiore de' Nobili, e Cittadini.*" The sale covered part of the cost of the prestigious building; and as for an apartment or a house, the owners had to pay a property tax for their boxes.[68] In 1867, of the forty privately owned boxes three belonged to the families of a prince (Hercolani, Spada, Simonetti), fifteen to a marquis, and seventeen to a count. One box belonged to a group of heirs and only one to a family mentioning no title of nobility.[69] Thus, the social profile of Bologna's box owners differed remarkably from that of other leading theatres in Italy, where the lists show "a mixture of nobles and professional men—lawyers, doctors, civil servants."[70] In Reggio Emilia, during the same year, less than half the boxes of the first and second tiers were occupied by titled families (Conte or Marchese), with the majority owned by professional families. Most of the boxes of the third tier in Reggio belonged to merchants, among them many Jewish families. The fourth tier was occupied by members of the middle class who did not belong to the establishment, but were too well off to join the lower middle class on the balconies.[71] The contrast between Reggio and Bologna could not be more striking. In 1884 thirty-six of Bologna's boxes were still privately owned, three by a prince, sixteen by a marquis, fourteen by a count, two by families with other noble titles; only two families without a noble title are mentioned. The municipality owned several boxes which were used by their own representatives; a few boxes were rented on an annual basis to private associations.[72] Those without access to a family box had to buy tickets for the stalls, the gallery or for the few boxes which were not privately owned. Seats in the stalls were usually not numbered and not infrequently the police had to intervene to settle disputes between spectators competing for the best places. Box owners and their guests could avoid these battles.[73] They could decide who and how many persons could use the box during a performance or how often they wanted to make use of it during the year. Their rights and duties as owners of the boxes were fixed in a contract with the city, which remained in force after the cardinal's departure. As mentioned above, in order to attend the *spettacolo regio* of the main or autumn season, the owners of the private boxes made use of their right of priority, usually by paying an annual fee or subscription. During the rest of the year and for any performance which was not defined as *opere eroiche o regie per drammi in musica*—what traditionally meant *opera seria* and a separate ballet—they could use their box free of charge, enjoying comedies, "*opere buffe, e gio-cose, anche in musica, opere in prosa, tragedie.*"[74]

As municipality and box owners shared the property of the theatre, the latter had considerable influence on the content of the main or autumn season. On the basis of their eighteenth-century contracts of ownership and their understanding of what *opere eroiche o regie per drammi in musica* were meant to be, the box owners insisted that every single performance of the autumn season should include a separate ballet in addition to an opera. In the words of Marina Calore this *coreodramma* was not considered a short supplementary "filler" for the evening, but an "imaginative combination of music, dance and scenery with the aim of evoking a specific atmosphere or telling a story."[75] This independent ballet was presented between two acts of the opera or at the end, as the climax of the evening. Sometimes it was framed not by a complete opera, but by a *potpourri* of popular arias and scenes from different operas. In France operas with integrated ballet scenes became fashionable from the late restoration period: Rossini's *Guillaume Tell*, first performed in Paris in 1829, contained *grandiosi ballabili;* likewise Meyerbeer's *grand-opéra*. Italy followed the French model with the so-called *spartito opera-ballo,* such as Marchetti's *Ruy Blas*. Verdi also integrated ballet scenes into some of his operas. These works were much appreciated, but Bologna's box owners insisted on seeing both an opera and a separate ballet in a single performance; otherwise they would not pay their annual fee.[76] Since the 1850s, these ballets had become more and more expensive, due to complex staging and the great number of dancers involved. A usual cast for the autumn season included a distinguished choreographer, a couple of first ballerinas *di rango francese,* a further eight solo dancers, up to forty dancers and a certain number of mimes for the bigger scenes.[77] Among Bologna's most expensive ballet productions were *La Capanna di Tom* (1858) and *Brahama* (1868) which both involved hundreds of dancers.[78] From the early 1860s a particular attraction for the staging of ballets was the use of electric light, as, for example, in Giuseppe Rota's *La Silfide del Pekino,* which was performed with "the greatest possible magnificence and splendour, as it seems appropriate for Bologna's municipal theatre."[79] The financial restrictions under the Moderate administrations of the early 1860s and the council's reluctance to approve a regular grant for the Comunale led to the first performances without ballets and in 1863, when the theatre's endowment was reduced from 30,000 to 20,000 Lire, the first thing the *impresario* Gaibi did was to abolish the ballet. Other theatres in Italy followed the example.[80] After the financial crisis of the early 1870s the employees of the Comunale planned to take over the theatre's management, suggesting once more abolishing the ballet.[81] As a report of the town council summarised the issue in 1875, the traditional evening programme of the autumn season—an *opera seria* and a separate ballet—

had become an obstacle to the maintenance of our theatre . . . It is no longer in demand and does not quite reflect the new tendencies in the arts and in the audiences. At the same time experience has demonstrated that the vast expenditure that it incurs is not matched by the results which are obtained.[82]

The modern opera repertoire—Meyerbeer, Verdi, Wagner—with its complex content and staging requirements hardly allowed for the traditional combination of opera and a separate ballet.[83] When the Teatro Regio in Turin wished to stage *Aida* in 1874, the publisher Ricordi insisted that the opera is presented "*tutta intera di seguito*" and that interruptions with ballet would be "firmly forbidden."[84] As the *Monitore di Bologna* wrote, "choreography had passed its days of glory," a natural consequence of "the law of progress":

A prima ballerina appearing on stage, coiffured and perfumed, turning round like a spinning top, can today only hope for some vulgar applause from the upper balconies and the impudent admiration of the occasional pretty countess, who stubbornly refuses to recognise the signs of the new times.[85]

However, interpreting the modern standards of performance as a breach of their contract, the private box owners were reluctant to pay their annual fee for the autumn season if no separate ballet was staged. Usually, if box owners did not use their box during the autumn season, they returned their keys to the *impresario,* who then had the right to sell the seats through the box-office. As the box owners considered performances without ballet as derogation from conditions specified in their ancient contracts, they not only refused to pay, they also retained their keys. This situation regularly provoked an outcry of anger in the local press and caused considerable financial loss to the *impresario* and the municipality: From the 1860s, whenever the box owners protested against the programme of the autumn

season, the theatre lost between 15,000 and 16,000 Lire.[86] The box owners, who sought in this way to resist the changes imposed by the new liberal
administration, included not only the old families of the Catholic opposition, the "black aristocracy" of the Malvezzi, Campeggi, or Ranuzzi, but
many Moderates of the local political establishment like the Bevilacqua,
Zucchini, Pepoli, Amorini.[87] Bologna's old noble families were conscious
that despite the political and social changes of recent years they had the
economic means to keep the theatre their own, to influence its artistic fate,
or just to resist change in a spirit of revenge against modern times and
their loss of status. Moreover, even if they did not attend the regular performances of opera during the autumn, the box owners still had the right
to use their box on all other occasions, making it impossible for the man-
ager to calculate in advance how many seats could be sold.[88] Last but not
least, if a significant number of boxes remained empty during the autumn
season, this not only resulted in an economic loss for the *impresario*, but
also made it more difficult to present the season as having been a success,
particularly when new operas were performed. The Comunale's change to
the performance of opera without separate ballet as well as the change of
repertoire reflected the ongoing transformation of society. Local politicians
fought for a "modern" performance without separate ballet and based on
operas which would bring Bologna to the attention of the international
press. Their determination illustrates the new impact of political representation on cultural policy under the liberal regime. The new style of performance without ballet made the evening at the theatre less glamorous and
less aristocratic, but attracted a new audience—"strange people with very
indecorous customs and behaviour," as some Moderate members of Bologna's town council complained in 1875.[89] The *impresari* who organised the
Comunale's balls, rather than counting on the traditional contribution of
Bologna's few noble and wealthy families, aimed at attracting a broad and
less exclusive public through unusually low entrance fees of only one Lira.[90]
Count Malvezzi criticised this system: "It is true that, as a consequence,
people come in droves, but what people! And how much unsuitable behaviour has occurred in the theatre and how much disorder? . . . It would be
desirable that this should be stopped by fixing the price of a ticket at no less
than two Lire."[91]

THE END OF EXCLUSIVITY

Confronted with increasing difficulties of municipal finance and the gradual transformation of social structures, the box owners' position in determining the fate of the theatre came under fire. The local administration
sought to address the financial loss which the *impresari* and indirectly the
citizenship suffered due to the box owners' reluctance to pay their annual
fees. Even if the box owners paid, their contribution was considered too

small to make a valuable opera season possible. As they occupied most of the tiers, the municipality was unable to generate significantly more income by increasing the prices for ordinary seats in the stalls or the upper gallery. Nevertheless, Bologna's Moderate administrations, relying on the support of the same noble families who owned the theatre boxes, hesitated to demand box owners for a higher contribution to the expensive autumn season. Instead, the Moderate councillors Bevilacqua and Minghetti suggested abolishing the municipal grant, encouraging the owners of the private boxes to form an association to take over the theatre without the participation of the municipality.[92] Thus, the city would loose its most important institution of cultural self-representation and the theatre would become the private business of a small number of noble families able to maintain a private box. However, "with a single voice" the box owners declared "their inability to commit themselves to any such project."[93] According to Prince Hercolani, who had previously served as a member of the Deputazione, local government had an obligation to the owners of the boxes: By acquiring the boxes they had enabled the municipality to build the theatre and in return had been promised regular performances, under the terms of their contracts. The box owners rejected the initiative, decisively and without much debate. Despite the Moderates' intention to reduce public spending, their attitude to the box owners' privileges had hardly changed. As part of the theatre's restoration during the 1860s parts of the corridor in the stalls were incorporated into the lateral boxes of the counts Malvezzi and Pallavicini, without the council being asked for its consent.[94] After the restoration councillors of the Right and the Left demanded that the prices for tickets be reduced, to make the theatre accessible to a larger portion of the population. Their proposal was rejected by the Moderate majority, who argued that the theatre's subsidy was insufficient to finance great performances and that the *impresario* should therefore be free to fix prices in line with his expenditure and in relation to the law of supply and demand.[95] Again, this decision favoured the box owners, whose annual fee remained unchanged. The theatre remained what it always had been, a *lieu de rencontre* for the local nobility.

Financial shortages at the beginning of the 1870s and Bologna's first Democratic administration brought the question of the box owners' financial contribution to the theatre's autumn season back onto the agenda. Since the local Left under Camillo Casarini had come to power, council debates were more strongly influenced by the representation and the arguments of the rising middle classes.[96] According to the municipal committee appointed to study the problem of the private boxes, the existing terms of the contract were intolerable. They made it "either impossible to find an *impresario* at all, which is very damaging to the city; or, if an *impresario* is found, his vast expenditure for the ballet prevents us from performing operas with artists who match the theatre's reputation."[97] Councillor Gustavo Sangiorgi, a local journalist, remarked that the existing contract with the box owners "is a century old and bears no relation to the changing circumstances regarding the quality, scale and cost of today's performances. There is an absolute need for change. This has been said many times, but nothing has ever been accomplished."[98]

The annual contribution of the box owners should not depend on their individual appreciation of the performance, he said; anyone who refused to pay should lose the right to use the box not only during the autumn season but for the entire year. Under the current circumstances even a much higher grant would not be sufficient to finance the theatre.[99] As Enrico Panzacchi pointed out, due to the small size of the permanent orchestra and choir, most of the municipality's annual grant was spent on the staging of the operas to which the box owners contributed too little.[100] Councillor Gualtiero Sacchetti suggested abolishing the ballet completely and concentrating resources on opera, regardless of the box owners' views; moreover, he wanted prices for tickets to be considerably lower, making the theatre accessible to new audiences. Sacchetti himself was not a Democrat, but represented the new generation of Moderates in the council, not a landowner, but a professional politician of middle class background with close links to local business. Camillo Casarini insisted that no reform should result in higher prices for tickets.[101] The box owners were asked to take account of "the changing conditions of our time and of performances in particular"; they had to pay their annual fees if they wanted to keep their boxes, whatever programme the administration would decide to stage. Although some councillors continued to defend the idea that "without a ballet the performance cannot be considered complete," the council had finally taken a firm position on the question and now sought a juridical solution to the conflict.[102]

The box owners' argument pointed to a problem of definition, raised by the stylistic transformation of opera, ballet and more generally the style of performances in Italian theatres during the past hundred years. With reference to the box owners' eighteenth-century contract and seeking a legal solution to the problem, the mayor asked the municipal librarian to research the "nature and character of ballets" performed since the theatre's inauguration with the aim of obtaining "an exact interpretation of the concept *opere eroiche* or *drammi in musica.*"[103] This approach encapsulates the difficulties both parties had in appreciating the fact that social change constituted the basis of this conflict. After several months of research the librarian Frati responded to the mayor's request with a detailed essay on the history of the concept "opera" since the eighteenth century, in which he tried to determine for which kind of performance the box owners were obliged to pay annual fees. Frati was an expert in historical research and the editor of Bologna's ancient statutes. His argument went back to Rousseau's critique of eighteenth century French theatre, explaining that dances were originally part of the drama itself and each act of an opera had its own ballet, even if the narrative itself did not require such scenes. "But good sense and reason would soon ban such feasts and entertainment, which not only interrupted the action and weakened its effect, but which roughly replaced the language of words with that of gestures and capers, destroying any *verisimilitude*."[104] Rousseau and later also Gluck turned against a form of *opera seria* whose principal idea had become to exhibit skill and "bravura of *castrati* and *prime donne*"—and of ballerinas. Instead, music was supposed to communicate dramatic action.[105] Therefore theatres increasingly presented ballets which were performed independently from opera. They gained in importance and became more expensive, in particular in respect to the number of dancers and the extravagance with which the works were staged.[106] In order to meet the costs and to avoid competition from other theatres, a prefectorial regulation of 1806 determined that "on the occasion of *opera e ballo serio* at the Teatro Comunale . . . any other performance [in the entire city] is forbidden, including private performances."[107] Based on this privilege, the Comunale's *impresari* were able to finance this form of performance until it was removed by the liberal regime. From 1819 the separate ballet was mentioned in the contracts between the municipality and the *impresari*;[108] but the ancient contracts between the municipality and the box owners were never adapted accordingly. Frati's report therefore concludes that the original terminology of the box owners' contract cannot be defined as a combination of opera and ballet, even if since the end of the eighteenth century such combinations had become fashionable and customary. If in the past the Teatro Comunale presented ballets between acts or after the opera, this was an additional splendour and entertainment which the Napoleonic and later the restored Papal regime offered to Bologna's social elite.[109]

Confronted with the committee's report, the box owners decided to change their legal strategy. They no longer insisted on their interpretation of the contract's terminology, but pointed to their prescriptive right of habit:

> For sixty years the fee has never been asked for when there was no ballet; and at no point has anybody maintained that a ballet can be replaced . . . by a dance as part of the opera itself. Moreover, it is manifest that if the ballet is abolished, the concept of *eroico e grandioso* would become vague and unclear; and at every performance the argument between commune and box-owners would arise again.[110]

The box owners reminded the mayor that even in 1867 the contract signed between the mayor and the *impresario* still defined the "*spettacolo regio*" as "*opera seria in musica e ballo grande*."[111] Although the municipality won the case in the first instance, the box owners still refused to give up and proposed that a committee composed of two representatives of each party (box owners and municipality) would decide from year to year if a season corresponded to the criterion of "grandiosity" or not. Moreover, they promised to pay an annual fee of 400 Lire if the council approved a grant of at least 40,000 Lire. Again, their argument was based on the idea that the municipality owed them an exclusive form of entertainment, notwithstanding the fact that the municipality's contractual obligation would violate the council's rights to fix the municipal budget from year to year. The proposal was rejected and, once again, the box owners' refusal to pay resulted in a loss of 12,950 Lire.[112]

A SOCIAL REVOLUTION

Another decade passed until in 1884 the court of appeal pronounced a judgement favourable to the municipality.[113] The sentence was of immense symbolic importance. As the liberation of the Papal Legations in 1859 had hardly been a social revolution, little had changed regarding Bologna's most famous theatre—apart from the suppression of censorship. With the law suit Bologna's nobility effectively lost its privileged position and its economic and legal power to insist on the traditional style of programme. Not private box owners, but political representatives of the citizens and professional experts were to determine the fate of the theatre as the principal institution of the city's self-representation. The judgement enabled the Comunale to follow a trend which throughout Europe characterised the opening up of opera houses to the middle classes: a transformation of the theatre's traditional style of performance and a modern differentiation of theatrical genres.[114] In Bologna this meant abolishing the expensive combination of opera and ballet, the theatre's focus on entertainment and effect, emphasising instead the narrative or symbolic content of a single work, its romantic, historical or realist meaning. By introducing these changes the political and cultural actors followed different motives: the conductor Angelo Mariani and his successors had artistic reasons, keen to extend the repertoire of an excellent orchestra; the *impresari* and publishers hoped to sell Verdi and Wagner in Bologna and avoid the costs of an additional ballet; for politicians like Camillo Casarini it was part of a social programme, marking the end of a socially exclusive cultural policy. With the 1884 judgement the question of who owned the theatre was finally resolved and an important barrier against modernisation was removed, allowing Bologna to be brought into line with European trends of nineteenth-century opera.

Is this an all too optimistic conclusion? The private boxes still occupied a considerable amount of space in the theatre. Although their owners were now obliged to pay their annual fees if they wanted to keep their box, some of them still deserted the theatre if the performance did not correspond to their taste. As the mayor Tacconi complained in an 1888 council meeting, many of their seats remained empty during Verdi's *Otello* or Wagner's *Tristan*, while the *impresari* and the municipality would have been keen to sell them to new audiences.[115] The relatively small number of seats sold through the box-office made it difficult to generate enough income to stage important works adequately. While the Comunale had not more than 1500 seats, the Corso counted over 2000 and the Nuovo Brunetti 2500 seats, the same number as the San Carlo in Naples. The Scala in Milan had a total of

4000 seats, enabling the *impresario* to reinvest some of his returns into the season.[116] In order to gain at least some additional rows of seats the administration decided to reduce the stage to its original size, as planned by Bibiena in the eighteenth century. This decision was open to objection, because in Bibiena's days the requirements to stage an opera were different from what was needed for Wagner, Puccini and Strauss in the early twentieth century.[117] The intervention increased the number of seats, but damaged the theatre's artistic potential. The owners of the private theatres took much more drastic measures than the municipality to adapt their houses to the changing conditions of the market. They gained considerable seating space in 1860, when the ecclesiastical, municipal and governmental authorities had to abandon their boxes.[118] Moreover, at the end of the century, the owner of the Teatro del Corso decided to modify the seating space of three balconies. Following a principle first applied during the French Revolution, only two balconies retained their individual boxes, while the others were transformed into open galleries, nearly doubling the number of available seats. The owner had to go through several years of bitter argument with the occupants of the boxes before they finally liquidated their contracts.[119] The opera house in Berlin did the same as early as 1789, Palermo in 1830, La Scala in Milan and La Fenice in Venice followed later on; at Bologna's Comunale this never happened.[120] Selling more seats helped to democratise theatres and the higher income allowed the *impresario* to finance more expensive productions.

According to Bologna's Democratic councillors, the Comunale remained an "eminently aristocratic theatre, because only a very small portion of the public can make use of it."[121] Their criticism was not directed against theatre in general, but against a cultural policy which favoured the "privileged classes of society." Their criticism remained unheard: shortly before the First World War the conservative mayor Marquis Tanari still described the Teatro Comunale self-confidently as "an ancient, an aristocratic theatre with a limited capacity. . . . All this . . . constitutes a serious and insuperable objection to the demand for a further reduction of ticket prices."[122]

3 Money and Culture

In most parts of ninteenth-century Europe urban planning and expenditure for cultural representation formed a central aspect of municipal administration. In Italy this remained a contested issue. While Florence, even before becoming the kingdom's new capital in 1864, witnessed its "urban revolution,"[1] other Italian cities lagged behind in developing infrastructure and cultural institutions. In Bologna one of the administration's first initiatives after the end of the Papal regime was a revision of the commune's finances. In May 1861 the councillor Fagnoli presented a report on the communal budgets between 1852 and 1858, leading the council not only to disapprove of the existing bureaucratic procedures as such, but also to note major irregularities in the city's public finance.[2] Already before the presentation of this report the municipality had raised a public loan of four million Lire to finance a series of urgent urban developments and to make a first step towards the transformation of the medieval town into a modern city. As Alaimo has demonstrated, these plans involved the expropriation of numerous ancient estates and aimed at building several prestigious avenues in the centre, to be flanked by modern apartment blocks.[3] The municipality hoped to make considerable profit from selling these estates, promising subscribers 6% interest for the loan. However, the expropriations were time-consuming and expensive, and some of them failed completely. Moreover, Bologna's prices for real estate after Unification did not develop as expected, ultimately obliging the municipality to sell their developments at a loss. An important chapter of the Moderates' policy in Bologna and part of their long-term financial planning thus resulted in a failure, limiting the city's capacity to pursue an active cultural policy.[4]

Due to the legal framework imposed upon the periphery from the centre, municipal autonomy was highly restricted in Liberal Italy.[5] Largely due to these pressures, the local Moderates adopted the financial doctrine of the governing Liberals, resulting in a severe savings programme and affecting in particular the spending on urban development and cultural institutions. The semi-official periodical *Rassegna settimanale* regularly criticized the

Italian cities' expenditure "*di lusso*" after Unification. The excessive trend towards local "embellishment" was regarded as "unseemly" for a country such as Italy, which had not even invested sufficiently in its national defence.[6] In Bologna the expenses for the wars of liberation and the subsequent increase in interest rates were repeatedly used to justify financial restrictions. The city's financial contributions to the nation's war effort were seen as a question of prestige, while spending for public gardens qualified as an extravagance of local administrators.[7] The mayor Marquis Gioacchino Pepoli repeatedly criticised "the unjustifiable and exorbitant pretensions of the big communes . . . *le feste, i teatri, i gaudi.*"[8] "I don't think it would damage the public administration if a mayor, deciding to descend into his grave, abstained from leaving traces of his reign in the form of monuments or public gardens."[9]

After Unification municipal theatres were especially under the attack of the Liberals. Leopoldo Franchetti, a Liberal from Tuscany close to Pasquale Villari and Sidney Sonnino, criticised in particular those mayors who considered building theatres before having built the public roads to which they were committed by law: "A good portion of the country's savings is buried in an eagerness for public works of luxury."[10] Gioacchino Pepoli himself "never understood why one pays for the theatre and its divine voices with the money of taxpayers, who themselves do not take part in these events for the recreation of the rich, who have to remain at home, in the cold, and probably hungry."[11] Their opponents, supporters of an active cultural policy, like the periodical *Nuova Antologia,* accused Cavour's party of "being largely responsible for the government's artistic absenteeism." The *Gazzetta Musicale di Milano* complained that "the Kingdom of Italy did nothing for its music."[12] In 1867 Italy ceded the last theatres it had inherited from its former states to the municipalities, with no obligation to support them with public subsidies. Numerous theatres had to close; others became the objects of long judicial battles.[13] However, according to the Liberals' view, theatres should be private and not operate on the basis of public subsidies. Social or cultural entertainment was not seen as a public responsibility. Culture was understood as serving the social representation of status, of social groups or families, but not of cities or the nation.

The Right's criticism of municipal "*spese di lusso*" was largely based on the notables' own economic interests in restricted taxation. In 1869 the prefect of Novara, Zoppi, argued polemically that "those voters paying the highest taxes had the honour of covering the bill for high and too often simply crazy expenditure [*spese pazze*]," making reference to bells and organs for churches, uniforms for the National Guards and subscriptions for monuments—all this "pure vanity."[14] The local Moderates in Turin and in particular Quintino Sella, member of the government as well as a local councillor in Italy's first capital, expressed similar views. At the beginning of the twentieth century economists such as Luigi Einaudi criticized Italy's static financial policies during these years.[15] As the examples quoted above illustrate, this financial policy was often coupled with a paternalistic attitude towards the lower strata of the population: Franchetti described the expenditure for "buildings of luxury" as a sign of the "unlimited and absolute power of the propertied class upon the poor"—socially and financially irresponsible because through the municipal tax on consumption the poor had to contribute to municipal expenditure without taking advantage of theatres or being interested in monuments. Franchetti understood his criticism explicitly as the Moderates' answer to the "social question."[16]

COMPULSION

The municipal law of 1865 introduced national uniformity in matters of municipal administration and restricted the communes' expenditure according to the Moderates' principles of financial policy. The principal position of any municipal budget was the "compulsory expenditure" (*spese obligatorie*) imposed upon the communes by central government and controlled by the prefect.[17] This position included expenditure for primary education, the administration and the police force, salaries for municipal employees, assistance to the poor, as well as the maintenance of public buildings, estates and infrastructure. The municipalities regarded the imposition of this expenditure as interference in their autonomy. Moreover, "compulsory expenditure" included positions that were described by critics as the responsibility of the State. "Facultative expenditure" (*spese facoltative*) only covered "services and offices of public utility,"[18] including nevertheless essential positions such as the lighting and paving of inner city streets and the costs of supporting voluntary fire brigades. The legislator defined these positions as "not compulsory". Depending on their individual financial situation, the communes could be forced to make savings on these positions. Under "spese facoltative" they were allowed to include expenditure for their cultural self-representation such as subsidies for theatres or exhibitions, the celebration of public events and commemorations, the municipal band or subscriptions for monuments. Keen to develop its profile as a place of learning and academic culture,[19] Bologna included under "spese facoltative" subsidies for the university, professional schools and the Liceo Musicale. A city like Bologna, with limited economic resources, depended for its own development on institutes of secondary and higher education, on libraries and museums.[20] The distinction between "facultative expenditure" and "compulsory expenditure" was not always clear and, especially during the first years after Unification, led to considerable debate in the council.[21]

Subsidies from central government, which used to be common under the *ancien régime,* were withdrawn after Unification. For Bologna this presented a matter of considerable concern. As the capital of the Legations and second city of the Papal States, the city was confronted with an enormous

expenditure for cultural representation and for services linked to its function as a regional centre, comparable to the situation of other cities which
after Unification lost their status as the capitals of the ancient Italian states:
Naples, Milan, Venice, Parma, Modena, (Turin and Florence, as temporary
capitals of the new kingdom, represent a different case). For many years
these cities had nothing to make up for "the courts, the bureaucracies and
the attendant luxury trades that once had made them relatively prosper-
ous."[22] Theatres were among the institutions which suffered most under
their loss of status after Unification. In 1868 their situation was further
aggravated when the government imposed a 10% tax on all theatre takings, making performances more expensive, at a time when most theatres
struggled with the growing costs of appropriate staging.

During the first years after Unification the national legislation regarding municipal income remained unclear and changes in the cities' financial
situation were difficult to foresee. Any expenditure had to be generated
by the cities' own sources of income: taxes on consumption (*dazio di con-
sumo*), local duties and, within certain limits, super-impositions on national
taxes.[23] To a large extent the communal budget—including spending on
cultural representation—was financed by consumers, including those who
were excluded from the suffrage or who would never attend a public performance at the Teatro Comunale or the Liceo Musicale. Therefore the tax
on consumption remained a major point of division between the political
groups represented in Bologna's town council.[24] Moreover, the "compulsory
expenditure," imposed upon the communes by the State, often exceeded
the total of the cities' income; and central government continued to extend
this position, raising regularly criticism of prefects, local politicians and
the legal profession.[25] Considering the growing burden of "compulsory
expenditure" during the first decades after Unification, any expenditure
beyond the positions imposed from the centre became extremely difficult.
As a symbol of prestige and despite growing financial pressures Pavia maintained its school of arts and its municipal band; other towns their local
lyceum.[26] Pisa allowed itself to build a new theatre, but reached the highest pro capita deficit of all the bigger Italian towns.[27] Cities like Florence,
Ancona and Rome were insolvent in the 1870s and obliged to ask the State
to intervene on their behalf, resulting in further loss of autonomy.[28] The
situation in Naples was similar, but here the municipality continued to contribute 180,000 and soon even 300,000 Lire to the opera's annual budget,
an amount Bologna's *mélomanes* could only dream of.[29]

MONEY AND MUSIC

Identifying closely with the Right's financial doctrine, for Bologna's Moderate administration savings on public expenditure were the order of the day,
even if it risked damaging the city's precious patrimony. Some councillors

suggested at regular intervals closing Bologna's prestigious conservatory, the Liceo Musicale, linked to famous names such as Donizetti and Rossini, arguing that this institution absorbed a considerable portion of the annual budget.[30] Similarly, the municipal band was often described as an unnecessary burden on the city's taxpayers. Originally part of the National Guards, which represented a revolutionary legacy unwelcome by the Moderates, the *Banda Civica* played for official celebrations and funerals, as well as giving weekly concerts on a central square during the summer months.[31] Together with the professors of the Liceo Musicale, the band formed the orchestra for the Teatro Comunale. Recognising the band's financial difficulties, some councillors suggested in 1863 a more substantial subsidy, but several Moderate councillors questioned the commune's obligations in this respect. Count Ercolani, belonging to the group around Minghetti, pronounced himself against any increase in the band's grant, reminding his colleagues of the expenditure for the conservatory and the theatre. Marquis Bevilacqua, likewise an old friend and collaborator of Minghetti, suggested privatising the band, supposed to then generate its own income through commercial activity.[32] The council remained undecided on this critical issue, until it realised that due to obligatory public celebrations, in particular the Constitutional day, it could not renounce having a band. As a matter of urgency the contract was finally renewed and the band was even allowed to appoint some new musicians.[33] After the short interlude of Casarini's Democratic administration, which invested considerably in the city's musical infrastructure, the band was again under threat of the Moderates' savings programmes. A few councillors made the case for the renewal of its grant: "Even the smallest villages maintain well instructed and disciplined corps of music, which on festive occasions provide a service." They reminded the council of their band's fame, hailed by people from all over the country during the inauguration of the monument for Gioacchino Rossini in Pesaro, and, just recently, by the international visitors attending Bologna's Conference on prehistoric sciences, when it had performed not only the usual Italian titles, but an international repertoire.[34] The historian of these debates has to consider that, at the time, attending a concert by the municipal band was one of the rare occasions when people could listen to music at all. Comparing Bologna to the smaller towns in the province, which were able to afford their own bands, brought local pride into play and turned the discussion in favour of the band's survival. As a condition for the renewal of its grant the council imposed new regulations, which brought the band under the control of the municipal *Deputazione dei pubblici spettacoli*.[35]

Theatres continued to be at the centre of debates on communal finances. As a member of Italy's early governments after Unification, Minghetti was well aware of the crisis of the Italian theatres after the disappearance of the ancient states, but he was equally determined that the nation-state as their successor would not take responsibility for their survival.[36] To enable an *impresario* to mount a successful season the subsidy of a leading theatre had to be roughly equal to the takings.[37] During the 1870s, when Bologna's Comunale had to live on a public subsidy of ca. 30,000 Lire, La Scala received Lit. 200,000; the Pergola in Florence Lit. 100,000 and the Apollo in Rome lit. 140,000.[38] La Fenice in Venice was often unable to find an impresario prepared to confront the financial risk of organising a season without adequate subsidies, and during the late nineteenth century, for eleven out of twenty-four years, its doors remained shut. Naples' San Carlo, used to generosity before and even after 1860, remained closed for three successive seasons during the 1870s; the Pergola in Florence ceased to produce regular performances of opera after 1877; and La Scala remained shut after 1897 due to conflicts with the box owners and because the commune was unable or unwilling to provide the *dote*.[39] In Naples, Parma and Modena the quality of the opera seasons declined during these years.[40] Why should a successful impresario run the risk of a season in an Italian theatre when government grants abroad were twice or three times higher than in Italy's best endowed opera houses? Moreover, in Paris the higher grants made it possible for prices to be about a third of the tickets at La Scala or the San Carlo, thus reducing the risk of performing in front of an empty house.[41]

During the Restoration period, Bologna was often able to attract the better *impresari* and companies due to its relatively substantial grant from the Papal government.[42] After the Liberation the new political regime called a committee to study the future of the city's municipal theatre. In January 1860 it urged the council to improve the funding for the theatre in order to respond to the increased expenditure of *impresari* and to allow for the modernisation of the Comunale's technical equipment. The annual contribution of the box owners should be increased to meet the costs of modern opera performances. Although the council thanked the committee for its efforts, any further investment in the city's cultural infrastructure was deemed inappropriate for a country at war.[43] Among the few initiatives in favour of the theatre was the acquisition of an organ, indispensable for the modern repertoire which the theatre's new conductor Angelo Mariani wished to perform.[44] The municipal subsidy of 7000 Scudi was maintained, but the grant was not increased and investment in the theatre's equipment was postponed. Subsequently, in November 1861, Marco Minghetti imposed his saving plans upon the council.[45] He was unable to justify the use of taxpayers' money for such purposes. Public subsidies would only lead to competition over which cities paid the largest grant and had the finest theatre. Theatres "do not even produce anything useful." Minghetti's position found support on the extreme Left, which viewed the grant as a subsidy for the entertainment of the rich.[46]

Although a number of councillors averted the risk of the theatre remaining closed, the annual grant was eliminated. Bologna's drastic decision alerted other administrations, equally keen to cut expenditure. In a reply to an enquiry from Piacenza, Bologna explained that it wanted its decision to be understood as "a proof of the system of free competition," which does not allow subsidies.[47] Only when it became virtually impossible to find an impresario, in 1863 and 1864, did the council discuss the issue again. Some councillors proposed compensating the members of the orchestra, usually paid by the impresario, as public employees with a monthly salary, but this turned out to be more expensive than paying the grant.[48] Privatising the theatre altogether was legally impossible, due to the municipality's obligations towards the box owners.[49] Presenting arguments "of economic order," the *Minghettiani* rejected once again the idea that the municipality had an obligation to finance a programme which corresponded to the city's prestige and musical tradition.[50] As a compromise the council agreed to contribute at least to certain items of the *impresario's* expenditure, to be agreed from year to year by individual contracts.

In cases when a mayor had a particular interest in opera, he would try to deal with matters regarding the theatre without involving the council. In 1861, the mayor Marquis Pizzardi was confronted with the urgent need to undertake restoration work at the theatre, in particular to the facade and the roof of the theatre's atrium, which according to the *assessore* Buggio could collapse at any moment.[51] The Papal administration would have contributed to such works. Under the new regime the mayor's enquiries in Turin were unsuccessful. During the debate Bibiena's original plans of the theatre were rediscovered, enabling the municipality to install modern technical equipment while respecting the theatre's original design.[52] Although a number of councillors insisted on discussing these projects,[53] the mayor asked for a free hand in this matter—otherwise, the "necessary speed of the intervention could not be maintained." Regarding the council as incompetent in these matters, the administration was authorized to undertake the necessary studies for the project and the discussion of the costs was postponed.[54]

The new budget included 65,000 Lire to repair the theatre's roof as well as the facade.[55] While the municipal engineers warned that any further delay might cause accidents, numerous councillors still wished to avoid this expenditure.[56] After a long debate the council approved the expenditure for the roof, but the work on the façade was further delayed. In the meantime, the theatre had to be closed.[57] When the commune finally started the work, the council immediately intervened, criticizing the administration for spending too much and for avoiding discussions in council.[58]

The local government was torn between its own economic principles and its responsibility for public safety. Enrico Bottrigari belonged to one of those old noble families who supported the Risorgimento, but who still conceived of the theatre as their own responsibility. He criticized the aesthetic limitations of the restoration works, but recognised that the project was conditioned by the commune's financial misery.[59] The Liberals' views on these matters were not shared by everybody. The debates in the council and among the citizenry reveal disappointment with the commune's limited capability to meet public expectations in cultural representation.

The administration relied on collaboration with cultural and professional experts and was therefore often more ambitious in this respect than the majority of the council members. At the same time numerous councillors felt that the administration tried to avoid confronting the council on these issues, coming close to violating the municipal statutes. Depending on a Moderate majority, the administration found it increasingly difficult to obtain the council's support for its cultural policies. Asking for consent only after *faits accomplis* seemed the only option, and there was no reason to fear that as a consequence the same old families would vote for the Democratic Left in the next elections.

While most Moderate councillors wished to reduce expenditure, very different were the views among Bologna's Democratic opposition: "Every other city is ahead of us; and Bologna still has a medieval system of public administration, with no proper building regulations, no covered market, no *passeggiata* for the public, no washing facilities, no public baths."[60] The cities with Democratic majorities were criticized by Liberals such as Alessandro Salandra: "A certain middling bourgeoisie, of limited means, which profiting from the power that has come to it from the false democratic movement of opinion, oppresses both the men of property on the one hand, and the poor on the other, and misuses its power in the local administrations."[61] Marco Minghetti, then prime minister, insisted in 1874 that "facultative expenditure . . . has the effect of unfairly burdening the landed property."[62] His assessment was marked by economic self-interest and a few decades later Giovanni Giolitti would come to a very different evaluation of the policies of past governments:

> The classes in power have been spending enormous sums of money on themselves and their own interests, and have obtained the money almost entirely from the poorer sections of society. We have a large number of taxes paid predominantly by the poor, on salt, on gambling, the *dazio* on grain and so forth, but we have not a single tax which is exclusively on wealth as such.[63]

The financial priorities of the Moderate political class help to explain why during the 1860s-Emilia-Romagna stayed poor, but at the same time figured among the regions with the lowest public deficit.[64] During this period Bologna missed the opportunity to give its cultural heritage—the arts, the Bibiena theatre, its medieval architecture—the political attention it needed to establish the city as one of the cultural centres of the new nation-state. As illustrated by the conflict on the boxes of the Teatro Comunale, the city's cultural institutions remained for a long time dominated by the city's traditional elites. The wider public, the middle classes, the city's academics and cultural experts only gradually came to participate in political decisions regarding the city's patrimony. As the debates with the box owners have demonstrated, the administration's influence on matters of repertoire and performance were limited and at least initially it was hardly in a position to use the theatre as an object of its cultural self-representation. The Moderates maintained an ambiguous position towards investment in the city's cultural infrastructure. While they needed institutions like the theatre to display their own social status, subsidies also meant public accountability and resulted in a limitation of their personal influence on what was performed and how.

Attitudes on public spending depended to a large extent on political preferences, as a comparison with Pisa illustrates. Pisa had an old eighteenth-century theatre which, similar to Bologna's Comunale, was partly owned by the local nobility. In 1865 a group of citizens, representing Pisa's rising middle class, established a society to build their own theatre.[65] The secretary of the association was Pisa's Democratic mayor. The *R. Teatro Nuovo* was not only to be bigger, offering a sufficient number of seats for the new social strata interested in opera, it also had to be built with the latest technical equipment, allowing for the performance of a modern repertoire. Both theatres were equipped with boxes. However, in the new theatre the best boxes were no longer occupied by the aristocracy, but by the city's commercial and industrial elite, most of them *"uomini nuovi."*[66] Many old families did not consider renting a box in the new theatre. The municipality's grant for the new theatre, 25,000 Lire annually, was smaller than Bologna's, but very generous considering Pisa's less important position among the Italian theatres.[67] With its *R. Teatro Nuovo* Pisa's middle classes celebrated their recently acquired social and political status as citizens of a rapidly developing economic and administrative centre. The local Moderates, representing the political opposition in Pisa, held their political meetings in the aristocratic *Settecento* theatre.

Was Pisa an exception? Even cities with a more urgent agenda of infrastructural developments, such as the maritime city of Syracuse in Sicily, allowed their urban middle class to build a new modern theatre after Unification. Initiated in 1872, due to continuous financial difficulties it took Syracuse until 1897 to open the House, but the project remained a priority throughout this long period.[68] The number of new public theatres in post-Unification Italy never came close to the peak of the Restoration period, but for many cities a new theatre was recognised as a symbol of pride for the rising middle classes. The decision to build a theatre in the first instance depended largely on the political majorities of the council and the social groups they represented.

A DEMOCRATIC INTERLUDE

In 1869 Bologna's principle newspaper during these years, *Il Monitore di Bologna,* summarised the first ten years of Moderate administration after the Liberation in bitter words: "Bologna, a city of over 100,000 inhabitants could have and should have done a lot: it did little, spent a lot, and did badly."[69] Similarly critical was the report of the central government's delegate, who led the interim administration after the resignation of the Moderate *giunta* in 1868 and produced a precise analysis of the city's financial situation, the structure of its administration and the development of the urban infrastructure during the previous decade.[70] Due to the failure of its urban development projects, and despite its reluctance to invest in the city's cultural representation, the Moderate administration left its successor a public deficit of 9,496,923 Lire.[71]

The years between 1868 and 1872, under the Democratic mayor Camillo Casarini, represent a short interlude within a long history of Moderate administrations. Casarini's administration was based on a majority of Democrats, Radicals and Republicans, which also included a few former supporters of the Moderate administration, who were not compromised by what was termed at the time the "*politica consortesca*" of the group around Marco Minghetti.[72] Casarini's administration distinguished itself through a new form of cultural policy aimed at strengthening local as well as national identity and Bologna's profile as a cultural and academic centre. A former leader of the *Società Nazionale,* member of the provisional *giunta* in 1859, governmental commissioner for the railways in Central Italy and a member of parliament, the lawyer Camillo Casarini represented in Bologna the politics of the new professional and educated middle classes. Most councillors of his group had been directly involved in the motions of 1848 or the liberation of the Papal Legations in 1858. Some of them had been loyal to Cavour's old party until 1867, when the Moderates refused to support Garibaldi's Mentana campaign. When Pepoli's Moderate *giunta* collapsed, Bologna and the Romagna were agitated by political uprisings and social unrest provoked by the region's economic crisis and by the imposition of new taxes, in particular the tax on flour. This regional crisis led repeatedly to parliamentary enquiries and deepened the gulf between the political ideas of Democrats and Moderates.[73] Compared to the politics of the Right during the first decade after the Liberation, Casarini's political priorities as mayor of Bologna illustrate an alternative approach to local administration.[74]

Numerous contemporaries and historians have commented on the disillusionment with the achievements of the Italian nation-state, a crisis which commenced shortly after Unification, most famously accentuated by Giosuè Carducci: "This is not Giuseppe Mazzini's Italy," the "Third Rome." Instead, the nation resembled a new Byzantium, a symbol of decline.[75] For the men around Casarini, who had invested their lives in the nation's resurgence and the liberation of the Papal Legations, the general mood of resignation was perceived as a national tragedy. Casarini spoke of a "*malcontento profondissimo,*"[76] which his majority confronted with a new approach to civil society and municipal administration. When the

Figure 3.1   Camillo Casarini. (Reproduction by Kind Permission of the Biblioteca dell'Archiginnasio, Bologna, Italy.)

Democrats took over, they presented their approach to the generally perceived crisis as that of a new generation of politicians, who were capable of introducing a fresh spirit not only to the concept of local administration, but also to the project of building the nation from its periphery. Only twenty of the sixty councillors elected in 1868 had been members of the previous council, and of the fifty-five councillors of whom a professional activity is known, only fourteen belonged to the category of *possidenti*, even if the number of landowners still exceeded the commercial or industrial middle class.[77] Born in 1830 and twelve years younger than Minghetti, Casarini was too young when he was first nominated for parliamentary elections and had to wait until 1865 to take up his seat. When he became mayor of Bologna, aged only thirty-eight, contemporaries commented on his *"grazia quasi infantile".*[78]

One of the reasons why the Right lost ground among the small local electorate was that voters lost confidence in their ability to solve the social crisis with which the region was confronted. After weeks of strikes and violent demonstrations, the new administration changed its system of local taxation, moving several positions from a proportional to a progressive system. While communal budgets everywhere in Italy suffered under the charges imposed by central government, Bologna's new system of local taxation increased the municipal income. Panzacchi, who as director of the *Monitore di Bologna* had bitterly criticized the years of Moderate administration, introduced a reform of local primary education which integrated a large portion of Bologna's children for the first time into the educational system, becoming a model followed by numerous other Italian towns.[79] Similarly, Casarini's administration restructured and refinanced local secondary and professional education. Casarini supported the constitution of a workers' cooperative and initiated a series of public works which created employment. Most of the Moderates' urban development projects had remained unfinished and continued to contribute to the city's financial crisis.[80] Now these projects were finally completed and several new streets improving access to the city centre were built, including the widening of the central axis of Via Farini, aimed at attracting new commercial activity.

Based on the new administration's professional background in finance and law, Casarini was able to demonstrate that there was room for political intervention in local administration.[81] His team started works for a new water supply system, built several markets and a municipal slaughterhouse, and created a new *Palazzo di giustizia,* thus freeing space under the city's central *Portico* for the expansion of its cultural institutions. Using his experience and his contacts as a former commissioner for the railways, he also lobbied for a new connection between Bologna and Verona, which, it was hoped, would create employment for the entire region. A reform of the local administration and public services, which had previously been characterised by nepotism and corruption, reduced expenditure while creating new employment in the public sector. The collaboration with politically independent professional experts became an integral part of the Democrats' political programme.[82] The Right and the *Gazzetta dell'Emilia* criticized this policy of public investment as unnecessary spending for the city's *decoro,* while the *Monitore di Bologna* defended the economic benefits of investments, taking the view that "this was not just about spending, but about spending well and productively."[83]

The administration's public works were integrated into a cultural policy which was aimed at injecting a new sense of urban and national identity into the municipality's public life. Among the most prestigious projects of the local government was the opening of the Museo Civico, which made the city's medieval and archaeological treasures, the Egyptian, Etruscan and Roman collections, accessible to a wider public. The administration financed the spectacular Etruscan excavations at the Certosa and local newspapers started reporting enthusiastically about every detail of the discoveries. The city sponsored the Fifth International Conference of Prehistoric Archaeology in Bologna, attended by several hundred visitors from all over the world. The mayor gave the event considerable publicity, hoping to boost the city's nascent tourist industry and to establish Bologna's reputation as a leading academic and cultural centre of the new Italy. Important funds went into the restoration, expansion and reorganisation of the famous municipal library in the Archiginnasio, a major symbol of Bologna's self-perception as a centre of academic life. The name of Casarini's electoral committee in 1868, "Galvani," after Bologna's famous eighteenth-century scientist, was a programme in itself.[84]

Within a few years Bologna changed its face. Beyond the municipality's investment in public works, the administration's activism stimulated private enterprise after a long period of economic and moral depression, after the council rejected some of the *giunta's* initial proposals for the direct management of public services. Despite an overall increase in expenditure and regardless of the fact that Casarini's period in office ended with a political scandal, the years 1868 to 1872 were remembered as a period of stabilization of municipal finance after years of mismanagement. Casarini inherited from the Moderate administration a current deficit of more than two million Lire and a debt of nearly seven million Lire in loans, most of which had to be repaid on short term, resulting in a considerable burden for the municipality's annual budget and paralysing local administration.[85] Both the current budget policy and the commune's loan system had to be revised. In order to resolve the problem of continuously having to cover expensive short-term loans, the administration arranged to balance the current accounts by transforming its short-term loans into a single long-term loan at a fixed interest rate. The idea behind this manoeuvre was to consolidate the annual budget, ending the permanent crisis provoked by short-term obligations and allowing for investment in the city's infrastructure, which would lead eventually to an increase in municipal income. Negotiations for this loan started in 1871, during a time when the banking sector, as a consequence of the Franco-German war, faced considerable difficulties in providing loans. The council supported Casarini's general approach to the city's financial problems, even if details of the arrangements were rejected. Within a year the annual deficit was reduced from 289,619 Lire to 167,059 Lire; and shortly afterwards the municipal budget was in balance, for the first time since Unification.[86] The municipality's public works were now controlled by politicians and administrators with professional expertise, marking a contrast to the approach of the Moderate administrations, which for too long had relied on civil servants usually without professional qualifications, still largely recruited under the Papal regime. The loans taken out under Casarini's administration were not agreed with the local banks, which were controlled by the same men who sat in the local or provincial councils, but were first negotiated with a number of international banks and finally agreed with an institution in Verona, offering the most advantageous deal.

From 1863 to 1867, and again from 1869 to his premature death in 1874, the *mélomane* Casarini also presided over the *Deputazione dei pubblici spettacoli*, which was in charge of the Teatro Comunale. His interventions in the management and the repertoire of the opera were among the most spectacular activities of his administration. Building on the ancient fame of Bologna's Bibiena Theatre, opera was at the centre of his cultural policy. Between 1868 and 1872 Bologna wrote important pages in Italy's history of music.[87] The reason for his particular interest in opera, contrasting so much with the Moderates' political priorities in Bologna, was rooted in his perception of Italy's moral crisis during these years. According to Casarini, the widespread consciousness of crisis during the years after Unification corresponded closely to the decline of Italy's lyric theatre, the nation's primary art form throughout the nineteenth century. An enthusiast of both French *grand opéra* and Wagner, he saw the reasons for the decline of Italian opera in the nation's *campanilismo* during and after the Risorgimento, in the nation's obsession with its own past and glory, and in the unwillingness to look beyond the peninsula. In a great speech in parliament he reminded the Italian people how much the greatest works of Rossini and Verdi owed to foreign influences, to unorthodox approaches, and to the courage to introduce new ideas into Italian music. Confronted with the criticism of his cultural policy in Bologna and with his emphasis on Wagner at the Teatro Comunale, he explained that Italy cannot "build a Chinese Wall around its temples of arts." He saw the cosmopolitan opening of Italy's theatres as a symbol for the nation's "*risveglio.*"[88] Patriotism and cosmopolitanism, for Casarini, were two sides of the same coin. At home, in the local council, Casarini accused the Moderates of lacking vision, of having nothing in mind but pettiness, of being incapable of appreciating his project of rejuvenating the city's spirit, of just serving an old party "which could not make peace with the fact that a *borghese* had the courage to hold up the banner of the city's dignity." After his resignation from office, Bologna's Left regarded the return of the Right as the "beginning of a war against science and the arts."[89] Their lack of a cultural policy was, for Casarini, a sign of the decline of patriotic spirit and civic virtue.

MONEY AND CULTURE IN THE LATE
NINETEENTH CENTURY

Towards the end of Casarini's administration rumours about financial mis-management and fraud emerged. As an official investigation revealed, sev-eral employees of the commune had passed a total of 33,886.67 Lire into their own pockets.[90] The centres of fraud were the population office, the communal slaughter-house and the cemetery; but the administration of the theatre was accused of irresponsible overspending. Too occupied with his projects for the city's cultural self-representation, it was alleged that the mayor had neglected control over his administrative body. According to the official report the members of the *giunta* were not personally involved in the scandals, but had entrusted the administration to an unreasonable degree. According to the auditors, by the end of Casarini's administration the commune was faced with a deficit of 55,000 Lire, hardly an extraordi-nary sum, but enough for the *giunta* to resign.

After Casarini's resignation, the returning Moderate *giunta* under Count Malvezzi first stopped most of the projects initiated under Casarini and even made some of the administration's new employees redundant. However, in the long term, Casarini's administration and the financial mechanisms he introduced became a model for subsequent local govern-ments. Bologna followed the example of other Italian cities by seeking international investment and contracting specialised international busi-ness to assume a whole new range of public services, which within decades turned Bologna into a modern city.[91] Although their political ranks were still dominated by the landed elite, the local Moderates started showing signs of a generational and social transformation. The engineer and uni-versity teacher Gualtiero Sacchetti, aged thirty-two at the beginning of Casarini's administration, became one of the most influential leaders of the local Moderates, abandoning his professional career to dedicate him-self to politics. Under the leadership of Sacchetti and Gaetano Tacconi, mayor from 1874, the Moderates increased their collaboration with Bolo-gna's professional classes, and Liberals belonging to the Progressive frac-tion occasionally accepted positions in their administrations. Despite their electoral defeat in 1872, Progressive and Democratic councillors, repre-senting the professional middle classes, continued to play a certain role in council decisions, marking a difference from the first decade of Moderate administration after the liberation.[92]

During the following years the growth of the local population and an increase in (taxed) consumption led to a continuous boost in the munici-pal income and allowed for a balancing of the municipal accounts.[93] Nevertheless, to a large extent cultural policy on the municipal level and investment in cultural representation were determined by the relationship the State had established with the municipalities and their cultural insti-tutions. As well as by council policies, Bologna's financial situation was

Table 3.1 Growth of Population and Municipal Revenue in the Commune of Bologna during the Years 1867 to 1897.[94]

	1867	1897	%
population	106,563	152,042	+ 42.7%
income from taxation	2,118,230 Lire	3,751,486 Lire	+ 77.1%

therefore marked by the general conditions of municipal finance created under the kingdom's early governments of the Right.[95]

Between 1867 and 1877 the commune of Bologna increased its income by 14.8 % and its expenditure by 25.2%.[96] However, nationwide municipal expenditure during this period increased by 50%. Marked by the financial policies of the city's Moderate administrations, Bologna's expenditure developed less strongly than the majority of cities under Democratic administrations.[97] During the following decade the pattern of expenditure in Bologna changed, becoming even more restrictive. While the city's income between 1877 and 1887 increased by 21%, its expenditure increased by only 10.8%. In the province municipal income increased by 17.6%, compared to an 18.2% increase in expenditure. Hence, despite providing services and infrastructure for the entire province, Bologna reduced expenditure in relation to its income. This policy reflected Bologna's need to reduce the public debt accumulated during the first years of the Moderate administration. Under pressure from central government to reduce "facultative spending," the short period of expansion in expenditure had come to an end. Nevertheless, both Bologna and the communes of the province made considerable efforts to invest in their cultural institutions. Between 1876 and 1886 municipal investment in cultural institutions increased by 35.2% in the province, more than the total expenditure during the period (+ 18.2%). *Spese facoltative* made up for 16% of the total expenditure in 1876, compared to 18.3% in 1886. This position was slightly higher than in most Italian towns.[98] In the city of Bologna we notice a similar trend. Expenditure imposed by the State, including for instance the salaries of teachers in primary education, increased by 28% between 1882 and 1892, while "facultative spending" for culture and education—including museums, the Liceo Musicale, subsidies for secondary education—increased by 35.4%.

Municipal finance in Italy was usually characterised by a structural deficit, due to the fact that expenditure exceeded the cities' income.[99] Contrasting with this national trend, the communes in the province of Bologna, in the 1870s and 1880s, were able to balance their accounts. This situation changed in the 1890s. In 1891 the province's communes

Table 3.2   Income and Expenditure of the Communes in the Province of Bologna for the
Years 1876, 1886, 1891, 1895 (in Million Lire).[100]

	1876	1886	(1876–86 in %)	1891	1895	(1891–95 in %)
Total income	6179.8	7272.5	(+17.6%)	7793.6	8605.9	(+9.4%)
Total expenditure	5961.4	7047.9	(+18.2%)	8174.6	8044.2	(-1.6%)
Spese obbligatorie	5005.8	5730.6	(+14.4%)	6661.1	6937.2	(+4.1%)
Spese facoltative	955.6	1292.3	(+35.2%)	1483.0	1079.6	(-27.2%)

reached a deficit of 381 million Lire or nearly 5%. In the city of Bologna,
in 1892, the deficit reached more than half a million Lire, or 16.7%. The
most important cause of this was the budget for Bologna's great exhibition in 1888. Increasing their income until 1895 by 9.4% and reducing
expenditure during the same period by 1.6%, the provincial communes
managed to balance their budgets, despite a further increase of centrally
imposed compulsory spending of 4.1% during the same period. The savings programme meant that *spese facoltative* had to be reduced—from
18.1% of the total budget in 1891 to 13.4% in 1895, a total reduction of
27.2%. The city of Bologna reduced its deficit during the same period,
but without balancing its accounts. Considering the high degree of compulsory expenditure imposed upon the communes by central government
(83.9% of the province's municipal budgets in 1876, reaching 86.2% in
1895), pressure to further reduce expenditure led to a rather questionable policy with regard to the local economy. During the period 1886
to 1895, when the entire region was confronted with an economic crisis
and an escalation of the "social question," the communes of the province
increased their income by 18.3%, but were obliged to keep their increase
in expenditure at 14.1%. Despite considerable financial pressure from
above, the communes did their best to keep *spese facoltative* up—the
only way to invest in their local development. However, having no influence on the compulsory requirements imposed by the state, the savings
programme reduced the overall proportion of *spese facoltative* between
1886 and 1895 by 16.4%—money that otherwise could have been spent
on infrastructure, urban planning and culture.

   When in 1876 the Italian State proudly reached a balance of income
and expenditure—to a large extent the work of Marco Minghetti as prime
minister and minister of finance—the Marquis Gioacchino Pepoli, former
mayor of Bologna, described this success as a "laughing mask, covering

Table 3.3   Income and Expenditure of the Commune of Bologna for the Years
1877, 1887, 1892, 1897 (in Million Lire).[101]

	1877	*1887*	*(1877–87 in %)*	*1892*	*1897*	*(1892–97 in %)*
Total income	2488.1	3019.7	(+21.3%)	3624.9	3751.4	(+ 3.5%)
Total expenditure	2974.7	3298.4	(+10.8%)	4129.8	4058.8	(- 4.2%)

Table 3.4   Expenditure for Public Education in the Commune of Bologna for the
Years 1882 and 1892 (in Lire).[102]

	1882	*1892*	*1882–92 in %*
Spese obligatorie	278,000	356,464	+28%
Spese facoltative:	243,000	328,973	+35.4%

a weeping face."[103] The balance was reached with the help of the hugely
unpopular tax on flour, introduced in 1868 and to be paid by farmers or
peasants when bringing their cereals, maize or chestnuts to the mill. However, part of the financial consolidation on the national level was also the
devolution of financial obligations from the centre to the periphery in the
form of numerous budget positions, which otherwise would have been the
responsibility of the State.[104] Minghetti saw his financial policy as one of
the great achievements of his political career, a marker of the success of
Italian unification. Pepoli, the Marquis from Bologna with the prestigious
ancient name, minister in the early governments of the Right and once himself an advocate of restrictive spending, distanced himself from the policies
of the Moderates. A principle architect of Italy's unification, his heart was
nevertheless with the peninsula's *cento città*. His "weeping" *patria* was the
old city of Bologna.[105]

Part II
Writing the Past

4 The Middle Class and the Historicising of the Present

Geschiedenis is de geestelijke vorm waarin een cultuur zich rekensc-
hap geeft van haar verleden.

(Johan Huizinga)[1]

HISTORICISING THE PRESENT

This chapter provides an introduction to the book's sections on Italy's nineteenth-century medieval revival and on the rediscovery of its pre-Roman
civilisations, chapters 5 and 6 respectively. In addition to presenting different local institutions involved in the writing of the urban, regional and
national past after Unification, the chapter discusses the role of historical
discourse in the construction of identity. The following two chapters then
examine the content of this historical discourse, drawing particular attention to Italy's medieval revival and to the wide-spread fascination with its
Etruscan past.

For Hobsbawm invented traditions are attempts to find re-compensation
for the feeling of loss associated with the experience of the present. The
socio-psychological mechanisms which come into effect through historical symbols include archaic elements, but they also operate within modern
forms of rationality.[2] Certain social groups perceive modernity as a negative and alienating challenge, as described by Engels, Tönnies and Simmel.
In this situation history offers "connective structures" to bridge social and
temporal discontinuities, offering the comfort of a common past.[3] As the
historian and anthropologist Sally Humphreys remarked, "the discourse
of modernity is incessantly involved, everywhere, in negotiating relations
between constructed pasts and imagined futures."[4] The experience of the
present depends upon the past; and "we will experience our present differently in accordance with the different pasts to which we are able to connect that present,"[5] as Paul Connerton argues. The complicity between past
and future explains why Italian society, in the process of making itself
"modern," paid so much attention to writing its past. Although Benedetto
Croce recounts how early nineteenth-century Italians deplored the "lack

of Italian (hi)stories conforming to modern concepts,"[6] the Risorgimento understood itself explicitly as an evocation of the past and, in order to justify its aims, made continuous references to historical events. Historical references produce effects even if they are used purely as a formula, if they are invented or based on wrong assumptions. The symbolic material used in myths constitutes something "like a reservoir of meanings" (Koselleck) which is available for possible use in numerous different structures.[7]

Based on similar assumptions Huizinga sees history as a form of the spirit rather than a science—a form of the spirit within which a culture produces its accounts of the past.[8] Each culture creates this specific historical form of the spirit, and regards it as true. In analysing this enterprise, Huizinga avoids a differentiation between the academic discipline of history and the arts. Also in Italy "historicising discourse" was not restricted to academia, but included other forms of expression as well—historicising literature from novels to children's books, political language, the arts and music. In particular Carducci's "historical-epical poetry" was fermented with "praxis," that is, political-historical sentiment. He insisted that "history is not exclusively made of political facts," but of arts and ideas as well.[9]

However, as André Malraux remarked, "*un cruxifix roman n'était pas d'abord une sculpture.*"[10] In creating museums, "we respond less to the intrinsic attributes of cultural goods, than to the symbolic meanings given to them."[11] Historicising discourse transforms objects into "sémiophores," defined by Krysztof Pomian as "objects bearing meaning," objects of aesthetic-historical experience used to interrogate the world.[12] The selection and presentation of objects in museums or in the urban landscape is "enacted within a power system," which contributes to the production of social systems. During this process the distance between historical object and contemporary observer, which Collingwood and Gadamer emphasise in their philosophical hermeneutic, is consciously ignored. Thus, the educational purpose of museums or monuments is largely determined by a contemporary agenda.[13] The historian is able to examine the historical production of semiophores, the meaning vested in them and their historical classification.

"Historical patrimony increases a nation's prestige."[14] With these words Count Gozzadini, president of Bologna's Deputazione di Storia Patria, justified in 1872 the need to commence a major programme of archaeological excavation in Italy. The excavation of sites, the foundation of museums and the preservation of historical architecture all help to create a sense of community, on a local, regional or national level. Recent historical writing tends to explore museums as shrines and schools of national significance. However, in Italy more particularly many museums are vested with regional and local meaning; and many local collections are older than the national museums. In the case of Bologna the modern history of its archaeological museum begins in 1871, while it took the government until 1889 to decree the institution of a National Archaeological Museum in Rome.[15] The Roman municipality, influenced by clerical opposition to the Italian nation-state and loyal to the Papal tradition of archaeological research, obstructed for years the creation of a national museum.

Not only the objects in municipal collections and museums, but also the city's historical and historicising architecture, monuments and infrastructure bear a symbolic meaning beyond their immediate significance. They are relics of the past: decorative accessories and built environment. Transformed into semiophores, they make the urban environment meaningful. Discourse about visual symbolism is constructed similarly to the formation of collective memory as defined by Maurice Halbwachs: Meaning changes over time and is continuously redefined according to the social and political needs of contemporary societies.[16] The prestige of a particular historical collection arises not from the objects themselves, but from an imagined, invisible world of the past with which they are associated.

The rediscovery of the past and the transformation of past objects into contemporary semiophores were based on the idea of progress, something to which contemporary society could easily relate.[17] Not only was the past read in a contemporary key, but also contemporary experiences were historicised. An interesting example of this historical contextualisation of modern experiences were the fake-historical buildings and villages at the world fairs—attempts to demonstrate where the modern world came from. Modern nation-states represented themselves not only through neo-classical pavilions, but also through "medieval" constructions such as Pugin's medieval court at the Great exhibition of 1851, the *"borgo medievale"* at Turin's 1884 exhibition, or the Flemish village at the 1910 exhibition in Brussels.[18] In post-Unification Bologna the past played a major role in the city's self-representation, not only through museums, excavations, or the preservation of the historical centre, but also through commemorations of historical events or debates on the local toponymy.

Within the construction of historically informed identities the past and the ways in which it was to be remembered always remained a matter of political debate. In these debates the Democratic middle class played a crucial role. According to Croce, Carducci's past was never

> an indifferent and cold narration of historical facts. . . . Carducci loves and hates: he loves ancient Rome and hates Papal Rome; he loves the people and hates the emperors. He loves and hates, because for him, unlike for the historian, the images of the past do not represent a sacred past; they are symbols of the future, ideal types of good and bad for which one has to fight.[19]

History meant debate. When asked for an inscription commemorating the battle of Legnano, Carducci had to return to his work many times "because the promoting committee wanted it in one way, the municipality in another and the Deputazione di Storia Patria in a third."[20] After Garibaldi's death Carducci received a total of forty invitations to compose epitaphs—from

Monarchists, Republicans, Socialists, and anybody who claimed the hero's legacy—each of them asking for the commemoration of a different Garibaldi.[21] Historical narratives were a literary genre, they were used for public speeches and as features for newspapers and magazines. Their authors were to a large extent of middle class origin. Academic reports on archaeological excavations or on the meetings of the Deputazione di Storia Patria were published on a regular basis in local newspapers.[22] Bologna's professors, men like Bertolini and Carducci, addressed large audiences on historical themes, most frequently with focus on the Communal age. The Republican Quirico Filopanti and the Catholic Alfonso Rubbiani lectured on medieval crafts to the local labour associations; the former mayor Carlo Pepoli spoke in schools to commemorate historical events; and Enrico Panzacchi gave lectures on the Renaissance in the Florentine Palazzo Ginori.[23] The cultural elite discovered a new sense of virtue behind the teaching of history. Carducci believed that even primary schools should teach "the duties and rights of the citizen, . . . sowing the seeds of a sense of their own dignity in the pupils. Pride creates good citizens." Such pride was to be based on local history, in Bologna with a preference for the period of "medieval freedom" before the "enslavement" under the Papal regime. The history of religion was to be taught not as catechism, but as part of young people's general culture and particular attention was to be paid to Jewish history, as the source of Christianity, in contrast to the anti-Jewish tradition of the former Legations, which still inspired parts of the Catholic-legitimist opposition.[24]

For the educated middle class the historicising discourse after Unification served three major aims: providing Bologna with a civic identity; legitimising the end of the Papal regime; and fostering Bologna's reputation as a major cultural and academic centre in the new nation-state. Historical consciousness, the "invention of a historical tradition," had to consolidate a consensus favourable to the new State and to the new municipal administration. The unification of Italy meant for Bologna first of all liberation from the Papal regime. Bringing about the end of this old-established state, the liberation was for Bologna almost a patricide. Accounts of the past had to justify it. The legacies of Papal dominion had to be erased; it had to be treated as an historical interlude. Positive traditions had to be found, representing the germ of a new identity, a substitute for the Papal past. In respect to the great medieval conflict between the supporters of the papacy (Guelphs) and of the Empire (Ghibellines), most Italian patriots during the nineteenth century took the side of the papacy. But unlike other North-Italian cities, Bologna obviously had difficulties in thinking of itself as a Guelph city.[25] As an important centre of the Risorgimento and the fight against the Austrian occupation, the city identified with historical narratives about "foreign" dominion, but the Risorgimento was also understood as a struggle for independence from the Papal regime. Confronted with these divided loyalties, the Bolognese historian Francesco Bertolini rejected the idea of using history for political aims altogether.[26]

BETWEEN CENTRE AND PERIPHERY

Bologna's Deputazione di Storia Patria played a major role in the creation of local historical narratives. Its constitution was decreed by the Piedmontese governor Luigi Carlo Farini in February 1860, following a proposal by the minister of education Antonio Montanari, himself professor at the University of Bologna. Its model was the Deputazione subalpina di storia patria, founded in 1833 by King Carlo Alberto. The aim of these historical institutes was to become "the intellectual and historical home from which Italy will resurge to new life."[27] This "home" was obviously furnished by men, "because professionalization and historical science developed at a time of separate spheres," when "the profession was virtually all male."[28] In this respect the modern institutions differed from Bologna's noble salons, in which, for instance, the countess Gozzadini had played an influential role. As will be demonstrated in chapter 6, many professional historians considered the historical interests of the local nobility as amateurish, even if for a long time men like Count Gozzadini were still able to play a dominant part in institutions such as the Deputazione. Due to the publication of its proceedings in the press, the Deputazione reached an audience which went far beyond the specialists working in the field, including political decision makers, the local administration, Bologna's intellectual elite and the educated middle classes. After Unification these groups were keen to see their city assume a historically distinctive identity.

In addition to the conservation and publication of historical documents, the Deputazione was assigned a role in the protection of ancient buildings and in taking care of archaeological excavations.[29] The first president of Bologna's Deputazione was Senator Count Giovanni Gozzadini, at the time already a corresponding member of the Deputazioni in Piedmont and Tuscany, of the Ateneo Veneto and the Archaeological Acadamies of Rome and Ercolano, and a member of the historical societies of the Liguria and Palermo. He seemed therefore an ideal candidate for the nomination. Carducci became a member of the Deputazione in 1863, its secretary in 1865 and its president in 1887. Although trained as a philologist, due to his position in the Deputazione, Carducci was regarded as an influential historian as well as being the most important poet of the post-Unification period. His editions of medieval documents in the *Rerum Italicarum Scriptores* were considered a major resource for Italian history and several of his former students became professional historians or archaeologists of major importance, like the later director of Bologna's museum, Gherardo Ghirardini.[30] As illustrated in the following chapter, the Deputazione played an important role in the preservation of historical buildings in Bologna. The architect Raffaele Faccioli, associated with the Deputazione since 1873, was director of the regional office for the Preservation of Monuments, an ideal position from which to voice the Deputazione's concerns for the city's historical heritage. He directed the restoration of Santo Stefano, one of Bologna's most remarkable ecclesiastical buildings and the Deputazione's most important restoration project during the second half of the nineteenth century. The Deputazione operated in collaboration with the prefect, who circulated its decisions to the relevant local and national authorities, and it applied on its own initiative for financial support to preserve or restore historic buildings.

Although the Deputazione could only make recommendations to public authorities, in a period of rapid transformation of the urban landscape it was often in a position to prevent injury to the city's patrimony. It represented a professional authority which the relevant decision makers could hardly ignore.[31] Moreover, the Deputazione made itself heard through the public role its members occupied in the local or provincial administration, or at the national level. Good examples of that are Gozzadini and Carducci, who at different times were members of the local council, but also of the parliament's first chamber. Nevertheless, their influence on local government decisions was limited and their relationship to the administration not without tensions. In the 1870s Gozzadini criticized the commune for failing to collaborate with the Deputazione over the Etruscan excavations at the Certosa, which were led by the municipality's chief engineer Antonio Zannoni. He was not a professional archaeologist, but mastered the modern methods of excavation better than Gozzadini himself.[32] After more than a decade of experience with excavations on his own lands Gozzadini saw himself as the leading expert in the field. Referring to the royal decree which regulated the Deputazione's role, Gozzadini was of the opinion that the Deputazione had to guide the commune in its excavation and conservation projects.[33] However, for the commune it was an issue of prestige that it should take care of its own sites. Moreover, there was also a political conflict behind this dispute, opposing Moderates and Democrats. Gozzadini and Bottrigari, *Il Monitore di Bologna* and the *Gazzetta dell'Emilia*, opposed the projects of the city's new Democratic administration under Camillo Casarini between 1868 and 1872.[34] While Zannoni, who also taught evening classes for local Labour organisations, had been promoted, the Democratic administration had made redundant numerous municipal employees, who had been employed by the Moderate administration or even before the political transition of 1859.[35] In 1875 Count Gozzadini was nominated royal commissioner for museums and excavations, which gave him authority over every site explored in the region. This position, which he occupied until his death in 1887, was unpaid and related to his existing public mandates, but it made him directly responsible to the minister of public education. The prefect told the mayors of the province to report on all excavations and work on ancient monuments to the commissioner, which had the effect of further strengthening the position of the Deputazione. The ministry's *Ufficio centrale della Direzione degli*

Figure 4.1 Zannoni's Excavations at the Certosa. (Antonio Zannoni, *Gli scavi della certosa di Bologna*. Bologna: Regia tipografia, 1876)

Scavi e dei Musei aimed to improve communication between centre and periphery, and to ensure that regulations were respected. Even on private property excavations now had to be authorised by the government. Gozzadini soon started complaining to the prefect about the municipality's lack of consultation in matters relating to its archaeological sites and it is not surprising that in particular Zannoni resisted the count's attempts to intervene in his municipal excavations.[36] Once Bologna's different collections of antiquities were united in a single site, Gozzadini also became the museum's first director general.

Rome provides comparable examples of conflicts regarding the authority over excavations and the protection of monuments. Denis Bocquet
describes a *"rivalité spatiale*," in which the Italian state sought to take control of the territory of its capital, against the elected municipal institutions,
which were in the hands of the "black aristocracy" and deeply hostile to the
new state. The minister of finance Quintino Sella, who had a strong personal interest in archaeology, succeeded in enabling the state to purchase
land from the municipality in order to promote his own projects, but some
of the former Papal archaeologists continued to represent their interests
through the Vatican and the town hall. In the long term the municipality
lost control over the territory with respect to archaeological matters.[37]

Despite these developments and conflicts, the Deputazione played a
major role in crafting Bologna's new historical identity after Unification. It
helped to arise an awareness of Bologna's ancient topography and encouraged local administrators to take part in the uncovering of the region's
ancient remains, of Roman streets and drainage systems or the Etruscan
burial places.[38] On certain projects, such as the controversial restoration
of the Teatro Comunale, the Deputazione was consulted directly by the
administration.[39] The Deputazione studied Bologna's medieval architecture, its churches, palaces and towers, and advised the municipality accordingly in matters of restoration. In most of its studies it emphasised the
quality of Bologna's early medieval architecture, in the period before the
domination under Papal government.[40] Dependent on central government
funding, the major constraints on the work of the Deputazione were of a
financial nature. Initially, after the liberation of the Papal Legations, the
Deputazione Romagnola had an annual budget of 8000 Lire, but in 1865
the grant was reduced to 2400 Lire, which reflected not only the kingdom's
financial difficulties at the time, but also the general luke-warm attitude of
the Moderate governments to "cultural" nation-building. These financial
restrictions made it difficult to maintain the Deputazione's prestigious editions of historical documents and to publish its proceedings, but it did not
prevent this committee of experts from voicing its concerns about the local
patrimony and the city's historical identity.[41]

For decades after Unification learned societies and institutions such as
the Deputazione were constituted to a large extent by the local nobility and
restricted in their membership through complex regulations. In Tuscany
the majority of members in academic institutions belonged to the nobility.
The marquis Matteo Ricci was described as "accademico residente" of the
famous Florentine Accademia della Crusca, a position similar to Count
Gozzadini's in Bologna.[42] However, after Unification academic institutions began to be influenced by the general trend towards professionalisation, with academics from middle class backgrounds gaining influence. In
Bologna's Deputazione this development can be illustrated by the role of
people like Carducci, Frati and Brizio. The municipal librarian Frati was
mentioned in chapter 2, in connection with the contracts of the theatre's

box owners. Brizio had studied classics with Ariodante Fabretti in Turin and graduated as one of the first students from the Scuola Archeologica Italiana, which had been created in 1866.[43] Gherardo Ghirardini was of modest origins and studied with Carducci, thanks to a municipal scholarship. After having obtained chairs in Pisa and Padova, he returned to Bologna in 1907 to succeed Brizio as director of the Civic Museum and superintendent of antiquities. In 1913 he became president of the Deputazione.[44] The Deputazione defended its academic freedom from government intervention until 1935, when the Fascist regime put it under the direct control of a government committee.

SHOWCASES OF THE PAST

One particular area in which the municipality was able to influence public perceptions of the past was the city's museums, emerging as public institutions in the modern sense during the 1870s and 1880s. James J. Sheehan has described the period between 1830 and 1880 as "the museum age."[45] While in the early-modern period museums were conceived as spaces for private scholarship, during the nineteenth century they became public leisure institutions and tools for the educational improvement of the masses.[46] These were the intentions of Bologna's administration when in the 1870s it made the municipal museum the city's most important cultural flagship after the Teatro Comunale—a policy started under the Democrat Casarini, but later continued under the Moderate administrations. Compared to Turin or the cities in the former provinces of the Habsburgs, Bologna was a latecomer in the creation of public museums and wished to make its museum one of the finest of the peninsula.[47] However, there were financial limitations to the municipality's pedagogical plans. In 1878 the Civic Museum started charging entrance fees, following the example of Bologna's state-run Pinacoteca, which during the previous years had generated about 8000 Lire per annum through the selling of tickets.[48] The Civic Museum, after its reorganisation and official inauguration in 1881, charged one Lira per ticket and made a total of 14,000 Lire during the first two months alone.[49] Considering the museum's educational objective of communicating a specific narrative of the past to a wider public, the decision to charge fees presented a problem which concerned successive municipal administrations. Since it had introduced fees, the museum counted a growing number of foreign visitors, but faced difficulties attracting the local population. As the mayor explained,

> Not even ten out of a hundred citizens know the Museum, despite the fact that it equals in importance the major museums of Italy and abroad. As this institution gives Bologna real prestige, it is truly saddening that the citizenry doesn't sufficiently appreciate an institution that does such honour to Bologna.[50]

Councillor Ercolani, the rector of the university, was mostly concerned about the people's "aesthetic education"—"helping to maintain a sense of beauty among the people and a sense for the good." He proposed that on at least one day of the week entry to the museum should be free.[51] As soon as the administration reintroduced free days the number of visitors went beyond the museum's capacity, obliging it to shut the doors during peak times. To cope with the problem the administration allocated additional funds to pay the municipal firemen to provide support for the wardens.[52] After the peak in the 1880s the number of visitors decreased to eight or nine per day in the 1890s. During World War I, under the first Socialist local government, there was a revival of interest in local museums, again creating difficulties for the administration due to the shortage of personnel.[53]

Despite the museum's international recognition and its initial popularity, the municipality's expenditure on this form of cultural self-representation was regularly criticised by Moderate as well as Socialist councillors. The Civic Museum, containing municipal collections as well as the state-owned collections of the university, required a coordination of the municipality's cultural policy with the university's academic objectives. In addition to the honorary position of the director general, the commune employed a director for the museum's medieval section; an "inspector" as head of the administration, who also taught Egyptology at the university; a ticket officer; seven wardens, two of whom also worked as conservationists; and an additional warden with residence at the museum. The central government paid for the director of the antiquities section, for a conservationist and two further wardens.[54] Staff who were professionally qualified or in academic positions frequently moved to other museums. (As late as 1912 women were still excluded from applying for any positions.) In addition to the salaries of the government employees, the minister of public education provided an annual grant for acquisitions and conservation, heating and lighting, the travel expenses of the archaeologists and the uniforms of the wardens. This grant amounted initially to 1500 Lire and was doubled in 1883. Hence, one of Bologna's most prestigious means of cultural self-representation depended on financial contributions from the State. Successive attempts to obtain additional financial means from the commune were blocked by the council. Not even the income from the sale of tickets—2654.50 Lire in 1889—was granted entirely to the museum. In debates on the museum's persistent financial difficulties, Bologna's mayors regularly pointed to the municipality's initial expenditure for the museum's inauguration in 1881 and to the general cost of excavations undertaken by the commune, which made it impossible to justify any further financial commitments.[55]

According to Kenneth Hudson modern public museums were largely "the creations of their directors," without much impact from visitors.[56] While it is true that in Bologna public response to the collections played only a minor role, the complex structures of administration and finance suggest that the power of academic directors over the management of their museums was relatively limited. As a later chapter will show, the local administration and the state were in a position to determine the content, arrangement and "reading" of the collections. Private benefactors who left their collections to the museum played an important part. The central government was keen to emphasise its role in the original creation of the museum and to mark out its property within the collections through printed catalogues and inventories.[57] In addition to the guidebooks of 1887 and 1914, produced for a less specialised readership, several scholarly catalogues provided an overview of the museum's different collections. However, once the catalogues had been completed, the minister showed no interest in covering the expenses. Their publication took several decades and the respective expenditure was routinely left to the commune. Despite these difficulties, the museum insisted on selling only its own publications and no books or guides produced by independent authors, thus keeping control over the historical narrative and the intended meaning of its collections.

Unlike the local Democrats, the Socialists commented rather critically on Bologna's cult of the past. They claimed that the municipal library, for instance, collected only books "which are useful for the study of old mummies, supporting an obscure cult of scholarship; there is nothing about contemporary culture, no books of modern literature, works on sociology and the economy, or about the colonies."[58]

MAL D'ARCHIVE

"Showcases of the past," but of a different kind from museums, were Italy's archives. In particular regarding the medieval period many Italian cities possessed archives which in quality and quantity were more important than the national archives of certain states in Northern Europe.[59] Archives played an important part in asserting the cities' role in the unified nation-state. Bologna's *Archivio di Stato* was created in 1874 and was originally located on the same site as the museum, before being moved to the Palazzo dei Celestini and arranged according to modern criteria. The main focus of the collection was on the period before the Papal administration, covering the history of the commune between the twelfth and the early sixteenth centuries.[60] The term "archive" refers to "commencement," where everything began, a central theme for a city setting out to search for its historical identity. But according to Derrida, the term also refers to "*commandement*," the exercise of authority, in this case authority over the past, an authority which could either be exercised by the municipality or by the State.[61] Even before the annexation of the Papal Legations by Piedmont the commune resolved in August 1859 that the *Archiginnasio* should be transformed in order to house the "*archivio patrio.*" Farini, then governor of the province, planned to return any archives not directly regarding the State to the local authorities.[62]

One of the Deputazione's objectives was to coordinate information regarding the location and content of archives, in particular the *Archivio Notarile*, the civil and criminal archives, the Papal State archives, the papers of the cathedral, and the documents of the military and the prefect. A first overview of holdings was undertaken in August 1860. Francesco Bonaini, superintendent of the Tuscan archives, was asked to develop a project setting out how the various collections should be organised. Bonaini was the first Italian to adapt the modern *"principe de provenance,"* organising the papers according to the institutions which created them, rather than by forming subject files.[63] Following these rules, Bonaini represented the avant-garde of the archival discipline, understood by archivists and historians alike as the key to a "scientific" reconstruction of the past. However, within a few months the municipality engaged in a long dispute with central government about the ownership of and access to the various collections; and in particular regarding the separation of "current" and "historical" archives. The state denied the commune access to any papers relating to the former Papal Legations, seeing itself as the only legitimate successor to the Papal regime and claiming to represent the continuity between the former states of the peninsula and the new Kingdom of Italy. The municipality wished to collect all papers relating to its past in one and the same location, if possible, linked to the site of its ancient university and library. They wanted to reorganise papers according to their institutional origins, create inventories and chronological tools for historical research. On this front Moderates and Democrats fought together against the central administration of the State: the nobility regarded the history of the city as the history of their own families; the middle class sought to provide the city with a historically informed local identity. The State denied the commune the right to declassify papers or to reorganise series of documents according to their historical origins. Only in exceptional cases was the government prepared to leave papers to the commune, that is, when in 1863 it closed Bologna's old mint and left its archives to the municipality.

Carducci described these years as "Bologna's re-awakening"; a period in which the entire Romagna competed to make its historical documents (many of them dating back to the thirteenth century) accessible to historians.[64] In this context a polemical article in the *Monitore di Bologna* signed C. and probably by Carducci, praised the German historical school: "Everywhere we encounter in the archives eager researchers from Germany. With admirable patience and skill they discover precious documents and reveal historical truth through their interrogation of the gigantic ruins of the past."[65] Repeatedly the Deputazione asked the government for permission to create the necessary means of access to documents, allowing historians to systematically research the city's and the region's past. "But ancient papers remain mixed up with current papers and the employees in the relevant offices are busy with other tasks. . . . In these archives it is pointless to even ask for a catalogue, or for any kind of rational organisation, not to speak of a scientific arrangement of the documents."[66]

In 1874 the *Archivio di Stato* established the State's authority over any papers relating to the former Legations and its predecessors, but at least access to documents was now regulated.[67] The conflict between municipality and central government regarding the documents mirrors the city's attempts to take possession of its past and to strengthen its historical consciousness. Bologna suffered from a *"mal d'archive,"* described by Derrida as the condition of a patient who searches for his identity in the past and tries to cure himself by rummaging for dusty documents.[68] In the case of Bologna the State denied the patient its self-prescribed cure. The city's "desire for memory" resulted in a tense relationship between city and State that lasted for decades. Being Italian also meant having a local identity which after the Risorgimento's completion did not simply vanish.

CRAFTING THE PAST

Historical discourse helped to legitimise the present by "crafting" the past, a local as well as a national past. Hayden White has demonstrated how "historical discourse seeks to explicate the relation between parts and wholes or between the phases and the completed structure of a process."[69] In his *Archaeology of Knowledge* Foucault depicted a similar process, pointing to the ways in which historians construct continuities and discontinuities. Like the writer of fiction, historians fashion their material, illustrating the struggles of the past and the triumph of the present, thus contributing to the creation of myths and collective identities.[70] In analysing such processes, most commentators draw attention to aspects of "national identity" and to nineteenth-century nationalism as a political ideology. Works on the emergence of the modern museum usually focus on the shift from the princely galleries and collections of curiosities to the creation of national museums.[71] However, the fashioning of national identities often went in parallel with the crafting of local or regional entities, or attempts to define national through regional and local identities. Museums, academies or universities became a focus of competition between provincial cities.[72] Carducci, during the 1880s, even feared that the interest in regional and local history would undermine the national sense of belonging:

> Alas, today there is hardly a town of any size which does not want to have its History Society and its own publications, which on the one hand shows the inexhaustible riches of our fatherland and the new generation's loving care for its past, but on the other it also presents fear lest our ancient vice of particularism comes creeping back and

lest each pursues his own interests with a narrow mind and heart: "*tre fratelli, tre castelli.*"[73]

In its efforts to craft a new municipal identity Bologna did not have to compete with an established capital. Turin was no longer the kingdom's capital and resentment against Piedmontese domination during and after the process of Unification made any such comparisons otiose. Florence was briefly the provisional capital but no more than that. Rome, from an institutional point of view, had a long way to go until it could fulfil the role of Italy's cultural capital. This put Bologna and other so-called "second cities" in a strong position. Bologna had to define its position not in relation to the capital but in relation to the nation as a whole and to a large number of cities, which competed with each other—historically, academically, culturally and institutionally.

THE RELATIVE AUTONOMY OF CULTURE

Camillo Casarini was the first mayor who fully understood the symbolic role of Bologna's cultural institutions in the search for the city's new civic profile after Unification. The Moderates' lack of a vision for Bologna, their reluctance, during the first years after the liberation, to develop Bologna's cultural infrastructure was for him a sign of "*impotenza cerebrale*," of aristocratic pettiness and the incapacity to appreciate the idealistic energies of the city's rising middle class.[74] The city's as well as Italy's public image abroad played an important role in his new cultural policy, an image of art and scholarship.[75] The historical patrimony was recognised as an important economic factor and towards the end of the century even Moderate mayors like Alberto Dallolio accepted these priorities.[76] The original initiative for this approach came from the middle class, the oppositional Democrats and Bologna's intellectuals.

What were the mechanisms by which members of the middle class occupied this position? Increasingly, the town council delegated cultural decisions to specialised committees of experts, concentrating its activity on financial issues and the municipal budget. During the first years of the Moderate administration restoration projects in the historical centre were to a large extent based on the initiatives of private citizens, those who owned large properties in the city, without comprehensive policies of urban planning coming into play. This administrative vacuum during the 1860s led to the destruction of substantial areas of the inner city, while the provision of public services and infrastructures was delayed.[77] Once the administration became aware of this problem, Enrico Panzacchi urged the council not to rely on common sense and good intentions regarding the city's future. As director of the Pinacoteca and a widely respected journalist, Panzacchi was an authorative voice when he intervened on these issues in council debates. He convinced the council to delegate important decisions to committees of experts, because, as he argued, "the local government or the office of civil engineering cannot fulfil this role."[78] Professional expertise was meant to balance the relationship between private and public interests, and to build barriers against decisions based exclusively on the economic and bureaucratic rationale of the administration. The works at the municipal cemetery, the demolition of the city gates or the project for the façade of San Domenico went beyond what individual councillors were able to evaluate. The delegation of decisions to professional experts was largely accepted, even if their recommendations were often thought to be "exaggerated" or even "pedantic," for example, when they made parts of the inner city inaccessible for traffic.[79]

As a consequence, the council debates on cultural policy and urban planning decreased in number, despite the fact that the council met more frequently and that individual sessions took more time. This trend started under the Democratic administration of Casarini. (Between Boxing Day and New Year's Eve of 1868 the council met every single day, closing its last session on the last day of the year at 11:00 p.m.) Rather than being concerned with aesthetic decisions and the city's cultural representation, the council spent most of its time debating the financial complexities of public services, the increasingly complicated annual budget and a greatly growing bureaucracy. Meanwhile, official control over urban space increased. In 1895 the government changed the code of public works, allowing local government to intervene against any private building project affecting artistic or historical monuments.[80] In addition to a national list, the municipalities produced their own lists of monuments which they wished to protect—according to councillor Ambrosini, "a weighty offence against the right of property."[81] The increase in administrative responsibilities led to a development in which more and more decisions were ratified by the council without debate. Between July and November 1912 about eighty proposals were passed in this manner. The reserve fund was used in a similar way, covering for municipal projects without prior discussion in council.[82]

The role of experts and intellectuals in determining the city's self-representation met resistance among other interest groups. A good example of that is the Exhibition of 1888, coinciding with the eight hundredth anniversary of the university.[83] Unlike comparable exhibition projects elsewhere in Italy, the event focussed on Bologna as a leading cultural centre of the nation. At the centre of the project was the International Music Exhibition, with a first-class programme of concerts and operas, coordinated by the composer Arrigo Boito and including the Italian premiere of *Tristan*. Although the exhibition also included an agricultural and an industrial show, the emphasis on music, academia and culture was criticized by the city's economic elite and by those Moderate councillors who opposed the narrow focus on culture in the city's public image. When subsequently the exhibition made a major financial loss, they were able to present strong arguments against the cultural elites:

I am sorry to say, but the deficit is the consequence of bad administration: the people at the head of the initiative were probably not sufficiently competent in drawing up contracts, organising deliveries etc. Without thinking, they assumed a responsibility which went beyond their abilities; and they failed.[84]

A few years earlier, the Milan exhibition of 1881 had generated the same conflicts, in this case opposing municipal committees against the Chamber of Commerce. While Bologna empowered its cultural elite to shape its exhibition, the event in Milan became a celebration of Lombard entrepreneurship, leaving the expectations of the cultural elite unfulfilled.[85]

Devolution from the level of politics to experts resulted in an increasing autonomy of public culture.[86] In their public role as experts men like Carducci, Panzacchi and Boito negotiated and moderated the relationship between politics, artists and the public, asserting the role of the middle class in the public domain. Narrating the past, the fostering of a historically informed civic identity, was at the core of this project. The following chapters provide telling examples of this process.

5   Medieval Revival

COMMUNAL FREEDOM AND PAPAL ENSLAVEMENT

For Thomas Mann the Germans' widespread "affinity with the Middle Ages" was a sign of reactionary mentality. However, considering options for a future Germany after the collapse of the *Kaiserreich,* Mann hoped that their nostalgia could be complemented by a new emphasis on the humanist values which the later Middle Ages also represented.[1] What this shows is that historicising references are based on complex connotations of meaning, which change over time and according to historical context. Since the late nineteenth century Germany attempted to amalgamate gothic with classical elements in creating places of worship for the nation.[2] Wagner's medieval opera *Parsifal* used modernist techniques, but was accomplished "in service of a social-cultural message" that was in its specific German context of reception anti-modern and regressive.[3] Raymond Williams has demonstrated how nineteenth-century Britain praised the social institutions of the Middle Ages as "a welcome alternative to the claims of individualism," a model of communal organisation, contrasting with the negative economic and social consequences of contemporary capitalism and industrialisation.[4] The circumstances of Italy's widespread interest in the Middle Ages were motivated by a different and at times explicitly modern agenda, even if its artistic expression assumed forms that were similar to the medieval revival in Britain and Germany. Part of what Lyttelton called the "Janus-faced nature of liberal romanticism, looking back to the Middle Ages and forward to the age of steam," Italy assumed the idea of the Middle Ages as an early modernity.[5] Along with Italian Humanism, a major point of reference in this enterprise was the year 1183, when in the Treaty of Constance Frederick Barbarossa granted the North-Italian cities self-government. The positive image of the Middle Ages contained two political references: The Middle Ages preceded the centuries of foreign intervention and political decline, which came to an end only with Unification. They also served to assert a tradition of self-government, protecting Italy's *cento città* from excessive centralisation and state intervention. In the specific case of Bologna references to the Communal Age, the period before the consolidation of Papal rule in the Lands of St. Peter, helped people to come to terms with the "patricide" of 1859, which marked the end of the Papal regime.

Reflected in the works of Francesco De Sanctis and Giosuè Carducci, Dante played a particular role in Italy's medieval revival. He had been the first to use the Italian *volgare* for complex academic and poetic treatises, thus laying the foundations for a cultural-linguistic understanding of the Italian nation. Through his emphasis on Italy's cultural unity Dante appealed thematically to nineteenth-century commentators, but also aesthetically, through a new style of representing historical realities based on "the dramatization of civic and political ideas." Petrarch was the other medieval poet who inspired the Risorgimento's imagination. However, as Andrea Ciccarelli has demonstrated, Petrarch symbolised a very different view of the Middle Ages. For Petrarch,

> memory (with its attachment to the past) represents the only faculty that can remove humanity from an ever-changing, uncontrollable reality. . . . Dante's cultural lesson . . . implies precisely the opposite point of view. The metamorphic nature of reality is not avoided but rather pursued. . . . The instability of experience includes the possibility of change from a negative to a positive mode of existence.[6]

It is this close relationship between the reference to the past and the dramatization of the present, not a conservative nostalgia of despair, which animated Bologna's medieval revival.

Since the 1860s the Communal Age became a major pedagogical instrument in the construction of civic identity. Numerous local history societies concentrated their activities on the medieval and early modern period, and on the history of the communes in particular.[7] In 1867 the national curriculum for secondary education prescribed seven and a half hours of medieval history weekly, twice as much as the time dedicated to the ancient and modern periods, justified by the fact that during this period "the modern Italian people was formed" and that history ceased to be "the history of a country but that of the nation."[8] The main reading room of Bologna's State archives collected the materials of the period *"detto del Comune o della Repubblica, dal 1062 al 1512."* The rediscovery of the Middle Ages was marked by a political climate in which the Church and the period of Papal government had become the antipode of the new nation-state. This context made the medieval revival in Italy rather different from the British experience. The medieval revival in Italy, as the Gothic style in Britain, was perceived as a national style and linked to a positive national identity. However, while in Italy the medieval revival was nurtured by anti-Papal and anti-clerical ideas, in Britain Gothic art and architecture were often understood as a positive reference to the Church, as an expression of "true faith," based on its "emotional appeal."[9] Romantically yearning for the splendour and mystery of the medieval Church, the convert Pugin and the pre-Raphaelite brotherhood made explicit references to Catholicism, to the point of challenging the protestant character of Britain's national identity.[10]

Alberto Banti has shown how historical fiction of the Risorgimento period assimilated unconnected historical events—the twelfth-century wars between Guelphs and Ghibbellines, the Sicilian Vespers of the thirteenth century, and the fights of the Florentine Republic in the sixteenth century—and invested them with "patriotic" meaning.[11] As autonomous segments of history these events anticipated the redemption of the nation, but they were not yet understood as part of a progressive-teleological development such as we find in modern, historicist narratives. The Risorgimental literature which Banti analyses—texts by Manzoni, Mazzini and Mameli, or Verdi's *libretti*—presented history not as an evolutionary process in which the nation progressively comes into being, but as a series of isolated moments, which for themselves anticipated the same promised and predestined event. The idea behind this schema is that the nation existed through a link of blood, but that its unfolding was hindered by adverse events. The protagonists of these "stories" of oppression and internal divisions were aware that the promise of a unified nation would one day be fulfilled.

In a similar fashion also Bologna's nineteenth-century preoccupation with the Middle Ages referred to a key event in the formation of Europe's political map, which became the starting point of a chain of "adverse events" hindering the unfolding of the nation for centuries. In 754 the Frankish king Pippin promised the pope to restore the lands of the Romans, referring to the forged *Constitutum Constantini imperatoris* by which Constantine the Great had supposedly granted the pope power over Rome and the Western Empire.[12] In return Pippin was solemnly anointed by Pope Stephen II as "king and patrician of the Romans." For centuries the significance of this donation remained contested between the pope, the Frankish-German Roman emperors, Byzantium, the cities of Northern Italy, and the countless local rulers of the Italian peninsula. In the Romagna, the Visconti from Milan, later the Borgia and the Venetians, as well as the Pepoli and the Bentivoglio from Bologna competed for influence and dominion, commonly conducting independent foreign policies.[13] As a consequence, Papal authority—like imperial government—in the region "was a fiction."[14] In the twelfth century Pope Innocent III had attempted to give the Papal territories a modern organisation, but at least in Bologna he was not successful in imposing his rule. In 1278 Rudolf of Habsburg ceded his imperial rights in the Romagna to the pope, leading to further friction among Bologna's elites. In particular, the period of the *signorie* was marked by civil war, famine and deprivation.[15] For Bologna, the conflict between the different powers was only resolved when in 1507 Pope Julius II defeated the *signoria* of Giovanni II Bentivoglio and his wife Ginevra Sforza. A former archbishop of Bologna, his defeat of the Bentivoglio gave Julius the reputation of a "warrior," a role hitherto unheard of for a pope.[16]

Rather as with the humanists' attack on "Papal tyranny," in the perception of Bologna's nineteenth-century discourse Julius' conquest marked the beginning of the city's "Papal enslavement," which was ended only three and a half centuries later with the liberation of 1858 and the annexation of the Legations by the kingdom of Piedmont.[17] Only once before, during the Napoleonic period, had Bologna obtained the reconfirmation of its ancient republican rights, from before the Papal rule.[18] In nineteenth-century historical and political discourse the pope's temporal dominion was more than an obstacle to the unification of Italy. In the words of councillor Regnoli, the Papal regime had been a "feudal anachronism . . . , absolutely incompatible with the principles of modern public law and with the present state of society."[19] Contrasting with these "three centuries of servitude," Carducci hailed the Communal Age for its republican freedom, an idea which reflected de Sismondi's influential account of the communes as a catalyst in the revival of European civilisation and which provided the narrative for many of Francesco Hayez' and Palagio Palagi's historical paintings during the Risorgimento.[20] Commentators such as Corrado Ricci, Gozzadini and Carducci perceived the Papal dominion since Julius II as "enslavement," but shared Mazzini's positive evaluation of the Papacy's earlier role.[21] The Catholic architect Alfonso Rubbiani described the fourteenth century, in a talk to the Association of Marble Workers, "as the period of greatest triumph for the working people," when "even the most brilliant knights had to be members of a corporation to obtain a vote and a voice in the public councils."[22] The use of the couple "tyranny and liberation" in political rhetoric was not an invention of the contemporary age. In 1506 Julius II had issued a coin for a Papal procession, carrying the inscription "Bologna freed by Julius from the tyrant."[23] However, even a man of cautious temperament like the Moderate prime minister Marco Minghetti described the period of Papal dominion that followed Julius' conquest of the city with the words "servitù, miseria, decadenza."[24] He presented the entire period as a history of continuous resistance and upheavals, culminating in the liberation of 1858.[25] On the same grounds, the Republican philosopher of history Quirico Filopanti integrated the Papal regime into a general theory of theocratic dominion. While the protestant nations progressed, a rich region like Latin-America, due to the impact of Catholic priests on education and sciences, fell back in its societal development.[26] These views reached a wide audience after Unification, from the readers of the Moderate press to the members of the local Labour organisations.

Bologna's nostalgia for the medieval communes differed from Cesare Balbo's view that communal freedom "was never complete" and represented an idea more than reality.[27] Representing the Sabaudian nobility and the Piedmontese Moderates, the author of the famous *Speranze d'Italia* feared that the historical mystification of the Communal Age after Unification would undermine the Piedmontese project of a centralized nation-state and encourage requests for municipal autonomy. Similarly, the prefects after Unification feared the recurrent references to the medieval communes. As the prefect of Turin wrote in 1868:

> Liberty is everywhere the cry, municipal autonomy, decentralisation, abstention of the government from *comunal* and provincial affairs. . . . In the municipalities many dream of the city republics of the Middle Ages, in ignorance of their history, their institutions, their character. The liberties once granted to the communes were the main cause of the evils, which are now so lamented.[28]

Hence, Piedmont and the fathers of the centralised nation-state presented a different account of medieval communal freedom than the advocates of Bologna's medieval revival, who hoped for increased municipal autonomy. Thus, the parliament, still dominated by Cavour's Piedmontese Moderates, rejected in 1861 Minghetti's bill on decentralization as "nurturing a cult of the past" and as "a threat to the political unity of the country."[29]

ARCHITECTURE FOR THE PEOPLE'S SOUL

Urban planning after Unification and the projects for the preservation of Bologna's city centre reflected the attempts to revive the municipality's historical identity. In this Bologna's urban development differed from cities like Turin, Milan and to some extent even Venice, which all sought for a "national style" in architecture.[30] The local Deputazione di Storia Patria played a major role in Bologna's urban development. Carducci defined architecture as "the walled history of a people's gestures, thoughts, and destiny," reflecting the idea that the urban environment represented for its citizens a link between the past and the present.[31] Reflecting the specific political meanings of Bologna's medieval revival, it became the Deputazione's official policy to clean any medieval building in Bologna from later architectural interventions, even if this meant destroying works of major importance from the seventeenth and eighteenth centuries. In the words of Gozzadini, Bologna had "to demolish any modern superposition on and extension of" its medieval architecture.[32] The return to the city's medieval origins also helped to rationalise and to modernise space—an example of "vernacular modernism," recognising "spatiality," along with temporality, "as a defining dimension of the modern."[33] On the occasion of the Great Exhibition of 1888 and the eight-hundred-year-celebration of the university Carducci provided the historical and aesthetic justification for this policy:

The projects of the priests and the Spanish during the seventeenth century, as well as the arcades built in the eighteenth century destroyed
Bologna, mortified her with bruises and covered her face with masks
and paint. Today, under the light of freedom, the bruises disappear
one after another, the masks fall, ceruse is taken off. Bologna's beauty
shines happily in the sun.[34]

In council meetings he argued that "streets, historical squares and monumental buildings have to be cleaned off the crusts of an uncivil transformation. . . . The clear lines, the forms, the joy and the pure beauty in
which they appeared during the times of the free Commune will finally
resurge."[35] These lines of Bologna's medieval architecture were to anticipate the modern industrial age.

This concept of preservation justified radical interventions against the
architectural relicts of the Papal period. The sixteenth-century Palazzo
Casali was sacrificed to build the modern Via Farini. Numerous buildings, including several churches and the eighteenth-century Palazzo Tazzi
Biancani, had to disappear for similar reasons.[36] In Bologna the aversion
against the architecture of the seventeenth and eighteenth centuries also
affected "the monstrosity" of decorating modern façades in the style of
these periods. The preferred style became the clear lines of the medieval
period.[37] Bologna does not represent a unique case in this form of radical intervention against historical architecture after Unification. Milan's
demolition of the Sforza Palace and the debates on San Giovanni in Conca
present similar examples.[38]

The Democratic councillor Ceneri proposed in 1867 replacing Bologna's
seventeenth-century monument for San Domenico with a statue of liberty
for the heroes of the Risorgimento.[39] The square in front of the abbey,
where the Saint had died in 1221, had just recently been named after Galileo, producing "an untenable dissonance between a simulacrum to venerate
the founder of the Inquisition and a square devoted to one of the greatest
heroes of democracy." Filopanti went beyond this proposal, suggesting that
the monument for San Domenico should remain in order to remind people
of "the precursor of persecution and of slaughter for religious fanaticism."
To educate future generations, then, a much bigger monument should be
erected next to the column, "paying tribute to the great forerunners of the
fatherland's freedom and independence." In his reply, the mayor warned
that no other commune would take such drastic decisions. "Nothing is
as unhealthy as the destruction of monuments caused by a change in time
or government." Referring to the ancient statues of Antonio and Marco
Aurelio which had been replaced by those of San Pietro and San Paolo, the
mayor sustained that "only the Popes have provided us with examples of
similar, anachronistic barbarism which history now deplores." Instead, he
wished to "remember barbarous and terrible periods" in order to illustrate
"the triumph of ideas and progress."[40] But Ceneri was not convinced:

Personally, I wait for the day when from this church, instead of the murmuring monotony of the monks, the joyous and merry singing of workers will be heard; when instead of incense we will smell the smoke of workshops; and when the times of superstition have given way to labour and industry.

Similar debates were common in Italy after Unification. In the Tuscan town Lucca several of the columns on the façade of S. Michele in Foro were decorated with busts of Garibaldi, Napoleon III, Pius IX, Vittorio Emanuele II and Cavour, placed there alongside saints and representations of wild animals dating back to the twelfth century. [41] Bologna's town hall was decorated with two plaques, one commemorating the coronation of Charles V and the other recording the first visit of Vittorio Emanuele II. After the restoration of the palace councillor Ceri suggested relocating the two plaques next to one another, "one remembering an oppressor of Italian freedom, the other a man who restored the fatherland and freedom."[42] Reminders of past oppression became negative *"lieux de mémoire"* and pedagogical tools in the civic mission of promoting the idea of freedom.

Bologna's architectural revival was partly inspired by the ideas of Viollet-le-Duc, the great French theorist of historical preservation and director of the Notre-Dame restorations in Paris. He was the preferred architect of the Impératrice and Charles Garnier's greatest competitor in building the French imperial capital. Going beyond the preservation of the historical substance, Viollet-le-Duc wanted to embellish the buildings by means of historicising imagination.[43] However, contrary to Bologna's "iconoclasts" who wished to destroy anything that was added to the original medieval architecture during later periods, Viollet-le-Duc maintained that "each part that has been added, during whatever period, must in principle be maintained, consolidated and restored in its own style."[44] Alfonso Rubbiani, the most important architect of Bologna's medieval revival, appropriated Viollet-le-Duc in his own way, appreciating the Frenchman's way of reading the past and reconstructing it where it had been destroyed, but without sharing his positive evaluation of successive interventions in a building's original design. Rubbiani's understanding of the medieval revival also contrasted with the political-historical concepts of the majority of Bologna's Liberals. As with the Catholic advocates of the Gothic style in Britain, Rubbiani's medieval revival included a spiritual dimension which was based on hopes of reconciling Catholicism with the idea of an Italian nation-state.

Rubbiani exemplifies the development of those Italians who struggled with the antithesis of legitimist convictions and a sense for *Realpolitik*. His intransigent newspaper *L'Ancora* was later absorbed by the Catholic paper *La Pace*, representing the Catholic opposition which realised that they had to integrate themselves into the political system if they wanted to influence the nation's rapidly changing political life and the transformation of society under the governments of the Left. Rubbiani started

---

Box 5.1　Alfonso Rubbiani

Born in 1848, the year of revolutions, and educated by the Jesuits in Reggio
Emilia, Alfonso Rubbiani was brought up to see the overthrow of the Papal
regime as a patricide. In his view these events provoked a trauma from which
the Italian people had to be cured through the careful reconstruction of its
historical consciousness. People should recognise themselves as Italians, but
also as Catholics and citizens of the former Papal State. Thus, he approached
the city's medieval revival from a perspective that was diametrically opposed
to the ideological foundations of the liberal and anti-clerical proponents of a
medieval revival. Rubbiani directed Bologna's *"intransigentissimo"* newspaper *L'Ancora*, which opposed the liberal nation-state on Catholic grounds.
For many years he was secretary general of the *Società della Gioventù cattolica italiana* and a representative of the *Opera dei Congressi Cattolici*, both
openly legitimist. In 1870 he interrupted his studies to fight on the side of the
Papal troops in Rome.

　　Considering this ideological background it might seem surprising that
Rubbiani, some years later, became one of Bologna's most influential architects during the liberal period, active in the city's public and political life,
secretary of the Accademia Filarmonica, a member of the Deputazione di
Storia Patria, later its treasurer, author of a textbook for primary schools and
other widely read works. In 1901, together with Count Francesco Cavazza
and the former mayor Gaetano Tacconi, he was one of the founders of the
Comitato per Bologna storica ed artistica, which promoted preservation
projects and took initiatives for the listing of historical buildings. Linked
to this circle, Rubbiani also became the leading figure behind the Arts and
Crafts movement *Aemilia Ars*.

---

describing himself as *"cattolico liberaleggiante."*[48] At about the same time
the Bolognesi Giovanni and Carlo Acquaderni, Achille Sassòli Tomba
and Luigi Fabbri, among others, turned to the transigent camp of the
Catholics and started defining themselves as "national conservatives."[49]
Rubbiani's political life between the fronts of Liberalism and intransigent Catholicism eventually led him to break with political Catholicism
altogether. His political conversion explains why he became one of Bologna's most influential architects and intellectuals, even if the moderate
Associazione costituzionale still refused to present him as a candidate
for the local elections. For the same reason also his membership in the
Accademia di Belle Arti was opposed by former Risorgimento activists.[50]
Nevertheless, he frequently attended council debates and from 1895 he
regularly wrote for Bologna's leading newspaper *Il Resto del Carlino*.[51]
Declaring himself in favour of a conservative national party, Catholic and

Italian,[52] on certain issues he was also close to the city's Democrats. He shared the Left's view of an active cultural policy and believed in the idea of forming a sense of citizenship through a strengthening of a historically informed municipal identity. Despite his nostalgia for the Papal regime, he shared Carducci's love for Bologna's period of communal government and frequently pointed to the later rivalry between the Roman Curia and Bologna. Sympathising with the concern for municipal autonomy, he maintained that "the real *patria* is the commune."[53] As Aldo Berselli explained in his study of Rubbiani's political past, it was here that "freedom and religion went hand in hand." For him the Middle Ages were "the era of Italy's great civil, cultural and religious renaissance."[54] This was the point at which Rubbiani was able to meet Carducci, the anti-clerical, but not atheist poet. Not religion, but the Church divided the two most prominent protagonists of Bologna's medieval revival.

The idea of the commune as *patria* was the guiding principle behind Rubbiani's restoration of the town hall, the people's palace. It had to offer something "to the people's soul," bringing together

> the squandered hearts of the dissolving citizenry, to inspire a new sense of collectivity. To reach these ideals . . . one has to use the arts, the glamour of the historical style, transforming the city's palace into a display of good citizenship, a symbol of union and continuity between past, present and future.[55]

Rubbiani's aesthetic message was not one of pure academic-historical accuracy in reconstruction, but one of civic education. At the same time, medieval and neo-medieval architecture had for Rubbiani a religious significance, evoking and restoring lost faith, which according to Rubbiani had once determined the lives of medieval men. "A few remains of medieval form are sufficient to provoke a hundred ideas."[56] For Rubbiani religious faith had a spatial and political notion; and the commune provided the institutional framework in which faith was practised. He also linked his preference for the medieval style in architecture to the idea of the medieval professional corporations, which Francesco de Sanctis described as an "organic" model for the organisation of social relations in contemporary society. Rubbiani's Gilda di San Francesco, a confraternity of craftsmen, explicitly referred to this model. Restoring the medieval environment meant to provide the conditions for a spiritual experience, a way of dealing with modernity.[57] Thus, Rubbiani formed a strategic-symbolic alliance with the anti-clerical forces for whom the Middle Ages predated the period of "Papal enslavement." Concerning the preservation of the medieval city, they formed a compromise, based on the shared appreciation of Bologna's medieval architecture and similar civic aims, despite a different understanding of the underlying aesthetic concepts of the medieval form: Like Rubbiani, Carducci had a poetic understanding of the medieval urban environment and was conscious of the aesthetic message the city was able to send out, but his reading of Bologna's medieval architecture emphasised the political freedom he associated with the Communal Age.[58] Carducci was uninterested in the religious attributes Rubbiani associated with Bologna's medieval remains, but understood the medieval city as a reference to the Communal Age and its political institutions, encouraging the people to experience their city as free citizens. Based on this contrast in the aesthetic appreciation of its architecture, nineteenth-century Bologna was restored as a medieval city.

Rubbiani's medieval Bologna, like Carducci's, was to a large extent an invented one. Already the new Porta Saragozza of 1859 was a work of historical fiction, designed by the engineer Brunetti-Rodati.[59] Speaking about his own work at San Francesco, Rubbiani revealed that he reconstructed the church as it "has been thought by its original architects."[60] For Rubbiani this meant to engage in a hermeneutic process during which he thinks and works with the mind of a medieval artist. "Phantasising about the remains of a single capital, he reconstructs an entire cathedral," a satirical journal commented on his work at the time.[61] Corrado Ricci spoke in this context about men who "from talking to the past learn things and get intuitions about form, which they take to be real (and often they are real), but for which one never will find a document . . . ."[62] However, in his pamphlet *Di Bologna riabbellita,* published as a spiritual testament in 1913, Rubbiani insisted that his approach was a scientific one, "comparable to history, which through the restoration of ancient facts and memories is also an art, but based on rational and scientific method."[63] Rubbiani's intuitive style has been described with horror by conservative philological preservationists and his tendency to entirely eliminate later transformations of historical architecture was opposed also by many contemporaries.[64] The lawyer Giuseppe Bacchelli, a Liberal member of parliament, voiced his concern about his project for Bologna's Palazzo del Podestà:

> Your historical and artistic concept is to restore the palazzo as it looked in 1500. "Let's eliminate what has been added in the seventeenth century." I doubt that this plan is based on good historical reasoning. The palazzo is not a building of 1500. Each century, every period of Bologna's history, has brought new buildings and has modified those which already existed. . . . Why therefore stop in 1500 and eliminate anything added in the seventeenth century? . . . Moreover, one cannot even say that you rebuild the palazzo as it looked in 1500, because you will have to build the northern part yourself . . . ; and also the open stairway will be your work. . . . Why therefore do we not respect the seventeenth century, which one day came to life in its own right?[65]

In particular, Bacchelli was concerned about Giambologna's Neptune, the city's famous fountain next to the Palazzo del Podestà, a monument of the second half of the sixteenth century, which would contrast too radically with a purely medieval façade as imagined by Rubbiani. Bacchelli described certain of Rubbiani's restoration projects as "massacres" in the urban landscape and its architect as more dangerous than the iconoclasts of previous centuries.[66] Usually, Rubbiani reconstructed Bologna's medieval architecture with features known from similar buildings elsewhere in Italy, without any proof that these elements had ever been used in Bologna. For the Palazzo del Re Enzo he added battlements to external walls. With a similar poetic imagination Carducci described Bologna's battlements,[67] but the local councillor and architect Giuseppe Ceri maintained that they were only "appropriate for cats to make love on the roofs, but not to assist soldiers in a battle." With reference to Rubbiani's role in the Arts and Crafts movement *Aemilia Ars*, Ceri suggested that he "should concentrate his time on designing lace underwear for elegant women rather than on great works of art."[68] The gendering of beauty and *Aemilia Ars* provided the argument to reject the movement as a whole. According to Bacchelli and the councillor Rivari, the aim of Rubbiani's Gilda di San Francesco was to render Bologna's monuments more beautiful than they are, "to complete and transform them!"

> The rigour of history and science is replaced by intuition. Objective examination is replaced by fantasy. One proceeds through guess, analogies, comparisons. The architect becomes an aestheticist and a reconstructivist. Historical precision is replaced with an arbitrary vision of romantic and scenic beauty![69]

Often recovering only fragments of original medieval features under layers of paint and plaster of subsequent centuries, Rubbiani appropriated these through a process of reinterpretation in medieval style.[70] Groups like his *Gilda di San Francesco* and *Aemilia Ars* developed a modern interpretation of medieval features, based on a new chromatic spectrum and floral patterns applied to the decoration of walls, windows and doorways, which anticipated aesthetically Italy's *Novecento* modernism. As a consequence, Bologna's Liberty was marked by the "recovery of pre-existing ancient forms of expression."[71] This approach allowed for an appropriation of the medieval urban landscape in a modern world and could be applied to entirely new edifices build in medieval style.

Despite the widespread critique of Rubbiani's medievalism, it is important to note that he was Bologna's most influential architect at the time, supported by a large alliance reaching from Republicans and Socialists to Liberals and Catholics. Medievalism had become a fashion which transcended ideological frontiers. He "constructed a mythic city stage on which the people of Bologna could reinvent themselves."[72] As

Figure 5.1 Palazzo del Podestà. (Reproduction by Kind Permission of the Collezioni d'Arte e di Storia della Fondazione Cassa di Risparmio, Bologna.)

the council remembers, "the entire city was in tears of sincere sorrow" when he died in 1913 and it was the Socialist majority which proposed to dedicate a street to Rubbiani, even if the opposition considered it too small for the protagonist of Bologna's medieval revival.[73]

COMMUNAL CHURCHES AND CIVIC PRIDE

Despite Rubbiani's popularity, anti-Papal iconoclasm was widespread in Bologna during the second half of the nineteenth century. Like Rubbiani, the local councillor and director of the academy Enrico Panzacchi was involved in Bologna's medieval preservation projects, but he came from the opposite end of the political spectrum, firmly representing Bologna's anti-clerical liberalism. The parts of Bologna's Palazzo Comunale originating from the centuries of Papal dominion were deemed by Panzacchi to be in open contrast to the city's historical and aesthetic development, reason enough for them to be knocked down "in honour of truth."[74] After the building had been restored according to its original medieval design, he complained that "there is a small spot which remains, which is the Madonna by Nicolò dall'Arca." Although Panzacchi was right that the majority of Bologna's sacred images in public spaces dated from the period of the Papal regime, the terracotta in question was produced in the late fifteenth century, under Giovanni II Bentivoglia's signoria. For similar reasons the art historian wished to eliminate the conch of San Petronio on the Palazzo's façade: "It shamelessly presents the pompous and discordant seventeenth century. Our town-hall will look revoltingly until it is taken away, presenting the entire front according to the rules of harmony and good taste." Piazza Maggiore had to present itself "as one of Italy's or even Europe's most beautiful squares," meaning that its original medieval design had to be reconstructed. Post-risorgimental Bologna had to be returned into a medieval city, eradicating three hundred and fifty years of Papal rule.

Like Rubbiani, Panzacchi supported the city's historicising embellishment, the recreation of a medieval environment, even where original medieval architecture did not exist. San Petronio, Bologna's municipal cathedral, played a central role in this project, a symbol of the city's medieval sense of *libertas* and its independence from Roman dominion. In size and magnificence San Petronio was more impressive than the city's Episcopal Cathedral San Pietro. In its original design the church should have been 216 meters long, 36 meters longer than Saint Peter in Rome, with a dome 152 meters high, one and a half times the size of the city's famous Asinelli tower. The church was never completed in these dimensions, but it was clearly more impressive than the Archbishop's church, located in a narrow street, with only one free-standing façade. Piazza Maggiore, with San Petronio at its head, was certainly among the most spectacular squares of the entire peninsula.

As "examples of sacred horror," Panzacchi wanted later modifications to the façade "to be removed," but he also campaigned for its completion—against the views of the so-called "dogmatists," who, like Carducci, understood the existing, fragmentary façade as a historical monument. According to Carducci, the cathedral's restoration should not result in its re-invention.[75] Since the fourteenth century Bologna had discussed projects to complete the façade of San Petronio. Some of the surviving sketches had been considered by the ecclesiastical and civic authorities, but were rejected for aesthetic or financial reasons. Before 1848 the composer Gioacchino Rossini and a group of local noblemen initiated a subscription for the façade's completion. Pius IX approved a contribution of 75.000 Roman Scudi (375,000 Italian Lire at the time), but the Italian Kingdom, as the inheritor of the Papal State, later ignored the promise.[76] In the 1880s Giuseppe Ceri became a major promoter of the idea. In 1887 he won a prize for a project to complete the façade in the Cinquecento style, corresponding to patterns of the existing façade. But the project was not taken further and Bologna's difficult budget situation protected the city from a romanticising completion in the fashion of the Florentine Santa Maria del Fiore. However, the committee for the completion of San Petronio survived and was later led by Count Giuseppe Grabinski, representing the city's most reactionary and anti-liberal facet of legitimist Catholicism. He saw the completion not as a project of urban development, but as a public testimony to the strength of the Catholic faith and as a manifestation against the patricide of 1859. The Fascist regime revived the idea once more, resulting in further polemics, but not in a project that could satisfy the various committees involved.

Panzacchi's outrage against the architectural legacies of the Papal regime was influential, but the political majorities in the council stopped his iconoclastic programme from being put into practice. As the liberal councillor Sacchetti remarked, "one epoch cannot pass judgement over others; the specific style which corresponds to our taste should not dominate everything, otherwise we run the risk of eliminating historical features which are valuable and interesting in their own right."[77] Hence, not everybody involved in the city's urban planning shared the medieval project. Similar to respective debates in Britain, proponents of the Classical style were ideologically strongly opposed to the medieval revival.[78] Coriolano Monti, the first head of the municipality's planning unit after 1860, favoured the neo-Renaissance for the new Bologna, but his views were opposed by the local Academy of Fine Arts, which was influential in the city's artistic decisions.[79] Giuseppe Ceri, who was greatly influenced by Monti, was inspired by Palladio's Venetian style. His own hatred against Bologna's medieval revival went so far that he wished Bologna's ancient towers to disappear from the urban landscape.[80] However, his ornamental style was considered a "return to the baroque, producing with the help of pretty details an effect which altogether is neither beautiful nor elegant."[81]

It might seem surprising that after the Liberation from the Papal regime Bologna showed any concern at all for the Church's architectural patrimony. However, many ecclesiastical buildings in Bologna were publicly owned, often by the municipality. Cathedral and church building during the Middle Ages "was first of all a civic undertaking" and churches were "symbols of civic majesty and freedom . . . dedicated to the glory of God and the commune."[82] Even anti-clericals like Carducci and Panzacchi had no difficulty associating themselves with this tradition. Local cults of saints were often civic creations rather than inventions of the ecclesiastical hierarchy. Instead of following the doctrines of the Church, the communes tended to devote themselves to their local saints, favouring civic cults of their patrons, "in many cases substituted for saints of older church tradition."[83] Despite its anti-Papal rhetoric liberal Bologna appreciated this legacy. The basilica of Santo Stefano, a complex of several churches traditionally referred to as "Gerusalemme" or "Sette Chiese," is among Bologna's most spectacular ecclesiastical buildings, due to its ancient origins, its reliquaries and its symbolic references to the New Jerusalem, the idea of representing the commune as a city of God.[84] A document by Emperor Charles the Fat from the year 887 refers to the basilica as *"qui dicitur sancta Hierusalem,"* a long time before the Crusades made similar symbolic references fashionable.[85] The number seven in the basilica's popular appellation "Sette Chiese" did not refer to a total of seven churches, but represented a mystical symbol, the idea of totality, used in the bible as a magical number of sacred powers.[86] Based on a pagan temple, Santo Stefano was the location of Bologna's first Christian cult. The square in front of the basilica was used as a central market from 1074, well before Piazza Maggiore became the commercial centre of the city. One of the basilica's four surviving edifices, the church of the Santo Sepolcro, was supposedly built with materials from the Holy Land and sustained by twelve columns from a Roman temple for the Egyptian goddess Isis. The church contained the reliquaries of Vitale and Agricola, the first known martyrs of Bologna, and of San Petronio, the city's patron, to whom the municipal cathedral was dedicated. Also, according to a local myth the body of Saint Peter was buried in one of the churches, a belief taken seriously enough to cause Pope Alexander VI to pronounce an edict which excommunicated anybody holding this view.[87] Hence, more than anything Santo Stefano was a place of communal worship, a tradition to which the Liberals also wanted to relate. Until the fifteenth century the bishop, together with the clerical and the civil authorities of Bologna, visited San Petronio's grave once a year to demonstrate that their spiritual and civic power over the city derived from the patron. Later it became customary that on the day before the patron's celebration the shrine with the Saint's head was brought from Santo Stefano to San Petronio. Then the relic had to be returned, in a solemn popular procession, to the monks of Santo Stefano. Each year notaries of the two institutions set up a new legal document for the transfer.[88] Only in the eighteenth century did the monks of Santo Stefano pass the relic to the Bolognese Pope Benedict XIV, who transferred the shrine to the Cathedral on a permanent basis.

The history of Santo Stefano closely mirrors the complex historical relationship between the institutions of the Church and the commune. In 1867 Count Gozzadini denounced the many transformations of the basilica during the early modern period, comparing the interventions of Alexander VI and Julius II to the devastations caused by the Hungarian invasions of the year 902. Playing on the double meaning of the word "pieta" as a representation of the mourning Virgin as well as a "wretched figure," he called the eighteenth-century Madonna of Santo Sepolcro "a pieta also from an aesthetical point of view."[89] The church had lost many of its ancient traces, but it still offered an impressive spectrum of the city's agitated history. The widespread public interest in the restoration of the basilica was also motivated by speculations that excavations could reveal an original "primitive" basilica under the crypt of SS.Vitale e Agricola, establishing Bologna as one of the very first centres of Christianity on the peninsula.[90] It was the early history of the basilica and the period before the fourteenth century which interested Bologna during its medieval revival. The Deputazione di Storia Patria took the initiative for the temple's restoration, applying in its own capacity for funding from the minister of education, the commune and the province.[91] For the commune the contribution to the project was part of its policy of civic regeneration under the administration of the Democrat Camillo Casarini, who, despite the explicitly anti-clerical tenor of his local administration, showed a greater interest in the issue than any of his Moderate predecessors. The intervention was indeed radical.

Most of the altars, built over the centuries by Bologna's best families in different parts of the basilica, had to disappear. The sixteenth-century portico on the back of SS. Vitale e Agricola and the Capella Banzi in the baptistery were suppressed. A portico in the Pilato Court and the terracotta columns of the fifteenth century around the sepulchre were removed. Hence, the works concerned to a large extent the interventions of the past three hundred and fifty years, restoring as far as possible the basilica's original medieval aspect. The square in front of the church was lowered to the original level of the Romanic period, resulting in a noticeable gradient between the buildings on one side of the square and the basilica on the other side, and offering an unusual and aesthetically fortunate perspective on the entire medieval complex. The works took until the 1920s to be completed, half a century after Carducci's and Gozzadini's first sod.[92]

TOWERS, PORTICI AND ANCIENT WALLS

Since the Middle Ages Bologna has been called the *"città portificata e turrita,"* referring to two unique characteristics of Bologna's inner city architecture: its thirty-eight kilometres of arcaded streets; and its towers, of which the two most famous examples assumed over the centuries a meaning as landmarks for the city comparable in their role to the famous *torre pendente* in Pisa.[93] The Torre degli Asinelli, ninety-eight meters high, was built in 1109, the forty-seven-meter Torre della Garisenda a year later. The latter, leaning impressively to one side and mentioned in Dante's *Inferno*, is recognisable in the earliest panoramic views of the city.[94] Bologna's towers represented the history of the city's old families and of their historical continuity from the end of the Roman Empire to the Unification of Italy. Many papers read at the Deputazione di Storia Patria dealt with the history of Bologna's noble families of that period and Count Gozzadini narrated the history of Bologna's one hundred and eighty-one towers as architectural monuments of the city's civil wars and its internal divisions.[95] For Gabriele D'Annunzio, in 1917, the towers became a symbol for Italy's "divine and ferocious war" against the Empire, an expression of the people's love "for every Italian wall, for every stone, for every brick, for the most humble home."[96]

A similar function was assumed by Bologna's *portici*, its arcaded streets in the inner city. Most of the *portici* had been constructed during the sixteenth and seventeenth centuries, but their origins were medieval and therefore seen as a characteristic feature of Bologna's communal

government.[97] The Roman origin of this unique feature of urban architecture was used to give legitimacy to Bologna's claim as one of Italy's
most ancient cities.[98] Nevertheless, in the context of Bologna's medieval
revival it seems not surprising that those *portici* constructed during the
sixteenth and seventeenth centuries, under the Papal government, were
described as less solid deviations from the original design. Bologna rediscovered the *portici* as a "mediator" between the city's public and private
space, between public streets and private homes, allowing pedestrians to
walk protected from rain, the sun, dirt, sewer drains or traffic. Therefore,
the *portici* were discussed as an original invention, perfectly adaptable to
the requirements of an expanding modern city. In the past, foreign tourists had sometimes remarked upon the dusky, dirty atmosphere of the
shops under the *portico,* with a reputation of inviting crime and dubious trades of all kinds.[99] After Unification Bologna reversed this image.
Architectural improvements and comfortable shopping facilities invited
for comparison with the nineteenth-century arcades of Europe's major
metropolis. Hence, the *portici* acquired a special status in the city's folk-
loristic representation, marketed as an original symbiosis of the ancient
and the modern.

Figure 5.2   Portico della Morte. (Reproduction by Kind Permission of the
Biblioteca dell'Archiginnasio, Bologna, Italy.)

The ancient city walls represent the third feature of medieval architecture that underwent a major re-evaluation after Unification. As in many other Italian cities, their demolition was at the centre of political debates, in particular since the city's development plan of 1889, aimed at reorganising urban space and preparing the city for the twentieth century.[100] While according to the plan the ancient walls had to disappear, most gates were preserved. Arguments in favour of the city's modernization were confronted with views which emphasised the walls' symbolic meaning, pointing to the sites of Bologna's heroic battles during the city's liberation from the Papal regime. Bologna was keen to have its own "Porta Pia," a reference to the Roman city gate at which in 1870 General Raffaele Cadorna defeated the Papal troops and entered the Holy City to make it the capital of the Italian kingdom. Bologna's respective site of memory was Porta di Galliera, the Northern city gate, used throughout the Risorgimento by Austrian troops, but also the site of their defeat in 1848 and again in 1858. In 1886 the local administration presented two plans to link the railway station with the city centre through a new "independence mall," Via Indipendenza. One of the plans involved demolishing the gate, while the other would result in a deviation of the new axis, maintaining the gate, but losing the direct connection between the city's central square and Bologna's station, the symbol of its modern development. According to the mayor Dallolio, "ancient monuments deserve respect, but this sentiment should not develop into fetishism. Moreover, neither the [municipal] committee for the maintenance of monuments nor the [national] Council for public works considered Porta Galliera an artistic monument."[101] However, for patriotic reasons Carducci considered the monument worth maintaining, even if it was not a medieval fabric but a construction of the seventeenth century. While councillor Sandoni insisted on the people's "patriotic sentiments" for Porta Galliera, the mayor explained "that the administration does not need to take lessons in patriotism. Everybody cares for and loves the memories of our Risorgimento; everybody feels the *religione della patria* of which one probably speaks too much today." The temporary liberation in 1848 "took place at the Montagnola—where the annual commemorations are celebrated—not at Porta Galliera, from where the enemy escaped and later re-entered the city. Hence, there is no patriotic reason to maintain the gate."[102] Despite the mayor's reservations the gate remained, and in 1926 it was integrated into a monumental square commemorating the city's liberation.

Among those opposed to the demolition of the walls was also the *Comitato per Bologna Storica-Artistica* of the Catholic Rubbiani. For him the walls were a "monument of most beautiful artistic and historical quality." In 1905, at a time when their demolition was already far advanced, he even rebuilt parts of a previously destroyed wall dating back to the year 1000 and bearing witness to the city's most ancient origins.[103]

COMMUNAL MYTHS

Neo-Guelph narratives represented the consensus of much historical writing in Italy. Municipal traditions and the *piccola patria* never ceased to be important for Italy's collective identities, despite the State's centralising approach to Unification after 1859. The emphasis on municipal autonomy in the neo-Guelph historiography stood for a feeling that with the decline of the communal liberties a central element of *italianità* had disappeared, an idea of the Italian nation which was based on the cities' cultural identity rather than on an ethnic concept. It was the loss of this notion of *italianità* which the people around Carducci deplored.[104]

While the neo-Guelph historiography in Italy, during and after the Risorgimento, explored the historical theme of defeating "foreign," imperial dominion, for Bologna the imagination of the Communal Age as an age of freedom was less focused on the idea of foreign dominion, but served as a contrast to the subsequent centuries of Papal rule. Despite this emphasis, Carducci made it clear that the collective memory of "Papal enslavement" did not lead him to assume a neo-Ghibelline or pro-imperial position. In a series of university lectures on "national literature," originally published in *Nuova Antologia* and reprinted in multiple editions, he explained:

> We do not sympathise with the Emperor or outrage the Pope. Let us leave these debates to the Arcadian poetry of the Ghibellines, who hate Peter as a consequence of their love of Caesar. Instead, let us admire the Italian people, . . . the people, which one fine day went in between the two adversaries [Pope and Emperor], to pronounce: I am here as well![105]

Early in the fourteenth century Petrarch had described Bologna as "defaced by war, slavery and famine, and recognisable only by its great churches and towers; singing had given way to sighing, and dancing troops of girls to bands of robbers and murderers." Thus, he introduced the concept of the Dark Ages into the periodization of history.[106] Carducci, an excellent connoisseur of Petrarch's work, made reference only to those sections of his work in which the poet "stigmatised the cardinals as rich, insolent, rapacious."[107] In Carducci's version of the Communal Age the focus is always on the people's victories and the "aura of freedom" which reigned in Bologna, praising the city as an idyll of academic scholarship: "Here, where the thoughtful commentator of the law was able to write without lifting his eyes from the desk, and where Bologna smiles, illuminated by the sun, with its red buildings in terracotta and its forest of new towers."[108]

Minghetti saw Italy's Communal Age in a similar way, "at the highest degree of prosperity and greatness," contrasting this period with the time after the surrender to the pope: "By the time of Charles V's coronation all this had disappeared: decadence reigned everywhere—incontestably, universally and dreadfully."[109] His coronation by the pope became one of the darkest days in the city's history, "expression of the idea of universal domination, material domination, spiritual domination. The church shook hands with the Empire . . . poor humanity."[110]

Although modern research acknowledges the city's stagnation under the Papal dominion, the Liberals presented a highly selective view of the period.[111] Bologna became an independent commune only during the twelfth century—as Max Weber put it, a "revolutionary usurpation" against legitimate powers, later legalised by manipulated documents, which during the nineteenth century were used as historical evidence for the glorification of communal freedom.[112] Already from the early thirteenth century, long before Julius II, life in the city could hardly be described as a Golden Age. Gina Fasoli speaks about "the myth of the Commune." Most of the communes in Emilia and Romagna "experienced republican moments and longer periods of tyranny."[113] Even Sismondi, who influenced most nineteenth-century reconstructions of the medieval past, acknowledged that "the political liberty of the Italian republics, like that of their classical ancestors, had its gravest shortcomings in the failure to protect the civil liberty of the individual." Participation in political life or eligibility for public office was based on income and property, leading Max Weber to describe the communes as a private club of wealthy citizens.[114] The Republican regimes were soon replaced by *signoria,* what usually meant despotic rule, more onerous than the direct rule of the Church and depending on protection through third forces—Venice, Milan, Florence, or fractions of these powers.[115] From the thirteenth century, life in the Italian city-states was dominated by fights between these factions, organised crime, fraud, tax evasion and the abuse of power by the holders of public offices. In Bologna, the fights between Ghibellines and Guelphs cost the lives of thousands of citizens and the rule of the changing seigniorial families was usually corrupt and burdensome for its citizens. The famous cry of the mob during these battles—"*carne! carne!* [meat! meat!]"—gives us a flavour of the atmosphere reigning at the time.[116] Increasingly, the cities suffered from poverty, declining birth rates, a lack of investment in public infrastructure—a picture far from the idealised image which the *Carducciani* presented in their glorification of communal freedom.[117] The nineteenth-century version of the past omits the fact that Julius II's triumphant entry into Bologna ended a period of despotic rule and decline, leading to political stability and eventually to Bologna's economic and cultural resurgence. Papal government did not replace the commune as such, but its rule by a single family. With its hierarchy of courts based on positive written laws and uniform procedures, some historians even argue that the transformation of the temporal dominion of the pontiffs into a principality made the Church into a "prototype for the modern State."[118]

FROM GHIBELLINES AND GUELPHS
TO LIBERALS AND SOCIALISTS

The post-Risorgimental historical narratives reflect the complexities of a city after centuries of Papal dominion. Bologna had an uneasy and often contradictory relationship to its past as a Guelph city. While Italy celebrated its Guelph past as an early attempt to liberate itself from foreign domination, Bologna had difficulties acknowledging that during most of the Middle Ages Papal power ensured independence from the Empire. Instead, the *Rivista Bolognese di Scienze* celebrates the Emperor Frederick II as a hero of religious tolerance.[119] Pontida, the village where the Lombard cities united against Barbarossa, hardly played a role in Bologna's official historical discourse.[120] In 1876 Bologna commemorated the seven hundred years since the battle of Legnano, the victory of the confederated communes over imperial rule, described by Carducci as "the first Latin revolution, the origin of the resurgent Italian people." However, Francesco Bertolini, a local history professor, rejected the idea that the battle had been fought for Italian interests, emphasising instead its benefits for the Roman curia.[121] When in 1876 the Workingmen's Society proposed a staging of Verdi's *La Battaglia di Legnano* the project was rejected.[122] Legnano presented the Liberals with too many contradictions and the Catholics were keen to remind the nation that Umberto III of Savoy had been an ally of Barbarossa, while Alessandro III, like Pius IX, was presented as an Italian patriot. Bertolini took his critique of neo-Guelph historiography so far as to describe the period as one of hatred between the Italian cities, with negative effects on the entire peninsula.[123]

A telling example of the ambiguity of Bologna's historical narratives and of the complex legacy of the fights between Guelphs and Ghibellines are the local stories about Re Enzo and the end of the Hohenstaufen in Italy. With the sudden death of Frederick II in 1250 the Church had lost its most important enemy. Frederick's son Konrad IV, the German king, was defeated by French and Papal troops and died in 1254. His other son, Enzo, king of Sardinia and commander of the imperial troops, had been captured by the Bolognesi. According to the myth, Enzo was the *stupor mundi's* preferred son and the very picture of his father. The last Hohenstaufen in a position to revive the Ghibelline cause, the young Enzo remained imprisoned in Bologna for nearly a quarter of a century, until his death in 1272. His domicile, later called the "Palazzo del Re Enzo," was located next to the town hall on Piazza Maggiore, permanently under the eyes of the pope's *cardinale legato*. Over centuries stories about Re Enzo remained popular in Bologna, far from being unsympathetic.[124] For the local school of painting Re Enzo became a much appreciated subject. Vittorio Emanuele II acquired Ippolito Bonaveri's *Enzo prigioniero in Bologna* for his local residence, Villa San Michele in Bosco; and Cesare Masini, secretary of Bologna's Academy of Fine Arts, sent his *Enzo re fatto prigioniere dai bolognesi alla battaglia di Fossalta* to the 1867 Universal Exhibition in Paris.[125] In 1905 Ottorino Respighi performed his first opera *Re Enzo* in Bologna. For Rubbiani the Palazzo del Re Enzo played a central role in returning Bologna into a medieval city, despite the architect's own Papalist-Catholic convictions.[126] According to the popular myth, "during clear nights the blond head of king Enzo still appears at the window of his prison, admiring the silence and the moon," looking out over Piazza Maggiore, which Carducci had once called "*la più bella piazza d'Italia.*"[127] From a symbol for the Ghibelline cause, Enzo had become part of Bologna's local patrimony.

In 1915, after Italy entered the war, the Socialist *giunta* suggested calling the square adjacent to Enzo's prison Piazza del Re Enzo. But was Frederick's son not a German, suggesting that the proposed denomination made explicit reference to the enemy? Was the Socialist proposal for the change meant to offend the Italian interventionists? Or was the name still a sign of the city's Risorgimental and anti-Papal spirit? Councillor Berti opposed the proposal, "because Enzo was not even Italian and moreover a vanquished," inappropriate for a nation in war. However, another councillor explained that the people of Bologna had always maintained their "sympathy for the handsome young man, who also had been an Italian poet, writing with great nobility in finest Italian."[128] "One can not really say that he was German, because he was the son of Frederick II, a born Italian and the grandson of Constance of Sicily, who Dante famously remembers as Italian." Also Bertolini associated Frederick II with the beginnings of Italian literature and Minghetti counted him among the fathers of a united Italy.[129]

Being Italian meant to be Guelph, aligned with the pope against a "foreign" emperor, but in Bologna it also meant opposition to the Papal regime. The emperor's defeat was a triumph of *Italianità*, understood as independence from the Empire, but the emperor himself was a born Italian who grew up in the streets of Palermo. With the collapse of Europe's old order in the Great War also the idealist historical narratives of the nineteenth century seemed to vanish. Confused, the council approved the proposal and ever since Bologna paid official tribute to Re Enzo, the son of a German emperor, who had been defeated by the pope. Did Bologna finally cease to be a Guelph city, bringing the Risorgimento to a conclusion? Or was the new denomination of the square an expression of the Socialists' Internationalism, a modern version of International Papacy? Again, the same history could have multiple meanings. An advocate of the strong centralised state rather than municipal autonomy, the Nationalist councillor Perozzi compared Bologna's "Municipal Socialism" and its support for the International League of Socialist Communes with the anti-governmental attitudes of the ancient Guelph cities.

> What was in the minds of the ancient Guelphs? Two ideas, one international, one *comunal*. The international idea was the Catholic idea. They stood with the Pope and wanted the action of the *Comune* to be subordinated to the Pope where the interests of Catholicism were concerned. The

comunal idea consisted in a lively sense of the identity of the *comune* and a desire for its autonomy. Armed with these two ideas, they declared war against the State, the only State that they could conceive of at that time, that is the Empire. . . . You [Socialists] have the same mentality. . . . You too have two ideas, an international and a *comunal* idea. . . . Armed with these two ideas you too go to war against the State. . . . I am a Ghibelline. For me, before the Pope, above the Pope, comes the King—meaning the Italian State. . . . And I reject vigorously and fervently anything which tends to diminish the sovereignty and the power of the Italian State.[130]

Even under the conditions of World War I the Middle Ages were still able to divide the council. However, historical allegations were also read as references to Bologna's long-lasting tradition of celebrating a cult of the past, an approach which the different political frictions shared and cherished. In their response to the Nationalist councillor, the Socialists happily admitted that Perozzi had pronounced *"un bel discorso"*![131] After Unification historicism constituted a major ingredient of local politics; with the new century historicism was merely perceived as *"un bel discorso."* The past continued to be reconfigured into local and national narratives. The crafting of these narratives, at a time when the nation struggled to come to terms with the experience of modernity, shows the inter-temporality of the post-modern, leading the historian to question the idea of a post-modern age as an epoch in itself. History, in its literary construction, is a momentum, not a fact: it is time passing, which acquires direction only in the hands of those who make use of it.

MODERNISM, THE PAST AND CRISIS

Frequently, we associate Italy at the time of its intervention in World War I with the aesthetic avant-garde. However, the emphasis on modernism and futurism in Italy's cultural debates around the turn of the century should not distract from the fact that narratives of the past were at the core of cultural politics. A society's interest in the past is often interpreted as an indicator of *crepuscolarism,* "when men sense the waning of a civilization."[132] In a similar line of argument, and with reference to the aesthetic concepts of Wagner and Nietzsche, many theorists point to the "social order, which has turned from the worship of ancestors and past authorities to the pursuit of a projected future."[133] However, as aesthetic experiences, past and future were closely connected, despite the fact that under modern conditions men lost the confidence to predict the future on the basis of past experiences. As Mikael af Malmborg argued, "modern Italian history stands out as particularly marked by the contrasts between an inherent archaic reality and abstract visions of the future."[134] What he describes as an "archaic reality" was the historical legacy of absolute monarchy and of municipal traditions reaching back to the Middle Ages; "visions of the future" were articulated not only in terms of political ideologies but also aesthetically, through modernism in the arts. Carl Schorske resolves this apparent contradiction by discussing modernism as the "antithesis" of the past, forming a dialectic relationship and confronting the present metaphorically through the exploration of historical legacies.[135]

This dialectic relationship also helps to explain the ways in which Italy, during the *fine secolo*, confronted crisis. Despite the gravity of Italy's political and economic development, culminating in the colonial disaster of Adowa in 1896, in General Pelloux' authoritarian response to the social unrest of 1899 and finally in the assassination of Umberto I, decay and moral decline are problematic categories when applied to the Italian *fine secolo*. As Ruth Ben-Ghiat has argued with reference to Gramsci, the "crisis of civilization was partly a projection of elites' fears over the loss of hegemony."[136] Social and cultural change was interpreted as crisis, in an attempt to conserve existing power relations. Moreover, applied to Italy's cultural development since the turn of the century, the concept of *Decadentismo* "erases the complex relationship between the pre- and the post-war period" with its multiple reactions to societal change, pre-determining aesthetic assessment through a moral judgement of the artistic experience.[137] Rather than giving itself up to decadence and celebrating its moral decline, *fine secolo* Italy confronted the crisis of the present by linking the consciousness of its past to expectations of the future.

According to the philosopher Hans Blumenberg myths are marked by the persistence of their narrative nucleus, implying that they are easily recognisable. Meanwhile, the variability of their outer shell allows for their assimilation to changing historical, social and cultural conditions.[138] What are the implications of these characteristics for the writing of urban and national pasts? Adrian Lyttelton argued that municipal identity and the *piccola patria* never ceased to be important in the "Making and Remaking" of Italy's "national past."[139] The example of Bologna shows that there was not one national past coexisting with many municipal pasts. Instead, individual municipal pasts generated different national pasts, each of which was characterised by specific regional and municipal experiences. Lyttelton challenges Ernest Gellner's assertion that nationalism "radically transforms" the "historically inherited proliferation of cultures" and the view that the "patches used by nationalism are often arbitrary historical inventions."[140] Emphasising the importance of tradition in the representation of the historical "repertoire," Lyttelton argues that the historical material which historians used in order to write the past did not leave much space for manipulation. Therefore, he rejects the term "construction" in the context of national histories, "because the materials were not new, only the uses to which they were put."[141] However, in the former Papal Legations the account of Italy's origins in the medieval conflict between Papacy and Empire was discussed in the light of subsequent historical developments and the assertion of the Papacy's temporal power in the territories, perceived and reconstructed as "Papal enslavement." As a consequence, regional and municipal experiences created new "versions" of the past, which overruled the "national" narratives. They were "constructed" according to very specific local or regional experiences and needs. Similarly, the narratives of Italy's origins in Republican or imperial Rome, or in the early Italic civilisations made different uses of the same material. Carducci and Rubbiani employed tropes of imagination to fill the gaps where historical evidence for continuity was lacking, similar to the way in which writers of Romantic opera librettos bridged historical events with dramatic content. The following chapter provides similar examples with regard to the rediscovery of the pre-Roman Italic tribes. The example of Bologna's medieval revival supports Lyttelton's conclusions that "the plurality of interpretations and their ideological significance does not imply that they are arbitrary," or that they are historically uninformed. However, imagination played a crucial role in this enterprise, which cannot be ignored and which often formed the cornerstone of the different local accounts of the national past. Moreover, the example of Bologna illustrates that 1848 was not the turning point "which determined the passage from a hegemonic narrative centred on the city to one centred on the monarchy," as Lyttelton argued. The plurality of municipal narratives persisted well into the *fine secolo* and was continuously supplemented by additional, national versions of the past.

6 Etruscans, Romans and Italians

*Es hängt vom subjektiven Nachleben, nicht vom objektiven Bestand
der antiken Erbmasse ab, ob wir zu leidenschaftlicher Tat angeregt
oder zu abgeklärter Weisheit beruhigt werden. Jede Zeit hat die
Renaissance der Antike, die sie verdient.*

(Aby Warburg)[1]

L'ANTICA SAPIENZA ITALIA

Hans Robert Jauss has demonstrated that the Enlightenment's disenchantment of the forces of nature went hand in hand with the creation of new
myths concerned with the origin of mankind, early forms of social organisation and religion.[2] Giambattista Vico and later the Republican writer
Vincenzo Cuoco, member of the 1799 Republican government of Naples,
revived the ancient myth of the Italian nation's Etruscan origins. A modern
Italian translation of Vico appeared in 1816 and we find the same theme
in Ugo Foscolo's verse and prose, in the works of Manzoni, Mazzoldi and
Berchet, as well as in the neo-Guelph idea of the Italians' moral primacy.[3]
However, interest in the Etruscans predated the Enlightenment and the
revolutionary period. When Napoleon turned the grand duchy of Tuscany
into the kingdom of Etruria, this was meant as a reference to Cosimo de'
Medici, the first grand duke of Tuscany, who in 1532 had assumed the title
Magnus Etruriae dux.[4] Petrarch, Cusanus, Florentine neo-Platonism as
well as the cabalistic writings of Pico and Reuchlin discussed Pythagoras'
Etruscan origins, the myth according to which the philosopher transmitted an ancient Etruscan-Italic knowledge, *l'antica sapienza italica*, which
was said to be at the origin of the Greek school of philosophy and science.
In this view the Etruscans rather than the Greeks were *fons et origo* of
European thought and civilisation.[5] The interest in ancient origins and
greatness was not an invention of nineteenth-century nationalism, but
widespread in early modern Europe from the fourteenth century. Four
centuries later, in the search for the origins of the Italian nation, these
ideas were integrated into a new context. Nostalgic invocations of past

greatness compensated for what was perceived to be Italy's civic decline during centuries of internal divisions and foreign domination.

From the seventeenth century historical consciousness was underpinned by a more systematic approach to archaeological research. The Lyonnais Jacob Spon (1647–1685) used the term archaeology to apply to a scientific discipline based on the methodical criticism of archaeological sources.[6] Cosimo II de' Medici (1590–1621) asked the Scottish Catholic émigré Thomas Dempster to compile *De Etruria regali*, a work rediscovered during the eighteenth century, inspiring a flow of books and dissertations on Etruscan Italy.[7] The Accademia Etrusca at Cortona was founded in 1726 and a decade later the noble cleric Mario Guarnacci started excavating the Etruscan remains at Volterra. The Scottish architect Robert Adam decorated the country houses of his English patrons in the Etruscan style, claiming that the characteristics of Roman architecture derived not from the Greeks, but from the indigenous Etruscans. Derby House in London was decorated in Etruscan style in 1773 and in 1830 the Kronprinzenpalais in Berlin received its *Etrurisches Kabinett*. In 1852 Carlo Alberto of Savoy invited the Bolognese painter Pelagio Palagi to design an Etruscan room for his Castello di Racconigi in Turin. Bologna's nineteenth-century *Etruscomania* started from Palagi.[8]

ROME AND THE REST

The humanists' early interest in the Etruscans focussed principally on the origins of ancient Rome. The learned societies, which sprang up from the eighteenth century, and which were made up predominantly by gentlemen, developed a "more complex" concept of the peninsula's ancient origins, an Italy profoundly marked by a variety of pre-Roman civilisations. These antiquarians were travellers and extended the historical evidence beyond the ancient literary sources used by the humanists; for them "Etruscan antiquities counted hardly less than Roman ruins" and made up for the fact that no Etruscan literature had survived.[9] Moreover, the idea that the Etruscans were the peninsula's most ancient civilisation could be turned against Rome, ancient Rome as well as the modern, Papal Rome. Eighteenth-century *Etruscheria* saw in ancient Rome "a conquering oppressor, and its modern counterpart as a centre of clerical reaction and an obstacle to nationalist aspirations."[10] It is no surprise that these ideas were welcome in Bologna. As Momigliano explained,

> Italian scholars were looking for a new focus for their patriotic feelings and cultural interests. Deeply rooted in their regional traditions and suspicious of Rome for various reasons, they found what they wanted in the Etruscans, Pelasgians and other pre-Roman tribes. Local patriotism was gratified by the high antiquity of pre-Roman civilizations.[11]

Winckelmann was influenced by such ideas when he explained the supposed superiority of the Florentine culture in terms of the city's Etruscan origins. Widely read in Italy, Winckelmann influenced Foscolo and Carducci; Minghetti studied him while preparing for his journey to Egypt, just a few months before the Liberation of the Papal Legations.[12] Theories about the Etruscan conquest of Rome in the late seventh century, though based on flimsy evidence, evoked passionate debates among historians. Inspired by Karl Otfried Müller's work, historians also believed the Etruscans to be at the origin of religious life in Rome.[13] Although concepts such as ethnicity, residence and origin might have been completely irrelevant in determining rule in early Rome, these were questions which mattered to nineteenth-century historians, operating with contemporary "scientific" concepts.[14]

Despite this widespread academic interest, the Etruscan past did not play an important part in the literature and iconography of the Risorgimento. Banti explains this hesitation to explore the paleo-Italian past for the poetic creation of a founding myth with people's lack of familiarity with the pre-Roman period and the distance to its historical content.[15] However, one might doubt if the same people were indeed more familiar with the history of the Huns, used for Verdi's *Attila,* or the kings of the Old Testament, as in *Nabucco.* Based on exotic themes, both operas became extremely popular. Moreover, specific references to Roman history, particularly to the imperial period, were also rare in the literary imagination which informed the Risorgimento. While Croce explained this by the patriots' desire to distinguish themselves from the symbolism of the revolutionary Jacobins, Banti argues that the internal divisions and the conquests, which characterised Rome's imperial period, were inappropriate for the construction of a national founding myth which was based on voluntarism. The Republican Quirico Filopanti explains in his *Storia Universale* how Rome became an oppressive power "*come tutti i conquistatori.*" In Southern Italy ancient Rome was perceived as a negative symbol for outside interference, hindering good government.[16] From the point of view of these arguments, it might seem surprising to find that the vicissitudes of the medieval or early modern periods occupied such a prominent place in the Risorgimento canon of literature, in Berchet's "civic prose," Verdi's operas, or the works of Manzoni. However, here it was assumed that the nation itself was already in existence and that the narratives about the peninsula's restless history during these periods presented the adverse circumstances which hindered the nation's political unfolding.

An important stimulus to reconsider the role of Rome in Italian history came from abroad. Theodor Mommsen famously viewed Rome as the predecessor of modern Italy, inspiring the Liberal Quintino Sella to illustrate the continuity from the "first" to the "third Rome" with help of archaeological excavations.[17] Giosué Carducci emphasised the role of Roman civilisation for the development of modern Italy and described Garibaldi as its "new Romulus." Bologna's Giambattista Gandino, a specialist on Cicero, disagreed with the German school, but emphasised the same continuities; and the leader of the Roman Republic in 1848, Aurelio Saffi, who during his exile had studied in Oxford, used the democratic revolution of the Gracchi as a model for his modern theory of revolution, based on a specifically Italian concept of freedom.[18] In a rather picturesque fashion the pantheist Quirico Filopanti established a cosmological relationship between 8 August 1848, the day when Bologna defeated the Austrian troops, and the foundation of the Roman colony of Bononia on 8 August 189 BC, which granted the city the right to hold free elections, to appoint councillors and to nominate a local government.[19] Bologna maintained these rights until the beginning of the Papal dominion in the sixteenth century, which ended only with the Unification of Italy. References to Rome were used not only in the context of national foundation myths, they were a reference to Europe, too. As Mikael af Malmborg has argued, Rome was inseparable "from the common European cultural heritage," underlining a "high degree of identity between Italian culture and general European or Western civilization."[20]

Standard works on the modern reception of antiquity differentiate between the *Etruscomania* of the eighteenth century and a supposedly more "scientific" approach to Etruscology since the nineteenth century.[21] Italy's nineteenth-century fascination with everything Etruscan makes this distinction questionable. Moreover, according to Momigliano the "municipalistic" agenda behind the antiquarian studies of the eighteenth and early nineteenth century was replaced, during the second half of the nineteenth century, by a more nationalistic emphasis, deriving from the Italian reception of Müller and Mommsen.[22] While later nineteenth-century references to the Etruscans were not necessarily used in an anti-Roman sense and were integrated into a more general discourse on Italy's national origins, Etruscology did, however, continue to foster local and regional identities, often following a clearly defined political agenda. When in 1866 the municipal authorities of Reggio Emilia asked for more administrative autonomy, they underlined their claims with historical references to the city's status as a self-contained administrative unit since pre-Roman times.[23]

A SINGLE RACE AND A TRUE CALIFORNIA

On 25 August 1869 Antonio Zannoni, the municipality's chief engineer, discovered an Etruscan tumulus at the Certosa, still today Bologna's central cemetery. This day became a notable date in the writing of the city's past. With its more than four hundred tombs, Zannoni's discovery is still considered a milestone in modern Etruscology. For the first time the municipality, as a public institution, directed the excavations itself, unearthing "day after day, treasures of art and antiquity."[24] Zannoni's excavations invited comparison with the famous site of Marzabotto, excavated by private initiative under Count Giovanni Gozzadini fifteen years earlier. Zannoni wanted

Figure 6.1   Sepolcreto Nord di Marzabotto. (*Congrès international d'anthropologie préhistorique. Compte rendu de la cinquième session de 1871.* Bologne: Fava & Garagnani, 1873)

people to believe in an ethnic continuity from Etruscan to contemporary times, in a common descent of modern-day Bologna from the region's earliest settlements. "Signori, the people of Marzabotto and Felsina [the Etruscan name for Bologna] were of a single race. Signori, after more than twenty centuries the race of the people of Felsina is still the same as that of modern day Bologna."[25] Zannoni stressed the sumptuousness of this pre-historic culture, for him characteristic of a sense of nationality.[26] "Not even Gods were dressed better than that; . . . Signori, do you see the accessories with which the women of Felsina made themselves look beautiful . . . ? Weapons, cloths, mores, everything expresses a sense of nationality, o Signori."[27] The aesthetic unity of material culture was to confirm the sense of nationhood. Moreover, the Etruscans' orientalising rather than geometrical decorations appear as an alternative to the classicist authority of Roman culture and an expression of their libertarian spirit.[28] The local newspapers wrote initially with a certain ironic distance about the excavations, sceptical that their old town could possess similar treasures. But as the discoveries progressed, they joined into the excitement for the Etruscan past and reported almost daily about the works of art unearthed. On the site of San Francesco alone fifteen hundred kilograms of metal objects were found.[29] Debates between professional archaeologists and popularising theories became regular features in the newspapers.[30] *Il Monitore di Bologna* described the Certosa and Marzabotto as a "true California for anybody excavating the ruins of a remote past."[31] Due to these sensationalist reports Bologna lived its Etruscan revival similar to a gold-rush and under the participation of large sections of its local population.

THE ETRUSCANS IN POETIC IMAGINATION

Pre-Roman cultures became an important source of poetic imagination, even for Carducci, who had hoped that the Risorgimento would bring about Mazzini's *"terza Roma."*[32] For Carducci Dante was Etruscan "rather than Roman or Italian," proved by his descent and physiognomy. In this context it might not seem surprising that he thought of himself as *"tarda etrusca prole"*; several decades later Puccini was also described as "sculpted from the ancient rock of Etruria."[33] The national sentiment which supposedly held the Italian cities together after the end of the Roman Empire was for Carducci a renewal of the Etruscan confederation of cities, to which he referred in a famous poem of 1872:

> Do you remember the widowed shores of the Tuscan sea,
> Where the feudal tower bends over the hazy fallow plain
> With long and dreary shadow
> And watches from the dark, burnt hills
> Over the sepulchral sleep of the Rasenna cities,
> Buried amidst the woods . . . ?[34]

Carducci was not simply Italy's most famous poet at the time: he wrote this piece also as secretary of the Deputazione di Storia Patria, for which he regularly produced minutes of meetings and summaries of proceedings, usually published in the local press and later included in his collected works. He was a close friend of the archaeologist Francesco Rocchi and regularly participated in student trips to local archaeological sites organized by Edoardo Brizio and Francesco Bertolini.[35] Bologna's Deputazione paid particular attention to archaeological research on the paleo-Italic period and among its early members were a number of influential archaeologists. Its president, Count Gozzadini, himself directed the excavations at his property in Villanova, the most important Iron Age site on the Italian peninsula, as well as at Marzabotto, which despite large scale destruction in 1944 is still today considered the most important excavation of an Etruscan city, although known now primarily as the site of one of the SS's most atrocious crimes against Italy's civilian population during World War II.[36] The Deputazione's vice president, Rocchi, had been Bologna's professor of archaeology since 1847. Other members included the archaeologists Achille Gennarelli from Florence, Giacomo Lignana from Rome, and Ariodante Fabretti, professor first in Bologna and then in Turin.[37] In particular Edoardo Brizio contributed to the wider dissemination of interest in Bologna's early settlements. Teaching both at the university, the *Studio,* and the popular university, he combined courses in primeval history, Etruscology and Egyptology with the teaching of Greek and Roman anthropology and history of art. Lecturing primarily in the city's *Gipsoteca,* which was modelled on similar examples in Bonn and Berlin, his experimental approach became a model for the modern university in Italy and was later continued by his former student Gherardo Ghirardini.[38]

The public interest in the Etruscans as well as the increasing number of excavations in the region inspired Carducci's poetic imagination and contributed to the creation of local historical myths around the Etruscan settlements. In his 1879 poem "Fuori alla Certosa di Bologna" he describes the succession of Bologna's pre-historic peoples: Umbrians, considered here as the fathers of the Villanovan culture, Etruscans, Celts, Romans and Lombards, reposing forever at the foot of the Apennine:

> Outside the Charterhouse of Bologna
>
> Here at the foot of the hill our Umbrian forebears sleep,
> Who first broke your divine silence with the sound of axes,
>   o Apennines:
>
> The Etruscans sleep here, who descended with the *lituus,*
> Their gaze uplifted to the green of those mysterious slopes,
>
> And the tall, red-haired Celts ran to wash themselves clean from
> The slaughter in the cold mountain stream which they hailed their
>   new Rhine,
>
> And the noble stock of Rome, and the long-haired Lombards
> Who were the last to make camp upon these wooded summits,
>
> They sleep with our more recent dead.[39]

In Carducci's historical imagination the Umbrians had been the first to interrupt the religious silence of the mountains. The Etruscans arrived as a people of warriors and colonizers, forming a civilisation which extended to both sides of the Apennines and therefore gave the Italian peninsula a political and cultural unity prior to the Romans.[40] He describes the Etruscans as arriving with the "lituo," used for the ritual division of space, and the defining of urban settlements, a reference to the foundation of "Felsina," as the city with the longest continuity of urban settlement in Europe. The Celts, depicted in Carduccci's poem as barbarians, with red hair and arriving from the Alps, called Bologna by its modern name—Bononia—before ceding it to the "noble race" of the Romans. The last to arrive were the Lombards, sleeping now alongside the other ancestors of modern-day Italians.

As Croce remarked with reference to Carducci's poem, "the thought of death provoked in him the strongest sense of life and love."[41] The physical presence of death inspired him to draw the spiritual connection between the past, present and future, between the ancient and the contemporary people of Bologna. His image establishes a trans-generational and interethnic sense of community between the different tribes and peoples of the Apennines, through which the contemporary people of Bologna originate anew.[42] As Homi K. Bhabha explains, "nations, like narratives, lose their origins in the myths of time and only fully realize their horizons in the mind's eye."[43] It is the narrative of the trope itself which brings the imagined community to life, here the community of Umbrians, Etruscans and modern Italians. Carducci influenced an entire generation of intellectuals with his poetic contribution to the pre-historic revival and still in 1912, Albert Grenier opened his important study on *Bologne Villanovienne et Étrusque* with a quote from the same poem.[44] In the case of Zannoni the same idea evoked an almost Messianic mission: "The people who lived here, and to whom Felsina owes its civilisation, slept and dreamed in the Certosa for twenty or more centuries. I awaked them, taking them out of their long and quiet asylum."[45] With the completion of the nation's Risorgimento and through the redemption by Zannoni's great deed Bologna's ancient peoples have come to life again, this time as Italians.[46]

In his conclusion to *Imagined Communities* Benedict Anderson outlined how national movements imagined their nations as "awakening" from "epochal sleep," opening up "an immense antiquity."[47] The literary origin of what Anderson describes can be traced back to Romantic poetry and even to Rousseau, summarised by de Man as "themes of sleep and waking, forgetting and memory, water and voyage."[48] In his memoirs of 1872, describing his first visit to Rome as a child, Garibaldi constructed a similar association between ancient Rome and the Papal city.[49] The ideas of "remembering" common descent and the notion of "social memory" were widespread in nineteenth-century Europe and linked to the observation of common cultural heritage, either in the form of similarity in material culture or cultural institutions, ways of life and thought. Burckhardt understood the "classical character" of Renaissance art as "heritage" rather than "direct imitation" and Warburg developed the notion of memory in aesthetic expression as the "deposit of an emotional experience which is derived from primitive religious attitudes." We find a similar disposition in a Rilke's *Letter to a Young Poet*: "These long forgotten, dwell within us as disposition, as a burden on our fate, as blood that courses and as gesture that arises from the depth of time."[50] Gombrich carefully discusses the "racialist" conviction behind many of these theories, quoting Moeller van den Bruck, who in 1913 argued for the legacy of "Asiatic racial karma" in Italian art, rooted in its Etrurian origins: "We know the forms created by Botticelli from the light steps of the dancing girls on the frescoes of Etruscan tombs."[51] While Warburg's writing emphasises "collective" rather than "racial" theories of memory, the idea of an inherited memory also informed the Bolognesi during the decades of their archaic discoveries. Thus, Carducci and Zannoni anticipated the notion of social and cultural memory when they employed the remembrance of the archaic age to endow their own present with meaning.[52]

The mystery of the Etruscans' life after death which Carducci evokes in his poem had its origin in the belief that the Etruscans formed a "sacerdotal race."[53] However, for Carducci this *teocrazia* also explains the decline of the Etruscan civilisation:

> Other peoples . . . revive themselves and develop a form of life of their own; not so the Etruscans. They live in the shadow and in its undefined contours they lose themselves in the thick air that surrounds them. They don't merit anything different: A people which always thinks about death had to die out.[54]

For Carducci, the anti-clerical Republican, it is the memory and experience of the Etruscans that justifies Bologna's "patricide" against the modern theocracy of the past Papal regime.

ETHNIC ORIGINS

Banti's influential book *La Nazione del Risorgimento* points to ethnic concepts of the Italian nation which earlier research, in particular Chabod's *L'idea della nazione,* ignored. According to Banti, it is too simple to identify Italian nationalism purely as a voluntaristic concept, based exclusively on political will, in contrast to Germany's ethnic nationalism.[55] Before the new empirical methodologies of nineteenth-century scientific research, the aim of Etruscology, as is the case for most scholarship at the time, was primarily the transmission of ancient literary knowledge.[56] This changed when historical, archaeological and anthropological research had to answer more general questions about human nature. Bologna's *Etruscomania* started at a time when the front pages of newspapers all over Europe reported regularly on spectacular Greek and Egyptian excavations, when the world fairs included showrooms illustrating national pasts along with the "civilizing mission" of colonial expansion and when Hegel's philosophy of history determined ideas about the rise and decline of civilisations and empires.[57] Archaeology played a major part in this and even the Papacy responded to the public interest in the discipline with a renewed impetus given to the excavations of Paleo-Christian Rome.[58] Moreover, the eighteenth-century discoveries of non-European civilisations set Greek and Italic cultures into a new perspective. As Benedict Anderson explains, the investigation of Sanskrit led to the realisation that the Indic civilisation is older than that of Greece and Judea. A similar effect followed the deciphering of cuneiform inscriptions and hieroglyphics in the early nineteenth century, further pluralizing extra-European antiquity.[59] This context explains the excitement when from the mid-nineteenth-century archaeologists became aware not only of neolithic cultures in the Bolognese, but also of paleolithic and mesolithic cultures, remains of civilisations dating back many thousands of years.[60] Bologna was particularly interested in the relationship between its Iron Age settlements, the so-called Villanova civilisation, and the Etruscans, and in the relationship between Felsina, as the Etruscans called Bologna, and the better known region of Central Etruria, south of the Apennines.[61]

Despite the discoveries of the so-called "protovillanovan period" (Tarquinia and Castellina, dating back to the tenth and eleventh centuries BC), Villanova remains the most ancient urban settlement in Italy, predating comparable sites in Tuscany and Lazio. Founded about 900 BC, the settlement was discovered by Count Gozzadini on his own estate in 1853; and it became the first large-scale pre-historic excavation in the province of Bologna—a necropolis of 193 tombs characterised by a funeral rite based on cremation.[62] When in 1848 the British consul in Rome George Dennis published his famous *The Cities and Cemeteries of Etruria*, Bologna was mentioned only once, referring to a few ancient authors, but to no archaeological evidence. After 1853, Villanova became a major point of reference for any discussion of the subject. Gozzadini identified his site in Villanova as the most ancient Etruscan settlement in Italy, assuming that anything predating the Roman period had to be Etruscan.[63]

Bologna came to be seen as the origin of a culture, which gave birth to the most important early art and craft, but also philosophy and science on the peninsula. Due to its Villanovan origins it appeared to be civilised and literate long before central Etruria and Rome. In this view the region was also the first to engage in trade relations with Greece, the first to adapt the Greek alphabet. The Etruscans assimilated the spiritual world of the Greeks—a process clearly documented in Bologna's archaeological collections of Greek and Etruscan artefacts, long before any other Italian people. It was through the Etruscans that Rome gained access to Greek culture; the Roman insignia of office—in particular the fasces—had their origin in the Etruscan administration.[64] No Etruria without Felsina, no Rome without Etruria. At the same time it was believed that Felsina brought the Hellenisation of Italy to a halt, underlining the strength of Etruria as a "national" civilisation in its own right. In this view Bologna became the centre of the civilized world. Etruscologists today would grant Villanova and Felsina an important place in the relationship between Etruria, Rome and Greece, but hardly the role nineteenth-century Bologna claimed for itself.[65] The former Moderate prime minister Marco Minghetti as well as the Republican Quirico Filopanti described Felsina as the "supreme capital city" of the Etruscan civilisation; councillor Pullé spoke of "Bologna's nobility and antiquity, which no other Italic town, not even Rome, has been able to equal;" and Alfonso Rubbiani referred to Bologna as the mother of the Italic tribes, "civilised well before Rome."[66]

For Count Gozzadini the nobility of Bologna's ancient civilisation lay in the fact that it was part and the origin of the famous civilisation of Etruria, which had fascinated Italian scholars since the times of the Medici. For Gozzadini the question of the Etruscans' ethnic and geographic origins was an issue of secondary importance. However, the following generation of professionally trained archaeologists paid greater attention to differences in material culture as well in ethnic origin. Their emphasis on difference and discontinuity is exemplary for the modern historiography of the nineteenth century, for Foucault's "*l'homme déshistorisé*," who requires the construction of a new historicity through innovative "scientific" approaches, in this case the ethnic matrix.[67]

Ethnic origins as well as the migrations of the early inhabitants of the Italian peninsula constituted a major issue of debate during the Fifth International Congress of Pre-historic Sciences which took place in Bologna in 1871. Each excavator was keen to present his own site as the most spectacular, using his own archaeological evidence as proof for the theories to which he adhered. Three major theories on the Etruscans' origins animated the debate at the time, of which nowadays at least two are regarded as myths. The "oriental theory" maintained that the Etruscans immigrated to Italy from Asia Minor and that they were of Lydian or pre-Greek Pelasgian origin. The "northern theory," today entirely rejected, argued that they had descended from the Alps. The "autochthonous theory" believed the Etruscans to be an indigenous population.[68] Francesco Bertolini summarised these theories in a paper for the Deputazione, the publication of which attracted attention well beyond narrow academic circles.[69] A history teacher at Bologna's *Liceo* and later professor at the university, he had been a member of the Deputazione since 1869 and wrote an influential *Storia d'Italia* from ancient origins to modern days. Unlike Gozzadini, the self-taught nobleman with antiquarian interests, Bertolini understood himself as a professional historian in the modern sense of the word, even if his expertise still covered all periods of history, from pre-Roman Italy to the Risorgimento. In his *Storia primitiva di Roma* Bertolini expressed his admiration for the source criticism of the German school, and his work on the Etruscans was based on the examination of those Roman and Greek historians who had been in personal contact with the Etruscan elites and still knew the "*auctores tusci*," who have not survived.[70] Bertolini dismissed the "oriental hypothesis" of the Etruscans' origins and in particular Herodotus' still very influential Lydian theory, which in Bologna was supported by Gozzadini, but also by Filopanti.[71] As the early historian of Rome Dionysius of Halicarnassus, a Greek writing at the time of Augustus, had pointed out, the Lydian and Etruscan peoples were of different religions, while Greeks and Romans seemed of common descent.[72] Many ancient and modern historians maintained that the Etruscans were Pelasgians, originating from Thessaly or from the islands Lemnos and Imbros, near Troy, from where they started the colonization of Italy, an idea to which Carducci often referred.[73] However, like the historians of the German school, Bertolini did not believe in the Etruscans' migration via the sea and he also dismissed Pliny's and Vico's Egyptian hypothesis, which was still very popular at the time and played a role in the concept of "*l'antica sapienza italica*." The scarabs and canobi in the Etruscan burial-grounds testified trade relations with the Orient and Egypt, he argued, but did not tell us anything about ethnic origins.[74] The common ground Bertolini shared with most speakers at Bologna's international congress of 1871 was that of the Etruscans' "Aryan origin." Count Giancarlo Conestabile divided the Aryan race into different branches, including a Celtic, a Germanic, a Greco-Italian and a Lithuanian-Slavonic branch.[75] However, regarding the Etruscan tribes, he still understood these to have migrated from Asia Minor, replacing the decadent Pelasgians and the Umbrians, who had come to Italy in earlier migrations.[76] Hence, Bertolini's rejection of the oriental theory complicated matters in Bologna. Autochthonous theories, already popularised by Michelet, added an Italian "nationalist" dimension to the debates and encouraged archaeologists to consider cultural differences between the various settlements, indigenous and immigrant, more carefully.

NATIONALITY AND MATERIAL CULTURE

Independently from the debates on their geographical origin, it was common in nineteenth-century Bologna to refer to the Etruscans in terms of race or nationality. Gozzadini used the terms *"genti tosche," "razza"* and *"stirpe etrusca."*[77] Zannoni frequently spoke about an Etruscan "nationality" of "oriental" origin, from which the modern-day Bolognesi descended. Grenier, who was strongly influenced by Zannoni, referred to the Etruscans as "conscious of their nationality."[78] However, while Zannoni agreed with Gozzadini on the Etruscans' oriental origin, he questioned that the region's most ancient settlements were indeed Etruscan. He saw the local Iron-Age settlements as an original and autochthonous Italian population. With emphasis on differences in their material culture he identified two distinct cultures, one Pelasgian and one Umbrian, and his four famous groups of tombs at the Certosa as a fusion of Pelasgian and Umbrian cultures.[79] Zannoni insisted on the originality of the Umbrians as an *Italian* culture, an idea supported by ancient literary sources. The Umbrian-Villanovan settlements were for Zannoni an indigenous Italian civilisation, which the foreign Etruscan "invaders" inherited: "yes, there is an Italic art, which existed independently in Italy before the arrival of oriental art from Asia and which predated the influence of any Greek culture."[80] He insisted that culturally the Etruscans learned from the Umbrians, which would explain the similarities in the funeral rites and certain decorative motifs. Moreover, based on his excavations at San Francesco, he insisted that the Umbrians of the Villanovan culture knew writing before, and independently of, the people of Central Etruria. He acknowledged the exotic wealth of the Etruscan civilisation, but at the same time he found a place for an even older, independent and highly developed Italic civilisation.

    Zannoni was not alone in pointing to differences between the various settlements. Edoardo Brizio worked in Bologna for the exhibition of local pre-historic excavations, organised on the occasion of the international congress of 1871. Later he spent several years in Rome and in Greece, making himself familiar with the German school of archaeology and classical *Kunstgeschichte*.[81] Influenced by both Niebuhr and Mommsen, and by the German Archaeological Institute in Rome, Edoardo Brizio initially adhered to the idea of the Etruscans' Northern or indigenous origin, before becoming a major advocate of their "oriental" provenance.[82] In 1876 he became professor of archaeology in Bologna and director of the university's collections in the museum, enjoying international recognition as a scholar. However, due to conflicts with Gozzadini he had to wait until 1881 to become a corresponding member of the Deputazione and until 1886 to become an active member.[83] After Gozzadini's death in 1887 Brizio succeeded him as director general of the museum and as royal commissioner for excavations and the museums of antiquities. Like Zannoni, he identified the civilisation of Villanova as Umbrian, constituting the main reason for his conflict with Gozzadini. Brizio paid considerable attention to differences in material culture, and tended to explain these by ethnic origin. Villanova was no longer seen as an early Etruscan culture and the Etruscans themselves became a separate ethnic group of warriors, which conquered the Umbrian settlements, later to be succeeded by Gallic and Roman conquerors. The Villanovans were identified as an indigenous Italic people, "un popolo di razza italica."[84] Even if Brizio speaks of a "fusion" and "assimilation" of the Umbrian and Etruscan peoples, recognising that conquest would not necessarily result in a complete disappearance of the indigenous culture,[85] there was no space for a cultural transition within specific ethnic groups. Instead, cultural change was determined by the succession of different ethnic groups, a view within which the Etruscans appear as carriers of a civilising mission, superseding a primitive Villanovan age. Observing differences between the material culture of orientalising Etruscans and the Villanovans' geometric decorations, he was also the first to propose a "scientific" explanation for the change from cremation to inhumation in local burial rites, recognising in the Etruscan invaders the bearers of an orientalizing and later Hellenizing civilization. For Brizio the cremating Villanovans were the Umbrians described by Herodotus, hence an Italic people. While the antiquarian Count Gozzadini was keen to link his own discoveries with the nobility of the Etrurian civilisation, discovering these Italic origins was for Brizio "a question of prestige and of national history."[86]

Brizio's ideas were based on "scientific" archaeological evidence, considered at the time an innovative empirical approach to the question. In this respect Gozzadini could hardly compete. Without producing detailed plans of the sites, he dismembered the objects found in the ground and reorganised them, in antiquarian tradition, according to typological criteria.[87] Thus, Gozzadini's approach to the organisation of knowledge still stands in the tradition of Rousseau, who to Foucault's astonishment, "*au cœur du XVIIIe siècle*," had nothing more important to do than to "*herborise*." As Sebald reminds us, Rousseau's objective of research was not to acquire knowledge about the place where he collected his plants, but to classify them according to a specific model of organisation.[88] Gozzadini applied a similar model of organisation to the objects he excavated, without much concern for cultural differences and change over time. Instead, Gozzadini's great opponent Zannoni, excavating for the commune at the

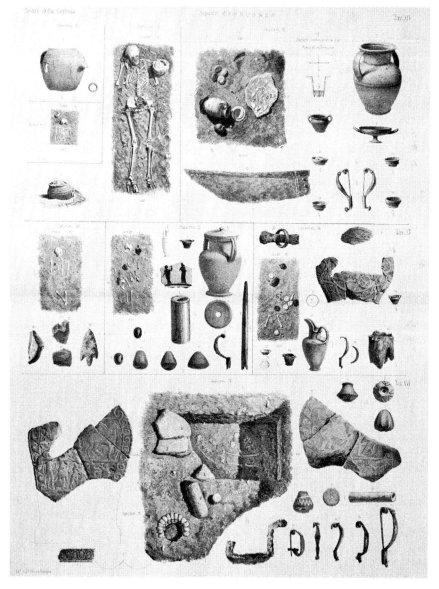

Figure 6.2 Excavations at the Certosa di Bologna. (Antonio Zannoni, *Gli scavi della certosa di Bologna*. Bologna: Regia tipografia, 1876)

Certosa, worked with focus on the specific place and its people rather than the unearthed material itself. Without a professional background in archaeology, the municipal engineer nevertheless revolutionised techniques and methods through scrupulous documentation, including inventories, detailed maps and photographs of the entire site as well as of each tomb. For his innovative methodology he was hailed at the 1871 congress; in 1887 he was awarded the prestigious "Premio Linceo"; and at the beginning of the twentieth century leading researchers in the field still recognised his extraordinary contribution to the subject.[89]

Zannoni was not alone in starting to question Gozzadini's assimilation of the Villanovan and Etruscan cultures. For Grenier, Ghirardini and Ducati the Villanovans were Umbrians, originally from Tuscany and Latium, who subsequently migrated North. Pigorini insisted upon the Villanovans' common "ethnic" origin with the people of the *terramare* in the region around Parma and Piacenza.[90] The difference between Gozzadini, the self-trained nobleman, and the subsequent generation of researchers lies in the attention paid to the ethnic interpretation of material culture and historical change. Scholars today are less critical of Gozzadini's interpretation, suggesting that the majority of the Etruscan cities were rooted in the Iron-Age culture of the Villanovans, understood as the most ancient period of the Etruscan culture.[91] Rather than speaking of ethnically different cultures, research emphasises the transition from the Villanovan to the Etruscan culture. Although comparisons of Villanova with the Etruscan Felsina demonstrate a watershed in cultural techniques—the development of urban structures, the large-scale import of "foreign" goods and the widespread use of writing—research today maintains that the Villanovans wrote Etruscan and therefore can be recognised as an early Etruscan civilisation.[92] Rather than searching for origin and migration, most Etruscologists today speak about the Etruscans' ethnic formation, which is believed to have happened in the different parts of Etruria itself.

ETRUSCOMANIA

Despite Gozzadini's "old-fashioned" and antiquarian approach to archaeology, most of the Deputazione's work demonstrates high academic standards, reflected in its methodology, source criticism, references to international debates and in a complex apparatus of footnotes and illustrations. Beyond the academic circles the fascination with Bologna's early civilisations obviously assumed a very different character. In 1870 *Il Monitore di Bologna* discussed the Etruscan origin and "strategic-astronomical" design of the city's famous towers, supposedly originating from Egyptian ideas about the architectural representation of the cosmos.[93] Referring back to the idea of *l'antica sapienza italica*, Egypt, Etruria and the early civilisation of the Bolognese were believed to have shared common religious roots. The remains of a Roman temple in the area of Santo Stefano, dedicated to the Egyptian goddess Isis and later used by the first local Christians, contributed to the belief in Bologna's special relationship with ancient Egypt.[94] The popular perception of these issues was rarely supported by Bologna's archaeologists, theologians and historians, but reflects the widespread public fascination with mythical origins. Zannoni contributed greatly to this popular interest. His presentations, in which he made for the first time use of photographs, attracted audiences well beyond academic circles: "Does it not seem to you, *o Signori*, as if you yourself were present during the excavations and as if you were looking into the trenches? Do you see the different positions of the skeletons and, as I told you, what they had with them?"[95] Very different in character were the expositions of Count Gozzadini, on which the newspapers only remarked that they were long and difficult to follow.[96]

Popular stories about the Etruscans as well as the official reports on excavations often pointed to the high status of Etruscan women in society; and to infect audiences with *Etruscomania* the archeologists constructed comparisons with contemporary society:

> *Signore,* the women of Felsina were as graceful as you and shared your love of beauty. Buckles for the garment, and ornaments, buttons, pins. See the bracelets and rings, necklaces and earrings; concerned about their appearance they used mirrors and nail-scissors. Cosmetics served to increase or to revitalise lost beauty.[97]

These comparisons became more delicate when Brizio, with reference to Plautus and Herodotus, maintained that Etruscan women, until getting married, prostituted themselves in order to collect a dowry. He insisted of course that "this was a rite absolutely foreign to Europeans," but underlined the progressive elements behind the custom: "*una specie di emancipazione di cui godevano le donne etrusche.*" Due to the difficulties of establishing paternity children acquired the name of their mothers.[98] Over years these lectures attracted huge audiences in Bologna.

Also the local carnival society *Duttòur Balanzòn* joined in the popular "*Etruscomania,*" celebrating in 1874 a great "*equepedemimodrammaticoetruscobalanzocurriculare,*" re-enacting the city's conquest by the Etruscans.[99] A song in local dialect explained what this was about:

> For three-thousand years they had been in the grave:
> The Etruscans. Only their name had remained,
> Some vases and some arid bones. . . .
> They were made to reappear, and I don't know how,
> Some say by virtue of spiritualism,
> Some say by help of magic, or magnetism . . . [100]

Each verse of the song describes a coach of the long procession that went through the streets of Bologna on 15 February 1874. A total of

30,000 Lire were spent on the show, equalling the municipality's annual subsidy for the opera house. The money was raised by selling seats from which to watch the final piece of the show and through contributions from the carnival society and private donors. A raffle for donkeys, pigs, geese, food and even a house made a surplus of 9,300 Lire. Moreover, the carnival society sold 10,000 copies of Anacleto Guadagnini's "*grande mascherata etrusca*," a souvenir with illustrations of the procession. The surplus funds from the event went into charity organisations for the poor.[101] Among the members of the carnival society were a number of distinguished citizens, who shared an interest in local Etruscheria, but who also played a role in Bologna's charitable welfare system: Count Malvezzi, Count Salina, the Marquis Francesco Albergati and Count Pompeo Aria, whose family owned the estate on which the site of Marzabotto was located. Among the members was also the painter Luigi Busi, who later produced a series of acclaimed Etruscan wall paintings for Bologna's museum. During the preparations for the event Count Gozzadini gave access to his private collection, allowing the organizers to study Etruscan decorations and dress. The day of the event the Museo Civico stayed open, giving citizens the opportunity to engage on different levels with the Etruscans. The carnival assumed an importance well beyond the city walls, with the railway society offering reduced fares for visitors to Bologna's Etruscan festival. Hotels and hostels were sold out days before, attracting especially visitors from the Marches, from Ferrara and various cities of Emilia.[102]

One of the *corso's* floats presented the historians and anthropologists who had visited Bologna in 1871 for the International Congress on Pre-historic

Figure 6.3   Anacleto Guadagnini, *Sfilata del carnevale 1874.* (Reproduction by Kind Permission of the Biblioteca dell'Archiginnasio, Bologna, Italy.)

Sciences. As an illusion to the evolutionist theories which they propagated, they were dressed as monkeys.[103] Other floats were occupied by Etruscan soldiers, priests, men and women and various imagined characters from Felsina and Etruria; the "Corps of Etruscan music" used instruments fabricated for this purpose after depictions in painted tombs at the Museo Etrusco Gregoriano in Rome, which the organisers had visited during their preparations.[104] All floats were decorated with vases and amphorae, Etruscan inscriptions and religious representations. The Etruscans themselves had dark faces and were meant to appear exotic: not only were they invaders, they also seemed to come from the East or the South. The term "truschi," in local dialect, came to signify dirty.[105] The parade took one hour to march from Santo Stefano to Piazza Maggiore, and a further thirty minutes to arrive at the "Etruscan castle" of the Montagnola, where the city's conquest was to be re-enacted.[106]

The narrative of the "grande rappresentazione *equepedemimodrammaticoetrusco-balanzocurriculare*" resembled other stagings of historical scenes popular at the time and was set out beforehand in the local press. The king of carnival was traditionally an academic, called in local dialect the *Duttòur Balanzòn*, a reference to the idea of *Bologna la dotta*, the learned, and reflecting with ironic distance Bologna's self-perception as a centre of academic study. On this occasion he guided the Etruscan visitors through the streets of the old city and offered them the opportunity to admire how beautiful Bologna had become since their departure many centuries ago. Arriving at the Montagnola, the Etruscans demonstrated their gratitude for the splendid welcome with a performance of traditional dances and sacred rites. Under the impact of this orgiastic Dionysian performance, Balanzòn's men fell passionately in love with the Etruscan women, requesting immediate marriage.[107] Not used to such a possessive understanding of sexual attraction, the Etruscans took up their arms to defend their wives and daughters, forcing the Balanzoni to retreat into their castle and setting it on fire. While the Balanzoni were rescued by the local fire brigades, the king of carnival took advantage of the general confusion, escaping with the Etruscan queen in a balloon.[108]

The performance of historical plays, mock sieges and battles represents a pattern of Italian carnival since the early modern period.[109] Mikhail Bakhtin's study on Rabelais, published in English in 1968, has often been used as a model for interpreting humorous manifestations of popular culture, independent of the specific historical context and in particular as a way to understand "excess" and the breaking of taboos.[110] However, Julio Caro Baroja insisted that the traditional idea of carnival was closely related to the Christian concept of a succession of collective emotions, of symbolically defined seasons throughout the cycle of the year. Thus, the *sfrenatezza* of the carnival season was framed by the *allegria familiare* of Christmas and the *repressione* of Quaresima, the *tristezza comandata* during the Easter week.[111] Traditional carnival was inherently linked to this cycle of contrasting emotions. If man stopped considering his life to be determined

Figure 6.4   Chariot of the Commander. (Emilio Roncaglia, *Balanzoneide: descrizione dell'ingresso degli Etruschi in Bologna nel carnevale dell'anno 1874*. Bologna: Zanichelli, 1874)

by supernatural forces and a prescribed cycle of order, the carnival lost its original function and meaning. These considerations invite us to be careful when reading modern, re-invented or commercial carnivals in the key of pre-modern societies. Carnivals staged by voluntary associations during the nineteenth century were integrated in modern concepts of charity and as public events connected to municipal policies and associational cultures, rooted in liberal concepts of the public sphere. They differ in their significance and meaning from the tradition which Baroja described as *"figlio del Cristianesimo."*[112] Bakhtin himself makes a clear distinction between the "culture of folk carnival humour" and "serious official . . . political cult forms and ceremonials." He asserts with reference to the medieval and early-modern tradition, that during the carnival there is "no other life" apart from the carnival itself, whereas Bologna's carnival in 1874 was principally an aspect of the city's political and civic culture, and a response to the city's societal transformation.[113] Rather than through a pre-modern ethnographical approach to popular culture, the events in Bologna should be read within the framework of a modern administration and the attempts of specific urban elites to negotiate complex webs of social identities and political interests. The carnival described by Rabelais was a symbolic destruction of authority and hierarchy, whereas in Bologna the authorities themselves staged the carnival.[114] While in Bologna the lay acting served the fostering of a sense of civic belonging, Rabelais' characters were more than just "comic actors."[115] His system of grotesque, bodily images of copulation, pregnancy, childbirth and death was symbolic of a cyclical concept of time, "the contrary to the classical images of the finished, completed man."[116] The Etruscans were represented as "oriental" but civilised and fashioned with an idealised sense of beauty. The references to Bologna's historic-ethnic debates commented on the idea of a linear progression from primitive to modern man, a story about man's perfection, picked with ironic undertones, as in the image of the monkey-historians. The anti-Papal tradition of carnival in the Romagna,[117] as well as the fact that the organizers represented the city's liberal establishment, make it unlikely that the depiction of historians as monkeys was intended or understood as an endorsement of the Church's anti-Darwinism.

The events were not a spontaneous expression of a popular sentiment, but an initiative to promote social cohesion, an expression of a *"panem et circenses"* policy towards the wider citizenry. This is also reflected in the criticism the carnival provoked among the Internationalists, who distributed manifestos throughout the city: "Shame on you! We want bread and work, not carnival! Down with your bourgeois privileges! Why don't you starve yourselves? The dirty *Monitore* never speaks out on our behalf. Instead, day in day out, it presents nice stories about the Etruscans, you imbeciles!"[118]

Other political groups distanced themselves from the event as well. The Republican Filopanti was concerned that Italy was perceived all over the world as a "carnival-nation." Moreover, he had objections against the parade's "indecent scenes"—warriors "with naked bottoms"; ballerinas "dressed only in long veils allowing the naked body to shine through," leading him to speculate whether this was the corps of the local prostitutes. Likewise he was concerned about the effect the public rape of the Etruscan women could have on young people watching these scenes.[119]

Several newspapers criticized the carnival society for problems in the organisation and for the uncontrolled behaviour of part of the audience, people fighting for access to the Montagnola and women fainting in the midst of the excited crowd.[120] Although this criticism was directed specifically against the carnival society, the Balanzoni were generally perceived as an organisation closely linked to the local administration. Occasionally they even assumed the *impresa* of the Teatro Comunale, the flagship of the city's self-representation. Many of their leading members belonged to the city's political elite and the association was widely perceived as an agent of the administration's cultural policy. With reference to the way power uses *"circenses* to keep the crowds quiet," Umberto Eco rejects romanticising projections on modern carnival as "unfortunately false."[121]

The organisers of Bologna's Great Exhibition in 1888 wanted to further explore the popular fascination with early civilisations, this time through an Etruscan exhibition explicitly designed for wider, non-academic audiences.

For Brizio the event was an occasion to present the region's "first class Etruscan objects, which were even more impressive than those of central Etruria."[122] However, the conservative senator Giovanni Codronchi, president of the 1888 committee, forced him to resign and the entire event was cancelled, a consequence of disagreements which went back to Brizio's ancient conflicts with Gozzadini.[123] Moreover, the concept of the exhibition had been to celebrate Bologna through comparison with materials from the entire region, but Brizio had difficulty obtaining objects from the other cities of Emilia Romagna.[124] For its first pre-historic exhibition in 1871 Bologna was able to obtain objects from all over Italy. But as Pomian remarks, collecting is a competitive business.[125] Times had changed since 1871 and the generous patriotic sentiment predominant during the period following the liberation of Rome had passed. Museums had become showcases of their own past, which any city tried to keep as treasures of their historical identity and their noble ancient origins.

RELIQUARIES OF THE PAST

In his anthropology of collecting Krzysztof Pomian establishes a close relationship between the sacred and the past, where relics "represented the sacred because they were supposed to have come from a personage belonging to sacred history."[126] Bologna's Museo Civico was an interesting hybrid between showcase of the past and reliquary, telling the story of the city's supposed origins through the exposition of funeral objects and sacred remains, which Carducci's poetry and Zannoni's public use of history had made into relics of a mystical past. However, it would be wrong to regard the museum too narrowly as a sacred shrine. As Kevin Walsh argues, "the foundation of modern museums is essentially a part of the emergence of modern ideas regarding order and progress, and the related experiences of time and space."[127] They represent a past employed to explain the present and the future. Bologna offers ample evidence for this Janus-headed relationship of the public with its modern reliquaries. The museum served the city to make the present meaningful. Since the 1880s, thanks to the research and the excavations of men like Gozzadini, Rocchi, Brizio, Zannoni and later Ghirardi, Bologna and its Museo Civico became Italy's most important centre for protohistoric studies. Until 1924, when the new *soprintendenza* excluded the Museo Civico from active participation in excavations, Bologna enjoyed an international reputation as a leading institution in the discipline. Subsequently, recognising Etruscology's particularistic potential, the Fascist regime moved away from pre-historic research, privileging instead excavations related to Ancient Rome, following the "desire to forge a mythic identity between the Roman past and fascist present."[128]

Most public museums have their origin in private collections, of which Italy, since the fifteenth century, was particularly rich.[129] The mode of transition from private to public collections illustrates the ways in which public agents engaged with the collective past. Bologna possessed several collections left to the commune during the eighteenth century, including the donations of the Salina family and the famous numismatic collection of the Bolognese pope Benedetto XIV. The university inherited the antiquarian collection of Count Luigi Ferdinando Marsigli (1658–1730), founder of the Istituto delle Scienze in Palazzo Poggi. In 1742 the institute obtained the collections of the scientist Ulisse Aldrovandi (1522–1605) and the *"museo delle meraviglie"* of Marquis Ferdinando Cospi (1609–1686). Between the late nineteenth and the early twentieth centuries Bologna added excavations from more than four thousand Villanovan tombs.[130] Long before the city was able to unite these objects in a single site, these collections attracted the interest of scholars from all over Europe and, since the eighteenth century, formed the basis for the remarkable development in the teaching of antiquity at the university, including specialised disciplines such as epigraphy, numismatics, iconography and early anthropology.[131]

In 1860, the Bolognese painter Pelagio Palagi, considered one of the city's most illustrious citizens, died at the age of eighty-five in Turin. During his time at the court of Carlo Alberto, in addition to his merits as a painter, he had acquired fame as an art historian and archaeologist. In his will Palagi offered the city of Bologna his collection of Egyptian, Greek, Etruscan, Roman and medieval artefacts, a treasure which was regarded at the time as one of Italy's, or even Europe's, most important private collections. Of particular interest for Bologna were the Etruscan objects, which the painter had collected with the help of the German archaeologist Eduard Gerhard.[132] For Bologna the acquisition of Palagi's rich collection marked the beginning of a new era regarding the ways in which artistic and historical treasures were used for the city's self-representation. The institution of a public museum became a major focus of municipal cultural policy. Palagi's will determined that Bologna would receive the value of one third of his collection as a gift, if it paid for the remaining two thirds, estimated at 213,876 Lire.[133] In addition, Bologna had to cover the custodian's salary. Hence, in addition to a political decision the commune had to take an important financial decision to acquire the collection. Palagi asked for a considerable sum of money in a period of economic constraints marked by the nation's war effort and at a time when other cultural institutes, like the theatre, lost their long-established public subsidies. Gozzadini later referred to Palagi as the "istitutore del Museo Civico."[134] However, in order to exhibit Palagi's material the commune's other collections also had to be reorganised and an appropriate site had to be found to house the new museum. Above all, a scientific rationale had to be developed, reflecting the historical and historicising discourse of Bologna's political and cultural elites. The museum had to illustrate Bologna's extraordinary historical and cultural heritage in the wider Italian and European context, providing the proofs of an early, pre-Roman *italianitá*, but also underlining the city's special role in relation to its "sister towns" and to Central Etruria.

After the discoveries at Villanova in the 1850s Bologna's excavations were discussed among academics all over Europe, attracting the interest not only of archaeologists, historians and art historians, but also of early ethnologists, anthropologists and, more generally, followers of Darwin's theories. As the geologist and later rector of the university Giovanni Capellini remembered, it was the association with Darwin's theories that for a long time hindered the investigation of the pre-historic world.[135] These ideological conditions changed with the liberation of the Legations from the Papal regime. Nevertheless, for more than a decade after Unification Bologna's various collections, including the Palagi heritage, were not exhibited in an appropriate public museum. Important parts remained inaccessible; others were shown under poor environmental conditions in various locations, without any historical or pedagogical rationale. Visitors had to rely on the goodwill of the university's academic staff or the municipal librarian to see the materials, as was the case for many collections, including some of the most famous museums of Europe, where entry was considered a privilege.[136] In 1859 Luigi Frati, municipal librarian and later nominated director of the municipal collections as well as secretary of the Deputazione di storia patria, presented a plan to the governor of the Legations, Luigi Carlo Farini, for a civic museum to be located in an extension between the Archiginnasio and the former Ospedale della morte.[137] Several years passed during which the council discussed a number of different projects for the museum,[138] but the Moderates' aversion to public expenditure resulted in general immobility. As the councillor Bordoni explained, "collecting archaeological objects goes beyond the municipality's mission, which is not to create museums."[139] Independent private institutions should engage in such projects. With similar arguments the municipal excavations were criticized, despite the international recognition the city gained for its archaeological projects. Important excavations in the province were financed privately: the sites of Benacci and De Luca, Villanova on the estates of Count Gozzadini, and Marzabotto, on the property of Count Giuseppe Aria. Even Zannoni undertook some of his excavations out of private initiative.[140] The Deputazione di Storia Patria endorsed a proposal made by Senator Luigi Torelli, that excavations should be financed by "società archeofile" of private citizens, who were prepared to commit themselves to such works in their local communities.[141] A change in the political circumstances was required should Bologna's museum ever become reality.

THE PAST AS SCIENCE

After years of debate the project for the Museo Civico was realised under the short-lived administration of the Democrat Camillo Casarini and inaugurated in 1871. The principal motivation for this initiative came from the city's decision to host the Fifth International Congress of Pre-historic Sciences, the most important international conference to have taken place in Italy since Unification and with the foundation of the *Bullettino di Paletnologia Italiana* in 1875, described as the most important catalyst for Italian research in the field.[142] Originally planned for 1870, due to the Franco-Prussian War the congress had to be postponed until 1871 to make possible the participation of French and German academics.[143] Casarini's administration enthusiastically supported the idea of holding this important meeting in Bologna and made considerable financial efforts to welcome the scientists from all over Europe with appropriate splendour. Casarini recognised the potential impact of this public celebration of science on the city's general climate of political and cultural change. The evolutionist credo of the congress, the idea that mankind had developed from primitive savages to modern man through a steady progression, was symbolic of the administration's vision of society and their positivist praise of progress. As Count Gozzadini remarked (in French) during the opening of the conference,

> The New Science has only recently emerged, but it has progressed at a speed worthy of the steam engine. Give it new life; add to it the intellectual means, comparable to the most powerful locomotives, which no obstacle can slow down. Make the train of science ever more quickly; this is the century of the telegraph: a curse on slowness![144]

This was not only a confession of progress but likewise a sign of what the philosopher Hans Blumenberg called the "pure fiction of historical economy," an attempt to make the experience of time meaningful.[145] Gozzadini, using his connections as member of the Upper House, and Minghetti, twice prime minister and Bologna's most influential politician during the years of the Right, lobbied for financial support from the Italian government. The town council released 12,000 Lire, the province and the municipalities of Modena and Ravenna contributed to the organisation of field trips, and the railway societies offered special fares to the members of the congress.[146] Bologna's citizenry followed the preparations for the congress with great interest and even details of the planning were discussed on a nearly daily basis in the local press. The prospect of the conference encouraged the administration to invest a further 5000 Lire in its own archaeological sites, aiming to present its international visitors with the latest excavations and to impress them with avant-garde methods of research.[147] Against critics the councillor Guadagnini underlined "the esteem and the inestimable value" of the objects which so far had been discovered. Numerous academics from all over Europe continuously approached the commune for more detailed information on the discoveries, representing a welcome publicity for the city and demonstrating how much these works were appreciated by the scientific community. Similarly, the question of appropriate funding for the museum was for many councillors a question of "prestige for our town" and a basis for making Bologna a modern centre of tourism.[148]

In addition to the opening of the museum, Capellini organised a temporary exhibition of pre-historic excavations from different regions of Italy, for the first time united on a single site and allowing scientists to study and compare materials for which they usually had to travel across the peninsula. The liberation of Rome, a few months earlier, enabled the organisers to include material from the new capital and from Lazio. Over fifty public and private collectors used this occasion to present their treasures.[149] For Bologna the congress and the exhibition offered a perfect backdrop for the inauguration of its museum, overshadowing the opening of the Etruscan museum in Florence the same year. Therefore, the organisation of the event was also marked by jealousy, *campanilismo* and municipal competition.[150] Museums in Parma, Florence and Turin refused to make their collections available for the exhibition or to cooperate with the conference organisers. The curator of the Museum of the Vatican, the Jesuit Padre Angelo Secchi was sympathetic, but did not obtain the necessary pontifical dispensation to send materials to the apostate former province.[151] Many cities did not even have municipal collections: Michelangelo had already been inspired by the painted tombs of Tarquinia, one of Italy's most important Etruscan sites, but its municipal collection was only founded in 1875, with catalogues of its holdings beginning to appear only during the twentieth century.[152] During the conference excursions to Modena, Ravenna, and Marzabotto underlined Bologna's self-perception as a new regional capital after the political borders between the Papal States and the former Duchies had been removed, but the implications of this change of status were not always welcome by the smaller towns of the region.

In contrast to the policies of Bologna's previous Moderate administrations, the Democrats around Casarini intended to promote the image of a modern, progressive city, understanding the events organised around the congress as part of a civic project to foster a historically informed local and national identity. However, its success was based on a local coalition of interests which transcended the traditional political milieus.[153] For instance, not all representatives of the new academic elite like Carducci, Ceneri or Filopanti were associated with the Left. A number of local academics had close contacts to the Moderate establishment and Bologna's nobility itself contributed considerably to the development of the municipal collections, keen to see them united in a proper museum, but at the same time as witness to their own cultural legacy and their social status. Giovanni Capellini, secretary of the congress, maintained close ties with Marco Minghetti as well as with Quintino Sella, himself a geologist and a minister in the Moderate government.[154] Gozzadini, Salina and others supported the idea of the museum for academic reasons, even if they were critical of the city's public commitment to excavations, which challenged their monopoly on interpreting the past.

The promoters of the congress and the museum had not only to convince Moderate councillors wishing to reduce public spending. Catholic opinion was opposed to the promotion of *"la Scienza Nuova"* and the evolutionary theories about anthropogenesis associated with the Congress. The first Italian translation of Darwin's *Origin of Species* had been published by the Bolognese house Zanichelli in 1864, only five years after the first English edition, making Bologna the symbolic capital of Italian Darwinism. Together with Luigi Bombicci, Capellini strongly supported scientific research along the lines of Darwin's theories, against the views of his own predecessor, Giuseppe Bianconi, who had resigned from his chair in order to avoid taking the oath to the Piedmontese government.[155] Bringing together historians, geologists, anthropologists and palaeontologists, most academics at the conference were convinced that the human race was several hundred-thousand years old.[156] Giustiniano Nicolucci, one of the fathers of ancient anthropology in Italy, presented a detailed account of "pre-historic men in Italy," which was perceived as an affront to Catholic doctrine. Rather than the academic debates about funeral rites and on differences between Umbrian and Etruscan decorations of pre-historic pots, Nicolucci's illustration of the impact of Darwin's theories on the reconstruction of the past attracted public interest.

> This was not the man we know today . . . He was less perfectly formed. His type and organisation was inferior to the type and organisation we know from the man of historical times. . . . From the small size of his skull we are able to conclude that the quaternary man was not very tall. He was small, but strong and vigorous. The shoulders demonstrate the strength of his muscles. He was obliged to fight for his existence, in constant battle with the elements, surrounded by all sorts of dangers to which he could only respond with the vigour of his body and the strength of his arms. As experience taught him to satisfy his needs more easily, man became less and less limited in his possibilities. Thus, ridding himself of his own barbarous nature, he arrived at the Neolithic age.[157]

At the time of this colourful and dramatic account of Bologna's Stone Age inhabitants, theological doctrine still posited a biblical chronology of some 10,000 years since the Creation. Rejecting the idea of evolutionary progress altogether, the Church maintained that since its initial creation mankind had fallen from a state of grace, rather than progressed. Newspapers like *Ancora, Rinnovamento Cattolico* and *L'Unione* responded to Bologna's sudden enthusiasm for pre-historic civilisations with long articles about "false sciences," denouncing "the enemies of Moses and Jesus Christ."[158] The liberal *Monitore di Bologna* contributed to the debate with a polemical front-page attack against "biblical legends" and Catholic *"ierofantismo"*:

> *Bologna la dotta*—in this city the opposition to superstition and the blind faith of the Vatican's tyranny is still very much alive. The city

wishes to support these learned men, who through their long study at our *alma mater* have revealed to us so many important pages of human history, pages which time had torn off the eternal book and which had been replaced with the stories of the bible.[159]

On the basis of the plans developed a decade earlier by Frati, the new museum occupied five rooms adjacent to the Archiginnasio, containing initially only the Palagi collection and materials from the Certosa, but not the university's collection. The curator of the first displays was Ariodante Fabretti, the famous professor of archaeology and director of the Museum of Antiquities in Turin, a corresponding member of Bologna's Deputazione. Fabretti was not only known as an expert in Etruscan language, but also as a collaborator of Filopanti and Mazzini at the times of the Roman Republic.[160] He developed his concept for the exhibition in close cooperation with the municipal administration, aiming to present Bologna's pride in its own history in relation to the other civilisations of the peninsula. Following the same criteria he had used for the organisation of the museum in Florence, Fabretti decided against the typological organisation of the material from Bologna, favouring instead a topological exposition, which constituted in two rooms "the nucleus of a museum of local antiquity."[161] Thus he broke with the antiquarian tradition represented by the noblemen like Gozzadini. Brizio compiled the catalogue and Zannoni a detailed report on the past excavations. Only Palagi's collection, originating from different places around the world, was organised according to typological criteria and kept separate from the local excavations. The showcases included many of Zannoni's photographs and maps indicating the sites of the various groups of tombs at the Certosa. In a spectacular operation he moved a number of tombs in their entirety, with original human skeletons and complete trousseaus, to the museum—something which was unprecedented and greatly admired by the international visitors.[162] Widely advertised through placards and the local press, the museum was opened on 2 October 1871.

Although Capellini maintained that the results of war did not overshadow the congress, the encounter between French and German scientists was a source of worry in Bologna and critically discussed in newspapers.[163] Despite the adverse diplomatic circumstances, the conference brought together academics from virtually every country in Europe and also the United States. Germany's delegation included one of the most prominent visitors, the pathologist and anthropologist Rudolf Virchow, collaborator of Schliemann in Troy, to whom Bologna offered a special banquet of honour, celebrating "the illustrious representative of positive sciences." His presence exemplifies the contemporary concept of pre-historic sciences as rooted in the natural sciences and the emergence of new academic disciplines leaving behind the literary approach which still encompassed the humanities.[164] Politically Virchow belonged to the left-wing liberals of the Prussian Chamber of Deputies and was internationally recognised as a public intellectual.[165] During the Prussian *Verfassungskonflikt* of the 1860s, when Bismarck violated the Prussian constitution by governing without the chamber, Virchow became the chancellor's most prominent opponent, to the point that Bismarck allegedly proposed to resolve the conflict outside the sphere of parliamentary politics in a duel. Virchow refused this invitation as a matter of principle, an event which was widely discussed in the international press, very much to the Iron Chancellor's embarrassment.[166] In the context of Bologna's conference and during this crucial period of Italy's political and societal transformation, Virchow stood for the academic's new public role and for a concept of scientific method firmly based on empirical research rather than preconceived doctrine.[167]

In opposition to the approach of Gozzadini's generation, Brizio's and Zannoni's insistence on detailed documentation and comparison of evidence in archaeological research made reference to the same "scientific" empirical method—a new "culture of truth," based on research methodologies that would allow the scientist to find the solution to specific problems through the observation of objective facts. Rather than pursuing the interest in particularities, symbolized by Gozzadini's typological approach, the scientist's aim was to understand and to explain the entirety of the natural and social environment.[168] The same scientific beliefs also influenced Virchow's approach to local politics during the transformation of Berlin into a modern capital—debates on public hygiene, water supply, and the creation of an appropriate urban environment for modern men, which similarly animated Bologna's council debates during Casarini's government. Modern science not only wished to understand the world, but also to identify the rules for normative action.[169] With Rudolf Virchow, Bologna had invited a political and scientific icon, paying witness to the idea of Italy's political, economic and cultural resurgence.

The local newspapers welcomed the international visitors on their front pages and the mayor published a manifesto reminding his citizens of Bologna's academic reputation and its sense of hospitality. After a parade across Piazza Maggiore the participants of the congress, led by the prefect, the mayor and other political representatives, entered the Archiginnasio's Aula Magna to the tunes of the municipal band, playing "L'inno delle Nazioni," which its leader Antonelli had arranged on the themes of various national anthems integrated into Italy's Royal March. The streets as well as the rooms where the proceedings took place were generously decorated with flowers, flags and coats of arms, and plaques commemorating the organisation's previous four conferences.[170] The city of Modena welcomed the congress for an excursion to the *terramare* settlement of Montale, offering a reception in the town hall, with bells ringing, music and speeches. The citizenry flanked the decorated streets to watch the fifty coaches carrying the visitors to the sites of the excavations, where after a guided tour each member was given permission to collect a number of objects as personal souvenirs.[171] In addition to guide books on Bologna and its new museum, participants were offered a historical map of the region and eight academic publications on recent excavations, two of which had been translated into French. The programme and summaries of the proceedings were published in the local press in French and Italian, even if some journalists criticized the "fashionable" use of French as the sole official conference language. Only the use of Latin, proposed by some of the German visitors, would have ensured the event's true "universal" character.[172] Crown Prince Umberto acted as patron to the congress and attended parts of the proceedings, as did the queen of the Netherlands, described in the press as a person of considerable education and academic culture.[173] Minghetti, too, and the minister of education attended several of the proceedings. For Capellini, the involvement of the royal family had been a priority, a sign of commitment to the national cause in the former lands of the Church. The radical newspapers and some Republican academics criticized these underlying monarchical tendencies, but without casting a shadow over the general tenor of the event.[174] In the mayor's words, for the first time in centuries a free Italy was allowed to present itself along with the other free nations of Europe, each of them "contributing to the progress of all."[175] For Casarini, the international meeting was the proof that the principle of nationality was not opposed to the common good of all, "because it is the sentiment of nationality which had been the great and true instrument of resistance against oppression; it is the brother, even the father of freedom and civilisation."

Bologna's citizenry took great interest in the proceedings of the conference, the opening of the museum and the way in which the municipality represented itself on this occasion. Ernesto Masi, a local historian and close collaborator of Casarini, described the event as a *"festa civile,"* "in which the free Italy honoured itself—and European science."[176] Thanking Capellini for the organisation of the event and alluding to the revived university, Casarini referred to Bologna as "the ancient mother of science." The *Gazzetta dell'Emilia* called the conference *"una festa della scienza,"* leaving behind the backwardness of the Papal regime.[177] Testifying to the extent to which the local council identified with this new image, all the members of the organising board were made honorary citizens, on the same day as Richard Wagner was given this honour. The first Italian performance of an opera by Wagner, after the conclusion of the conference, but with many of the participants still present, was for Casarini a similar sign of the city's cosmopolitan and modern identity.[178] The council commented with great satisfaction on the publication of a volume commemorating the conference—published by the Portuguese historian G. da Silva and underlining Bologna's great efforts in welcoming its international visitors.[179] The following year Giovanni Capellini presented the official proceedings of the conference to the council.[180]

A MODERN MUSEUM IN AN ANCIENT SHELL

With the sudden end of Casarini's administration in February 1872 and the return of the Moderate *giunta*, the initiatives for the creation of a scientific and historically informed local identity lost their most eminent proponent. The museum still exhibited only parts of Bologna's antiquities. The collections of the municipality and the university were still separate, and important excavations were not yet completed. Hence, for many a bigger museum represented a priority in discussions about the city's self-representation as a cultural and academic centre. However, the returning Moderate administration was determined to make savings in the area of the city's cultural policy, even if the Left continued to lobby for the project. Shortly after his resignation Casarini declared "that the decision to suspend the excavations is not well considered. During the recent pre-historic conference our excavations attracted the attention of Europe's entire scientific community and a suspension could bring the commune under serious criticism." With reference to Italy's emerging tourist industry Casarini also pointed to the museum's commercial value for the city as a whole.[181] In response to his passionate intervention a large group of councillors drawn from different political groups deliberated further funding for the excavations and in 1873 the council took the decision to amplify the Archiginnasio and Palazzo Galvani to locate in a single site the municipal collections, the collections of the university, the historical archives and the library.[182] The two new wings of Palazzo Galvani were designed by Zannoni. In 1878, after considerable bureaucratic hurdles, the formal unification of the municipal collections with the university's collections was finalised by royal decree, thanks to the direct intervention of the new minister of education Francesco De Sanctis, who recognised in the museum a major vehicle for the fulfilment of the State's educative and moral role in relation to the population as a whole.[183] Through the unification of the collections the museum was transformed from a semi-private institution restricted largely to specialists, into an institution for the instruction of the general public, a process that marked the development of many public museums during the second half of the nineteenth century.[184] In one respect Bologna's Civic Museum differed considerably from similar projects in other parts of Europe. In France cities like Bordeaux, Marseilles and Rouen all constructed their museums *ex novo*, monuments for and symbols of a particular idea of the respective cities. The same was true for the new museums of German or Austrian provincial capitals like Leipzig or Laibach.[185] In Bologna, however, the new museum was housed in a historical building. The site itself, the Archiginnasio and Palazzo Galvani, represented the monument and the symbol, the city's centuries-old site of study, the shrine of ancient as well as the laboratory of modern knowledge.

Bologna abolished the division of the different collections according to their original owners and, following a modern plan, exhibited all objects according to historical periods and geographical origin. The various "*stanze della antichità*" and "museums of wonders" of the old private collections were transformed into one of Europe's most important historical museums. The new rooms also allowed for the exhibition of the most recent excavations, material from 991 Villanovan, Gallic and Roman tombs discovered at Porta Sant'Isaia (Benacci), the necropolis of the Arsenal and that of the Margherita Gardens, five hundred Villanovan habitations, as well as Etruscan and Roman houses discovered by Zannoni during road works in the Western city. Most recently more than 14,000 Villanovan bronze objects had been excavated in Piazza San Francesco, which were exhibited in a separate room.[186]

The new and enlarged museum opened on 25 September 1881, and Bologna chose once more an important international event for the inauguration, the second *Congresso Internazionale di Geologia*. On the same occasion the new Geological Museum opened its doors to the public, coinciding with the founding of Italy's *Società Geologica Italiana*, several decades after similar institutions had come to life in Britain, France and Germany.[187] This coincidence of events followed the same scheme as ten years before and gave the opening of the museum a remarkable international resonance. As the press underlined, even scientists from the United States and India came to Bologna for the occasion, and several Australian representatives participated in the conference as corresponding members. Through these initiatives the scholars anticipated the formation of a transnational and cross-continental academic community,[188] and Bologna, only a decade after the completion of Italy's national Unification, was proud to be at the forefront of this process.

No comparable museum project had been conceived during the two decades since the Unification of Italy, making Bologna's museum a model for similar projects in numerous other Italian cities. Seven rooms were divided into Egyptian, Greek, Roman and Etruscan sections. The remaining three rooms were reserved for excavations from Bologna, including a general pre-historic section, presenting the local Villanovan and Etruscan cultures, and a room for the materials from San Francesco. Objects were rigorously organised according to Brizio's scientific criteria and didactic intentions. The university's Institute of Archaeology with its Gipsoteca was integrated into the museum.

Particular attention was paid to the decoration of the walls in *Salone X*. Seventy-two meters long, this was by far the biggest room of the museum, decorated with scenes of daily life taken from Etruscan tombs. Here, the showcase became part of the museological concept itself. Similar scenes had been conceived in 1837 for the Museo Gregoriano Etrusco in Rome and for the British Museum, which was well known to Bolognesi such as Carlo Pepoli, Minghetti, Filopanti, who had spent their exile or periods of study in London. The wall paintings were the work of Luigi

Busi. A native of Bologna, professor of the Accademia di Belle Arti and, since the 1870s, one of Bologna's most famous painters, he was regularly employed for public commissions, including local churches, the Teatro Comunale and the Teatro del Corso. However, despite the fact that the room hosted the objects relating to the local pre-historic cultures, the wall paintings were entirely based on artefacts from central Etruria in Tuscany and Lazio, from Tarquinia, Chiusi, Orvieto, Veio and Cerveteri. As the local material culture did not offer a similar polychromatic spectrum, the idea was meant to underline the links between Bologna's Etruscan settlements and those of central Etruria, a programme on which the different archaeologists in Bologna were able to agree.[189] During the following years the museum's public and political recognition as an academic institution of international prestige led to exchanges of duplicates and objects with other museums, and to several important donations. Count Salina presented the museum with an acclaimed mineralogical collection.[190] Countess Gozzadini Zucchini, daughter of Giovanni Gozzadini, left the city the family's library, their armoury and the archives as well as finds from Villanova.[191] On his deathbed the count had determined that his private collection would be kept in a separate room, marking his contrast with Brizio's interpretation of the material.[192] In the 1890s the museum displayed the Roman funeral inscriptions found in the river Reno, and obtained the private collections of Giovanni Ercolani (native American objects) and Giovanni Capellini (3355 pre-historic objects from various Italian and European sites).[193] In 1911 Ghirardini, the museum's new director, bought Zannoni's personal archives and a sample of his archaeological objects.[194]

CRAFTING THE NEW ITALY

Rather than objective representations, reconstructions of the past are obviously always specific to the period in which they were crafted and therefore provide a major source for researching the spirit of an epoch, reflecting the social, political and cultural structures of societies. Lucien Goldmann's work on the *"vision tragique"* in the writings of Pascal, Kant and Racine shows how the spiritual structures of a particular age determine perceptions as a quasi inescapable way of seeing the world.[195] Without denying human agency, structures specific to the nineteenth century influence the tropes we encounter in researching the writing of Italy's past after Unification and the crafting of national and local identities. As Stuart Hall explained,

> identities are about questions of using the resources of history, language and culture in the process of becoming rather than being: not "who we are" or "where we come from," so much as what we might

become, how we have been represented and how that bears on how we might represent ourselves.[196]

This applies to the idea the new generation of professional archaeologists had about Italy's past. What nineteenth-century research in early civilisations shared was the ethnic significance attributed to the cultural phenomena discovered in excavations and through linguistic studies.[197] Each culture had to belong to a distinctive ethnic group which was preceded and succeeded by another ethnically defined culture. Each people presented its own culture, and cultural change or progress came about quasi mechanically, as the consequence of the imposition of an ethnically and culturally different population. While change through conquest and assimilation cannot be excluded, models based on the parallel development of separate communities, on cultural-historical evolution or local ethnic formations, as discussed in modern Etruscology since Pallottino, only slowly gained ground in Italian research on early civilisations.[198]

The meta-structure behind explanations of historical change in nineteenth-century historical tropes can be traced back to the influence of Hegel on European narratives of the nation. However, the ethnic key employed in constructing links with the ancient past developed from the encounter between the human sciences, to a large extent still antiquarian, and the natural sciences, in particular Darwin's evolutionary theory.[199] While the Romans were known through the literary tradition, which represented a more general European legacy, the pre-Roman tribes were researched through an ethnic interpretation of their culture. In this respect it is significant that the 1871 conference was not dominated by Gozzadini's approach to collecting or Bertolini's philological school, but by anthropologists, who took the positivist agenda of the medical and biological sciences as a model, reflected in the public attention given to Virchow's visit. Understood to be modern and scientific, this trend was clearly favoured by the Democratic administration in charge of staging the event. The new approach to the study of ancient cultures therefore corresponds to what Thomas Kuhn has described as "an occasion for retooling": the traditional approach proved no longer capable of solving the problems posed by the changing context of research.[200]

Although aimed at fostering social cohesion and identity, Italy's writing of the past after Unification demonstrates that this process often provokes passionate debates within society. The writing of national histories does not necessarily reflect a primacy of national identities over regional or local identities. Moreover, different versions of the past were openly contested in Bologna after Unification. The Moderate aristocracy, the *notabili* around Count Gozzadini, enjoyed an almost hegemonic position in the region's political and economic structures. However, the impact of the professional middle class on the crafting of historical identities illustrates how the politics of culture served to undermine the Moderates' position. These politics of culture formed the basis for creating the new Italy.

Part III

The City, the Nation and European Culture

7 Urban Space and Civic Culture
Representing City and Nation

*Che ricordi, che glorie, che presagî di nobile avvenire non contiene
per gl'Italiani questo vocabolo di Municipio!*

(Aurelio Saffi)[1]

CITY, REGION AND NATION

In December 1866 Bologna's councillor Ercolani made a recommendation
to the local administration, that the "municipal clocks should be adjusted
to the Mean Time of Rome."[2] However, after Unification the cities did
not simply have to synchronise their clocks. They had also to define and
to negotiate their relationship as cities to the nation. Bologna claimed a
prominent place in the young nation-state and within the history of the
Risorgimento. According to its mayor Gaetano Tacconi, "the Unification
[of Italy] came into being the day that Vittorio Emanuele officially accepted
the annexation of the Papal provinces."[3] In this perspective the liberation
of the Legations from the Papal regime appears as the key to Unification
and the point of departure for redefining Bologna's municipal identity, a
historically strong but, during most of the nineteenth century, a politically
suppressed identity.

Carlotta Sorba redefined the "century of nationalism" as a "century of
municipalities."[4] The Milanese Republican Carlo Cattaneo saw the cities as
the principal agents of Italian history and Quirico Filopanti, in his 1882 *Sintesi di Storia Universale*, acknowledged their role even in terms of world history. For the *Gazzetta dell'Emilia* "*il sentimento municipale*" stood against
the triumph of the "*principio nazionale*."[5] Municipal identities in Italy were
traditionally fostered by conflicts with other cities and have always existed
alongside and sometimes in competition with regional identities, defined
either politically, in relation to Italy's ancient states, or culturally through
local customs and the use of regional dialects. While modernisation theory
assumed that national identities would one day replace local identities and
parochial loyalties, recent work on the relationship between the national and
the local tries to understand not only "how the nation penetrated the local

level," but also how localness can become "a shaper of nationhood." Historians ask about the ways in which "the locality and the concept of localness altered, even forged national belonging" (Alon Confino).[6] Celia Applegate has described the German *Heimatverbundenheit* and the Germans' regional identities after the Unification of 1871 as something private and often explicitly non-urban.[7] While the concept of Heimat usually imparts a moral or emotional connotation to identity,[8] municipal allegiances in Italy have a strong public and political connotation, fostered through history and ancient documents rather than custom and folk tradition. Both regional and municipal identities define and re-define themselves also through their respective relationship to the nation. Although the relationship between national and local identities has only recently become the focus of specific historical studies, the two are undoubtedly connected. Ilaria Porciani has argued that local identities, based either on municipal traditions or on the peninsula's ancient states, did not necessarily conflict with the formation of national identity. This argument tallies with the German experience, where local identities often helped to familiarise the population with the new nation, understood as a "nation of provincials." In the case of Italy we can speak about a "nation of municipalities." In this sense local identities become a metaphor for the nation.[9]

The historical legacies of the Papal States complicated the formation of regional identity in the former Legations. Local identity, after 1860, had to make reference to the city of Bologna rather than to the administrative tradition of the Papal State. Even if the Restoration after 1814 did much to humiliate the city's pride, Bologna had a strong tradition of municipal identity. However, after the liberation Bologna had to adapt to the Savoyard system of communal administration, which in 1847 had eliminated the notion "city" from its constitutional vocabulary, erasing the nuanced historical distinctions between *citta,' borgo* and *villaggio* and referring to a single institution, known as the *commune*.[10] From an administrative point of view this relegated cities like Bologna to the same level as the numerous smaller towns in the region, and thus represented a dramatic change in their juridical and political status. The new institutional uniformity was presented as a step towards administrative modernisation, but de facto it was a challenge to the cities' pride and to their traditional desire for autonomy. In many parts of the peninsula the cities had long since lost their constitutional privileges. Annexation by Piedmont did not reverse their loss of status; indeed, a careful negotiation between municipal and national identities was required. Rather than representing the end of particularism, the administrative "abolition of the cities" resulted in new forms of local particularism.[11]

One of the protagonists of Italy's Unification provides us with a concise definition of the nation. In a speech delivered in 1879 at a secondary school for girls, the former Italian prime minister and Bologna's most influential Moderate politician, Marco Minghetti, answered Ernest Renan's famous question: "What is a nation?" His statement is representative of the Right's abstract approach to the issue of national identity, ignoring the people's subjective and lived experience, in which municipal traditions usually counted more than the newly imposed national identity. A nation

> is a people which inhabits a naturally configured territory distinct from other territories; which shares a language; which is of the same race, which feels in itself the same traditions, customs, affections. Therefore the principle of nationality is referred to as the right and sometimes even the duty of a nation to form a single, autonomous and independent state. Nationality, one could say, is the civil personality of a people; manifesting itself only when the people is conscious of its personality.[12]

However, this consciousness of the people's personality was not strongly developed among Italians. Minghetti's speech was more the expression of an ambition than an empirically based descriptive definition. Moreover, his reference to race and culture contradicts Chabod's theory of Italian nationalism as a voluntary pact of foundation, differing in this regard from the concepts of ethnicity, blood and soil that informed German nationalism.[13] Several of Minghetti's criteria can be applied only with difficulty to the Italy of his time; especially the common language, traditions, customs, affections; the presence of Slavs, Greeks or Albanians in various parts of the peninsula would probably not fit Minghetti's own concept of a common race. The idea of natural borders was also not unproblematic. While his emphasis on customs and tradition might be understood as leaving space for regional identities, no mention is made of Italy's deep-rooted municipal identities.

Unlike the statesman Minghetti, Carlo Pepoli, a former mayor of Bologna, emphasises the relationship between municipality and nation, which had mattered so much to the local protagonists of Unification: "One can only be proud of one's native city if this contributes to the universal pride of the nation."[14] Local and regional identities had to be continuously reconciled with national identity, as a letter by Carducci to the Deputazione di Storia Patria likewise illustrates:

> History of the Commune, of the province, of the region means for us to maintain and explain the great tradition in which Roman and local elements were mixed, a way to always return and adhere to the great mother Italia. She is everything for us and we are all part of her and for her. That's the way one thinks in Bologna and in the Romagna.[15]

Both Pepoli and Carducci show here the extent to which the nation was understood as a multiplicity of municipal identities. In the case of the Bolognesi, municipal identity was certainly stronger than regional identity. Unlike Tuscany, Emilia-Romagna had never been a self-contained unit in an administrative or political sense. The so-called provinces of Emilia, which were united "for reasons of contingent political necessity" during the course of Unification, comprised three different political entities: the former duchies of Parma and Modena as well as the Romagna, historically divided by one of the most ancient frontiers in Europe, the border between the Papal States and the Empire. While the Romagna was largely defined in cultural terms and through the use of dialect, its territorial extension had been contested since the fifteenth century. Some observers included the cities of Bologna and Ferrara, while others restricted the Romagna to the provinces of Ravenna and Forlì and to parts of the provinces of Pesaro and Florence. The Papal style of government did little to foster a common sense of citizenship among its constituent communities; and the relationship between centre and periphery was characterised by a complex network of special relations between individual communes and Rome.[16] The French administration had created the Department Reno, which also included Bologna. Ambitions to incorporate new territories, such as the ancient rivals Modena and Ferrara, were rejected by the French authorities. After Unification attempts were made to strengthen regional identity by supporting dictionaries and literature in dialect, but for the most part the local elites described the language of the Romagna as semi-barbarous.[17] A link between the former duchies and the Romagna was only created when the ancient horizontal line of communication, the river Po, was supplemented by the vertical railway link between Milan and Bologna.[18] As a consequence Bologna never identified with Emilia-Romagna in the same way as Florence did with Tuscany.

While Bologna could be proud of its cultural legacy, the Romagna had the reputation of a region of violent, backward and bloodthirsty peasants. Only gradually did the nation start to revise this image, in particular after the visit of Umberto I in 1888; but a "tradition of subversion" remained and not long after the royal visit the events of the *"settimana rossa"* seemed to reinforce the ancient stereotypes.[19] This is why municipal identity, in the case of Bologna, hardly had to compete with regional identity. Only the rare advocates of legitimist reaction to the nation-state still deplored the disappearance of the Papal regime and saw the former Legations as part of the historic land of Saint Peter.

When in 1860 Marco Minghetti, at the time minister of interior, tried to alter Piedmont's centralised administration and to introduce more regional autonomy, not even the Moderates from Bologna supported his plans. Despite being an example of failed legislation, his project for a decentralised administration based on independent provinces and regions, represents an interesting attempt to reconcile regional and national identities. "French centralism is a product of [France's] history," Minghetti wrote, while the history of Italy seems to indicate a different development . . . . "[20] In his view, the trend towards the oppressive centralisation of state and territory, already visible under the *ancien régime,* served to destroy the life of the cities and provinces. Instead, he proposed the region as a new administrative unit, "a permanent consortium of provinces," in charge of the maintenance of streets and rivers, responsible for public works, higher education, artistic institutions, archives, and so on.[21] However, the project was opposed by the Piedmontese and got only half-hearted support from Cavour, who died before the debate in parliament. At a time when the government feared to lose the *mezzogiorno,* any idea of regional autonomy seemed out of place.[22]

At home in Bologna Leone Carpi criticized the plans for administrative decentralisation out of fear of political extremists on the periphery, believing that Italians lacked the necessary sense of responsibility for self-government.[23] Moreover, there was no historical-political basis for a regional identification with Emilia-Romagna. Bearing in mind Bologna's strong municipal tradition the proposal still contained too much central control, while the former duchies of Emilia resented the idea that Bologna would assume the role of a regional capital.[24] These disputes over the administrative role of specific cities had traditionally flared up throughout Italy, for instance in Sicily, where Noto and Modica challenged the role of Syracuse as *"capoluogo."*[25] Even the Liberals in Florence, despite their strong Tuscan identity, rejected the idea of the region as an administrative unit, seeing it as an impediment to the kingdom's unification and as a threat to communal freedom.[26] Instead, the centralising and authoritarian Piedmontese law of 1859 was extended to the entire kingdom. La Marmora's 1865 legislation on the communal administration further reinforced centralisation and imposed a rigid control over the periphery. Both laws were passed without discussion in parliament. Romanelli called this the "liberal dictatorship," which for the following decades characterised the relationship between cities and state without taking account of local or regional particularities. In Bologna both the democratic and the clerical opposition criticized the Moderates in parliament for this "mortification of local identity."[27]

With no constitutional basis for the development of regional identities and despite the suppression of the cities' desire for autonomy, municipal identity assumed an important role after Unification. For the local political elites an emphasis upon the nation's municipal tradition became the only way to reconcile local and national identities. In the cities' official rhetoric after Unification the nation's municipal entities recovered a natural relationship between each other, which in the imagination of the Risorgimento had once existed, but had then been destroyed as a result of foreign dominion. Carducci illustrates this idea, recalling the times "when evil dominion more than the Apennines kept us, people from Bologna and Tuscany, divided, and on both sides of the Apennine the ruling law was the will of foreign weapons."[28] *"L'Italia delle cento città,"* an idea dating back to Ancient Rome, informed national identity after Unification, understood as the experience and heritage of the nation's cities.[29] However, the Italian cities had a long tradition of competing for administrative and judicial authority. Not far from Bologna, during the times of the Cisalpine Republic, Reggio Emilia wanted to cast off the rule of Modena, and Piacenza that of Parma. In 1808,

Napoleon integrated the Marches into the Kingdom of Italy, but divided the provinces of Urbino, Ancona, Macerata and Camerino into three departments. This merely served to exacerbate entrenched *campanilismo* and municipal discontent. Ancient arguments were employed to oppose the new administrative units: Recanati argued against the attachment of Porto Recanati to the province of Loreto, invoking privileges originally obtained under Frederick II. As Steen Bo Frandsen has shown, most of Napoleonic Italy was driven by similar struggles for influence.[30] Unification provoked and revived exactly the same animosities. Marco Minghetti regretted these struggles and hoped that instead "the Italian cities would compete to surrender their ancient privileges."[31] The general situation of the Italian cities after 1860 was characterized by their subordination to the centre. Local politicians, who shared liberal convictions and had no choice but to accept Unification, strove to build a relationship between their cities and the monarchy, regularly referring to the contribution their cities had made to the political Unification of the nation. The predominant view was that not the people, but the cities of Italy had fashioned the nation-state.

In October 1861, Bologna's first mayor, Marquis Luigi Pizzardo, offered the commune a portrait of King Vittorio Emanuele II, "to commemorate the day on which, for the unity of Italy, Bologna gave itself to its elected king."[32] Similar ideas emphasising the cities' role as the historical actor of the Risorgimento were expressed on the occasion of Vittorio Emanuele II's death in 1878: "Like the other Italian cities, Bologna owes its freedom to him. Thanks to him Bologna was in a position to join the other cities forming together the unity of the nation."[33] During the funeral in the Roman Pantheon the cities of Italy were central to the national symbolism and, in the shape of banners and coats of arms, dominated the official iconography of the ritual.[34] References to Italy's ancient states were avoided, despite the fact that the plebiscites had been held within the borders of the former states and not on a municipal basis. The only exceptions permitted were references to the ancient origins of the Savoyard dynasty, despite the fact that at the court, for a long time, the use of French dominated over Italian or Piedmontese. As Minghetti declared in a commemoration for Victor Emanuel in 1879,

> beneath the lowering rocks of the Alps, a dynasty, more ancient and illustrious than any other in Europe . . . remembered the spirit of Italy, which had long been dead elsewhere. It began to prepare the long way ahead for better times, thoughtfully and with military discipline. . . . During the three centuries of our decline and foreign domination, this dynasty had nurtured its people and cultivated its native virtues.[35]

Bologna had to secure its place within this young nation-state, and to win recognition as one of its leading cultural centres. In this enterprise it found itself in competition with Florence, the kingdom's political capital after

1864.[36] Milan was more inward-looking than Florence or Bologna, but with its print industry and its sixteen theatres it constituted a major cultural centre.[37] Turin remained strongly associated with the monarchy, even after it lost its status as the kingdom's capital, an event violently opposed by the local population. The ensuing protests left two hundred people injured and several killed during confrontations with the army.[38] Even Naples, despite being disparaged as backward and "un-Italian" by the fathers of Unification, could claim a special status as the peninsula's only city that during the eighteenth century had the feel of a capital, one of the most splendid in Europe.[39] In order to assert its place Bologna's administration sponsored municipal representation at national or international exhibitions, for instance in Nürnberg (1884), Rome (1886), Turin and Dresden (both in 1911). In 1888, on the occasion of the eight-hundred-year celebrations of its university, Bologna promoted its own great exhibition, pitted against the international Vatican exhibition the same year. As the Milanese example of 1881 demonstrates, the objective of such exhibitions was not just to present industrial progress, but also an idea of "urban modernity" generated through civic and municipal institutions.[40] At the 1884 *Esposizione Generale Italiana* in Turin, Bologna put the emphasis on its prehistoric cultures, presenting itself as the origin of the Italic civilisations.[41] In 1899 one of Bologna's first cinematographic events was the performance of a short film about the third exhibition of fine arts in Venice, predecessor of the famous Biennale. According to the audience, the film's most remarkable scene was a brief appearance by Bologna's town mayor, Alberto Dallolio.[42]

MEN, WOMEN AND CIVIC CULTURE

Croce argued that after Unification associations constituted a vital element in the country's political and moral life.[43] Bruno Tobia, in his analysis of the 1884 national pilgrimage to the tomb of Vittorio Emanuele II, has demonstrated how the municipality became a voice and an organisational link between the nation and the organisations of civil society, in particular voluntary associations.[44] Voluntary associations are typical forms of middle class sociability, representing a fertile ground for the emergence of a public sphere. Moreover, membership in associations is often regarded as an entrance ticket into local politics.[45] However, in many parts of Italy these structures of civil society took a long time to develop or they disappeared shortly after Unification; and even if associations included "*aristocratici*" as well as "*borghesi*," they often "reinforced the persistence of two parallel but distinct classes."[46] Rifle clubs, or "*societá di tiro a segno*," created in the years immediately after Unification, were socially more inclusive in their membership, even if they were presided over by the local *notabili*.[47] As democratic institutions of civic education and inspired by Garibaldi's concept of a nation in arms, initially they were strongly represented in the province of Bologna. However, in his groundbreaking study Gilles Pécout has demonstrated the decline, since the mid-1860s, of this particular form of voluntary associations. Remerging during the 1880s, they had lost their progressive and democratic ethos in representing the nation. In 1868 *Il Monitore di Bologna* complained that the "total lack of associational culture" represented a vital problem for the nation.[48]

Before Unification the Papal regime hindered the development of associational forms of sociability in the Papal States. Felicité de Lamennais described Rome during the restoration period as a "city of death": "Public life does not exist; there is nothing that could animate any noble activity, nothing social. . . . Going to church represents the principal form of sociability for Italians. Their society is constituted by their churches. . . . Is this a people? Is this a *patria?*"[49] Leopardi provides us with similar accounts of his experiences.[50] Despite the liberalisation under Pio IX, the Papal States missed the social structures that according to Maurice Agulhon are responsible for the conversion of a passive and reactionary society into a politicised and revolutionary one. While since 1848 *"circoli popolari"* and institutions of political socialisation developed to some extent in the smaller towns of the Romagna,[51] Bologna was more strongly affected by police control. In his memoirs Minghetti mentions the reading room of the *Società medicochirurgica*, which tried to evade the spies of the Papal police and provided access to political newspapers. But censorship set narrow limits to freedom of expression and even references to Galileo Galilei were still forbidden.[52]

Emilia-Romagna had a tradition of freemasonry, of mutual aid and professional organisations.[53] Nevertheless, compared to other European societies a wider ranging associational culture remained underdeveloped. It was the aristocracy rather than the middle classes which animated clubs, *salotti di cultura* or *circoli*. The *Società Agraria*, for example, was an exclusive meeting point for Bologna's most distinguished families.[54] Since the 1830s Minghetti had organised a fortnightly academy of literature in his parents' home, called *Amatori delle muse*, but this remained a private circle for the offspring of the better families.[55] In most cases recreational or cultural associations, such as the *Società del Quartetto* or the *Società del Casino*, were restricted to Bologna's notables. As an Austrian police report noted, the Italian casino had little in common with the politically advanced circles in Germany or England. According to this same report, Italians rarely received at home, and used the generally very expensive casino for their evening entertainments, to play games, to smoke and to laugh.[56] Due to its un-political character the casino contributed little to the formation of a public sphere. Many Italians knew modern forms of sociability only from journeys to France, Britain, Germany and Switzerland. It was on the basis of this experience that Filippo Buonarroti wrote in 1831 his *Principij fondamentali di Sociabilità*.[57] In Rome, even after the liberation, setting up a *salotto* proved difficult, as the majority of noble families remained loyal to the pope and saw this kind of sociability as a habit of the northern cities, associated with the national movement.[58] Before the times of Queen Margherita, literary circles or *salotti di cultura* were practically unknown in Rome; and in the Legations the situation was not much better.

Fear of crime also hindered the development of sociability and the public sphere. The mysterious secret society of the Settembrini, which allegedly was founded during the 1848 revolution, was credited with over two thousand murders in the region.[59] As Minghetti remembers in his memoirs, during the summer *in villa* they were regularly menaced by brigands headed by the famous Passatore, who "emptied houses and castles, violated the women and committed any crime imaginable. . . . The Austrian commanders showed little interest, the Papal troops were impotent, a motley crowd without discipline and order, ridiculed by the people."[60] As a result of this general feeling of depression Rodolfo Audinot feared for the ultimate success of the Legations' liberation. During the early summer of 1859 he wrote to his friend Minghetti about the atmosphere that marked the last weeks of the Papal regime:

> I no longer recognised our home. Discouragement and humiliation reigns, so that any endeavour, any thought is determined by the same sad feeling, which is fear. The disillusionment of the past, the lessons of ten years of police-courts now show results: People have no faith. Rather than enthusiasm it is mistrust which determines the situation. In addition to these general conditions we have the problem that the inspired youth is away now, fighting in the Italian army. . . . You will understand that . . . discouragement is a natural reaction. It is the fear of falling back into the clutches of the priests, as has happened so many times before.[61]

Minghetti himself wrote to Cavour about the "utterly subdued" mood prevailing in the Legations.[62] Lacking basic structures of sociability, it was hard to involve wider strata of society in the project of Unification. This explains why the liberation of Bologna was in the end marked by anarchy and an implosion of all structures of public order, a situation which Minghetti's diaries vividly depict.[63]

Since Unification the number of associations increased throughout Italy. With the development of political parties the region around Bologna became the "laboratory of the country's politicisation."[64] However, many associations listed in the prefects' registries represented primarily economic interests, often defending the hegemony of the landed aristocracy against the rising middle classes.[65] Others were associations for mutual assistance, craft corporations and workers cooperatives, not necessarily an expression of middle class sociability. The Republican and Socialist associations from the Romagna politicised rural workers and artisans, with a limited effect on the cities. The associations which were open to the middle classes were usually dominated by the influence of patricians. In 1886 Bologna's association of engineers organised only 50% of the profession. Only 33%

of the local medical doctors belonged to the medical profession's mutual aid association.[66] According to a national statistic of 1894, only about 15% of a total of 9,379 registered voluntary associations pursued leisure activities; the large majority were mutual aid organisations.[67] In Bologna the opening of a number of traditionally aristocratic associations, like the *Società di Casino*, tended to attract only the upper strata of the middle classes, which in their cultural habitus were sufficiently assimilated to the aristocratic life style.

Efforts to win municipal backing for attempts to stimulate civil society were often rejected, on the grounds that the commune could not afford them. In 1864 the Society for the Protection of Fine Arts, headed by Count Giovanni Malvezzi Medici, asked the commune for financial support, but the mayor Marquis Gioacchino Pepoli took the view that such initiatives were not the municipality's business. Moreover, "if we give in to one such request, we can hardly refuse similar ones which will follow."[68] Under these circumstances it seems remarkable that the society, between its foundation in 1854 and 1866, displayed a total of 869 works. The minister of education and the king bought several works of art at the association's exhibitions. Unlike similar associations in other Italian towns Bologna's *Società Protettrice* invited artists from all over Italy, symbolising, in the words of its president, the "political fraternization of the Italian peoples" through the arts.[69] Nevertheless, as with so many of Bologna's associations, the *società* remained throughout its lifetime an exclusive circle for the better families.

The council was more easily persuaded to support civic initiatives if "*panem et circenses*" was offered to the lower strata of society. The carnival society Duttòur Balanzòn, known from the Etruscan carnival mentioned in the previous chapter, was founded in 1867 and presided over by Count Malvezzi, a former head of the provisional administration during the transition of 1859 and mayor in 1872. The local carnival gained a new lease on life in 1860 when the government conceded the use of masks, previously forbidden by the Papal regime.[70] As the mayor explained, the society's festivities would be "much appreciated by the popular classes" and would "stimulate local industry. Their honest activities do not only lighten the public mood, they also foster the material development of the popular classes."[71] As outlined in its programme, the society aimed at "promoting and co-ordinating public entertainment, to favour commerce and industry and to co-operate with public welfare."[72] As the monthly membership fee of one Lira was not sufficient to provide the funds for its vast programme of activities, the council contributed 1000 Lire to its initiatives, including carnival parades as well as banquets and masked balls for the wealthier citizens.[73] Not only the Church, but also the Left criticised this kind of public entertainment. For the Internationalists it was a waste of money;[74] the Republican Filopanti suggested investing these sums in public welfare;[75] and Aurelio Saffi thought that carnival should be abolished altogether, as it "corrupts people . . . and underlines the contrast between those who enjoy and those who suffer, between those who laugh and those who cry, those who see their lives as an orgy and those dying of starvation and hunger."[76]

Compared to England, France and Germany, chamber music associations or amateur orchestras were less developed in nineteenth-century Italy. However, Bologna was an important centre for brass bands.[77] In addition to the municipal band and several bands belonging to the Church, there were three professional bands of about forty-five musicians each, which performed an average of forty-five concerts per year, providing an income of between sixty-five and seventy Lire for each musician.[78] In 1868 the municipal firemen formed a brass band, an initiative welcomed by the council, although no subsidies were forthcoming.[79] The concerts of these bands were the most important popular entertainment Bologna had to offer throughout the year.

Sport clubs for the middle and lower classes developed later than in England or Germany.[80] In 1860 the municipality offered a prize for the horse races organised by the *Società per le Corse dei Cavalli*.[81] However, when in 1862 and 1863 the society asked again to assign a prize for the races, the council refused to see "any utility in this initiative."[82] Bologna had its own ancient ball game, *giuoco del pallone,* and in 1822, mainly for this purpose, the municipality had built a proper arena, designed in classical style by the architect Giuseppe Tubertini. The same arena was also used for popular entertainments with acrobats, exotic animals, or for aeronautic performances.[83] However, in the council's view the ball game resulted in too many injuries. In particular the spectators needed to be protected

> from the dangers of veritable misfortunes. . . . It is correct that the game might not impress peoples who are used to much more ferocious entertainments, for example bull-fights. Nevertheless, in Italy, with its more gentle customs, security measures are to be recommended.[84]

While the relevant municipal Deputazione wished to abolish the games altogether, the council, after controversial debates, decided to invest into fences to protect the spectators.

Following the example of the German *Turnvereine* and supported by the Republicans, Bologna had two gymnastic societies. Since Francesco de Sanctis' early interest in physical education,[85] it was traditionally the Left which supported public sports and in particular gymnastics. However, for the Moderate municipality in Bologna it became a question of prestige to be involved in regional and national gymnastic competitions, leading the local government to sponsor the organisation of such events.[86] The Moderates' support altered the meaning of public exercise, which Mazzinians and the Socialist Labour movement now attacked, shouting "*Abbasso lo sport!*" and ridiculing organised sport as "the body's violent response to the unproductive idling of the propertied classes."[87] At the end of the 1890s the municipality gave Bologna's Gymnastic Society 1000 Lire to build a swimming pool on the Reno Canal, equipped with hundred-meter lanes and changing facilities.[88] According to the Moderate mayor Dallolio, the clubs: "give the town confidence in its own strength . . . and encourage other forms of private initiative, which a forward-looking administration should support."[89] By the 1880s Bologna's Moderate governments understood the importance of leisure activities and associational culture for the city's well-being. If only for economic reasons, Bologna now also showed an interest in equestrian sport as a support for local animal breeding, cattle trade and fairs. Such initiatives would strengthen private enterprise, encourage the tourism industry and foster the economic development of the population. Bologna's bicycle club *Veloce* was originally an aristocratic initiative, similar to the clubs in Florence or Turin, but unlike most societies, open to women.[90] Only when the middle classes and the lower strata of society discovered the bicycle was this new sport redefined as an activity for the common people and unsuitable for the female body.

From the late 1880s new associations of middle class initiative emerged, such as Alberto Barberi's association for the protection of animals.[91] The Society for Cremation initiated during the 1880s a lively public debate on the societal advantages of cremation. Supporters included *Il Resto del Carlino*, which saw cremation as a modern response to a major social problem, but also the eccentric Catholic Giuseppe Ceri.[92] The public authorities praised the hygienic implications of the practice and eventually also the criminologists withdrew their initial opposition. The main opponent remained the Church.[93] In the council debate on subsidies for a Crematorium Count Zucchini maintained that the commune should not support initiatives which clashed with the customs of its own citizens. Only one in a thousand Italians would wish to be cremated.

> The general feeling is against this, a feeling, which is rooted in customs, in traditions, in religious beliefs, as proved by the penultimate census in which an impressive majority, 99% of the population, described itself as Catholic. If Catholicism gradually diminishes in daily life, this changes when it comes to questions of death. Bologna never has more than ten or twelve purely civic funerals per year.[94]

Nevertheless, founded in 1880, the society soon boasted two hundred fifty members and after 1889 the number of cremations in Bologna quickly rose to about twenty-five per year.[95] As to its social composition, it was one of the few societies in Bologna dominated by the middle classes. Of 622 cremations between 1889 and 1914, a total of 96 bodies were registered as deceased landowners, compared to 265 representatives of the liberal professions, civil servants, businessmen and academics. Jews and free-masons represented an important group among the first cremations. Many members were known to be Democrats or Republicans and had close links to the *Società Operaia*, which in line with the majority of the European Labour movement declared itself in favour of cremation. The name of Andrea Costa, Italy's first Socialist deputy in parliament, appears in the society's register of 1910 in red ink.[96] The inauguration of the Crematorium was attended by representatives of the *giunta*, the council, the public authorities and other crematory societies. The mayor himself was not present, fearing confrontations with the Church at a time when the first Catholics were about to join the council's Conservative majority. Nevertheless, the municipal band played on the occasion, as if to mark the inauguration's official character.[97] In 1899 the council recognised the society's status as a registered charity, against the will of its own cleri-cal-conservative council majority.[98] Only the Fascist regime declared itself explicitly against cremation. The society was also one of the few associations which allowed women to join, even if prior to 1914 only 123 women were cremated as against 499 men.

Women only slowly assumed a more visible position in public life. Perhaps unsurprisingly, Bologna's politics of culture were strongly gendered. Cultural politics were made by men and produced an image of the city and the nation created by men. This was not only the consequence of the way in which politi-cal representation was organized, but also of the gendered character of the emerging public sphere. Only gradually, towards the end of the century, was the public position of women strengthened, partly through their role in the educational system. In 1870, of seventy primary teachers in Bologna thirty were female, corresponding to the national trend in the provision of primary education. However, for the commune this was also a way of saving money, as salaries of female teachers were legally bound not to exceed two-thirds of the salaries of equally qualified male teachers.[99] Several new women's associations were founded, most of which were engaged in charitable activities or in public welfare, just as aristocratic women during the Risorgimento had been.[100] In 1912 the Bolognese councillor Manaresi argued for the first time that for each street named after an illustrious man another street should commemorate a woman noted for her achievements in the arts or the sciences.[101]

So far as political associations are concerned, we find women largely confined to the extreme Left, with figures such as Violetta Dall'Alpi, Giuseppina Cattani, Argentina Bonetti and most prominently Anna Kulis-cioff, playing an important role in the local Internationalist and Social-ist organisations.[102] At the start of the 1890s the Propaganda Committee for the Improvement of the Female Condition exerted some influence on public debates in Bologna, but the group also included several influential men.[103] Although its political tendency was described as *"filosocialista,"* many of its activities attracted women of middle class background. Among its initiatives were lectures on women's history, female suffrage, and on the role of women in the liberal professions. Although in 1881 the first Italian woman passed her juridical exams, women were still excluded from exer-cising the profession. From 1882 onwards Carducci accepted women for exams in the humanities and the Committee's treasurer, Elisa Norsa Guer-rieri, became the first Bolognese woman to graduate with a higher degree in science (1894), but these women only played a limited role in shaping the city's image of itself. The Committee maintained close links with *Il Resto del Carlino*, which shared its concerns and regularly reported on its meetings. The newspaper was the first to publish a regular column for female readers, written by a woman signing herself Miss Liza; and from 1886 the paper's frontispiece featured a smoking woman reading a newspaper.[104] Among those who attended the Committee's meetings were well-known Republicans and Socialists, like Aurelio Saffi and Andrea Costa, Carducci and Pascoli. However, the Committee's political orientation and its relationship towards the Church led to divisions on the question of whether women should be advocates of revolutionary change or guardians of tradition. Beyond Socialist and academic circles the Committee hardly enjoyed any influence and was therefore dissolved after three years, its outstanding funds going to a professional school for women.

Considering that even Italian coffeehouse culture was described by contemporaries as a largely masculine affair,[105] women scarcely had any place at all in Bologna's public sphere. As a typical meeting point between private and public spheres, coffeehouses offset the general lack of associational culture in Bologna and they had the advantage of not having to comply with Italy's restrictive law on associations.[106] While Paolo Macry's analysis of prefectorial records in Naples suggests that politics hardly played a role in the coffeehouse conversations, in Bologna they tended to divide along social and political lines.[107] Since the Risorgimento the *Caffè della Fenice* had been a meeting point for Italian patriots. The former *Caffè Ungherese*, renamed the *Caffè dei Cacciatori* after the end of the Austrian occupation, was a meeting point for the educated middle classes, Democratic or Republican academics and artists, including Carducci, Panzacchi and later Pascoli. Although the clientele was predominantly male, its owner was a woman. Carducci's circle of academics, journalists and poets also met in Zanichelli's bookshop, under the Portico of the *Archiginnasio*. [108] The *melomanes*, Wagnerians, Rossiniani and supporters of Verdi, fought in the *Caffè delle Scienze*,[109] while the *Caffè dell'Arena*, orginally attracting the artists and employees of the surrounding theatres, became a meeting place for the critics of "Crispi's dictatorship." Other coffeehouses in Bologna fulfilled the function of small groceries, attracting a wider mixture of social classes.[110] Considering how difficult it was for Bologna's middle classes to break into the political hegemony of the local Moderates, these informal structures of sociability assumed particular importance. Discussions in these circles helped to coordinate political strategies and to strengthen local and social identities. The circle around Carducci, initially hardly interested in music, became the nucleus of the local Wagnerians and it was Carducci's friend Zanichelli, who in 1872, during the most controversial debates about *la musica del futuro*, published Panzacchi's influential pamphlet in favour of Wagner.[111] Thus, informal circles laid the groundwork for a major shift in musical taste among the cultural elites.

NATIONAL CRISIS AND MUNICIPAL SOLIDARITY

For the municipalities, one important way of communicating a sense of belonging to the nation was solidarity with the victims of natural disasters in the different regions of Italy. As Dickie and Foot have demonstrated in their study on social, political and cultural responses to disasters in modern Italian history, such moments "test the social fabric and the political system to their limits."[112] While most research in disaster studies concentrates on the reactions of the immediate victims or the initiatives of the state in such situations, these moments also offer insights into the "imagining" of national communities through acts of solidarity.[113] Cities would compete for the honour of being the first to help or the most generous. Floods, earthquakes and volcanic eruptions allowed the nation to develop a sense of responsibility for people about whom they knew hardly anything and whose regional languages or dialects they were often unable to understand. Not the nation, but the municipalities became the main political actor in these situations and even cities far removed from the disaster accepted these situations as a symbolic challenge to which they had to respond, immediately and with generosity, in most cases starting with an emergency meeting of the council to allocate funds to assist the victims. In February 1862 and in May 1872 Bologna's council approved budgets of 5000 and 1000 Lire respectively to help the victims of the eruptions of the Vesuvius, substantial sums considering the legal constraints on municipal budgets imposed by central government.[114] In 1908, earthquakes in Messina and Reggio Calabria, described as "the world's most lethal ever seismic event," resulted in an urgent meeting of Bologna's town council, during which the commune wished

> to give an example of practical and effective solidarity with the unfortunate populations. Today there are two pressing necessities: first, to meet the most urgent needs of our unhappy brothers . . . , the second that the whole town expresses its solidarity with the unfortunate people.[115]

A similar initiative was taken in 1915 after earthquakes in large parts of Central Italy, when Bologna's town council allocated the sum of 20,000 Lire to help the families of the victims.[116] These situations demonstrate that practical assistance was as important as the municipalities' symbolic expression of solidarity, especially when the state and the military were charged with incompetence in face of the suffering.[117] It is in historical moments such as these that the imagined community was felt to be a reality. During the first years after Unification some municipalities also supported the victims of *brigantaggio* and of organised crime in the South, for which Bologna set up a special committee chaired by Count Malvezzi. This activity not only fostered feelings of solidarity, but also confirmed negative stereotypes of the South, despite the fact that at the time the press reported almost daily on the same forms of crime in the Romagna.[118]

TERROR AND NATIONAL IDENTITY

The assassination of the French president Sadi Carnot in 1894 by the Italian Sante Caserio aroused heated emotions in Italy. As Bologna's council remarked,

> After the French, we are offended the most by this dreadful deed. It seems natural and legitimate that honest condemnation of such an atrocity should be more vivid here than anywhere else, and that we communicate openly and rigorously our sorrow for the victim and our horror at the murderer. . . . People like this might have been born under our skies, but they do not represent Italy![119]

Italy, and Bologna in particular, had to come to terms with the reputation for politically motivated crime on an unprecedented international scale. Already before Unification, Italian anarchists had made several attempts on the life of the French emperor. In 1858, Felice Orsini, a student from Bologna who was personally acquainted with Minghetti, was held responsible for the attempt on the life of Napoleon III.[120] Carnot's assassination had been preceded by an unsuccessful attempt on the Italian king Umberto I shortly after his accession to the throne in 1878 and was followed by a whole series of similar events involving Italian terrorists. The same month several bombs exploded in Roman government buildings and an anarchist from Lugo, near Bologna, attempted to kill the prime minister Crispi. When Russian Socialists assassinated Alexander II in 1881 Italy feared that public manifestations of sympathy for the Tsar might provoke anti-monarchical demonstrations.[121] The following year the Republican Guglielmo Oberdan from Trieste attempted to assassinate the Austrian emperor Franz Joseph and in 1897 Italian anarchists undertook a second unsuccessful attempt on the life of Umberto I, followed a few months later by the assassination of the Spanish prime minister Antonio Canovas and of Empress Elizabeth of Austria. Two years later, in 1900, Umberto I was assassinated.

Bologna had the reputation of being a local centre of anarchist activity and terrorist plots. In 1874 Bakunin led a failed uprising in the Romagna and in 1877 Bologna was one of the organisational centres when Malatesta and Cafiero attempted to revolutionise the peasants in Southern Italy. In 1892 anarchists exploded a bomb in Bologna's telegraph office. Also the bombing of the Barcelona opera house in 1893, during a performance of Rossini's *Guillaume Tell*, which killed twenty-two people and wounded thirty others, was linked to the activity of Italian anarchists.[122] Although Bologna's Democratic and Republican milieu, traditionally, has had close links with the anarchists, after Carnot's assassination the Left echoed the public condemnation of the terrorists. The Republican Filopanti paid tribute to "the years when France was seen as a beacon of freedom and hope in the whole of Europe." Carducci praised the president's "true Republican virtues which gave him the dignity to fight for his fatherland, with his blood and until his death."[123] With similar emphasis, speaking for the Extreme Left in parliament, Felice Cavallotti lamented that Caserio had wounded the Latin brotherhood between France and Italy.[124]

Considering the role of Italian anarchists in this international wave of terrorism, it is not surprising that the first international anti-anarchism conference in 1898 took place in Rome. Although "not all the alleged 'anarchist' terrorists were anarchists" and "neither Proudhon nor Bakunin called for assassination attempts," their activity served as a pretext to undermine civil liberties.[125] As Bologna's council pronounced in 1897, "murderers have no party, murderers have no fatherland."[126] The experience served to bind the nation together; and the municipal elites used these occasions to speak on the nation's behalf. Meanwhile, political assassinations represented an aspect of the Italian *fine secolo* which did much to exacerbate the nation's sense of crisis, seriously undermining popular trust in the stability of the nation's political institutions. For Derrida terrorism is the symptom of a traumatic element intrinsic to the experience of modernity. In Koselleck's terms, it reflects a modernity permanently concentrated on the future, pathologically understood as a promise, a hope and an affirmation of the self.[127]

NATIONAL AND MUNICIPAL GLORIES

The municipalities' role as architects of the nation was fostered, symbolically, through the honouring and commemoration of famous Italians, through monuments and the naming of streets. Urban space was invested with civic meaning. The inauguration of public monuments in Italy reached its peak in the 1880s, in part because of the sudden death of Victor Emanuel II in 1878.[128] The Milanese conservationist and municipal councillor Camillo Boito defined monuments as "a historical synthesis, a philosophy of history embodied in ideal representations."[129] Monuments for dead heroes, like the Pantheon in Rome or the Montagnola in Bologna, are sacred places, creating symbolic links between generations. The argument here was that the present generation owed their lives to the sacrifice or martyrdom of the dead; martyrs were the price the community paid for its survival or victory.[130] The Italian state played a crucial role in the transmission of the Risorgimento's foundation myth, responding to a "crisis of legitimacy" that over the years had produced a "social-psychological trauma."[131] Part of this response was the fostering of a patriotic religion—a religion of politics defined by Emilio Gentile as the sacralization of politics, understood as "the prerogative to determine the meaning and fundamental aim of human existence for individuals and the collectivity."[132] Within a functionalist reading, as proposed by Durkheim, this religion elevates people to a superior life either through self-sacrifice, as exemplified by the heroes of the Risorgimento, or through the worshipping of their sacrifice. On the level of religious practice the sacralization of the *patria* was reflected in the erection of patriotic monuments. Although a national project, this monumentalisation of legitimacy was crafted to a large extent by the municipalities. While in his work on Germany Mosse pointed to the role of monuments in the "nationalization of the masses,"[133] Italian cities formed "national citizens," educating them through monuments of predominantly local and regional significance. As Pierre-Yves Saunier has demonstrated, for Florentine liberals their city was the political key to the Unification of Italy, a view clearly reflected in the city's cultural self-representation.[134] Commemorations and celebrations for famous Florentines helped to illustrate the role of the city and its elites in the process of national Unification.[135] Similarly, in 1868 Milan embarked upon a programme of inaugurating commemorative plaques for its martyrs of the Risorgimento.[136] Bologna's political elites understood their role to be that of constructing the link between local and national identity through the city's self-representation.[137]

The municipality participated in subscriptions for monuments, named city streets after famous Italians and placed commemorative plaques on buildings to create *lieux de mémoire*, thus writing its glories into the urban landscape. Commenting on Europe's nineteenth-century *statuomanie*, a concept introduced originally by Maurice Agulhon,[138] Roberto Balzani has pointed to differences between France, with its endless variations on the same Marianne, and Italy, where every patriot, martyr or "proto-martyr" of the Risorgimento, every local poet, musician or political thinker got their individual monument or at least a commemorative plaque in their town of origin, and not infrequently several more in other cities.[139] These commemorations helped Italy's post-Risorgimento middle class to develop their civic consciousness, and offered symbolic points of reference for a new civil religion, which was at least partly a response to the secular concept of the liberal regime. Moreover, through monuments for the heroes of the Risorgimento the middle class was able to celebrate itself, underlining its political role during the process of Unification and its sacrifices for the fatherland. With the help of these monuments the middle class inscribed itself in the urban and national landscape.

Italy's *statuomanie* was a local expression of national sentiment, but sometimes took the form of *campanilismo*. It enabled the local history of the Risorgimento to be inserted into a national context, providing an opportunity to reconcile local and national identities. Apart from the Montagnola, *lieu de mémoire* of 1848 and 1859, Bologna's most remarkable example of *statuomanie* is undoubtedly the municipal burial ground of the Certosa, with its pantheon of several hundred busts of the city's most illustrious citizens and many professors of the university, providing a living for generations of sculptors and marble workers. A *Valhalla*, but to celebrate local rather than national pride.[140] Despite this general commitment to the commemoration of local glories, every subscription for a monument, every denomination of a street or square, every plaque placed on a public building provoked controversy, even if it was only in relation to the sum of money invested in a monument, compared to the expenditure for another hero or to the generosity of other cities. The money spent on these occasions varied according to the role of the person to be commemorated and the town in question. Carducci deplored the fact that considerable sums of money went into this monumentalisation of history, while local administrations often forgot to invest in their existing historical patrimony, the treasures of their museums or the architectural remains of past glories.[141]

Even though individual towns were usually able to raise the sums required for such initiatives, other municipalities sought to participate in these subscriptions, expressing their commitment to the cause of their sister towns. In 1865 Bologna contributed 500 Lire to a monument in Milan for the Lombard Enlightenment philosopher and economist Cesare Beccaria.[142] When in 1868 the towns of Noale, Montanara and Curtatone invited contributions to monuments for Pier Fortunato Calvi and the victims of the 1848 battles, the council kept its coffers closed:[143] Calvi, a veteran of the Venetian Republic, had been a supporter of Mazzini, which for the Moderate majority was reason enough to be sceptical; the other two towns were not important enough to justify the expenditure during a period of major financial restrictions. When in 1904 the council proposed to contribute 100 Lire to a monument for Francesco Petrarch in Arezzo, celebrating the sixth centennial of his birth, the sum was considered too small compared to the 500 Lire which Bologna had given for a monument of its late councillor Quirico Filopanti in Budrio.[144] Given the fact that Petrarch had once been a student in Bologna, the council agreed to increase the subscription to 300 Lire.[145]

In 1859 a journal in Turin discussed the German *Schillerfeiern* as a model for celebrating Dante.[146] The father of the Italian language played an important role in defining the relationship between Italy's *cento città* and the nation. During the 1860s the commemoration of Dante led repeatedly to competition between Ravenna, where Dante had lived during his exile, and Florence, his native city. In 1865 Florence unveiled its Dante monument outside Santa Croce, claiming that his remains should be buried in the Tuscan capital. Since the sixteenth century the monks of the Dante church in Ravenna feared that the Florentines would steal the poet's ashes. Somewhat overshadowed by the battle between Florence and Ravenna, Bologna was keen to point out that it had repeatedly hosted the poet during his political struggles and that it was here that the first edition of his *Divina Commedia* had been published. Luciano Scarabelli dedicated his famous commentary on the *Divina Commedia* to the city of Bologna and was thanked with the award of honorary citizenship. The poets Carducci, Pascoli and Guerrini were praised as the spiritual successors of Dante and Petrarch.[147] Only the conductor of the Teatro Comunale, Angelo Mariani, betrayed Bologna by writing an *Inno a Dante* for the Teatro Alighieri of his native Ravenna.[148] Commemorations of Dante not only celebrated the Italian language, but also stood for irredentism and the territorial completion of the fatherland. Debating the subscription for a Dante monument to be erected in Trento, still belonging to the lands of the Austrian enemy, Carducci remarked that Bologna had "a special responsibility" to contribute to this cause and that Florence had already offered 500 Lire.[149] The initiative was a response to a monument for the medieval Minnesänger Walther von der Vogelweide, unveiled by the German population of Bozen. Later the name of Dante assumed still more complex meanings: In 1903 Alfonso Rubbiani rejected an invitation to speak at the imperialist *Società Dante Alighieri,* explaining that "for Dante the Empire was in its idea and in its time a concept that went beyond geographical and ethnic divisions, aspiring to a universal order of mankind."[150]

Committees for the subscription of monuments were usually presided over by members of Bologna's cultural or intellectual elite, or well-known veterans of the Risorgimento, men in a position to negotiate with council majorities. The anti-Austrian feelings associated with the monument for Guglielmo Oberdan—sentenced to death in Trieste in 1882—were considered to be politically sensitive; but it was difficult to reject the proposal of a committee consisting of Carducci, Aurelio Saffi, Giuseppe Ceneri, Olindo Guerrini and Raffaele Ghelli, which at the time had already collected contributions from all over Italy.[151] Reflecting the Moderates' policy of reconciliation with the Church, Bologna did not participate in the subscriptions for the Giordano Bruno monument in Rome, which was considered to be a symbol of anticlericalism. Only the *Società Operaia* gave 25 Lire for the subscription—a small sum compared to the 100 Lire which it contributed to the local monument for Ugo Bassi, but still an important symbolic gesture considering its limited resources. Among individual subscribers for the monument were Minghetti, Carducci and Saffi, but also Hugo and Renan.[152] Some prefects and councillors maintained that a municipality was only allowed to contribute to works of public utility, and not to the erection of public monuments. Carducci opposed this "materialistic utility of pennies" arguing for a "moral interest in the cult of the fatherland and the national idea."[153]

THE DEATH OF ITALY'S FIRST STATESMAN

As Gramsci has pointed out, official funerals and obsequies, due to their public and sometimes even popular character, played an important role in creating national cohesion, with their specific "melodramatic" rhetoric contributing to "a conformity of taste and language."[154] Comparative studies of memorial preaching suggest that the rhetoric used on such occasions does not only have the function of lamentation and of praising the deceased. "Sermons on the dead" constitute a genre which informs us also about attitudes to the office the individual held—in the case of modern Italy providing an opportunity to define constitutional realities.[155] Funerals present an occasion on which political rulers invite the nation to adopt a collective identity: through the celebration, the citizen is supposed to feel part of the nation and to identify emotionally with its representatives.[156]

An early occasion to review Bologna's relationship to the nation's Risorgimento, or to a specific version of it, was the sudden death of Count Cavour in 1861. With Marco Minghetti present at his death bed, Bologna felt in a particular way part of the event.[157] Even Bologna's Left spoke of the prime minister with the highest respect. Thus, in Casarini's letters to Pinelli, Cavour appeared transfigured, a super-human being, and the count's death was presented as putting at risk the entire project of the nation-state, suggesting that office and person were intrinsically linked.[158] As Ernesto Masi, a historian and local politician close to Casarini, remembered: "Among the Italian people the death of Count Cavour produced a feeling of anguish mixed with terror, similar to the feeling of a blind man whose hand suddenly notices the departure of his faithful guide to whom he was used to entrusting himself entirely."[159] The prime minister's death became an occasion to define the symbolic meaning of the office. As a consequence of this process, one of Cavour's legacies was a moral obligation on the part of any successor to guard that same office.

Bologna's council decided to participate in the national subscription for a monument to be erected in Turin, to name a street after Cavour, to place a plaque to remember the "painful event" of his death and to celebrate a requiem in the local cathedral.[160] These signs, which the people of Bologna perceived as the formal expression of grief, at the same time left space for diverse individual and collective interpretations. A contribution of 10,000 Lire to the subscription, a colossal sum at the time, as well as the location of a plaque on a public building and the service in San Petronio did not even need further discussion in council. However, the council was not satisfied with the idea of naming an ordinary street after Cavour but wished to inscribe its devotion to the state's founder more prominently into the local topography. Rather than a street, a central square should carry the name of the count[161]; and the square should then be dignified with Bologna's own monument to Cavour. Two alternatives were discussed, representing two different views of the city's priorities in the process of creating Bologna's post-Papal identity. One proposal set the commemoration of the state's founder before any other consideration; the second wished to celebrate Cavour, but without any sacrifice to local pride. A very prominent location for Bologna's Piazza Cavour would have been a square, which was to have been named after the famous local scientist Luigi Galvani, remembered as one of the discoverers of electricity. The square was adjacent to the university at which Galvani had taught and where he undertook his path-breaking research. Dedicating this square to Cavour would require Bologna to forego the commemoration of a prominent local citizen. As an alternative proposal, a new square could be named after Cavour, a square to be built as part of a major inner-urban development project, close to the planned Via dello Statuto [Constitutional Avenue]. The new square had yet to be built and the inauguration of the monument for Cavour would probably be delayed by several decades. The councillors favouring the first proposal wished to demonstrate the city's loyalty to Cavour's idea of national unification, and thereby to undermine the habitual association of Bologna with clerical opposition to the nation-state. Considering the city's national reputation in this regard, they had, they felt, to communicate this message without further delay. Conversely, their opponents maintained that Bologna had to give priority to the commemoration of its own prominent citizens, helping the city to create a specific profile within the nation-state, built upon its academic tradition as the site of Italy's and Europe's most ancient and famous university. After a long discussion the council decided in favour of the second option—a monument and a square for Cavour, but without compromising its local pride.

The death of the statesman offered an opportunity to renegotiate local and national identities. Similar occasions occurred after the death of the poets Alessandro Manzoni and Francesco Domenico Guerrazzi.[162] Occasionally these commemorations assumed an international dimension. The death of Victor Hugo in 1885 thus became a major event. Numerous local associations and the council wrote to the poet's family and in the ensuing weeks the press presented anecdotes of his life, impressions of his last hours and reports on the commemorations in France. The university marked Hugo's death with an official mourning at which Carducci delivered the address.[163] Bologna identified with a citizen of the world.

TOPONYMY

Similarly important for the relationship between city and nation were the changes in Bologna's toponymy. In Milan, the local government's initial proposal for changes in the denomination of streets had to be reviewed after stormy public debates. Ultimately, the names of forty streets were changed and twenty-five new ones were created, but one hundred ninety-two streets and squares from the original list maintained their traditional name.[164] Most cities had completed their topographic revision by 1863.[165] Bologna took a different approach, not changing names at once, but over a longer period and in smaller numbers, when the occasion arose. In many cases the naming of streets was meant to place the city in relation to the nation, to compare the city with its sister towns and to negotiate between local and national identities. In 1864 the mayor Count Pepopli invited Bologna to repay its debt of gratitude to the memory of the many prominent men who in all times made the city's name known. . . . Bologna should follow the example of other towns which compete in erecting monuments, putting up epigraphs and naming central squares and streets after their most famous citizens.[166]

The councillors themselves regularly reminded their local government that Bologna should honour "the illustrious names associated with the arts, the sciences, and in particular its patriots."[167] If the council decided to dedicate only a minor street to a relevant person, sympathetic councillors regularly evoked the example of other towns which had chosen more prestigious avenues. This was the case with a street for Aurelio Saffi, who for Bologna's Right was too closely associated with the Roman Republic, but honoured without hesitation by other cities. Five years after his death Forlì and Ravenna had named major streets after the hero, while Bologna was still awaiting a decision. Whereas Genoa named the boulevard along its famous seafront after Saffi, Bologna's mayor eventually proposed a street in one of the new residential areas outside the centre.[168]

Patriotism was not the only driving force in the process of renaming streets. At times the argument was made that names of streets had to be changed because they sound "too ancient or are too long . . . others have meaningless or just not very nice names. Streets like *Vault of the poultries* or *Cabmen Street* should be changed for modern and shorter names."[169] Many streets and squares in Bologna were traditionally named after the saints of the local churches. In these cases the Left aimed at eradicating religious symbols in favour of the new "patriotic religion." The Left's ideological approach could lead to rather amusing misjudgements, for example, when in 1880 a councillor proposed changing *Via dei Preti* into *Via del Progresso*, not realising that the street was not dedicated to the "priests" but to a family called Preti.[170] From the mid-1890s the general trend for change was reversed and it became council policy to maintain the historical names of the streets in the centre and to honour famous citizens with new streets in the recently created residential areas of the periphery.[171]

CONTESTED PATERNITIES

In 1864 Bologna named a square after its most famous citizen, Gioacchino Rossini.[172] In 1869, three months after his death and thirty years since he had assumed the honorary direction of the Liceo Musicale, a bust was placed in the Pantheon while a tablet on the wall of the Archiginnasio served to commemorate the first performance of his *Stabat Mater*, conducted by Gaetano Donizetti, another alumnus of Bologna's conservatory.[173] Considering the fame which Rossini brought to Bologna, one might regard this commemoration as rather modest in scope. The relevant deliberations were taken under

Casarini's Democratic administration, when the focus of Bologna's musical life definitely shifted from *bel canto* to Wagner. An administration of the Left was reluctant to draw too much attention to a man who under the nickname *"tedeschino"* had been too close to the Austrian occupier and who had left Bologna to escape from the 1848 revolution. His lover and later wife Olimpia Pelissier had been famous for her anti-liberal views and her open support of the Austrians. Minghetti had known Rossini privately since his early years and had no doubts that he had been a man of the restoration regime. The 1830 revolution had marked the end of his epoch. Appalled by Bologna's revolution, Rossini had decided to leave his fortune to a new institute in Pesaro rather than to Bologna's Liceo Musicale.[174]

In 1886, by parliamentary decree, Rossini's ashes were transferred to Santa Croce in Florence, which had become Italy's "Pantheon of Glory"[175], the burial place of Michelangelo, Machiavelli, Galileo, Alfieri, Cherubini, Leonardo Bruni, Ugo Foscolo and others. However, Bologna protested about the transfer of Rossini's ashes. Although Bologna was not Rossini's place of birth, it was his *"patria musicale,"* because "the real patria of a famous man is the place where he learned, studied and flourished." To publicize its claims, Bologna sent a garland to the ceremony in Florence, carrying the words "Bologna to its adopted son."[176] For the centennial celebrations in Pesaro Panzacchi referred to the composer as his "concittadino." He also reinvented Rossini as a patriot and a composer of "revolutionary music."[177] After Florence, Pesaro and Bologna, Lugo in Romagna was the fourth town to make claims on Rossini, the place where the composer had spent his early formative years and where his father owned a house, for the local council reason enough to argue that Lugo was the composer's real home town, at least in the legal sense of the term.[178] Rossini was proud to be called *"il cigno* [swan] *di Pesaro,"* calling his own father *"il cignale* [boar] *di Lugo."* Nevertheless, in a document concerning his paternal house he addressed the Lughesi as his *"concittadini."*[179]

Verdi considered Bologna to be Rossini's *"vera capitale musicale"* and it was here that the performance of the famous Requiem for Rossini should have taken place.[180] The organising committee, which Verdi chaired, had hoped the city would provide its choir, orchestra and soloists free of charge, but the impresario of the Teatro Comunale, Scalaberni, refused to act as a patron of the arts, considering himself "a businessman with six children, who is not well off."[181] Ultimately, the project collapsed due to Verdi's personal conflicts with the conductor Angelo Mariani.

A similar competition for paternity rights marked the debate surrounding the commemoration of Ugo Bassi, a former chaplain of the revolutionary army and a veteran of the battles of Treviso, Rieti and Velletri. Arrested in Bologna by the Austrians on 7 August 1848, he had been sentenced by a tribunal of priests and was shot the following day. Having lived and studied in Bologna, the city considered him its principal revolutionary martyr.[182] However, until Filopanti came up with the compromise of referring to Bassi

Figure 7.1 Teatro Rossini, Lugo. (Reproduction by Kind Permission of the Fondazione Teatro Rossini and the Comune di Lugo.)

as "*martire italiano,*" veterans of the revolution from Cento, where Bassi was born, insisted that he was not "*bolognese.*"[183] Animosities of this kind were the order of the day, but occasionally commemorations also helped to overcome competition between cities. In 1861 Cesare Masini from the Academy of Fine Arts launched a subscription for a monument to Luigi Galvani, but the committee failed to collect the necessary amount; instead, only a bust was placed in the Pantheon.[184] Once the council had decided to dedicate the square next to the Archiginnasio to Galvani rather than Cavour,[185] a new committee started a subscription for the "*celebratissimo.*" Many local Moderates formed part of the committee, including Count Agostino Salina, Count Giovanni Malvezzi and Marquis Luigi Pizzardi, all members of the parliament's first chamber; but local politicians of the Left, such as Cesare Lugli and Quirico Filopanti, also supported the initiative—despite the fact that in 1797 Galvani had pronounced himself against the Republic, subsequently lost his university chair and was denied a public funeral.[186] However, for Bologna's Republicans Galvani's name stood for modern empirical sciences and for the role of academia and the middle class in public life.

The mayor Tacconi declared with pride that this was the first "civil monument" inaugurated in Bologna, a reference "to genius and science."[187] The committee approached numerous international statesmen for a contribution and wrote to the Brazilian and German emperors, and to the French president. The provincial council, several Italian and international scientific bodies, and the municipality all subscribed. Panzacchi supported the initiative with a poem.[188] The monument was inaugurated on 9 November 1879 in the presence of the king's minister, the minister of education, members of Galvani's family, military authorities and many citizens. The last to speak at the inauguration was a representative of the city of Como, Zanino Volta, himself a descendant of Alessandro Volta, Galvani's contemporary and the inventor of the battery. Despite early manifestations of mutual respect, the two scientists had denied each other's contributions to the discovery of electricity. Officially representing the city of Como, Volta insisted that Bologna should be proud of a genius like Galvani, just as Como was proud of its Volta—both honouring the glory of the fatherland.[189] Twenty years later, on the centennial of Galvani's death, the university and municipality celebrated the idea of progress and a name standing for "one of the most important discoveries of modern civilisation," "a man who knew to combine morality, the religion of life and intensive study."[190]

At the start of the twentieth century animosities fostered by local pride and *campanilismo* took on an international dimension. Bologna's most famous monument, erected three hundred years before the Unification of Italy, was the "Fontana del Nettunno" by Giambologna, between Piazza Maggiore and the town hall. Inspired by Giambologna's Flemish origins, the Belgian king Leopold II, in 1903, placed a copy of the fountain outside his residence in Laeken, near Brussels. This led to embittered debates in Bologna's local press and the town council,[191] which claimed Bologna's exclusive right of property regarding its patrimony. For Bologna, Belgium had no right to produce a copy of its famous landmark and the monument in Laeken was regarded as an illegal reproduction. Originally, the Belgian king had asked the city of Bologna for a copy of the entire fountain, which the *giunta* refused to provide. Impudently, the agents of the Belgian king took the copy of the Neptune from a reproduction at the Pinacoteca in Parma, asking Bologna only for copies of the Sirens. Belgium was thus able to reproduce the complete monument, without explaining its intentions. In Bologna, a committee of citizens drew up a petition, signed by the city's most illustrious professors and artists, asking the mayor to intervene and the popular *giunta* of Enrico Golinelli welcomed the chance to criticize the previous (Moderate) administration for neglecting the city's interests.[192] The fake Neptune remains to this day squeezed between the walls of the royal domain and the exit of Brussels' motorway.

The examples mentioned above demonstrate the role of the municipality in creating a sense of national belonging, but they also illustrate that, where questions of national prestige were concerned, relations between Italian cities were often marked by competition and tension.[193] Subscriptions for monuments, mutual assistance and recognition of the "sister cities" contribution to the nation's advancement all helped to create the nation on the symbolic level. For the citizens involved in this process, the nation assumed both a symbolic meaning and a territorial dimension. Bologna and Italy as a whole urgently needed to develop awareness of the nation's territoriality. Like many leading politicians at the time, the most famous of the *padri della patria*, Count Camillo Cavour, had visited France, Switzerland, England, Belgium and Germany, without ever seeing Rome and Naples; and he made his first visit to Bologna, Florence and Pisa just a year before his death.[194]

CELEBRATING THE NATION

Paul Connerton differentiates between the collective memory of "small face-to-face societies" and "territorially extensive societies" forming communities that mostly exist as imagined entities, without its members knowing each other personally.[195] This distinction is crucial to the study of historical commemorations and their relationship on a local and a national level. Immediately after Unification, popular perceptions of the liberation and celebrations of the nation were not yet influenced by the governmental decrees and parliamentary decisions which since 1861 had imposed a compulsory calendar and a specific liturgy to commemorate these events. Celebrations emerged in the periphery rather than at the centre, staged by local political actors, following models and forms which were rooted in local experiences, occasionally reaching back to the Republican period of the late eighteenth century. Moreover, the ancient states of the peninsula had traditions whereby the monarchical power of their sovereigns was displayed in public celebrations.[196] This might explain why manifestations of patriotism and celebrations of the nation in the early years differed from the official celebrations of the Savoyard constitution, the *Festa dello Statuto*, which after the annexation by Piedmont became an official public holiday for the entire nation, celebrated according to centrally planned prescriptions.[197]

Carlo Alberto's proclamation of the *Statuto* in 1848, which transformed Piedmont-Sardinia into a liberal constitutional monarchy, represented an event which to most people in Bologna meant very little. The celebration was centred on a legal document written in French, the official language of the court. Instead, locally, the most important events to commemorate were revolutionary in character, like Bologna's defeat of the Austrian troops in August 1848 or the liberation from the Papal regime in 1859. The 1861 celebration of the 8 August was an expression of popular enthusiasm for the population's triumph over the occupying army, considered to be among the strongest in Europe. Moreover, the event was understood as a political demonstration marking the civil legitimization of the new state but also calling for the completion of the Risorgimento and for the liberation of Venice,

Rome and the provinces remaining under foreign occupation. Hence, the celebration was not free of revolutionary undertones, contrasting with the government's approach to the national question.[198] In this sense the popular expressions of freedom displayed a semantic link between past and future, similar to Mona Ozouf's analysis of the *fête révolutionnaire*.[199] In August 1861 Bologna invited its citizens to a *"rustica festa popolare"* commemorating the glorious battle of 8 August 1848.

It is nearly thirteen years since the AUSTRIAN invaded our city and the surrounding plains. Quickly he fled, daunted and defeated, by the unexpected awakening of this people, almost without arms, but roused by a great and terrible anger! Facing the gardens which had been the principal theatre of this memorable event, the illustrious municipality put up a marble inscription, solemnly inaugurated, to commemorate the name of all those valiant men who fell in this holy battle of freedom. Not long ago our populace came together with exiles from Venice and Rome, their flags hung with black, in a fine procession, to protest at this inscription and to pray for the peace of the dead heroes. But once these rituals, a religious consecration of great virtue, have been completed, it seems only fitting that we celebrate the victory of the people, that the people comes together for its own celebrations, to delight in honest entertainments and to rest from harsh labour; and that it is able to secure its mutual and fraternal affections, to take heart, and thus to prepare itself for further honourable ventures.[200]

The schedule included patriotic music, games and competitions, *tableaux vivants* and dances. The announcement concludes with a triumphant "Oust the foreigners! Long live the one, free and independent Italy! Long live the king, a good and honest man!" The explicitly anti-Austrian tenor of the manifestation, the emphasis on the Risorgimento's popular and revolutionary dimension and on the battles to come contrast with both the government's official representation of the events and the Moderates' national programme. This is despite the fact that the local administration in Bologna was still dominated by the same Moderates who shaped national politics in Turin and feared the revolutionary legacy of 1848. In 1860 Minghetti, Bologna's most influential Moderate, remembered 1848 as the "year of the great catastrophe." He revived the image of disorder and anarchy, and expressed fears that the revolutionary party might still resume its activities:

This party exists; it has a programme; it is on the move; it is a threat; and this is sufficient to instigate violence. It wishes to repeat the French revolution and wants to adorn itself with its different phases. The committee of public safety is its type of government. Its dogma is the omnipotent state which immolates the individual, the family and the nation. And while it confounds any right, any guarantees into a vague and artificial cosmopolitism, it cherishes the ideal of Sparta and Rome, up to the point of ostracising the most valuable citizens and praising political assassinations. . . . Gentlemen, our memory of the upheavals of 1848 and 1849, of the dangers which society had to overcome, has not yet faded![201]

There are two explanations for this contrast between the official Moderate voices in parliament and their toleration of public commemorations at the local level. In the case of Bologna, only months after the liberation, politics were not yet marked by the confrontation between Right and Left that had characterised the 1860 conflict over the South between Cavour and Garibaldi. Bologna maintained a patriotic consensus between its diverse political forces.[202] Another reason for the contrast was that Bologna's celebrations were still organised by a committee of citizens and the Deputazione degli pubblici spettacoli, without interference from central government.[203]

The programme for the first anniversary of the 1859 liberation was similar in style. Rather than highlighting the annexation by Piedmont, Bologna celebrated the defeat [*sgombro*] of the Austrians,[204] the foreign occupiers. The celebration did not refer to the departure of the cardinal, which was difficult to explain and to justify in an event that was popular in character. In September 1860, twelve hundred Papal troops, arrested as prisoners of war, passed through Bologna. The streets were filled with people who had left their workplace to witness the event in real time.[205] From the sources it is hard to gauge how this event was experienced by the local population. Like the Austrians, the Papal troops were to a large extent foreigners, but had the role of protecting the Holy Father. A few days before Bologna had marked the fall of Fort Ancona and Garibaldi's entrance into Naples with fireworks, events which later would disappear from the official agenda of national commemorations.[206] The emphasis on the commemoration of local or regional events during the first years after the liberation, and the anti-Austrian sentiments voiced on such occasions, do not mean that Bolognese lacked loyalty towards the monarchy or that they only celebrated their liberation from an oppressive regime. Most of these events paid tribute to the king of Piedmont and in March 1861, when Bologna's deputies in parliament telegraphed the mayor about the proclamation of Vittorio Emanuele II as king of Italy, the municipality celebrated the event with fireworks and music. Large parts of the local population took part in the event.[207]

STAGING THE CONSTITUTION

Events involving the local populations dominated commemorations immediately after Unification. They were characterised by spontaneity and imagination, and were designed to include the populace in its social diversity without drawing attention to social hierarchies. Many of these events were organised by committees of patriotic citizens, some of them all but supervised by the local authorities. The very dense calendar of these early celebrations bears comparison with Bologna's Napoleonic years.[208] However, the popular and revolutionary character of commemorations changed with the government's official deliberations concerning national holidays. In 1868, the Moderate establishment remembered the 8 August 1848 not as the people's revolutionary liberation of their city, but as a "tribute of blood to the fatherland."[209] The *Festa dello Statuto* became the focus of official celebrations, and served to symbolise "Italy's regeneration." Local and popular celebrations of the nation disappeared from the municipal agenda.[210]

In the early years after Unification the municipality still enjoyed a certain freedom regarding the organisation of the *Festa dello Statuto*. A circular of the minister of interior of May 1860 explained that the new provinces of Piedmont were legally obliged to celebrate the proclamation of Carlo Alberto's 1848 constitution, but "the law leaves it to the single municipalities to organise the celebration and to cover the expenses."[211] The minister merely reminded the local authorities to celebrate a Te Deum in the principal church. Considering the conflict between Church and State precipitated by the liberation of the Legations, the celebration of a Te Deum represented a difficult task for local governors and for Bologna in particular. Earlier popular celebrations focused not on the liberation from the Papal regime but on the departure of the Austrian troops, thus avoiding religious connotations. The commemoration of 8 August included a Requiem for the fallen patriots, but the service took place not in a church, but in the Montagnola gardens—as to give less offence to the ecclesiastical authorities.[212] Although public and religious spheres remained officially separate after Unification, the sacred legitimisation of the new state was a priority, despite the pontiff's reluctance to recognise the Italian State.[213] Some bishops did not oppose the celebration of a mass in their churches, but refused to take part. On these occasions the relationship between State and Church was often marked by a schism between higher and lower clergy; and, as Illaria Porciani has shown, most municipalities could find a priest prepared, with or without the bishop's authorisation, to read the Te Deum.[214]

In May 1861, a more detailed ministerial circular instituted the *Festa dello Statuto* as the kingdom's only official national holiday.[215] The circular stressed that no other anniversary—not the 8th of August nor any event linked to the liberation of Central or Southern Italy—had the status of a national holiday. Celebrating these latter anniversaries assumed an almost subversive character. In 1874 the anarchists had planned an uprising in the Romagna, to commence on 8 August and so to recover the symbolic meaning of the liberation's revolutionary character.[216] Ideological connotations aside, reducing the number of public holidays, and of religious festivals in particular, was also understood as a measure to modernise state and society. Shortly after the proclamation of the *Statuto*, the city of Turin reduced the number of celebrations for the patrons of local churches at which the municipality would be officially represented, a measure viewed as part and parcel of the "*laicizzazione della vita pubblica.*" In the Po region most processions for the local saints, who were supposed to protect the population from floods, disappeared.[217]

The 1861 circular on the *Festa dello Statuto* specified that not only the constitution itself, but also the unity of Italy was to be celebrated. Hence, the proclamation of Carlo Alberto's *Statuto* was interpreted as the most important event leading to the Unification of Italy, representing "the completion of all the partial facts." Therefore, "the government of his majesty recommends banning any other celebration commemorating ancient municipal divisions, partial triumphs or victories, which only damage the nation as an entity." No other event "merits being celebrated as much as this one, encapsulating the three major achievements of a people—its unity, its independence and its freedom."[218] Thus, the new law imposed a specific reading of this event, and of the Risorgimento as a whole. The constitution of Piedmont was presented as the catalyst of the process of Unification, overshadowing the contribution of Garibaldi's volunteers, local revolutionary uprisings or the plebiscites. The manner in which the *Statuto* was to be celebrated was intended to deflect attention from any later episodes of the Risorgimento, from the risks and ambiguities of Cavour's policy and from his differences with the king.[219] The policy of the Piedmontese liberals during the 1840s and 1850s was presented as the principal factor leading to Unification. Neglecting local battles of liberation, Piedmont's annexation of the pre-unitarian states since 1859 became the logical consequence of the Liberals' policy.

The celebration of the *Statuto* was fixed on the first Sunday of June and the event was to be financed by the municipalities themselves. A further ministerial circular outlined in greater detail the way to mark the new national holiday, which was supposed to unite "all peoples of Italy into a single family under the rule of the constitutional monarchy of Vittorio Emanuele II and his successors."[220] The ceremony itself had to be agreed to by the prefect as the local representative of central government and mayors were asked to invite the ecclesiastical authorities, but not to insist on their presence should they refuse.[221] A review of permanent troops stationed in the area and of the National Guards became an official requirement for any national celebration. The Guardia Nazionale, purportedly a link between the armed forces and civil society, had been in decline since 1860, and its outdated equipment regularly provoked the laughter of local populations during parades. There was little that was popular about such celebrations, save perhaps the awarding of prizes for target practice and occasional exhibitions of local crafts and industry.[222]

In Bologna, until 1865, the military parade for the *Festa dello Statuto* took place on the Prati di Carprara. Since it started in the early hours of the morning, there was little chance of the local population attending.

For the staged celebrations of the British nation masses in the streets were part of the state ritual. In Britain the focus of celebrations was the monarch, whereas Italy celebrated a piece of paper and the abstract idea of the nation's unity. In later years Bologna's parades moved into the city, to Piazza Maggiore, where benches were allocated to selected authorities, thus maintaining the exclusive character of the event.[223] After the first celebrations Bologna's Moderates themselves were surprised that the *Festa* had assumed the character of a quasi-military event, without any participation of civil society.[224] Sedan-Day celebrations in Germany were also militaristic rituals, but they were organised by local notables rather than by municipal administrations acting on behalf of the state. Moreover, the German event was never sanctioned as a national holiday, underlining the idea of an initiative of civil society. Although in many parts of Germany Catholics, Socialists, Democrats and particularists opposed or boycotted the national holiday, local associations, school children, women and even kindergartens played a major role in the organisation and used it as an occasion "to shape national identity in their own image," even if this could be regarded as a voluntary militarization of civil society.[225] In 1758 Jean-Jacques Rousseau had explained that in order to evoke emotions and the passion necessary to foster a community's spiritual and moral cohesion certain symbols of self-recognition were needed, in particular a choreography that transformed the audience for celebrations into active participants.[226] This aspect was certainly underdeveloped in Italy's official celebrations of the constitution.

Bologna's council, in order to modify the nature of the event and make it appeal to larger sections of society, decided to combine the celebration of the *Statuto* with acts of public charity, distributing money to the families of serving soldiers, to poor children, and to the Venetian and Roman exiles based in Bologna.[227] Nevertheless, the way the *Statuto* was celebrated emphasised hierarchies of power and excluded important social groups that formed part of the nation, ressembling what Ozouf defined as the "*fête dynastique, qui fixe avec un raideur exemplaire l'ordre des rangs et des corps.*" Rather than celebrating civil society, or the political institutions representing it, the *Festa* transmitted the idea of an "*Obrigkeitsstaat.*"[228] Women were to be excluded from official representation for some time to come; it was not until 1915 that female primary teachers were officially invited to take part in the celebrations.[229] Hardly anywhere did the press record the participation of wider sections of the population. Only towards the end of the century did Bologna's Jewish community take an active part in the celebrations, with prayers for the House of Savoy, tricolours in the synagogues and the setting of national lyrics to Jewish chants. The Florentine synagogue was inaugurated by Queen Margherita on the day of the *Festa dello Statuto.*[230]

Apart from the *Festa dello Statuto*, the few remaining national festivals changed in character or became more exclusive. Throughout the 19th century parts of Italian society nourished a cult of Napoleon, regarded as the first to grant freedom and some form of unity to the population of Italy. Bologna commemorated Napoleon's brother-in-law and king of Naples, Gioacchino Murat, who took Bologna in 1801 and was one of the first to advocate Italy's unification under one crown.[231] When the returning Papal regime deprived the Legations of their constitutional privileges, this was the price they had to pay for having supported Murat until 1814. Literary glorifications of the Napoleonic period, as in the works of Stendhal and Chateaubriand, and biographies of the emperor, enjoyed a wide circulation. Songs, devotional pictures and anecdotes about Napoleon's life resembled Béranger's *Légende Napoléonienne* in France or the cult around Garibaldi.[232] When Bologna, in May 1861, commemorated the fortieth anniversary of Napoleon's death, the celebration was organised by a local committee of notables who had been decorated with the emperor's Medal of Saint Helena. Invitations were addressed exclusively to the local nobility, the military and to the civil authorities, representatives of the French imperial administration in Bologna and members of Napoleon's wider family, like the future mayor of Bologna, Marquis Gioacchino Napoleone Pepoli, cousin of Napoleon III.[233]

The council decided in February 1872 to double the funds for the *Festa dello Statuto* from 1000 Lire to 2000 Lire and to add a further 500 to celebrate the birthday of King Vittorio Emanuele on the same occasion.[234] However, the local populace was left out and according to the oppositional press the celebrations of the Statuto remained unpopular. *Il Resto del Carlino* mocked in 1885:

> The *Festa dello Statuto* was extremely animated. A cannon on . . . Via Panoramica outside Porta d'Azeglio was fired with the usual shots, breaking numerous windows and destroying other belongings of the pacifist inhabitants, who fired back with frightful oaths against the military authorities. Can't these good citizens be cheered up by firing the cannon at the Monte della Guardia? And who pays for the broken windows?

The only other episode worth mentioning was "a soldier of the Fifth Cavalry, found completely drunk in Via Indipendenza."[235] The newspaper's attitude towards the kingdom's principal holiday reflects the distance of the wider public from the political system as a whole.

Because these celebrations had no impact on society, local associations invented their own political and civic traditions, often of a more popular character and occasionally adopting patterns from traditional religious rituals. On 19 March, the day of San Giuseppe, the Democrats honoured the two "lay Giuseppe," Mazzini and Garibaldi. Until the 1880s, they regularly organised meetings, outdoor activities for families and banquets, celebrated in the spirit of a new civil religion. Later, the Socialists refused to celebrate the religious name-day and decided instead to mark the respective birthdays of the two heroes.[236] Contrasting with the gaiety of the name-days and birthdays, the Socialists' commemorations for the death of Mazzini on 10 March were marked by religious piety and the sacrilisation of ritual.[237]

STATE AND NATION

During the Umbertian era the authorities understood that they had to make the *Festa dello Statuto* more popular. Moreover, the political trans-formation of local representations and the new parliamentary majorities served to alter the social background to the event. The fiftieth anniversary of the *Festa* in 1898 was celebrated in connection with the International Exhibition in Turin, co-financed through a subscription by Italian munici-palities and designed to transmit the image of a modern and industrious society, represented through its municipalities.[238] However, even in 1898 there was still a need to explain the *Festa dello Statuto* to the nation.

> Italy was made the day that in Piedmont a magnificent sovereign granted the *Statuto* and thus sanctioned civil equality, freedom of thought and political representation; the day that the Piedmontese army hoisted the tricolour. From that day forth the hope of so many centuries had only to be fulfilled. The *Statuto* is for us not just this fundamental, inviolable pact between the people and its king, to whom we convey today a devout and affectionate salutation. The granting of the *Statuto* also precipitated the great events which in the end gave us a fatherland.[239]

For liberal Italy the focus of national celebrations remained Piedmont and the granting of the constitution, a concept of the nation predominantly based on the Savoyard monarchy. The celebration of other events which led to the nation's resurgence in 1860 was perceived as a potential threat to the political status quo attained at Unification. However, in celebrat-ing the *Statuto* the municipalities created a link between State and civil society. The local elites in the council and the *giunta* represented the stra-tum of society that identified with both municipal traditions and the new nation-state. They understood their public role to be that of negotiating the relationship between local and national identities. The attempts of the State to promote national identity through celebrations of the Piedmon-tese constitution stifled local and spontaneous expressions of national sentiment and failed to foster popular identification with the nation-state. However, during the Umbertian age, the concept of the nation gradu-ally assumed a more concrete meaning for Italians. Whereas towards the end of the century the nationalism of the Italian government increasingly assumed an aggressive and anti-liberal character,[240] the idea of a "century of municipalities"[241] survived—expression of a civil society constituted on the basis of municipal identities.

8 *Margherita*
Umbertian Italy and its Monarchy

RITUAL AND MONARCHY

"*Je ne veux absolument ni adresses, ni remerciements, ni fêtes,*" replied King Carlo Alberto—in French—when the town council of Turin asked for permission to thank the monarch for granting the *Statuto*, the constitution of 1848. Instead of giving permission for a public celebration, the king complained that his family's blue *cocarde* had been replaced with the new Italian *tricolour* as the official symbol of the monarchy. The Savoy's blue appears today exclusively in connection with Italy's national football team, the *squadra azzura*. Conscious and proud of its dynastic conventions, the House of Savoy had a tradition of avowed unease concerning symbolic celebrations of the Italian nation. Only in 1890 had the Savoy's coat of arms, the red cross, become an official symbol of the Italian State, finally creating a symbolic link between the nation and its monarchy, between the ancient Kingdom of Piedmont-Sardinia and the new Kingdom of Italy.[1] But did these symbols matter to Italians? Crispi's newspaper *La Riforma* observed in 1896:

> When the national flag is raised in France, England, Germany, and Russia, people stop talking, and every citizen, whatever his party, bows his head in conformity with his national duty. In Italy, on the other hand (where there is never any serious talk about anything) people begin talking precisely when the national flag is raised.[2]

Ritual, as a form of standardized "symbolic behaviour," plays an important political role "in bringing about solidarity where consensus is lacking."[3] Among Democrats, especially since the interwar crisis of the twentieth century, this aspect of ritual has often caused suspicion, but it did help to develop an analytical framework for understanding how the social psychology of symbolism works. What Cannadine calls the "secular magic of monarchy," elsewhere described as the monarch's sacredness, depends on popular sentiment rather than the legislator and is largely created by ritual.[4] As Kertzer has demonstrated in his comparative analysis of political power, ritual is a "means of influencing people's ideas about political events, political policies, political systems, and political leaders."[5] Thus, ritual becomes a means of communication. Percy Ernst Schramm described this process of communication as a "conscious act" aimed at provoking a specific psychological reaction among the different social layers of the people.[6] In Italy not the monarchy itself, but the institutions of the liberal State—parliament, government and the municipalities—assumed the role of transforming the monarchy into a symbol for, and embodiment of the nation. Royal parades, weddings and funerals, State visits or the monarch's own visits to the different parts of his country provide opportunities for investing the external world with meaning, "in part by linking the past to the present and the present to the future," thus providing "a sense of continuity."[7] For the Italian monarchy after 1860 most of these symbolic forms had to be invented. Often they were improvised on the basis of existing symbols, in the hope that formal familiarity would help to convince or even to seduce spectators and audiences. As the previous chapter has suggested, after Unification the municipalities played a major role in fostering civic identities. By inventing, performing and standardizing rituals they created a link between the monarchy and the nation. The municipalities put the monarchy on stage and made the monarchs into symbols of the nation.

THE KING-SOLDIER

In 1868, the *Rivista Bolognese* published an article by Angelo Camillo De Meis claiming that the monarchy, in addition to its constitutional function, had to fulfil a social role as mediator, contributing to the process of nation building. These ideas sparked a debate in which Carducci, at the time still a fervent Republican, played a leading role.[8] Although Vittorio Emanuele's part in the Unification of the country was widely acknowledged, commentators were conscious of the distance between the crown and the people. Like other cities, Bologna's authorities devoted great attention and ceremonial effort to the unexpected death of Vittorio Emanuele II in January 1878. The fact that the king was not buried in Turin came as a shock to the people of the Piedmontese capital.[9] However, the government's decision in favour of Rome represented an attempt to strengthen the nation's bonds with the monarchy. Vittorio Emanuele was popular, among the middle classes as well as the lower strata of society, but it was a popularity almost exclusively linked to his role as a military leader during the Risorgimento and the wars of liberation.[10] The nation had difficulties expressing its feelings towards the monarchy once Italy had been united. When Umberto I visited Bologna, shortly after his coronation, only two or three shops in the centre displayed the tricolour. The streets remained empty and the people silent. Since the crown prince's wedding with the beautiful princess Margherita, a previously unknown cult around the royal family had started to develop, but in the former Legations the people's relationship with the monarchy continued to be almost cold.[11] Despite the king's popularity as Italy's first soldier, the ritualistic concentration on military achievements and Piedmontese tradition had created a distance between Vittorio Emanuele and the nation, and this hindered the formation of national identity after Unification.

Since the end of the eighteenth century patriotic paintings and illustrations on nationalist pamphlets represented *Italia* as a woman, usually with bare breasts, "ready to feed her children."[12] In the literature of the Italian Risorgimento—the works of D'Azeglio, Guerrazzi, or Verdi's librettist Solera—Italian women appear as the defenders of morality and of the purity of Italian blood, fulfilling their role as good wives and mothers by holding the offspring together. Hence, women were indispensable to representing the honour of the fatherland.[13] "Feeling ourselves to be sons of the same mother" had been an important theme in the lexicon of patriotic language, introduced in Italy through national discourse in poetry, prose and drama. This discourse of the nation as a family had influenced a growing audience of patriots and later formed the basis for national subscriptions assisting the victims of natural disasters, political exiles and prisoners, or the orphans of the wars of liberation.[14] For the patriot Montanelli "Italy became a dear mother" and Minghetti, explaining the motives behind the solidarity with the Roman refugees, spoke about "our Italian brothers" and the "sacrament of the common family," making direct reference to the nation of the "*fratelli d'Italia*" common in political language since the 1840s.[15] A few decades later Carducci broke with the romanticising idealization of the Italian woman. According to Croce, Carducci's women lose the nimbus of the saint and "go back to being simply women."[16] Nevertheless, they retain an important role as mothers, sisters and wives in the nation's imagination. Conversely, Vittorio Emanuele II represented the nation not as a father but as a soldier, "*il primo soldato dell'indipendenza*," as *La Gazzetta dell'Emilia* wrote on the occasion of his death. Whereas the queen was scarcely ever present in public, popular representations show the monarch frequently on the battlefield, always armed and in action.[17] Carlo Alberto supplied the template, as is evident from the description given by Minghetti, one of his great admirers and at the time part of his general staff, in 1848:

> The king is of a tall and thin stature, of a leaden colour, with two big and sparkling eyes. His life, in its sobriety, devotion and austere habits, greatly resembles that of a medieval knight; he never smiles. . . . His cold blood and his courage are indeed miraculous. He is always in the thick of the fight and often ahead of all soldiers.[18]

Vittorio Emanuele had no wish to challenge the image his father had created of the monarchy, and when, in 1869, he refused to reprieve a young soldier sentenced to death for the murder of a major, after having been subject to humiliation and bullying, even the Moderate *Monitore* took a critical stand against the regime's "uncivilised" military ethos. During the execution two soldiers of the firing squad fainted, leaving the victim injured and alive on the ground, before finally being shot in the head.[19] Apart from his army, Vittorio Emaunele enjoyed outdoor pursuits, hunting in particular. He resented the life of the court and lacked the ability to sense the importance of public ritual, so much so that even the city of Turin was increasingly disappointed with its monarch.[20] Queen Victoria found him "startling in the extreme in appearance and manner"; "his bristling mustachios and swaggering air left a vivid impression on all who recorded their recollections of him."[21] The French newspapers described him as a "proud man of the sword."[22] Despite being the most ancient governing dynasty in Europe, the legitimacy of the Savoy as kings of Italy could be questioned and their position had not been sanctioned by the princes of the former Italian states, as in the case of the German unification.[23] This represented a problem for the Italian nobility and widened the gap between the crown and its lands. Although Vittorio Emanuele continuously asked for an increase in spending for his army, it was difficult to build a military tradition in Italy and to make this the basis of a new national identity. The image of the army had been seriously damaged by the failure of its military strategy against Austria in 1848 and the weakness of the campaign in 1866; and Garibaldi's revolutionary volunteers were not allowed, at least not during the first years after Unification, to play any important role in representing and legitimising the nation.[24] Moreover, in many parts of Italy the public image of armed forces had been associated for too long with foreign occupation and the Piedmontese army was frequently seen as just the same. Giolitti once remarked that "only boys with whom nobody knew what to do, rascals and idiots, were chosen for a career in the military."[25] Without a "popular" army even the idea of a king-soldier could not readily serve to foster national identity.

THE "GOOD KING"

In rites of initiation, Cassirer claims "a man is given a new name because what he receives in the rite is a new self."[26] When becoming king of Italy Vittorio Emanuele had refused this new self and continued to call himself Vittorio Emanuele II, following the Savoyard succession, rather than inaugurating a new Italian line. Similarly, the sessions of the new Italian parliament followed the Savoyard numbering. Crispi insisted that Umberto, who would have been Umberto IV in the Savoyard succession, called himself Umberto I.[27] Like Vittorio Emanuele, Umberto loved his uniforms, his horses and hunting dogs, but at least he would now and then forsake the

uniform for a suit.[28] With Umberto's accession to the throne the representation of the monarchy and the court changed. Now, the monarchy had
to represent the nation; and the State carefully constructed a new public
image of the king. During the Umbertian age charismatic "involvement"
with the nation characterised the monarch's rule.[29] Bologna's changing
attitude to the monarchy illustrates the impact of this transformation in
the symbolic representation of the nation.

During Umberto's reign the *leggenda del re buono* replaced the image
of the king-soldier, epitomised by his early visits to the scenes of the
floods in Polesine in 1882 and the earthquake on Ischia in 1883, and
by his visit to Naples during the cholera epidemic a year later.[30] These
images of the monarchy became an exercise in nation building: "By joining the people in its moments of mourning as in its moments of rejoicing,
the king has shown that a single heart beats in the chest of every Italian"
wrote Crispi's newspaper *La Riforma* after Umberto had inspected the
floods that struck the Po region in September 1882.[31] During the cholera
epidemic in Naples he refused to make use of disinfectants after visiting
the wards and he remained in the city until the situation showed signs
of improvement. "Every inch a king," *The Lancet* commented.[32] There
was an element of constructed and perceived (rather than "real") irratio-
nality behind the king's public demonstration of compassion. As Mary
Douglas suggests, in the nineteenth century "humans were thought to
be risk averse, because they were supposed to be making their choices
according to hedonic calculus."[33] Thus, exposing himself to the contami-
nated poor of Naples, without actually being in a position to help, the
king broke with a basic pattern of human behaviour. The visit resulted
in an unprecedented wave of popular support for the monarchy, winning
large-scale backing even from Socialist and Republican organisations:
"Never was Italy so morally united as she is," commented *The Times*.
Even the Church had to recognize the king's charismatic reaction to the
crisis, which led to a sudden rapprochement with the Liberal State.[34] Ide-
alising Umberto's role and passing over the long period of crisis towards
the end of his reign, Croce inscribed this image of the king into the history of the new Italy:

> King Umberto has always been close to his people, in every misfortune.
> When in 1884, in Naples, he walked amongst those marked by the
> cholera, when the evil raged worst, the Italians' gratitude met with the
> civilised world's admiration for the Italian king, who still deserves to
> be called "the good king."[35]

The "good king's" nation even included "semicivilised" *meridionali*.
Ironically, even at the time the prevailing view was that the cholera in
Naples was the consequence of the State's failure to prevent the epidemic
spreading across the Mediterranean in its early stages.[36] But in people's

perceptions the king, visiting even the poorest and most dangerous neigh-
bourhoods of Naples, had assumed a position that was above the State
and its responsibilities.

PATRIOTTISMO FISIOLOGICO

Part of the process of renegotiating the relationship between the nation
and the crown was to translate official representations into a language
accessible to the people. The gendering of the nation through the public
image of the crown as a family played a major role in this process, forging
the alliance between "nationalism and respectability," which according to
George Mosse marked the nineteenth century.[37] Vittorio Emanuele, due to
his adventurous love-life and the early death of his wife Maria-Adeleide,
was unable to represent the nation through a royal family. His open competition with Cavour for the former ballerina Bianca Ronzani certainly did
nothing to enhance the king's reputation as a family man.[38] His affairs,
and finally his morganatic marriage to Rosina Vercellana, the daughter of
a palace guard, just weeks after the marrying of his own daughter to the
son of the French emperor, nearly led to a diplomatic crisis with France.
"*La bella Rosina*," made countess of Mirafiori, remained a queen "without throne and without crown."[39] Through her assumption of a new public
role Queen Margherita did much to create a different image of the monarchy, and in time she became an object of intense popular admiration, and
not only for the "*simpatica fisionomia*" to which *Il Monitore di Bologna*
referred during one of her early visits.[40] Daughter of Vittorio Emanuele's
brother, the Duke of Genova, and of a princess of Saxony, Margherita
had an upbringing that contrasted with the severe etiquette of the court of
Savoy and in some respects even resembled a bourgeois life-style. Her public attitudes were influenced by the relatively liberal and modern education
she received under the guidance of her Austrian teacher, Rosa Arbesser,
for whom literature, arts and the humanities assumed a greater importance than the catechism which was customarily the focus of female education at the court. Remaining intellectually a dilettante, she nevertheless
acquired during these years a taste and love for literature and the arts,
and became fluent in French, English and German, (less so in Italian), an
important condition for her later relationship with intellectuals and artists
frequenting the court.[41] Again, in Croce's assessment myth and historical
observation were mixed:

> Queen Margherita lived during these years the great season of her
> life, adding to her sweet piety and her enchanting smile a love for the
> arts and for poetry. She seemed herself a creation of poetry, who had
> come to incarnate the perfect ideal of the queen of Italy, the land of
> arts and beauty.[42]

The public role she assumed after her marriage to Umberto, which even led her on occasions to represent the crown at naval manoeuvres, was unusual for the Savoy and not foreseen in the constitution. Her new style of court culture, although open towards certain strata of the middle classes, was described at the time as the most splendid in Europe.[43] Margherita's personality profoundly marked the perceptions of Italy's *fine secolo*. This image survived the king's assassination and lived on until the early years of the Fascist regime. Without wishing to idealise the feminine element in the representation of the monarchy during the Umbertian age, by contrast, Luisa Passerini's *Mussolini Immaginario* demonstrates how the Fascist regime reversed this idea.[44] While until then Margherita had played a central role in representing the Italian nation, from the 1920s commentators affirmed that *"il fascismo è maschio."* Mussolini's Italian was "a modern barbarian."[45] The contrast to the monarchy's public image under Umberto is striking. After Vittorio Emanuele's death the newspapers reported that during the parade of the troops, on the eve of the funeral, "[Umberto's] eyes were red from weeping. . . . Even the vigorous currassiers were deeply moved."[46] Faced with the destruction wreaked by the earthquake on Ischia and its two thousand victims, *La Capitale* reported: "Every so often the king, who was extremely moved, wiped away a tear. . . . The King was pale. No one remembers having seen him more moved. His voice trembled." What these reports show is that the idea of the monarchy as a family had an impact also on the particular representation of the king's masculinity. In 1865 Vittorio Emanuele had visited the victims of cholera in Naples, but no one had seen him weep.[47]

In Italy, the physiological appearance of public figures and their body language were openly and frequently referred to in public discourse. Luciani Milani, on the first anniversary of Minghetti's death in 1887, gave a physiological and quasi erotic description of the statesman, constructing a relationship between his moral qualities and his bodily appearance.[48] Newspapers regularly commented on Minghetti's *"mezzi vocali,"* and the *"sonorità chiara e piacevole"* of his voice; and even his old adversaries on the Left joined in.[49] Minghetti himself recorded his impressions of the already ageing Lord Palmerstone as a man *"di bellissimo aspetto,"* which in a different national context might have been regarded as a rather inappropriate comment on another statesman.[50] Similarly Enrico Panzacchi was remembered in official obituaries and commemorations for his masculine beauty:

A tall and strong personality, carrying a Roman head on his broad and robust shoulders . . . Free of any common aspects, his huge and open face was marked by constantly moving eyes, as if lost or immersed in an enchanted dream. But if his black and lucid eyes fixed on an individual, an audience or the masses, he was able to communicate support, love and devotion with a mix of benevolence and reserve, of courtesy and frankness, the herald and the spirit behind a voice which perfectly matched this vigorous body.[51]

An even more explicit register of language was used during the Fascist period in relation to Mussolini. Marinetti described the frequent references to Mussolini's physical, virile image as "*patriottismo fisiologico*," which became a literary genre at the time. During a visit to Bologna in 1927 the ecstatic masses greeted their "*duce*" with the words "*sei bello.*"[52] As Sergio Luzzatto has demonstrated, the politicisation of the body's physiological appearance produces multiple and different meanings, depending on the social-political and historical context.[53] The symbolic meaning of both the person and the office is constructed through its physiological dimension.

While historians usually trace the origins of Fascism's physiological dimension back to the experience of slaughter and bloodshed in the trenches of World War I, the phenomenon has semantic roots in the imagination of the Risorgimento as well as in the symbolic construction of the nation during the Liberal period.[54] In 1878, during the sovereigns' visit to Bologna, Marquis Gioacchino Pepoli welcomed the queen with the words "*Salve Madre pietosa! Ave Stella d'Italia.*" Previously Italians did not have a queen to whom to direct such a "*dolce salute.*"[55] Margherita began to cultivate life at the court, a fact that fascinated the nation at large. Representing the ideal of the "mediating princes," Umberto and Margherita sought to overcome the isolation to which the crown had been driven by the character and life-style of Vittorio Emanuele II[56]. Paternalism, maternalism and charisma played an important role in this mediation, allowing wider strata of society to identify more readily with the royal family than with the nation's political class. A model for this relationship was the public image cultivated by Queen Victoria after her marriage to Albert von Sachsen-Coburg-Gotha. Victoria herself, at least until her consort's death, invoked the idea of the queen as mother and housewife.[57] Already in 1868, on a first visit to Bologna, ten years before Umberto's coronation, the then crown prince and his young wife represented themselves as the nation's first family. Inspecting a local school, the royal couple hugged a four-year-old girl presented to them by the mayor. As *Il Monitore* reports with astonishment and delight, Margherita kissed the girl and then knelt down in front of the entire class to exchange kisses with all the children present: "This spontaneous gesture of true affection deeply touched everybody and moved not a few of those present to tears." For a long time images such as this overshadowed the rumours about Umberto's numerous extra-conjugal relationships before and during his reign.[58]

POPULAR ROYALISM AND THE NEW COURT

Italy's first king was a constitutionally powerful king, representing Italy in foreign policy, with a cabinet responsible only to him, not the parliament, and the right to issue royal decrees without further consultation. He was commander-in-chief of the army, having the sole right to declare war. He appointed town mayors and the members of the senate. After Cavour's early death in 1861 the king assumed even greater political power.[59] However, as an institution the monarchy remained strange to most Italians. Also Umberto was a soldier and much praised for his bravery in battle. But his manner was different, more reserved, less bold. After the accession to the throne, parliament and cabinet increased their powers, and reduced the king's constitutional role. Representatives of the court disappeared from government and the administration of the royal household was delegated to a minister.[60] At the same time, without any formal change in the constitution, the king's ceremonial office became more important. Undoubtedly, Umberto had a conservative and often reactionary approach to the emerging social question as well as to foreign policy, symbolised in the 1882 Triple Alliance with Germany and Austria against Republican France. However, his attitude towards the nation and to the cultural elites in particular made it possible for critical intellectuals to be drawn to some degree into a commitment to the liberal State. The king displayed a paternal tolerance, which allowed the cultural elite to identify with the monarchy and to contribute to the nation's cultural development. When travelling the Romagna, aware of its associational culture, the king allegedly declared that "the dynasty must become democratic or it will fall." Even if his policy clearly illustrates the limitations of his understanding of democracy, such affirmations, combined with the monarchy's new public image, had an important impact on the nation's relationship with the monarchy.[61]

Giovanni Capellini, who dedicated one of his early geological maps to Umberto, described in his memoirs how the princes Amedeo and Umberto differed from their father in their attitude to Italy's academic elite. This attitude led even a fervent Republican like Filopanti to write to Umberto about his scientific discoveries and to ask for subsidies in support of his research.[62] Whereas Vittorio Emanuele's visit to Bologna in 1861 did not even include a reception for the professors of the university, Crown Prince Umberto honoured the city with his participation in the International Conference of Pre-Historical Sciences of 1871. In November 1878 the new king met the entire academic body and Carducci had his first personal encounter with Umberto, at a time when the poet was beginning to moderate his earlier political radicalism. Carducci's account of the event in a personal letter illustrates his perception of the young king's attitude towards Italy's cultural elite, but also the way in which formerly critical intellectuals were impressed and subsequently drawn into the system.[63]

> "I am delighted to shake hands with you and to get to know you personally," the king said approaching Carducci. "Since when have you been teaching here?"

> "Since 1860, Sire."

"And you are still so young! This notwithstanding, you have already brought great honour to the arts and to our country. . . . I am serious, you know. Greatly though our political opinions may diverge, I admire your genius which brings so much honour to the fatherland. . . ."

"Sire, I feel deeply honoured by the praise that H.M. grants me and for having the opportunity to express the feelings of exaltation and hope with which I regard the high and civilised principles of H.M.'s reign."

"I have not yet done anything. If you speak of my intentions, you can be assured, they are all for the better and the honour of the fatherland: in this we will always agree."

Later Carducci remembered: "Everybody was impressed. But really, the first time the king spoke to me with such excitement and emotion, and the second time he shook my hands with such cordiality, that it nearly seemed as if he would be grateful to me. The archaeologist Professor Brizio observed that 'it looked as if he told you that he regards you as an old friend.' Today this episode was on everyone's lips. Everybody spoke about Umberto's affection for me."[64]

Bologna was even more impressed by Carducci's encounter with the queen on the same occasion, when Her Majesty surprised everybody by quoting

Figure 8.1 King Umberto and Queen Margherita Visiting Bologna in 1878. (Author's Collection.)

from memory the poet's *Odi barbare*.[65] Other encounters with the royal family followed, and in 1889 Carducci was invited to their holiday resort in Gressoney, where he spent several hours reading poetry with the queen. In 1902 Margherita acquired Carducci's personal library to make it accessible to the public and in 1906 she bought his house, leaving it to the municipality as a museum.

During Umberto's 1878 visit to Bologna meetings with representatives of the Labour organisations were as cordial as the reception for the city's academic elites had been. Bologna and the former Papal Legations were regarded as the most difficult leg during the monarch's first official journey across the nation, when he visited most of Italy's important cities and regions. Bologna was a stronghold of legitimist Papalism, whereas the Romagna was marked by Socialist and revolutionary unrest. Despite the initially rather cold welcome, Bologna, after this first visit, radically changed its attitude to the royal family and the queen in particular. As a witness close to the court noted in his diary, "the success that the queen has here in Bologna, as a woman and as sovereign, can hardly be described."[66]

Referring to Italy's enthusiasm for Napoleon, Adolphe Thiers had commented that "Italians are extremely sensitive and sometimes moved even by sovereigns they don't love. Like all peoples, they are easily seduced by the impression of great staging."[67] What seduced Bologna on this occasion was the sovereigns' openly displayed charm. In the popular imagination King Umberto's first official tour of the country assumed particular significance through the dramatic events in Naples, only a few days after the visit to Bologna. Naples had a special relationship to the royal couple, since they had taken official residence in the city after their wedding in 1868. The hereditary prince was born here and created Prince of Naples. According to an anecdote, when leaving the palace for the first time after her accouchement, Margherita had presented the young prince to the women of the local market.[68] In 1878, during the enthusiastic welcoming of the royal couple in the streets of Naples, the unemployed cook and assumed anarchist Giovanni Passanante emerged from the throng with a knife and tried to assassinate the king. The prime minister Benedetto Cairoli threw himself on the murderer and saved Umberto's life. Paying no heed to the injuries suffered, the sovereigns continued their parade smiling and greeting, until they reached the royal palace. Cairoli, who had received a deep leg wound, became a national hero.[69]

Famous Republicans such as Aurelio Saffi and Alberto Mario condemned regicide as an insane crime. In Rome spontaneous manifestations demonstrated solidarity with Umberto, while numerous churches celebrated the Te Deum to thank God for having saved the king.[70] The popular expressions of solidarity with the king caused unexpected fatalities, when a bomb thrown into the crowd in Florence killed four bystanders.[71] The history of anarchism often refers to popular publications celebrating the perpetrators. However, there also existed another genre of pamphlet literature condemning these acts

Figure 8.2   Attempted Assassination of King Umberto in Naples. (Author's Collection.)

of violence. Cesare Causa, a retired officer of the army, published in 1879 an illustrated volume about the event.[72] In the course of 127 pages, mostly through quotations from official documents and witnesses, Causa described Passanante's life, the attempted assassination, the trial and the reactions, arguing a passionate case against regicide and in favour of applying the death penalty to Passanante. All this contributed to widespread identification with the monarch.

It would be wrong to assume that modern societies need less myth and ritual than traditional societies.[73] Depending on how monarchical power is staged, the royal family is in a position to respond to these popular needs for myth and ritual. It was with the entrance of the young Queen Margherita into the public sphere that Italy—and Italian women in particular—became familiar with the monarchy. The crown was for the first time represented as a family. Press reports on Vittorio Emanuele's death devoted much time to the public appearance of the princess, presenting the picture of a mourning daughter.[74] In the South, where the Piedmontese were regarded as a foreign regime, peasants began crossing themselves at the mention of the queen's name; the fashion magazine *Margherita* became a best-seller; Naples invented its famous Pizza Margherita; by the year 1901 more than two hundred poets had dedicated their verses to her; and the queen was largely held responsible for the new flavour of court life in Rome. For a British commentator she became "a *beatrice* in the crusade to clean up Italian politics."[75]

Even before Umberto's accession to the throne, in 1876, the masses in Rome referred to her as "the people's queen." Not infrequently support for her went hand in hand with the request for a constitutional strengthening of the monarchy or with the voicing of anti-parliamentary sentiments. For the queen's name-day in 1881 the *Gazzetta dell'Emilia* wrote:

> The twentieth of July is a date that every Italian remembers with true love—the name-day of Her Majesty, our gracious queen. Her name evokes affection, devotion and enthusiasm among every Italian. Everywhere her presence is celebrated with spontaneous ardour, with real admiration for her outstanding virtue. We too send this majestic woman our sincere blessings, convinced that her felicity will always be linked to the well-being of the patria.[76]

On that day the streets of Bologna were decorated with flags and flowers; music played in the squares. The newspapers published the letters of congratulation from numerous associations and circles, as well as the replies by the queen's *cavaliere d'onore*.[77]

Public perception of the court and popular royalism changed dramatically during the Umbertian age, due in large part to the ways in which the queen transformed the court into a cultural and social centre. Margherita's relationship to artists and intellectuals, who for the first time were prominent at the Savoyard court, played a key role in effecting this alteration. Once the queen had opened a great ball at the Quirinale with the German historian Gregorovius as her *cavaliere*, the local nobility and the military understood that they were to take second place. This decision not only represented a breach of etiquette; it was also a remarkable gesture considering that the Vatican had placed the German's *History of Rome* on its index of forbidden books.[78] Likewise conduct at the queen's salon demonstrated how the monarchy wished to be perceived. For Nicolaus Sombart the social dynamic of a salon depended on the "influence and the attractive strength" of its central figure, usually female, which "laid the basis for the group's cohesion."[79] Erotic tension complemented the institution's classical culture. In Italy contemporaries remarked how many "wise men" and how few officers were seen around the queen, another break with Savoyard tradition. Her salon resembled in some respect that of the Princess Mathilde, Napoleon III's illustrious cousin, bringing together nobility, artists and men of letters.[80] The intellectual centre of the *salotto* was until his death in 1886 Marco Minghetti, a further reason for Bologna to feel privileged in its relationship to the queen. Not only Margherita's adviser on art, music and occasionally on politics, Minghetti also became her Latin tutor, teaching her grammar and ancient literature, taking her through a programme that corresponded to that of Italy's Liceo Classico. The public perception of the queen's relationship with the nation's men of letters became a central element of Italy's popular royalism.

BRITISH IMAGININGS

The gendering of the monarchy during the *fine secolo* was also influenced by foreign perceptions of the Italian nation, especially in the former Papal States with their many political exiles. Long before Umberto and Margherita began to represent the nation as a family, British public opinion had analysed the peninsula in gendered terms, in thrall to what Maura O'Connor has termed the "Romance of Italy."[81] Numerous examples may serve to illustrate these imaginings. The Italian landscape became the backdrop for the famous romance between the poets Elizabeth Barrett and Robert Browning, a relationship previously prohibited by societal and climatological conditions in London. Born in Camberwell into a wealthy family with an intense interest in the arts, a graduate in Greek and Latin from University College London, Robert had formed his idea of Italy long before his first visit to the Mediterranean. The cliché of Italy as "the home of all the arts" made the country "particularly suitable for ladies" a fair number of whom were fascinated by, and politically involved in the Italian Risorgimento. Famous figures included Aurelio Saffi's wife Lady Crawford and Jessie White, an English nurse who travelled with Garibaldi's "Thousand" and married the Mazzinian Alberto Mario. Another woman of the "Thousand," Crispi's wife Rosalia Montmasson, was admired by British public opinion for the courageous fashion in which she faced her years of exile in Malta and England. A similar part was played by the baroness Maria Espérance von Schwartz and by the Countess Maria Martini della Torre, who met Garibaldi in London in 1854.[82] Many of these women were able to influence diplomatic circles. Mazzini, during his exile in England, likewise relied on a network of women and the debates among the "Friends of Italy" became for many English women an important political forum. According to Maura O'Connor, the political concerns of these women were expressed "in a language closely associated with their feminine values and positions"[83]. Their role as the "moral guardian of the English family and nation" formed the basis for their maternal-political struggle in favour of an imagined Italy. They perceived Italy as a backward country, whose women were not yet morally prepared to do their duty, a perception in stark contrast to the image of uncontaminated purity with which the authors of the Risorgimento themselves described their female heroes. Victorian women volunteered to perform this role, practicing charity as a leisure activity and keen on adventure as distraction from their humdrum everyday existence. In Italy, however, contemporaries tended to describe Garibaldi's British nurses as eccentric, unattractive and domineering.[84] In acts of charity, as Mary Douglas observed, "the recipient does not like the giver."[85] Broad swaths of Italian public opinion rejected the patronising role of the foreign female observer.

Despite all restrictions, women had not been absent from public life. Bologna's newspapers regularly ran stories about local women supporting

Garibaldi or the Guardia Nazionale with collections and nursing the wounded during the wars of liberation.[86] As one article stated, "the women of these lands [Emila and Romagna] are demonstrating to the rest of Europe that they know how to live for those who sacrifice every-thing on the altar of the *patria*."[87] After Unification both the Left and the Right emphasised the importance of women in the construction of a national community, even if they excluded them from important areas of public life.[88] The case of Adelaide Cairoli, imagined as the grieving mother of the Cairoli brothers, may be taken to exemplify the manner in which liberal Italy fashioned its female guardians of the nation. The *"Cornelia dell'età nostra,"* as she was remembered in Bologna, had lost four of her five sons during the wars of the Risorgimento, while a fifth had risked his life in the streets of Naples to save King Umberto from the assassin's dagger. "Mamma Adelaide," came to be represented as "a moral example for entire generations of Italians."[89] Carducci honoured her with a hymn, published in his *Giambi ed Epodi*. Anita Garibaldi, who lost her life during the campaign, played a yet more dramatic role as the mother of the nation. There is no doubt that the fathers of the Risorgimento attributed to women a reactionary role as agents of domes-ticity, but this hardly differed from the Victorian model. Only exception-ally did these women abandon their traditional role for the sake of the nation. The new role of Queen Margherita in representing the monarchy has to be viewed against this general backdrop.

THE PEOPLE'S QUEEN, THE PEOPLE'S NATION

Since 1876 the governments of the Left had sought to fashion a new patri-otic religion, to promote "political education" and so to give "Italians a fatherland"[90]. In the same spirit Umberto appointed for the first time a Southerner as prime minister, Crispi, a former collaborator of Mazzini and Garibaldi, and a representative of the middle class. Crispi played a major role in strengthening national identity and in imposing a new image of the nation upon the Italian people. An Italian *Giacobino*, Crispi feared a political class emerging directly from civil society. Instead, he regarded it as legitimate for the political class to forge its own civil society in accor-dance with the politicians' own values. Under Crispi, the popular heroes Garibaldi and Mazzini were absorbed into the State's official representa-tion of itself, part of a general effort to foster national identity and to create social cohesion.[91] Since the 1860s, under the impact of the official celebrations of the *Statuto*, the commemoration of 8 August had in general been neglected in Bologna. When celebrations did take place, the event was organised by various associations and committees of veterans, such as the league for popular education, the Workingmen's Society and the mutual aid societies. The municipality, still governed by the Moderates, did not play an active part in such events.[92] However, since 1878, civil society and the popular associations had grasped that the monarchy and the new government supported their initiatives and shared the popular image of the Risorgimento that they wished to transmit. Fifty years after the revolution the king granted Bologna the gold medal "to reward its citizens for their military endeavours." On the same occasion the council finally approved the budget to erect a monument recording this event, a project first proposed by the Left in 1867.[93]

The most significant step towards a new idea of the Risorgimento, taking account of the people's role in the national revolution, was the "Risorgimento-Temple" exacted at the 1888 exhibition. The temple collected "the most remarkable proofs of the sacrifices we have made and of the unutterable sorrows we endured for Italy."[94] The museum's emphasis on traces of sacrifice corresponded closely to Mazzini's concept of "political education," ideas to a certain extent implemented by Crispi as minister of interior. A year after the 1888 exhibition the commune housed the temporary exhibition in a permanent Museum of the Risorgimento and approved, unanimously, a budget of 1200 Lire to order and catalogue the material and to build up a specialised library.[95]

Changes are also noticeable in the way Bologna represented itself on public occasions. During the opening of the 1871 museum and the International Congress of Pre-Historical Sciences only the authorities had taken part in the festivities, organised by the municipality with the greatest splendour; the people of Bologna had to observe the dignitaries from the streets. In 1881, for the opening of the new Civic Museum and the inauguration of the International Geological Congress, voluntary associations, the Workingmen's Society, veterans' organisations, women's and trade organisations played an active role in the programme and were represented on the organising committee.[96] Forty Labour associations welcomed the participants of the congress with banners, music and a parade in Piazza Rossini. During the inauguration of the Geological Museum the representatives of the *Società Operaie* were formally introduced to the minister Quintino Sella, honorary president of the congress. The minister, himself a geologist, elaborated upon the symbolic meaning of this encounter when he explained that "we geologists, like the humblest of workers, use hammers. I value a democracy which strives to better itself and which reaches out to those who study and work in the sciences."[97] This emphasis on the encounter between academic and political elites and Bologna's civic organisations reflected the changing political climate in Umbertian Italy, even if Bologna's cultural policy was still dominated by a Moderate council majority. In particular the emerging middle class insisted on creating symbolic links between the city and the monarchy, as demonstrated during the celebrations for the eight hundred years of Bologna's university in 1888 and the Great Exhibitions organised on that occasion, combined with the inauguration of the monument for Vittorio Emanuele II and the opening of the *Giardini Margherita*, a huge park with lakes outside the former city walls named after the queen.[98] For the event Margherita visited Bologna once again. Considering her popularity, the Church was ill-advised when it received the queen, on her visit to the cathedral, according to the ceremony for foreign princes, thus demonstrating, a decade after the death of Pius IX, that it still refused to recognise the Savoy as legitimate rulers of the Legations and of Italy.

During these years the life of the royal family was increasingly made public. In 1866 the death of Prince Ordone had merited just twelve lines in Bologna's principal newspaper; and unlike the Piedmontese capital, Bologna did not go out of its way to celebrate the crown prince's wedding in 1868.[99] This changed after 1878. The queen's name-days and the monarchs' twenty-fifth wedding anniversary in 1893 were marked as major events in the life of the nation and the city. Through charity events the cities used these occasions to create an image that presented the sovereigns as deeply committed to the nation's well-being. To celebrate the sovereigns' wedding anniversary, the commune gave 3000 Lire to a home for children whose parents had been mutilated or killed at work; the council contributed 50,000 Lire to a children's hospital in Bologna and a plot of municipal land was designated as the site of an infant school. As the council proclaimed, "the welfare of poor children is the best greeting Bologna can send to the king."[100] The total sum spent on these initiatives exceeded Bologna's investment in the commemoration of Vittorio Emanuele II fifteen years earlier. Moreover, at the time the emphasis was not on charity but on the commemoration of the king-soldier: 10,000 Lire were given for the national monument in Rome and 50,000 Lire for a monument in Bologna to the nation's first soldier. Only 1000 Lire went to the local poorhouse, named after the first king of Italy.[101] From the 1880s onwards other members of the royal family were accorded considerable public attention. In 1890 the council commemorated the death of the king's brother Prince Amedeo as a hero of the Risorgimento. A street was named after him and his bust was placed in the local Risorgimento museum.[102] For the wedding of the Duke of Aosta in 1895 the council sent telegram greetings to the royal family and announced the event in the local press. The birth of Princesse Jolanda Margherita was worth 2000 Lire to help foster-children.[103] Frequently, these initiatives were meant to convey a particular political message. For the engagement of the crown prince with Princess Elena of Montenegro the council pronounced its gratitude for the fact

> that the young prince chose his consort from a country which, like ours, owes its independence to the virtue of its people. Like Italy, this country is a new state, with a right to exist, an idea kept alive through indomitable virtue, the force of weapons, and the strong, determined and continuous will to become a nation.[104]

Bologna thus interpreted the engagement as an opportunity for the nation to identify with the Savoy's dynastic policy.

The changing public representations of the monarchy in Italy corresponded to a wider European trend and went hand in hand with the gradual retreat of many European monarchs from active politics. Meanwhile, Victorian Britain, since the late 1870s, had created an image of its monarchy that was more splendid than anything Britain had seen before, thereby enhancing the monarchy's popularity among the wider population. Two generations earlier the expenditure for George IV's coronation in 1821, the most extravagant and expensive in history, had outraged public opinion and provoked a sharp reaction. Public perceptions of Queen Victoria's coronation in 1838 were markedly different. Likewise, in 1877, when Disraeli made Queen Victoria Empress of India the population stood behind the event. Similar public support was expressed for the Viennese celebrations of the six-hundredth anniversary of the Habsburg monarchy, for the millennium of the kingdom of Hungary and for the jubilees and birthdays of Emperor Franz Joseph. The invention of an imperial court in Berlin followed a similar course, based on numerous new rituals and a sophisticatedly staged ceremony. Robert Musil's notion of the *Parallelaktion,* a few decades later, mocked the extent to which the European courts had entered into a competition regarding the splendour of their monarchical ritual.[105]

On 28 June 1896 the royal family—the king, in the company of the queen and the prince of Naples—visited Bologna yet again, this time to unveil Giulio Monteverde's monument for Marco Minghetti and to open the Orthopaedic Institute in the former monastery of San Michele in Bosco. They also inaugurated the new Montagnola gardens, the scene of the revolutionary defeat of the Austrians in 1848. The prospect of the visit plunged Bologna into a state of *"fantasmagoria."*[106] The streets of the city were decorated with hundreds of flags and flowers, the city-gates were illuminated, bands played in the squares. The celebrations started at 11:00 a.m. in Piazza Minghetti, followed by a great banquet with representatives of the city in the council hall. The event culminated in popular merry-making at the Montagnola, continuing throughout the night. With the inauguration of the monument for Minghetti the sovereigns paid tribute to Bologna's most famous politician, an intimate friend and tutor of the queen and one of the founders of the State. At the Montagnola the sovereigns acknowledged the people's contribution to the national revolution; and with the inauguration of the hospital they underlined once more their image as the nation's first benefactors, playing upon the idea of the *"Re buono."* Eight hundred seats on the tribunes of the Montagnola were reserved for the workers who had been employed in this major project of urban development. "An unforgettable day for Bologna" ran the headline of the *Gazzetta dell'Emilia* the following day, a feast for the nation as well as for the city, in striking contrast to the traditional celebrations of the *"Festa dello Statuto."* Illustrating Bologna's special relationship with the sovereigns, the calm and friendly atmosphere contrasted sharply with the somewhat mixed welcome the city of Milan accorded the king a few weeks earlier, an event coloured by political tensions and by the hostile demonstrations staged by Republicans and Socialists.[107]

REGICIDE

The last governments under Umberto I were formed around authoritarian conservatives like Pelloux and Sonnino. They combined a compassionate social policy with fiercely anti-Socialist repression. For a majority of Italians the king represented an authoritarian father-figure, trying to temper his government's harsh approach to the social question. Social and political tensions deteriorated dramatically during the *fine secolo*. In the agricultural sector alone, the year 1897 involved 24,135 workers in strikes, with a total of 322,020 days of labour lost. Attempts to pacify society through a strengthening of national consciousness largely failed.[108] According to Fulvio Cammarano this policy offered "national identity without political identity." The *"mancato colpo di Stato"* against the Left in parliament, and the repressive policy in the South and against the Labour movement caused Radicals, Republicans and Socialists to forge a common front, a political development mirrored in Bologna's council alliances since the 1880s.[109] Increasingly, the government's reactionary conservatism led to criticism even within the ranks of the Right, to protests among intellectuals, in the press, and even within the Chamber of Commerce, which was keen to pacify Labour relations. However, the idea of an authoritarian but paternal king, combined with the image of the sovereigns as a family transmitted by the queen, supplanted in popular memory the darker moments of Umberto's reign—the uprisings in Sicily and Milan, the violent confrontations with the Labour movement, the financial scandals and the colonial disasters. The crown's positive public image also served to deflect the occasional rumours about Umberto's affairs with certain ladies of the court as well as with less noble women, rumours that threatened to tarnish the carefully crafted image of the sovereigns as the nation's first family.[110]

On 29 July 1900, during the sovereigns' habitual holiday in Monza, the anarchist Gaetano Bresci killed Umberto I with three shots of his revolver. He was the first member of the house of Savoy to be assassinated in seven hundred years and his death was widely perceived as the end of an epoch, a real *fine secolo*.[111] According to a legend numerous times reiterated in the press, the queen captured the event in the words: "this is the greatest crime of the century." Just minutes after the assassination Bresci himself offered an equally powerful trope: "I didn't kill Umberto. I killed a king. I killed a principle!"[112] At the time the terrorists active in Europe were often described as mad or psychologically disturbed. Allegedly, Passanante's mental health deteriorated in prison; Bresci and other anarchists committed suicide or were assassinated in captivity. Conversely, Errico Malatesta explained their actions as a consequence of the "infamous persecutions" and the "social injustice" they had to endure.[113] Bresci, a thirty-two-year-old highly skilled silk weaver from Tuscany, was educated and of lower middle class background. He had lived for several years in Paterson, New Jersey, where he had two children with an Irish woman and worked, not badly paid, for a silk company. Paterson was not particularly hostile to its working class and since the 1880s streets had been named after William Tell and Karl Marx.[114] It was here that Bresci became acquainted with Malatesta, an influential leader among Italian anarchists, less demagogic than most Socialists at the time.[115] His personal circumstances differed considerably from the image of Italian workers in the USA that Malatesta himself transmitted in his writings. The Italians, Malatesta claimed, were treated as "an inferior race just a little above the negroes."[116] Bresci's motive in returning to Italy was to avenge the victims of the Milan uprisings. According to the local press, anarchist circles in New York had spent months preparing the assassination, though contemporaries as well as later generations of historians insist that he had acted alone.[117] Shortly before his return to Italy, Bresci had also been in contact with anarchists in Paris. Like Luccheni, the murderer of Elisabeth of Austria, he became an object of admiration among anarchists all over the world and despite being officially condemned by the Socialist parties, parts of the European Labour movement interpreted the assassination as a comprehensive reaction to the social tensions mounting in Italy during Umberto's reign.[118]

The popular image of the monarchy was surprisingly unaffected by the social and political developments during the last years of Umberto's reign, thus reflecting the ambivalent nature of identification as a specific form of emotional tie.[119] While the anarchists referred to the dead monarch as "Machinegun King" or "Umberto-dirty hands," public perceptions of the events in Monza made Umberto a "martyr king." Pascoli and D'Annunzio, certainly not unsympathetic to the social question, dedicated hymns to the dead king, while Matilde Serao wept for Margherita, who so "gladdened our lives."[120] In a booklet published shortly after the assassination, Fernanda De-Amici identified with the grieving queen: "An entire people joins her in prayer and weeps with her."[121] Even the Socialist *L'Avanti* described the murderer as "mad and a criminal." Leo Tolstoi was one of only a few to express sympathy for Bresci, explaining that this kind of violence came from above and was provoked by colonial wars, repression and torture. The intense reaction to the king's death reinforced the myth of the popular and "good king," and caused many to forget that towards the end of his reign this image had been more than a little tarnished.[122] As Arturo Labriola wrote a few years later, this public reaction to the assassination demonstrates that "the liberal revolution, which should have transformed subjects into citizens and the king into the state's first civil servant, had never permeated Italians."[123] Cathérine Brice has demonstrated how in the public responses to their death both Vittorio Emaunele II and Umberto I were associated with the people, *il popolo*. In the case of Vittorio Emanuele this people was the Risorgimento's social body; with Umberto, however, it was the working people, "the man of the street, the poor." Umberto represented the "good king always close to his people." Thus, the monarchy became a popular institution, with a clearly defined social mission.[124]

The king's funeral, in the Pantheon, in Rome, was staged with the greatest splendour and attended by pilgrims from all over the country, including many Bolognesi. With some weeks delay a film documenting the funeral was presented in Bologna's Teatro Eleonora Duse and attracted a great throng of citizens from various social backgrounds, one of the city's first spectacular cinematographic projections, a media event extending the community of mourners well beyond the pilgrims present in Rome.

During the official commemorations in Bologna's council, the first thoughts went to the widow:

> There, in the sad palace of Monza, a majestic woman, a paragon of gratitude and virtue, is oppressed by a grief for which there is no comfort. We will not disturb the tragic keenness of this grief by empty words, but the Augusta Donna should know that the whole of Italy suffers and weeps with her.[125]

Then the mayor lauded the successor to the throne, Vittorio Emanuele III, "who takes the crown during such an anguished moment." His name, a reference to the kingdom's founding father, was interpreted as a symbol of comfort for the nation. The orations of the councillors made reference to the kinship between king and people, the idea of the nation as a family, headed by the monarch.[126] "This sad and wicked murderer did not commit a regicide, but a patricide, because Umberto I was not the king, he was the loving father of his people." The parties of the Left used the occasion to confirm their commitment to the constitution and to condemn the anarchists' methods in the strongest possible terms:

> Between honest popular parties and assassins there is only an abyss, there is only infinity. . . . The assassin and the cowards who belong with him have no family, no fatherland, no party, no nation, they are unworthy of belonging to humanity. . . . They deprived the people, the workers and the poor of their greatest friend and of their beloved benefactor.[127]

The commemorations also reveal the extent to which Bologna prized its special relationship with Italy's second sovereign. The monarch's numerous visits to the city were recorded in the courtyard of the town hall. As on previous occasions, "this good and benevolent king" was commemorated through an act of charity, a further 50,000 Lire for the local children's hospital.[128] When a century later the anarchists of Carrara wanted to erect a monument to Gaetano Bresci, in an age when public monuments had almost gone out of fashion, the request provoked a scandal and was rejected, leading Mario Isnenghi to conclude that at least in a negative sense the cultural mechanisms of public monuments still work.[129]

CIVIL RELIGION AROUND THE TURN OF THE CENTURY

Vittorio Emanuele III and Queen Elena broke with the splendour of Margherita's court life. They left the Quirinale for less spectacular residences and endorsed the notion of a democratic king living a bourgeois life-style, challenging the public image of the Italian monarchy once more. Unlike his father and his grandfather, Vittorio Emanuele III was interested in literature and the arts and emphasised the administrative duties of his office, spending long hours at his desk. Politically, the years before World War I were a period of consolidation for the monarchy and in many respects also for Italy as a whole. Economic consolidation went hand in hand with attempts at social pacification.

The commemorations for Garibaldi between his death in 1882 and World War I illustrate both the government's changing attitude towards the legacy of the Risorgimento and the persistence of a politically divided memory. "The invention of the hero" had started several decades before his death, but after 1882 the institutions of the liberal State assumed an active role in this process. The municipalities in particular rallied to the new cult around Garibaldi, a name "rooted in the history of every city and town," as the catalogue of the 1884 *Esposizione nazionale* in Turin noted.[130] From the moment the news of Garibaldi's death broke, shops and theatres all over Italy closed. Public buildings were decorated with mourning drapes and the newspapers appeared with black margins. The mayor's official declaration stood in marked contrast to the Moderates' earlier utterances regarding Garibaldi's contribution to the national revolution:

> The history of Giuseppe Garibaldi's glorious deeds and his noble sacrifice are written . . . into the heart of every Italian. Remembering this sublime figure of a hero, our profound gratitude will remain imperishable. Together with a great king and a great minister he formed the sacred triad to which Italy owes the fulfilment of its unity and independence, the realisation of the longings of so many martyrs and illustrious thinkers, including, more than anybody else, Giuseppe Mazzini.[131]

Now even Mazzini figured among the Risorgimento's officially recognised heroes. In the city's largest and most popular theatre Bologna's students organised a commemoration for Garibaldi, with a weeping Carducci as the main speaker. The audience openly displayed its despair. The council celebrated its own commemoration and contributed 40,000 Lire to a local monument for Garibaldi—four times the sum provided for Cavour's monument in 1861 and only 10,000 Lire less than the commune had paid for its monument to Vittorio Emanuele II.[132] Count Grabinski was the only councillor who voted against the motion and who remained seated during the mourning. Subsequently the council discussed a proposal of the Workingmen's Society. Instead of using the approved sum to erect a monument, they wished to build a public bath bearing the hero's name. Their approach was characteristic of the Left at the time: On the first anniversary of the General's death Cavallotti explained that "*Garibaldi non si commemora: si sente.*"[133] Although some councillors expressed doubts as to whether "a warrior like General Garibaldi should be honoured with dirty water," Filopanti, himself a veteran of Garibaldi's campaigns, explained that "if the hero was still alive and consulted on his preference, he would opt without hesitation for the first choice. Although the water of the pool will get dirty, it then has the merit of having cleaned human bodies." After lengthy debates the commune built the bath in addition to erecting a monument, designed by Carlo Parmeggiani and placed on Bologna's most prestigious street, the new axis leading from the station to Piazza Maggiore.[134]

The monarchy also assumed an important role in celebrating the new cult around Garibaldi, and the king presided over the national commemorations for the centennial of his birth. On this occasion Bologna presented a prize for the best book on the "Expedition of the Thousand" and distributed historical accounts of Garibaldi's life among the pupils of the local secondary schools. The mayor pleaded for a commemoration that might overcome political divisions, but the Socialist councillors questioned whether this was possible, considering that the clerical members of the majority "have always been Garibaldi's most bitter enemy."[135] With reference to the municipal prize, councillor Grossi maintained that the administration had chosen the theme of the "Thousand" because the event "culminated in the donation of a monarchy," while a more general treatment would have to discuss the Roman Republic of 1849 and the unsuccessful Mentana campaign. Any other topic would have produced clashes within the conservative-clerical majority.[136] Three years later, in 1910, on the fiftieth anniversary of Garibaldi's Expedition, the mayor Marquis Tanari remembered "the immortal *Duce* Giuseppe Garibaldi," while the opposition celebrated a mission whose motto had been "*Roma o Morte!*" The Socialists reminded the council that the Redshirts had a "vision," "postulating a new society."[137] Memories remained divided. There were at least two Garibaldis—the official hero representing the nation *super partes* and the popular hero of the Democratic and Socialist tradition. The popular Garibaldi assumed a function comparable to the cult of the Madonna invented during the Middle Ages, belonging first to the people and only second to the institution of the church.[138] Despite the efforts to create a hero *super partes*, for the Left Garibaldi was never completely identified with the institution of the liberal State.

The occasions for public commemorations changed over time. In 1905, commenting on the dates on which the municipality flies the national flag, the Socialists asked why the anniversary of the Roman Republic and the 1 May were not listed among the official dates. According to the mayor the 1 May did not mark any historical or patriotic event; and while the commune commemorated Mazzini and Garibaldi for their contribution to the Unification of Italy, the Roman Republic represented "a form of government which the *giunta* does not wish to celebrate." When a few months later the opposition sought to clarify if the clerical members of the majority subscribed to the celebration of Mazzini, the mayor interrupted the debate.[139] Ten years later, the Socialist council majority set the dates on which the flag should be flown. The list no longer included the king's birthday, provoking protests among the monarchical opposition. In their view the outbreak of the war meant a defeat of Socialist Internationalism and required solidarity between the peoples and their monarchs.[140] May Day was celebrated with financial contributions from the municipality and after Italy entered the war the Socialist mayor published a manifesto describing "how the barbarities of a terrible war undermine civic life." Therefore, "Bologna's proletariat" should commemorate May Day as "a manifestation of faith in a better future":

> Despite these unexpected events, the men of Labour know . . . that in every corner of the world there are other men who suffer the same obstacles and nurture the same hopes. . . . The capitalist order is the political and economic expression of an aggressive imperialism. It re-vives conservative tendencies, violently suppresses freedom of thought and action, and does not answer to the needs of the labouring classes. The various forms of militarism cannot foster healthy social and civil relationships. The proletariat . . . requests that all peoples, without pressure of weapons, unite in freedom under those forms of govern-ment which correspond best to their traditions, to their interests, to their history. . . . Citizens! Strong in our convictions, on this first of May we raise our voice for a most fervent invocation of peace, a peace which . . . promotes the triumph of the workers' International and the exaltation of human civilization.[141]

However, the more confident the Socialist administration became in stak-ing its claim to the municipal territory of cultural self-representation, the more the local representatives of central government took fright. Without notification or justification, the chief of the police halted the distribution of the mayor's manifesto, thus demonstrating the institutional barriers against the establishment of a new civic culture based on Municipal Socialism.[142]

9 "*Viva Rossini—Morte a Wagner*"?
From *Campanilismo* to the Future

Nineteenth-century Italian opera is often equated with the combination of La Scala and Verdi, regardless of the fact that between 1845 and 1887 not a single opera by Verdi was premiered in Milan;[1] and despite extensive research on the repertoire of Italian theatres, for most people "opera in Italy" still means the middle and later Verdi, some Rossini, Bellini and Donizetti, as a curiosity possibly Giordano's *Andrea Chénier* and Ponchielli's *La Gioconda*, and since the *fine secolo* Puccini, Leoncavallo and Mascagni. While this is an accurate reflection upon "Italian opera in the world," it is a distortion of what was happening on the Italian stages between Unification and Fascism, contributing to the stereotype of Italians obsessed with their own operatic, culinary and criminal culture, mentally sealed off from what is happening outside the peninsula.[2] There were countless Italian stage composers whom we have forgotten (often for good reasons); and *impresari* as well as local administrations were keen to internationalise the repertoire of their theatres.

The example of Bologna's Teatro Comunale illustrates how Italian culture was shaped through a constant dialogue with the international repertoire, and, more generally, with intellectual and aesthetic developments from all over Europe, particularly France and Germany. Starting from the cultural stagnation of the late Papal regime under Austrian occupation, during the *fine secolo* Bologna became one of the centres of Italy's musical avant-garde. While it might be argued that Bologna's Teatro Comunale constitutes a special case, at the same time it had a major influence on the Italian opera scene as a whole; and the city was not alone in promoting the non-Italian repertoire. At the 1884 *Esposizione Italiana* in Turin, conceived as a showcase of the nation, the musical programme conducted by the young Giuseppe Martucci included works by Mozart, Beethoven, Mendelssohn, Schumann, Berlioz and Wagner, but no Verdi; and the only Italian composers on the programme were Cherubini, Boccherini and Scarlatti.[3] The international profile of the repertoire was frequently criticized, for instance by the futurist composer Balilla Pratella,[4] but in an age which increasingly saw cultural self-representation as a means to articulate national pride, the image emerging here is that of a nation which understood its cosmopolitan orientation as an integral part of its cultural value system, its intellectual ambition and its humanist legacy.

IMPRESARI, PUBLISHERS AND CULTURAL POLITICS

Any analysis of the role of music and opera in the cultural self-representation of Italian cities has to take into account the relatively small impact of politicians on the content of the repertoire.[5] The number of *impresari* in a position to propose a project for the season of Bologna's Teatro Comunale was limited. The theatre was too prestigious for small travelling companies. Although its annual endowment and potential turnover were lower than those of the San Carlo, La Fenice or La Scala, it signed contracts with the same *impresari* or their associates: Lanari, Scalaberni, Tinti. The *impresaris'* impact on the programme was usually more important than the aesthetic views of the local government or the theatre's administrators. As Panzacchi observed, not "platonic love for the arts," but the *impresario's* commercial considerations determined decisions.[6] Often there was no significant variation between the programmes presented by the different *impresari*; and before the *Repertoire-Theater*, with its focus on historical works, this meant mostly music of the past few decades by a small number of fashionable composers.[7] Publishers also intervened in the negotiations between *impresari* and local government. In 1878, Ricordi obliged the agency Gaibi-Scalaberni to stage Gaetano Coronaro's new opera *La Creola* as a condition for obtaining the scores of Verdi's *Don Carlos* and Massenet's *Roi de Lahore;* and as Bologna wanted to be in the headlines for Italy's first performance of these works, it had to accept Ricordi's conditions.[8] At the time most musical periodicals belonged to theatre agents or *impresari* and therefore did not necessarily represent an independent and disinterested opinion. Often they concentrated on gossip about famous divas currently on stage. Many of these periodicals disappeared shortly after the publication of their first issues.[9] In Bologna the agent Raffaele Vitali published *L'Arpa*, founded in 1853 by Carlo Gardini as a paper for the theatre industry.[10] Not until after Unification, when Gustavo Sangiorgi and later Count Albicini took over the paper, did *L'Arpa* become an independent musical journal (which published, among other articles, the proceedings of the R. Accademia Filarmonica). Earlier, the weekly *Teatri Arti e Letteratura* directed by Gaetano Fiori played an important role in Bologna's musical life, but it ceased its activities in 1863. The major newspapers for music criticism were the *Monitore di Bologna* and the *Corriere dell'Emilia*, later fused with the *Gazzetta dell'Emilia*, and from 1885 *Il Resto del Carlino*, which absorbed *La Patria* a few years later. A number of smaller and satirical papers also published reviews of concerts and operas.

   Despite the role of *impresario* and publishers, theatres were not exclusively governed by market forces. Rather than commenting on the works to be performed, local administrators discussed in surprising detail the cast of singers and dancers, and occasionally the staging.[11] Moreover, politicians could determine the quality of performances by granting a generous subsidy and by ensuring that the financial contributions of the box owners were paid. They could decide to invest in the cultural infrastructure: improving the contracts of musicians and choruses; using local conservatories and municipal bands to enlarge the orchestra; modernising the theatre's technology, lighting and stage machinery. Direct political intervention in questions of repertoire increased during the *fine secolo*. Examples are Bologna's first Italian staging of Wagner in 1871 (*Lohengrin*) under the administration of Camillo Casarini, described in a Moderate newspaper as part of the Democrats' political agenda;[12] or the city's 1875 revival of Boito's *Mefistofele,* an initiative of the influential Salina family after the opera's 1868 fiasco in Milan. The internationalisation of Bologna's repertoire was clearly driven by political, aesthetic as well as commercial considerations. The most important factor in securing a season's success depended on the ability to attract—by way of financial inducement and musical resources— a good *impresario.* Only a wealthy theatre was able to maintain the new style of ballet which had become fashionable since the Napoleonic period, the French innovations of *grand opéra,* or later the staging of Wagner. The *impresario* had to fill the theatre in order to cover his expenses; and for Bologna, where most of the seats belonged to private box owners who often refused to pay their annual fees, this meant seeking new audiences, also from outside the city. Rather than with *bel canto,* performed everywhere, visitors were attracted by events like the Italian premiere of Verdi's *Don Carlos,* spectacular works such as Meyerbeer's *Africana,* Gounod's *Faust* or by Wagner.[13]

ITALIAN OPERA AND THE CRISIS OF A NATIONAL CULTURE

Gramsci described Italian opera as an "authentic product" of national culture, translating the themes of a literature intended for the educated elites into a universally comprehensible language.[14] Its audiences included people of different social backgrounds, from the nobility in the private boxes to less solvent *mélomanes* and the *petite bourgeoisie* in the *loggione.* In smaller theatres the popular element in the audience was greater. They performed mostly vaudevilles, but also *opera buffa.* Brass bands and itinerant musicians performed potpourris of the current repertoire in the squares, under Bologna's *portici* and in local coffee-houses. Giuseppe Mazzini played Ferdinando Carulli's Rossini-arrangements on his guitar in London; Angelo Mariani reduced entire operas into versions for string quartet, to be performed at private venues; and almost all of the instrumental music appearing in the advertisements and lists of Italian music publishers at the time "was directly inspired by operatic scores, and was designed to make those scores more readily available."[15] Piano recitals almost always included extracts from operas. During the years of the revolution and the Cisalpine Republic the propagandistic use of opera and performances of patriotic works, often in the open air, represented another form of popular theatre through which different social strata participated aesthetically in the emergence of modern society.[16] According to John Rosselli, in 1871 there existed 940 theatres in 699 Italian towns; in 1907, Italy counted over 3,000 theatres. Most of them did not perform opera on a regular basis, but many saw at least occasionally a touring company of musicians. By 1913 131 towns had an opera season of some sort. Many of these theatres were new and offered cheap tickets, affordable to craftsmen, shop assistants and white collar workers.[17]

While the relationship between opera and politics during the Risorgimento is often romanticised and not infrequently distorted, after Unification audiences used the theatre as a space for political manifestations, at least occasionally. In October 1868, when the Roman question was acute, and there had been revolution in Spain, performances in Bologna were interrupted by shouts of "*Viva la Spagna! Viva Roma! Fuori lo straniero!,*" and later also "*Viva la Repubblica! Viva* Mazzini! *Viva* Garibaldi!" Although they began in the stalls, orchestra and choruses also joined in these commotions. To calm down the restless masses, the authorities had to allow the "Inno a Garibaldi" to be played, and it was repeated twenty times.[18]

Alberto Banti's study on concepts of the nation during the Risorgimento established a catalogue of literary works which had marked the first generation of Risorgimento patriots. The operas in this catalogue include works by Rossini, Bellini and Donizetti, all presumably associated with a national or patriotic agenda: *L'assedio di Corinto, Mosè* and *Guglielmo Tell* by Rossini; Bellini's *Norma;* Mercadante's *Donna Caritea.*[19] Verdi's early operas also figure prominently in the catalogue: *Nabucco, I Lombardi alla prima crociata, Ernani, Attila, Macbeth, La battaglia di Legnano,* written during the years between 1842 and 1849.[20] However, as we saw in chapter seven Rossini himself favoured the *ancien régime;* and although Mazzini liked playing Rossini on his guitar, in his *Philosophy of Music* he rejected Rossini's operas for representing "man without God . . . unconsecrated by an eternal faith."[21] Bellini and Donizetti were hardly interested in politics; and the view of the early Verdi as the bard of the Risorgimento has been rejected as a myth, an image constructed to a large extent *a posteriori.*[22] In order to assess the relationship between opera and politics we have to examine the contemporary reception of these works. The reviews of Bologna's *Nabucco* in 1843 and 1855 show no sign of a patriotic reading of the opera, likewise, the 1860 performance of *La Battaglia di Legnano.* Usually seen as an example of Verdi's identification with the Risorgimento, this work was criticized in Bologna for the apparent "*discordanza*" between the historical-national theme and what Verdi did with it—for the fact that Verdi's music did not correspond to the "patriotic affection" of Berchet's poetry on the same subject. Instead, the critics said, the work was no more than a "private story about love and jealousy."[23] This is not to deny that in the context of later political developments many of Verdi's works acquired a national meaning. However, analysing the content and reception of these works, it is difficult to establish a relationship between cause and effect: to see if the works helped to politicize the audiences or rather if the historical-political context of the time transformed the works into patriotic operas. Moreover, the Italian intellectuals who identified with the Risorgimento might have read these works very differently from the wider audiences or indeed the critics: on the basis of Leopardi's contemporary observations, Mary Ann Smart characterizes opera-going as "essentially passive, a herd activity like promenading through the *piazza* before dinner."[24]

Whatever the exact nature of the relationship between work, audiences and political context was at the time, Verdi's music was extremely popular in European theatres during most of the nineteenth century. However, after the success of Verdi's *triologia* (*Rigoletto, Trovatore, Traviata*) in the early 1850s, the decades after Unification were marked by a profound crisis of Italian opera—a surprising development considering the extent to which Italian culture, since the eighteenth century, had defined itself through the lyric theatre.[25] Rossini's last opera had been *Guillaume Tell* in 1829; Bellini had died in 1835; Donizetti in 1848. Verdi wrote *La forza del destino* (1862) for St. Petersburg, keeping Italy waiting for a revised version until 1869. *Don Carlos* (1867) was a French opera, written for the stage in Paris, with a libretto based on Schiller. *Aida* (Cairo, 1871) was commissioned by the Ismail Pasha, the Khedive of Egypt, and instead of celebrating the completion of the Risorgimento after the liberation of Rome, the work inaugurated the Cairo Opera House, built in connection with the opening of the Suez Canal.[26] Verdi's last two operas, *Othello* (1887) and *Falstaff* (1893), already belonged to a different epoch in the history of music. Hence, since Unification Verdi almost ceased to contribute to the consolidation of a national culture through new operas. In the view of many the *Schaffenskrise* of Italian opera composers was part of a larger intellectual crisis which hit Italy profoundly during the years between 1871 and 1890.[27] Although about a hundred new Italian operas were staged during this period, the only works to make a considerable impact were those of the later Verdi, Boito's *Mefistofele* and Ponchielli's *La Gioconda*. None of them was able to revive the general euphoria with which the operas of the first half of the century were often met. The international comeback of Italian opera did not start until the 1890s, with the *Giovine Scuola* of Puccini and Mascagni as its protagonists.[28]

CAMPANILISMO

Bologna has not always been at the vanguard of European music. Although during the four decades between 1820 and Unification the Comunale staged every year about six different operas, very few foreign works were performed, seemingly confirming Berlioz' view that Italian audiences hated innovation.[29] Frequently the Comunale presented three operas by Rossini in a single season, or a combination of Rossini with Bellini and Donizetti.[30] As discussed in Chapter 7, Bologna had a special relationship to Rossini. The son of a local soprano and of a horn player, Rossini was known in Bologna from an early age, first as a soprano, then as keyboard player. After he became a composer of international fame, Bologna regularly marked his visits with sumptuous receptions in the palaces of the Hercolani, Malvezzi, and Poniatowski. On these occasions members of the local aristocracy, accompanied by Rossini at the piano, sang arias from popular *bel canto* roles. Anecdotes about the composer's life in Paris contributed further to the myth surrounding him. Meanwhile, a number of important chapters in the history of European music remained almost unknown to Bologna's audiences—Cherubini, although he had studied for a while in Bologna, Spontini, a native of the Papal States, but celebrated mostly in Paris and Berlin, even Mozart, Beethoven's *Fidelio* and Weber, at a time when most European theatres were concentrating more and more on historic repertoire.[31] Ethnic and racial stereotypes served to justify prejudice against "foreign" music; and even in 1869 *Il Monitore di Bologna* remarked, bizarrely, that Mendelssohn was "German and Jewish, a severe figure in the arts . . . one with his tribe, not one of us."[32] Liszt wrote *"musica senza musica"* and a theatre magazine commented on Meyerbeer that "a German opera does not go together with Italian taste." He was described as *"più filosofo che maestro."*[33] What such criticism failed to remember was that Rossini too had once been charged "with having adulterated the pure fount of Italian melody by bringing in far too much noisy German harmony," a legacy of his German-trained teacher in Lugo, with whom he had studied the works of Mozart and Haydn.[34] Panzacchi reminded Bologna that Father Mattei, professor at the Liceo Musicale, was called "il tedeschino," for his love of Mozart and Haydn.[35] Moreover, between the late eighteenth and early nineteenth centuries German composers enjoyed remarkable success in Italian opera houses, including Adalbert Gyrowetz, Peter von Winter, Joseph Weigl and Johann Simon Mayr, who wrote over seventy works for all the major Italian stages and who counted Donizetti among his students.[36] Verdi was influenced by Meyerbeer and his recurring themes were sometimes criticized as copies of Wagner's leitmotivs.[37] Catalani, Giordano and Puccini all learned from studying French and German scores. Mazzini discovered Beethoven, Mozart and Wagner in London and greatly appreciated their work, which had a major impact on his philosophy of music.[38] Although he was concerned about the decline of Italian opera, he certainly can not be criticized for undermining Italy's cultural tradition.

Not only "foreign" composers were rejected: Bologna's response to Verdi was complex too. During the 1840s the city had gone through a period of enthusiasm for the master from Busseto. *Nabucco* reached the Bolognese stage later than the secondary theatres of Piacenza, Faenza, Cagliari and Como; but then it was performed more than thirty times.[39] After the election of Pius IX *"una variante filopapale* of *Ernani,"* transforming the hymn for Charlemagne into one for the new liberal pope, was hailed in the theatres of the Papal Legations.[40] However, Bologna's *La Farfalla* as well as the local periodical *Teatri Arti e Letteratura* disliked the *"troppo assordante rumore* of *Nabucco"* (1843), the volume of his music and the use of declamation, which *Il Mondo Illustrato* (1847) also found distasteful, considering that one went to the opera for distraction and entertainment.[41] After 1848 Pius introduced a rigorous regime of censorship directed explicitly against the composer. In an article published in 1853 the Jesuit *Civiltà Cattolica* referred to his works "as bad examples of taste in matters of politics, religion, or morality."[42]

Although during the first decade after Unification Verdi appeared regularly on the Comunale's programme, the end of the Papal regime did not silence his critics.[43] On the occasion of Vittorio Emanuele's first visit, on the 4th of May 1860, the theatre presented *I Lombardi*, followed during the autumn season by *Un Ballo in Maschera*—"difficult music" according to the city's principle newspaper.[44] For *Il Monitore* the opera was well performed, but based on "abstruse harmonic and melodic combinations." One of Bologna's most well-known commentators on the life of the Teatro Comunale, Enrico Bottrigari, opined that the work "lacks vigour and imagination. The first act is poor, the others contain effective moments, but altogether hardly anything is new, a mosaic made up from various other scores." Of *I due Foscari* Bottrigari wrote that the composer "has not yet the spark of genius," that he "lacks thought and has no sense of melody"; *Rigoletto* was again just too "loud"; *Stiffelio* artificially "forced."[45] The *impresario* who in 1861 staged *La Battaglia di Legnano* blamed the audience for what turned out to be a fiasco, causing him a major deficit.[46] On the occasion of Crown Prince Umberto's visit the Comunale presented *Simon Boccanegra*, but the citizenry did not appreciate its "abstruse and complicated" tunes, favouring still the "paradise-like music of Rossini."[47] The local officer corps even refused to renew its subscription for the season.[48] *La forza del destino* was welcomed, but its success was overshadowed by a dislike for the complicated libretto.[49]

As a consequence, although several of Bologna's smaller theatres presented Verdi regularly, the Teatro Comunale staged many of his operas only once or twice, and with several years delay after their Italian premiere: *La Battaglia di Legnano* had to wait twelve years after the *prima* in Rome and was staged only once in the composer's lifetime; *Simon Boccanegra* was staged once, five years after the premiere in Venice; *La forza del destino* once, seven years after the premiere in Saint Petersburg; *Aida* had to wait six years. *Oberto*, *Un giorno di regno*, *Alzira* and *Il Corsaro* as well as *Stiffelio* and *Jérusalem*, which are different versions of *Aroldo* and *I Lombardi*, never made it onto the stage of the Comunale during his lifetime. Bologna did of course also have "Verdian periods," like the year 1850, when Verdi himself conducted *Macbeth* and *Luisa Miller*, or 1856, when *Luisa Miller, Rigoletto, I Due Foscari, I Vespri* and *La Traviata* were all on the programme, but especially between 1870 and World War I there were many years without a single Verdi opera on the Comunale's programme.[50]

Bologna was not alone in criticising Verdi. Throughout his career the composer had "a difficult relationship with the Neapolitan public," accusing it of being "fussy any time you present it with something different."[51] In particular the nobility favoured *bel canto* over Verdi's new style. A literary reference to the nobility's views on Verdi appears in Giuseppe Tomasi di Lampedusa's *Il Gattopardo*, describing the moment when the mayor Don Calogero welcomes the family of Prince Salina on its arrival at its Sicilian estate with *"l'imperversare della musica di Verdi e del frastuono delle campane."*[52] Visconti, in his film of the novel, illustrates with a fine sense of irony the prince's reaction to the mediocrity with which Don Calogero decided to mark the transition from the old to the new regime at Donnafugata, a statement symptomatic of his view of the mayor for decades to come.

Florence was more open towards Verdi's aesthetic challenges and to the supposedly patriotic operas which became a success around 1848.[53] Florentine audiences and the influential *Rivista musicale di Firenze* also appreciated the German and Austrian style more easily and engaged seriously with the European tradition of symphonic and chamber music. The 1843 Italian *prima* of Weber's *Freischütz* had been a great success at the Pergola. Four years later, during the first presentation of *Macbeth*, Florence discovered Verdi's new emphasis on the psychology of his protagonists. Although certain observers speculated that a German composer would have been better equipped to represent the witches, the Florentines appreciated Verdi's new drama for what they called its "philosophical" content, clearly in line with Weber's innovations in opera.

What Florence enjoyed as "mysteriously fascinating" remained for Bologna still "too foreign."[54] In 1863 the local councillor and editor of *L'Arpa*, Gustavo Sangiorgi, tried to bring *La Forza del Destino* from Reggio Emilia to the Comunale, but due to restoration works the project was abandoned.[55] On other occasions the *giunta* considered the staging of Verdi too elaborate and expensive.[56] In September 1867 Bologna signed a three-year contract with the famous *impresario* Luigi Scalaberni,[57] to include the Italian premiere of Verdi's *Don Carlos*. However, the liberation and national symbolism of the work, based on Schiller's drama, proved unable to inspire Enrico Bottrigari. With the great Franco Faccio as conductor and with Teresa Stolz as prima donna, the occasion was described by Sangiorgi as *"una vera festa artistica,"* but Bottrigari was "rather bored" by the opera.[58] Different, though, was the reaction of the outside observers, who recognised and praised the recent developments of Bologna's theatre: Filippo Filippi, director of Milan's influential *Mondo Artistico*, wrote on the occasion that Bologna should be proud of its premiers: "The Teatro Comunale has presented extraordinary stagings of *Un Ballo in Maschera, Faust, L'Africaine* and now of *Don Carlos*. Its perfection—and I say this without exaggeration—will not be found in any other theatre."[59] However, *Luisa Miller*, staged in 1881 at the Teatro Dal Verme, provoked again discontent among the local audience, to the point that the police had to intervene.[60] Although most papers praised the *Aida* of 1877, the frequent comparisons with the music of Wagner were not necessarily understood as a compliment and *Il Nuovo Alfiere* called it *"un aborto d'un colosso."*[61] Corrado Ricci reports in his *Ricordi Bolognesi* an encounter between the municipal engineer Leopoldo Lambertini and the writer Edmondo De Amicis, who was visiting Bologna with his children. On the question why he would not be at the theatre that night, Lambertini shocked the famous author of *Cuore* with the words *"perchè fanno quella cretinata dell'Aida!,"* and going on with a harangue against the composer's orchestration, his vulgarity and his choruses *"da osteria":* "The romance *Eri tu che macchiavi quell'anima* is stuff for heavy drinkers," he said, "though one couldn't tell if the drinkers took it from Verdi or Verdi from the drinkers."[62]

Meyerbeer's work also had a difficult time in Bologna. For most of the nineteenth century his operas were applauded in theatres all over Europe, with the exception of his native Germany, where despite the composer's official position at the Prussian court his work was often criticized. Florence, from the 1820s through to the 1850s, had been *"la città meyerberiana per eccellenza."* The Milanese music critic Filippo Filippi hailed Meyerbeer for the fruitful influence of different German traditions on his music, from Bach and Handel to Beethoven and Weber. Mazzini admired Meyerbeer for moralising musical drama, "making it an echo of the world and its eternal vital problem." In Bologna his success came late, just before his death in 1864.[63] In 1820, 1824 and 1826 his Italian operas, *Semiramide, Margherita d'Anjou* and *Il Crociato in Egitto* had been performed. Twenty years later, in 1846, the arrival of the new cardinal legate was celebrated with *Roberto il Diavolo*, the work which had sealed the composer's success in Paris. But Bologna's aristocratic audience rejected it.[64] Of *Gli Ugonotti*, an extremely popular work at Covent Garden and by 1900 performed a thousand times in the French capital, *Il Monitore* wrote in 1860 that "the music is heavy, philosophical, a product of study, all based on harmonies [rather than melody]."[65] The scale of the work did not allow for the performance of a separate ballet during the same evening, with the consequence that Bologna's box owners deserted the theatre: although *Gli Ugonotti* was explicitly defined as *"opera-ballo,"* its ballet scenes did not count as *"ballo eroico,"* reason enough to withhold the annual contribution to the autumn season.[66] Staging *grand opéra*, such as Meyerbeer, which was usually in five acts, presented musical, financial and technical challenges. Citing the burdens imposed upon the orchestra, the musicians asked for better working conditions. (Meyerbeer himself had been known for improvements to the conditions of his musicians during his years in Berlin.) Although most of them had regular incomes as professors of the Liceo Musicale or as members of the municipal band, they wished to become a stable orchestra with monthly salaries. When the council rejected this request, the orchestra went on strike.[67] This occurred only a year after a major dispute with the chorus, settled only after the *impresario* promised to increase the singers' wages.[68] Hence, staging Meyerbeer presented a considerable challenge.

Nevertheless, during the 1860s, Mariani established Meyerbeer as an integral part of the local repertoire, convincing the audience by his own professional genius and the continuously improving quality of the productions.[69] Soon, the composer appeared in the popular open-air potpourris of the municipal band and during the local 1848 commemorations.[70] Influential sections of the cultural and political elites resisted the local musical conservatism. The Deputazione degli spettacoli wrote to Meyerbeer, congratulating him on the "triumphant" success of his *Profeta* and on the symphonic parts of his new opera, *Le Pardon de Ploërmel*.[71] For the 1866 celebrations after the liberation of Venice Mariani presented a programme exclusively based on works by Meyerbeer and Verdi.[72]

Two years later, in 1868, Verdi was made an honorary citizen of Bologna and a fellow of the Accademia Filarmonica,[73] but during the entire year Bologna staged not a single one of his works, presenting instead Mercadante's *Giuramenti,* several works by Donizetti, Halévy's *La Juive,* Lionello Ventura's *Alda,* Louis Ferdinand Hérold's *Zampa* and in *prima assoluta* Dall'Argine's *Barbiere.* Had Verdi gone completely out of fashion? While Eric Hobsbawm contrasted the cosmopolitan taste of the aristocracy with the bourgeoisie's search for national resurgence through the arts,[74] the situation in the Italian theatres seems more complex. The nobility in their private boxes were fans of Bellini, Donizetti and Rossini, while the middle class quickly moved from Verdi towards the international repertoire, in particular towards the works of French and German composers.

MODERN TIMES AND MODERNIST AESTHETICS

Meyerbeer died during the rehearsals for his last opera, *L'Africaine,* completed by François-Joseph Fétis and premiered posthumously in Paris in 1865. In 1868 Bologna's first Democratic mayor, Camillo Casarini, assumed the responsibility for the staging of the work, extending the existing contract with the *impresario* Scalaberni to add the opera *"in prima italiana"* to the programme for the Quaresima season.[75] The enthusiastically received performance was described by *Il Monitore* as "one of the greatest musical events of our time," a judgement shared by the press all over Italy. The opera marked a turning point in the Comunale's history: "Ever since *L'Africaine,* the theatre has been growing in reputation and importance," the local council commented.[76] A first step towards a more cosmopolitan opening of the Comunale had been achieved and Bologna was now widely acclaimed for the extraordinary quality of its theatre. This new fame was appreciated even by those Bolognesi who regretted the cancellation of the separate ballet during opera evenings and who did not identify with the foreign departures from their beloved *bel canto*.

The personal prestige of Bologna's conductors contributed to the theatre's part in the city's self-representation. Angelo Mariani was one of the first conductors in Italy whose role was distinct from that of the leader, a consequence of the growing technical complexity of the repertoire. Following the methods of Berlioz (*L'art du chef d'orchestre*) and Wagner (*Über das Dirigieren*), he concentrated his work on welding the orchestra's players into a unified body and on emphasising his interpretation of the score.[77] For Bologna Mariani was one of themselves—a compatriot from the former Papal States, born in Ravenna, with an early career as *maestro di musica* in Macerata and Faenza.[78] As early as the 1840s Rossini had conducted Mariani's symphonies in Bologna, before the latter started his career in Milan, and went on to Stradella, Vincenza, Copenhagen and Constantinople. After experience with the Florentine orchestra of the Pergola, Mariani went on to transform the Genoese orchestra into one of the finest in Italy. Then, from 1860 until his death in 1873, he directed ten seasons at Bologna's Comunale. Many of his compositions had been published and performed in Paris and London as well as in Italy. Bologna's administration knew that the theatre's recent international recognition was closely linked to his name and undertook every effort to bind him permanently to the Comunale. As an international star he became a major attraction of Bologna's musical life.[79] He was the first Italian conductor comparable to such giants as Hans von Bülow, Arthur Nikisch and Hans Richter. He became a model for the generation of Weingartner, Mahler and Schalk, and an icon for Toscanini, when aged only twenty-seven he started to conduct the Comunale in 1894.

Earlier the cult of the star had focussed mainly on violinists, pianists and opera singers. But now it extended, with its associated trivia, to the conductor—himself a new phenomenon in the history of music. A notorious example of the public interest in the private life of great conductors is Hans von Bülow, married to Liszt's daughter Cosima de Flagney, who later left him for the conductor's own greatest idol, Richard Wagner.[80] But with Mariani Italy had an even more dramatic story to offer. Since the 1840s Mariani was not only Verdi's most important conductor, but also, in the words of Rosselli, his "willing slave"; and Verdi knew how to exploit Mariani's veneration for him.[81] The slightest criticism by Verdi of one of his performances left the conductor shattered, but at the same time it further increased his admiration for the master from Busseto. The relationship between the two men became even more complex when Verdi started taking an interest in Mariani's fiancée, Teresa Stolz, one of the most applauded sopranos of the time, known in Bologna for the 1864 staging of *Ernani* and for the first Italian performance of *Don Carlos*. Differences over the commemorations

Figure 9.1   Angelo Mariani. (Author's Collection.)

for the death of Rossini in 1868 served Verdi as a pretext to break up his relationship to Mariani. In 1871 Verdi refused to offer his best conductor the *prima* of *Aida*; but when he was later obliged to fall back on Mariani, he was not available.[82] Stolz broke her engagement with the conductor and spent the following months with Verdi and his wife Giuseppina Strepponi at Sant'Agata, in a curious *ménage à trois*. Personally humiliated, Mariani took his revenge with greatest possible insult to the composer: on the first of November 1871 he conducted the Italian *prima* of Wagner's *Lohengrin* in Bologna. They never spoke again. Seriously ill with cancer, Mariani died shortly afterwards. This "private life" drama contributed considerably to

Mariani's "celebrity," and there was widespread public interest in the personal tragedy of the international star. It also increased the national and international attention paid to Bologna's theatre. As Casarini remarked after the conductor's death, Mariani's and the Comunale's reputation—if not quite in the way just described—were one and the same.[83]

Meanwhile, a new generation of local politicians began to reverse the Moderates' economizing policy and their neglect of Bologna's cultural representation. The concept of an Italian *Kulturnation* represented through its cities, challenged the Moderates' principles, but even among the Moderates themselves these ideas started taking hold. Apart from Count Agostino Salina, who had an influential role in the Deputazione, Gustavo Sangiorgi was an important supporter of the theatre's modern and international orientation.[84] Through his role as editor of *L'Arpa* and critic for *Il Monitore*, the Moderate councillor was regarded as a cultural expert in a political milieu that was still dominated by the landed nobility. The cultural elite among the local Moderates joined the Democrats in their efforts to strengthen the city's cultural image and contributed to the symbolic construction of the nation as a whole. Bologna wanted to be considered "second only to Paris." Following the example of the city's major private theatres the council decided in 1865 to install modern gas-lightening in the Comunale. The expense of 50,000 Lire for the new chandeliers, designed by Luigi Samoggia, was approved by a majority of ninteen out of twenty-eight.[85] The council now also provided the money to complete the restoration of the theatre itself.[86] Renewing the municipal subsidy for the autumn season became a matter of course: local government discovered the economic advantages of a flourishing opera house. Confident in attracting visitors from outside, the mayor negotiated special fares with the railway company for the 1867 premiere of *Don Carlos*.[87]

In contrast with the situation in the early 1860s, when the council was reluctant to provide funds, municipal subsidies could now be increased still further. In order to ensure a more splendid staging for Meyerbeer's *Dinorah*, Verdi's *Macbeth* and *La forza del destino* during the autumn of 1870, the Democratic mayor Casarini convinced the council to supplement the agreed *dote* by a further 5000 Lire.[88] For the following autumn season he brought the grant up to 45,000 Lire and completed the remaining wall paintings, gildings and woodwork in the theatre, which added up to a bill of over 52,000 Lire.[89] In spring 1871 central heating was installed and the stage was now also equipped with modern lighting.[90] An additional 6000 Lire were spent to install an organ, which came from the former convent of the Annunziata, which the city had inherited from the state.[91] As could be expected for such a splendid theatre, chorus and orchestra were also of high standard. "I have heard the world's most famous orchestras, but I declare that I have never seen similar perfection" wrote the critic of *Il Monitore*, about the opening of the autumn season of 1871.[92] Everything seemed ready for an operatic event of extraordinary importance and ambition: the first Italian staging of an opera by Richard Wagner, *Lohengrin*.

WAGNERISM AS METAPHOR FOR THE FUTURE

Coinciding with Bologna's grandly staged International Congress of Pre-Historic Sciences, the premiere of *Lohengrin* took place on 1 November 1871, the year of the opera's New York premiere. As the editor of *L'Arpa* remarked, "for a prehistoric congress the 'music of the future' seems appropriate."[93] A reference to the savants' positivist convictions, the remark was not meant as an ironical observation: by explaining the past, they thought they were able to fashion the future. Prior to the premiere, a performance of *Lohengrin* in Munich was attended by an official delegation from Bologna, consisting of the mayor Casarini, Wagner's Italian publisher Giovannina Lucca, the stage engineer, the orchestra's leader and a number of delegates from Florence.[94] Wagner himself had supervised the Munich production, but he had doubts about staging the opera in Italy: *Lohengrin* did not present the same difficulties as *Tristan*, but even for German theatres the work posed major technical challenges and for the *impresario* a considerable financial risk. In the end it was decided that the preparations for the Italian premiere would be supervised by the young Bavarian Kapellmeister and composer Ernst Frank; and Casarini's financial arrangements allowed the Comunale to employ an excellent cast.[95]

Arguments between supporters and opponents of Wagner started long before the premiere. Two years earlier, after a concert of the Liceo Musicale with extracts from *Tannhäuser, Il Monitore* had maintained that the German composer abolished melody in favour of absurd harmonic constructions: music for mediocre amateurs and "pseudo-artists." However, these concerts helped to strengthen the Liceo's cosmopolitan profile, at a time when the Conservatory in Naples, under Mercadante's direction, was widely regarded as a bastion of reaction.[96] Bologna's principal newspaper prepared for the premiere of *Lohengrin* with a biographical *feuilleton* on the composer. It called for freedom of opinion in questions of art and defined the opera as "*un mostruoso aborto dell'ingegno umano.*" Other critics voiced their opposition to Wagner with cries of "*Viva Verdi! Viva Rossini!*" before rehearsals had even started.[97] On the first night the theatre was sold out to the last seats in the upper balconies; it was filled with foreign visitors, ambassadors and politicians, among them Marco Minghetti, critics from all over Italy as well as abroad, and experts following the performance with the score on their knees. Enrico Panzacchi recorded his impression of the first performance:

> The theatre clock points exactly to eight: in the hall there is immediately a silence as of the tomb. And look, Angelo Mariani has climbed on to his conductor's podium; slowly turns his handsome head to left and right; nods to Camillo Casarini with a calm smile, who responds from his mayor's box with a nervous smile; enters into the prelude with the orchestra ... A choir of angels slowly descends from the heavens and

restores to earth the miraculous chalice in which the Saviour blessed the wine during the last supper with the Apostles.[98]

The account reveals the tension in the theatre, the mystical atmosphere created by the staging and the extent to which the musical event was perceived as a cultural challenge of political significance. When Lohengrin entered with the swan people rose in their seats, overcome by the enchanting power of the music and the visual effects of the scenery. Concluding the last chord, Mariani "throws back his leonine head, turns round—pale and deeply moved, but with a smile on his lips. Then he thanks the audience for its approval." At this point Casarini had won his battle. After the powerful effect of the opening the performance developed into a celebration of Wagner and his music, creating an extraordinary, almost sacred atmosphere in the theatre.

Referring to Wagner's famous article "*Zukunftsmusik*," Panzacchi compared Bologna's debates on the composer explicitly with the eighteenth-century battles between *Gluckisti* and *Piccinisti*.[99] Baudelaire explored the same argument in his review "*Tannhäuser* in Paris," calling Wagner "the consolidator of an old idea."[100] The eighteenth-century debate was perceived as a dispute about national character, even if the German Gluck stood here for France, while Piccini represented Italy.[101] Wagner's concept of *Gesamtkunstwerk* was perceived to be of similar revolutionary importance for the history of musical drama as Gluck's reforms a century earlier. In the battles between *Piccinisti* and *Gluckisti*, Bologna had supported Gluck. Piccini triumphed in Paris, but was soon forgotten. Would Bologna, with its Wagnerism, set again on the right card?

On the day of the *prima* the box office made a surplus of more than 6000 Lire, which was considered an extraordinary result; and this financial success continued through the whole run, making it difficult to present economic arguments against Casarini's theatre policy.[102] Hans von Bülow attended one evening and even Verdi came incognito to one of the last performances. Enthusiastic letters reached Wagner, including letters from the chorus and the orchestra.[103] Often in the past overshadowed by Florence, Bologna was now in a position to export its culture to the Tuscan capital. The entire production, including sets, cast and orchestra, was transferred to the Teatro Pagliano, known today as Teatro Verdi, and welcomed on its arrival at the station by the National Guard.[104]

Panzacchi supported Wagner, in spite of the fact that he disliked his anti-Semitism and his attitude of constantly passing judgement on the work of others.[105] He considered Wagner's work the most important innovation in music since Monteverdi.[106] *Il Monitore*, always a strong supporter of Mariani but initially in the anti-Wagnerian camp, admired the magnificence of the *Lohengrin* staging as well as the excellent preparation of orchestra, choruses and cast: "Anybody who has travelled the world," it wrote, "will admit that one could not expect more."[107] Disapproving of the opera's long recitatives, without rhythmic structure or melody, the newspaper emphasized the numerous connections between Wagner and the traditional school of opera, seeing the future in a fusion of the styles of Mozart, Wagner and Rossini, Gounod, Meyerbeer and Verdi, considered to be the most innovative composers of the modern age. Sangiorgio did not consider himself a Wagnerian, but acknowledged in his journal L'Arpa the audience's responsiveness to the music's "supernatural effects," in particular during the first scene and the Vorspiel to the third act. He perceived a difference between the universal language of Italian music, speaking immediately to the soul, and Wagner's music, requiring an additional intellectual effort in order to be comprehensible. He considered Wagner's complex symphonic structures, which the listener could only grasp through reason, to be an expression of Germany's positivist science. But this made his music revolutionary, in contrast to Italian convention. He refers to certain parts of Lohengrin as "innegabilmente bello," but misses melodic elaboration. Wagner "satisfies the thinker's brain but does not always deliver for the heart."[108] To a large extent comments concentrated on the narrative elements of the passionately presented story. When Lohengrin exclaimed "Elsa io t'amo!" the audience was enthused. However, "Wagner was wrong" when the violins take the lead in the duet between Ortrud and Elsa, because "the melisma of the human voice should always stand out from the other musical elements."[109] The vocal narrative is what matters, not individual psychology expressed by means of absolute music.

Hence, the extraordinary success of the premiere did not put an end to the debate. Certain commentators spoke of "musica da matti"[110] and a correspondent from Naples could not understand why Bologna performed the works of a man who hated Rossini, Bellini, Donizetti and whom he considered the greatest enemy of Italian music.[111] The influential critic Torelli-Viollier compared Bologna's audience to "an enormous oistrich, for whom everything is good; who swallows everything—whether a stone or a doughnut—whose indefaticable stomach digests anything— . . . even Wagner's Lohengrin."[112] For Bologna anything would be good as long as it was new. The Gazzetta dell'Emilia expressed its worries about the adverse effect upon European music as a whole. Wagner represented a particular German problem, reflecting the late development of a specific German genre, which had nothing to do with what was going on in other countries: "Wagner has written, first and for all, for Germany, rather than for Italy," the paper wrote. "And I do not think Wagner himself desired or asked for a performance of Lohengrin at our principal theatre." Why then were Italians getting so excited about him?[113] For Bottrigari the preference for German operas was nothing more than a fashion, motivated by the ambition to show that Bologna, came second only to Paris in staging these works. He resented the fact that the local councillors, and also Mariani supported the performance of foreign music at Bologna's principal theatre. Mariani, he complained, no longer knew how to conduct Rossini, Bellini and Donizetti.[114] The debate over Lohengrin shows that Italian anti-Wagnerism was very different from the opposition against the composer for instance in Munich, where the Church, the bureaucracy and important sections of the middle class pointed to the "immoral" content of his operas, to the composer's adulterous and extravagant lifestyle and his attempts to meddle in Bavarian politics.[115] These issues did not seem to play any role in Bologna.

WAGNER AND THE LEFT

Bologna's *Lohengrin* was undoubtedly the brainchild of Casarini's Democratic administration. On what grounds did Bologna's Left support the performance of Wagner? How were the Risorgimento traditions compatible with the internationalisation (and "Germanisation") of the Comunale's repertoire? According to the historian Emilio Gentile a "variety of nationalisms" emerged in Italy from the beginning of the nineteenth century. Italy's "modernist nationalism" of the early twentieth century, associated mostly with futurism in the arts, originated aesthetically from "cosmopolitan nationalism," which permeated Italian culture during the *fine secolo*.[116] The opening of Bologna's theatre towards the European repertoire can be read in this key, as a conscious commitment to what was perceived as aesthetic progress, going hand-in-hand with the modernising ideology of nationalism. Everywhere in Europe the followers of Wagner saw themselves as an avant-garde, as "an intellectual cadre supporting works that it claimed were progressive and, by definition, controversial."[117] Moreover, the Democratic and Radical middle class in Italy still considered Wagner the composer of the 1848 barricades, a personal friend of the Russian Anarchist Bakunin and a former political refugee in Switzerland and France. Of *Lohengrin* the local press maintained that Wagner had composed the opera during his exile. As a matter of fact the work was completed in April 1848 and the warrant for his arrest was issued more than a year later, in May 1849.[118] However, the myth surrounding the work's completion appealed to those protagonists of Bologna's Risorgimento who themselves had spent years in exile.[119] At least verbally Wagner continued to identify with the peoples' spring of 1848, even after the Unification of Germany. Meanwhile, the Italian Left "welcomed Bismarck as an anticlerical and exponent of state socialism."[120] The Democrats understood the revolution of 1848 as a crucial stage in the history of the Risorgimento, at a time when the government still tended to minimise its contribution to the nation's Unification. The local Wagner Society in Bologna was largely made up from the Democratic middle class rather than the Moderate aristocracy, which dominated most of the city's cultural associations.[121] Parts of the local Party of Action maintained close contacts with Bakunin, whom Wagner himself compared to his Siegfried.[122] Among the most influential supporters of Wagner in Italy was Giosuè Carducci, at the time still a convinced Republican with close contacts to the anarchists in the Romagna.[123] Of particular interest also to Bologna's Democratic middle class was Wagner's *Rienzi*, performed there in 1876 and read in an anti-clerical key and as a popular attempt to break aristocratic hegemony. This Democratic and even Socialist reading remained an important constituent of Italian Wagnerism. In the 1890s Bologna's *Cronaca Wagneriana* (comparable to the *Revue Wagnerienne* in Paris and *The Meister* in London), remembered Wagner as "conspirator of 1848" and friend of Bakunin, who had lived the straitened existence of a political refugee in Switzerland. During that time, so the paper, the composer "familiarised himself with the socialist theories of Proudhon and Saint-Simon" and wrote for popular periodicals.[124] Comparing Wagner to Zola, icon of the *"artiste engagé,"* the *Cronaca Wagneriana* reported the Frenchman's conviction that no composer could ever write greater music than Wagner.[125] The Italian contextualisation of Wagner corresponds to the general European reception of his work. Zola's praise was shared by Mallarmé and recalls Baudelaire's impressions in the famous article "Richard Wagner and *Tannhäuser* in Paris" or Dorian Gray's reaction in Oscar Wilde's work.[126] The political sympathies of Hans von Bülow contributed to the association between Wagner and the Left. Bülow was not only the most important conductor of Wagner, but also the composer of the "Bundeslied" for Lassalle's German workers' party.[127] Jaurès praised Wagner as a "communist" and "some of the early Soviet Wagner stagings were among the most radical Soviet opera productions of the time." In this context it comes as no surprise that Gramsci confirmed the Left's appreciation of Wagner.[128] Arturo Frizzi's popular *"Galleria di famiglia socialista"* presents Wagner along with portraits of Hugo, De Amicis and Zola, as well as Marx, Lenin, Bissolati, Turati, Trotzky and Jaurès.[129]

The Italian Left engaged also with Wagner's theoretical writings, which until the 1870s were better known than his music.[130] Historically, Wagner's project for a reform of the theatre, dating back to 1848, could be linked to the idea of *"un buon Teatro Nazionale"* serving *"l'educazione del popolo,"* which had played an important role during Italy's Napoleonic period, when for instance Bologna's *Teatro Marsigli* changed its name to *Teatro Civico*.[131] Mazzini's *Filosofia della musica* (1836) anticipated in many ways Wagner's later writings, criticising Italian opera for having lost its "social mission" and for being reduced to "mere formula."[132] Sangiorgio's *Arpa* referred to the proximity of Wagner's and Mazzini's ideas: rejecting the Italian stress on melody as expression of an "egoistic individualism," Mazzini wanted to revolutionise opera through the "integration of the different arts," by "identifying the main characters through musical themes" and "by using the chorus as an independent actor."[133] Much of this can be found in Wagner.

Disillusioned with Italy's musical institutions and the state of culture after Unification, the Milanese *scapigliati* movement, which is discussed later in this chapter, sympathised with Wagner's analysis. Most of them were Mazzinian Republicans.[134] Considering this context, it is not surprising that D'Annunzio, as the country's most prominent nationalist intellectual associated with the avant-garde, showed a strong interest in Wagner,

approving in particular the idea of "art as a direct reflection of the people's will," again a concept not far from Mazzini's *Philosophy of Music.*
Writing in *La Tribuna* and a number of other newspapers, from 1892
D'Annunzio defended Wagner against Nietzsche's famous pamphlet, and
showed his contempt for Italy's *Giovine Scuola.* In 1898 he came to Bologna to attend the symphonic concerts with extracts from Wagner's works,
but about this time he had a change of mind, now claiming that Italian
music was superior to anything Wagner had ever written and praising on
the pages of *Figaro* the Italian origins of paleo-Christian music and the
melodic culture of the *race latine.* Nevertheless, particularly through his
novels *Trionfo della Morte* (1894) and *Il Fuoco* (1898) D'Annuzio had an
important impact on Wagnerism in Italy. The strata of Italian society he
reached included mostly the advocates of an anti-egalitarian and authoritarian nationalism.[135]

EUROPE, THE MODERN AND THE FUTURE

Even after the eighteenth-century *"querelle des anciens et des modernes"*
and Baudelaire's famous article on Constantin Guy and *"la vie moderne"*
Europeans hardly used the term modernism in aesthetic debate and it was
Rubén Darío who introduced the concept in Latin America in 1888.[136] The
term used almost exclusively in Italy was *futuro*; as an aesthetic concept it
emerged from the debate about Wagner. Beyond references to various fictitious (socialist or anarchist) Wagners the Italian debate on the composer is
characteristic of a society marked by social transition and cultural change.
It reflects the search for a response to the experience of modernity in aesthetic modernism, as demonstrated by an article on *Lohengrin*, published
two days before the opera's premiere in the *Gazzetta:* "It is beyond doubt
that our epoch is characterised by the fermentation of ideas, of battles
between the most disparate principles—an epoch of transition, what con-
ducts us straight to the great question, which is if reaction will prevail or if
progress reaches apotheosis."[137]

The future, in the form of *"musica del futuro,"* became the key to inter-
pret the modern present. Baudelaire called "music of the future" an expression "as inexact as it is currently heard on all sides"; the same could be
said concerning the use of the concept in Bologna, but it nevertheless had
a determining impact on intellectual debate.[138] "Music of the future" stood
for the opposite of everything the *"esclusivisti* of the music of the past"
referred to.[139] While most of the press analysed the conflict about Wagner
in terms of nationality, the *Gazzetta dell'Emilia* referred explicitly to the
"modern school" in opposition to tradition.[140] This was not a conflict about
the music of a particular country or one particular composer, who claimed
that his music was the future, but about the concept of aesthetic progress
itself and about the question whether the idea of progress and future could

be associated with music.[141] Ultimately, the question was whether there was a legitimate place in Italian society for a philosophy of history in the Hegelian sense. Wagner stood for a modernist aesthetic response to the modern experience of time. This modernity was perceived as a European phenomenon. Associating Italian interest in German music with aesthetic progress does not mean to subscribe to a germanocentric view on the history of music, as criticised for instance by the Czech musicologist Vladimir Karbusicky.[142] Instead, it is a reflection upon a historical debate; and contemporaries in Italy used similar arguments to defend French repertoire on Italian stages.

For Casarini and the Democrats the nation's cosmopolitan opening was part of a political project to overcome Italy's "intellectual isolationism." Rejecting the idea that Italians had much to learn "from foreigners," the *Rivista Bolognese di Scienze, Lettere, Arti e Scuole* maintained in 1867 that Italy should focus on "its own genius, its institutions, its rich history."[143] However, the following year, in 1868, the musical correspondent of the *Rivista* compared Italian theatres to those in Germany, America and in Paris, despairing about Italy's narrow focus on Verdi, Donizetti and Bellini. A few issues later the same periodical claimed that the listener thirsts "for new things, new combinations, wishing to hear strong and innovative counterpoints, to be moved by original and unexpected melodramatic moments," words that resemble Baudelaire's and Wagner's writings on music and modern aesthetics.[144] A year after the *Lohengrin* premiere the Italian parliament discussed the state of the country's music schools, with certain deputies voicing their concern about the presumed dominance of German innovation over Italian tradition. Replying, Casarini denounced Italy's "ecstatic state of contemplative isolationism" in everything regarding music. In his view Italy was out of step with the general progress of modern times. With reference to the "*italianissimi* Rossini and Verdi," he maintained that Italy's musical genius had always been inspired by contacts with ideas from abroad. Should one really deprive Italian students and audiences of Meyerbeer, Beethoven, Gounod or Mozart? Of Haydn's and Händel's oratorios?[145]

UNCERTAINTIES

Bologna's musical springtime came to an abrupt and dramatic end in February 1872. Casarini had pursued his projects without increasing the price of tickets, absorbing a considerable portion of the municipal budget for the city's cultural self-representation.[146] From early on the council had criticised that the municipal budget privileged "certain arts and industry." Councillor Osima wondered if Bologna really needed to take a lead in international opera life. Other opponents of Casarini's policy compared the expenditure for the theatre with that for hospitals and public education. If the wealthy parts of the citizenship and local business really had an interest in opera and saw an economic advantage in the existence of a theatre, they should participate in a public subscription which would allow them to run the theatre out of their own means.[147] Casarini's *giunta* resigned as a consequence of the fraud scandal discussed in Chapter 3, but also due to a sudden deficit in the municipal budget, which had been produced by his investment in the fabric of the theatre and the expenditure for the 1871 autumn season, which went 17,400 Lire beyond the agreed subsidies.[148] How did this happen, considering that *Lohengrin* had been a great success?

Keen to impress with splendid performances, Casarini made all necessary funds available to achieve them, in terms of quality of staging and performers. The cost could not be recuperated by the box office. As a consequence, the theatre had been insolvent since Meyerbeer's *Dinorah*, only the first of three works on the programme of the 1870 autumn season.[149] The carnival balls, but also the remaining operas of the autumn, Verdi's *La forza del destino* and *Macbeth*, were expected to bring financial recovery. From the start of the following season, 1871, Casarini had repeatedly granted the *impresario* advances of several thousand Lire, which did not even cover the daily expenditure for the musicians engaged in Gounod's *Faust,* the work preceding *Lohengrin* in the season's programme. While the mayor was in Munich, his *assessore* passed a further 8000 Lire to the theatre. The administration spent a total of 24,000 Lire beyond the agreed subsidy, of which only 7000 were covered by the *impresario*'s deposit. Even the success of *Lohengrin* could not make up the difference of 17,000 Lire. From a financial point of view the theatre should have been closed, which was not uncommon for Italian theatres. But for Casarini this was not an option. The city's cultural representation was at the core of his political programme for a civic reawakening. Due to the grandeur of his plans with their cosmopolitan and modernist profile, mistakes in the financial management became a natural point of attack for his conservative critics. Casarini carried his programme through, hoping that the spectacular effect of an Italian staging of Wagner would save the situation both financially and morally. Whether his expenditure was unreasonable remains debatable. While Bianca Blume, the first Italian Elsa, received 5000 Lire for the entire season, Teresa Stolz, at La Scala, received 43,000 Lire for a similar period.[150]

Casarini continued to be seen as an expert in cultural policy after his resignation and the return of a Moderate *giunta,* a reputation that extended well beyond Bologna's city walls. As an elected member of the council he had been in charge of the theatre since 1865 and it was largely due to his initiative that after years of debate the restoration of the Comunale had been completed. As founder of the local *Società Nazionale* and a member of the region's provisional government after the departure of the cardinal, he was widely respected well beyond the Democratic milieu. Moreover, a number of local Moderates started questioning the savings policy imposed by their own administrations and were concerned about the role the Italian cities should assume within the new *patria*.[151] While the returning Moderate *giunta* at first cancelled the theatre's subsidy, those councillors in favour of an active cultural policy were able to mobilise a lobby outside the council. After five months of public debate on the issue and considerable criticism of the Moderates' economizing policy in the press the council reversed its decision and renewed the subsidy.[152] Rossini, Bellini and Wagner were programmed for the next season. The council was determined to follow the cultural emphasis of the past years, trying to maintain Bologna's distinctive profile among the peninsula's major opera houses, Milan, Naples and Venice.[153] Milan presented its first opera by Wagner two years after Bologna, in 1873, Naples in 1881 (both *Lohengrin*). Venice staged *Rienzi* in 1874 and its first *Lohengrin* in 1881.[154] Bologna on the contrary presented a Wagner opera twenty-three times between 1871 and 1914, while Verdi appeared only twelve times on the programme. Bellini, Donizetti and Rossini were given only a total of eleven times during this period.[155] *Lohengrin* became the most frequent opera on the schedule, well ahead of *La Traviata* and with *Tristan* following in third place.[156]

Bologna's second Wagner was *Tannhäuser,* performed a year after *Lohengrin* in 1872. During the first night protests and whistling came to a head during the third act, when a desperate Elizabeth fainted under screams of "*Viva* Rossini! *Morte a* Wagner!," bringing Tannhäuser's narration after his return from Rome to an abrupt end.[157] Rubbiani, in the Catholic *L'Ancora*, commented that this is "a mad story of the middle ages mixing historical and fictitious characters . . . ; the usual confusion of periods." He was convinced that after this fiasco the work would be "buried for ever" and that Bologna would finally "remain Italian. . . . One cannot impose the aesthetic sentiment of German art on the Italian people."[158] He was wrong. The scandal only further increased the interest in the work. Panzacchi, in a series of letters to the press, publicized the fact that after the second evening the anti-Wagnerians had abandoned the theatre, allowing the audience to appreciate and applaud the work. In fact, after only eight performances the box office had made more money with *Tannhäuser* than with Rossini's *Mosè* the previous month.[159] While the prominent Milanese critic Filippo Filippi insisted that Wagner's music required an "educated audience," Panzacchi maintained that in Bologna, unlike elsewhere, this was indeed the case.[160] Rejecting the idea of a pro-German plot of the cultural-political elites against Italian audiences, he claimed that in order to maintain the theatre's fame and to attract new audiences, Bologna could not afford just duplicating the programmes of previous seasons or of other leading theatres.[161]

Not only political and aesthetic reasons influenced the local debate on Wagner; commercial considerations also played a role. The director of the Catholic *Ancora* had himself presented a programme for the *impresa* of the Comunale, which included *Tannhäuser*,[162] a work easily presented as a Christian-Catholic opera. The fact that the administration favoured Scalaberni's project was reason enough to attack the staging of *Tannhäuser* with the usual polemics against German art. Commercial considerations were also behind the strong anti-Wagnerian position of Ricordi's *Gazzetta musicale di Milano*. In 1861 Ricordi refused Wagner a contract for the publication of his works in Italy, causing him to turn to Giovannina Lucca, who rather unexpectedly enjoyed a commercial success with the German composer and became a major figure in Bayreuth circles. Obviously, Ricordi's *Gazzetta* had no interest in writing favourably about Wagner, even if this dislike was expressed through references to *italianità* and loyalty to Verdi, which contributed to the 1873 fiasco of *Lohengrin* at La Scala.[163] Subsequently, very much to Ricordi's satisfaction, La Scala did not put any Wagner on until 1889.[164] During that time the Comunale produced *Rienzi* in 1876, *Holländer* the following year, its first complete *Ring* in 1883 and *Tristan* in 1888. Then Ricordi bought the publisher Lucca and his attitude toward Wagner's work began to change.[165]

THE SEARCH FOR AN ITALIAN WAGNER

But was there an Italian Wagner—a composer who would put an end to the "national" polarization of the debate? In November 1873 the premiere of Stefano Gobatti's opera *I Goti* was encored continuously and got fifty-one curtains at the Comunale, probably the greatest success of any opera in the history of Italian theatre. For weeks after every performance, the composer was accompanied home by a cheerful parade of enthusiasts and the city walls were plastered with sonnets in praise of his celebrated talent.[166] Soon after, the opera was repeated at La Scala, in Turin, Genoa, Parma, at the Pergola in Florence and the Apollo in Rome, as well as in smaller theatres. From modest social origins in the Romagna, taught by Lauro Rossi in Milan and Giuseppe Busi at Bologna's Liceo Musicale, the young composer was recognised by Casarini, Golinelli and Panzacchi as well as by Anton Rubinstein as a Wagnerian genius. Carducci described the evening of the first performance as the beginning of a new future for Italian music, the end of the long crisis of Italian opera. The king bestowed a knighthood upon Gobatti, he became a member of the Accademia Filarmonica and Bologna's council awarded him honorary citizenship, placing him alongside Verdi and Wagner, before anyone even knew who he was.[167] But in Rome *I Goti* failed to convince the critics and musical circles in Milan were sceptical about the sudden success of the previously unknown composer, with Verdi calling *I Goti* "the most monstrous musical miscarriage ever produced."[168] The press started to speak about the "*caso* Gobatti," a reaction perceived by many Bolognesi as a humiliating reflection on their musical judgement. His next work, *Luce*, clearly failed to live up to the public expectations and by now the composer divided the press in just the same way as Wagner did. Count Salina defended *Luce* as a work written for the purpose of entertainment, but in fifty-three

Figure 9.2   Stefano Gobatti, 1873. (Reproduction by Kind Permission of Pàtron editore.)

complaints to the mayor the box owners deemed the season's *spettacolo* "neither heroic nor *regio* or *grandioso*." Refusing to pay their annual fee, they caused the theatre a financial loss of nearly 13,000 Lire.[169]

It was difficult, however, to convince the composer of his limitations and the administration itself also still hoped for his come-back. *Cordelia* in

1881 was an even greater fiasco. In 1886 Gobatti conducted a concert of his works at the Comunale and hoped to save the fate of *I Goti* by approaching a French playwright with the suggestion for a translation of his first opera. When Milan's Teatro Dal Verme presented a revised version of *I Goti* the musicians refused to play the work, but in 1898, twenty-five years after the opera's first success, Gobatti presented the work once more at Bologna's Politeama D'Azeglio, without making it into the repertoire. In March 1912 Giacomo Puccini joined a local campaign in favour of Gobatti's last opera, *Massias,* but the project was aborted before the score had been completed. Gobatti never gave up and lived over the decades as a singing teacher for the local primary schools, later playing the organ at the famous Santuario della Madonna di San Luca.[170] He died poor, disillusioned and mentally deranged in December 1913, a few days before Bologna's Italian premiere of *Parsifal.* As the obituaries suggest, Bologna had never abandoned the hope of presenting the nation with an Italian Wagner, but in vain.

The city demonstrated much better instincts with its campaign for Arrigo Boito's *Mefistofele,* after the opera's 1868 failure in Milan. Reviving the opera in 1875 was certainly a controversial decision and in many ways a political statement. Thereafter Boito played an important role in Bologna's musical life, not just because of the local popularity of *Mefistofele*—programmed six times by the Comunale up to 1920—but also through Boito's collaboration with Luigi Mancinelli and events such as the International Exhibition of 1888. Together with the writers Emilio Praga and Antonio Ghislanzoni, and the composer Franco Faccio, Boito formed the core of the so-called *scapigliati* group, the "dishevelled" or "unkempt heads," who cultivated a strong sense of generational identity. Rejecting academic tradition and subscribing to the spirit of Nietzsche, their collective projects of symbolist poetry, theatre and music enlivened the intellectual and artistic scene in post-Risorgimental Italy. They shared Baudelaire's interest in experimenting with hashish, under the influence of which they read *Les fleurs du mal* together.[171] In 1866 Faccio and Boito had volunteered under Garibaldi and politically they were rooted in the Risorgimento's Party of Action, combining nationalist with socialist ideas, despite their elitist attitude. By the time of Boito's success in Bologna the group's youthful radicalism had calmed down, but their names still stood for innovation and experiment.

According to his own writings, Boito "enjoyed fighting with the audience, . . . fighting for progress and for the future of the arts."[172] In his theoretical writings he tried to create a symbiosis which many considered impossible—bringing together Wagner, whose theoretical works he translated into Italian, and Verdi, with whom he worked for thirty-seven years, from the *Inno delle nazioni,* performed in 1862 at Her Majesty's Theatre in London, until the completion of *Quattro pezzi sacri* in 1898. His concept of a "new melodrama" was intended as a response to the crisis of Italian music after Unification, overcoming the banality of the *usé* and meeting the aesthetic objectives set out in Wagner's theoretical writings. Boito expressed his belief in musical progress as well as his boredom with the continuous repetition of the same repertoire in Italy's principal opera houses.[173] However, later he seemingly embraced Nietzsche's critique of Wagner, referring to the composer as *"un falso apostolo."*[174] Boito's aesthetic ideas were marked by an extraordinary cosmopolitan ambition, rooted in his own upbringing and his early travelling. Son of a Venetian father and a Polish mother, Boito left Italy together with Faccio at the age of twenty to live in Paris, at the time of the French premiere of *Tannhäuser* and Baudelaire's most influential writings as an art critic. He was introduced to Rossini, Gounod, Auber and later Hector Berlioz; and it was here that he first met Verdi.[175] For eleven years Boito lived in a romantic relationship with Eleonora Duse, with whom he tried to introduce modern stagings of Shakespeare in Italy, before the actress left him for D'Annunzio.[176] Ambitious as a theorist, Boito was less successful in applying his aesthetic principles to his work as a composer: after half a century, he left his second opera *Nerone* incomplete. It was performed posthumously in a revised version by Arturo Toscanini.[177]

Why did Bologna, after the recent failures with the musical experiments of Stefano Gobatti, show an interest in Boito? The *scapigliati's* centre had been Milan, but through the publisher Sommaruga and the Roman newspaper *Nabab* Carducci and Panzacchi were linked to the group and Faccio regularly conducted the Comunale. Martucci also was in contact with the group from an early age.[178] The decision to stage *Mefistofele* was a controversial statement. After the premiere in Milan Bologna's *Monitore* had described the work as *"un mostruoso aborto;"*[179] but once Bologna understood that a revised version of the opera might rescue the composer's reputation and renew the Comunale's fame, the local elites were quick to embrace the opportunity.[180] Although parts of the audience voiced discontent during the first night, Boito was repeatedly applauded and called on stage. For the local connoisseurs *Mefistofele* was a success, in spite of the fact that Verdi still disapproved of the work.[181] The press criticized the staging, costumes, the orchestra's as well as the chorus's performance, but acclaimed the composer, and Erminia Borghi-Mamo in the role of Margherita and Elena.[182] All performances were sold out well in advance and there was widespread interest among critics, musicians and conductors from all over Italy and abroad. Despite animosities between individual critics from different parts of Italy, the *Gazzetta d'Italia* and the *Fanfulla* praised Bologna for its courage in restaging the work. The influential Marquis d'Arcais reported in the pages of *L'Opinione* *"un successo immenso, incontestabile"*; *Il Rinnovamento* from Venice wrote about *"entusiasmi trionfali"*; and even Milan praised Bologna's performance as the work's "resurrection."[183] This was the start of the opera's international success, with performances in Rome, Turin, London, Boston, New York, Lisbon, Barcelona, Warsaw, St. Petersburg,

Hamburg, Vienna, Brussels and Madrid, followed by Paris after several years delay.[184]

As could have been expected, the courageous initiative of the cultural elites provoked criticism in the council. De Simonis complained that Bologna had become the laboratory for all kinds of operatic experiments rather than presenting music to the taste of its own citizenry.[185] Instead of sponsoring such controversial works, the administration should consider closing the theatre altogether. However, in contrast with the debate on Wagner, this time the Democrats could not be held responsible. Instead, keen to keep Bologna's theatre in the public eye, the returning Moderate *giunta* decided to maintain Casarini's approach, trying to develop Bologna's reputation as a stage for innovative and challenging works. While the season was not to the mayor's personal taste, "nobody would accept this as a reason for not presenting new operas," as he confessed himself.[186] Count Salina explained the audience's mixed response as a result of the theatre's financial situation, having made it impossible for the *impresa* to pay for better singers and sets. As for the operas by Boito and Dall'Olio he claimed that "no moderately cultured person . . . could fail to recognize the imposing nature of those two works."[187]

Another example of the search for an Italian Wagner was the debate about Alberto Franchetti, a Piedmontese nobleman who had studied in Turin, Venice, Dresden and Munich, and who attempted to blend "national-historic subjects" with Germanic techniques of composing.[188] Bologna played an important role in promoting this unusual composer. His *Asrael* combined themes inspired by *Mefistofele* (hell and heaven) with the geographical setting of *Lohengrin* (medieval Brabant). The opera was premiered in Reggio Emilia in 1888, before coming to the Comunale during same year. Resembling in its dramatic structure Meyerbeer's *grand opéra*, the work is based on a libretto by Ferdinando Fontana, author of Puccini's *Le villi,* who represented an Italian current of interest in Nordic mythology and German fairy-tale plots, known mostly through Catalani's operas. Franchetti's *Cristoforo Colombo,* on a libretto by Luigi Illica, was commissioned by the city of Genoa and premiered under Mancinelli at the Carlo Felice in 1892, followed two years later by presentations at the Teatro Sociale in Treviso and at the Comunale under Toscanini. Bologna's third Franchetti opera, *Germania* (1902), was also based on a libretto by Illica and set during the time of the Napoleonic wars. After the premiere at La Scala with Toscanini and Caruso, *Germania* came to Bologna the same year. In addition to the predominantly non-Italian themes much of Franchetti's music was rooted in Germanic *sinfonismo* and Nordic folk songs. Despite *Colombo*'s focus on Italy's humanist genius and the struggle against the obscurantism of the Church, Franchetti's work could hardly pass as Italian *Nationaloper*. In order to stand out through its repertoire Bologna had to turn to imports from abroad.

FROM AVANT-GARDE TO *LEITKULTUR*[189]

Following a proposal by Casarini, Wagner and Mariani were given honorary citizenship under the returning Moderate administration. Wagner was also elected a member of Bologna's Accademia Filarmonica, for a long time seen as the bulwark of musical tradition.[190] In 1876 the mayor Tacconi invited Wagner to visit Bologna and to attend a performance of *Rienzi* in celebration of the new citizenship.[191] *Rienzi* was Wagner's most popular opera in Leipzig, but as a French style *grand opéra* it was in many respects the opposite of what the composer stood for in the 1870s. The work was conducted by Marino Mancinelli, who despite his comparative youth had already established himself as one of the greatest Italian Wagner specialists.[192] (A dramatic coincidence, putting the entire enterprise at risk, was that the *impresario* Luigi Scalaberni died on the day of *Rienzi*'s first performance.[193]) The following year Bologna presented *Der Fliegende Holländer*, combined with Bologna's first performance of *Aida* and Donizetti's *La Favorita*, followed by Gustavo Ruiz' new opera *Vallenstein*.[194] Wagner was now established as part of the repertoire and closely identified with Bologna's theatre. A new production of *Lohengrin*, conducted by Luigi Mancinelli in 1882, ran for twenty performances.[195] Wagner's death in 1883 was marked by a performance of *Gotterdämmerung* and a separate *Ring* under the Austro-Hungarian conductor Anton Seidl. Panzacchi spoke at the city's official commemoration for its honorary citizen and Carducci described the music he heard on the occasion to his friend Dafne Gargiolli:

> "Isoldes Liebestod" is for me the most extraordinary music I have ever heard. What greatness, what longing, what stitch for the soul, what holy pain! "Walkürenritt": fantastic, beyond every human creation and at the same time a product of perfect technique. All this is a miracle. Finally, the opening of the *Meistersinger*, a treasure of music, not even to mention *Tannhäuser* . . . !196

Angelo Neumann described Bologna's performance of the *Ring* as a celebration for the *Meister* which went beyond anything he had ever seen in Germany.[197] Originating from an initiative of Wagner himself, Bologna's *Ring* was preceded by a premiere in Venice, where the composer had died, and was followed by stagings in Rome, Turin and Trieste.[198] The Roman *Vorabend* was attended by the king, while Queen Margherita attended three entire evenings. The Italian railway company supported the event with a 75% reduction on the transport cost for the entire cast.[199] Five years later Bologna celebrated the *Mostra Emiliana* with the Italian premiere of *Tristan*, conducted by Giuseppe Martucci, in the presence of Boito, Catalani, Marchetti, Faccio and the young Toscanini, Carducci and D'Annunzio, the local Wagnerians Panzacchi, Luigi Torchi and Corrado Ricci, the mayor

Alberto Dallolio as well as political representatives from all over Italy and the *crème* of the nation's musical press.[200]

Bologna had established itself as the Italian capital of Wagnerism, with a major influence on Italy's musical life as a whole. Between 1871 and 1893 the *Cronaca Wagneriana* listed a total of 993 performances of Wagner in Italy, including 705 performances of *Lohengrin*. By 1900 the opera had been staged 93 times in Italy, and not only at the Scala (1873) or San Carlo (1881), but also in smaller theatres like Treviso (1885), Piacenza (1889), and Cagliari (1899) and in cities not far from Bologna, like Ferrara (1889) and Modena (1890). Since 1871 Bologna had seen six stagings of Italy's most popular Wagner opera, not only at the Comunale (repeated in 1882, 1887, 1889), but also at the Brunetti (1884, 1891).[201]

The Comunale's profile required first-class conductors. With Marino Mancinelli at the head of the Comunale Bologna had hoped to have appointed a permanent successor for Angelo Mariani. However, during a concert tour to Rio de Janeiro the young conductor committed suicide and the position again became vacant. For a year the Scala's principal director Franco Faccio conducted the season and in 1881 the *giunta* appointed Luigi Mancinelli, Marino's brother, to lead both the theatre and the Liceo, with the aim of offering Bologna's music students the opportunity to gain practical experience at the Comunale.[202] Bologna had known Luigi Mancinelli since 1878 as conductor of the *Concerti Popolari* at the Brunetti (later Teatro Eleonora Duse).[203] Having started his career unexpectedly, replacing a drunken conductor for *Aida,* by the time of his appointment in Bologna he was already an international star. While only two of his own operas, *Isora di Provenza* and *Paolo e Francesca* were presented in Bologna, he became one of the Comunale's most successful conductors.[204] In September 1886 Giuseppe Martucci, aged only thirty, succeeded Luigi Mancinelli at the head of the Liceo and the Cappella di San Petronio. He had been celebrated as pianist, composer and conductor in the major capitals of Europe and his talent had been recognised at a young age by Rubinstein and Liszt. Since his first appointment in Naples he regularly conducted symphonies by Beethoven and Schumann, at the time hardly known to Italian audiences. The admiration for him was linked to the modesty of his origins as son of an impoverished musician from Capua as well as to his relationship to Queen Margherita.[205] Bologna's capacity to attract musicians of Martucci's fame helped the city to maintain its status as a leading centre of musical life in Europe.

FINE SECOLO CRISIS AND THE
PROFESSIONALISATION OF CULTURE

Mancinelli's position as director of the theatre, the Liceo, the Cappella of San Petronio and the *Società del Quartetto* had been criticized as a "musical dictatorship."[206] His appointment had led some councillors to question spending such an important part of the municipal budget on music: in 1882, 105,000 Lire for the Liceo, the municipal band and the theatre.[207] The Extreme Left questioned the financial implications of the city's political emphasis on theatre, weakening the Democrats' position on cultural politics. Quirico Filopanti spoke against the "artificial character" of opera, the exaggerated demands of publishers for the staging of works for which they held the copyright and the ridiculously high number of employees in modern theatres. At the same time he deplored the social conditions of those employees, who as a consequence of the theatre's frequent closure could suddenly lose their incomes.[208] However, Italy's parliamentary revolution of 1876, when the majority changed from the Moderate Right to the Democratic Left, and the government's new emphasis on the cultural construction of the Italian nation encouraged cultural initiatives at the municipal level. Rather than criticizing the city's expenditure, *Il Resto del Carlino* blamed *impresari* and the *deputazione* for making bad use of public money through cheap stagings and bad casts.[209] Italy was hardly in a position to compete with the fees paid to singers abroad and many international stars refused to work under the poor conditions of Italian opera houses—too few rehearsals in draughty, unheated theatres; too many performances per week; unprepared orchestras; no replacements for leading roles in case of illness.[210] When Mancinelli left Bologna for an international career, it was to a large extent out of discontent about the lack of resources. Covent Garden, where he conducted the premieres of *Otello* and *Falstaff, Cavalleria rusticana* and *Tosca*, as well as most of Wagner's works, operated on a different scale.[211] For the rest of his career he appeared mostly in New York, Buenos Aires and Rio de Janeiro, visiting Italy only occasionally for a few spectacular premiers. Due to the limits of its subsidies, the Comunale was in a difficult situation compared to other theatres, where the grants were approved for periods between three and five years, allowing the *impresari* to make better use of their budget, employing famous singers for longer periods and under better conditions.[212]

Considering these circumstances, did Italian opera ever overcome its post-Unification crisis? While according to Panzacchi the success of Verdi's *Aida*, Boito's *Mefistofele* and Ponchielli's *Gioconda* demonstrated that Italian composers did not have to fear international competition, others were convinced that the high season of opera had come to an end: "There are not many valuable composers in Italy or indeed anywhere; and since Verdi stopped it seems as if any musical genius has vanished," as one of Bologna's mayors remarked.[213] Meanwhile, councillors unhappy with the repertoire of their local theatre were increasingly sidelined in favour of experts. Town councils are "not the place to discuss taste and musical aesthetics; and there is no doubt that we lack competence in this respect," Bologna's mayor Tacconi maintained.[214] Theatre "is not just a question of entertainment . . . but of art," Dallolio explained. Bologna had started "a revolution in music" which according to the responsible *assessore* influenced Italy as a whole. "The history of theatre will certainly register this event as a glorious achievement. Bologna occupies a position in the arts which has to be maintained," irrespective of the taste of individual councillors.[215]

In 1885 the international reputation of Bologna's orchestra was acknowledged through an invitation to the world fair in Antwerp.[216] Another sign of public recognition was Luigi Mancinelli's nomination as "Officer of the Crown of Italy" the same year.[217] Boito, closely associated with Bologna's theatre, was honoured with a special performance of his *Mefistofele* at the Hofoper in Vienna.[218] Bologna's autumn season started with the great success of another work qualified as "Wagnerian," *La Regina di Saba* by Karl Goldmark, followed by Puccini's *Le Villi*, *La Traviata* and Meyerbeer's *Dinorah*. *Il Resto del Carlino* remarked upon the German and French influences on Puccini's first opera, praising his departures from the Italian tradition.[219] Goldmark's *Regina di Saba* was deserted by *"le signore"* in the private boxes, but welcomed by a crowded *parterre*.[220] *Il Resto del Carlino* explicitly supported the modern turn in Bologna's musical life:

> In recent years opera has made impressive progress and the younger generation was happy to welcome the works of Thomas, Boito, Wagner, Massenet, Goldmark, in short the works of the Moderns. They combine grandeur with the aim of escaping old, conventional and stale forms.[221]

The 1880s were also marked by the triumph of Sarah Bernhardt on the Bologna stage and by an interest in naturalism, realism and Verga's *verismo*.[222] While social realism in literature "greatly increased public awareness of social issues," the poet of idealist classicism, Carducci, opposed these modernist tendencies.[223] And although he was among the first to contribute to a subscription supporting Zola during the Dreyfus affair,[224] he had only contempt for the writer's literary success in Italy. For Carducci these modern trends in literature were the aesthetic counterpart to the positivism which prevailed among the bourgeoisie, a sign of its decadence and the end of any hopes in Mazzini's *"terza Italia,"* the resurgence of Italy to the greatness of Ancient Rome. Despite his role in Italy's literary and aesthetic debates since the 1860s, Carducci's polemical arguments were powerless when confronted with the preferences of the new middle class. Rejecting his idealist classicism, aesthetic positions were no longer perceived as independent of historical context, but as an expression of the historical situation. Carducci had become a poet of another epoch, of another Italy.[225]

> *Imbeciles!* . . . What rubbish to tell us stories about what we do and see every day! Isn't that boring enough? . . . Run, fat citizens of Bologna, run noble ladies; run to hear Mademoiselle Bernhardt tonight! It is the end of everything, both high and popular art! The bourgeoisie, which prides itself with having killed the epic with the novel, tragedy with melodrama, is itself now dying, dying with the operettas of Offenbach. Advance, positivist democracy, American realism. No more theatre,

but spectacle; no more drama, but the assise court; no more art, but production.[226]

The Socialist *Critica Sociale* complained about the bourgeoisie's decadent preference for the pleasures of the French-style Café-Concert.[227] The escapism associated with these new forms of commercialised entertainment as well as the general intellectual and aesthetic opening towards wider European trends of debate in the arts went hand in hand with a sense of disillusionment regarding the content and significance of Italy's cultural identity. Since the expectations associated with the Risorgimento had not been fulfilled, the Italian nation seemed to have little to offer, even in the field of music and theatre. As Francesco d'Arcais bemoaned in an obituary for Amilcare Ponchielli, Italy's young composers were interested exclusively in eclecticism. They had lost the sense for what Italian music was all about: melodic invention. Looking for recipes abroad, they were enthused by European modernism. Regarding its relationship to the "foreign" schools he wrote "Italy gives little and takes much . . . , a servant and slave of other peoples."[228] Franco Faccio, who had been associated with Garibaldi and the Risorgimento, returned to Bologna, but to conduct a French classic, Bizet's *Les pêcheurs de perles*, and Wagner's *Tristan*. Was there a solution to this crisis of Italian music? Deploring the "decline of musical culture," Enrico Panzacchi suggested raising the nation's consciousness of its own musical heritage through the teaching of and research into the history of music. A new musical historicism should inspire Italy's intellectual and cultural reawakening.[229]

MUSICAL HISTORICISM

Bologna's interest in the historical repertoire followed developments that elsewhere in Europe had started several decades earlier. As William Weber has demonstrated, since 1850 over 60% of the Leipzig Gewandhaus repertoire and 90% of the music played by the orchestra of the Paris Conservatoire was written by composers who were no longer alive. Vienna had reached a figure of 75% as early as 1827, the year of Beethoven's death. From the 1870s 80% of the London Philharmonic Society's repertoire was by composers who had already died. All over Europe symphony concerts became "musical museums." As in the case of Bologna's *Concerti Popolari*, this phenomenon was linked to a new musical "middle-class culture."[230] However, in Italy this trend started later than in the rest of Europe, partly due to the focus of musical life on opera and the weakness of a proper symphonic tradition. Italy lacked the necessary orchestral infrastructure and the respective emphasis in musical education. Due to the same circumstances Italian cities had not seen the same expansion of concert halls and audiences as cities like Vienna, Paris, London or Leipzig.

Italy of course had not always concentrated so exclusively on operatic music. Until the eighteenth century musicians from all over Europe came to Italy to study the rules of harmony and counterpoint. At the time when the young Mozart visited Padre Giovanni Battista Martini in Bologna, the Accademia Filarmonica was a centre of Europe's musical life. However, the rise of opera in Italy during the second half of the eighteenth century coincided with the decline of sacred and instrumental music. Religious orders, which had played an important role in sponsoring sacred music were dissolved; most churches were unable to maintain choruses and *castrati*. Not even the Sistine Chapel in Rome was in a position regularly to provide music for services. In Venice, Naples and elsewhere the famous musical orphanages were closed. Italian composers of instrumental music mostly worked abroad: Cherubini in France, Boccherini in Spain, Viotti and Clementi in England. One of the consequences of this decline was the shortage of good viola and cello players, as Rossini and later Verdi remarked.[231] Italian composers continued writing sacred music, but the best musicians and composers made a better living by working for the opera. Clerics like Padre Stanislao Mattei continued to teach at Bologna's Liceo Musicale, but his best students, Rossini and Donizetti, became famous as composers of operas. Mercadante and Carlo Coccia retired to positions financed by the Church only once their operas had turned unfashionable.[232]

Hence, a condition for the raising of Italy's own historical consciousness in this sphere was the development of a new musical infrastructure and acquaintance with the European symphonic repertoire. In his *Concerti Popolari* Luigi Mancinelli included the Viennese classic, works by Schumann, Brahms, French composers as well as extracts from Wagner's operas. Likewise, Martucci, from his position at the Liceo, introduced Bologna to French, German as well as English and Irish composers.[233] The audience of the *concerti popolari*—which were affordable for almost everyone—accepted this repertoire without preconceptions, which contributed to the popularity of Mancinelli, who was commonly known as *"il buon Gigi."*[234] Meanwhile the Teatro Comunale developed its profile as *Repertoireoper,* concentrating, but not exclusively, on a number of great works which were permanently inscribed in the programmes of European opera houses.[235] Bologna's *bel canto* operas did not disappear from the Comunale's programme, but were "historicised." Bellini's *Puritani* for example figured on the programme for the Mostra Emiliana of 1888, but given that its libretto was by the former mayor Carlo Pepoli (written during his exile in Paris), it was understood as a special reference to the city's history. The beginnings of this new musical culture were often marked by difficulties with the repertoire. The famous violinist Verardi promoted the performance of Beethoven's string quartets at the *Società del Quartetto,* but considered certain movements to be "completely mad" [*musica da matto*], replacing them with extracts from other works by the same composer. For example, he performed as a single work the first three movements of opus

59, number 1, replacing the fourth movement with the last movement of opus 59, number 3.[236] Changes of key, or the fact that the last movement of opus 59, number 1 takes up certain themes of the first movement apparently seemed irrelevant.

Bologna's academic institutions contributed to this historical revival. After studies in Germany, Luigi Torchi taught history and aesthetics of music first in Pesaro, then at Bologna's Liceo. In 1894 he founded the *Rivista musicale italiana* in Turin.[237] Giuseppe Busi, son of the composer Alessandro Busi, researched the local history of sixteenth- and seventeenth-century music and donated an important collection of historical scores to the commune.[238] A major role in the city's musical revival was played by the Accademia Filarmonica, which dated back to the year 1622 and was chaired by influential representatives of the local nobility: from 1860 to 1878 Count Gaetano Zucchini, then until 1887 Marquis Giuseppe Mazzacorati, and from 1903 Count Ferdinando Ranuzzi.[239] The Accademia organised its first *"concerti storici"* with works of Palestrina, Monteverdi, Frescobaldi and the Bolognese Bagnara in 1886.[240] Some of these concerts reconstructed important pages of local history: Monteverdi was involved in a passionate dispute with the conservative Bolognese music theorist Giovanni Maria Artusi, a monk of the order of San Salvatore. In 1599 Monteverdi replied to Artusi's pamphlets against *"la musica moderna,"* "heresy" and "barbarism" with the *Fifth Book of Madrigals,* which was even more radical than his earlier works.[241] The concerts presenting this repertoire were well attended.[242] The academy's musical director Gaetano Gaspari was also the Comunale's *direttore dei cori* (1848–1855), Maestro of San Petronio and librarian of the Liceo Musicale. In 1866 he started a cycle of lectures at the Deputazione di Storia Patria on local medieval and Renaissance music, lasting over several years. He played a major role in editing and printing early music from the vestry of San Petronio, in particular the *policorali* for up to eighteen or twenty voices.[243] Gaspari reconstructed bibliographical information and dates of performances, the origin of musicians, details about salaries and their years of service as organists, chorus masters and trumpeters. Along ecclesiastical and liturgical aspects, his work looked at the social and civic context of this music, contributing to the already widespread interest in the history of Bologna's Communal Age. With pride Gaspari explained that during the sixteenth century Bologna's cathedral counted thirty-six *cantori,* while Milan had only twelve.[244]

On the basis of its historical revival Bologna took the lead in organising Italy's contribution to the 1892 international music exhibition in Vienna. The Italian committee, chaired by the president of Bologna's Wagner Society Count Salina, included delegates from Bologna's Liceo, San Petronio, the Accademia Filarmonica as well as the Academy of Fine Arts.[245] Prior to this, an important forum for ancient music had been the Emilian exhibition of 1888, for which Arrigo Boito coordinated the musical programme. Its emphasis on religious music was not a sign of a political opening towards Bologna's growing political Catholicism. To a large extent religious music meant in fact

Protestant music; and despite the renewed interest in sacred music, San Petronio's once famous Cappella halved in size between 1886 and 1896 and by 1920 it had disappeared. The interest in religious music was connected rather to the medieval revival, and even more to an interest in aesthetic experimentation among the Italian avant-garde.[246] The intellectual circles interested in the historical, religious and symphonic repertoire overlapped to a large extend with the Wagnerians and with those looking for musical innovation. This was not surprising considering that Wagner shared the concerns of the so-called musical idealists.[247] Wagner invented the term "absolute music" to describe a music that was autonomous, a value in itself, a metaphysical experience without narrative function or programme, all of which, as Carl Dahlhaus argues, added up to a "aesthetic paradigm-shift" in the evolution of music during the nineteenth century, for which symphonic music was exemplary.[248] Within the tradition of German romanticism, the rediscovery of early religious music was an important element in this "aesthetic paradigm-shift," pointing toward the parallel between religious and musical contemplation.[249] This connection between religious music and absolute music might explain the absence of anticlerical protest against this aspect of Bologna's musical historicism. Reviving Italy's lost instrumental tradition became a cultural mission for the musical avant-garde, with Mancinelli, Martucci and Boito as its protagonists, who later also included Toscanini and Busoni.

After the performance of Mendelssohn's *Elias* in 1888, Bologna witnessed in 1913 Bach's *St. Matthew Passion*, performed by the Berlin Philharmonic and the Sing-Akademie. After the concert the mayor thanked the musicians in a personal letter expressing his "admiration for the perfect technique, the masterly manner and the admirable blending which distinguished this splendid performance."[250] The concert had been a secular event, featuring Protestant music, but its spiritual content made an impact also on Bologna's political Catholicism. Rubbiani remained "profoundly touched by Bach" and expressed his admiration for the asceticism of his music: "This is not *l'art pour l'art*, but art for religion," he wrote.[251]

Carl Dahlhaus has shown how musical historicism is rooted in the tradition of performance, making historical objectivity almost impossible.[252] The rediscovery of historical music, by audiences, performers as well as composers was part of the modern experience, a historicist modernism that is not necessarily nostalgic or conservative in the traditional sense. While Dahlhaus sees this trend as "an educated fashion among despisers of musical fashion," Bologna's supporters of musical historicism were driven not only by an interest in the documentation of ancient music, but also in its aesthetics as a response to the experience of modernity, aiming "to establish a dialogic relation with tradition." With a particular focus on the study of form and material, Italian modernism sought "to mediate between the necessity of giving formal expression to the sense of alienation and futility of artistic practice," associated with the experience of modernity, "and the desire to recuperate in a critical fashion the cultural tradition."[253] The

enthusiasts of ancient music were mostly those who at the same time introduced Bologna to aesthetic modernism and the European avant-garde.

SOCIALIST INTERNATIONALISM VERSUS
AESTHETIC INTERNATIONALISM

In 1903, at the start of the "popular" government under the Republican
Enrico Golinelli—the first administration of the Left since Casarini—the
theatre's season had to be cancelled due to a financial shortfall.[254] The citizenry was alerted and, by responding to this situation, challenged the traditional structures of Bologna's cultural life. As president of the *Società per
il risveglio della vita cittadina* Prince Hercolani staged a performance of
Francesco Cilea's new opera *Adriana Lecouvreur*.[255] Cilea had been Martucci's best pupil in Naples and the work had been hailed at its premiere
in Milan. The *Società per pubblici divertimenti* proposed Wagner's *Meistersinger*, to be produced in conjunction with a work by the winner of the
Liceo's competition for young composers. Events such as these were aimed
at renewing Bologna's role as the "fulcrum of modern music," but also
to support the local theatre industry.[256] *Die Meistersinger* had never been
presented in Bologna; but considering its current crisis, would the theatre
be able to attract a director capable of conducting the opera? Faccio, who
had conducted the 1889 Italian *prima* in Milan, had died of tertiary syphi-
lis in 1891.[257] Concerned to restore the theatre's fame, the council itself
took charge of the choice of the conductor—either Hans Richter, who had
recently enthused Bologna with a concert of the Berlin Philharmonic, or
Arturo Toscanini. The commune was unable to provide the necessary funds
before 1904, but then it staged the opera with Toscanini, the conductor's
last public appearance in Italy before departing for the United States.[258]

　　Despite financial constraints the council approved 10,000 Lire to celebrate the Liceo's centennial with publications and concerts, explicitly aimed
at attracting visitors from outside Bologna.[259] The *Società del Quartetto* as
well as the *Società di risveglio* contributed 12,000 Lire to fund new instruments and prizes for distinguished students.[260] Toscanini returned, conducting Martucci, Wagner and Verdi, along with Italian premiers by Debussy,
Sibelius, Elgar and Strauss. The international stars taken under contract on
the occasion included Alessandro Bonci and Enrico Caruso, shortly after
his celebrated debut at the Met.[261] Although these events took place under
an administration of the Left and included concerts for as little as 0.75 Lire,
some councillors still rejected them as a "class-based commemoration to
which the working class had not been invited."[262] On cultural issues numerous Socialist councillors voted against their own administration—"because
the arts have to contribute to everybody's education . . . whereas for ordinary people the tickets of the Teatro Comunale are never affordable."[263]
For Zanardi, who later became Bologna's first Socialist mayor, "the theatre

must be accessible not only to the aristocracy, but also to those who dispose of lesser means."[264] When the Republican mayor Golinelli used the theatre to host the 1904 congress of the Italian Socialist Party, his decision led to bitter protests by the box owners.[265] They did not intervene when a few years later the Italian Naval League invited the Nationalist De Martino to speak at the theatre about "*la Somalia Italiana*."[266]

Despite increasing ideological tensions in the council, the popular administration's emphasis on cultural politics was supported by many oppositional Moderates and Catholics. The Republican mayor justified votes based on floating majorities with the view that "in the arts there are no parties."[267] During the first decades after Unification the Moderates had opposed public investment in the city's cultural development; now the Socialists rejected this form of expenditure—one reason for the instability of Golinelli's *giunta*—in spite of the fact that the administration regularly underlined the material benefits of the subsidies for the "numerous proletariat of singers and musicians."[268] The Moderate councillor Luigi Tanari asked why the bourgeoisie should support a subsidy of 6000 Lire for the *Camera di Lavoro*, "which serves the interests of the proletariat," if the Socialists refused to subsidise the theatre, which served the interests of all citizens. In his reply the councillor Sarti declared that

> the Socialist group is not opposed to developing the arts; on the contrary, he and his friends would wish that the arts become even more popular, allowing the people to take part in them. But there is no hiding . . . that the Teatro Comunale, for the way it is built and due to the usual price of its tickets, only serves the rich. The Socialist group is convinced that the arts can be and must be to the benefit of all social classes.[269]

The "popular administration" came to a sudden end after just a few months in office, during the summer of 1904. No major transformation in Bologna's cultural life had taken place and the government delegate who took over the administration temporarily limited his intervention to a review of the Deputazione's internal regulations. A committee, including Toscanini, was set up to review ticket prices.[270] However, the returning Conservative administration reminded the council that "first class performances and popular prices represent two concepts which . . . are absolutely opposed to one another."[271] Plans to increase the Comunale's capacity were rejected on the grounds of the existing theatre's architectural value.[272] In their cultural policies, local administrations continued to rely on artistic prestige, the judgement of cultural experts and on the national or international reputation of stars. Toscanini conducted *Siegfried*, *Madama Butterfly* and Vittorio Gnecchi's controversial *Cassandra*, based on Greek modes, as well as Humperdinck's *Hänsel und Gretel*. The 1911 autumn programme included Dukas' *Arianna e Barbablù*, on a libretto by Maeterlinck, recently performed in Paris, as well as Musorgsky's *Godunov*, criticized as an index of "the decline of our city's musical tradition," but defended by the administration for its "clamorous success with echoes all over Italy."[273] After *Lohengrin* and *Mefistofele*, Gounod's *Faust* was together with *Aida* the work that the Comunale revived most frequently between 1871 and 1922; and between 1901 and 1913 twenty-one Italian operas competed with nineteen "foreign" operas. Bologna's emphasis on the international repertoire had a major impact on Italy as a whole. Even the Teatro Regio in Parma, "sanctuary of the Verdi cult," performed *Lohengrin* five times between 1870 and 1915, as well as a number of other Wagner operas. At La Scala foreign imports outnumbered native composers and Milan's major prose theatres preferred French to Italian works. While occasionally Massenet was able to dominate the repertoire in France, Verdi never came close to a similar position in Italy. Italian culture during the decades around the turn of the century was profoundly cosmopolitan. Contrary to claims emphasising the role of opera in the nationalisation of European society, internationalisation was an important aspect of its aesthetic as well as its commercial success.[274]

With Wagner appearing increasingly even on smaller Italian stages, Bologna had to enhance its profile as the Italian capital of Wagnerism. In 1907 the tablet commemorating the first Italian performance of *Lohengrin* had been replaced by a big inscription in bronze with a marble frame, financed through public subscription and a municipal subsidy of 1000 Lire.[275] The same year the Comunale had restaged *Tristan* under Luigi Mancinelli, combined with the premiere of the conductor's own opera *Paolo e Francesca* and Tchaikovsky's *Iolanta*.[276] While between 1900 and the beginning of World War I the Comunale presented an opera by Verdi five times, with altogether 39 performances, Wagner appeared eleven times on the programme, with a total of 122 performances.[277] Remarkably, it gave an opera by Puccini only twice: *Tosca* in 1900 and *Madama Butterfly* in 1905. Two further stagings of Boito, Humperdinck's *Hänsel und Gretel* and Strauss' *Salome* led the commentators to categorise the programme as "Germanic" and "futurist." Even Berlioz' *Damnation de Faust*, staged in 1906, was considered as belonging to the same category, regardless of Berlioz' own dislike for Wagner.[278]

1914: THE *PARSIFAL* YEAR

The musical correspondent of the *Gazzetta del Popolo* named 1914 "the *Parsifal*-year."[279] Shortly before his death in 1883 Wagner had determined that for thirty years his *Festspielhaus* should have the exclusive right to present the opera, a rule broken only by stagings in London (1884) and New York (1903 performed in German; 1904 in Yiddish).[280] On the earliest permissible occasion, the 1st of January 1914, Bologna vied with Rome to present the first Italian *Parsifal*, a major event in the history of opera in Italy. Bologna got ahead only thanks to the decision to start the performance a few hours earlier, but it was beaten by Barcelona, which opened its *Parsifal* fashioned as a Catalan national opera, at midnight on New Year's Eve, staking its claims as a modern European metropolis. Prague even offered two *Parsifals* on the first of January, one in German, the other in Czech.[281] Comparable only to the efforts made for Casarini's 1871 *Lohengrin*, Bologna undertook major investments to launch the work with the most advanced stage technology, including a new orchestra pit and facilities for polychrome electric lights. Although conservationists and art historians criticized the changes to Bibiena's house, for local politicians a spectacular staging of *Parsifal* presented a priority, aimed at ensuring a broad coverage in the international press. The mayor appointed a special advisory committee for the building works, including again Arturo Toscanini. While some Wagnerians hoped to transform Bibiena's theatre into a Frankish Festspielhaus, a less ambitious version of the original plans was in the end approved. The reallocation of funds within the municipal budget, by direct intervention of the Moderate *giunta* without prior consultation of the council, clearly resembled the financial manoeuvres of the Democrat Casarini for the staging of *Lohengrin*.[282]

The Futurists rejected *Parsifal* for its historical theme as well as its aesthetic techniques. Admirers of Wagner in their early years, by the time of World War One Giovanni Papini and Filippo Tommaso Marinetti shouted "down with Wagner; long live Stravinsky!"[283] However, for Bologna the 1914 *Parsifal* represented an ideal synthesis between cosmopolitan modernism and medieval pride. In a public commemoration for the architect of Bologna's medieval revival, Alfonso Rubbiani, the councillor Rivari interpreted Bologna's enthusiasm for *Parsifal* as showing the extent to which Rubbiani's mission "of disseminating the desire for early medieval beauty" had been successful: "We recently saw the evidence—this great mass of citizens coming together to hear the grave and solemn *Parsifal*. . . . The emotions arising from the music fused with those evoked by our embattled facades and the mullions of the palace."[284]

The medieval imagination of Wagner's last opera was assimilated to the colours and figurative representations of Bologna's medieval architecture and Rubbiani's *Aemelia Ars*. Rubbiani's own devastating rejection of Wagner, forty years earlier, had been forgotten. Again, Bologna read Wagner within its own scheme of interpretation, an assimilation of European modernism, which attempted to come to terms with the city's own experience of modernity, in the specific social, cultural and historical context of post-Risorgimental Bologna as the former capital of the Papal Legations. This contextualisation was not without roots in Wagner's work itself. Bayreuth's original staging of *Parsifal* had been inspired by Italian medieval architecture, or at any rate by the nineteenth-century version of it. Although the opera itself is set in Spain, Paul von Joukowsky's *Gralstempel*, emblem of the greatest Good, reproduced the spatial effect of the Cathedral in Siena,

following Wagner's own idea. Wagner's main source, Wolfgang von Eschenbach's poem "Parzival," dates back to 1210, the period of communal Italy,
idealised by Panzacchi, Rubbiani and by Carducci, who had described "the
myth of the Holy Grail as a Eucharistic symbol," a symbol of thanksgiving, which had acquired a dedicated place also in the secular history of
European literature.[285] What the Liberal- and Democratic-minded Wagnerians in Italy admired was not the religious content of the narrative, but
its form, its language and its symbolism. As a modernist form of aesthetic
expression, Paul de Man understood symbolism as a reaction to the modern experience of rupture, in which the poetic language is used "to restore
the lost unity," a kit to repair the injuries caused by modernity.[286] While in
Germany *Parsifal* was often seen as a work for the Easter period, Wagner's
symbolism sufficiently integrates pagan elements to perform the opera as
Ersatz- or *Kunstreligion.*[287] Thus, aesthetic modernism gave meaning to
modern times—including commercial satisfaction: A local photographer
created a souvenir postcard to commemorate the first Italian *Parsifal,* of
which the municipality ordered one hundred copies. Bologna sold cosmet-
ics named after Wagner's main characters as well as ice cream *Ortruda,*
biscuits *Volfrano* and cakes called *Parsifal* and *Saint Gral.* Given names
in Bologna around the turn of the century included not only Aida and
Radames, but also Lohengrin.[288]

Shortly before Bologna's spectacular *Parsifal* the council had appointed
Ferruccio Busoni as director of its Liceo Musicale.[289] His appointment
was perceived as a radical opening towards new aesthetic horizons.[290] He
had been a famous *Wunderkind* of Rubinstein's school, with a spectacular career in Europe and the USA. He was born in Tuscany of a Corsican
father and an Austrian mother, grew up in Trieste, married a Swede and
was primarily at home in Germany. But Bologna saw him as one of its
many adopted sons. His works had been published and premiered in Bologna since 1880 and, aged fifteen, he had become a member of Bologna's
Academy. In 1883 Luigi Mancinelli produced his Cantata "Il Sabato del
Villaggio" at the Comunale.[291] Subsequently, he studied with Sibelius in
Helsinki and premiered numerous works by Delius and Bartòk. In 1907
he had published the first edition of his *Entwurf einer neuen Ästhetik
der Tonkunst,* dedicated to Rainer Maria Rilke—a manifesto for a musical avant-garde.[292] Although anticipating certain aspects of Schönberg's
Dodecaphony, he rejected the twelve-tone harmonic system as well as
complete atonality, proposing instead 113 new modes based on sixth tones
and the electrical generation of sound.[293] The year before his appointment
in Bologna his opera *Die Brautwahl* had been presented in Hamburg,
a city widely associated with the aesthetic avant-garde. At the Musik-
hochschule in Berlin he later prepared the ground for the appointment of
Arnold Schönberg, who would become his successor.[294] The actual reason
for Schönberg's move to Berlin had been anti-Semitic attacks in Austria.
The relationship between the two men was not free of tensions and in

the text of his *Ballad of Lippold the Jew-coiner* Busoni himself showed signs of anti-Semitism, at a time when T. S. Eliot produced what has been described as "anti-Semitic modernism."[295]

By offering the chair of the Liceo to Busoni the local administration took a well-considered and a courageous decision, demonstrating the extent to which the city wished to engage with the international avant-garde. In the words of the musicologist Edward Dent, it was a "liberal-minded" appointment, well paid from an Italian point of view, with little administrative or teaching duties and flexible in its duration: "Bologna desired his presence as leader of musical life," making the city "once more a great European musical centre."[296] A few months after Busoni's appointment the municipality decided to adapt the Liceo's regulations to those of the (national) conservatories of Naples and Milan, the so-called conservatories "*di prima categoria*," distinguishing the institute from those in Parma, Florence and Palermo.[297] However, feeling lonely and homesick for Berlin, Busoni frequently stayed away from his new position. He left Bologna initially for a tour in the USA,[298] before taking refuge in Switzerland during the war.

Bologna was widely considered the Italian capital of musical modernism and many of Italy's new composers were linked to Bologna. Apart from Boito and Martucci, Balilla Pratella dominated *futurismo* in nearby Lugo, trying to strengthen Italy's "musical sensibility" and experimenting with atonality and microtones. His *La Sina d'Vargöun* was based on local scenes from the Romagna and was premiered at the Comunale in 1909.[299] The following year Ottorino Respighi, a pupil of Martucci and Rimsky-Korsakov, presented his opera *Semirama* in Bologna. The works of the Liceo's former director Marco Enrico Bossi also contributed to Bologna's reputation abroad. Nevertheless, the "dusty Bolognesi" appeared to Busoni "as old as their institutions," unable to understand modern theatre and music.[300] According to the *Weltbürger* Busoni, who was at home in Vienna, Paris, London and Berlin, Italians were deprived of the ability to appreciate modernist responses to modernity, due to their lack of experience of modern life. Was he right? Were the Italian cities too small, too much rooted in their traditions to fully engage with modernist art? Wagner in 1871 certainly represented a challenge, but his Bolognesi identified with *Lohengrin, Rienzi* and *Tannhäuser* rather than the more advanced *Tristan* or the *Ring*.[301] What Bologna liked about Wagner were not necessarily the "modern" elements of his music, his harmonic system and the structure of his musical drama. Instead, they based their judgement on the narrative and on selected melodic and romantic passages which corresponded to their own expectations of lyric theatre. Bologna wished to be seen as one with the modern developments in European art, but in order to do so it constructed its own Wagner and its own modernism, independent from the aesthetic meanings associated with modernism elsewhere in Europe. A reflection of multiple modernities, modernisms also vary according to historical experience and aesthetic traditions. Italians developed an appreciation of the modern which allowed them to reread their own heritage in a new key and to set a period to traditions that no longer corresponded to their own political and social transformation since Unification. Bologna's experience of modernity contrasted dramatically with that of the *Weltbürger* Busoni, but subjective perception is one of the distinctive features that characterises the modernist response to the changing world.

10 Conclusions and Epilogue
Modernity, the Political Power of Culture and the Collapse of Liberal Democracy

MODERNISM AS FUTURISM

The semantic content of Italy's modernism was futurism. Futurism started well before 1909, when, with the publication of Marinetti's *Foundation and Manifesto of Futurism*, the term was used to denote a specific aesthetic-political movement.[1] Like Baudelaire's *Painter of Modern Life*, Constantin Guy, the Italian futurists were concerned with the aesthetic problem of representing time, the motion of time. However, the principal art-form for the aesthetic representation of time is music, because sound is by definition concerned with and dependent upon the passing of time. A painting, by contrast with music, is primarily static whereas text, as a form of aesthetic representation, is less abstract than music. If, according to Koselleck, the experience of modernity is grounded in a specific semantic of historical time, music was bound to assume a particular role in the aesthetic representation of that experience. Busoni was recognised as one of the masters of musical futurism; and the influential pamphlet *Futuristengefahr* [*The danger of Futurists*, 1917], by the German composer Hans Pfitzner, was a direct reply to Busoni's theoretical writings and his new aesthetic.[2]

As has been shown in the previous chapter, aesthetic debates in Italian music theory were primarily concerned with melody and rhythm, the horizontal dimension of music. By the same token, participants in those debates had often reacted with perplexity to the Germanic (and to some extent French) emphasis on developing music's vertical dimension through experimentation with the harmonic system and the symphonic structure of sound.[3] Owing to the changing social context of opera in nineteenth-century Italy, the aesthetic expectations associated with music theatre changed after Unification. For certain parts of the audience the works of Rossini, Bellini and Donizetti no longer fitted the experience of societal change and before long even Verdi only partly lived up to their expectations. The appeal of Wagner's operas lay in the fact that they did not correspond to any established genre. Wagner's music drama challenged harmonic conventions, but in addition to that it pioneered a new approach to music's horizontal dimension through "orchestral melody" and through

what Dahlhaus calls "motivic working," the "development of formal associations."[4] Thus, new political and cultural actors, men like the Democrat
Casarini, the critic Panzacchi and the conductors Mariani and Martucci
were able to introduce Wagner as the composer of a new aesthetic, capable
of generating meaning through new musical forms. The Italian Democrats were not alone in recognising the potential of Wagner to respond to
the experience of societal change. Long before the Nazis, but almost half
a century after Bologna's *Lohengrin* of 1871, the first Russian Wagner
staging after the October Revolution in 1918 was a "futurist" production
of *Lohengrin* by Fyodor Komissarzhevsky at the *Theatre of the Workers
Soviet*, in which he radically broke with the historicizing naturalism of
conventional opera production, proposing instead an abstract and timeless
interpretation of the work.[5] These examples demonstrate that *musica del
futuro* acquired a double meaning: on the one hand the term referred to
a technically innovative apparatus; on the other, the term referred to an
aesthetic capable of making the contemporary experience of modern time
meaningful. Modern time was marked by the sense that the past and the
future no longer coincided. Through this new temporal dynamic the future
was perceived as open and unpredictable. The music of the future was to
be a music of infinity.[6] It is only by exploring the reactions to both of these
aspects of *musica del futuro* that we can fully understand this form of
modernism in relation to the experience of modernity.

ITALY AND EUROPE

Before Futurism became linked with nationalism, Italian aesthetic concepts of the future were European and cosmopolitan. As late as 1910
anarchists and syndicalists, who were generally sympathetic towards the
futurists, interrupted a lecture by Marinetti in Milan with a chorus of
Evviva l'internazionalismo.[7] Italy's interest in German music was part of
a general European phenomenon, since Wagnerism was just as much celebrated in nineteenth-century France, Belgium, England and Spain.[8] Likewise, Wagnerians in Italy were often accused of undermining the national
foundations of Italian opera. Such charges call to mind the German polemics against the "alien element in art" and the condemnation of movements
such as the Berlin Secession as un-German.[9] Italy's cosmopolitan enthusiasm for European modernism was rooted in an earlier commitment to
European thought, evident in the heroic idealism of the Risorgimento as
well as the liberal founding of the nation-state. "From the Risorgimento
on, the highest aspiration of the Italian patriots had been to raise Italy to
the level of the great modern nation-states," turning Italians into truly
"modern men," or as de Sanctis claimed, "to convert the modern world
into our world."[10] Referring to the Republic of Letters, the patriotic poet
Giovanni Berchet had declared that Shakespeare, Racine and Schiller were

as Italian as Dante, Ariosto and Alfieri.[11] Italians set aside the idea of the foreigner as the occupier of the *patria* and embraced Europe as a cultural model: "The reasons for the political hatred of the past have ceased; today the Italian should measure himself against the foreigner . . . and his aim must be to reach one day the level of any other civilised people," as Michele Lessona argued in his 1869 "self-help-guide" for Italians, *Volere è potere*. In the words of Marco Meriggi, "it was time to look abroad."[12] By means of a specifically Italian reading, this looking abroad also included the cosmopolitan engagement with modernism, understood as an aesthetic response to the general European experience of modernity of which Italy wished to be part.

As the previous chapters have demonstrated, Italians engaged confidently with the transnational phenomenon of European modernism. Openly discussing moments of crisis at home, they fostered their new identity through the embrace of an artistic and intellectual culture which they perceived as modern, but no longer as "foreign." References to Italy's past, like the monuments for Galvani in Bologna, for Beccaria in Milan and for Bruno in Rome, underlined the degree to which Italy saw itself as part of a European modernity. Bologna's musical futurism was embedded in a wider European context of aesthetic debate and likewise the literary culture of Florence. The city of D'Annunzio and the literary magazines *Leonardo*, *Il Marzocco*, *La Voce* attracted figures such as Fyodor Dostoyevsky, Arnold Böcklin, Stefan George, André Gide, Georg Lukács, Thomas Mann, Rainer Maria Rilke, and Oscar Wilde. The parallels with Munich, the capital of avant-garde theatre, are striking, but despite the presence of Ibsen and Kandinsky its artistic milieu was probably less cosmopolitan than Florence.[13] The aesthetic concepts of Ardengo Soffici, Papini and Prezzolini were rooted in their reading of Bergson and their experience of intellectual and artistic life in *fin-de-siècle* Paris. Unlike the *letterati* of the younger generation, Carducci did not enjoy travelling and spent most of his adult life within the parameters of Bologna's city-walls. As the international press remarked at the time, in 1906 he even rejected the invitation to Stockholm to receive the Nobel Prize. He opposed many of the modern international trends in literature. Nevertheless, on the occasion of his death, in February 1907, Europe celebrated him along with the names of Dante, Rabelais, Heine and Hugo as "the greatest lyricist of the Romanic peoples, . . . a name known all over the world."[14]

The Italian engagement with (and assimilation of) European modernism obviously provoked intellectual and political debate. In line with the nationalistic credo of the time certain sections of the avant-garde continuously referred to concepts of Italian primacy. However, the image of *fine secolo* Italy as a nation enclosed in its own traditions, obsessed with Verdi and proud of a history which set them apart from the rest of Europe, is utterly misleading. Bologna's patisseries baked from old recipes of the Romagna, but naming their *confiseries* after Wagnerian characters such as

Ortrud and Elsa demonstrated the extent to which this culture was inter-linked with Europe as a whole. Did Bologna's modernism reach beyond the confines of the Italian peninsula?[15] This question might best be answered with an example: During the years just before World War I a most power-ful symbol for the transnational dimension of European modernism was Gustav Mahler's work as a conductor in New York. During his last concert at Carnegie Hall, shortly before his death, Mahler conducted (in the pres-ence of Toscanini) the world premiere of Busoni's *Berceuse élégiaque*, Mar-tucci's second piano concerto and the *Intermezzi Goldoniani* by Marco Enrico Bossi. All three names were closely connected with Bologna: this was Italian modernism "made in Bologna," performed in New York.[16]

CROCE'S ROLE

Modernism represented one way of making the experience of modernity meaningful; Italy's very specific and unique reading and appropriation of idealism, positivism and Marxism since the turn of the century was another way. Naples played an important role in these philosophical debates, which provide us with a key not only to the relationship between Italian and European thought, but also to the connection between Italian modernism and the collapse of liberal democracy. Bertrando Spaventa and Francesco De Sanctis, who both died in 1883, the same year as Wagner, attempted to connect Italian culture with the principles of Hegel's dialectical philosophy of history. They established a new framework of debate, which profoundly marked Italian intellectual life until the middle of the twentieth century. Bologna took part in this. Supporting the Neapolitan philosophers, the *Rivista Bolognese* published articles by Spaventa and Filippo Masci on Hegel, and adhered in 1869 to the subscription for a Hegel monument in Berlin.[17] In the context of these debates Benedetto Croce's work is of par-ticular relevance, because he analyses aesthetic techniques within a wider framework of problems of European history, presenting a synthetic account of Europe's modern experience since the Enlightenment. Croce's contribu-tion to projects such as the *Encyclopaedia Britannica* was an important recognition of his widely acknowledged role in European debate and the fruit of an intellectual project he had broached several decades earlier.[18] Unlike most other thinkers of his time Croce treated Europe as a cultural unity. Due to his failure to recognise the relationship between the crisis of liberalism and the advent of Fascism, Croce's *History of Italy* and his *History of Europe* have rightly been challenged by post-war historiogra-phy.[19] However, born of his own opposition to Fascism, in their theoretical conception these works present themselves also as synthetic products of the debates that marked Europe's intellectual life between the end of the nineteenth and the early twentieth century, standing alongside his treatises on aesthetics and literature as monuments to the defence of the European culture of his time. During the first half of the twentieth century it is difficult to think of any theorist more representative of Europe's liberal values and better aware of its philosophical and intellectual concerns than Benedetto Croce. Too often post-war historians have seen Croce only as a historian rather than as a source for Italy's intellectual debate around the turn of the century. Belonging to the intellectual milieu which Stefan Zweig, shortly before his suicide in 1942, described as *The World of Yesterday*, he collaborated with André Gide, Aldous Huxley, Heinrich Mann, Romain Rolland, Jean Cocteau, Boris Pasternak and many others for Klaus Mann's anti-Fascist periodical *Die Sammlung*, representing a Europe which refused to surrender its humanist values.[20]

What were the philosophical foundations of Croce's Europeanism? Croce confronted himself with the challenges of both Marxism and idealism, an encounter which had a major impact on Italian intellectual debate at the turn of the century. Croce questioned the Enlightenment's belief in humankind as well as Hegel's faith in progress. He also rejected the scientific positivism which characterised the Italian reception of Marxism and much of nineteenth-century debate in Europe. However, he engaged critically with Hegel's idealism and the concept of history as a meaningful process, and made the dialectical method the basis of his historical and philosophical enquiries. Like Hegel, Croce placed history at the centre of his new humanism, but his was an "absolute historicism," a history without God. As a consequence, and despite his confrontational relationship with the social sciences in Italy, he had a lively interest in European social theory and socio-economic reform, reflected in his collaboration with the Italian publisher Laterza and in the latter's publication of Max Weber's and Walter Rathenau's works in translation. On similar grounds he engaged closely with Windelband, Simmel and Durkheim, but he also showed interest in Freud's *Die Traumdeutung*.[21] To varying degrees, Italy's Socialist Left as well as parts of the Right engaged with Hegel and Marx in a dialogue which was as original as it was controversial. Labriola's critique of capitalism was based on Marxist theory, but the liberal prime minister Giolitti also studied *Das Kapital*. Hence, Marxism influenced Italy's philosophical debate well beyond the often rather narrow readings of the nascent Labour movement. Interest in the principles of Socialist internationalism spread even among its most prominent political opponents, including Gentile and Volpe, who later aligned themselves with Fascism.[22] The synthesis between the Marxist consideration of material conditions and Hegel's idealist belief in the generative power of the human spirit led to the rejection of any form of positivist-evolutionary determinism, both on the Right as well as among sections of the Left. This "philosophy of praxis" had a direct effect on the ways in which Italy addressed the experience of modernity, and of World War I in particular: Although economically shattered, marked by deep social and political fissures, and unsatisfied with the compensation it received from the victors for its intervention in 1915, Italy avoided the state of mental depression which characterised Austria, for instance, after its long *fin de siècle* crisis and the loss of its empire.[23] The broad conceptual foundation of this philosophical enterprise was also reflected in the ideological heterogeneity of the Italian mass movements during the early twentieth century. It affected Gramsci's critique of the Socialists' economic determinism as well as the activism of Futurists, Interventionists and Fascists, whose "politicisation of aesthetics" Croce himself found distasteful.[24]

Despite its inherent ideological contradictions, Italy's aesthetic and intellectual debate since the turn of the century appears to have been the most synthetically European answer to the experience of modernity, with a major impact on Italian society as a whole. Although Italy still suffered from one of the highest rates of illiteracy in Europe, it also had the highest rates of university attendance. Within this perspective, the historiographical tradition of depicting Italian society as a deviation from general European developments, or as a people, in Trevelyan's terms, wholly absorbed in its own instincts and traditions, seems barely plausible. Italy's intellectual life at the turn of the century was at one with the wider European experience of modernity.[25]

MODERNISM AS A CHANGE OF PERSPECTIVE

As Adamson in his study of the Florentine avant-garde has demonstrated,

> modernism was by no means an embrace of the modernity of industry, science, and technology. It was, on the contrary, an "adversary culture" or "other modernity" that challenged the "modernizing" forces of science, commerce, and industry, usually in the name of some more "spiritual" alternative."[26]

Modernism is not a thematic mirror of the modern, but an aesthetic expression of its experience, which operates principally on the symbolic level. Perceptions of the past and of the future share fluidity as their principal attribute. Since modernism emerges out of the relationship between past and future, it is no easy matter to come up with a historical definition of the term. In 1924 the American philosopher and literary historian Arthur Lovejoy claimed that the term romanticism had become so vague and meaningless that it had better be abandoned.[27] Should the same concern apply to the term modernism?

The ideological ambivalence of modernity is reflected in the aesthetic ambivalence of modernism. Ambivalence is perceived as an uncomfortable disorder, but according to Zygmunt Bauman this is the "normal condition" of the process in which we create categories to make the experience of the modern world meaningful. Thus, ambivalence appears as "the alter ego of language"[28], including aesthetic language in the Crocean sense. As my account of the Italian reception of Wagner was designed to show, modernism gives aesthetic expression to the experience of the modern condition.

George Kubler associates modernism with the "abrupt change of content and expression at intervals when an entire language of form suddenly falls into disuse, being replaced by a new language of different components and an unfamiliar grammar."[29] T. J. Clark identifies these changes with Jacques-Louis David's *Death of Marat* (1793). The painting was displayed for the first time on the occasion of the martyr's carefully staged funeral, which fell on the same day on which Marie-Antoinette was guillotined. What this "moment of picture-making" means for Clark is "the fact that contingency rules." Modernism "is the art of these new circumstances."[30] For Simmel and Tönnies these new circumstances are marked by the structural transformation of social networks and of the individual's place within them. According to Baudelaire such changes offer new opportunities: the perception of the modern emerges from a new relationship between viewer and viewed.[31] However, at the same time the new webs of social relations become so complex that an aesthetic analysis of macro-social structures following classical-universal patterns seems no longer possible. Under these circumstances the experience of modernity results in disenchantment, in new forms of mystification, or simply in fragmentation, alienation and derangement.[32] Having lost the capacity to make universal claims, we turn our attention to smaller scale social realities, as discussed in the work of Walter Benjamin, or as exemplified by Rilke's and Kafka's aesthetic change of perspective. But this is not the only possible response to the experience of modernity. As the "moment of picture-making" described by Clark demonstrates, modernism is not necessarily a pessimistic reaction to the experience of change. On the philosophical and symbolic level, the aesthetic challenge is often perceived as a new beginning and a radical break with the past, a language which attracted thinkers of the Right as well as of the Left. Thus, the idiom of modernism gave expression to a wide range of revolutionary expectations, which marked the modern age.[33]

The European experience of modernity gave rise to multiple modernisms. The engagement with and assimilation of modernism in the arts implies that recipients undertake subjective appropriations of the modernisms circulating in Europe, depending upon the particular socio-political context in which modernity is experienced. Esra Akcan speaks in this context about *translation*, a conceptual framework pointing to "interaction" as well as to "mutual dependence" between different national contexts. The trans-nationality of both modernity and modernism continuously produces "new hybrids and dialectical relations," with the result that "the definition of the local is always in flux."[34] Modernism was international and transnational, but did not speak a single language, even when it was concerned with the same object of symbolic representation: the same modern opera or style could have different meanings depending upon the social context of its location. More specifically, in Bologna in 1871 the music of *Lohengrin* represented a stronger "antithesis" of the past than was the case in Germany or France, where by that time the repertoire had already evolved in a different direction. The perceived modernist content is always dependent on the specific context of reception. Ernst Bloch's concept of *Ungleichze-itigkeit* or non-synchronicity, as well as recent work on metamorphoric modernism (Russia), provincial modernities (Hamburg) or multiple and/or alternative modernities (in the case of Fascist Italy or Latin-America), presents similar phenomena.[35]

MODERNISM AND CONFLICT

In Italy the change of perspective was linked to the growing socio-political conflict which marked the Italian experience of modernity. The following sections of the conclusions present an epilogue, discussing the social, political and institutional crisis in Italy since the turn of the century in order to assess its impact on the politics of culture and on municipal identities. Giolitti's governments and the reliance of Vittorio Emanuele III on parliamentary methods before World War I brought a period of political consolidation, which coincided with the reform of the banking system, the emergence of the Genoa-Milan-Turin "industrial triangle," the growth of income and the pacification of labour conflicts.[36] For Italy this was a missed opportunity. Italian intervention in World War I not only divided Italian society, it also proved to be a turning point in the relationship between Italians and the State.[37] It was the beginning of the end of the parliamentary system. Socialists and Catholics found new reasons to question the legitimacy of the State. Meanwhile, they were divided about which political groups to collaborate with or whether to collaborate at all. In this situation, despite the fact that Italy found itself on the winning side of World War I, it was easy for the new forces of reaction to destroy the liberal-democratic state.

Obviously, modernist aesthetics cannot be seen as instrumental to or as a by-product of the consolidation of liberal democracy. Some theorists even argue the opposite, questioning the legacy of the Enlightenment and maintaining that the modern condition was founded upon the link between reason and terror. The Italian quartet of modernism, futurism, interventionism and Fascism seems to reflect these complexities. However, such views are often based on a reductive understanding of the Enlightenment, which paved the way for various possibilities, including totalitarian as well as emancipatory social models. The aesthetic expressions of the modern experience were as heterogeneous as modernity itself, serving multiple political and ideological ends, which changed over time. Therefore, it does not seem surprising that throughout the Age of Extremes modernist aesthetics featured both in totalitarian regimes and in democratic societies. As Adrian Lyttelton has argued, one should keep in mind that "Fascism was, after all, more characteristic of an age than of any one nation or people."[38]

Analysing the modernism of Fascist Italy would require a different book on a topic which is no longer neglected.[39] Nevertheless, in order to understand the changing context of Italian modernism around the turn of the century, this book must close with an analysis of the circumstances which led to the collapse of the liberal institutions. While throughout the book Bologna has served in the main as a case study of Italy's socio-political transformation since Unification, in the conclusions the focus on Bologna is particularly justified by the exemplary character of local events for developments in Italy as a whole. Bologna was the first city in which Fascism removed a democratic administration, two years before the March on Rome; and nowhere did the collapse of the liberal regime generate a higher degree of violence than in Emilia Romagna.

SOCIAL CRISIS

What were the circumstances under which liberal democracy collapsed in Bologna? As explained in chapter 1, until the late 1880s the region largely maintained its pre-modern structures in agriculture and Bologna could hardly compete with the international trend towards capitalist and mechanised farming methods. The agrarian crisis encouraged a diversification of the regional economy, but the Bolognese had to start from such a low level of industrialisation that even during the Giolittian years only 10% of the population worked in the industrial sector.[40] Although Bologna itself produced virtually nothing for the national or international market, products from outside the region increasingly arrived in the region's urban centres, putting the prices paid for local products under pressure. Meanwhile, an oversupply of labour resulted in extremely low salaries and a hesitant technological modernisation.[41] During the economic crisis of the early 1890s day-labourers were the first to suffer. The average number of working days went down to about a hundred and twenty days per year, and in bad years it would fall still lower. In 1902 the average labourer found eighty-six days of employment with wages well below those of the 1870s.[42] Their lives were characterised by grinding poverty, with a majority of families sleeping all year in stables side by side with animals which were not even their own. The low level of income made any provisioning for the winter impossible. Paternalistic forms of assistance, as advocated by Moderate Liberals and Catholics, could no longer ease the misery of large sections of the rural population. Even the prefects, who tended to blame the Socialists for protest and violence, admitted that the landowners did too little to improve the redistribution of profits.[43] Instead, as Anthony Cardoza writes, "Bologna's elite of large landowners and commercial farmers took the lead in creating strong employer associations," providing the personnel and the ideas for the agrarian interest organizations that arose at the start of the new century.[44]

Bologna, as the urban centre of a huge agricultural, non-industrialised region, felt the pressure of this crisis more acutely than most Italian cities.

Faced with hunger and bad weather conditions, the rural proletariat fled the countryside, hoping to find occasional employment in the urban centres. The municipal administrations created some jobs through public works, but were unable to provide solutions. The entire region was shaken by strikes and protests, resulting in violent confrontations with the police during which even women and children were among those arrested. Bologna's economic, social and political crisis became a matter of national concern.[45] During the years between 1888 and 1897 the province saw thirty-seven strikes, amounting to a total of 178 days of industrial action and involving at least 20,000 workers. In 1901 alone twenty-six peasant strikes involved a total of 17,478 workers.[46] The province came close to social collapse.

Confronted with the escalation of the social question and the growing strength of the Labour Movement, Nationalism and Catholicism furnished the Bolognese with the framework for a new form of Conservatism, which had little in common with Cavour's or Minghetti's Moderate Liberalism.[47] Given that the region's first phase of industrialisation had been almost entirely based on the agrarian sector, the new economic elites were still agrarians, even if they now used capitalist methods to exploit their properties. In their eyes the Democratic middle class was politically discredited by their local alliances with the Extreme Left. This hindered attempts of social pacification as encouraged by Giolitti. The Nationalists represented agrarian-capitalist interests, while forming a powerful instrument of propaganda to recruit broader sections of society. Understood as a modern form of Risorgimento irredentism, Nationalism was able to attract intellectuals and parts of the local student population, which had previously sympathised with Socialism and Radicalism. Meanwhile, they recognised in the Church a bulwark against Socialism, enabling them to integrate important sections of Catholics into the nation's political life.[48] Under Pope Pio X political Catholicism became a reactionary and conservative force, very different from Romolo Murri's efforts to create a Christian Democracy. Under pressure from the organisational advance of the Freethinkers, who during these years held international meetings in Rome, Bologna and Milan,[49] the pope eliminated any progressive tendencies inside the organisation of the Church. The *Unione elettorale cattolica italiana* under the leadership of Count Ottorino Gentiloni found a new social base among rural workers, the petite bourgeoisie and primary-school teachers. Recognising Liberalism's failures to drive a wedge between the lower classes and the Socialists and Radicals, Liberals, Catholics and Nationalists were forced into a new alliance.

AN ITALIAN EMPIRE

In 1911 the principal voice of propaganda for the *Associazione Nazionalista Bolognese* became the newspaper *La Nuova Italia*. A similar line was taken by *Il Resto del Carlino*, a paper owned since 1909 by a consortium of local Agrarians, who subscribed to the alliance between Catholicism and Nationalism.[50] Since the Abyssinian War of 1895–96 Italy's national question had been linked to colonial ambitions, the idea of completing the Risorgimento through territorial aggrandisement in Africa being seen as a way to compensate for the disillusionment associated with Unification. An earlier form of colonialism found expression in the activities of the *Società Geografica Italiana*, founded in 1867 to pursue predominantly political and military interests, with academic geographers representing only 11% of its members.[51] In Bologna the writer and journalist Alfredo Oriani (1852–1909) became an important supporter of these ideas, declaring in local coffee-houses or in the pages of Panzacchi's Roman newspaper *Nabab* that Italy needed colonial expansion as a "test" to prepare the nation for an even bigger conflict, which would eventually enhance Italy's prestige as a great power in Europe.[52] Colonial war became the continuation of the nation's Risorgimento.[53] Dropping their old battle-cry *"Roma o Morte,"* the new *"Garibaldini del Mare"* suddenly became knights of the pope, crusaders, fighting in the name of "Christian-Latin civilization."[54] Ancient imperial Rome provided the nation with a recipe for survival. For Bologna's nationalist councillors the Italian blood shed in Africa was "holy and fertile for the fatherland's future."[55] Thus, the Libyan War anticipated the Italians' experience of the Great War.

Bologna's Conservative council majority was gripped by a new patriotic and imperial fervour. Municipal employees volunteering for the Red Cross in Africa continued to be paid during their mission; the council contributed 10,000 Lire to the development of a national air force;[56] and the appointment of Carducci's successor as chair of Italian literature became a search for a bard of war: Giovanni Pascoli. According to the mayor, his words gave notice to Europe of Italy's "right and its mission, . . . writing the chant of our victory, the hymn of our resurgent patriotic greatness."[57] The thousands of civilian deaths, the air raids against villages and the deportation of thousands of Arabs to Southern Italy found no echo in the mayor's words. Only the Socialists were uneasy about Pascoli's appointment. They interrupted the council meeting, shouting "down with the war!" and describing the Libyan campaign as a "mad enterprise . . . and a return to barbarism," contradicting the most basic principles of civilisation.[58]

INTERNATIONALISM

Hence, nationalism and imperialism were far from capturing all sections of Italian society. Traditionally, *"anticolonialismo"* had been stronger in Italy than in most parts of Europe, starting with opposition to Crispi's policy in Ethiopia, some years earlier. During the defeat of Amba Alagi and the disaster of Adowa 7000 Italian soldiers had been killed, which was about as many as during all three wars of liberation. The events were followed by demonstrations all over the country, with people from very different social backgrounds screaming *"Abasso* Crispi! *Viva* Menelik!"[59] While parts of the Catholic spectrum recognised in the colonial defeat a revenge for the injustice on which the Italian kingdom was founded, many Radicals and the Socialists understood imperialism as a contradiction of their Mazzinian and internationalist beliefs. Crispi's departure after nearly half a century at the centre of Italian politics was to a large extent a consequence of not only the failure, but also the unpopularity of his colonial policy.

Socialism offered many Italians solutions to the crisis of the *fine secolo*, attracting in particular the younger generation. Contrary to most European workers' parties at the time, Italian Socialism was still to some extent rooted in anarchism, and therefore implied a profound aversion to the state.[60] However, the principal background to the growth of internationalism and Socialism in the region were the dramatic social conditions of the rural proletariat. In November 1901 the representatives of eight hundred leagues, representing 152,122 members, assembled for the first time at a national congress of agricultural workers in Bologna. The Romagna was one of the movement's strongholds, with eighty different leagues representing 11,399 labourers.[61] In the course of that year Italy had witnessed a total of 629 agricultural strikes, amounting to 2,931,766 lost working days. In response to the unrest the farmers reduced rice production by about 50%, replacing it with labour-saving crops. The same logic led them to intensify mechanisation, in order to undermine the position of the peasant leagues. A web of new organisations under the leadership of Count Giovanni Enrico Sturani and Marquis Giuseppe Tanari started defending their interests and imposing coordinated labour contracts on the rural population. As a local agrarian committee stated in a document, "machines were introduced principally to avert strikes." According to the *Federconsorzi*, "two years of strikes have been more valuable [for the spread of agricultural machines] than twenty years of technical propaganda."[62]

The modernisation of the agrarian economy failed to halt the advance of the Left. In 1892 Italy had introduced uninominal elections for parliament, which assigned thirty-nine seats to Emilia Romagna. Initially, twenty-six Liberals sat alongside thirteen representatives of the Extreme Left (Radicals, Republicans, Socialists). Over the following elections the Liberals gradually lost ground and by 1900 the groups' respective strength was reversed, with only thirteen Liberals elected alongside twenty-six successful candidates of the Extreme Left (including eleven Socialists).[63] While most *mezzadri* of the Romagna voted for the Republicans, *braccianti* tended to support the Socialists. The Republicans, who traditionally had been strong, lost ground to the Socialists and the Nationalists. In the parliamentary elections of 1904 the entire zone of the plains was won by the Socialists and only two out of eight seats went to the Liberals.[64] In 1912, more than forty years after Germany, Italy finally introduced universal manhood suffrage. This strengthened the Extreme Left, but also altered the balance between Radicals, Republicans and Socialists. While in 1903 Giolitti still favoured Bologna's alliance between Democrats, Republicans and Socialists, from now on, confronted with the growing impact of the Socialists, Giolitti attempted to form a Liberal bloc which would unite the Right with the Democrats. However, in the national election of 1913 Bologna's Socialists gained 15,098 votes, against 13,183 votes for all the other parties. In reaction to these results, the local government resigned. In the subsequent local election the PSI gained 12,689 votes against 11,370 votes for the Liberal-Catholic list and 1,473 votes for the Radicals.[65] Speaking of "Bologna *la rossa*" no longer referred to the city's traditional use of red bricks, but to the political orientation of the majority of its inhabitants.

MUNICIPAL SOCIALISM

In June 1914, on the day of the local elections, armed troops opened fire against a non-authorised anti-war demonstration in Ancona and killed two people. The Chamber of Labour declared an open-ended strike; trade unions and the Socialist party organised manifestations. In Bologna and the Romagna insurrections led to occupations of public offices and train stations, and to the capture of officers and civil servants. A Republic was proclaimed, although it was to prove short-lived. In disagreement over the meaning of these events and the direction to take, trade unions and the party lost control of the situation, but Mussolini, through the party's official organ *Avanti!*, welcomed the violent confrontation with the state. The *settimana rossa* in Romagna "represents the culmination of social dissidence against the liberal state" and the "last great proof" of the region's subversive strength.[66] This was the climate in which the middle class perceived the Socialist victories in Bologna, Milan and many other towns of the North. The commemoration of the victims of the *settimana rossa* was one of the first initiatives of Bologna's new council majority.[67] The events overshadowed the Austrian ultimatum of 1914, of which Italy was informed only retrospectively, freeing it from any obligation towards the purely defensive Triple Alliance. Instead of joining the Central Powers, nine months after the start of the conflict Italy entered the war on the side of the Entente.

With a university degree and as the owner of a small pharmaceutical company, Bologna's first Socialist mayor Francesco Zanardi himself belonged to the middle class, but in the new municipal council he was surrounded by twenty-one blue-collar- and five white-collar workers, who shared their seats with seventeen representatives of the liberal professions, three businessmen and two accountants. The nobility was no longer represented. For the Catholic *Avvenire* Bologna had fallen "under the hegemony of illiteracy and the Chamber of Labour."[68] "Let's occupy the communes" had been Andrea Costa's answer to the attempts to outlaw Socialism. Thus, "municipal socialism" became a significant step towards gaining power at the national level. As Fabio Rugge has outlined, this experience was not just a specific form of Socialism, but also a model of administration.[69] Their main agenda consisted in changes to local taxes, the municipalisation of services, the formation of cooperatives for public works as well as support for the organisations of the Labour movement. Bologna's public bread factory was described as "a true monument of this new civilisation."[70] In order to cover their expenditure the Socialist administration did not increase taxes on consumption, as previous local governments had done, but taxes on property—according to the opposition a measure aimed at "increasing taxes above revenue," thus destroying income and corroding capital.[71]

THE WAR

The Romagna had long been seen as a region populated by violent, vindictive and impulsive people of backward mentality, a stereotype regularly evoked in the national press, but also cultivated in the region's own literature, in poetry written in local dialect and popular vaudevilles. World War I allowed the people of the Romagna to present their supposed ruthlessness in a positive light, contributing to the defence of the fatherland. Sacrifice for the Great War offered an opportunity to participate in the nation's resurgence.[72] Meanwhile, however, Bologna also became known as an important centre of Syndicalist and anti-interventionist activity.[73]

In August 1914 the council voted unanimously to subscribe to the *Società Dante Aligheri,* "supporting the fight for the propagation of the Italian language and hindering the Slavification and Germanisation of Italian territories." However, a debate on subsidies for Belgian refugees evolved into a discussion about a possible Italian intervention in favour of "[our] French brothers."[74] Despite the Socialists' official anti-interventionist position, the mayor commemorated the Italian volunteers fallen in France as proletarian internationalists, paying tribute to a "Garibaldian tradition" and "fertilizing with proletarian blood the justice of labour!"[75] Throughout the war the Socialists' anti-militarist stance—contrasting with the attitudes of most other Socialist parties in Europe—was at the centre of local political debate. Because the Socialists formed the local government, the issue was to prove highly contentious, causing more heated debate than elsewhere in Italy. Meanwhile, many interventionists also saw themselves as revolutionaries, hoping that war would create the conditions for a social and political revolution.[76] As a Socialist island in a country increasingly divided on the issue of the war the municipality was determined to take the lead in formulating the Left's opposition to an Italian intervention:

> As Socialists we do not believe in a war of emancipation and we think that militarism will grow even stronger after the war, among both the defeated and the victors. Awaiting further developments, we confirm our faith in the Workers' International; . . . In case the fatherland needs us to defend our borders we will do our duty. After that we will rejoin the path which leads to holier and more humane claims.[77]

The war cost the lives of 578,000 Italian soldiers, not counting victims among civilians. 500,000 soldiers returned home wounded. Tens of thousands of cases of tuberculosis were registered, largely attributable to the physical exhaustion of the population and comparable to the impact of the "Spanish influenza" at the end of 1918. The ratio of deaths to births among the civilian population exceeded the pre-war years by 600,000. The total cost of the war has been estimated at 148 billion Lire, twice the sum of the entire government expenditure between 1861 and 1913.[78] To a large extent it was financed by inflation, with devastating consequences for the economy and large parts of the population. Meanwhile, the war was a period of Labour protest in Italy, expressing discontent not only about the social conditions of the urban masses, but also about the sacrifice they had to make for a war with which many Italians did not identify. For Italy the war brought a period of phenomenal expansion in industrial production, making Fiat the leading vehicle producer in Europe and creating an army which had more cannons in the field than Britain and an aircraft industry which started from scratch to become a major exporter.[79] Although based on a large state bureaucracy, industrial demand produced a technological revolution, which can at least partly be explained by the fact that the country did not possess coal and had only limited access to raw materials. While industrial profits reached unprecedented levels, the factory workers, often supervised by armed soldiers, witnessed a decline in their purchasing power and an increase in working hours to seventy-five a week.[80] Figures for Turin and Milan reveal that households had to rely on at least two wage earners to cover the expenses for basic necessities. Despite that, consumption of calories fell dramatically during the war and the housing shortage remained acute. In Socialist Bologna 15,000 relatives of soldiers were entitled to bread, flour and other subsidies; many women without regular occupation found work in the arsenals.[81] Apart from rationing, the municipality took drastic measures to improve the living conditions of the masses, including the requisitioning of basic consumer goods from manufacturers and warehouses in an attempt to regulate prices.[82] The harsh winter of 1916–17 provoked widespread popular discontent, in particular among women. Increasingly, the war was seen in terms of class conflict, fought with proletarian blood in the interests of industry and capital.

WAGNER, VERDI AND THE WAR

In 1901, the year of Verdi's death, Bologna had been acclaimed in the international press for a spectacular *Traviata* and for a *Rigoletto* featuring Enrico Caruso. However, in 1913 Bologna decided to celebrate Wagner's rather than Verdi's centenary. The mayor and the administration discussed plans for another great performance of *Rigoletto*, but were unable to find an appropriate cast.[83] A few days after the Italian premiere of *Parsifal*, discussed in the previous chapter, a committee of local Wagnerians, supported by the Liberal councillor and senator Enrico Pini, proposed the commissioning of a new plaque to be located under the theatre's portico, commemorating the Italian premieres of all Wagner operas, clearly aimed at underlining Bologna's leadership in Italian Wagnerism. A letter—written in poor Italian and signed by 112 citizens—protested in no uncertain terms against this "plaque for Vagner" [sic], urged Bologna to look to its "artistic and national honour," and reminded the city of its duty to avoid such an offence "against the very patriotic Verdi in the year of his centennial anniversary." It concluded by asking for "a last blow to be struck against the camorra which infects Bologna's musical environment."[84] Despite this counter-petition, the Wagnerians lost no time in informing the mayor that the subscription for the plaque was complete and that the funds for its installation were now available. In order to avoid a desecration of the plaque during the war against Germany, the municipality suggested locating the inscription inside the theatre rather than under the portico. However, the local Wagnerians took umbrage and the project stalled once again.[85]

The 1914 autumn season opened with Meyerbeer's *L'Africaine*, followed by Catalani's "Germanic" *Loreley*. But once Italy had entered the war only Italian operas were performed: Rossini, Donizetti, Puccini—and finally in 1918 two operas by Verdi, *Aida* and *La Traviata*.[86] Puccini played a role in representing "the nation in arms," with a committee of volunteers organising fourteen performances of *Tosca* and *La Bohème* to collect money for local war orphans. However, the Italian premiere of *La rondine*, in 1915, was met with harsh criticism from the press.[87] As early as 1920, Wagner was back on the bill. The autumn season opened once again with *Lohengrin*.[88] Shortly after, the Wagnerians reminded the mayor of the abandoned project for their plaque and finally, in November 1920, the proposal was approved—not by a Socialist council majority, but under the Fascist *giunta* which in the meantime had taken power.[89]

SOCIALIST CULTURE

Despite their recurrent criticism of the theatre's "aristocratic" tradition, the Socialists recognised the importance of the city's musical life, looking for ways to assimilate it to their own political programme. Some of the new Socialist councillors, like the journalist and music critic Francesco Tonolla, were experts in the field, and did all they could both to preserve and to reform Bologna's musical institutions.[90] Busoni's attempts to reform the Liceo Musicale were thus backed by the Socialists, "because a feeling for the arts exists and vibrates even among the most humble people . . . ; music had a great influence on the national resurgence and hopefully will also have the virtue of creating feelings of love and fraternity between different peoples."[91] For *Concerti Popolari* the municipality opened the theatre free of charge.[92] The Socialists supported the restoration of the Liceo, installed fire and burglar alarms in its library, and launched a new annual piano competition, the prize of the "Fondazione Mugellini." After Tonolla's death the municipality established a prize in his memory.[93] Two council-lors of working-class background, who, according to the mayor, "were not without artistic intuition," were appointed members of the Deputazione.[94] In accordance with government policy, the theatre stayed open for most of the war, despite falling audiences and growing financial difficulties.[95] At the end of the war the Socialist municipality addressed the problem of the private theatre boxes. By 1918 the market value of a box was down to about 5,500 Lire. Considering the number of seats available in a private box and the general demand for tickets, the municipality could redeem the acquisition of private boxes without difficulty.[96]

In 1919 the municipality also started discussing the construction of a "Popular Theatre."[97] Following a proposal from a private investor, the "Society for Theatre and Entertainment" presented an idea which the *giunta* took as a basis to develop its concept of a Socialist cultural pol-icy, so as "to offer the people better opportunities to attend theatrical and musical performances" and to create a stage for its children's theatre, the "Teatro dei Piccoli." Socialist municipal policy was meant to be technologi-cally advanced, leading the administration in 1920 to install *théâtrophones* for the transmission of performances from the Liceo and the Comunale.[98] Compared to even medium-sized European cities, Bologna was several decades late in adopting the technology, but it was the Socialist administra-tion which undertook the necessary investments.

Public space became Socialist. The conservative council majority had dedicated five streets to the Libyan War, creating the *"quartiere libico."* In secret initiatives the names of these streets were soon replaced by others, intended to commemorate fallen soldiers as well as men "valuable to the Socialist party."[99] The Socialist administration took up this idea, naming streets after local politicians, popular writers and the heroes of the Risor-gimento—Giuseppe Ceneri, Edmondo de Amicis, Felice Cavallotti. "Carlo

Marx" also got a street within the very first year of the Socialist administration.[100] In 1914 the council commemorated Jean Jaurès and August Bebel, the former for "defending the principles of the Socialist International," the latter as the "Red Kaiser." After the war the administration named streets after "Giovanni Jaurès" and Andrea Costa, the first Socialist member of parliament.[101] However, in many respects Bologna's Socialists were less dogmatic in the representation of the past than the post-Risorgimento Democrats and Republicans, anti-clericals like Carducci or Panzacchi had been. In 1915 the Socialist administration named several streets after local artists from the communal period, such as Lorenzo Costa, who had decorated the famous *Salone dei mesi* in Ferrara and died in Bologna at the time of the Black Death, or Jacopo della Quercia, who had been in the employ of the cathedral of San Petronio. They also considered artists of the later period, who had worked for the Papal regime: Elisabetta Sirani, a female painter of the seventeenth century; Alessandro Menganti, who in the sixteenth century sculpted Bologna's famous statue of Pope Gregorio XIII; and Michele Angelo Colonna, who decorated parts of the town hall during the seventeenth century.[102] Previous generations of anti-clerical councillors had refused to commemorate these artists, tainted by their association with the Papal government, and had sought to create a "modern" city by cleansing public space of religious references. In August 1917 the municipality welcomed an official delegation of the Russian "Soviet," an event perceived as an international recognition of Bologna's model for Socialism. Workers marched in solidarity with the Russian guests and several thousand delegates of the local Labour organisations assembled for the occasion in the Teatro Comunale, which Zanardi, not long before, had denounced as an aristocratic theatre.[103]

Bologna saw itself as the prototype of municipal socialism. Popular libraries and evening schools became a priority for the Socialist budget.[104] Events like May Day assumed an official character, a showcase for the Socialist movement elsewhere in Italy, but a violation of the monarchical principle for the opposition, which branded such events anti-constitutional. To the horror of the Liberal councillor Perozzi even teachers at the local primary schools participated with their pupils in the parade, "a day of sorrow and anguish for all who share a vivid sense of the people's unity."[105] For the opposition,

> a municipality which declares itself against the constitution ceases to act as a municipality of the state: it becomes a body politic in itself, which separates itself from the national body politic. . . . You set the Republican municipality against the Monarchical state; you set Bologna against Italy. . . . This is a most disgraceful act of revolution![106]

For councillor Perozzi a Socialist could no longer be considered Italian. But as Zanardi argued, under these circumstances neither Garibaldi, nor Mazzini and Saffi would count as Italians.[107]

REACTION

After the war municipal Socialism had precious little time to consolidate itself in Bologna. The war left the workers more conscious of their rights, the Liberals divided and the Socialists isolated by their decision not to contribute to a stable majority in parliament.[108] The elections of November 1919 were probably the most democratic in the kingdom's history, a consequence of the new electoral system and of the government's decision not to manipulate the election. For the first time the composition of parliament seemed to reflect the country's political diversity. However, the result made it impossible to form a majority and to establish parliamentary control of government. The elections were a fiasco for the liberal forces which had governed the country since Unification, but they did not offer any viable alternatives ether. The Socialists, as the biggest group, won 156 out of 508 seats, the Catholics 100. Stable coalitions became impossible. Almost two thirds of those elected had no previous parliamentary experience.[109]

In Emilia Romagna the conservative-agrarian forces had to enlarge the basis of their alliance. As a consequence of the interventionist campaign Nationalism had gained new support. Enthusiasm for Italy's moral renewal through war was popular among sections of the lower classes and the petite bourgeoisie, as well as in certain intellectual circles.[110] The *fasci* included workers as well as intellectuals, artists associated with the avant-garde as well as young reserve officers, referred to by Mussolini as "trenchocracy."[111] They also recruited veterans with a rural background, who after their return from the front were unable to reintegrate into a world on the verge of disappearing. In cities like Milan and Bologna students and also small shopkeepers, opposed to the Socialists' social and fiscal policy, were attracted to the new political milieu of the Fascists. The movement included Republicans, Monarchists, Catholics, former Radicals as well as former Socialists, who were disappointed with their party's pacifism.[112] For many of them the lodestar was not Benito Mussolini but Gabriele D'Annunzio, hailed by General Pietro Badoglio as the "new Garibaldi."[113] As Lyttelton explains, "the open-ended character of Fascist ideology, in contrast to the coherence of the Nationalists, facilitated the winning of converts."[114]

Until 1921 Bologna was the province with the second largest membership in Fascist organisations. Local Fascism was characterised by a relatively low proportion of rural and industrial workers, but a high proportion of employees, sharecroppers and students.[115] According to Mussolini, the *fasci di combattimento* were "armed groups composed of 200–250 tried and tested and well-armed individuals," with an unambiguously subversive, *putschist*, revolutionary function.[116] Backed by nationalist students and parts of the urban middle classes, they were in general financed by the region's agricultural entrepreneurs, who later formed the upper echelons of the Fascist *Federazione italiana sindacati agricoltori*, born in Bologna in 1922.[117] The agricultural elites viewed the takeover as a Fascist restoration of the state or, in Gramsci's words, as identical with the "legalisation of violence."[118] Before it came to this, the advance of "municipal Socialism" was confirmed by the administrative elections of October and November 1920, which took place in an atmosphere marked by the agricultural strikes and the occupation of the factories a few weeks earlier. Armed intervention of the *fasci* during the electoral campaign was widespread.[119] Membership in the National Federation of Agricultural Workers had risen to 845,635, with Emilia the strongest regional organisation and Bologna the second strongest provincial affiliation after Ferrara.[120] Nationally, 2022 out of 8327 municipalities and 26 out of 69 provinces elected Socialist majorities. In Emilia seven out of eight provincial councils and 65% of the communes became Socialist. In the town councils of Genoa, Naples, Messina and Palermo the PSI managed to further increase their seats. Milan, Bologna, Livorno, Turin, Venice and Florence were governed by Socialists. "Socialism had become the sum of several thousand local Socialisms." (Angelo Tasca)[121]

A soon as the red flags were waved from the balconies of the town halls political reaction assumed a new quality. It was in Bologna, on 21 November 1920, that Fascism for the first time eliminated a democratically elected government.[122] During the inauguration of the new administration, when the Socialist mayor Ennio Gnudi addressed the citizenry outside the town hall, the Fascist militia, supported by parts of the police, entered the square and started shooting. From a window of the town hall a bomb was thrown into the crowd, killing nine people and leaving more than fifty injured—all of them Socialists. Inside the town hall the Nationalist councillor Giordani was shot dead. The massacre of Palazzo D'Accursio marked the end of Bologna's *socialismo municipale*. The democratically elected council was suspended and the administration replaced by a prefectural commissioner. Within a few weeks, the Fascists took all the major towns along the old Via Emilia: Modena, Reggio Emilia, Parma, Cremona, Pavia. From Ferrara they moved north in the direction of Mantova, and through the Veneto, taking Rovigo, Padova, Verona, Vicenza. Similar moves followed in Tuscany and Umbria. Everywhere the premises of the *Camera del Lavoro* were burned down. *Case del popolo* and the headquarters of peasant leagues were destroyed and later taken over by the Fascist organisations themselves. Leaders of the Left were murdered, executed by Fascist militia men, who were paid 20 or 30 Lire per day. Depending on the different localities, between 53 and 72% of the funding for the Fascist militia came from industrial, agrarian and other business organisations.[123]

Italian Fascism was grounded in economic interests as well as in the new context of nationalist ideology which emerged with the campaign for intervention in the war. However, in order to understand the direction which Fascist violence took we have to take into account the role of municipal institutions, traditions and politics in fostering the identity of Italians since Unification. The example of Bologna shows that the democratically elected Socialist administrations and the success of *socialismo municipale* were the main target of the Fascist assault, despite Fascism's agrarian background. Liberal Italy struggled to establish a *cultura nazionale* after Unification, which would have allowed Italians to identify themselves with the nation-state. However, there existed in Italy a *cultura municipale*, which was the source of a positive civic identity, creating a strong link between the urban selves and the liberal democratic institutions of the municipalities. This was not the case everywhere in Italy; but where these bonds existed, they were also the result of a municipal politics of culture since Unification, which had fostered a sense of identity and which corresponded to the tradition of *l'Italia delle cento città*. Italy's *Socialismo municipale* was rooted in these traditions. Therefore, in order to conquer Italy, the Fascists had to start with the cities, even if the Labour conflicts at the time to a large extent involved the countryside.

The 1925 meeting of the Italian Society for the progress of science (Sips) took place in Bologna and was inaugurated by Mussolini. On this occasion he confirmed the new regime's commitment to modern scientific research:

I need science. . . . Science has to tell me if there is an even stronger poison gas and, in particular, what is to be done to fight the others' gas. You have seen the development of chemistry during the last war. . . . Science confronts me with many problems, which are linked to fundamental phenomena of physical life, for obvious reasons.[124]

The rector of the university, Pasquale Sfameni, welcomed the fact that "Mussolini has adopted a principle of ancient philosophy—the link between political power and science . . . the union between knowledge and action."[125] Given its ancient academic tradition, Bologna had no difficulty defining its role in relation to these new challenges of the modern world, thereby seemingly confirming the racialising stereotypes of another "reactionary modernist," Werner Sombart, who said of the Italians' national character: "mediterraneans are quicker to make up their minds, but also quicker to come to an agreement with one another and to commit themselves to action in common."[126]

Notes

NOTES TO THE INTRODUCTION

1. For an excellent and insightful study of the events in Parma see Basini 2001. For the general context Parker 1997b: 102–3. Guarnieri Corazzol 1988: 28. Parma, once part of the Papal States, became a separate dukedom of the Farnese family, then of the Bourbons. After the Napoleonic period it was ruled by Marie-Louise of Habsburg Lorraine.
2. According to Croce 1891: 334, it was the opening of the Teatro di San Carlo which transformed Naples from a provincial into a capital city. For the impact of culture and society on the formation of institutions see Eder 1997.
3. On Verdi's centenary see in particular Morelli 1998: 43–113.
4. Using these categories to describe the work is evidently problematic, not least because the completion of *Parsifal* had coincided with some of Wagner's last essays, which were both anti-semitic and anti-modern. However, what matters for this introduction is the context of Bologna's *Parsifal* reception in 1914. Dahlhaus and Deathridge 1984: 62ff.
5. Exemplary, Drake 1980, and more recently, Griffin 2007: 196–97. More balanced, Emilio Agazzi et al. 1980. See in this context the debate in Riall 2004: 437–38. On the increased use of the concept of crisis to describe a specific sense of time see Koselleck 2006: 358.
6. For a critique of this approach see Corner 1986: 12–13.
7. On Catholic power see Chadwick 1998: 109–14.
8. This critique of Gramsci's comparison between the French Revolution and the Italian Risorgimento was initiated by Romeo 1959. See also Gerschenkron 1962: 92.
9. For these concepts see Charle and Roche (eds) 2002. Frandsen 1998: 83–106. Gerbel et al. (eds) 1996. Kannonier and Konrad (eds) 1995. Umbach 2005.
10. The most important study of early popular celebrations of the nation is Pécout 1995.
11. Gramsci 1975: vol. 3, 2108.
12. Porciani 1997a: 11 sq. Banti 2000: 56. For "the Reasons of Misrule" see Zemon Davis 1975. Also Henningsen and Beindorf (eds) 1999.
13. Philippe Poirrier, a pioneer in research on municipal cultural policy, defined the term in the form of a Weberian ideal type, capturing a wide range of cultural objectives and means, put into practice by municipal authorities on the basis of an explicit, politically legitimising discourse. Poirrier 1990: 12.
14. Anderson 1991.
15. Figures refer to the territory in its modern extension (1971) and are based on Istituto Centrale di Statistica 1976: 13.

16. Frandsen 1998: 99.
17. Castronovo (ed.) 1977: 49. Levra (ed.) 2001: xix. Ghirelli 1973: 261–78. For Bologna's military role: Segretariato Generale della Camera dei Deputati 1971: vol. 1, 49–50.
18. On the stereotypes of the South see Dickie 1999. Riall 1998a: 5–8. So far as Italy's economic development is concerned it is important to emphasise its regional diversity, which Gerschenkron was among the first to analyse, 1962: 72.
19. Cazzola 1997: 54–55. Pollard 2005: 24. Romanelli 1979: 74. Zamagni 1997: 127.
20. Quine 2002: 36, 182. Cattini 1997: 8. As a consequence of poor diet, the illness of pellagra, widespread in Italy, was particularly fatal in the region.
21. Cammelli and di Francia 1996: 15. Bergonzini 1966: 284, 291. (These numbers include only the population which could neither read nor write. Those who read, but were unable to write, counted as literate.) See also Berselli 1980: 269. Vigo 1993: 43, 50.
22. *La Nazione,* quoted in Avellini 1997: 662. Cammelli 1995: 74ff. On the university during the transition Simoni 1947: vol. 2, 209ff.
23. Melis 1996: 17.
24. Adani and Bentini (eds) 1996: vol. 4, 254–55.
25. Bellocchi 1977: 356.
26. Zangheri 1986: 23.
27. For the political development of administration in Bologna see Körner 2005.
28. Davis (ed.) 1979. Also Riall 1998a: 8 sq. Riall 1994.
29. Davis 1994: 304.
30. Körner 2007.
31. For instance, Isnenghi 2004: 161, tells us the story of the Cuccoli family, which from a hut on Piazza Maggiore entertained Bologna for seventy years with vaudevilles, popular anecdotes and street theatre, without representing the city's official cultural policy.
32. Williams 1976: 137. See in this context also Gramsci 1975: vol. 3, 2109.
33. Kneif 1971.
34. I refer in this context to the approach of Jauss 1970: 10.
35. Davis (ed.) 1979: 16.
36. Kocka 1989: 9. Conze and Kocka 1985: 11.
37. Weber, M. 1988a. On this process see also Perkin 1989: 2. On the contrast with the educated notable see Charle 1990: 11. Malatesta, M. (ed.) 1995: 9, 14. Also Malatesta, M. 2006a: 84ff. Most of the ancient Italian states preceded the rest of Europe in the efficient regulation of the professions, and earlier than anywhere else Italy required university degrees as the basis for professional recognition. This explains in part the numeric strength of Italians with a university degree in relation to the high quota of illiteracy.
38. Bourdieu 1979: 549.
39. Croce 1928: 8.
40. Bigaran (ed.) 1986: 23. Aurelio Alaimo has analysed the professionalisation of Bologna's administration in the field of urban planning, helped by the role of the new school of engineering, which was favoured by the urban elites, but which received only half-hearted support from the State: Alaimo 1990a. See also Malatesta, M. 2006b. Simoni 1974: vol. 2, 220–21. Romanelli 1989. Filippo De Pieri describes the nineteenth-century city as one of professionals, civil servants, artists and academics: De Pieri 2005: 11–12, 19ff. Bocquet and De Pieri 2002: 144. In "Paris, Hauptstadt des 19. Jahrhunderts" Walter Benjamin discussed the role of the professional engineer: Benjamin 1955, vol. 1, 406–22.

41. Charle 1990: 12. For intellectual professionalisation see Charle 1996. Bourdieu 1979: 490.
42. Janik and Toulmin 1973: 247ff. The professionalisation described by Janik and Toulmin produces the "expert" as defined by Walter Benjamin. See "Distraction. Walter Benjamin and the Avant-Garde," in: Schwartz 2005.
43. Schmitt 1954: 9.
44. Gramsci 1975: vol. 3, 1793. See in this context Gramsci's discussion of the Jacobins during the French Revolution: Gramsci 1975: vol. 2, 763. Also Koselleck 1992: 68.
45. Charle 1990: 11–12. Pasolini 2005: 127. See also 7–8. See also Hübinger 1993: 202. For a recent empirical case study under conditions not dissimilar to Bologna see Pietrow-Ennker 2005: 172.
46. Ragionieri 1979c: 269. Benda observes the *"trahison des clercs"* in the 1890s, when they leave objective and interest-free analysis as described by Weber behind, in order to enter the political arena: Benda 1927. Weber, M. 1988b: 148. Charle 1990: 7.
47. Mayer 1981.
48. Salvemini 1973: 55–68.
49. See in this context Forgacs' argument that Fascism "was not so much an onslaught on the working-class movement in its revolutionary manifestations . . . but an onslaught on the reformist working-class movement as part of the legal apparatus of the liberal state." Bologna's "municipal socialism" provides an example for this integration of reformism into the apparatus of the liberal state: Forgacs 1986b: 26. On the concept of Fascism as a "cultural revolution" see Morgan 2004: 3, 18. Also Ben-Ghiat 2001.

NOTES TO CHAPTER 1

1. Gramsci 1971: 20.
2. Zangheri 1986: 20. Similar, Fincardi 2004: 216.
3. Mayer 1981. Izenberg 1979 presents a similar argument. For the Italian debate on Mayer see Caracciolo; Cervelli; Fohlen; Woolf 1983. Also the special issue of *MRSSS*, 19, 1994 (January) and in particular Banti 1994. A more nuanced position is taken by Macry 2002: 13–14. Jocteau's description of Mayer's book as "an intelligent historiographical provocation" and Meriggi's discussion present exceptions in this debate: Jocteau 1997: vii; Meriggi 2000b: 209–10. The debate as a whole leads to the question as to whether Italy after Unification can be defined as liberal. Contrasting with the Gramscian tradition, Roberto Vivarelli sees the core of this problem not in the social composition of the political elites after Unification, which changed on the national level under the governments of the Left, but in their departure from liberal values after 1876: Vivarelli 1995.
4. For Sheehan's review of Mayer see *SH*, 8, 1983, 111–12. My work investigates this problem in relation to networks of local power as encouraged by Gall 1990: 5.
5. As Raffaele Romanelli remarked during the debate, when analyzing historicising style in nineteenth-century architecture the historian needs to take into account the ambivalence of the relationship with the past and the changing aesthetic meanings of cultural representations: Romanelli 1982: 1102.
6. Aimo 1997: 27, 55. It should be noted that the administration by aristocratic elites was usually based on liberal principles. See in particular Kroll 1999.
7. Ferraboschi 2003: 52 sq.

8. Croce 1928: 94–95. As Neumann 2004 has pointed out, due to political and constitutional changes it is difficult to differentiate between the concepts nobility and aristocracy. For the persistent role of patricians in municipal administration see also Van Dijk 1988: 458–59.
9. Cited in: Cammarano 2004: 39–40. For Bologna see Maestri 1984: 181–208. Similar, Preti and Tarozzi 1988: 54.
10. Banti 1996a: 51. Banti 1994: 14–17.
11. Cardoza 1997: 55. Montroni 1996: 415, 419. Romanelli 1995a: 14. Petersen 1990: 245–46, 253. Banti 1996a: 52. Banti 1990: 72. Also France had after 1815 an "aristocracy without privileges" and many titles were not recognised in heraldic documents: Mayer 1981: 126 sq.; Haupt 1989: 129. In Prussia membership in the Herrenhaus was granted: Wehler 1995: 168, 807.
12. Montroni 1996: 424. Zangheri 1986: 40. Cardoza 1997: 57 speaks of a de facto aristocratic control of the Senate. On the composition of the Senate, also Jocteau 1997: 4. Members of the Senate were appointed for life. One hundred members were high civil, military and judicial officials; 100 members were appointed among former members of the second chamber who had served at least six years; 100 members were wealthy notables paying at least 3000 Lire in taxes; between 60 and 100 members belonged to learned societies, universities or had served the nation as individuals: Mayer 1981: 160.
13. Banti 1996a: 53. In the lower chamber this trend was also a consequence of the electoral system: Niccolai 1995: 84. Within this group the Piedmontese nobles accounted for more parliamentary deputies, senators, statesmen and army officers than any of the other old titles: Cardoza 1997: 6.
14. Cardoza 1997: 8, 55 sq., 71–72.
15. Croce 1928: 94–95. Macry 2002: 35 speaks about the "*logica del cognome*" in local elections. Also Macry 1990: 33. Macry 1984: 361–62.
16. CdE, 09 September 1860.
17. Romeo 1990: 215. Ullrich 1978: 51. On the aristocracy's role in the Associazione Costituzionale delle Romagne see Cuccoli 1974/1975: 278. In Bologna the representation of *nobili* in the associazione costituzionale was less important than in the rest of the Romagna.
18. Cammarano 2004: 22. Cammarano 1995a: 28. Romanelli 1979: 26. Cardoza 1997: 44.
19. Giovanni Codronchi, quoted in: Cardoza 1997: 40. On the dominating role of the nobility in the Associazione costituzionale of the Romagna also Brice 2005: 154.
20. ACC, 23 November 1896, consigliere Putti.
21. Mack Smith 1969: 39. See also Ragionieri 1979c: 95.
22. Romeo 1990: 41. On the tradition of nobles in the local administration Cardoza 1997: 37.
23. Alaimo 1990b: 6. D'Attore 1986: 65–66.
24. Zangheri 1986: 41. Alaimo 1990a: 41–42. D'Attore 1986: 66. Albertazzi 1990.
25. Casarini (1830–1874) was a leading member of the Società Nazionale and a member of parliament since 1865, first for Castel San Pietro, later for Castelmaggiore and finally Budrio. Initially belonging to the Terzo Partito, he then voted consistently with the opposition. Piretti and Guidi (eds) 1992: vol. 2, 73. Masi 1875: 137, 152, 155. D'Attore 1986: 72. D'Attore 1991: 92. Preti and Tarozzi 1988: 59. Alaimo 1990b: 9. Marquis Luigi Tanari was a veteran of 1848 and in 1859 he was part of the provisional government, later a member of parliament and senator. ACC, 24 March 1904.
26. Colombo, E. 2005: 19.
27. Spadolini 1993: 233.

28. Pepoli 1862. On the following see Lindon 1998 and Spini 1956: 144. For Bellini's libretto he received detailed instructions from the composer: Parker 1988: 297.
29. Hale Bellot 1929: 121ff. Considering that the *Principles of Political Economy* were placed on the Papal Index, his contacts with Mill were certainly not appreciated by the Papal administration: Pollard 2005: 24.
30. Other works included *Il nobile e il cittadino*, *Lucia di Treviglio*, *L'onore di una figlia*, and *La scuola delle giovani spose*. Calore 1982: 60, 79, 85–86. Calore 1998: 61ff. On nobility and literature and the nobility's representation in post-Unification fiction see Jocteau 1997: 173–249.
31. Minghetti 1888–90: vol. 3, 153.
32. Mayer 1981: 26.
33. Veroli s.a. Masi 1875: 54.
34. Zangheri 1986: 7, 10. D'Attore 1986: 70. On the role of the press in organizing local politics see also Sorba 1993: 29.
35. Two thirds of the Italian diplomats abroad belonged to the aristocracy: Petersen 1990: 249. The number seems to be higher than the respective number for Germany: Lequin 1978: 315.
36. See in particular Pepoli 1864. On the perception of his role Albertazzi 1990: 24–25. Veroli s.a.: xii–xiii. For the quote: Casarini to Pinelli, 13 June 1861, reprinted in Franzoni Gamberini 1961: 239. This adds an interesting aspect to the political attitudes of the aristocratic liberal movement, which generally was rather critical of the Napoleonic legacy: Meriggi 2000a: 50.
37. Veroli s.a.: xvii. On the repercussions of this event in Bologna see Körner 2005.
38. On his complex relationship to the Moderates D'Attore 1991: 89–90. Also Caracciolo 1973: 29. On the role of the nobility in the Labour associations: Gianni 2006: 130.
39. Alaimo 1990a: 138. For comparison, in Turin, until the early 1880s, the nobility occupied a quarter of the seats in the municipal council; thereafter numbers began to shrink: Cardoza 1997: 70. For Parma Sorba 1993: 22–23.
40. Likewise Bianconcini, Bonora, Carpi, Fagnoli, Loup, Lugli, Maccaferri, Massei, Mazzacorati, Sacchetti, Scarselchi, Silvani, Zabban, Zorzi. See Masulli 1980: 33. Cazzola 1997: 77.
41. See for the period 1861 to 1895 the biographical appendix in Randeraad 1997: 289–307. Fried 1963: 126.
42. Cardoza 1997: 50. Not an uncommon phenomenon in Northern Italy: Fincardi 2004: 216–18.
43. Romanelli 1995a: 3–21.
44. Jones 1997: 18, 83–84. See also Cardoza 1997: 4.
45. Croce 1928: 91–92. See also Romanelli 1979: 27.
46. *Il Paese*, 5 November 1861, quoted in: Berselli 1980: 263.
47. Banti 2000: 33 describes the Risorgimento as a "generational phenomenon." In his sample of memoirs and correspondence he includes men and women born between 1783 and 1843, a period of ca. two generations. On the problem of loyalty Ullrich 1978: 51. For Palagi see Tovoli 1984a: 191.
48. Hearder 1983: 157. Banti 2000: 3–4. On the municipality as the principal producer of collective identity see Balzani 1997a: 599.
49. Banti 2000: 5.
50. Banti 2000: 10, 47–48.
51. ACC, 15 January 1903, sindaco Golinelli.
52. Macry 2002a: 22.
53. Minghetti 1888–90: vol. 2, 148. Balzani 1997a: 600 sq. Berselli 1980: 258. Meriggi 1997: 51. On the links between Bologna's nobility and the Papal regime see also Cavazza and Bertondini 1976: 15, 325.

54. Minghetti 1888–90: vol. 1, 105, 164ff., vol. 3, 15–16. Banti 2000: 16. Woolf 1981: vol. 1, 236–37.

55. Marco Minghetti, "Ordinamento amministrativo dello Stato," 13 March 1861, in: Minghetti 1988: vol. 1, 89–105. Minghetti 1865: 5. Lipparini 1942: vol. 1, 234. For an outline of his later, more critical views on the Church see his letters to Emile de Laveley of 16 July 1878 and 21 January 1882, in: Dumoulin (ed.) 1979: 21–22, 60–61.

56. Marco Minghetti, "Facoltà al Governo di accettare e stabilire con decreto reale, l'annessione allo Stato di nuove provincie italiane," 10 October 1860, in: Minghetti 1988: vol. 1, 72–73. On the weakness of legitimism: Ragionieri 1976: 1678–79. D'Attore 1986: 75. Porciani 1993: 213. In Naples the urban aristocracy and the former officers of the army celebrated in 1884 the silver wedding of Francesco II and Maria Sofia of Bavaria: Macry 1984: 351. Randeraad 1997: 58–59, 254. Zangheri 1986: 6. Even Piedmont knew a black aristocracy: Cardoza 1997: 78ff.

57. Ragionieri 1976: 1730; Randeraad 1997: 65ff., 228. On the "social role assigned to the landed elites since the beginning of unification" Romanelli 1995b: 103.

58. Prefect of Bologna, government inquiry 1869, quoted in Romanelli 1995b: 129.

59. Cardoza 1997: 38. D'Attore 1992: 237.

60. Alfonso Rubbiani, quoted in: Bignardi 1963: 42.

61. Pollard 2005: 1–15.

62. Randeraad 1997: 86. These numbers were significant considering that in 1865 only 3.9% of the local population had the right to vote (and even after the reforms of 1889 only 11.2%). On the national level, where between 2 and 8% of the population had the right to vote, participation ranged between 45 and 60%. On abstention see also Pombeni 1995: 80–81.

63. *L'Unione*, 28/06/1879, quoted in: Maestri 1984: 193. For Bologna consider also Minghetti's position towards the Church: Jemolo 1965: 17, 37–38.

64. Ragionieri 1976: 1731. In this election (1870) 2% of the national population had the right to vote. On the reactions in Bologna on 20 September see for instance *MdB*, 21 September 1870.

65. ACC, 25 January 1868. As late as in the 1890s the conservative councillor Ambrosini replies to a democratic councillor speaking in favour of lay education that a number of councillors who officially take an anti-clerical position in council send their own sons to Bologna's religious schools: ACC, 18 December 1895, consigliere Ambrosini.

66. Polsi 1986: 113–14.

67. Cavazza and Bertondini 1976: 277, 316. D'Attore 1992: 236–37.

68. Defining themselves in opposition to the middle-class Democrats, they often represented local and regional interests in parliament, even if these differed from the government's ideas. Berselli 1980: 264, 271. For the Right's "*consorteria*" in Milan see Colombo, E. 2005: 22.

69. See in this context Caracciolo 1973: 12.

70. Izenberg 1979. Mosse, W. 1988.

71. Woolf 1981: vol. 1, 290ff. Banti 1990: 46–50. Cardoza 1997: 32. Morabito 1988: 169. Meriggi 1988: 146, 150. D'Attore 1991: 88. Cardoza 1997: 30. Cattini 1997: 12. Malatesta, M. 1999: 11.

72. Cazzola 1997: 80. Banti 1990: 52, 89. Only a century later, after 1915, the number of small landholders around Bologna started to increase dramatically.

73. Numbers in Masulli 1980: 15. Mayer 1981: 31. On the last decades before Unification and for a comparative view see Meriggi 1994: 163 sq.

74. Minghetti 1888–90: vol. 3, 25. Berselli 2001: 17. See also Zanichelli 1896: vi, x. Several items of the British Library's collection of Minghetti's pamphlets and writings carry personal dedications to the British prime minister. Mosse, W. 1988: 295–96 analyses the Gladstones as a model of social and political promotion in a European context. On the influence of Italian Moderates on Gladstone's attitude towards Unification Spadolini 1960: 12–13.
75. On the following Albertazzi 1986. Baioni 1994: 47.
76. D'Attore 1986: 89–90. Aurelio Alaimo, "Bologna," 15.
77. Baioni 1994: 47.
78. Meriggi 1988: 148. Petersen 1990: 249. Among the general staff the aristocracy still occupied 33.6% during the 1880s. Jocteau 1997: 6.
79. Malatesta, M. 2006b: 90–91. In general see Mayer 1981: 12. Cammarano 1995a: 19. Romanelli 1991: 726–27. Petersen 1990: 244. Siegrist 1988: 100. On the role of voluntary associations in this process: Banti and Meriggi 1991: 360–61. Kocka; Macry; Romanelli; Salvati 1990: 32. Ridolfi 1987: 31. More critical, underlining the limits of this symbiosis Cardoza 1997: 162 sq. The openness of the aristocracy to the upper middle class and the trend of the urban rich to acquire land was a general European phenomenon: Kocka 1995: 789, 802.
80. Roberto Michels, quoted in: Lyttelton 1991: 232.
81. Minghetti to Laveleye, 2 July 1880, in: Dumoulin (ed.) 1979: 42–43.
82. *MdB*, 28 February and 1 March 1869. Cavina 2005: 238. Also Banti 2000: 144. A report on a duel between two *borghesi* in *MdB*, 05 July 1870 still refers to "*strette regole di cavalleria.*"
83. Mack Smith 1969: 64–65.
84. Banti and Meriggi 1991. For Minghetti's socioeconomic background see Berselli 2001.
85. Bourdieu 1979: 190.
86. Meriggi 1988: 147. Lyttelton 1991: 219. For more detailed data see Cammarano 1995b: 281. Cammelli 1995: 28. Siegrist 1992: 146. Siegrist 1988: 94–95.
87. Siegrist 1994: 233–34. On the problem of categorizing professionals in parliament Cammarano 1995b: 278.
88. Cammarano and Piretti 1996: 529. Masulli 1980: 23, 33. Cavazza and Bertondini 1976: 326. For similar examples Banti 1995: 240–41. Alaimo 1990a: 210. Alaimo 1992 a: 24. Ferraboschi 2003: 69. The idea of the aristocratic lawyer goes back to the Middle Ages: Waley 1988: 14, 61. Oexle 1985: 61. For the modern period Petersen 1990: 247. Lyttelton 1991: 219–20, 223. Montroni 1996: 418, 422. Siegrist 1988: 114, 120. Siegrist 1992. Cardoza 1997: 221. During the nineteenth century the number of Italian lawyers of noble origin decreases, but until well into the twentieth century law remained the most popular degree among the aristocracy. Before Unification, 11% of the practicing lawyers in Florence belonged to the nobility; in Milan, in 1888, 4%. In Naples it was common for the nobility to hold a degree in law, but the number of aristocrats exercising the profession was negligible. Also in other countries the nobility attended university whether or not they completed a degree: Neumann 2004: 164–65.
89. Siegrist 1994: 227.
90. Siegrist 1994: 235–36. Siegrist 1988: 123. Finzi and Tasinari 1986: 207.
91. Lyttelton 1991: 231. Macry 2002a: 259. Musella 1995: 332. ASCB: CA, 1861, Tit. XVI, Adunanza dei Palchisti del Teatro Comunale, 22 December 1861.
92. Marco Minghetti, "Commemorazione di G.B.Ercolani. Discorso pronunziato nell'Archiginnasio Bolognese il 23 Novembre 1884," in: Minghetti 1896:

367–99. Minghetti 1888–90: vol. 3, 159. Porciani 1981: 118. In France the noble university teacher practically disappeared after 1860: Charle 1994: 107.

93. Romanelli 1991: 723ff. estimates that the borghesia ranged from 300,000 to 350,000 persons between 1881 and 1921, of which about 200,000 were property owners or entrepreneurs. Lyttelton 1991: 224 includes shopkeepers and comes to about one million members, or 6.7% of the total population, less than half of the percentage for France during the same period. For the earlier period see Davis 1988: 94, 112–13. Also in other parts of Europe the *borghesia umanistica* remained subordinate: Kocka 1995: 791. Concerning differences in the structure of wealth see Charle 1991: 42. Lequin 1998: 499.

94. Jemolo 1965: 10. Romanelli 1979: 136. For similar evaluations see Leone Carpi writing in 1878 or Francesco S. Nitti in 1901, both quoted in Banti 1996b: 491–92. Cavour's remark probably reflected the difference in income of the liberal professions in rural areas compared to the urban centres: See for this Banti 1996b: 507. In 1880 the South counted twice as many solicitors and barristers as the centre of Italy: Siegrist 1994: 230. The majority of lawyers from the North and the Centre belonged to the Right, while those from the South sat on the Left: Cammarano and Piretti 1996: 527.

95. Spadolini 1960: 11ff. Battistini 1986: 322–23.

96. Vinciguerra 1957: 21 sq., 36. Minghetti did not support the freemasons. Piromalli 1988: 58. Biagini 1961: 194–95.

97. Marco Minghetti to Luigi Carlo Farini, quoted in: Romanelli 1979: 36. Faucci 1976. Dunnage 1995: 382. Davis 1988: 217 sq.

98. Codronchi to Minghetti, 15 June 1874, quoted in Berselli 1980: 284. For a portrait of this political milieu see the Bologna Trial of 1876, following the failed anarchist insurrection two years earlier: Pernicone 1993: 101ff.

99. Alaimo 1990b: 45–49. On this function in the administration Romanelli 1989: 68–69. Tubertini seems to contradict Romanelli's idea that many *segretari* were "*intellettuali deracinés*," 71.

100. Cammarano 1993: 142–43. Varni 1997: 563.

101. Albertazzi 1985: 227. On his political activity see Carducci 1935–1968: vol. 25. On Carducci as political journalist: Cristofori 1985.

102. D'Attore 1986: 76. On the symbolic importance of these celebrations Conti 2000: 15. Isnenghi 2004: 77.

103. On the relationship between the Radical Left and freemasonry in Italy Conti 2003: 50 sq. See in particular Filopanti 1858; (for the quote see p. 4). On Filopanti see Preti (ed.) 1997.

104. Bourdieu 1979: 16 sq. See also Carpi 1981: 447.

105. Petersen 1990: 247. Albertazzi 1987: 31. Cucchiella 1993: 134. In this respect the Italian situation differs profoundly from Germany, where subsequent to Stein's reforms of 1808 municipal administration became the almost exclusive domain of *Bildungsbürger*: Reulecke 1989.

106. Macry 1984: 358–59 showed that qualified civil servants in Naples lived in complete poverty. For Bologna Spadolini 1960: 16 sq. Battistini 1986: 322.

107. Meriggi 1988: 141. Meriggi 2000b: 203–209. Also Banti 1996a.

108. See for example the criticism of Count Jacini (1889), Caracciolo 1976: 53. Also Salvemini 1976: 71.

109. Romanelli 1979: 49–50. Cammelli 1995: 35. For a general overview of the changing electoral system Ballini 1988.

110. Kelikian 1996: 378. Romanelli 1995b: 89–90. Cammarano 1995a: 41.

111. Romanelli 1991: 723. See also the situation in the nearby city of Piacenza, where the "*possidenti*" represented the biggest group among the electors (20.2%). They were followed by the liberal professions (13,8%), which included again a considerable number of "*possidenti*." Banti 1989: 203.

112. Alaimo 1990a: 45.
113. Romanelli 1979: 136. On the impact of the electoral reform also Ullrich 1978: 55. For a West-European comparison see Kocka 1995: 791–92. On the difference between these categories see Meriggi 1988: 144.
114. Zangheri 1986: 43ff. Finzi and Tassinari 1986: 208. Masulli 1980: 140. Malatesta, M. 2006b: 53.
115. Carlo De Cesare, quoted in Randeraad 1997: 229. See also Romanelli 1995b: 104. Malatesta, M. 1989: 53.
116. Urbinati 1996: 202. On the limited effect of this reform Jocteau 1997: 5.
117. Carli was unable to form a stable majority. Alaimo 1990b: 9. For a summary of the elections see Lotti 1980. See also Körner 2005. The case of democratic administration in Parma was very different: Sorba 1993.
118. Berselli 1980: 289. On *trasformismo* Sabbatucci 2003. Musella 2003.
119. Cucchiella 1993: 273. Cavazza, G. 1984: 49ff. Masulli 1980: 51. On the electoral alliances see in particular Istituto per la storia del Risorgimento 1968.
120. Orata 1968: 72. Berselli 1980: 288–89, 293, 292. Straziota 1968: 119ff. Cucchiella 1993: 135.
121. D'Attore 1991: 93 sq.
122. Polsi 1984. Similar to the example of Bologna, a number of councillors appearing in the statistics as lawyers also owned large properties. However, for the majority of the political representatives law and academia were the principle sources of income; revenue from property became the exception.
123. Preti and Tarozzi 1988: 46–50. Sorba 1993. Berselli 1980: 300.
124. Mazzonis 2001: 445, 488. In Milan the anti-Moderate alliance of Radicals, Republicans and Socialists won the municipal elections in 1899, but subsequently the majority went back to a Moderate-Catholic alliance: Meriggi 2001: 27, 33.
125. Adorno 1998.
126. On the decline of the aristocracy: Meriggi 1988: 156–57. Petersen 1990: 245–46 also emphasises the decline of the aristocracy after Unification. Other historians state that notions concerning the alleged triumph of the bourgeoisie were exaggerated and that the impact of the Revolution on the distribution of wealth was more limited than previously thought. See also "the close proximity and interconnection between aristocratic and bourgeois elements" in the elite of notables in France: Kocka 1995: 789–90. Mosse, W. 1988: 278 underlines the poor economic basis of the majority of the European aristocracy and states that only a minority belonged to the societal elites. Lequin 1978 shows how the society of notables knew to defend their economic and social status; quote on p. 314. The picture of Germany in Wehler 1995: 167 sq. differed from the situation in Italy. For a European comparison Malatesta, M. 1999.
127. Jardin and Tudesq 1973: vol. 1, 157–58. Daumard 1987: 256–57. On the history of the concept Haupt 1989: 115–16. Also Kocka 1988: 25.
128. Meriggi 2000b: 209. Sorba 1993: 21, 25. Aimo 1997: 53. Ponziani (ed.) 2000. Cammarano 2004: 38. Cammarano 2002. Pombeni 1993: 72–73. Analysing Bologna's political situation during the second half of the nineteenth century, Maestri 1984 speaks about "*una politica di notabili.*" Alaimo 1990b: 7 speaks about *notabili-politici*. Also Conti 1994. For Spadolini 1993: 228 Minghetti represented the model of a *notabile*.
129. Weber, M. 1982: 15, 38–39. See also Haupt 1989: 116. The professionalisation of municipal politics was also the consequence of the opening of council debates, a process the local press did not necessarily welcome: *GdR*, 11 March 1865.
130. Ragionieri 1976: 1723.

131. Ridolfi 1989. Ridolfi 1990. Ridolfi 1992. Davis 1988: 192 sq.
132. Maestri 1984: 207. Pombeni 1993: 45ff.
133. For these concepts see Bobbio 1990a. Cotta 1979: 7 defines the political class as the "concrete actors of the political life." For von Beyme 1993: 7 sq. this is a phenomenon of the modern *Parteienstaat*, which is the reason why Pareto and Mosca do not differentiate between the two concepts. Political party organisations in the modern sense emerged only with the Socialist movement. On political parties in Italy: Pombeni 1993: 45. Ullrich 1980: 403–50. Finelli and Fruci 2000. Cioli 1993: 429ff. For comparison see Koshar 1986: 59.
134. Zanichelli 1896: xlvi. Before World War I Tranfaglia 1995: 23 still defines the Liberals as "*gruppi notabiliari che si collegano tra loro.*"
135. See "I deputati" in: Mosca 1974: 80.
136. See von Beyme 1968: 110–12. D'Attore 1992: 235.
137. Marx and Engels 1962: 62. Engels 1962: 165ff.
138. Romanelli 1979: 70.
139. Romanelli 1979: 278. Masulli 1980: 16–19.
140. Zangheri 1986: 44, 47ff. Finzi and Tassinari 1986: 202. Zamagni 1986: 248. Cardoza 1982: 15. Alaimo 1990b: 3. Finzi 1997: 44.
141. Carpi, quoted in Romanelli 1979: 137. *GdE*, 05 October 1871. See also Preti 1992: 294. Lyttelton 1991: 217, 229.
142. Masulli 1980: 138. Romanelli 1979: 138. See also Lyttelton 1991: 224.
143. Castronovo (ed.) 1977: 12.
144. Marco Minghetti, "Intorno alla tendenza agli interessi materiali che è nel secolo presente" (1841), in: Minghetti 1896: 35. See also Fincardi 2004: 211. This picture contrasts with the emphasis on the propertied elites' industrial interests, e.g., Malatesta, M. 1999: 87 sq.
145. Marco Minghetti, "Nuove osservazioni intorno alla tendenza agli interessi materiali che è nel secolo presente in risposta alla lettera del sig.A.Pizzoli" (1841), in: Minghetti 1896: 93–94, 105.
146. Minghetti 1888–90: vol. 3, 159. For the other quotes see Berselli 1980: 267. Preti 1992: 289–90.
147. On the teaching agronomy in Bologna: Finzi (ed.) 1992.
148. Regarding the technological development see similar Banti 1989: 15ff.
149. During the first decade after Unification the mezzadria in the entire region increased from 34.07% of the rural population in 1861 to 36.25% in 1871: Berselli 1980: 266. In the province of Bologna, in 1881, 44.9% of the population employed in agriculture were *mezzadri*, compared to 35.4% *braccianti*: Zamagni 1986: 249–50. In 1901 sharecroppers were still the largest single peasant group in the Bolognese: Cardoza 1982: 19.
150. Zamagni 1986: 248. Porisini 1978. Finzi 1990. Cazzola 1997: 61 sq.
151. During the eighteenth century the region had benefited from increasing international demand and the stagnant economy of Naples. Brötel 2002: 114ff. Chorley 1965: 13. Finzi 1997: 42–43. Castronovo (ed.) 1977: 13, 74. Zangheri 1986: 44.
152. Finzi and Tassinari 1986: 203. Masulli 1980: 8–9, 16. Precapitalist structures were still quite common among aristocratic landholders: Lequin 1978: 313. See similar already Sombart 1893: 213–18, 226.
153. Zamagni 1986: 247ff. Meriggi 1988: 149.
154. On the following Masulli 1980: 23–29. For comparison see for instance Castronovo (ed.) 1977: 46–47.
155. Zangheri 1986: 54.
156. Preti 1992: 278. Finzi and Tassinari 1986: 203–4.
157. Masulli 1980: 28–31. Zamagni 1986: 255. Romanelli 1979: 240. Zangheri 1986: 53. Alaimo 1990b: 4.

158. Cesare Orsini, *Le Romagne*, quoted in: Balzani 1997a: 606. Similar Pacifico Valussi, "Le piccole città," *NA*, 3 (7), 1868, 541–595.
159. Alaimo 1990b: 15. Masulli 1980: 116–17, 136. Zamagni 1997: 127ff. Also Finzi 1997: 23–50.
160. Banti 1990: 79.
161. Cardoza 1982: 47 sq.
162. Count Francesco Massei, quoted in: Cardoza 1982: 83–84. On the opposition towards "modern" farming within the Società Agraria see also D'Attore 1992: 239.
163. Zamagni 1986: 251ff. Cardoza 1982: 16–53.
164. Macry 1984: 341–42.
165. Schnapper 1971.
166. Banti and Meriggi 1991.
167. Schnapper 1971: 95.
168. *MdB*, 1 October 1871.
169. Quoted in Bertozzi 1997: 64. Alaimo 1990a: 156.
170. Bottrigari 1960–63: vol. 4, 204–5.
171. *MdB*, 2 October 1871. Sardanapalus was a legendary Assyrian king associated with the fall of the Empire. Less critical was the *GdE*, linked to the Moderate establishment: 2 and 5 October 1871.
172. Zu den Architekten Cipolla und Mengoni siehe: Bernabei, Gresleri, Zagnomi 1977: 24ff., 34ff., 295, 298.
173. Masulli 1980: 28. Zamagni 1986: 251, 255.
174. Minghetti 1888–90: vol. 1, 135–36.
175. Bottrigaro 1960–62: vol. 3, 9.
176. Morabito 1988. Cavazza and Bertondini 1976: 16. On the social exclusiveness of these forms of sociability: Ridolfi 1997a: 297. For a comparison with other Italian cities see Banti and Meriggi 1991.
177. D'Attore 1992: 236. Alaimo 1992b: 313. For Bologna's professional organisations in general see Malatesta, M. 2006b: 59 sq.
178. Minghetti to Cavour, quoted in: Lipparini 1942: vol. 1, 212.
179. Pepoli, C. 1875: vol. 1, 26. Capellini 1914: vol. 2, 39, 80. Vitali 1984: 224, 235.
180. Palazzolo 1984: 24, 48, 90–91.
181. Ricci 1924: 189. Among the first musical events mentioned in the records were Gluck's *Orfeo ed Euridice* and *Alceste* as well as Haydn's *Schöpfung*: Morabito 1988: 169. Calore 1982: 46. See similar also Cardoza 1997: 20. Galli della Loggia 1998: 106–7. For a detailed study of these forms of sociability see Meriggi 1992: 87 sq. He notes a decline of aristocratic membership in the city's principal associations, but with 23% at the end of the century their role still exceeded by far their proportion of the population (pp.186–87).
182. Ferraboschi 2003: 155. Cavazzana Romanelli and Rossi Minutelli 2002: 1109ff.
183. ACC, 12 February 1916, consigliere Ghigi.
184. Dahlhaus 1980. Weber, W. 1975: 16 sq. Weber, W. 1979: 109–21. Kannonier 1984: 170ff.
185. Basso 1976: 343. Rosselli 1991: 124ff.
186. See for instance the description of a concert in Count Hercolani's theatre of October 1860: Bottrigari 1960–63: vol. 3, 132. Also Brice 2005: 164.
187. Flora 1960: 121.
188. *RdC*, 27 April 1885. The focus on the audience's self-representation rather than the music itself was not uncommon in the musical press. See for instance D'Annunzio's first article on Wagner in 1884: Guarnieri Corazzol 1988: 7–8.
189. See the review of the series' last concert in 1885: *RdC*, 18 May 1885.

296   *Notes*

NOTES TO CHAPTER 2

1. Plato 1952: 247–48.
2. ACC, 5 February 1870. Count Giovanni Bentivoglio, not to be mistaken for the typographer and president of the Workingmen's Society Paolo Bentivoglio. Bottrigari 1960–63: vol. 2, 521.
3. Rubbiani 1981: 613. On the comparison of the Teatro Comunale with other European opera houses see Pierre Patte and Paolo Landriani, *Storia e descrizione dei principali teatri antichi e moderni* (1830), quoted in Schiavina 1982: 402. Ironically, under Bentivoglio's signoria theatre played only a minor role in Bologna, contrasting with nearby Ferrara under Ercole I d'Este: Vecchi 1976: 423. On the history of the Teatro Comunale see in particular Trezzini 1987; Calore 1982; Gavelli and Tarozzi (eds) 1998; and for the historical context of Risorgimento theatre the fundamental study by Sorba 2001. For the management of Italian opera during the period Rosselli 1987.
4. Shaw 1993: 48–49, 149 sq., 204 sq. On the discussion about Julius' Caesarean image see Nesselrath 2004.
5. Fernàndez 1999: 141–42, 153. Shaw 1993: 12ff., 189. The pope's references to the Empire in the representation of power were not new: Since the early Middle Ages the ceremony of the Roman church was partly borrowed from the late Empire, which, nevertheless, in Italy was perceived as Greek and "foreign." (Partner 1972: 15–16.)
6. Jones 1997: 636ff. Dean 1995: 147. Shaw 1993: 148.
7. Elias 1999: vol. 2, 362.
8. Lenzi 1977: 738, 741. On the rights and duties of the *palchettisti*: Rosmini 1872: 228 sq. Also Sorba 2001: 68. For a nice description of the distribution of boxes at Naples' San Carlo see Croce 1891: 327–28. On the concept of the aristocratic theatre see Ther 2006: 343 sq.
9. Davis 2006b: 573. Macry 2002b: 18.
10. On the opening of the Comunale see Levi 1987: 3. On the origin of municipal theatres Sorba 2001: 17–22. On Galli Bibiena's theatres see Bignami 2002a: 966–67. Bignami 2002b: 979ff. Also Croce 1891: 738ff. The family built theatres in Vienna, Mantova, Verona, Mannheim, Bayreuth, Lisbon and Pavia among other major cities. While *Il Trionfo di Clelia* belongs to the operas Gluck composed in the traditional style, before his reform of the opera, in 1771 and 1778 Bologna saw performances of his new-style operas *Orfeo e Euridice* and *Alceste*. Bologna's first musical drama had been performed in 1605 in the palace of count Ridolfo Campeggi, *Il Filarmindo* by Giramolo Giacobbi. A century prior to the opening of the Comunale Monteverdi's *Il Ritorno di Ulisse* was performed in Bologna. Vecchi 1976: 429–30, 438. Vatielli 1976: vol. 2, 97–132.
11. See the projects and contracts of the impresari collected in ASCB, Deputazione dei pubblici spettacoli, 1860–61; since 1863 ASCB, CA, Tit. X, 4; and in ASCB, SP. For the local carnival see Sobrero 1995: 120.
12. Rosmini 1872: 191 sq. Also Alonge 1988: 19.
13. See for example ASCB, CA, 1864, Tit. X, 3, 4, allegato 8971, Condizioni speciali pel capitolato d'appalto del Teatro Comunitativo di Bologna, 4 March 1864. From the second half of the 1860s the *impresario's* duty during carnival was usually to present "*sola opera in musica*," without obligation of a ballet. ASCB, SP, 1867, no. 26, Appalto per un triennio 1867–68–69 dell'impresa del Teatro Comunale, 19 September 1867, Allegato, Capitoli per l'appalto.
14. ASCB, CA, 1860, Tit. XVI, 2, Badini to the sindaco, 7 June 1859.

15. Presented exclusively in theatres of a certain prestige and by the most celebrated "virtuosi," *opera seria* was traditionally regarded as a musical genre superior to *opera buffa* (Mila 1979: 3).

16. See for instance the debate ACC, 5 February 1870.

17. Alonge 1988: 6. Levi 1987: 4. Basso 1976: 318–19. Soloists usually made between 45 and 55% of the entire budget of a season, but during the 1870s and 1880s their fees varied between a poor 6 Francs a night for the principal tenor in Assisi and 10,000 Francs paid for a star in the category of Adelina Patti in Turin. One reason for increased costs was the opening of commercial theatres abroad, in particular in the Americas, which led from the 1830s on to a steep rise in fees. Nevertheless, despite complaints, in the long-term they rose no faster than other costs. See on this point the statistics in Rosselli 1987: 58–59, 65, 78.

18. Rosselli 1987: chapter 6.

19. See for instance Jules Massenet on the occasion of Bologna's staging of his *Roi de Lahore* in 1878: ASCB, CA, 1863, Tit. X, 3, 4, 9943, contract Cesare Gaibi, allegato, 5 September 1863; and CA, 1878, Tit. X, 3, 4, 7417, allegato, Massenet to the impresario, 18 July 1878.

20. Alonge 1988: 20. Rosmini 1872: 51–52.

21. Due to the administration's and the box owners' specific expectations concerning the autumn season, Bologna's impresari had to fight against this tendency throughout the second half of the nineteenth century. See for example Ercole Tinti: "[I]t has been proved that in Bologna the autumn always results in a loss for the contractor, even if the performances go well . . . ." ASCB, CA, 1860, Tit. XVI, 2, Appalto del Teatro Comunitativo per gli Spettacoli d'Autunno 1860 deliberato a Ercole Tinti, 28 May 1860. As illustrated in chapters 3 and 9, the financial difficulties of the theatre during the autumn season of 1871 contributed considerably to the resignation of Casarini's local government.

22. ASCB,CA, 1866, Tit. X, 3, 4, 2988 sq., allegato, Ristauro del Teatro Comunitativo. See the following example: ASCB, CA, 1861, Tit. XVI, 4, Osservazioni al Progetto di Appalto del Sig. Ercole Tinti, Stagione di Autunno. ASCB, SP, 1867, no. 26, Appalto per un triennio 1867–68–69 dell'impresa del Teatro Comunale, 19 September 1867.

23. Masini 1867: 28. In 1861 Ercole Tinti was obliged to commission at least six scenes from local "professors or their students": ASCB, CA, 1861, Tit. XVI, 4, Scrittura fra l'Ecc. Municipio di Bologna ed il sig. Ercole Tinti per l'Impresa del Teatro Comunale delle due stagioni d'autunno e carnevale; and ASCB, CA, 1861, Tit. XVI, 4, Osservazioni al Progetto di Appalto del Sig. Ercole Tinti, Stagione di Autunno. ASCB, CA, 1861, Tit. XVI, 4, Patti addizionali o modificati del capitolato generale.

24. Mariani 1985. For his influence on the staging of opera Busmanti 1876: 17–18.

25. ASCB, CA, 1861, Tit. XVI, 4, Avviso d'Appalto, 13 May 1861.

26. Parker 1989: 136, 144 sq.

27. See for example the project discussed between Ercole Tinti and the municipality in 1860: ASCB, CA, 1860, Tit. XVI, 2, Appalto del Teatro Comunitativo per gli Spettacoli d'Autunno 1860 deliberato a Ercole Tinti, letter by Tinti to Pizzardi, s.d; Tinti alla Nobile Deputazione dei Spettacoli, 3 July 1860.

28. See for example, ASCB, CA, 1875 [sic], Tit. X, 3, 4, Capitolato per l'Appalto del Teatro Comunitativo di Bologna, Regia Tipografia, 1884, art. 32, Modo di pagamento delle spese serali.

29. See for example the view of the impresario Alessandro Sartori for his project in 1861: ASCB, CA, 1861, Deputazione dei pubblici spettacoli, Miscellanea, Progetto d'Appalto per un Sessenio pel Teatro Comunale.

30. On the following see ASCB, CA, 1863, Tit. X, 3, 1—allegato 10138, Regolamento Provvisorio per la Costituzione della Direzione Civica dei pubblici Spettacoli (for the period 1863–1867); for the period since 1867 see idem, X, 3, 2, 3446, Regolamento della Deputazione dei Pubblici Spettacoli nei Teatri Civici di Bologna; in 1904, again, new regulations were approved: idem, 1904, Tit. X, 3, 1, Regolamento per la Deputazione Comunale degli spettacoli in Bologna.

31. These procedures are outlined in the triennial contract between the municipality and the impresario Scalaberni: ASCB, SP, 1867, no. 26, Appalto per un triennio 1867–68–69 dell'impresa del Teatro Comunale, 19 September 1867. As an example of the often controversial relationship between municipality and impresari see for instance Basso 1976: 263 sq.

32. ASCB, CA, 1860, Tit. II, Deputazione dei pubblici spettacoli, III, 2, Copia lettera anonima scritta al sig. Sindaco in ordine alla Direzione degli spettacoli, 28 May 1860. Members of the Deputazione itself, in particular Prince Hercolani, also complained about the bad functioning of the committee: ASCB, CA, 1863, Tit. X, 3, 4, 1 September 1863, letter by Hercolani to the Deputazione.

33. ASCB, CA, 1867, Tit. X, 3, 2, letter by Cesare Masini to sindaco G. Pepoli, 18 April 1867 and reply; letter by Gioacchino Malaguti and Alessandro Brentazzoli to the sindaco, 30 September 1867 and copy of reply. For the composition of the Deputazione in Rome under the Papal regime see Giger 1999: 239ff.

34. Hughes 1994.

35. For the members of the Deputazione see the (incomplete) lists in the CA under X, 3, 1.

36. ASCB, CA, 1867, Tit. X, 3, 2 letter by the mayor to the Deputazione, 12/03/1867. In 1913 the mayor Nadalini sought to professionalise the Deputazione further by appointing the director of the conservatory as a permanent member: ASCB, CA, 1914, Tit. X, 3, 1, 25164, Atto separato di deliberazione della Giunta Municipale, 23 September 1913.

37. See for example the relevant explanations in the triennial contract between the municipality and the impresario Scalaberni, outlining the process of decision-making: ASCB, SP, 1867, no. 26, Appalto per un triennio 1867–68–69 dell'impresa del Teatro Comunale, 19 September 1867.

38. At times this could be an important argument in favour of investment in the city's cultural infrastructure: ACC, 29 August 1903, sindaco Golinelli. The Deputazione, presided over until 1867 by Count Salina, counted among its members representatives of the Historic Left, but also a Radical with Republican sympathies like the professor Giuseppe Ceneri. ASCB, CA, 1867, Tit. X, 3, 2, 3446, Estratto del Verbale della Giunta. The Deputazione counted among its members a number of medical doctors, to be present at public events organised by the municipality and monitoring the artists' sick-leave.

39. At times the municipality even forbade organising balls in private homes if the Comunale had scheduled a ball for the same evening: ASCB, CA, 1861, Tit. XVI, 2, Tinti to the mayor, 4 February 1861. For the Teatro Comunale between 1806 and 1859 see the report by Badini, owner of Bologna's most important private theatre, the Teatro del Corso: ASCB, CA, 1860, Tit. XVI, 2, Badini to the mayor, 7 June 1859. Badini wanted to oblige the municipality to cover for his economic loss due to the past privileges of the Comunale, but was unsuccessful: The new local government was not held responsible for actions of the previous regime. In 1861 the current impresario of the Comunale, Ercole Tinti, was still granted an exclusive right to organise balls on days when other theatres had to remain closed: ASCB, CA, 1861, Deputazione dei pubblici spettacoli, Miscellanea, Osservazioni al progetto d'Appalto del sig.e Ercole Tinti, 31 May 1861. In other cities monopolies were less important: see Rosselli 1987: 24.

40. ASCB, CA, 1860, II, Deputazione dei pubblici spettacoli, Miscellanea, III, 3, Delegati Amministrativi e Provinciali, Intendenza generale della provincia di Bologna al Questore di Bologna, 9 May 1860; and 1860, Tit. XVI, Intendenza generale della provincia di Bologna al Questore di Bologna, 15 May 1860. On censorship during the Restoration: Davis 2000. On the later period Bianconi and Pestelli 1987: 170. On the Piedmontese legislation see Piazzoni 2004: 77–78.
41. ASCB, CA, 1860, Tit. XVI, 2, Appalto del Teatro Comunitativo per gli Spettacoli d'Autunno 1860 deliberato a Ercole Tinti, 28 May 1860.
42. ASCB, CA, 1860, Tit. XVI, 2, Questura del Circondario di Bologna al Sindaco, Soppressione della Direzione dei pubblici spettacoli, 28 September 1860.
43. ASCB, CA, 1860, Tit. XVI, 2, Gaetano Badini to the mayor, 08 May 1860. Badini made his first request on 7 June 1859, even before the cardinal and the Austrian troops had left the city behind. The "free lists" were in deed very common under the *ancien régime* and a real hindrance to an *impresario's* earnings: Rosselli 1987: 91–92.
44. Rosmini 1872: 81–88.
45. ASCB, CA, 1860, Tit. XVI, 2, Regolamento pei Teatri. Disposizioni speciali del servizio interno dei teatri di Bologna; and 1860 II, Deputazione dei pubblici spettacoli, III, 2, Questore, Rainoni, Disposizioni speciali pel servizio interno dei teatri di Bologna, 28 September 1860.
46. Rosmini 1872: 113.
47. Ricci 1888. Alonge 1988: 5.
48. Calore 1982: 24. Calore 1998: 26.
49. Ricci 1888: 302. Calore 1982: 103. For details of the restoration see *MdB*, 16 February 1865. Giosuè Carducci, "In aspettazione d'una recita di Sara Bernhardt" [*Don Chisciotte*, Bologna, March 1882], in: Carducci 1935–68: (*Confessioni e battaglie* II), 124.
50. Alonge 1988: 4, 193. Bianconi and Pestelli 1987: 171. For the regional distribution of theatres see Sorba 2001: 49–50.
51. ACC, 4 July 1861. *MdB*, 5 January 1870.
52. Calore 1982: 24–31.
53. ACC, 23 February 1887, consigliere Ceri and assessore Dallolio. On Ceri see Gottarelli 1977.
54. Surian 1980.
55. De Angelis 1982: 7, 19, 45. Rosselli 1987: 26 refers to Bartolomeo Merelli as the "Napoleon of Impresari."
56. Calore 1982: 9–12. It was also for economic reasons that Bologna's smaller theatres altered expensive opera seasons with drama and other entertainment like masked balls, the exposition of animals or living images. For an overview of the different kinds of performance see the register of taxes paid by Bologna's theatres: ASCB, CA, 1860 Tit. II, Deputazione dei pubblici spettacoli, Miscellanea, III, 2 a 2, Delegati Amministrativi e Provinciali, Registro delle tasse pagate dei teatri nei anni 1859/1860; also ASCB, CA, Tit. IV, 3, Veglioni, Feste di ballo e trattenimenti vari. Occasionally the Corso was able, without subsidies, to produce first class performances, like the much appraised *Aida* of 1886. *RdC*, 5 and 9 April 86. The performance was staged by Cesare Gaibi, who regularly worked with the Comunale. (Rosselli 1987: 117 is mistaken when he describes the Corso as "a minor theatre.")
57. ACC, 27 December 1888, consigliere Baratelli. ACC, 30 December 1911, consigliere Zanardi.
58. Vecchi 1966.
59. For a comparison see Staffieri 135–36. For the Comunale see the lists of the orchestra and the correspondence with the Deputazione: ASCB, CA, 1861,

Deputazione dei pubblici spettacoli, Miscellanea, 1861–62, Stazione di Carnevale. For the spring season of 1860 the regular orchestra was composed of twenty-one first and second violins, six violas, four celli, two doublebass, nine wood-winds and ten brass. The honorarium per evening varied between 1.40 and 0.50 Lire. In 1867 the orchestra counted seventy-six men whose honorarium varied between 6.50 Lire and 2.50 Lire; conductor and leader received 25 Lire per evening. ASCB, CA, 1860 Tit. II, Deputazione dei pubblici spettacoli, Miscellanea, IV, Tabella d'orchestra per la primavera 1860. ASCB, SP, 1867, no. 26, Appalto per un triennio 1867–68–69 dell'impresa del Teatro Comunale, 19 September 1867. On earlier arrangements for Bologna's orchestra see Rosselli 1987: 57, 114–15. The size of the chorus increased over the years from thirty members in 1855 to sixty in 1871 and one hundred in 1914.

60. ASCB, CA, 1861, Deputazione dei pubblici spettacoli, Miscellanea, Regio Teatro in Parma, 6 December 1861; idem, 1871, Tit. X, 3, 4, 9676, 9787, the sindaco of Florence to Casarini, 17 November 1871. Salvarani 2002.

61. Giger 1999: 237.

62. Sobrero 1995: 120. Rosselli 1987: 4, 12, 28ff. A main purpose of the spacious foyers in eighteenth-century opera houses was to allow the upper classes to gamble, an additional source of income for governments and *impresari*.

63. ASCB, SP, 1867, no. 26, Appalto per un triennio 1867–68–69 dell'impresa del Teatro Comunale, 19 September 1867.

64. ACC, 21 December 1883, consigliere Azzolini; 22 December 1884, consigliere Salaroli; 27 December 1888, consigliere Fusconi.

65. Alonge 1988: 3. Sorba 2001: 57, 93. For a general overview see Rosselli 1996. For a literary account of the opera as backdrop for staging social status see Franz Werfel, *Die Geschwister von Neapel* (1931). For Naples Macry 1984: 341. For Milan Santoro 2004. For Turin Cardoza 1997: 38–39. For Europe as a whole Lequin 1978: 317.

66. Rosselli 1991: 57. Of about forty privately owned boxes seventeen were bought within the first decade of the theatre's existence by families which more than a century later were still in their possession: ASCB, CA, 1876, Tit. X, 3, 4, 7091, allegato, Nota indicativa delle famiglie che hanno diritto d'uso o prelazione dei palchi. Concerning the decoration of the ceilings Schiavina 1982: 414.

67. Pepoli 1871: 8. Vatielli 1921: 11.

68. ASCB, CA, 1867, Tit. X, 3, 4, 1969, allegato: Notificazione d'invito a chi volesse acquistare Gius Privato dell'Uso, e pertua Prelazione ne' Palchi del Nuovo eretto Teatro Pubblico, 18 December 1762. Trezzini 2000: 1037.

69. ASCB, SP, 1867, no. 26, Appalto per un triennio 1867–68–69 dell'impresa del Teatro Comunale, 19 September 1867, Pianta indicativa delle Famiglie che hanno diritto d'uso, o prelazione dei Palchi del Teatro Comunitativo a seconda degli Spettacoli che vi si rappresentano.

70. Rosselli 1987: 42. On other systems for the administration of the boxes: Parmentola 1977: 490–91. For a comparison with La Scala in Milan Santoro 2004: 110–11, 114: in 1862 43.2% of boxes belonged to the borghesia. Hence, the history of the Comunale contrasts to some extent the *Verbürgerlichung*, which characterised many European theatres since the eighteenth century: Steinhauser 1988: 313. The Comunale, with its privately owned boxes, was "public" only to a certain extent, even after Unification.

71. Ferraboschi 2003: 159, 285–86.

72. See for details of these contracts ACC, 18 January 1920, no. 87 all'ordine del giorno. The associations are also mentioned in the contracts between the municipality and the *impresari*. At the time the Romagna counted among its nobility 9 princes, 9 dukes, 56 marquis and 184 counts: Jocteau 1997: 22.

73. The questore's regulations of 1860 determined that the first person arriving had the right to occupy a seat; it was not permitted to reserve the seat by leaving a hat or other objects, as customary in other theatres: ASCB, CA, 1860, Tit. XVI, 2, Regolamento pei Teatri. Disposizioni speciali del servizio interno dei teatri di Bologna. See also the letter of assessore Ulisse Cassarini to the mayor of Piacenza: ASCB, Carteggio Amministrativo, 1861, Tit. XVI-2, 10479, 21 November 1861.

74. ASCB, CA, 1867, Tit. X, 3, 4, 1969, allegato: Notificazione d'invito a chi volesse acquistare Gius Privato dell'Uso, e pertua Prelazione ne' Palchi del Nuovo eretto Teatro Pubblico, 18 December 1762.

75. Calore 1982: 50. Similarly, the box owners in Turin insisted on *opera seria* and a separate ballet, even if the opera already included ballet scenes: Rosselli 1987: 111. On nineteenth-century conventions regarding the combination of opera and ballet see in particular Everist 2005: 11.

76. ASCB, CA, 1863, Tit. X, 3, 4, 9333, project by Cesare Gaibi, 7 September 1863. Their argument was different from that of the rioters during the Parisian premiere of Tannhäuser in 1861: Large and Weber (eds) 1984: 21. For a general discussion of the genre during the 1860s in Italy see Roccatagliati 1993.

77. For an example see again the project of the impresario Alessandro Sartori for 1861: ASCB, CA, 1861, Deputazione dei pubblici spettacoli, Miscellanea, Progetto d'Appalto per un Sessenio pel Teatro Comunale. Before signing a contract with an impresario the theatre's administration insisted on knowing the name of the choreographer—remarkable in so far as the names of the conductors for the season and even parts of the works to be staged were often announced only at the beginning of the season. ASCB, CA, 1861, Deputazione dei pubblici spettacoli, Miscellanea, Osservazioni al progetto d'Appalto del sig.e Ercole Tinti, 31 May 1861.

78. *MdB*, 25 September and 18 October 1868; Calore 1982: 52.

79. ASCB, CA, 1860, Tit. XVI, 2, Appalto del Teatro Comunitativo per gli Spettacoli d'Autunno 1860 deliberato a Ercole Tinti, 28 May 1860.

80. Bottrigari 1960–63: 316. ASCB, CA, 1863, Tit. X, 3, 4, 9491, Progetto Gaibi, 12 September 1863. Alberti 2002: 1042.

81. ASCB, CA, 1874, Tit. X, 3, 4, 9564, Progetto per l'Impresa, 4 September 1874.

82. ASCB, CA, 1875, Tit. X, 3, 4, 3439, Rapporto della Commissione incaricata di studiare i diritti dei palchettisti nel Teatro Comunale, 28 March 1875.

83. ACC, 16 December 1872. Similarly, theatre productions became increasingly a commercial activity involving rising costs for impresari: Piazzoni 2004: 64.

84. Basso 1976: 357.

85. *MdB*, 6 October 1870.

86. *MdB*, 4 October 1875. ACC, 21 December 1883, sindaco Tacconi. Concerning the financial loss see also the sentence in the case between the city and the Marquis Annibale Banzi concerning the charity concert on 17 October 1864, ASCB, CA, 1866, Tit. X, 3, 4, 1125, rapporto del avv. Sarti al sindaco G. Pepoli, a proposito della causa Marchese Cav. Annibale Banzi, 28 March 1866. See a similar example idem, 1874, Tit. X, 3, 4, 12905, Rapporto del Archivio Generale, 18 January 1875.

87. ASCB, CA, 1875, Tit. X, 3, 4, 8661, letter by the Società del Duttour Balanzon to the sindaco, 25 September 1875, allegati.

88. See the sentence in the case between the city and the Marquis Annibale Banzi concerning the concert of 17 October 1864, ASCB, CA, 1866, Tit. X, 3, 4, 1125, rapporto del avv. Sarti al sindaco Pepoli, a proposito della causa Marchese Cav. Annibale Banzi, 28 March 1866. Similar, idem, 1874, Tit. X, 3, 4, 12905, Rapporto del Archivio Generale, 18 January 1875.

89. ACC, 28 December 1875, consigliere De Simonis.
90. The benefit of these evenings—in particular through lotteries—went to charitable organisations. Lotteries, like horse-races, etc., played at the time an important role in public entertainment; see for details ASCB, CA, 1861, Deputazione dei pubblici spettacoli, Miscellanea, Estrazione di Tombola, Regolarmento delle Tombola in occasione di feste. Bologna also publicised similar events in other cities of the region: ASCB, CA, 1861, Tit. XVI, 3.
91. ACC, 21 March 1884, consigliere Malvezzi.
92. ACC, 13 November 1861, consiglieri Bevilacqua and Minghetti.
93. ASCB, CA, 1861, Tit. XVI, Adunanza dei Palchisti del Teatro Comunale, 22 December 1861.
94. ACC, 23 July 1867 and 6 September 1867.
95. ACC, 17 January 1868, consigliere Osima; 5 February 1870, consiglieri Ceneri and Rossi. Apparently the entrance fee is slightly below the price in comparable theatres: ACC, 29 February 1872.
96. See for the approach of Casarini's *giunta* to the problem of the box owners: ASCB, CA, 1871, Tit. X, 3, 4, 975, Atti della Commissione nominata dal consiglio nella seduta del 19 Maggio con facoltà di prendere intelligenze colla Giunta in ordine all'assegnazione della Dote al Teatro Comunale. In particular: "Progetto d'Appalto pel Teatro Comunale di Bologna presentato all'onorevole Giunta ed Ill.tre Consiglio il 30 Gennaio 1871." Before any of these proposals were discussed in detail Casarini's *giunta* resigned.
97. ASCB, CA, 1874, Tit. X, 3, 4, 12300, Commissione incaricata di esaminare il diritto dei Prelazionisti dei palchi di godere senza pagamento di canone gli spettacoli che ivi si danno all'infuori del caso di rappresentazioni di opera seria con Ballo grandioso, 7 November 1874, 4. As the minutes of the local government during the 1870s reveal, Bologna had indeed difficulties to find *impresari* for its theatre: ASCB, CA, 1876, Tit. X, 3, 4, 2838, Estratto del Verbale della Giunta.
98. *MdB*, 28 October and 10 November 1867, 28 June 1868.
99. ACC, 27 February 1872, consigliere Sangiorgi.
100. *MdB*, 10 April 1875.
101. ASCB, CA, 1871, Tit. X, 3, 4, 975, Atti della Commissione nominata dal consiglio nella seduta del 19 Maggio con facoltà di prendere intelligenze colla Giunta in ordine all'assegnazione della Dote al Teatro Comunale, Adunanza del 24 Maggio 1871, consigliere Sacchetti, sindaco Casarini. Alaimo 1990a: 147.
102. ACC, 28 December 1875, consigliere Malvezzi; 30 April 1875. See also ASCB, CA, 1875, Tit. X, 3, 4, 3439, Rapporto della Commissione incaricata di studiare i diritti dei palchettisti nel Teatro Comunale, 28 March 1875.
103. ASCB, CA, 1874, Tit. X, 3, 4, 12906, letter by the mayor Tacconi to the municipal librarian, 30 November 1874.
104. ASCB, CA, 1874, Tit. X, 3, 4, 12906, report of the librarian Frati, 7 February 1875. On "*ballo analogo*," "*ballo grande*" and the changing role of dance in the theatre see Dahms 1998: 307.
105. Mila 1979: 4. With similar intentions Benedetto Marcello had already criticized Vivaldi's operas in his *Il teatro alla moda*, published in 1720. On Rousseau's philosophy of music see in particular his "Lettre sur la musique française" and "Examen de deux principes avancés par M. Rameau" in Rousseau 1993. Rousseau's critique was inspired by a presentation in Paris of Pergolesi's *La serva padrona* in 1752: "music based on the observation of life and characters, a music able to increase . . . and to deepen the sense of the words, following closely the action and exploring the psychology of the characters." Quoted in Mila 1979: 5–6.

106. The committee's reading of Frati's report differed slightly from the original: ASCB, CA, 1874, Tit. X, 3, 4, 12300, Commissione incaricata di esaminare il diritto dei Prelazionisti dei palchi di godere senza pagamento di canone gli spettacoli che ivi si danno all'infuori del caso di rappresentatzioni di opera seria con Ballo grandioso, 7 November 1874, 13.
107. Regolamento del Mosca, Prefetto del Dipartimento del Reno, 15 November 1806, quoted ibid., 14.
108. ASCB, CA, 1874, Tit. X, 3, 4, 12300, Commissione incaricata di esaminare il diritto dei Prelazionisti dei palchi di godere senza pagamento di canone gli spettacoli che ivi si danno all'infuori del caso di rappresentazioni di opera seria con Ballo grandioso, 7 November 1874, 16.
109. We know from other Italian theatres, for instance in Lucca, that the French regime had a major impact on the style, content and social significance of theatrical productions. Biagi Ravenni 1992.
110. ASCB, CA, 1874, Tit. X, 3, 4, 6779, R. Tribunale civile e correzionale di Bologna, 31 July 1875.
111. ASCB, CA, 1876, Tit. X, 3, 4, 2430, Associazione dei Palchettisti to the mayor, 19 March 1876.
112. ASCB, CA, 1875, Tit. X, 3, 4, 8401, Palchettisti to the mayor, 18 September 1875, and committee report, 21 September 1875; 8661, Società del Dottour Balanzon to the mayor, 25 September 1875.
113. ACC, 21 December 1883, report by the sindaco Tacconi to the council; 21 March 1884, assessore Dallolio. On similar debates at La Scala see Bianconi and Pestelli 1987: 184.
114. In Milan it was Toscanini who abolished the ballet at the end of great operas. Santoro 2004: 133.
115. ACC, 27 December 1888, sindaco Tacconi.
116. Rosmini 1872: 581, 587ff. These numbers reflect the situation in 1872.
117. ACC, 23 July 1913. The same restorations provided new electric equipment for the stage lighting, as required for modern scenery.
118. ASCB, CA, 1860, Tit. XVI, 2, Restituzione ai proprietari dei diversi Teatri in questa città dei rispettivi Palchi che erano stati assegnati alla N.Direzione dei pubblici speattacoli, dapresso la soppressione di quest'ultimo. Non che degli altri di Lubione nel Teatro del Corso che servivano in uso dei Famigli delle autorità Governativa, Municipale, ed Ecclesiastica. See also letter by Badini, owner of the Teatro del Corso, to the mayor, 12 April 1860.
119. Steinhauser 1988: 317. Calore 1982: 12–13.
120. Rosselli 1991: 59; Rosselli 1987: 43. Bianconi and Pestelli 1987: 192. Alberti 2002: 1042.
121. ACC, 27 December 1888, consigliere Baratelli.
122. ACC, 30 December 1911, sindaco Tanari.

NOTES TO CHAPTER 3

1. Mori 1986: 136.
2. ACC, 6 May 1861.
3. On the following Alaimo 1990b: 12 and for a more detailed account Alaimo 1990a.
4. These difficulties were not unique to Bologna. See for instance Tobia 1998: 93.
5. Aimo 1997: 37–43.
6. *Rassegna settimanale*, 1869 and 1878, quoted in Romanelli 1995b: 62. The case of Parma is similar: Sorba 1993: 56–57. On the relationship between laissez-faire liberalism and a weak state see also Quine 2002: 38–39.

7. ACC, 29 August 1866, "Riferimento della Giunta sul rapporto della Commissione pei Lavori Straordinari", Allegato B del vol. 1861–67. See also Romanelli 1995b: 62.
8. Gioacchino Pepoli, "All'illustre commendatore Benedetto Cairoli", in: Pepoli, G. 1880: vol. 1, 70.
9. Idem, "I comuni e la questione sociale", in: Pepoli, G. 1880: vol. 1, 124.
10. Leopoldo Franchetti, quoted in Romanelli 1995b: 69. On the issue of public subsidies see the legal regulations and political debates in Rosmini 1872: 161 sq.
11. Gioacchino Pepoli, "I comuni e la questione sociale", in: Pepoli, G. 1880: vol. 1, 123–24. However, in Milan, in 1897, the Centre-Left and the Catholics voted for the suppression of municipal subsidies for La Scala. The vote led to the temporary closure of the theatre. It reopened in 1899 as a private entreprise: Marco Vitale, "La Scala e gli scolari poveri. Nel 1897 il comune tolse i fondi al teatro: già allora la cultura era considerata un lusso", in: *Il Sole—24 Ore*, 27 March 2005, no. 85.
12. Quoted in Bianconi and Pestelli 1987: 170.
13. Rosmini 1872: 164–72. Also Bianconi and Pestelli 1987: 169–70. Kimbell 1991: 537. For the transition of Turin's Teatro Regio after Unification see Basso 2001: 996–97.
14. Franchetti quoted in Romanelli 1995b: 106, 109.
15. Bracco 2001: 533. Mazzonis 2001: 440–41.
16. Franchetti to Sidney Sonnino, quoted in: Romanelli 1995b: 113. Croce 1928: 81.
17. Aimo 1997. Romanelli 1989: 15 and Romanelli 1986: 90–91. For the implications of the law see also Denis Bocquet and Filippo De Pieri 2002. On the following see the important study by Randeraad 1997: 176 sq. Also Fried 1963: 133–34. Romanelli 1995b: 53 sq. Melis 1996: 77–78. Von Krosigk 1999. Giannini 1976. Randeraad used the province of Bologna as one of his three case studies. Ried's work is mostly based on the analysis of the legal framework. Romanelli discusses the political and legal debate at the time. With regard to the prefectorial control over municipal expenditure on culture compare also the French system: Sherman 1989: 122–23.
18. Romanelli 1995b: 64.
19. See for example the debate in ACC 7 December 1863. For a wider perspective see Mozzarelli (ed.) 1992, in particular 9.
20. Alaimo 1990b: 22. Mascilli Migliorini 1988: 51.
21. ACC, November 1863. On the increase of communal expenditure in Bologna see also the contemporary account Maccaferri 1881: 6.
22. Rosselli 1991: 137.
23. Alaimo 1990b: 12. Randeraad 1997: 174. Romanelli 1995c: 140–41.
24. The town council discussed this question from November 1863. For the position of the local Left on the tax on consumption see ACC, 18 December 1895, consigliere Albertoni. See also Körner 2005; for a general critique of the tax see Antonio Salandra in *Nuova Antologia* (1878), quoted in Romanelli 1995b: 62. Also Sorba 1993: 57ff, 83 sq., 139 sq.
25. Romanelli 1995b: 53–54, 59–60. Randeraad 1997: 182–83. Romeo 1990: 499.
26. See the case studies in Mozzarelli (ed.) 1992.
27. Polsi 1984: 498. Randeraad 1997: 181.
28. Romanelli 1995b: 55.
29. Macry 1984: 341. For a comparison of communal deficit at the start of the twentieth century see Sorba 1993: 107–8. Leading the table with the highest deficit are Rome, Naples and Milan; Bologna occupies the ninth place, after Pisa and before Catania.

30. See for example the arguments presented in ACC, 7 December 1863, consigliere Ercolani.
31. ACC, 27 February 1872, consigliere Osima. On the political role and the social function of municipal bands see Isnenghi 2004: 39 sq., 153 sq. Like many other municipal institutions, from the beginning of the twentieth century the bands were under threat of being abolished. See for instance the example of Pavia: Liva 1992.
32. ACC, 11 December 1863, consiglieri Ercolani and Bevilacqua.
33. ACC, 4 April 1865.
34. ACC, 27 February 1872, consigliere Osima.
35. ACC, 13 May 1873. From 1878 the contracts with the band were renewed every three years, but for several decades the salaries of the musicians remained the same, despite wage increases for other categories of public employees: ACC, 7 December 1909, Progetto di riordinamento della civica Banda musicale. Whenever the band demanded additional subsidies—as, for instance, in 1881, when it wished to participate in an international brass band competition in Turin—the council refused to give money, claiming that its only obligation was to entertain the citizenship once a week, "without further artistic ambitions": ACC, 7 May 1881, consigliere Bacchelli.
36. In November 1860 he presided over a meeting with members of parliament to discuss the question. See his diary: Minghetti 1955: 286. On transition of the institutions of the former states see Romanelli 1995c: 126–27.
37. This subsidy usually included the box owners' fee and the municipality's grant. Rosselli 1987: 75.
38. Bianconi and Pestelli 1987: 180.
39. Rosselli 1987: 78. Santoro 2004: 115–16. Bianconi and Pestelli 1987: 180.
40. Rosselli 1987: 138.
41. Rosselli 1987: 76.
42. De Angelis, 51.
43. ACC, 09 January 1860, Riferimento della Commissione incaricata degli studi per la dotazione e illuminazione a gas del Teatro Comunale; see also consigliere Ulisse Cassarini. The wars of liberation presented indeed a major financial issue for the Italian state: The war of 1848 49 had cost some 200 million Lire, the war of 1859 250 million and an additional 50 million Lire were spent on the Crimean War. The annual revenue was only about 480 million Lire per year. In 1861 the public debt stood at 2,540 million Lire. The war of 1866 would cost 600 million Lire. Mack Smith 1969: 85.
44. ASCB, CA, 1860 Tit. II, Deputazione dei pubblici spettacoli, Miscellanea, Tit. IV, letter by Angelo Mariani to Count Agostino Salina, 12 November 1860. A second organ was installed in 1871, originally placed in a former church owned by the municipality (Chiesa dell'Annunziata, Porta Mamolo): ASCB, CA, 1871, Tit. X, 3, 4, 4856, 7808, 8706, 1 June 1871.
45. Bottrigari 1960–63: vol. 3, 225.
46. ACC, 12 November 1861, consiglieri Minghetti, G. Pepoli, Ceneri. On the Left's widespread critique of the *dote* during the Finesecolo see Piazzoni 2004: 62.
47. ASCB, Carteggio Amministrativo, 1861, Tit. XVI-2, 10479, letter by the assessore delegato of the mayor of Piacenza to the mayor of Bologna, 16 November 1861, and reply 21 November 1861.
48. ACC, 13 November 1861. The same issue comes up with certain regularity in council debates: ACC, 30 December 1878; 29 December 1880; 21 December 1883.
49. ASCB, Carteggio Amministrativo, 1861, Tit. XVI, Adunanza dei Palchisti del Teatro Comunale, 22 December 1861.

50. ACC, 7 November 1862, consigliere Baldini and assessore Minghetti.
51. ACC, 20 June 1861. See also Bottrigari 1960–63: vol. 3, 315.
52. ASCB, CA, 1861, Tit. XVI, 2, Teatro Comunale, Necessità di rinnovare il Tetto, nota dell'Ingegnere in Capo, 5 November 1861.
53. ACC, 20 June 1861, consigliere Cocchi.
54. ACC, 20 June 1861, consigliere Ceneri.
55. ACC, 17 November 1862.
56. See in particular the views of assessore L. Berti ACC, 17 November 1862.
57. ACC, 9 May 1863.
58. ACC, 10 September 1863, consiglieri A. Montanari, Baldini, Bevilacqua, L. Berti, assessore Buggio, sindaco C. Pepoli.
59. Bottrigari 1960–63: vol. 3, 315 (September 1863).
60. *MdB*, 13 July 1869.
61. Antonio Salandra, quoted in Romanelli 1995b: 74, and for similar examples 109–11.
62. Marco Minghetti, quoted in Romanelli 1995b: 71. Banti 1990: 76 f. Similar principles divided Moderates and Democrats in other North-Italian towns. See, for instance, Banti 1989: 202.
63. Giolitti in September 1900, quoted in: Mack Smith 1969: 214.
64. Romanelli 1995b: 72.
65. Polsi 1984: 498.
66. Polsi 1984: 499. Similar Ridolfi 1987–88: 10.
67. Polsi 1984: 500.
68. Trigilia 1998: 222ff.
69. *MdB*, 26 February 1869. Originally close to Minghetti, after changes in its administration the paper's orientation was towards the Centre-Left: Berselli 1963: 237.
70. ACC, Relazione letta dal delegato straordinario, 7 November 1868.
71. The municipal finances during that period have been analysed in detail by a local councillor and member of Casarini's *giunta*, the engineer Maccaferri 1881: 18. See also Casarini 1872: 5 sq.
72. Berselli 1980: 276.
73. Davis 1988: 191. Körner 2005. Masi 1875: 172 sq.
74. On the following see Masi 1875: 182–83 and in more detail Maccaferri 1881: 28 sq.
75. Drake 1980: 21–22. See also Romanelli 1979: 210. The theme was taken up by numerous commentators and poets, see for example Pascoli 1910: viii; and the poem for Mazzini in Panzacchi 1910: 157–58.
76. Camera dei Deputati, 18 April 1868, quoted in Masi 1875: 176.
77. Alaimo 1990a: 143–44.
78. Masi 1875: 184. On the following see also Maccaferri 1881. Alaimo 1990a: chpt. 3; Alaimo 1988.
79. In 1869 Bologna spent 150,000 Lire for its 85 primary schools and 3494 pupils: Malvezzi 1905: 12.
80. Alaimo 1990a: 142; Alaimo 1990b: 7, 12.
81. On the new role of professionals in local administrations see Musella 1995: 324.
82. Alaimo 1990a: 148 sq., 168 sq. Alaimo 1990b: 30. D'Attore 1986: 71–72.
83. See the summary of the debate in *MdB*, 6 July 1870.
84. The committee met at the Liceo named after the famous scientist, but "Galvani" was also the name of a local freemasons' lodge. The lodge played an important role in the local Left and sympathised openly with Democratic and "Garibaldian" positions: Preti 1997: 17. D'Attore 1986: 76.

85. Alaimo 1990b: 12–13. On the following Alaimo 1990a: 169 sq. On the Moderate critique of Casarini's municiple finance see Alaimo 1988: 281.
86. Maccaferri 1881: 23. On the reluctance of successive administrations to take over the management of services or building projects Cesari and Gresleri 1976: 106.
87. See Chapter 9 and Körner 1996b: 85–120.
88. Masi 1875: 187. Casarini's view regarding the decline of Italian lyric theatre after Unification corresponds to evaluations of today's musicologists, see Della Seta 1993: 277–78.
89. Casarini 1872: 19–20.
90. See the report of the inquiry committee: ACC, 5 February 72.
91. Berselli; Della Peruta; Varni (eds) 1988.
92. Alaimo 1990b: 9. Alaimo 1990a: 204.
93. Maccaferri 1881: 5, 45–46. Alaimo 1990b: 13–17.
94. Based on Alaimo 1990b: 16–17.
95. In order to analyse the development of Bologna's expenditure in the long term and to compare the relationship between "compulsory" and "facultative spending," Bologna's budget will be considered in the context of all the municipal budgets in the entire province of Bologna. The mayors of the smaller towns in the province often belonged to Bologna's ancient elite of notables and were resident in Bologna. Through the provincial council they controlled the communal budgets of the entire province, and the spending of the smaller communes was considered in relation to the expenditure of the provincial capital, which had to provide the infrastructure for its periphery, in particular with regard to cultural institutions and education. The province of Bologna counted fifty-eight communes (sixty-one since 1884). In 1881 the city of Bologna alone counted 126,178 inhabitants, the size of some of Italy's smaller provinces, compared to 461,000 inhabitants of the entire province. Of that population 27.3% lived in the provincial capital, where the pro-capita income was considerably higher than in the smaller communes of the province.
96. The following figures are based on the statistics in Randeraad 1997: 184ff.; Alaimo 1990b: 11–12 and Finzi and Tassinari 1986: 192–93.
97. Romanelli 1995b: 60–61.
98. In 1878 the "facultative spending" of all Italian communes corresponded to 15% of the total public expenditure. Romanelli 1995b: 63.
99. Randeraad 1997: 179. During the 1870s this was the case for almost half of the Italian communes. Gioacchino Pepoli, "I comuni e la questione sociale", in Pepoli, G. 1880: vol. 1, 111.
100. Table based on Randeraad 1997: 184ff.
101. Table based on Alaimo 1990b: 16.
102. Table based on Alaimo 1990b: 21–22.
103. Gioacchino Pepoli, quoted in Randeraad 1997: 181. On the circumstances of the balance Romanelli 1979: 193–94. Taxation was one of the major preoccupations of Pepoli's social policy; see for instance Pepoli, G. 1880.
104. Romanelli 1979: 87, 155. On the regional agitation about the *tassa sul macinato* Berselli 1980: 279. D'Attore 1986: 76.
105. On the local discontent with centralisation Berselli 1980: 261–62. D'Attore 1991: 89.

NOTES TO CHAPTER 4

1. Johan Huizinga, "Over een definitie van het begrip geschiedenis" (1929), in: Huizinga 1995: 66–67.

2. Hobsbawm and Ranger (eds) 1983. For Italy see similar Isnenghi (ed.) 1998: viii. For Karl Löwith the idea of "recollection" as part of a new beginning characterised in particular the Jacobin tradition and later the European dictatorships: Löwith 1986: xvi. See also Koselleck 1984 and Arendt 1963. Also Jauss 1989: 59ff.
3. History becomes part of cultural memory. See in this context Assmann 2000: 16.
4. Humphreys 2004: 13.
5. Connerton 1995: 2. Also see Sheehan 2000: 84–85.
6. Croce 1926: i, 2. The philosopher refers here to the "*mancanza di storie italiane conformi ai concetti moderni.*"
7. Koselleck 1989: 38–66. For an anthropological definition Schlesier 1997. Connerton 1995: 56.
8. Huizinga 1995: 66.
9. Croce 1914: ii, 52. Carducci, "Delle cose operate dalla R. Deputazione su gli studi di storia patria per le province di Romagna, 27 maggio 1875," in: Carducci 1913a: 429. Also Porciani 1988: 173 sq.
10. Malraux 1951: 11. See also Hudson 1975: 11–12.
11. Prior 2002: 13.
12. Pomian 1997. Pomian 1999, 167–170. Pomian 1990: 5–6. See also Alpers 1991: 27. Malraux 1951: 601.
13. Karp 1992: 1, 7. Gadamer 1990. Collingwood 1999. McClellan 1994: 4 sq.
14. Quoted in Carducci 1913b: vol. 2, 112–13. Also Pomian 1990: 10–11. Clemens 2004. On the conservation of historical patrimony in Italy see Troilo 2005.
15. Bruni 2001.
16. Halbwachs 1968. For a critique of the over-employed concept in the analysis of nationalism see Bell 2003: 65.
17. Croce 2001: 299–300.
18. Auerbach 1999: 171–72. Kretschmer 1999: 143, 169. Porciani 1988: 168. Serra, R. 2001: 602.
19. Croce 1953: 109.
20. Carducci, "Epigrafi, epigrafisti, epigrafai" [*Cronaca Bizantina*, Rome, 18 October 1881], in Carducci 1921: 119.
21. Carducci, "Arcadie della gloria e della carità" [*Cronaca Bizantina*, Rome, 16 October 1882], in: Carducci 1921: 126. On the wide-reaching political appeal of Garibaldi see Riall 2007a.
22. At the time only few academic journals showed an interest in pre-historic archaeology. Desittere 1984: 78.
23. Foratti 1940: 2.
24. ACC, 19 November 1869, consiglieri Carducci, Panzacchi. Under the Papal government the cardinals even removed Jewish singers from the cast of the opera, as in the case of Fanny Goldberg at the Fiera di Senigallia in 1842. De Angelis 1982: 88. On anti-Semitism in Italy during the second half of the nineteenth century see the review article by Bernardini 1996: 296–97.
25. Porciani 1988: 185. For a more specific analysis Manselli and Riedman (eds) 1982.
26. Porciani 1988: 186. Although Bertolini's position against the use of history for political aims seems plausible regarding the example of Legnano, there is less evidence for this in his schoolbooks or in his political speeches. See for instance his commemoration for Garibaldi, where he compares the Italian hero with George Washington: Bertolini 1882; for his widely circulated popular history books see Bertolini 1895 and Bertolini 1880.
27. Quoted in Morigi Govi 1984b: 259. Ridolfi 1990: 57–58. For their role in local politics see Sorba 1993: 44. Clemens 2004: 1. Levine 1986.

28. Smith 1998: 3. The distinction between separate spheres does not necessarily mean that their semiotic content is clearly distinguished: Gal 2004.
29. Carducci, "La R. Deputazione di Storia Patria per le province di Romagna" (1872), in: Carducci 1913b: vol. 2, 76–77. On the history of the Deputazione see Deputazione di Storia Patria per le Province di Bologna 1989. Cencetti 1962. Fasoli 1984. Clemens 2004: 128 sq. On the outreach of academic history during the nineteenth century see Ash 2002.
30. Chabod 1969: 154.
31. Fasoli 1984: 34. Tovoli 1984c.
32. See for an authorative appraisal of his work Grenier 1912, introduction.
33. ASCB, CA, 1862, Tit. IV, 1452, 1453, 1508, 1825.
34. Vitali 1984: 227; (see here in particular the correspondence between Gozzadini, his wife and Capellini in n.8). Morigi Govi 1984b: 265. Tovoli 1984c: 300. Similar conflicts arose from the Benacci excavations: Morigi Govi (ed.) 1996: 4.
35. Alaimo 1990a: 154.
36. Bermond Montanari 1984: 55. Desittere 1984: 80. Tovoli 1984c: 301. On the new legislative framework also Troilo 2005: 69. Vitali 1984: n.8. Morigi Govi 1984a: 244.
37. Bocquet 2001: 763–64. Bocquet 2004: 98.
38. Carducci, "La R. Deputazione di Storia Patria per le province di Romagna" (1872), in: Carducci 1913b: vol. 2, 77.
39. ASCB, CA, 1863, Tit. X, 3, 4, 9252, Consultazione della Deputazione di Storia Patria per lavori al Teatro Comunale, Rapporto del Sindaco; 9278, Rapporto Gozzadini per la Deputazione di Storia Patria.
40. Giovanni Gozzadini, "Delle torri gentilizie di Bologna" and "Della architettura civile in Bologna da' principii del medio evo al sec.XVI," in: Carducci 1913b: vol. 2, 129–227 and 281–90. Enrico Bottrigari, "Delle due più antiche catedrali di Bologna," in: ibid., 237–40.
41. Carducci, "La R. Deputazione di Storia Patria per le province di Romagna" (1872), in: Carducci 1913b: vol. 2, 86.
42. This is best illustrated by the annual lists of members published in the association's proceedings. See also Clemens 2004: 65 sq. and Levra 1992. According to Clemens 2004 nine out of fifty-seven members of the Florentine Deputazione belonged to the nobility. See also Porciani 1981: 118.
43. Gran-Aymerich 2001: 111.
44. ACC, 10 July 1920. Sassatelli 1984a. On the development of modern archaeology in the context of the creation of new national institutions after Unification: Barbanera 2001.
45. Sheehan 2000: 83.
46. Crane 2000: 107. Georges Bataille, quoted in: Sherman 1989: 2.
47. Serra, R. 2001: 589.
48. ACC, 28 December 1878. On the legal framework see Emiliani 1973: 1642. Since 1885 entrance fees to museums, galleries and archaeological sites were regulated by a royal decree, aimed at avoiding fraud and evasion: R. D. 11 novembre 1885, n.3191. Regolamento generale per la ricossione e pel conteggio della tassa d'ingresso nei Musei, nelle Gallerie, negli Scavi e nei Monumenti nazionali.
49. Morigi Govi 1984c: 356.
50. ACC, 20 December 1882, sindaco Tacconi.
51. ACC, 30 November 1881, consigliere Ercolani.
52. ACC, 28 December 1887; 18 October 1889, consigliere Baratelli; 24 October 1889.
53. ACC, 23 December 1894. Appello publicato da Antonio Zannoni per la commemorazione del 25.o anniversario dell'inaugurazione del Museo Civico di

Bologna, Marzo 1906, Archiginnasio 17 Sez. Antica, cart. Ba 2 n.13. ACC, 31 December 1914 and 12 February 1916, consigliere Lanzi.

54. Mandrioli Bizzarri and Meconcelli Notarianni 1984: 407ff.

55. Mandrioli Bizzarri and Meconcelli Notarianni 1984: 411. In this respect the situation differed considerably from that, for instance, in French municipal art museums during the same period, which were able to regularly purchase new objects: Sherman 1989: 134 sq.

56. Hudson 1975: 6. A rather different view is that of Bazin 1967: 421, who emphasises the extent to which the modern museum tries to respond to public opinion.

57. Mandrioli Bizzarri and Meconcelli Notarianni 1984: 421.

58. ACC, 12 February 1916, consigliere Giommi.

59. Frandsen 1998: 86.

60. D'Angiolini and Pavone 1973: 1668. The first modern archives in Italy dated back to the seventeenth century and shared the *"gusto del collezionismo"* of the then fashionable collections of curiosities.

61. Derrida 1995: 11.

62. D'Angiolini and Pavone 1973: 1664. On the following Fasoli 1989.

63. On Bonaini and the Tuscan school of archives: Lodolini 2001: 173 sq.

64. Carducci, "La R. Deputazione di Storia Patria per le province di Romagna" (1872), in: Carducci 1913b.

65. *MdB*, 28 August 1870. Although leading archivists in Italy frequently made references to German methodology, Bonaini corresponded mainly with Böhmer, who at the time still suggested creating subject files rather than following the *"principe de provenance"*: Lodolini 2001: 176.

66. Carducci, "La R. Deputazione di Storia Patria per le province di Romagna" (1872), in: Carducci 1913b: vol. 2, 74.

67. Carlo Malagola, *L'Archivio di Stato di Bologna dalla sua istituzione a tutto il 1882*, quoted in Lodolini 2001: 200.

68. Derrida 1995: 1.

69. White 1975: 54.

70. See also Penny 1995: 344, 367. Penny 1998: 157.

71. Prior 2002: 21, 37. See also Haupt, Müller, Woolf 1998.

72. For comparison see again Penny 1995: 351; Penny 1998: 158ff.; Penny 1999.

73. Carducci, quoted in Porciani 1981: 107–8.

74. Casarini 1872: 19-21.

75. See also ACC, 23 December 1893, consigliere Fusconi. Concerning the city's image abroad *Il Resto del Carlino* was particularly concerned about the impression ambulant dealers made on Bologna's foreign visitors: *RdC*, 24 August 1885.

76. According to a municipal study, about eight hundred people lived directly from the theatre, in addition to the economic benefit derived from the theatre's attraction for visitors from outside. ACC, 11 September and 17 December 1897; 27 December 1898, sindaco Dallolio; 27 November 1899, consigliere Sanguinetti. ASCB, CA, 1903, Tit. X, 3, 4, Deputazione dei pubblici spettacoli, no. 33, 16 May 1903; and idem, 4910, 5669, 6125, 6371, 6705, 6836.

77. Onofri 1988: 500–501.

78. ACC, 13 May 1875, consigliere Panzacchi.

79. ACC, 30 December 1889, consigliere Filopanti.

80. ACC, 1 July 1895.

81. ACC, 1 July 1895, consigliere Ambrosini.

82. See for example the meeting ACC, 25 November 1912.

83. For the experts involved in the organisation of the exhibition see ASB, 4506 Esposizione Emiliana. 1: Comitato Provisorio poi generale; and for the members of the different commissions ASB, 4506, 35–67.
84. ACC, 29 April 1889, consigliere Grabinski.
85. Colombo, E. 2005: 134 sq., 180.
86. Kannonier and Konrad 1995: 13. Kannonier and Konrad 1996: 15–16.

NOTES TO CHAPTER 5

1. Mann 1979: 200–201 (17 April 1919).
2. Mosse, G. 1975: 33–34.
3. Frisch 2005: 34–35.
4. Williams 1976: 19, 187–88. Dixon and Muthesius 1985: 21. J. Mordaunt Crook defined revivalism in opposition to "survival" as a "self-conscious use of antique forms": Crook 1978: 27.
5. Contrary to the argument in this chapter, Bordone 1993: 63 provides a rather anti-modern interpretation of Italy's medieval revival, going back to the eighteenth century. See also Lyttelton 2001: 33.
6. Ciccarelli 2001: 79–80, 86.
7. Porciani 1988: 108. The nineteenth-century rediscovered the Middle Ages as the origin of Italy's existence as a nation. Clemens 2004: 247–55. See also Croce 2001: 292 sq. Banti 2000. Soldani 2004: 152
8. Porciani 1988: 180–81. See also Marcelli 1989: 47.
9. Dixon and Muthesius 1985: 21.
10. Williams 1976: 131. Dixon and Muthesius 1985: 182ff. For an early discussion of this issue Eastlake (ed.) 1978: 117ff. Auerbach 1999: 171–72. Himmelfarb 1952: in particular Chapters 2 and 3.
11. Banti 2000: 76. What the romantic-historical novels share is the idea that history has a sense, even if the particular philosophies of history underlying these works differ from author to author. See also Lützeler 1988: 235. Much of the literature on the early modern period followed Stendhal's model. See, for instance, Stendhal 1973.
12. On the origins of the Papal State: Partner 1972: 20ff.
13. Concerning the claims on the Romagna: Fasoli 1976: 365. Partner 1972: 123. Shaw 1993: 140.
14. Jones 1997: 345. Partner 1972: 298. Vasina 1976: 710.
15. Vasina 1976: 743. Colliva 1977: 15–16. This view contrasts with Burckhardt's idealisation of this period. Buck 1989.
16. His contemporary critics included local despots as well as Erasmus of Rotterdam. Shaw 1993: 149.
17. On the humanist attack on Papal "tyranny": Skinner 1978: 148. On the "deformation" of the Renaissance during the Risorgimento and the liberal period see Dionisotti 1989: 159. The same idea was applied to Southern Italy, whose rulers the pope regarded as feudal vassals. Davis 2006a: 25–26.
18. Frandsen 1998: 88.
19. ACC, 1 July 1895, consigliere Regnoli.
20. ACC, 21 November 1889, consigliere anziano Carducci. Carducci, "Risposta ai soci della Deputazione di Storia patria," *RdC*, 14 July 1896. Piromalli 1988: 84ff. Lyttelton 2001: 42. Poppi (ed.) 1989: 30–31.
21. Carducci, quoted in: Della Peruta 1995: 40. See also Lyttelton 2001: 65n. Gozzadini, "Note per studi sull'architettura di Bologna al secolo XIII al XVI," see Gozzadini 1862: 1. Gozzadini, "Del restauro di due chiese

monumentali nella basilica stefaniana di Bologna," see Gozzadini 1864:
47. Ricci 1924: 102.
22. Alfonso Rubbiani, quoted in: Fanti 1981: 119.
23. Shaw 1993: 205.
24. Minghetti 1888–90: vol. 2, 145.
25. Minghetti 1879.
26. Quirico Filopanti [1864], quoted in Tarozzi 1997: 112.
27. Ciliberto 1989: 72. Soldani 2004: 173.
28. Quoted in Romanelli 1995b: 82.
29. Fried 1963: 84.
30. Gabetti 2001: 326. Serra, R. 2001: 578.
31. Carducci, "Delle cose operate dalla R. Deputazione su gli studi di storia patria per le province di Romagna, 27 maggio 1875," in: Carducci 1913a: 430.
32. Giovanni Gozzadini, quoted in: Dezzi Bardeschi 1979: 13.
33. Umbach and Hüppauf (ed.) 2005.
34. Carducci, "Esposizione di Bologna" [*Il Secolo*, Milan, 10 July 1888], in: Carducci 1921: 329–30.
35. Quoted in: Gottarelli 1985: 190.
36. Gottarelli 1985: 177.
37. ACC, 15 May 1895, consigliere Zannoni, sindaco Dallolio.
38. Colombo, E. 2005: 33 sq.
39. ACC, 27 December 1867, 30 January 1868, consigliere Ceneri.
40. ACC, 30 January 1868, consiglieri Ceneri, Filopanti; sindaco marquis Pepoli.
41. Tobia 1998: 163.
42. ACC, 10 December 1888, consigliere Ceri.
43. Dezzi Bardeschi 1981. Choay 1998: 211. For his impact on the Italian debate see also Camillo Boito, "I nostri vecchi monuments. Conservare o restaurare?," *NA* Terza serie, 1, 1866, 11, 480–506. For similar debates in Germany see Crane 2000: 38 sq.
44. Quoted in Choay 1998: 212–13.
45. Berselli 1981: in particular 32 sq.
46. Calore 1981a. Porciani 1981: 169. For a detailed list of his architectural works see the catalogue in *SSB* 31, 1981: 21ff.
47. Bertozzi 1997: 71. Marchetti 1981. Acting as a mediator between the public and the private sector the committee also gave very specific guidelines to local craftsmen on the use of colours and on the preservation of historical features. See for instance Tacconi et al., Lettera aperta indirizzata dal Comitato per Bologna Storica e Artistica ai Capimastri, Decoratori e Imbianchini, 1902, in Solmi and Dezzi Bardeschi (eds) 1981: 248–49. The association still exists today.
48. Mazzei 1979: 26–27. Bignardi 1963: 41, 44.
49. Berselli 1981: 37.
50. Gottarelli 1976: 193–94.
51. ACC, 29 September 1913, sindaco Tanari. From 1879 to 1888 Rubbiani was councillor and assessor in Budrio, in 1883–1884 with the function of sindaco: Mazzei 1979: 28. Masetti and Branchetta 1981: 245.
52. Bignardi 1963: 45.
53. Rubbiani 1981a: 603. For the quote Fanti 1981: 118.
54. Berselli 1981: 38. Fanti 1981: 116.
55. Rubbiani, quoted in: Fanti 1981: 120.
56. Rubbiani, quoted in: Bertozzi 1997: 61. See also Dezzi Bardeschi 1981: 34.
57. Prociani 1988: 170. Bertozzi 1997: 66. On De Sanctis' medievalism Asor Rosa 1975: 864. See also ACC, 29 September 1913, consigliere Albini.
58. Ricci 1924: 111.
59. Dezzi Bardeschi 1979: 13.

60. Alfonso Rubbiani, quoted in: Scalise 1981: 506. Bertozzi 1997: 75ff. Also Bordone 1993: 64.
61. Quoted in Dezzi Bardeschi 1979: 18.
62. Ricci 1924: 100.
63. Rubbiani 1981a: 603. On this document see also Dezzi Bardeschi 1979: 10–11.
64. Gottarelli 1976: 191.
65. Bacchelli to Rubbiani, 30 January 1908, in: Solmi and Dezzi Bardeschi (eds) 1981: 250, 259.
66. Bacchelli 1910: 616.
67. Giosuè Carducci, Nella Piazza di San Petronio [1877], in Carducci 1994a: 165. The poem has been described as his most imaginative lines: Croce 1914: vol. 2, 30.
68. Giuseppe Ceri, quoted in: Mazzei 1979: 123, 133.
69. Bacchelli 1910: 620–21. ACC, 29 September 1913, consigliere Rivari.
70. Bertozzi 1997: 63, 65. Masetti and Branchetta 1981: 246.
71. Bertozzi 1997: 69. On the relationship to Arts and Crafts: Solmi and Dezzi Bardeschi (eds) 1981: 18, 25.
72. Kirk 2005: 216.
73. ACC, 29 September 1913, consigliere Faccioli; 5 December 1915, consigliere Ciamician.
74. ACC, 16 January 1889, consigliere Panzacchi. Interventions against sacred images in public space were common during the period. Papal Rome counted 2739 images of the Madonna or various Saints in its streets, of which only 535 remained in 1939: Tobia 1998: 97.
75. ACC, 16 January 1889, consigliere Panzacchi. Carducci, quoted in: Fanti 1976: 160.
76. Fanti 1976: 159. ACC, 10 December 1888, consigliere Ceri; articolo 94 della legge comunale.
77. ACC, 16 January 1889, assessore Sacchetti.
78. Dixon and Muthesius 1985: 22. Crook 1978: 18.
79. Bertozzi 2000: 131.
80. Gottarelli 1977: 213–16. Gottarelli 1976: 195.
81. ACC, 10 December 1888, consigliere Ceri, assessore Sacchetti.
82. Jones 1997: 124, 438.
83. Jones 1997: 439. Jones refers explicitly to the example of San Petronio in Bologna.
84. Theodor Mommsen must have been one of the very few foreign visitors not to appreciate the unique history and beauty of the place when he remarked after his visit in 1845 that "da ist nichts Interessantes": Mommsen 1976: 178.
85. Gozzadini 1878: 25.
86. Vianelli 1997: 98.
87. Gozzadini 1878: 3, 13.
88. Foschi 1997: 23–24.
89. Gozzadini 1878: 14, 29.
90. ACC, 23 December 1892, consigliere Zannoni.
91. Carducci, "Delle cose operate dalla R. Deputazione su gli studi di storia patria per le province di Romagna, 26 maggio 1869," in: Carducci 1913a: 381–82. Idem, "Delle cose operate dalla R. Deputazione su gli studi di storia patria per le province di Romagna, 1 giugno 1870," in: Carducci 1913a: 399. Gozzadini 1878: 6ff. Further expenses, only partly covered by additional government and municipal funding occurred through the demolition of edifices belonging to several noble families from Bologna.
92. ACC, 28 December 1887, 30 December 1889, 28 February 1894, ACC, 23 December 1892. Gottarelli 1985: 183.

93. ACC, 25 July 1911.
94. See for example the painting by Cristoforo da Bologna, "L'orazione nell'orto e Santi," Bologna, Pinacoteca Nazionale. Dante Alighieri, *La Divina Commedia, L'Inferno,* xxxi. The Torre della Garisenda was renovated in 1887 by Rubbiani's teacher Tito Azzolini. In 1904 Baron Raimondo Franchetti passed the property on to the city of Bologna, under the condition that it would be maintained as a monument: ACC, 24 June 1904. Masetti and Branchetta 1981: 245.
95. Giovanni Battista Sezanne presented his research on Taddeo Pepoli, a professor of law who assumed the *signoria* after the defeat of Cardinal Del Pogetto in 1334: Giovanni Battista Sezanne, "Di Taddeo Pepoli conservatore della Repubblica bolognese," see Carducci 1913b: vol. 2, 253–54. In a series of five lectures Count Albicini presented the chronicle of Galeazzo Marescotti, dealing mostly with the history of the Bentivoglio family between the fourteenth century and the early sixteenth century: Cesare Albicini, "Di Galeazzo Marescotti e della sua cronaca," see Carducci 1913b: vol. 2, 257–75. Also Corrado Ricci gave popular lectures on the history of Bologna's towers, explaining their origin in the battles between Guelphs and Ghibellines: *RdC,* 13 and 15 January1886
96. Del Vecchio 1917: 47. *RdC,* 8 May 1916. Gabriele D'Annunzio, quoted in: Del Vecchio 1917: 50–51.
97. On the origins of the porticoes: Ricci 1989: 50. Bertozzi 1997: 99.
98. Giovanni Gozzadini, "Della architettura civile in Bologna da' principii del medio evo al sec. XVI," see Carducci 1913b: vol. 2, 281–90, 281ff.
99. Miller 1879: 358. Strang 1863: 168. Ricci 1989: 75.
100. See for instance Dufour 1998 and Voza 1998.
101. ACC, 22 December 1893, sindaco Dallolio.
102. ACC, 22 December 1893, consigliere Sandoni, sindaco Dallolio.
103. Gottarelli 1985: 192. Ricci 1924: 104–5. ACC, 28 December 1905. Mazzei 1979: 122.
104. Jones 1997: 91. On neo-Guelph historiography in nineteenth-century Italy also Soldani 2004. Without providing a clear definition of its meaning, the concept of *Italianità* was frequently used by Carducci. See also ACC, 16 March 1907, consigliere Albini.
105. Giosuè Carducci, "Dello Svolgimento della Letteratura Nazionale. Discorsi tenuti nella Università di Bologna MDCCCLXVIII—MDCCCLXXI" (Discorso Primo: Dei tre elementi formatori della letteratura italiana: l'elemento ecclesiastico, il cavalleresco, il nazionale), in: Carducci 1913a: 27–187, 32–33.
106. Petrarch, quoted in: Partner 1972: 355. Calinescu 1987: 20.
107. Giosuè Carducci, "Presso la tomba di Francesco Petrarca, Discorso tenuto in Arqua il XVIII Luglio MDCCCLXXIV," in: Carducci 1913a: 237–63. Carducci mentions the poet's concern about the civil wars only briefly. See also Croce 1914: vol. 2, 92. Hay 1966: 277.
108. Giosuè Carducci, "Lo Studio di Bologna. Discorso tenuto nell'Archiginnasio di Bologna il dì XII Giugno MDCCCLXXXIII alla presenza di Umberto I Re d'Italia," in: Carducci 1913a: 1–26, 16–17.
109. Marco Minghetti in a letter to Count Radowitz, Berlin, 12 April 1853, quoted in: Minghetti 1888–90: vol. 3, 413.
110. *MdB,* 9 October 1871. See also Piromalli 1988: 87.
111. Colliva 1977: 13.
112. Waley 1988: 33ff. Fasoli 1976: 375. Weber, M. 1980: 749.
113. Fasoli 1976: 377. Also Jones 1997. Hay 1966: 177.
114. Lyttelton 2001: 43. Fasoli 1976: 378. Weber, M. 1980: 750.
115. Jones 1997: 519–18, 636–37. Partner 1972: 208, 282, 440. Prodi 1987: 9. Fubini 1995: 178. Hay 1966: 178.

116. Jones 1997: 606. Partner 1972: 276, 317. Shaw 1993: 5. Burke 1978: 186 discusses the semantic vicinity of the Italian terms "meat" and "sex," indicating that the battle-cry was also an invitation for sexual abuse of the opponent's wives and daughters.
117. Jones 1997: 233–34, 527–28.
118. Colliva 1977: 22ff. See also Volpi 1983: 50–51. As Paolo Prodi has demonstrated, in the Church-State the authority of the bishops was subordinated to the rigid laws of temporal dominion, placing Papal government "at the head of the secularisation process of the modern State": Prodi 1987: 2, 156.
119. *Rivista Bolognese di Scienze, Lettere, Arti e Scuole*, I, 1867, II, 2, 101–14. See also Marcelli 1989.
120. Brunello 1998: 21.
121. Epigraph by Carducci on the Palazzo Comunale, see Carducci 1913b: vol. 2, 62. Bertolini 1876. Concerning Bertolini's essay see also Croce 1926: vol. 2, 143 and Porciani 1988: 186. However, in his later works Bertolini returned to a more traditional Risorgimento historiography: Croce 1926: vol. 2, 171. On the Risorgimento's mystification of Legnano: Fasoli 1982. Fasoli 1976: 379. Shaw 1993: 4.
122. ASCB, CA, 1876, Tit. X, 3, 4, 3576, 3829, 4138, 4139.
123. Bertolini 1892: vol. 2, 37–38, 58. On the historiographical debate see Manselli and Riedmann (eds) 1982 and in particular Brezzi 1982.
124. Filopanti 1882–83: vol. 3, 313ff. idem, *RdC*, 7 August 1885. According to Filopanti the Bentivoglio were descendents of a romantic relationship between Enzo and a Bolognese maiden.
125. Masini 1867: 13, 19.
126. Rubbiani 1981b: 251.
127. The story is referred to by the councillor Albini: ACC, 16 March 1907. Albini tells the same story on the occasion of the council's commemoration for Alfonso Rubbiani: ACC, 29 September 1913. See also Bacchelli 1910: 618.
128. ACC, 5 December 1915, consiglieri Berti, Vancini.
129. Bertolini 1892: vol. 2, 50. Marco Minghetti, "Commemorazione di Vittorio Emanuele fondatore della nazionalità italiana" (*NA*, 15 January 1879), in: Minghetti 1896: 288ff.
130. ACC, 31 December 1916, consigliere Perozzi. See in this context also Giovanni Gentile's critique of the Renaissance in his essay "Che cosa e' il fascismo": Asor Rosa 1975: 1408–9. For the nationalists particularistic interests constituted one of the many reasons for the weakness of the State: De Grand 1978: 5–6, 14–15. Contrary to the imperialist sympathies of the Italian nationalists, the German nationalists during the first half of the twentieth century frequently favoured the Guelphs over the Ghibellines: while Heinrich der Löwe pursued a policy of Baltic and Eastern expansion, Frederick II was accused of concentrating his interest too much on Italy. See Firnkes 1983: 345.
131. ACC, 31 December 1916, sindaco Zanardi, consigliere Bentini.
132. See for instance Bazin 1967: 6.
133. Clark 1999: 7. See in this context Wagner 1873. Friedrich Nietzsche, "Wagner in Bayreuth," in: Nietzsche 1983. Also Charles Baudelaire, "The Painter of Modern Life" and "Richard Wagner and Tannhäuser in Paris," in Baudelaire 1992.
134. Af Malmborg 2002: 52.
135. Schorske 2006: 676, 681.
136. Ben-Ghiat 2001: 2.

137. On the critique of decadentismo as an analytical category Somigli and Moroni (eds) 2004: 9.
138. Blumenberg 1979: 40.
139. Lyttelton 2001: 27–28.
140. Gellner 1998: in particular 55–56. On the construction of meaning see also Crane 2000: 18.
141. Lyttelton 2001: 28–29.

NOTES TO CHAPTER 6

1. "It really depends on the subjective make-up of the late-born rather than on the objective character of the classical heritage whether we feel that it arouses us to passionate action or induces the calm of the serene wisdom. Every age has the renaissance of antiquity it deserves." Aby Warburg, quoted in: Gombrich 1986: 238.
2. Hans Robert Jauss, "Mythen des Anfangs: Eine geheime Sehnsucht der Aufklärung," in Jauss 1989: 23–66.
3. Giovanni Battista de Vico, *Dell'antichissima Sapienza Italica* (1710), in: Vico 1953: 244. This is largely an anti-Cartesian work on the origins of Latin language. According to Arnaldo Momigliano Vico "contributed nothing to the study of the fashionable Etruscans," but his ideas played a significant role in subsequent debates: Momigliano 1966b: 154. See also the introduction by Lucia M. Palmer in Vico 1988: 1–34. See also Banti 2000: 73–74, 112–13. Croce 1926: vol. 1, 14–15, 55. For a general evaluation of Cuoco and his influence ibid., vol. 1, 9 sq.; Carpi 1981: 433; Davis 2006a: 94–106.
4. Casini 1998: 202. In a similar spirit, during the early seventeenth century, the Swedish king Gustav II Adolf promoted the idea of Scandinavia as the cradle of the Goths, from where they conquered the world: Hillebrecht 1997.
5. On the Etruscans as the origin of European civilisation: Robertson Ridgway 2003: 510–11. On the political context of neo-Platonism in Florence Flasch 1988: 553–54. On the origins of early modern etruscology and the role of etruscheria: Pallottino 1957. Pallottino 1975: 24. Moses Finley, "Etruscheria" (1964) in: Finley 1972: 99–109. Briquel 1999: 273–301. Roncalli 1993. Wolfzettel and Ihring 1994: 444ff. As example for the reception of these ideas among the wider public after Unification see the *appendice* "Sulle età preistoriche," in *MdB*, June / July 1870; also Michelet 1843: 7.
6. Gran-Aymerich 1998: 23.
7. First published by Filippo Buonarroti, a Florentine senator and descendant of Michelangelo: Dempster 1723. See Casini 1998: 205. Cristofani 1983.
8. Prayon 1999a; Prayon 1999b. Beard 1978: 12. I am grateful to Luke Rosier for introducing me to Adam's work. Tovoli 1984a: 191. Already Adam employed Italian painters for his Etruscan decorations: Beard 1978: 23ff. On the role of archaeology in imagining the Italian nation see the introduction to Díaz-Andreu and Champion (eds) 1996 and Guidi 1996. Troilo 2005: 69. On Palagi see Bernardini (ed.) 2004. Poppi (ed.) 1996. Poppi (ed.) 1989. Museo Civico di Bologna 1976. The duchess in Stendhal's *Charteuse de Parme* remained deeply impressed by her encounter with Palagi: Lucchese 1996: 19–25.
9. Momigliano 1966e: 1. On Momigliano's understanding of the antiquarians Cornell 1995b. Also Calaresu 1997: 643. Schnapp 2002. On the distinction between antiquarians, historians and archaeologists: Schnapp 1993. Unlike

the historians of their time, the antiquarians did not confine themselves to materials relating to political and military events, showing a particular interest in religious texts and private documents: Cornell 1995a: 24. On nineteenth-century antiquarians also Salmeri 1993. Only few historians deny that the Etruscans represented a distinctive pre-Roman civilisation: e.g., Dumézil 1970: appendix on the religion of the Etruscans.

10. Cornell 1995a: 151.
11. Momigliano 1966e: 18–19. Momigliano 1988a: 11. Surprisingly, certain histories of archaeology still ignore this context of Italian antiquarianism: Trigger 1989. For a review of recent historiography on the relationship between municipal identity and antiquity see Brice 2001: 486–87. (See also the contributions by Simona Troilo, Carlo Franco and Stefania de Vido in the same volume.) It should be noted that at the same time antiquarians also showed a great deal of interest in the Roman past: Haskell 1993: 13 sq.
12. On Winckelmann's influence see Settis 1993: 304–5, 311–12. Marabini Moevs 1971. Cristofani 1983: 142–76. Schnapp 1993: 262ff., and Petronio 1970: 558–59, 582, 768.
13. Pallottino 1975: 143, 154. Crawford 1992: 16–17, 19. Cornell 1995a: 152, 153 sq. Prayon 2001: 9, 112. Similarly, in eighteenth-century Naples the Samnites were seen as "the most powerful people before the emergence of the Romans": Calaresu 1997: 651. On the impact of Müller's and other German scholars see Canfora 1998; Isler-Kerényi 1998: 256ff. Agostiniani 1993: 35ff.
14. For a particularly popular account see Michelet 1843: 52 sq. For the contemporary debate see Francesco Gamuttini, "Della recenti scoperte," *NA*, 3 (5), 1868, 170-179. Confronted with the widespread interest in the Etruscans, most historians of Rome, headed by Niebuhr and Mommsen, tended to minimise their role. The early twentieth century rediscovered the Etruscans' role in early Rome, an argument combined since World War I and the Fascist period with attempts to redefine the Etruscans' *romanità* as an expression of native Italian genius. Only since the second half of the twentieth century historians described Etruscan settlements as "open cities" in which ethnic origin, citizenship or residence did not play a significant role. Cornell 1995a: 151, 157–58.
15. See for instance Jean-Charles-Léonard Sismonde de Sismondi in a letter to the Countess of Albany, quoted in Banti 2000: 113.
16. Banti 2000: 73–74, 112ff. More complex on this issue is the evaluation by Momigliano 1988a: 16. Filopanti 1882–83: vol. 3, 23. The comments in the *GdR* about Napoleon III's biography of Caesar seem rather uncritical, although the paper at least suggests that this work might be the key to the emperor's future policy: 4, 5 and 6 March 1865. See also Brice 2001: 480. Calaresu 1997. On the "romantic revolt against classicism" see also Lyttelton 2001.
17. Momigliano 1988a: 16–17. Bocquet 2001: 762. Lyttelton 2001: 29, 31 argues that the Roman dominion over Italy as well as the Empire's fall before the Barbarians were "critical for defining the sense of a national history." Sally Humphreys 2004: 13 argues that "the new discipline of Classics, at the beginning of the nineteenth century, imagined antiquity as the inspiration for a modern future, counterposed to a past seen as Christian." The classical world as imagined in the nineteenth century had rejected religion and discovered national thought and modern secular administration. See for instance the example of Munich under Maximilian II, where classicist architecture served as a secular alternative to Catholic baroque: Jelavich 1985: 19–20.

18. Giosuè Carducci, "Dello Svolgimento della Letteratura Nazionale. Discorsi tenuti nella Università di Bologna MDCCCLXVIII—MDCCCLXXI" (Discorso Primo": Dei tre elementi formatori della letteratura italiana: l'elemento ecclesiastico, il cavalleresco, il nazionale," in Carducci 1913a: 42–43. On the role of Rome as a "lyrical symbol" for the "new Italy" in Carducci see Croce 1914: vol. 2, 80–81. Piromalli 1988: 6–7. On Gandino: Battistini 1986: 323. Momigliano 1988a: 19. Giosuè Carducci, "Aurelio Saffi" [1890], in Carducci 1921: 363.

19. *RdC*, 7 August 1885. See also 8 August 1885. Filopanti already maintained this theory in his earlier work: Filopanti 1858. See also Battistini 1997: 81–82.

20. Af Malmborg 2002: 52. The issue of European civilisation likewise posed the problem of Italy's strong legacy of Greek authentic culture: Momigliano 1988a: 10.

21. See for instance Prayon 1999a and Prayon 1999b. Also Thomson de Grummond 1996.

22. Momigliano 1966c: 804.

23. Ferraboschi 2003: 42.

24. *MdB*, 25 August 1869. See also Giosuè Carducci, "Delle cose operate dalla R. Deputazione su gli studi di storia patria per le province di Romagna, 1 giugno 1870," in Carducci 1913a: 395. On Zannoni Gran-Aymerich 2001: 736–38 and Alaimo 1990a: 154. For a similar reaction on the part of a municipality see the discovery of forty-two tombs in Alfedena (Abruzzi): Troilo 2005: 67.

25. Zannoni 1871: xxvi. Gentile 1997: 37 maintains that the national myths circulating in nineteenth-century Italy did not refer to a positive Italian race. (This issue requires re-examination.)

26. Zannoni 1871: xlviii. See also Gozzadini 1871: 5ff. and Filopanti 1882–83: vol. 1, 317. The unity of an Etruscan "national culture" goes back to Müller: Isler-Kerényi 1998: 256.

27. Zannoni 1871: xiii. For similar reactions see also Troilo 2005: 96.

28. Wolfzettel and Ihring 1994: 447.

29. Grenier 1912: 4.

30. *MdB*, 10 April 1870 on Gozzadini's excavations; 26 April 1870 on the Certosa.

31. *MdB*, 12 July 1869.

32. For Carducci's reference to Mazzini's "terza Roma" see Carducci 1888: 24. On this idea Gentile 1997: 46 sq. Piromalli 1988: 45. Drake 1980: 6. Also Marabini Moevs 1971: 10 sq. Biagini 1961: 139.

33. Giosuè Carducci, "Delle cose operate dalla R. Deputazione su gli studi di storia patria per le province di Romagna, 8 luglio 1866," in Carducci 1913a: 346. Braccesi 1984: 52. Piromalli 1988: 42. Also Nicolucci 1866: 8. Wilson, A. 2007: 188.

34. Giosuè Carducci, "Avanti, avanti!" English translation in: Pallottino 1975: 105.

35. Marabini Moevs 1971: 86–87. Chiarini 1901: 345.

36. Mansuelli 1979: 354. On Carducci's relationship to the local archaeologists Marabini Moevs 1971: 43ff.

37. Fasoli 1984: 33–35. On Rocchi's revolutionary past Brizzolara 1984a: 163.

38. Susini 1984: 38. On the local developments of these academic disciplines Mansuelli 1984 and on Brizio as teacher Sassatelli 1984a: 446; Brizzolara 1984b. Troilo 2005: 91. On the early school of archaeology: Settis 1993.

39. Giosuè Carducci, "Fuori alla Certosa," in: Carducci 1994b; translation in Carducci 1994a: 167–68.

40. According to Braccesi's interpretation of the poem, the link between the Etruscan settlements on both sides of the Apennines is explicit, "gli occhi ne l'alto a' verdi misteriosi clivi" being a reference to the poet's own native Maremma, in the centre of Etruria near the Etruscan Populonia, referred to in a poem four years later, where he created a link between Tuscany and his second patria, the Padania: Braccesi 1984: 52–53.

41. Croce 1914: vol. 2, 75.

42. This process is similar to Paul de Man's idea of the "intentional structure of the romantic image," where poetic language constitutes origination: see the chapter "Intentional Structure of the Romantic Image," in de Man 1984: 1–17. On the past's poetic creation see also Walsh 1992: 16–17.

43. Bhabha 1990: 1.

44. Grenier 1912. On Grenier see Gran-Aymerich 2001: 312–13. Gran Aymerich 1998: 320–23, 355. Schnapp 1996.

45. Antonio Zannoni, quoted in: Sassatelli 1984b: 328.

46. On the following see in particular the interpretations of the poem by Braccesi 1984; and Sassatelli 1984c: 387.

47. Anderson 1991: 195. On metaphors of dreams and sleep in relation to historical consciousness see also Crane 2000: 5–6. The theme of reawakening from death appears also in other historical contexts evoked by Carducci in his poetry: Piromalli 1988: 9.

48. Paul de Man, "The Image of Rousseau in the Poetry of Hölderlin," in de Man 1984: 21. This shows the extent to which the neo-classicist Carducci is rooted in the imagination of European romanticism.

49. Capozza (ed.) 2002: 5.

50. Gombrich 1986: 239–40. Rilke to Kappus, Rome, 23 December 1903, in Rilke 1998: 33.

51. Gombrich 1986: 240–41.

52. The same theme is still present in Giorgio Bassani's prologue to *Il giardino dei Finzi-Contini*, in which a child reminds a party of weekend excursionists that there is no reason to love the Etruscan ancestors less, only because they died so long ago, causing the novel's hero to conceptualise his feeling of loss for the Jews of his native Ferrara. As Marcel Detienne recently demonstrated, this idea represents a major pattern of contemporary historiography: Détienne 2005: 18.

53. Carducci frequently referred to this idea: "Dello Svolgimento della Letteratura Nazionale. Discorsi tenuti nella Università di Bologna MDCCCLX-VIII–MDCCCLXXI" (Discorso Quarto e Quinto); "L'opera di Dante. Discorso tenuto nell'Università di Roma il dì VIII Gennaio MDCCCLXXX-VIII," in: Opere di Giosuè Carducci, Discorsi letterari e storici, 119–87, 123 and 160; 203–36.

54. Giosuè Carducci, "Delle cose operate dalla R. Deputazione su gli studi di storia patria per le province di Romagna, 26 maggio 1869," in Carducci 1913a: 378. This anti-theological emphasis anticipates Eduard Meyer's thought: See Schlesier 1994: 70 sq.

55. On the idea of the Italian nation as "ethno-biological community" in the literature of the Risorgimento see Banti 2000: 56–57, 66 sq., 83 sq. and in particular 92. Already Croce demonstrated Carducci's emphasis on the nation's blood and the "harmonic spirit of an ancient race": Croce 1914: 39. Asor Rosa 1975: 864 emphasises De Sanctis' reference to the role of blood in making Italians. The origin of this might be partly the legacy of the Italian reception of Müller, to which Arnaldo Momigliano has pointed us: "K.O.Müller's Prolegomena," in Momigliano 1984: 272, 283.

56. Stichweh 1999: 162.

57. On the place of history at international exhibitions: Wilson, M. 1991: 145 sq. Rydell 1984.
58. Pollard 2005: 10.
59. Anderson 1991: 69–70. Trigger 1989: 39–45. On the study of Sanskrit in Italy see Croce 1926: vol. 2, 127.
60. See for instance Tubertini 1871. Gozzadini 1881: 6–7, 20. Also Bagolini and Vitale 1988.
61. Giosuè Carducci, "Delle cose operate dalla R. Deputazione su gli studi di storia patria per le province di Romagna, 8 luglio 1866," in Carducci 1913a: 348. Modern research maintains that the Etruscan civilisation emerged directly from the Villanovan phase, representing the Etruscans' Iron Age: Cornell 1995a: 46.
62. Morigi Govi 1984b: 259. On the content of the site Tovoli and Sassatelli 1988b. For his own work on the site: Gozzadini 1865. See also the review in *RB* 1867, vol. 1, 4, 428–36.
63. As a matter of fact, many archaeologists today believe that Villanovan culture was an Iron-Age Etruscan culture. Grenier 1912: 18.
64. On the insignia Pallottino 1975: 129. Cornell 1995a: 165–66. See the quote by Dionysius of Halicarnassus in Crawford 1992: 19–20, and Poseidonios of Apameia, quoted in Prayon 2001: 7–8.
65. Barfield 1971: 113 argues that contacts between Felsina and Etruria diminished after 700 BC. Only towards the end of the sixth century did the Etruscans take control of the Po plan.
66. Minghetti 1879: 255. ACC, 10 May 1907, consigliere Pullè. Filopanti 1882–83: vol. 1, 314. Rubbiani 1981a: 604.
67. Foucault 1966: 380. On the structures of nineteenth-century scientific explanations of human civilisation see Stoczkowski 2002.
68. For Vincenzo Gioberti the superiority of the Italians could be attributed to their Pelasgian descent. See Laven 2003: 259. On the "northern theory" Pallottino 1975: 75 sq. Livy mentions Alpine populations speaking a language similar to Etruscan, a theory developed by Nicolas Fréret in 1753. On the "oriental theory" (supported in particular by Bachofen) and on Dionysius of Halicarnassus Pallottino 1975: 64. He wrote at a time when Etruscan families enjoyed great influence in Rome: Casini 1998: 200. On the Lemnos theory Casini 1998: 20 and Dumézil 1970: 629. Excavations on Lemnos seemed to reveal that people on the island operated in a language that was not related to Greek or any Anatolian language, but very similar to the language used in archaic Etruria. Modern Etruscology tends to consider these similarities to be a consequence of early Etruscan expansion. Despite the use of the Greek alphabet, Etruscan does not belong to the Indo-European languages, but could be described as a "pre-Indo-European language," dating back to the time before the Indo-Europeanization of language in Italy. Pallottino describes the pre-Indo-European language as "a kind of ethnic island": Pallottino 1975: 51–56, 65, 68. Also Cornell 1995a: 46. On the Pelasgen theory Briquel 1984: 55–81. For a summary of recent theories on ethnic origins, including the autochthonous argument, see Briquel 1999: 51–80.
69. On the following see Carducci's summary of Bertolini's paper: Carducci 1913b: vol. 2, 95–97. For a popular history version of these debates see Filopanti 1882–83: vol. 1, 312. See also the contribution by Count Giancarlo Conestabile from Perugia in: Congrès international d'anthropologie préhistorique 1873: 181 sq. For the stage of nineteenth-century Etruscology in Italy Agostiniani 1993: 31–77 and Roncalli 1993.

70. Bertolini 1860: 5, 30. On the transition from an erudite-aristocratic-private to a public archaeology after Unification see Troilo 2005: 68ff. On the ancient authors Crawford 1992: 14. Prayon 2001: 13. However, Momigliano reminds us that most ancient authors were prevalently interested in the facts of their own recent past, which limits their use for researching earlier periods: Momigliano 1972: 280.
71. On Quirico Filopanti's critique of Niebuhr see Battistini 1997: 73n.
72. Bertolini 1860: 21. On Dionysius of Halicarnassus' role in ancient Etruscology Briquel 1999: 13–14.
73. Braccesi 1984: 50.
74. Carducci 1913b: vol. 2, 97. Bertolini 1892: vol. 1, 7. The only city on the sea was Populonia, which was founded later. Today the argument is considered not very plausible, as the Etruscans maintained important fleets for commerce and war. Modern historiography on Etruscan settlements gives strategic reason for the founding of cities on plateaus at least a kilometre from the sea: Prayon 2001: 22, 45 sq. Already Brizio dismissed this argument with reference to Greek naval cities which were not located directly on the sea: Brizio 1885: 14–17. According to Vico the Etruscans had transmitted Egyptian thought and knowledge to the Latin peoples, before coming under Greek influence. Casini 1998: 193–94.
75. Congrès international d'anthropologie préhistorique 1873: 183. See also Pallottino 1975: 64 sq. Originally concerned with philological questions, since Renan these debates assumed a racial significance: Olender 1989. On the Aryan myth in nineteenth-century Italy and its influence on Carducci see Raspanti 1999: 77–82.
76. Congrès international d'anthropologie préhistorique 1873: 188ff.
77. Gozzadini 1865: 79, 83. The concepts "race" and "nation" were often used interchangeably: Smith, A. D. 1998: 10.
78. Zannoni 1871: xlix. Brizio 1885: 86–87 also emphasises the similarity between the different centres of Etruscan civilisation.
79. Morigi Govi 1984a: 247.
80. Zannoni, quoted in: Morigi Govi 1984a: 249.
81. On Winckelmann's approach Gran-Aymerich 1998: 32 and on the impact of the German school on Italian scholarship 163–64. Also Brice 2001: 477. Barbanera 2001: 501–2. Arnaldo Momigliano, "Gli studi italiani di storia greca e romana dal 1895 al 1939," in: Momigliano 1979: 278.
82. Sassatelli 1984c: 383. On the differences between Niebuhr and Mommsen: Christ 1976: 32–33.
83. Sassatelli 1984c: 392. On Gozzadini's relationship to Brizio and Zannoni see Susini 1987.
84. Brizio 1885: 40, 50ff. Sassatelli 1984c: 389. See in this respect also the organisation of the huge Salone X of the 1881 museum: Morigi Govi 1984c.
85. Brizio 1885: 21.
86. Brizio quoted in Sassatelli 1984c: 386. For a summary of his thesis see Pallottino 1975: 66. Also Morigi Govi 1976: 63. From an archaeological point of view the distinction is not obvious, as tombs dating from different periods can often be found on the same sites: Gualandi 1976: 88.
87. Vitali 1984a: 225, 229. On a critique of Gozzadini's theories see also Vitali 1984c: 283. In the case of Marzabotto Gozzadini's questionable methodology might be explained by the fact that the site had been explored for several centuries before he initiated his excavations. Gozzadini 1865 includes two maps, but no detailed plan.
88. Foucault 1966: 138. Sebald 2003: 62–63. Concerning the "totalitarian" ambition of the "gardening state" see Bauman 1991: 26 sq.

89. Morigi Govi 1984a: 245. Morigi Govi 1988: 5. Susini 1987: 378. Grenier 1912: 15 testifies his admiration for Zannoni, referring to the "*grande et austère figure de l'homme excellent et archéologue passionné.*"
90. Morigi Govi 1976: 63. Much later Pallottino recognised in the Villanovan culture an archaic phase of the Etruscan culture, which started in the ninth century BC and survived until the first half of the sixth century BC. On Pigorini see Guidi 1996: 111.
91. Briquel 1999. Mansuelli 1979: 365. Morigi Govi (ed.) 1996: 5.
92. Tovoli and Sassatelli 1988b: 222, 255–56. Sassatelli 1988: 272.
93. M. Sibaud, in *MdB*, 24 July 1870. Astronomical design and ritual purposes are considered an important aspect of Etruscan town planning: Mansuelli 1979: 354. Very little is known about Etruscan religion and some authors see it as a Roman rather than Egyptian tradition: Dumézil 1970: 626.
94. Foschi 1997: 7. Temples for Isis were not uncommon in the Ancient Mediterranean and the cosmology of this cult usually incorporated other cults and deities, including the worshipping of Venus, Minerva or the Magna Mater: Beard, North and Price 1998: vol. 1, 281; vol. 2, 297. In this context it is interesting to note that Bologna's most popular Verdi opera was *Aida*, based on a scenario by the Egyptologist Auguste Mariette, including scenes in the temple of Isis. Mariette had created the exhibition for the Egyptian pavilion at the 1867 Paris Exposition Universelle, with which Ismail Pasha, the viceroy of Egypt, wished to represent his country as "a major player on the modern world stage." Contrary to Said 1993: 145 sq., who accuses Verdi of orientalising Egypt in imperial fashion, the opera actually seems to equate Egypt with Europe (representing a major military power) and depicts Ethiopia as a non-European other, a division of roles evident in the dramatic action as well as the music. The fact that the plot associates Egypt with the role of the Habsburg Empire, Italy's oppressor, and therefore in a negative light, suggests that audiences in Bologna were not necessarily very receptive to the scenario's moral complexity. Robinson 1993: 135–36. Bergeron 2002.
95. Zannoni 1871: xxi.
96. *MdB*, 4 October 1871.
97. Zannoni 1871: xliii. He presented his talk on the occasion of the inauguration of the Civic Museum in 1871, and the newspapers at the time remarked upon the presence of women in the audience. For the historical context Pallottino 1975: 178–79.
98. Brizio 1885: 6ff. It is likely that on this issue Brizio was influenced by Johann Jakob Bachofen, who had known Pellegrino Rossi and many of the Italian exiles in England, although he himself opposed the end of the Papal regime: Momigliano 1988b and Arrigoni 1988.
99. *MdB*, 9 February 1874. Calore 1982: 75–76. Sassatelli 1984b.
100. E. Roncaglia, quoted in Sassatelli 1984b: 332.
101. *GdE*, 11, 13, 14 February 1874. *MdB*, 3 February 1874. See also Crane 2000: 93–94.
102. *GdE*, 14 and 15 February 1874. Sassatelli 1984b: 330. On modern carnival and the tourist industry see Fincardi 1995: 13.
103. In contemporary caricatures Darwin was frequently represented as a monkey. Schnapp 1993: 314.
104. *GdE*, 13 February 1874.
105. Sassatelli 1984b: 343.
106. *GdE*, 16 February 1874.
107. On the origins of Etruscan dance and music Pallottino 1975: 157. Two generations later, and based on his concept of social memory, Aby Warburg

maintained that contact with ancient symbols, cults and rites permits to experience "the *mnemic energies* with which they were charged." Gombrich 1986: 244. The events in nineteenth-century Bologna seem to express a rather ironic distance to such beliefs.

108. *MdB*, 3 February 1874. The performance at the Montagnola was scheduled to be repeated a few days later, but the event had to be cancelled due to bad weather conditions: *GdE*, 17 and 22 February 1874.
109. Burke 1978: 185.
110. Bakhtin 1984.
111. Baroja 1989: 13. Also Burke 1978: 179–80. Similar concepts are known since antiquity and common in many different cultures. Köpping 1997: 1048–50.
112. Baroja 1989: 19–20.
113. Bakhtin 1984: 5ff., 15.
114. Bakhtin 1984: 8ff. See Umberto Eco's definition as "connected with comedy" and a "situation in which we are not concerned by rules": Eco 1984: 2–3. For modern examples of subversive carnival see Kertzer 1988: 146–47.
115. Bakhtin 1984: 197. There is a risk of romanticising popular culture: Burke 1978: 184, for instance, describes examples based on a clear distinction between actors and spectators, where the former were principally recruited from the upper classes.
116. Bakhtin 1984: 25. Burke 1978: 186.
117. Ridolfi 1990: 108.
118. *GdE*, 17 February 1874. See in this context also Handelman 1982: 166.
119. *MdB*, 4 February 1874. The English perception of Italy as a "carnival nation" was further discussed *MdB*, 10 February 1874.
120. *MdB*, 16 February 1874.
121. Eco 1984: 3, 6. For Eco an important difference between traditional and modern carnival is its spatial limitation: modern carnival is "reserved for certain places, certain streets," representing a paramount example of "law reinforcement," reminding us "of the existence of the rule."
122. ASB, 4506 Esposizione Emiliana, 67. Commissioni ordinatrici: Etrusca-Universitaria, letter Brizio to Codronchi, 5 March 1887.
123. On Edoardo Brizio's role in the local politics of history see his commemoration in the council: ACC, 10 May 1907. Difficulties of this kind were common at the great exhibitions of the nineteenth century: Auerbach 1999: 38 sq.
124. ASB, 4506 Esposizione Emiliana, 67. Commissioni ordinatrici: Etrusca-Universitaria, letter to Codronchi, 8 December 1887.
125. Pomian 1990: 16.
126. Pomian 1990: 22. On archaeological objects as sémiophores see also Schnapp 1993: 12.
127. Walsh 1992: 31.
128. Morigi Govi 1988: 10. Fogu 2003: 23. Gentile 2003: 60. See also Manacorda 1982.
129. Pomian 1990: 2, 35.
130. Tovoli and Sassatelli 1988b: 222.
131. Susini 1984.
132. Caranti Martignago 1995. Tubertini 1871. Tovoli and Sassatelli 1988a. Gerhard was the author of important catalogues for the Royal Museum in Berlin and the founder of the Istituto di Correspondenza Archeologica, the predecessor of the German Archaeological Institute in Rome. Like Karl Otfried Müller he was a pupil of August Boeckh and enjoyed a similar influence on Italian scholarship. See Schnapp 1993: 304–10. Borbein 1979: 119–23.

133. ACC, 27 October 1861. For a transcript of the will see the report of the *segretario comunale* Tubertini 1871. Tovoli 1984a: 191.
134. Tovoli 1984a: 191.
135. Capellini 1914: vol. 2, 4, 8. On the academic reception of Darwin's theories in Bologna see Giovanni Franceschi, "La Natura o L'origine delle Specie di Carlo Darwin," in *RB* 1868: vol. 2, 12, 1025–37. Also Paolo Mangegazza "Carlo Darwin e il sui ultimo libro," *NA*, 3 (5), 1868, 70–98.
136. Hudson 1975: 8 sq.
137. Tovoli 1984b.
138. ACC, 19 February 1865; 5 March 1868; 25 May 1868. Even the commission set up to buy equipment for the display of the Palagi inheritance was dissolved: ACC, 13 November 1862.
139. ACC, 23 January 1871, consigliere Bordoni.
140. See for instance on Marzabotto *MdB*, 7 November 1862. Also Gozzadini 1881: 4. Morigi Govi (ed.) 1996: 6.
141. Tovoli 1984c: 300.
142. Capellini 1914: vol. 2, 195–96. The institution's origins go back to the meeting of the Société italienne des Sciences Naturelles in 1865. The first international meeting took place in Neuchâtel in 1866, the second during the Exposition Universelle in Paris, 1867, a third meeting in Norwich and London in 1868. See Congrès international d'anthropologie préhistorique 1873: vii–viii. Also Kaeser 2002.
143. Jean Capellini and Jean Gozzadini, "À Messieurs les correspondants et adhérents du Congrès international," *MdB*, 6 August 1870.
144. Congrès international d'anthropologie préhistorique 1873: 10. For the positivist context of the debate see in particular Patriarca 1996: 185 sq.
145. Blumenberg 1966: 435, also 204.
146. Gozzadini 1871: 3–4. *MdB*, 6 September 1871. *GdE*, 26 September 1871.
147. On the municipal planning see ACC, 25 May 1870. The first important contribution (2000 Lire) to the excavations was released in June 1870: ACC, 11 June 1870. On the subsidies for the conference ACC, 21 July 1871. Vitali 1984c: 278.
148. ACC, 23 January 1871, assessore Guadagnini, consigliere Sassoli.
149. Capellini 1914: vol. 2, 211. Vitali 1984c: 284 sq.
150. On the Florentine museum: Delpino 2001.
151. Vitali 1984c: 287–88. *GdE*, 10 October 1871 underlines the importance of this first attempt to bring together materials from the various parts of Italy, including the Trentino and Istria, still under Austrian domination.
152. Serra Ridgway 1996: 1072–73.
153. The composition of membership in the Deputazione di Storia Patria, which was very much in favour of both the project for a museum and the excavations themselves, mirrors this trend: among the officers and active members during the academic year 1870–71 we find representatives of the Moderate elite like the Gozzadini, Enrico Bottrigari, Antonio Montanari, but also Carducci, who served as secretary, and Pietro Ellero. Similarly, in the relevant council debate several eminent councillors of the Right, like the Marquis Bevilacqua, supported the public excavation project of Casarini's administration: ACC, 23 January 1871. For the concept of the "political milieu" see Lepsius 1973.
154. On the relationship between Capellini and Sella see Vitali 1984b: 270–71.
155. Avellini 1997: 665–66. On anthropogenesis and science see Stoczkowski 2002: 29–67.
156. They were of course still far from today's approximations. Vitali 1984c: 278–79, 282, 293. See on this debate also the *MdB*'s front-page for the inauguration:

1 October 1871. On the impact of this insight on the archaeological profession see Schnapp 1993: 321.

157. Giustiniano Nicolucci, "Sur l'homme préhistorique en Italie," in: Congrès international d'anthropologie préhistorique 1873: 235–36. On Nicolucci Fedele and Baldi (eds) 1988.

158. See also Artigas, Glick and Martínez 2006. It should be noted that religious opposition to Darwin's theory was not confined to the Catholic world: Caullery and Leroy 1965: 477–78.

159. *MdB*, 1 October 1871.

160. Morigi Govi 1984b: 260–61. Sassatelli 1984c: 381. Also Gran-Aymerich 2001: 253.

161. Ariodante Fabretti to Casarini, quoted in Morigi Govi 1984b: 261.

162. Congrès international d'anthropologie préhistorique 1873: 265. For a detailed description of Zannoni's revolutionary engineering works on the site see Morigi Govi 1984b: 263. Also Delpino 2001: 635–36.

163. *MdB*, 28 September 1871. Ten years later Gozzadini still refers to *"una guerra titanica"*: Gozzadini 1881: 3. See also Schnapp 2001 and Gran-Aymerich 2001: 575. Gaehtgens 2002: 245–46. A more complex picture emerges from Schlesier 2003: 128.

164. *GdE*, 5 October 1871. On Virchow's interest in anthropology and pre-history see Gran-Aymerich 2001: 688. On the German academic model Malatesta, M. 2006a: 9–13. The scientific vicinity between medicine, anthropology, psychology and ethnology was not unusual at the time. Until the first half of the nineteenth century "men of science" were expected not to be "mere specialists," but to pursue "cosmological interests": Knight 1998: 23. Schlesier 1999: 220–21. Also Schnapp 2002. Charle 1996: 207–8. Also Sherratt 2002.

165. Use of this term started only during the 1890s: Charle 1996: 17, 257. These Italian sympathies with Virchow challenge the argument that admiration for Bismarck was in the centre of Italian *"germanofilia."* See Schiera 1997: 27–28.

166. Goschler 2004: 236–37.

167. Goschler 2004: 224.

168. Goschler 2004: 221, 225. On this definition of modern research and the role of observation Stichweh 1999: 164. Stoczkowski 2002: 1. On these developments in modern archaeology also Walsh 1992: 15.

169. Blumenberg 1966: 18. Reulecke 1989: 132.

170. *GdE*, 1 and 2 October 1871.

171. *GdE*, 4 October 1871: *"ogni forestiere pote' farsi la sua piccola raccolta!"*

172. Morigi Govi 1984b: 264.

173. *MdB*, 4 October 1871. *GdE*, 5 and 6 October 1871.

174. Capellini 1914: vol. 2, 210. *MdB*, 9 and 11 January 1870. Not only was *Il Monitore* critical of the scientist's devotion to the royal family (*"una cortigianata volgare"*), it also resented the fact that Capellini privileged the *Gazzetta dell'Emilia* when communicating information on the congress.

175. Camillo Casarini in his opening speech, quoted in Masi 1875: 190.

176. Masi 1875: 189.

177. Capellini 1914: vol. 2, 215. *GdE*, quoted in Pancaldi 1986: 361.

178. Capellini 1914: vol. 2, 216.

179. ACC, 23 May 1872.

180. ACC, 1 May 1873.

181. ACC, 1 March 1872, consigliere Casarini.

182. ACC, 6 July 1873.

183. R.D. of 29 November 1878; ACC, 19 May 1882. Gozzadini 1881: 5–6.

184. On this process Bennett 1988: 63–64.

185. Sherman 1989: 154 sq. Kannonier and Konrad (eds) 1995. Gerbel et al. (eds) 1996.
186. Morigi Govi 1988: 7. Tovoli and Sassatelli 1988b: 222. On the Benacci excavation see also the catalogue of the 1996 exhibition: Morigi Govi (ed.) 1996.
187. Furon 1965: 345.
188. Stichweh 1999: 194–95.
189. For a complete list and descriptions see Sassatelli 1984d: 365 and Sassatelli 1988: 271.
190. On the donations during the 1880s and 1890s see Vitali and Meconcelli Notarianni 1984. ACC, 5 December 1873.
191. ACC, 28 December 1887. As a condition for the donation certain rooms and the museum's library had to carry Gozzadini's name.
192. Vitali 1984a: 234. Not until 1960 was the Villanovan collection integrated into the museum.
193. ACC, 11 November 1891 and 6 March 1895. On Cappelini's collection, which occupied a separate room, see Vitali 1988.
194. Morigi Govi 1996: 7.
195. Goldmann 1959.
196. Hall 1996: 4.
197. On the importance of establishing ethnic and racial distinction see also Banti 2002.
198. Pallottino 1975: 37. Also Gualandi 1976: 85–86. Tovoli and Sassatelli 1988b: 222, 255–56. Barfield 1971: 107. For a critique of theories of cultural evolution see Nippel 1990: 361.
199. Darwin discusses the absorption of tribes and the concept of cultural exchange in *Origin of Species* (1859) and in *The Descent of Man* (1871): Darwin 1994: 102, 180–81.
200. Kuhn 1970: 76. Even at that time some ethnologists rejected the term "anthropology" for its "biological" content: Schlesier 1999: 220.

NOTES TO CHAPTER 7

1. Aurelio Saffi, *Il Popolo d'Italia*, Naples, 14 May 1861, in: Saffi 1901: vol. 7, 142–46.
2. ACC, 17 December 1866, consigliere Ercolani.
3. ACC, 25 January 1878, sindaco Tacconi. Cavour himself recognised this role in a reply to the member of parliament Rodolfo Audinot, 25–27 March 1861: Segretariato Generale della Camera dei Deputati 1971: vol. 1, 30–31.
4. Sorba 1997: 154. See also Ferraboschi 2003: 48ff. Raffaele Romanelli 1986: 80 speaks about the "*pregiudizio anticentralistico*" and Simonetta Soldani: See "Prefazione" in Kroll 2005: xx. Clemens 2004: 316 sq. Also Woolf 2004: 28. For a classical examination of the relationship between the Italian State, its citizens and civil society see Caracciolo 1977. See also Prociani 1997: 14. The discourse on patrimony as municipal treasures presents an interesting case study of the role of municipal identity after Unification: Troilo 2005: 29. Regarding the relationship between opera and urban identity see Ther 2006: 19.
5. Filopanti 1882–83: vol. 1, 293. GdE, 26 September 1871.
6. Confino 2001: 8–9. On the political context and the historiographical tradition of this debate see Applegate 1999. For a critique of traditional approaches and the interpenetration of national loyalties with loyalties towards other territorial units such as regions, cities or villages see also Haupt, Müller and Woolf 1998. Also the conference report Petri 2003a. On the ritualistic

mechanisms relating the local to the national see Kertzer 1988: 21 sq. On the "pivotal relationship" of identity to "politics of location" see Hall 1996: 2.

7. Applegate 1990: 3, 9. See in this context also White 1977. The case of the German cities is somewhat different: see Jenkins 2003: 146 sq. On the role of *Heimat* in the construction of national identity: Cuaz 1998: 608.

8. According to Petri "the central symbol of Heimat is not the community but rather man facing his own existential loneliness": Petri 2003b: 308.

9. Porciani 1997b: 146. Likewise in the case of France see Saunier 1998: 133. Applegate 1990: 10 sq. Confino 1997. See also Tacke 1995. Haupt, Müller and Woolf 1998: 12.

10. The significance of the "abolition of the cities" becomes clear if one considers that in Prussia, until the early twentieth century, fifty-one cities were represented in the Herrenhaus. Rugge 1993: 52.

11. Rugge 1993: 55.

12. "Commemorazione di Vittorio Emanuele fondatore della nazionalità italiana," in Minghetti 1896: 279–320.

13. Banti 2000: 56. Banti 2005: 160.

14. "Allocuzione a Giovani Alunni del Ginnasio Premiati," in: Pepoli, C. 1880: vol. 1, 5.

15. Giosuè Carducci, "Risposta ai socii" [*GdE*, 14 February 1896], in: Carducci 1921: 518.

16. Lyttelton 1996: 34–35. Volpi 1983: 265. Cavazza, S. 1998: 79. For the general context see also Cole (ed.) 2007.

17. ACC, 27 May 1800. Pepoli 1862. Capellini 1914: vol. 2, 76.

18. Frandsen 1998: 88. Volpi 1983: 15ff., 48 sq. Ghisalberti 1997: 103. On the comparison with Tuscany and Florence see Saunier 1998: 147. Cazzola 1997: 53.

19. Isnenghi 2004: 191. Cavazza, S. 1998: 79–80. On Umberto's visit to the Romagna see Brice 2005: 750–51.

20. "Centralità o discentramento amministrativo," 8 June 1860, in: Minghetti 1988: vol. 1, 45 sq. See also Berselli 1980: 258 sq. On the rejection of the French in favour of the English model: Ragionieri 1979b: 83. Patriarca 1996: 195ff. Meriggi 1997: 51. Schiera 1997: 36.

21. Marco Minghetti, quoted in: Lipparini 1942: vol. 1, 234. See also Marco Minghetti, "Ordinamento amministrativo dello Stato," 13 March 1861, in: Minghetti 1988: 89–105. Also Minghetti 1865: 5. Caracciolo 1977: 16.

22. Fearing the possible impact of the Democrats, most Moderates opposed the idea of regional autonomy, but tended to support Minghetti on the issue of municipal and provincial self-government. Romeo 1990: 503. Romanelli 1988: 685. Romanelli 1979: 43. See also Porciani 1997b: 168; and on Cavour's view Ragionieri 1979b: 93.

23. Ragionieri 1979b: 96–97.

24. Berselli 1980: 262. For the administrative debate in the former *ducato* see Ferraboschi 2003: 29, 38 sq.

25. Russo 1998: 13–33.

26. Saunier 1998: 152.

27. D'Attore 1991: 90. Romanelli 1979: 46. See also Meriggi 1997: 49.

28. ACC, 21 November 1889, consigliere anziano Carducci. See in this context also Troilo 2005: 31.

29. Galli del Loggia 1998: 37. Soldani 2004: 168ff. Woolf 2004: 19. Della Peruta 1995: 34. See also Ghisalberti 1997: 103. Avellini 1997: 652.

30. Frandsen 1998: 89, 91ff.

31. "Petizione della Città di Siracusa per essere reintegrata a capoluogo di Provincia," 20 May 1861, in: Minghetti 1988: vol. 1, 227. See also Avellini 1997: 654. On the more general issue see Frandsen 1998.

32. ACC, 2 October 1861.
33. ACC, 11 January 1878, sindaco Tacconi.
34. The most important study of reactions to Vittorio Emanuele's death is Levra 1992: 1–298. On the symbolism of the obsequies for Vittorio Emanuele: Tobia 2000: 77. Tobia 1993. See also Duggan 2002: 379ff. Porciani 1997b: 147. Nasto 1994: 99 sq.
35. "Commemorazione di Vittorio Emanuele fondatore della nazionalità italiana" (1879), in Minghetti 1896: 291, 303.
36. Mori 1986: 266 sq.
37. Acerboni 2001: 388.
38. Frandsen 1998: 102.
39. Davis 2006a: 27ff. Of the major Italian cities only Venice played for a long time a rather negligible role, partly as a consequence of the fact that it did not contribute much to its liberation in 1866, but the reasons for this are complex: Infelise 2002.
40. Colombo, E. 2005: 125.
41. Mandrioli Bizzarri and Meconcelli Notarianni 1984: 426–27.
42. The episode referrs to the Sala Emiliana at the Esposizione di Belle Arte in Venice: ACC, 30 June 1905. See also Calore 1982: 122.
43. Croce 1928: 89–90.
44. Tobia 1998: 100ff.
45. On the association of private individuals attempting to form a civic public sphere see Habermas 1990: 86–121. On associational culture in Italy: Banti and Meriggi 1991: 358. On the relationship between associational culture and politics see also Conti 2000: 193 sq. For the social and political functions of male associational culture see Davidoff and Hall 2002: 416, 446.
46. Cardoza 1991: 385.
47. Pécout 1990: 581.
48. *MdB*, 20 February 1868. See on this issue Ridolfi 1990: 25 sq.
49. Felicité de Lamennais, quoted in: Boutry 1988: 66.
50. Giacomo Leopardi, quoted in: Cavazza and Bertondini 1976: 16.
51. Ridolfi 1990: 112–13.
52. Minghetti 1888–90: vol. 1, 41, 47.
53. Ridolfi 1990: 40ff. Pombeni 1984: 31. For the Italian and European comparison see Palazzolo 1984: 69–70. Meriggi 1988: 152. Meriggi 2001: 13. Less critical Ridolfi and Tarozzi (eds) 1987–88. Siegrist 1988: 116.
54. Minghetti 1888–90: vol. 1, 124–25.
55. Minghetti 1888–90: vol. 1, 53.
56. Quoted in Galli della Loggia 1998: 106. See also Meriggi 1994: 194ff.
57. Boutry 1988: 70.
58. See the introduction by Lilla Lipparini in: Minghetti 1947: 7. On the slow development of the *salotto* in Italy: Salvati 1998: 179.
59. Davis 1988: 188–89. For a general account of crime and policing in the area during the Risorgimento see Hughes 1994.
60. Marco Minghetti to Terenzio Mamiani (1851), quoted in: Minghetti 1888–90: vol. 3, 5–8. See also idem 217. On the problem of security in the region see Hughes 1994. Minghetti's evaluation was probably based on the perceived contrast between the tensions associated with the Risorgimento period and the tranquillity of the previous century. See Davis 1988: 17.
61. Rodolfo Audinot to Minghetti, 7 July 1859, quoted in Lipparini 1942: 310–11.
62. Marco Minghetti to Cavour (1856), quoted in Minghetti 1888–90: vol. 3, 92.
63. Minghetti 1955: 293 sq. (27–29 December 1860).

64. Ridolfi 1990: 47ff., 61, 68, 104 sq. Gianni 2006: 131–34.
65. Banti and Meriggi 1991: 360. See for Turin Cardoza 1991. For a comparison with Forlì: Balzani 1987: 56.
66. Banti 1996b: 510–11.
67. Ridolfi 1990: 64.
68. ACC, 3 May 1864, consigliere Pepoli.
69. Masini 1867: 11, 13.
70. ASCB, CA, 1860, Tit. XVI, Avviso del municipio di Bologna in seguito e di conformità alla Governativa Notificazione in data 20 corrente per la concessione dell'uso della Maschera, e dei corsi delle Carozze, 28 January 1860.
71. ACC, 30 January 1872.
72. Quoted in Calore 1982: 75. See for a summary of activities *MdB*, 2 and 27 January as well as 20 February 1868.
73. Calore 1982: 75.
74. *GdE*, 17 February 1874.
75. *MdB*, 4 February 1874.
76. Sobrero 1995: 124–25.
77. Habermas 1990: 101. Weber, W. 1979: 109–21. Ridolfi 1987: 37. Brice 2005: 385.
78. ACC, 17 December 1897, report by the town mayor.
79. ACC, 25 March 1868.
80. Pivato 1987: 169.
81. ASCB, CA, 1860, Tit. XVI and 1861, Tit. XVI, 3, letter of 30 September 1861.
82. ACC, 14 May 1863.
83. ASCB, CA, 1861, Deputazione dei pubblici spettacoli, Miscellanea, Arena del Giuoco del Pallone, stazione estiva, 28 June 1861. ASCB, CA, 1861, Tit. XVI, 3, Eugene Godard to the sindaco, 15 June 1861 and 20 July 1861. 1861, Deputazione dei pubblici spettacoli, Miscellanea, Arena del Giuoco del Pallone, stazione estiva, 5 November 1861. Francesco Zambeccari became famous for his ascent in 1804, recorded in a print by Pio Panfili: Calore 1982: ill. 1.
84. ACC, 11 June 1873, consigliere Ercolani.
85. Croce 1928: 91.
86. In 1885 Il Resto del Carlino covered the regional gymnastic festival in great detail: *RdC*, 30 May 1885.
87. Pivato 1987: 177–82. The 1909 Socialist Youth Congress in Florence decided that membership in sport associations was incompatible with membership in the *Federazione Giovanile Socialista*. Only shortly before World War I did the attitude of the Socialist Labour movement towards sport begin to change. See for example Imola's "Ciclisti Rossi."
88. ACC, 22 June 1889, assessore Sacchetti.
89. ACC, 23 May 1899, sindaco Dallolio.
90. Even Princess Agnese Hercolani did not hesitate to ride a bicycle at the club: Raccagni 1988: 235ff.
91. *GdE*, 2 and 5 September 1889.
92. Il Resto del Carlino refers to the association as a "useful, civilised and philan-tropical institution": *RdC*, 11 May 1885. See also 19 August 1885 and 2 July 1886. On Ceri see the report on his talk at the Teatro Brunetti in *RdC*, 28 June 1886.
93. Gavelli and Tarozzi 1987: 119. The foundation of the association in Bologna coincided with the time when Naples, for reasons of public hygiene, prohibited bearing the dead without coffins along the streets of the city:

Macry1984: 350. The issue of public hygiene also played a major role in the discussions about urban planning and the modernisation of Bologna's infra-structure, promoted by the progressive middle classes. See for instance Carducci's speech on the 1889 piano regolatore: Gottarelli 1985: 190. For similar debates in Turin Mazzonis 2001: 475–76.

94. ACC, 24 August 1886, consigliere Zucchini.
95. Numbers based on Gavelli and Tarozzi 1987.
96. Gavelli and Tarozzi 1987: 129, 133.
97. GdE, 6 July 1889.
98. Gavelli and Tarozzi 1987: 126–27.
99. ACC, 28 September 1870 and 1 October 1870. Soldani 1993, in particular 83. Soldani (ed.) 1989.
100. During the liberation Brigida Tanari, together with other women of Bologna's better families, raised funds for "the national cause," but without much impact on wider strata of society. Cavazza and Bertondini 1976: 18. Marco Minghetti describes in his memoirs the female support for the Guardia Nazionale in 1831. Minghetti 1888–90: vol. 1, 12, 187. Bottrigari 1960–63: vol. 3, 245–46. See also the role of Letizia Pepoli, daughter of Gioacchino Murat: Letizia Pepoli Murat to Minghetti, 19 July 1858, quoted in: Lipparini 1942: 294. To demonstrate their loyalty to the Piedmontese monarchy, the Comitato delle signore dell'Emilia, in 1860, produced a bandage for the king's horse: see MdB, 16 March and 12 April 1860.
101. ACC, 12 July 1912.
102. Zangheri 1997a: vol. 2, 189–90.
103. On the following Dalla Casa 1987. For similar associations see De Giorgio 1992: 397 sq.
104. RdC, 19 July 1885; 1 January 1886. On women journalists in Italy De Giorgio 1992: 484–94.
105. See on this the chronicler of coffeehouse culture in Udine, Giovanni Andrea Ronchi, quoted in: Francfort 1988: 136. On the role of the coffeehouse in the emergence of a public sphere Habermas 1990: 105–6.
106. On the botega del caffè as a place of sociability see Malatesta, M. 1997. Isnenghi 2004: 37 sq.
107. Macry 1984: 342. Sani 1922: 6–32, 73–110. This was not unique to Bologna: Francfort 1988: 135.
108. Flora 1960: 121.
109. Santini and Trezzini 1987: vol. 1, 128.
110. Malatesta, M. 1997: 57.
111. Santini and Trezzini 1987: vol. 1, 120–23.
112. Dickie and Foot 2002: 3.
113. On the concept of community see Körner 1999.
114. ACC, 3 February 1862; 23 May 1872.
115. ACC, 31 December 1908. Figures for the number of victims are difficult to assess and vary between 50,000 and 200,000, with 40% of the population of Messina killed. For a detailed study of the narratives created in the aftermath of the event (and for the first quote) see Dickie 2002: 238ff. On the damage to the urban infrastructure Oteri 2005.
116. ACC, 18 February 1915. I am grateful to the late Giulia Quercettini whose personal account stimulated my initial interest in the event.
117. Dickie and Foot 2002: 23.
118. MdB, 19 January 1863. On the perception of the South during Unification see Riall 1998a.
119. ASCB, ACC, 26 June 1894, sindaco Dallolio. On Sante Caserio see Masini 1981: 39–54.

120. Romeo 1990: 371–72. In December 1863 three Italians had been charged with the attempted assassination of Napoleon III, covered in detail by the Italian press. See for instance *MdB*, 28 February 1864. Minghetti 1888–90: vol. 3, 210. Calore 1982: 81–82.
121. *Ill. Ital.*, 27 March 1881. The tsar was assassinated just a few hours after announcing "a timid first step toward the participation of elected representatives in legislation." Hosking 2001: 317.
122. Toda 1988: 41. Berti 2003: 190. Pernicone 1993: 90–91. Macedo 1998: 98.
123. ACC, 26 June 1894, consiglieri Filopanti and Carducci. In his *Letture del Risorgimento*, which appeared the following year, Carducci underlined the French role in stimulating national sentiment among Italians.
124. See Della Peruta 1995: 58 and Masini 1981: 52. The same notion of a *fratellanza latina* would still influence the debate on intervention in 1914 and 1915: Isnenghi 1997: 279.
125. Bach Jensen 2004: 117, 122. Masini 1981: 36, 55–59. Cammarano 2004: 507. An element rarely taken into consideration when explaining the roots of Italian anarchism is the influence of Proudhon's "federalist patriotism," which as an anti-Jacobin and anti-centralist ideology contrasted with the Italian concept of state after Unification: Levy 2004: 333.
126. ACC, 23 April 1897.
127. Derrida, Habermas, and Borradori 2004: 16–17. Koselleck 1992.
128. Brice 2005: 668. Levra 1997: 61ff. Luciani 1997: 150. On the first wave of monuments after Unification see Isnenghi 2005: 330ff.
129. Camillo Boito, quoted in Porciani 1993: 230. On Camillo Boito see also Colombo, E. 2005: 96–97. He had a major impact on his brother Arrigo, who lived most of his life in the same household: Helbling 1995: 63–64.
130. See in this context the introduction to Koselleck and Jeismann (eds) 1994.
131. Tobia 1998: v. Levra 1992: 299 sq. See similar Baioni 1994. Duggan 1997. Duggan 2002: 432 sq. Even with regard to individual monuments the liberal state appears occasionally as the promoter: Porciani 1993: 214 sq.
132. Gentile 2006: xiv–xv. In defining "religion of politics" Gentile differentiates conceptually between secular, civil and political religion.
133. Mosse, G. 1975: 47 sq.
134. Saunier 1998: 149.
135. Cerasi 2000: 15 sq.
136. Porciani 1997a: 41.
137. However, as the nation's temporary capital Florence never assumed the same importance as Turin and Rome: Porciani 2002: 46.
138. Agulhon 1978.
139. Porciani 1993: 215. Balzani 1997b: 302.
140. On the Bavarian Walhalla Mosse, G. 1975: 53ff.
141. Balzani 1997b: 303.
142. ACC, 12 May 1865.
143. ACC, 26 March 1868.
144. ACC, 5 May 1904.
145. ACC, 5 May 1904, consigliere Nadalini.
146. Tobia 2000: 68.
147. Nicolucci 1866. ACC, 12 May 1865; 26 April 1890, consigliere Carducci; 10 June 1910, consigliere Albini (Carducci); 3 May 1912 (Pascoli); 7 May 1915 (Guerrini).
148. Mariani 1985: 29.
149. ACC, 26 April 1890, consigliere Carducci. In 1860 a bust of Dante had been unveiled in a civic library in Trento. For detailed information on this battle of monuments I am grateful to Laurence Cole.

150. Rubbiani, quoted in: Fanti 1981: 120. On the *Societa' Dante Alighieri* during this period see also Cerasi 2000: 152 sq.
151. Giosuè Carducci, "Rogito della consegna," *RdC*, 28 June 1886. On local commemorations for Oberdan see "La Lapide a Guglielmo Oberdan," in: *Vita Citt.*, II, 9/10, 1916, 25.
152. *RdC*, 21 July 1885 and 22 February 1886. Carducci sent "a small sum" to the committee in respect of his opposition to "papal tyranny," but remained sceptical towards the thinker and writer Bruno: Carducci, "Commemorazione di Giordano Bruno" [1889], in: Carducci 1921: 318–19.
153. ACC, 14 January 1891, consigliere Carducci.
154. Antonio Gramsci, "Letteratura popolare. Il gusto melodrammatico," in Gramsci 1975: vol. 3, 1676–77.
155. My thinking about obsequies in the context of this chapter owes much to discussions with David d'Avray and to his book on medieval memorial preaching: D'Avray 1994.
156. Ackermann 2000: 90.
157. Minghetti 1955: 374 sq. (2–6 June 1861). On local commemorations for Cavour see Pécout 1995: 70–71.
158. Pinelli and Casarini both feared that the recently united nation could lose the support of Napoleon III. It was hoped that in this respect Gioacchino Pepoli, future mayor of Bologna and cousin of Napoleon III, would have some positive influence on the emperor. Franzoni Gamberini 1961. Also Masi 1875: 142 sq.
159. Masi 1875: 143.
160. ACC, 13 June 1861, sindaco Pizzardi.
161. ACC, 13 June 1861, consiglieri Berti, Ramponi, Zanolini, Cassarini.
162. ACC, 23 May 1873 and 26 September 1873.
163. *RdC*, 28 May 1885.
164. Tobia 1998: 95.
165. Raffaelli 1998: 219.
166. ACC, 2 October 1864, sindaco Pepoli.
167. ACC, 26 March 1868, consigliere Filopanti. Similar Enrico Panzacchi on 26 September 1873.
168. ACC, 18 November 1895, consigliere Regnoli and sindaco Dallolio; 31 May 1897, consigliere Ghelli.
169. ACC, 26 March 1868. Similar developments took place throughout Italy: Raffaelli 1998: 217–18.
170. Raffaelli 1998: 220.
171. ACC, 18 November 1895. Among the first to criticise the modernising tendencies was the German historian Ferdinand Gregorovius: Raffaelli 1998: 221.
172. ACC, 2 October 1864.
173. ACC, 11 February 1869. The idea of this tablet had first been discussed in 1844 and only much later was it noticed that the Stabat Mater had seen an Italian "ante-prima" in Florence in 1842. De Angelis 1982: 50–51.
174. By contrast with Rossini's father, who was expelled from Pesaro by the pontifical police and, once in Bologna, again imprisoned for revolutionary activity: Vatielli 1928: vol. 2, 143, 173–74. Minghetti 1888–90: vol. 1, 56–57, 92. For a balanced view: Weinstock 1968: 243–47.
175. Tobia 2000: 70, 73.
176. *MdB*, 20 November 1868. ACC, 22 December 1886 and 12 April 1887.
177. "Gioacchino Rossini. Discorso detto a Pesaro nell'aula grande dell'Istituto Rossini, per il centenario rossiniano," in: Panzacchi 1895: 110, 116, 131 sq.
178. *MdB*, 22 November 1868. Also Alessandro Biaggi, in *NA*, 3(12), 1868, 745–746. I am grateful to Daniele Serafini for introducing me to these *lieux de mémoire*.

179. *MdB*, 16 December 1868.
180. Quoted in: Vatielli 1928: vol. 2, 133.
181. Rosselli 1987: 101.
182. *RdC*, 9 May 1885. On similar conflicts over "paternity claims" in Germany see Confino 1997: 44.
183. *RdC*, 9 May and 9 August 1885, letter by Filopanti.
184. *MdB*, 21 August 1862. Mesini 1979: 255.
185. ACC, 13 June 1861.
186. Mesini 1979: 246–49, 256.
187. Mayor's manifesto printed for the occasion see ACC.
188. Enrico Panzacchi, "A Galvani," in Panzacchi 1910: 59–61.
189. Quoted in Mesini 1979: 259.
190. ACC, 12 December 1898, sindaco Dallolio, consigliere Merlani.
191. ACC, 18 April 1903.
192. Letter of 7 March 1903, see ACC, 18 April 1903.
193. Similar tensions were known since the Middle Ages and resulted in competition for the highest tower, the cathedral with the richest decorations, etc.: Isnenghi 2004: 20. New tensions between Bologna and the Tuscan capital arose in the 1880s, when both cities competed for connections with the Italian railway network (*RdC*, 23 June 1885) and when Florence completed the façade of its cathedral: Gottarelli 1977: 212. Moreover, the two cities competed for intellectual recognition, with Florence described as "the Italian Athens" and Bologna pointing to its status as having Europe's oldest university: Cerasi 2000: 25 sq.
194. Romeo 1990: 21.
195. Connerton 1995: 1.
196. Ridolfi 2003: 11–12, 16–17.
197. See for the celebrations of the *Festa dello Statuto* in particular the excellent and detailed study Porciani 1997a. Also Meriggi 2000b: 214. On the role of the *Statuto* in the political life of the nation Caracciolo 1977: 15. Soldani 2000: 147ff.
198. ASCB, CA, 1861, Deputazione dei pubblicci spettacoli, Miscellanea, Feste popolari alla Montagnola, 11 August 1861.
199. Ozouf 1976: 276.
200. ASCB, CA, 1861, Deputazione dei pubblicci spettacoli, Miscellanea, Feste popolari alla Montagnola, 11 August 1861.
201. Marco Minghetti, "Facoltà al Governo di accettare e stabilire con decreto reale, l'annessione allo Stato di nuove provincie italiane" (10 October 1860), in: Minghetti 1988: vol. 1, 77. For similar observations on the French Revolution and on Italy's secret societies see Minghetti 1888–90: vol. 1, 71. On another occasion, in 1862, Minghetti repeated: "Italy remembers sorrowfully the damage provoked by the circles of 1849, and under no circumstances would Italy wish that the events of 1849 repeat themselves." Marco Minghetti, "Arresti di Sarnico e di Palazzo" (5 June 1862), in: Minghetti 1988: vol. 1, 467.
202. For a close analysis of this change in the relationship between Right and Left see Körner 2005. On the division of national movements into separate political groups see Clifford Geertz, "After the Revolution: The Fate of Nationalism in the new States," in: Geertz 1993a: 245.
203. ASCB, CA, 1861, Tit. XVI, 4, Anniversario della cacciata de' Tedeschi e della morte di Ugo Bassi su initiativa di un comitato di citadini; lettera del comitato al sindaco, 10 July 1861.
204. ASCB, CA, 1860, Tit. XVI, Festa nazionale e popolare nei pubblici Giardini della Montagnola in commemorazione dello sgombro degli Austriaci da questa città avvenuta il 12 Giugno 1859.

205. *MdB* 25 September 1860.
206. ASCB, CA, 1860, Tit. XVI, Fuochi di gioia nei giardini della montagnola, 30 September 1860. *MdB*, 11 September 1860.
207. ASCB, CA, 1861, Tit. XVI, 4, 13 March 1861.
208. Porciani 1997a: 27ff. Porciani 1996: vol. 2, 337–60.
209. Quoted in Porciani 1997a: 41–42.
210. Carlo Pepoli, "Allocuzione ai premiati alunni delle scuole serali," in Pepoli 1881: vol. 2, 5. On the Festa dello Statuto Porciani 1997a and Brize 2005: 454–59. The process described corresponds to the model offered by Ozouf 1976: 284–85. See likewise the celebrations in Rome after 1870: Nasto 1994: 81.
211. ASCB, CA, Tit. XVI, Circolare del Ministero dell'Interno ai signori Governatori ed Intendenti del Regno, 3 May 1860.
212. ASCB, CA, 1860, Tit. XVI, invitation of the sindaco Pizzardi to the Gran Comando Militare.
213. Ridolfi 1995: 86–87. Porciani 1995: 155. Porciani 1997a: 17, 173.
214. Porciani 1997a: 174, 180–81.
215. ASCB, CA, 1861, Tit. XVI, 4, Festa nazionale per celebrare l'Unità d'Italia e lo Statuto, Circolare della Legge per l'Istituzione di una festa nazionale, 5 May 1861.
216. Berti 2003: 41–42.
217. Fincardi 1995: 11–27. Turnaturi 1996. Ozouf 1976: 8–13. Ridolfi 1995: 87. Ridolfi 2003: 17.
218. ASCB, CA, 1861, Tit. XVI, 4, Festa nazionale per celebrare l'Unità d'Italia e lo Statuto, Circolare n.39 del Ministero dell'Interno ai sindaci, gonfalonieri e autorità comunali del Regno, 6 May 1861.
219. Romeo 1990: 406–7, 432.
220. ASCB, CA, 1861, Tit. XVI, 4, Festa nazionale per celebrare l'Unità d'Italia e lo Statuto, Circolare n.39 del Ministero dell'Interno ai sindaci, gonfalonieri e autorità comunali del Regno, 6 May 1861.
221. See also Marco Minghetti, "Istituzione di una festa nazionale per celebrare l'unità d'Italia e lo Statuto del Regno" (2 May 1861), in: Minghetti 1988: 221. Likewise "Interpellanza dell'on.Petruccelli ad una circolare diretta dal Ministro Minghetti ai Sindaci del Regno" (24 May 1861), in: Minghetti 1988: 241–42.
222. Porciani 1997a: 69. On the distance between the Risorgmento's voluntaristic tradition and the role of the Piedmontese army Riall 2007b.
223. Colley 1992: 215–16, 223ff. Porciani 1997a: 77, 58–59.
224. ACC, 14 May 1861.
225. Confino 1997: 27 sq., 46. In Germany national festivals offered citizens an opportunity to articulate themselves politically and symbolically: Hardtwig 1990: 270. As an initiative of civil society, the Sedan-Day never assumed the same importance as the official Kaiser or military parades: Vogel 1995.
226. Ridolfi 2003: 12.
227. ASCB, CA, 1861, Tit. XVI, 4, letter of the mayor to the Comitato di Emigrazione in Bologna, 16 May 1861; and Nota del Sindaco, 29 May 1861.
228. Porciani 1997a: 18ff. Ozouf 1976: 11. See also Handelman 1982: 166. On the lack of identification between people and military in Italy Riall 2007b.
229. Porciani 1997a: 95.
230. Porciani 2000: 62ff.
231. See for instance Bertolini 1887: 9. On Murat Davis 2006a: 139–274.
232. On the popular cult in France: Körner 1997: 258–64. On Garibaldi: Riall 1998b and Riall 2007a. Della Peruta 1995.

233. ASCB, CA, 1861, Tit. XVI, 4, Quarantesimo Anniversario della morte di Napoleone Primo, a cura dei Decorati della Medaglia di S. Elena, 28 May 1861.
234. Already in 1864 the fund for the celebration had been brought from 1000 to 1200 Lire, but was reduced again to 1000 Lire under the left-wing administration of Camillo Casarini, in 1868. ACC, 11 January 1864; 29 December 1868. These funds were minimal compared, for instance, to the expenditure in the capital Turin in 1861, where a total of 21,000 Lire were spent. Porciani 1997a: 3940.
235. *RdC*, 10 June 1885.
236. Ridolfi 1995: 88–89. Ridolfi 1990: 122. Ridolfi 1997b: 12ff. Liakos 1995: 108. Also Pécout 1990: 551. On rituals of civil religion in the Labour movement see Unfried (ed.) 1999.
237. Ridolfi 1995: 89. Mengozzi 1999.
238. Bologna participates with 2000 Lire in the subscription: ACC, 31 May 1897.
239. ACC, 28 February 1898.
240. Vivarelli 1995: 29–30. On the changing concept of nationalism in Italy also Agnelli 1994: 15–36.
241. Sorba 1997: 154.

NOTES TO CHAPTER 8

1. Ridolfi 2003: 24ff.
2. Quoted in Duggan 2002: 432.
3. Kertzer 1988: 8–9, 78. For the theoretical debate see Fehrenbach 1971: 298ff.
4. Cannadine 1983: 102. See also Colombo, P. 1999: 33–34. The Italian celebrations on the occasion of the Unification's anniversary 1909–1911, coinciding with the anniversary of Mazzini's death, provide an excellent example for the sacralisation of the fatherland: Gentile 1997: 16ff. The poet Giovanni Pascoli played a major role in evoking and constructing the relevant foundation myths.
5. Kertzer 1988: 78–79.
6. Schramm 1956: vol. 3, 1063.
7. Kertzer 1988: 9–10. Also Cannadine 1983: 105.
8. Mazzonis 2003: 134ff. See in this context also Luciani 1997.
9. Mazzonis 2001: 469–70.
10. Levra 1992: 8. Levra 1997.
11. Spadolini 1960: 33. See for a comparison the splendid welcoming of 1868 in Florence: Casalegno 2001: 43–44. For the role of the monarchy in Italy after 1860 see Mazzonis 2003 and Brice 2005.
12. Banti 2000: 15, 67. See for a broader investigation De Giorgio 1992: chpt. 1.
13. Banti 2000: 83–93, 97–102, 140–41.
14. Banti 2000: 151. Soldani 2004: 150.
15. Quoted in: Banti 2000: 151.
16. Croce 1914: vol. 2, 43.
17. *GdE*, 10 January 1878. See similar ACC, 23 April 1894, sindaco Dallolio. Also Croce 1928: 43. Nasto 1994: 85. Luciani 1997: 151.
18. Minghetti, quoted in: Banti 2000: 188.
19. *MdB*, 1 February 1869. However, Umberto took an equally hard line on similar issues: Mazzonis 2003: 162.

20. Colombo, P. 1999: 116. Casalegno 2001: Introduzione di Filippo Mazzonis, 11. On his distance to "ordinary citizens": Mack Smith 1989: 32, 37, 64. Mazzonis 2001: 438–39.
21. Drake 1980: xviii. For similar international statements see Brice 2005: 38.
22. See the dispatches in *GdE*, 13 January 1878.
23. Croce 1928: 42. Ragionieri 1976: 1684, 1729.
24. Mack Smith 1989: 34. Romeo 1990: 160–61.
25. Giovanni Giolitti, quoted in Ragionieri 1976: 1729.
26. Ernst Cassirer, quoted in Kertzer 1988: 25.
27. Vallauri 1971: vol. 1, 184. Duggan 2002: 380.
28. Ragionieri 1976: 1745. Brice 2005: 182–83, 415. On Umberto's and Margherita's "image-making policy" see Brice 2001: 61–79.
29. For Clifford Geertz charismatic rule is identified with "involvement with the animated centre of society": See "Centers, Kings, and Charisma: Reflections on the Symbolics of Power," in: Geertz 1993b: 124.
30. Brice 2002a: 65 sq. Dickie 1999: 97–98. Snowden 1995: 163–64.
31. Quoted in Brice 2002a: 66.
32. Snowden 1995: 164.
33. Douglas 1992: 21.
34. Snowden 1995: 165–66.
35. Croce 1928: 84. Mack Smith 1989: 71 rejected Croce's assessment of "the good king" and "good man" without considering the more positive evaluations of contemporary observers.
36. Dickie 1999: 99. Snowden 1995: 100ff. Brice 2002a: 70.
37. Mosse, G. 1985: 10.
38. Romeo 1990: 522.
39. Gigliozzi 1997: 26. Romeo 1990: 394. Mack Smith 1989: 46.
40. *MdB*, 30 April 1868. De Giorgio 1992: 183–84. Brice 2005: 64 sq.
41. Casalegno 2001: 26 sq. For a contemporary account and related documents see in particular Roux 1901.
42. Croce 1928: 85.
43. Porciani 1997a: 152. On the changing role of Rome also Brice 2002b: 141 sq.
44. Passerini 1991: 23, 35–36.
45. Passerini 1991: 61, 101. Gentile 2003: 61.
46. *GdE*, 14 January 1878.
47. *La Capitale*, August 1883, quoted in Brice 2002a: 68.
48. Milani 1887: 6. Regarding homoeroticism in eighteenth- and nineteenth-century Italian literature see also Cestaro (ed.) 2004: 7–8.
49. *GdE*, 12 February 1874. Duggan 2002: 435–36.
50. Minghetti 1888–90: vol. 3, 26.
51. Foratti 1940: 1.
52. Passerini 1991: 62, 102.
53. Luzzatto 1998: 5.
54. Luzzatto 1998: 6. Banti 2005.
55. Gioacchino N. Pepoli, "Indirizzi presentati alle LL.MM.," in: Pepoli, G. 1880: vol. 1, 18.
56. Ragionieri 1976: 1684.
57. Banti 2005: 194–95.
58. *MdB*, 30 April 1868. On the role of children in the symbolic representation of monarchical power see Geertz 1993b: 126–27. For an anecdotal account of Umberto's love-life see Gigliozzi 1997: 30–36.
59. Mazzonis 2003: 53–79.
60. Colombo, P. 1999: 118.
61. Mack Smith 1989: 73.

62. Capellini 1914: vol. 2, 10–37, 161ff. Preti 1997: 19.
63. Brice 2005: 7 speaks in this context about "*une monarchie médiatrice.*" About the meeting Piromalli 1988: 31–32. See also Vinciguerra 1957: 16–20.
64. Quoted from a contemporary letter by Carducci in: Carducci 1994b: 62–63. On his changing relationship to the monarchy Alatri 1995.
65. Capellini 1914: vol. 2, 260.
66. Quoted in Casalegno 2001: 66.
67. Quoted in Porciani 1996: 339.
68. On the relationship of Naples with the Umberto and Margherita see Gigliozzi 1997: 37–38.
69. Duggan 2002: 391–92. Casalegno 2001: 68–69. Benedetto Cairoli received one of Italy's highest decorations and became an honorary citizen of Bologna. A victim of the Left's *trasformismo*, the growing fear of anarchism and his supposed failure in Italy's early colonial adventures soon brought his political career to an end. Spadolini 1993: 191. Ragionieri 1976: 1741 called his government "the only experiment of a democratic administration of power." See also Conti 2000: 88. After his death in 1889 a street in one of Bologna's new residential areas was named after him and the council decided to place a tablet for him at the town hall: ACC, 10 and 24 October 1889.
70. Nasto 1994: 105.
71. Pernicone 1993: 147–54.
72. Causa 1879.
73. Cannadine 1983: 102.
74. GdE, 11 January 1878. On the public reactions to the succession Levra 1992: 6. See also Colley 1992: 219.
75. A document full of mostly not very plausible anecdotes is Bordeux Vahdeh 1926. See also Drake 1980: 18, 131.
76. GdE, 20 July 1881.
77. GdE, 21, 22 July 1881.
78. Casalegno 2001: 72. On the changing role of the court in the representation of the monarchy and as a stage of ritual see Brewer 1979: 3–28.
79. Nicolaus Sombart, quoted in Frevert 1993: 126.
80. Martin-Fugier 2003: 188.
81. O'Connor 1998: 5. Also Cavaliero 2005: 10. Rosselli 1991: 15.
82. Duggan 2002: 124, 176–77. Drake 1980: 134. Mack Smith 1957: 64ff.
83. Besides Jessie White Mario, O'Connor 1998: 5 mentions Emilie Ashurst Venturi, Caroline Ashurst Stansfeld, Harriet Hamilton King. Mack Smith 1994 analyses this network in similar terms. See also Mack Smith 1957: 64.
84. Banti 2000: 83–93, 97. O'Connor 1998: 7. Cavaliero 2005: 172. See also Wenk 2000: 63–77; and for a comparison Banti 2005. More favourably was Carducci's image of Jessie White Mario, the only politician of the Left seriously interested in the social question: "*La democrazia conta un solo scrittore sociale: ed è un inglese, ed è una donna; la signora Jessy White Mario . . . .*" [*Il paese*, 28 February 1879], in: Carducci 1921: vol. 2, 80. See also Spadolini 1993: 180, 183.
85. Douglas 1992: 155.
86. MdB, 8 August and 16 August 1860.
87. MdB, 17 August 1860.
88. Re 2001: 159, 164.
89. GdE, 21 September 1889. Spadolini 1993: 186. See also Isnenghi 2005: 133–34. On Carducci and Cairoli Biagini 1961: 204–5.
90. See for example Tobia 1998. Baioni 1994. See also Duggan 1997: 146 sq.
91. Pombeni 1993: 43–44. Levra 1992: 299 sq. Duggan 2002: 393 sq., 432 sq. Riall 1998b. Baioni 1994: 27. Porciani 1993: 219 sq. For a striking local

example Panzacchi 1882. The emphasis here is on the soldier and citizen, and on Garibaldi's famous "*obbedisco.*"

92. *RdC*, 7, 8 and 9 August 1885.
93. ACC, 12 December 1898. Baioni 1994: 77. See also Soldani 2000: 147 sq. ACC, 27 December 1867; 30 January 1868; 28 February 1898; 30 March 1898.
94. ACC, 22 June 1889, consigliere Rossi. For press reports on the "temple" see *RdC* between 20 May and 10 June 1888. For a first-hand account of the museum from its director see Cantoni 1916. The model for the temple and the museum was the *Padiglione del Risorgimento* at the 1884 *Esposizione nazionale* in Turin. Baioni 1994: 13, 23.
95. ACC, 24 October 1889. In 1906 there existed a total of twenty-nine Risorgimento exhibitions, mostly in the North and the centre of Italy, the majority in the form of dedicated sections of local civic museums. Trevelyan, who visited many of these during the research for his book on Garibaldi, singled out Bologna's museum for particular praise. Baioni 1994: 39, 128–29. For a discussion of Mazzini's notion of national sacrifice see Urbinati 1996. For Crispi's concept of "political education": Duggan 1997.
96. *GdE*, 26 and 27 September 1881. In 1898 the royal family even attended a football match in the Cascine gardens in Florence, demonstrating the involvement of the wider citizenry during the official celebrations of the Umbertian period; See Laura Cerasi, *Gli Ateniesi d'Italia*, 22–23.
97. *GdE*, 27 September 1881.
98. *Bologna e le sue Esposizioni* 1888. See similar *L'Esposizione illustrata delle provincie dell'Emilia in Bologna* 1888. Capellini et al. 1892. Carducci 1888. Panzacchi 1888. Illustrazione Italiana 1888. See also Tega (ed.) 1987. The monuments for Italy's first monarch were usually inaugurated by the king: Tobia 1998: 150. However, the debate on the monument for Vittorio Emanuele II on Piazza Maggiore was controversial. The colossal equestrian monument was at odds with a square whose great beauty lay in the fragmentary character of its many buildings, dating from a wider range of different periods. See Ricci 1886. *RdC*, 8 February 1886. Ricci's view was shared by Carducci, Edoardo Brizio, Olindo Guerrini, the painter Raffaele Faccioli, Cesare Albicini, Alfonso Rubbiani and many others: *RdC*, 11 February 1886.
99. *MdB*, 23 January 1866. ACC, 26 March 1868.
100. ACC, 8 April 1893.
101. ACC, 25 January 1878.
102. ACC, 27 January 1890.
103. ACC, 1 July 1895; 18 June 1900.
104. ACC, 12 September 1896, sindaco Dallolio. Similar arguments to praise this alliance are made by Giosuè Carducci, "Nozze Reali" [*Tribuna*, Roma, 11 October 1896], in: Carducci 1921: vol. 2, 320.
105. Cannadine 1983: 120, 128. Nipperdey 1995: vol. 2, 79. Strong 2005: 374, 417. Musil 1990: 77ff.
106. Vianelli 1965: 272.
107. Quoted in Vianelli 1965: 274. Tobia 1998: 150–51.
108. Zangheri (ed.) 1960: xxx. Salvadori 2001: 9–10. For the Southern question during these years see Lumley and Morris (eds) 1997. Dickie 1999.
109. Cammarano 2004: 520. Ragionieri 1976: 1842, 1849. Körner 2005.
110. Casalegno 2001: 91 sq. In this respect Umberto seems to have followed the tradition of "*libertinaggio aristocratico*" of an earlier period: Banti 2005: 33 sq.
111. Malvezzi 1905: 12 remembers the assassination as "*la fine di un epoca.*" Similar Panzacchi 1900 and Panzachi 1901. De-Amici 1900. Also Berti

2003: 304–23. On reactions to the assassination see also Brize 2005: 515ff. According to Cannadine 1983: 115 "a royal funeral might be a thanksgiving and celebration for a monarch" or "it could be interpreted as a requiem, not only for the monarch himself, but for the country as a great power." In the case of Umberto the two cannot be separated.

112. Casalegno 2001: 179. Galzerano 1988: 37.
113. Causa 1879: 86–87. Errico Malatesta, "Anarchia e Violenza," in: Malatesta, E. 1936: vol. 3, 108. This view is still held by Bach Jensen 2004.
114. Although Italians were considered as "new immigrants" in the lucrative Paterson textile industry, the sector's labour relations were characterised by mutual respect, the high professional standard of the workers and their influence on the management's decision making. This situation changed first during the 1890s, but economically the workers remained in a relatively strong position. See Ramella 1999. On the local anarchic communities see Berti 2003: 286ff. On Bresci see Galzerano 1988.
115. *RdC*, 1, 2, 3 August 1900. Levy 1998.
116. Errico Malatesta, "Gli Italiani all'estero," in: Malatesta, E. 1936: vol. 1, 251.
117. *RdC*, 1 August 1900.
118. Paris 1973: 550.
119. Hall 1996: 3.
120. Berti 2003: 309.
121. De-Amici 1900: 22.
122. Masini 1981: 158–59. Mack Smith 1989: 139.
123. Arturo Labriola, quoted in: Berti 2003: 309. On Labriola's relationship to the anarchists see Masini 1981: 12.
124. Brice 2005: 516.
125. ACC, 31 July 1900, sindaco Dallolio.
126. ACC, 31 July 1900, consigliere Pini. These commemorations differed clearly from the tone of the tributes to Vittorio Emanuele II. See for example Marco Minghetti, Commemorazione di Vittorio Emanuele fondatore della nazionalità italiana (*NA*, 15 January 1879), in: Minghetti 1896: 279–320. See also the council debates ACC, 11 January 1878 and 25 January 1878.
127. ACC, 31 July 1900, consigliere Bedetti.
128. ACC, 26 November 1900.
129. Isnenghi 2005: 322.
130. Quoted in Baioni 1994: 27. On the notion of a divided memory see Soldani 2000. For the "popular politics" of the cult of Garibaldi see Riall 2007a.
131. ACC, 6 June 1882, sindaco Tacconi.
132. See Corrado Ricci's colourful description of the event: "Carducci per Garibaldi," in: Ricci 1924: 3–8. ACC, 25 January 1878. Over the last twenty years prices had increased by about 10%: based on G. Sabbatucci and Vidotto (eds) 1994–95: vol. 2, 584. The municipality of Turin contributed 100,000 Lire to its Garibaldi monument, supplemented by another 8,000 Lire from a public subscription: Isnenghi 2004: 331.
133. Felice Cavalotti, quoted in: Della Peruta 1995: 45.
134. ACC, 27 December 1888, consiglieri Rossi and Filopanti; 9 April 1900.
135. ACC, 28 June 1907, sindaco Tanari and consigliere Zanardi.
136. ACC, 28 June 1907, consigliere Grossi.
137. ACC, 9 May 1910, consigliere Pulle. See for a similarly divided memory the debates about the national monument for Mazzini in Rome, authorised in 1890, but inaugurated in 1949 only: Lescure 1993: 177–201.
138. Galli della Loggia 1998: 48.
139. ACC, 20 February 1905, consigliere Grossi, sindaco Tanari; 30 June1905, consigliere Francia.

140. ACC, 26 November 1914, consigliere Ghigi.
141. ASCB, CA; 1915, Tit. X, 3, 3, 10416 and allegati. Pupils received a free magazine, medals were distributed, and the mayor addressed the people of Bologna assembled in front of the town hall. ASCB, CA, 1916, Tit. X, 3, 3, 7678, Manifesto della Giunta per il 1.o Maggio.
142. ASCB, CA, 1916, Tit. X, 3, 3, 7678, allegato: R. Questura di Bologna, divisione prima n. 1784, 29 April 1916.

NOTES TO CHAPTER 9

1. The only exceptions were the Milan premieres of the revised versions of *La forza del destino* (1869), *Simon Boccanegra* (1881) and *Don Carlos* (1884).
2. For the distinction between "opera in Italy" and "Italian opera in the world" see John Rosselli's review of Kimbell 1991, in: *COJ*, 4 (1992), 1, 87–90.
3. Perrino 1992–96: vol. 2, 131.
4. Balilla Pratella 1915 is a manifesto against Germanic and French influences in Italy.
5. This position questions Marxist interpretations of the "function of music in the superstructure," but also the historiographical emphasis on the elites' political-idealist use of opera, mostly in France or Germany, for purposes of societal education in the sense of Schiller. Kneif 1971: 62. Ther 2006: 17, 36 sq.
6. Panzacchi 1872: 8.
7. This phenomenon was not restricted to theatre. Regarding the repertoire for piano solo the works of Beethoven, Liszt, Chopin, Schubert, Schumann and Mendelssohn-Bartholdy were hardly known: Mainardi 2004: 230.
8. ASCB, CA, 1878, Tit. X, 3, 4, 7417 and allegati, Progetto dell'Agenzia teatrale Cesare Gaibi ed imprese Scalaberni, 27 July 1878 and letter to the sindaco, 29 July 1878. During the liberal period Massenet appeared only four times in the repertoire of the Comunale. On the changing role of publishers see Kimbell 1991: 539–40.
9. Calore 1982: 78–79. On the early history of music journalism in Bologna see Calore 1988. For the new approach to opera criticism see Parker and Smart (eds) 2001. Also Parker 1989: 16 sq. Italy saw an explosion of musical journals in the 1820s, but their number declined again after 1848: Rosselli 1987: 144.
10. The paper demanded that "articles for insertion must be paid for in advance." The impresarios' advertisements had to indicate "contracts already concluded, seasons available, and repertoire of operas." Quoted in Rosselli 1987: 145.
11. ASCB, CA, 1860, Tit. XVI, 2. Direzione degli Spettacoli al sindaco, 20 June 1860.
12. MdB, 25 and 28 August 1869. On Wagner as a "cultural power" see Theodor Schieder, "Richard Wagner, das Reich und die Deutschen," in: Schieder 1980: 111.
13. ASCB, CA, 1871, Tit. X, 3, 4, 975. Atti della commissione nominata. . . . Also *MdB*, 4 November 1865 and 5 January 1870. *RdC*, 22 December 1885.
14. Antonio Gramsci, "Letteratura popolare," in: Gramsci 1975: vol. 2, 1136–37. At the same time he questioned the political implications of opera as an art form. See also Tedeschi 1973: 1170; Sorba 2001: 14. On the identification between national character and opera Chiappini 2007.
15. Sciannameo 2004: 2. Parker 1989: 45. Perrino 1992–96: vol. 1, 44.
16. Charle 2002: 403. Rabb 2006. Davis 2006b: 569. Ther 2006: 13, 356–57. Hailey 1986. Salvarani 2002: 138. Alliegro 2003. For the Romagna: Ricci

1888: xvi–xvii. Rosselli 1991: 27. Calore 1998: 8–9. The opening of the-atres to the lower strata of the bourgeoisie started in France with Mercier and Beaumarchais, and soon reached the Comédie Française, as discussed in Diderot's and d'Alembert's *Encyclopédie*. See the essays in Boyd (ed.) 1992. Steinhauser 1988: 297–98. More generally on the role of audiences Sorba 2006a.

17. Rosselli 1991: 139–40. Rosselli 1987: 173.
18. *MdB*, 12 and 14 October 1868. See similar Rabb 2006: 322.
19. Banti 2000: 45. On the role of these works in Italian theatres see Sorba 2001; and for Bologna in particular Gavelli and Tarozzi (eds) 1998.
20. Banti 2000: 45.
21. Mazzini 2004: 46.
22. Parker 1989: 10 sq., 135 sq.; Parker 1997a. Parker 1997b: 20–41. Also Ashbrook 1996: 128. Smart 2001. Similar Davis 2006b: 570ff., 577; Castelvecchi 2006: 619. For the traditional view of Verdi as the bard of the Risorgimento: Martin 1979.
23. For *Nabucco* see Verdi (ed.) 2001: 4–5, 73. For *La Battaglia* see *MdB*, 28 December 1860.
24. Davis 2006b: 572. Calore 1998: 7. Smart 2006. In the context of Smart's argument see also Sennett 1977: 73, who argues that the society of the *ancien régime* was actually more likely to politicize performances than nineteenth-century audiences.
25. Della Seta 1993: 277–78. Nicolaisen 1980. For Mazzini in London this decline even started with *Il Trovatore*: Mack Smith 1994: 26.
26. Budden 1981: vol. 3, 163–64. Also Robinson 1993: 134.
27. See for instance Croce 1928: 133.
28. Della Seta 1993: 178. Francfort 2005 points to an even more dramatic perio-disation of the crisis, emerging with Verdi's death (1901), in which not even Puccini's operas are able to stop the decline.
29. Quoted in Rosselli 1987: 153.
30. See for instance the autumn seasons of 1828, 1829 and 1836. Still in 1863 Bellini's *Sonnambula* was performed along with *Lucia di Lammermoor* and *La Favorita* by Donizetti during the same season: ASCB, CA, 1863, Tit. X, 3, 4, 9490, 12 September 1863. However, for the local taste even *La Favorita* was too close to French *grand opéra*: Bottrigari 1960–63: vol. 3, 130.
31. Levi 1987: 5.
32. *MdB*, 11 June 1869.
33. *Teatri, Arte e Letteratura*, quoted in: Vatielli 1921: 14–15. *MdB*, 24 March and 10 November 1869. Similar debates go back to the 1850s: Roccatagliati 1993: 293ff.
34. Rosselli 1991: 52.
35. Enrico Panzacchi, "Gioacchino Rossini. Discorso detto a Pesaro nell'aula grande dell'Istituto Rossini, per il centenario rossiniano," in: Panzacchi 1895: 116–17.
36. Everist 2005: 87–88.
37. Rosselli 1991: 131.
38. Mack Smith 1994: 26.
39. Levi 1987: 10. Parker 1997a: 106–7. In its early years *Nabucco* was mostly per-formed in provincial theatres and nowhere south of Rome. Parker 1989: 135. As stated earlier, Verdi was not necessarily read in a patriotic key at the time.
40. Parker 1997a: 25–26. Sorba 2002: 143–44.
41. *La Farfalla* and *Teatri Arti e Letteratura*, quoted in Verdi (ed.) 2001: 3–4; *Mondo Illustrato*, quoted in Tedeschi 1973: 1171.
42. Giger 1999: 233.

43. Between 1860 and 1870 Verdi was on the programme of the Comunale (including revivals) seventeen times, but already during the second half of the 1860s the interest in Verdi had declined. At the time Donizetti was the second most popular composer, followed by Meyerbeer. Rossini (as well as Bellini) appeared only three times on the programme, very much to the regret of the more conservative opera lovers. During this period a total of fifty-two works were staged.
44. *MdB*, 5 October 1860.
45. Bottrigari 196063: vol. 3, 115. He was similarly severe on Rossini: Weinstock 1986: 243. See also Panzacchi's summary of the public response to Verdi's later works in: *MdB*, 12 October 1875. Also Panzacchi 1872: 25.
46. ASCB, Carteggio Amministrativo, 1861, Tit. XVI-2, 595, letter by the impresario to the mayor. See also Sorba 2002: 147. Tedeschi 1973: 1172.
47. Bottrigari 1960–63: vol. 3, 219; vol. 4, 79. *MdB*, 7 October 1861. This was despite the fact that Rossini's operas were increasingly performed only on minor stages and in provincial theatres, and that the most influential critics considered his music no longer appropriate for the new era of history that had started in Italy. Antolini 1994: 128.
48. ASCB, CA, 1861, Deputazione dei pubblici spettacoli, Miscellanea, Ufficiali del Battaglione di Bologna al Cav. Delegato per i pubblici spettacoli, 8 November 1861.
49. Verdi (ed.) 2001: 178, 181, 188–89.
50. Verdi (ed.) 2001: viiiff. For an early historical reflection on Bologna's Verdism see Romani 1880: 9.
51. Sorba 2006a: 601.
52. Tomasi di Lampedusa 1974: 43.
53. De Angelis 1982: 86, 97–98. The Florentine premiere of Verdi's *Lombardi* in 1843 was one of the greatest commercial successes in the history of opera, even if the critics disagreed with the operas positive reception.
54. De Angelis 1982: 86, 90–93, 115–120, 129.
55. ACC, 8 May 1863. ASCB, CA, 1863, Tit. X, 3, 45615, 5616.
56. ASCB, CA, 1876, Tit. X, 3, 4, 5446, Estratto del verbale della Giunta, 20 June 1876.
57. ASCB, SP, 1867, no. 26, no. 263, Appalto per un triennio 1867–68–69 dell'impresa del Teatro Comunale. Atto notarile tra Agostino Salina per il Municipio ed Luigi Scalaberni, 19 September 1867.
58. *MdB*, 28 October 1867. Bottrigari 1960–63: vol. 3, 494. See on the performance also Levi 1987: 15.
59. Santini and Trezzini 1987: 108.
60. *GdE*, 23 September 1881.
61. Verdi (ed.) 2001: 201–31, for the quote 210.
62. Ricci 1924: 31–35. On Lambertini also Vatiello 1921: 32.
63. Everist 2005: 177. Becker 1989: 12ff. De Angelis 1982: 21, 81. Roccatagliati 1993: 300. Mack Smith 1994: 26. He had a major impact on Italian opera, even if his influence on Mercadante "amounts to little more than a rumour": Wittmann 1993: 117.
64. *Teatri, Arte e Letteratura*, quoted in: Vatielli 1921: 14–15. The opera was repeated during Mariani's first Bologna season and evoked some enthusiasm thanks to the celebrated Adelaide Borghi-Mamo, a born Bolognese and the star of sixty-five evenings as *La Favorita* at the Paris Opera.
65. *MdB*, 19 November 1860. Vatiello 1921: 20. Becker 1989: 12.
66. ASCB, CA, 1861, Deputzaione dei pubblici spettacoli, Miscellanea, Osservazioni al progetto d'Appalto del sig,e Ercole Tinti, 31 May 1861. We know that the officers of Bologna's battalion did not consider *Gli Ugonotti*

a sufficient attraction to renew their subscription: ASCB, CA, 1861, Deputazione dei pubblici spettacoli, Miscellanea, Ufficiali del Battaglione di Bologna al Cav. Delegato per i pubblici spettacoli, 8 November 1861. On difficulties with Meyerbeer in Italy also Jung 1974: 18.

67. ASCB, CA, 1861, Tit. XVI, 4, 157, sentence of the commercial court, 28 April 1862.
68. Rosselli 1987: 119.
69. See for instance the positive assessment of Meyerbeer in *MdB:* 19 and 23 November 1861.
70. *MdB*, 23 November 1861, 4 August 1864.
71. ASCB, CA, 1860, Tit. II, Deputazione dei pubblici spettacoli, Miscellanea, Tit. III, 2, Delegati Amministrativi e Provinciali, Direzione della Deputazione dei spettacoli a Meyerbeer, 26 November 1860.
72. Extracts from Meyerbeer's *Stella del Nord* and il *Perdono di Ploermel*, and from Verdi's *Alzira* and his *Inno delle Nazioni*. ASCB, CA, 1866, Tit. X, 3, 4, Atti della Commissione per la Festa da darsi al Teatro Comunale a pro del Consorzio Nazionale, Manifesto, 25 April 1866.
73. ACC, 25 March 1868.
74. Hobsbawm 1989: 311.
75. ASCB, SP, 1867, Appalto per la stagione di Quaresima 1868, 10 December 1868 [sic].
76. *MdB* 5 November 1865. ACC, 29 February 1872. In 1876 a second performance of *L'Africaine* was again a great success, even more appreciated than Marchetti's Hugo opera *Ruy Blas* during the same season: ASCB, CA, 1876, Tit. X, 3, 4, 11028, Report of the Deputazione to the mayor on the past autumn season, Count Salina, 20 December 1876.
77. Schünemann 1913: 253, 256. Honigsheim 1973: 61, 70. Fellerer 1984: 58. Rosselli 2000: 134. De Angelis 1982: 22. Kimbell 1991: 561.
78. Mariani 1985: 15ff. In 1844 Mariani had also conducted in Trento, belonging at the time to the Austrian crown land of Tirol. When he was offered a contract to conduct the following season at the theatre in Messina the orchestra refused to play under "*un forestiere ragazzo.*"
79. ACC, 16 July 1873, consigliere Casarini. This became a political issue between the cities of Bologna and Genoa, where the conductor was still under contract. ASCB, CA, 1860 Tit. II, Deputazione dei pubblici spettacoli, Miscellanea, Tit. III, 2, Delegati Amministrativi e Provinciali, letter of 16 November 1860.
80. *CW*, II (2), 1 April 1894: 9ff. Large and Weber (eds) 1984: 26.
81. Rosselli 2000: 135–41. Verdi's letters to Mariani constitute an interesting document concerning their emotional relationship: Mariani 1985: 62–67. For the different stories recounting Verdi's breach with Mariani see Walker 1982: 283 sq.
82. Both Ricordi and Faccio apparently helped Verdi to arrange the affair with Stolz. See Verdi to Ricordi, 2 September 1871; Ricordi to Verdi, 2 September 1871; Verdi to Faccio, 10 September 1871, in: Busch (ed.) 1978: 211ff., 220. The uncertainties surrounding the first performance are reason enough to question Edward Said's claim that the composer's total control over the production was part of the opera's "imperial notion." See Said 1993: 116.
83. ACC, 16 July 1873, consigliere Casarini.
84. *MdB*, 28 June 1868.
85. ACC, 25 August 1865.
86. ACC, 26 February 1866 and 24 March 1866.
87. ASCB, CA, 1867, Tit. X, 3, 4, 12152, 12319, letter by the mayor, 29 October 1867.

88. ACC, 3 September 1870. The original grant in the publication of the contract was 35,000 Lire: ASCB, CA, 1870, Tit. X, 3, 4, 2202, Avviso per l'Appalto del'Esercizio del Teatro Comunitativo per la stagione autunnale 1870, 2 April 1870.
89. ACC, 30 January 1871. ASCB, CA, 1866, Tit. X, 3, 4, 2988 sq. [As the document refers to the performance of *Lohengrin*, which took place in 1871, the date of the reference must be wrong.]
90. ASCB, CA, 1871, Tit. X, 3, 4, 2568, 9423, 1 March 1871 and idem, 7999, 8346, 8710, 8830, 1 September 1871.
91. Casarini 1872: 9.
92. *MdB*, 2 October 1871.
93. Santini and Trezzini 1978: 119.
94. Casarini 1872: 11.
95. Wagner, C. 1976: 451. (22 October 1871). Neumann 1907: 4, 9ff. For the same reason, in 1863, *Tristan* was removed from the programme of Vienna's Hofoper. On Frank see Münster 2007.
96. *MdB*, 5 June 1869. For Mercadante and Naples see Kimbell 1991: 538. Of major importance for this debate was an article by Francesco d'Arcais, which referred to "*false teorie dell'avvenire propugnate dal Wagner*": NA, 1, 1866, 115.
97. *MdB*, 9 August and 4 December 1871; 1 November 1870. The most detailed works on the reception of Wagner in Italy are Guarnieri Corazzol 1988. Jung 1974. Manera and Pugliese (eds) 1982. See also Miller, M. 1984. Purely anecdotal but with many photographs: Panizzardi 1914. For Bologna see Santini and Trezzini 1987. Perazzo 1983.
98. Panzacchi 1883: 65–66.
99. Panzacchi 1872: 14–15. Panzachi 1883: 163–64, 174, 177. On conflicts between Gluckisti and Piccinisti see Vatielli 1928, vol. 2, 97132.
100. See "Zukunftsmusik" in: Wagner, R. 1887–88, vol. 7, 102. "Richard Wagner and Tannhäuser in Paris" in: Bauelaire 1992: 335.
101. Vatielli 1928: vol. 2, 101, 114ff.
102. *L'Arpa*, 11 November 1871; *GdE*, 2 November 1871. For a detailed account Panzacchi 1883: 65 sq. Despite the considerable cost involved in the staging of Wagner, the performances were usually an economic success. The premiere of *Lohengrin* at La Monnaie in Brussels, a year before Bologna's premiere, produced the second highest box office return any European opera house had ever produced. Gubin and Van der Hoeven 1998: 8.
103. Wagner, C. 1976: 456 57, 461 (5, 7 and 20 November 1871). Cosima's diaries report on an almost daily basis about the success of the opera, making reference to Italian press cuttings.
104. ASCB, CA, 1871, Tit. X, 3, 4, 9676, 9787, the mayor of Florence to Casarini, 17 November 1871. See on this event also Jung 1974: 133–34. Manera and Pugliese (eds) 1982: 114. Wagner, C. 1976: 467 (10 December 1871).
105. Panzacchi 1883: 7 sq., 170–71.
106. Panzacchi 1883: 161.
107. *MdB*, 2 November 1871.
108. Gustavo San Giorgio, *L'Arpa*, 11 November 1871.
109. *L'Arpa*, 11 and 20 November 1871.
110. Quoted in: Perazzo 1983: 202.
111. Quoted in Jung 1974: 30. Wagner himself presents a more complex picture of his relationship to Rossini: "Eine Erinnerung an Rossini," in: Wagner, R. 1887–88: vol. 8, 220–25. Rather than condemning the composer himself, he holds the epoch responsible for the shortcomings of his music. On the encounter see also Weinstock 1968: 284–99; Weber, W. 1984: 48.
112. *MdB*, 9 October 1875.

113. *GdE*, 30 October 1871.
114. Bottrigari 1960–63: vol. 4, 207–8.
115. Jelavich 1985: 23.
116. Gentile 1997: 91. In this context it is interesting to remember that Meinecke rejected the concept of the mutual exclusiveness of "Nationalgefühl" and "Weltbürgertum": Meinecke 1969: 24.
117. Weber, W. 1984: 29.
118. Deathridge, Geck and Voss 1986: 305. Deathridge and Dahlhaus 1984: 32.
119. *MdB*, 4 October 1871. On Wagner and the Left also 28 August 1869.
120. Mack Smith 1969: 121.
121. Of the one hundred thirty-five members only twenty-one belonged to the nobility, seven of which were female. *CW*, 1 (4), 1 December 1893, 33. While Wagnerism in Turin was based on similar political references, the Democratic press in Milan joined the anti-Wagnerian camp.
122. See the Vorwort by Dietrich Mack and Martin Gregor-Dellin in Wagner, C. 1976: 12. Pernicone 1993: 88.
123. He met his later lover Carolina Cristofori Piva at the premiere of *Lohengrin*. She received almost 600 letters by the poet and appears as Lidia or Lina in some of his most famous poems. Piromalli 1988: 30–31. The reception of Wagner's work at the time corresponded largely to that of Carducci: Chiarini 1901: 66–67.
124. *CW*, 1 (2), 1 August 1893, 9–10 and 2 (6), 1 December 1894, 43. I am grateful to Patrick Chorley for pointing me to this source.
125. Quoting an article by Zola published in *Le Journal*: *CW*, 1 (4), 1 December 1893, 27–28. On the Italian echoes of the Dreyfus affair after 1898 Gentile 2003: chpt 1.
126. "Richard Wagner and Tannhäuser in Paris" in Baudelaire 1992: 325–57.
127. *CW*, 2 (2), 1 April 1894, 9ff. On Bülow and Lassalle see Körner 1997: 96. The choral societies linked to the German Labour movement regularly included Wagner in their repertoire: Lidtke 1985: 97ff.
128. Bartlett 1995: 221. Large and Weber (eds) 1984: 16. See also Gramsci's "Tendenze della cultura italiana," in: Gramsci 1975: vol. 2, 717–18. The USA too had a tradition of associating Wagner with democracy, at a time when German opera dominated the theatres and Verdi was neglected: Peretti 1989: 30ff. In 1904 a Russian émigré *impresario* presented *Parsifal* in Yiddish translation in Manhattan's Lower East Side. Perlmutter 1952: 104–6.
129. Isnenghi 2004: 169–70. On the Italian Left's association with "creative intellectuals" see also Levy 2001.
130. Miller, M. 1984: 189.
131. *Il Repubblicano*, quoted in: Calore 1998: 11.
132. Tomlinson 1986: 50. Miller, M. 1984: 172–73, 175. Rather different is the approach of De Angelis 1977: 27, who emphasises the differences between Wagner and Mazzini.
133. Miller, M. 1984: 168–69. Risorgimento opera and Verdi in particular responded to these ideas: Gossett 1990. Soldani 2001. Also Swales 2000: 61–62. Parker 1997a questions some of these assumptions.
134. Miller, M. 1984: 170–71. See also Drake 1984. Likewise in Belgium, where one of the most important promoters of *Wagnérisme* and the translator of *La Walkyrie* was Henri La Fontaine, a senator for the Parti Ouvrier Belge. He held a chair in international law, wrote for radical periodicals and was a committed internationalist and pacifist. I am grateful to Daniel Laqua for this information.
135. D'Annunzio 1914. The most important study of D'Annunzio's view of Wagner is Guarnieri Corazzol 1988: 7 sq. Mosse, G. 1975: 109–10. Miller,

M. 1984: 188–91. Angelini 1988: 10. Jung 1974: 121, 387 sq. Associating D'Annunzio's Wagnerism with his Fascism is more problematic, as by that time he had turned away from Wagner: Schoffman 1993. The musical avant-garde in Italy did not necessarily have much respect for D'Annunzio. See for instance Busoni 1935: 54 (letter of 4 April 1902).

136. Habermas 1987: 8. Calinescu 1987: 69. Miller, N. 2007: 12.
137. *GdE*, 30 October 1871.
138. Richard Wagner, "Zukunftsmusik," in: Wagner, R. 1887–88, vol. 7, 101. Charles Baudelaire, "Richard Wagner and Tannhäuser in Paris," in: Baudelaire 1972: 335. Wagner's own attitude to modernity is still a topic of debate. See for instance Deathridge 1992.
139. *GdE*, 30 October 1871.
140. *GdE*, 3 November 1904.
141. For a critique of the idea of progress in music see Pfitzner 1917: 16–17.
142. Karbusicky 1995. The essay is a critique of Eggebrecht 1991. See also Gerhard 2000.
143. *RB*, 1, 1867 (1), 5.
144. *RB*, 2, 1868 (4), 331 and (6), 556.
145. Camera dei Deputati, 6 February 1873, quoted in: Masi 1875: 185–88.
146. ASCB, CA, 1871, Tit. X, 3, 4, 975, Atti della Commissione nominata dal consiglio nella seduta del 19 Maggio con facolta di prendere intelligenze colla Giunta in ordine all'assegnazione della Dote al Teatro Comunale, Adunanza del 24 Maggio 1871, sindaco Casarini.
147. ACC, 30 January 1871, consiglieri Sacchetti, Osima, Bordoni, Pizzoli.
148. ACC, 4 July 1872. See for details ASCB, CA, 1866, Tit. X, 3, 4, 2988 sq., Teatro Comunale. Ristauro del medesimo and 1871, Tit. X, 3, 4, 2568, 9423, Installazione di un riscaldamento. ACC, 5 February 1872. On the more general context of the theatre's overspending see ASCB, CA, 1871, Tit. X, 3, 4, 2992, 4634, 5750, 6502, 6618, 9007.
149. ACC, 4 July 1872.
150. Bianconi and Pestelli 1987: 179.
151. See for instance ACC, 27 February 1872, consiglieri Bevilacqua, Sangiorgi and Panzacchi.
152. ACC, 3 July 1872.
153. ACC, 21 July 1873, consiglieri Bellenghi and Casarini.
154. The Scala staged Wagner twenty-four times before the war, but the total number of the theatre's performances was much higher than in Bologna. Manera and Pugliese (eds) 1982.
155. Bellini and Donizetti appeared four times each, Rossini twice.
156. This last figure concerns the period 1882–1950, covering the modern history of the theatre from the year in which the exact number of performances per season is known. *Lohengrin* was played on 76 evenings, *La Traviata* on 57 and *Tristan* on 54.
157. Santini and Trezzini 1987: 133.
158. Alfonso Rubbiani, quoted in: Calore 1981b: 583. See also Panzacchi 1883: 34–35 and Jung 1974: 34.
159. Another supporter of Wagner's music in Bologna, Zanichelli, published Panzacchi's articles on the topic as a book: Panzacchi 1872. See also Panzachi 1883: 39. For the year 1871 Bologna's *Lohengrin* constitutes Wagner's most important source of income: Wagner, C. 1976: 341 (16 January 1871).
160. Panzacchi 1872: 24. He later qualified this through a distinction between *Holländer, Tannhäuser, Lohengrin* and *Meistersinger*, considered to be accessible to wider audiences, and *Tristan*, the *Ring* and *Parsifal*, requiring an expert audience: Panzacchi 1883: 10. On Filippi see Miller, M. 1984: 185.

161. Panzacchi 1872: 2, 6.
162. Panzacchi 1872: 7.
163. Miller, M. 1984: 174.
164. Piazzoni 2004: 69–70. Miller, M. 1984: 180–81. Although Verdi pronounced himself occasionally against "the invasion of foreign art," on other occasions he also showed an interest and admitted being impressed by Wagner's work.
165. Mainardi 2004: 223. Schnitzler 1954: 210.
166. For a detailed documentation of Gobatti's career see Zaghini, Ferri and Verdi (eds) 2002. Miller, M. 1984: 179. Santini and Trezzini 1987: 135. Sani 1922: 129–32. On Gobatti see also Vatiello 1921: 34–35. (A CD with extracts of various works is available from Bongiovanni, GB5057–2).
167. ACC, 19 December 1873. Cagli 2001: 65.
168. *MdB*, 19 February 1874.
169. ASCB, CA, 1876, Tit. X, 3, 4, 2255, letter by Salina to the mayor, 11 March 1876. Gobatti continued to find supporters in Bologna and his works occasionally appeared in recitals: See "Musica Odiosa" in a concert organised by the *Società Felsinea*: *RdC*, 9 December 1885. ASCB, CA, 1875, Tit. X, 3, 4, 8661, letter by the Società del Duttour Balanzon to the mayor, 25 September 1875.
170. Zaghini, Ferri and Verdi (eds) 2002: 200–201, 223–24, 243–44.
171. Pöschl 1939: 36.
172. Boito 1942: 1078. On the relationship to his teacher Mazzucato see Boito to Carlo Schmidl, 15 February 1889, in: Boito 1932: 31. On the general musical context Kimbell 1991: 571.
173. Boito 1942: 1093. See also Ashbrook 1988: 274. On Verdi's *Inno* see Sorba 2001: 263.
174. Guarnieri Corazzol 1988: 36ff. Her evaluation of Boito's anti-Wagnerism seems exaggerated considering for instance Boito's role in Bologna's Italian *prima* of *Tristan* in 1888. See also Tedeschi 1973: 1174–75. Helbling 1995: 12–13, 51ff. Busoni 1954: 32.
175. Walker 1982: 447 sq.
176. Istituto di Studi Verdiani 1978: vol. 1, xxiii. Helbling 1995: 64–80.
177. Helbling 1995: 109ff.
178. Drake 1984: 34, 86. Perrino 1992–96: vol.1, 111.
179. *MdB*, 4 June 1869.
180. Enrico Panzacchi, in: *MdB*, 4 October 1875. Trebbi 1918: 233. Ashbrook 1988: 270–71.
181. Istituto di Studi Verdiani 1978: vol. 2, 331. Among the more influential critics was also Giulio Ricordi: Roccatagliati 1993: 340.
182. *MdB*, 5, 6 October 1875 and Panzacchi, 9, 15 and 19 October 1875. *L'Arpa*, 18 October 1875.
183. See Panzacchi's review in *MdB*, 9 October 1875.
184. Basso 1976: 369. Helbling 1995: 37. As a condition for the Bologna staging Boito agreed to renounce any royalties; after that the work became Boito's major source of income.
185. ACC, 28 December 1875, consigliere De Simonis.
186. ACC, 28 December 1875, consigliere Sangiorgi, sindaco Tacconi. Trebbi 1918: 231. Calore 1982: 98.
187. ASCB, CA, 1876, Tit. X, 3, 4, 2255, letter by Salina to the mayor, 11 March 1876.
188. Maehder 2007. Zoppelli 1996.
189. On the concept of *Urbane Leitkultur* see Kannonier and Konrad (eds) 1995.
190. ACC, 29 March 1872, 31 May 1872 and 16 July 1873.

191. ASCB, CA, 1876, Tit. X, 3, 4, 7408, letter of the mayor to Wagner (22 September 1876), and 11028, Report of the Deputazione to the mayor on the past autumn season, Count Salina, 20 December 1876.
192. ASCB, CA, 1876, Tit. X, 3, 4, 11028, Report of the Deputazione to the mayor on the past autumn season, Count Salina, 20 December 1876. On Wagner's mixed impressions of the city see Wagner, C. 1976: 1004–5, 1017ff. Also Jung 1974: 38–39.
193. ASCB, CA, 1876, Tit. X, 3, 4, 11028, Report of the Deputazione to the mayor on the past autumn season, count Salina, 20 December 1876.
194. ASCB, CA, 1876, Tit. X, 3, 4, 5272, Deputazione degli Spettacoli to the mayor, 9 June 1876 and 1877, Tit. X, 3, 4, 8407, Deputazione dei pubblici spettacoli to the mayor, 4 September 1877. Florence lost the competition for *Holländer*, presenting the opera only ten years later. Manera and Pugliese (eds) 1982: 100. While for technical reasons the first evening of *Holländer* resulted in a complete fiasco, the audience's appreciation improved from the second evening. Panzacchi 1883: 19ff.
195. ACC, 21 March 1884, assessore Dallolio.
196. Quoted in: Flora 1960: 121.
197. Neumann 1907: 304.
198. Jung 1974: 171 sq. Deathridge and Dahlhaus 1984: 65. Neumann's *Ring* cycle started with a performance in Berlin in 1881.
199. Neumann 1907: 298–99.
200. Levi 1987: 26.
201. CW, I (3), 1 October 1893. Rostirolla 1982.
202. ACC, 21 March 1884, assessore Dallolio. A decade earlier Camillo Casarini had presented the same point of view in parliament: Camera dei Deputati, 6 February 1873, quoted in Masi 1875: 186–87.
203. Calore 1982: 99. From 1885 also theatre tickets for students of the local secondary schools and the university were reduced. *RdC*, 22 September 1885.
204. Vatielli 1921: 5. Silvestri 1966: 14, 30, 183ff. Mancinelli's opera *Ero e Leandro*, on a libretto by Boito, was a great success in Britain as well as in several other theatres of both worlds.
205. ACC, 7 June 1886 and 16 January 1888. Ricci 1924: 77–93. For Martucci's first contact with Liszt and with the princess Margherita see Perrino 1992–96: vol. 1, 62–63. For the appointment in Bologna see *RdC*, 17 May 1886.
206. ACC, 27 March 1886, consigliere Panzacchi. Similar: ACC, 23 December 1895, sindaco Dallolio.
207. ACC, 2 December 1881, consigliere Zorzi.
208. ACC, 19 October 1874, consigliere Filopanti. He saw the opera as an unnecessary object of luxury; this general attitude was already present in his contributions to the debates on the constitution for the Roman Republic in 1849: Cavazza 1997: 213.
209. *RdC*, 27 and 28 December 1885, 6 and 26 November 1885, 22 December 1885.
210. See for instance ACC, 2 December 1881 and 24 October 1889, sindaco Tacconi; *RdC*, 26 April 1885 and 22 December 1885. Also Rosselli 1987: 8–9, 50. Rosselli 1991: 76ff., 83.
211. Silvestri 1966: 31–44, 53. While he was admired by Cosima Wagner, Weingartner and Elgar, G. B. Shaw seemed rather critical of him.
212. When in 1867 Bologna had offered Scalaberni a contract over three years, the result was "the most splendid episode in the entire history of our theatre," with several works by Verdi which had never been presented on Bologna's stages, operas by Halevy, Mercadante, Gounod and Meyerbeer to quote only a few: ACC, 21 March 1884, assessore Dallolio.

213. ACC, 21 March 1884, consigliere Panzacchi; 30 December 1885 and 24 October 1889, sindaco Tacconi.
214. ACC, 22 December 1884, consiglieri Salaroli and Pedrini, sindaco Tacconi.
215. 21 March 1884, assessore Dallolio.
216. *RdC*, 6 May 1885.
217. *RdC*, 18 September 1885.
218. *RdC*, 17 November 1885.
219. *RdC*, 9 November and 10 November 1885. The critic F. Tomolla speaks of a "Wagnerian taste" in certain passages of the music. Goldmark got twenty curtains after the premiere: Vatiello 1921: 40.
220. *RdC*, 4 October 1885. The governor of Gmünden in Austria, Goldmark's residence, attended a performance of the opera, congratulating the composer on the success of his work: *RdC*, 14 October 1885. Despite these contested beginnings, Goldmark was elected honorary fellow of Bologna's R. Accademia Filarmonica in 1899, together with Saint-Saëns, Boito and Puccini. *L'Arpa*, 28 November 1899.
221. *RdC*, 26 April 1885.
222. Panzacchi, Bologna's most famous critic of literature, was one of the many admirers who dedicated a poem to her: "A Sarah Bernhard," in: Panzachi 1910: 48–50. On the general impact of Bernhardt see Sennett 1977: 211–12.
223. Grew 2000: 232.
224. Battistini 1986: 323.
225. Giosuè Carducci, "Alla lega per l'istruzione del popolo" [1873], in: Carducci 1913b: vol. 2, 33–44. On the advance of naturalism and realism in Italy, the debates on Zola and the links between positivism and naturalism see: Asor Rosa 1975: 966–72.
226. Giosuè Carducci, "In aspettazione d'una recita di Sara Bernhardt" [*Don Chisciotte*, Bologna, March 1882], in: Carducci 1935–38: vol. 25, 206–9.
227. Mosconi 1896: 156. See also Sorba 2006b.
228. Francesco d'Arcais, quoted in Rosselli 1991: 103. Also *NA*, Serie terza, 1(3). 459–474.
229. ACC, 30 December 1885, consigliere Panzacchi. *RdC*, 31 December 1885.
230. Weber, W. 1984: 38, 49. Weber, W. 1977: 6.
231. Rosselli 1991: 43, 49, 124.
232. On Martini and Mattei Vatielli 1928: vol. 2, 44.
233. *CW* I (1), 1 June 1893, 4. Levi 1987: 24–25. Vatiello 1921: 47.
234. *RdC*, 18 May 1885.
235. In the history of music this trend is usually dated at the beginning of the twentieth century: Dahlhaus 1978b: 115.
236. Sani 1922: 162–63.
237. Bologna's first chair in music had been established in 1420, two centuries before the foundation of the Accademia Filarmonica, Italy's most famous musical academy: Venturi 1977: 469. Surian 1980: 4–5. ACC, 26 June 1891.
238. ACC, 27 January 1887, assessore Dallolio. On Busi's role see ACC, 17 August 1895, assessore Pini.
239. Accademia Filarmonica di Bologna 1966.
240. *RdC*, 24 March 1886; 27 February 1886. Palestrina played a crucial role in Boito's plans for a new syllabus for Italy's musical academies: Boito to Verdi, 4 and 5 October 1887, in: Istituto di Studi Verdiani 1978: vol. 1, 127ff.
241. Gaetano Gasparri, "Di Ercole Bottrigari e G.M.Artusi, teorici musicali bolognesi," see Carducci 1913b: vol. 2, 327.
242. On the third "historical concert" with music by Durante, Pistocchi and Lotti, see *RdC* 3 April 1886. For the fourth concert with music from Bologna by Martini and Marcello see *RdC*, 10 April 1886.

243. See the lectures by Gaetano Gasparri: "La musica in San Petronio," "De' mae-stri di cappella alla basilica petroniana," "Di Ercole Bottrigari e G.M.Artusi, teorici musicali bolognesi" and "De' compositori di musica bolognesi nella seconda metà del sec. XVI," in: Carducci 1913b: vol. 2, 300–338. On Gasparri and the Cappella also Vecchi 1976: 418. Vatiello 1921: 16.

244. Gaetano Gasparri, "Di Ercole Bottrigari e G.M.Artusi, teorici musicali bolognesi," in: Carducci 1913b: vol. 2, 330.

245. ACC, 28 March 1892.

246. Hence this musical historicism differs considerably from, for instance, the German Palestrina revival, which was explicitly religious with an important impact on new church music: Garratt 2002.

247. Likewise "Schönberg was adamant in his insistence that the only way to learn to write music was by a thoroughgoing study of the older masters." See Janik and Toulmin 1973: 107. Boito 1942: 1172–73. Weber, W. 1984: 40–41. Mack and Gregor-Dellin, in Wagner, C. 1976: 11. One of the local protagonists of the historical revival was Luigi Torchi, who also translated Wagner's theoretical writings and wrote a major work on him: Torchi 1890.

248. Dahlhaus 1987: 7, 24, 43–44. For Busoni's critique of the concept of "absolute music" see Busoni 1954: 12ff.

249. Dahlhaus 1987: 81–82, 87.

250. ASCB, CA, 1913, Tit. X, 3, 4, 8604, 8899, letter of the mayor to the German consul, 4 May 1913.

251. Alfonso Rubbiani, quoted in: Fanti 1981: 129. On the Bach Renaissance in Germany after 1829 see Applegate 2005. See also Frisch 2005: 144–49.

252. Dahlhaus and Krummacher 1996: 337, 340–41. For the concept of histori-cist modernism see Frisch 2005: 138–39.

253. Somigli and Moroni (eds) 2004: 10.

254. ASCB, CA, 1903, Tit. X, 3, 4, 17950 and alleagti, progetto Bolcioni Bordasso, 17 November 1903, and 18355, letter by the mayor to the prefect, 25 November 1903.

255. ASCB, CA, 1903, Tit. X, 3, 4, Deputazione dei pubblici spettacoli, no. 33, 16 May 1903, and 4910, 5669, 6125, 6371, 6705, 6836.

256. ASCB, CA, 1903, Tit. X, 3, 4, 4173, Alesandro Rossi to the mayor, 18 March 1903.

257. Rosselli 1991: 127. Ashbrook 2007.

258. ACC, 29 August 1903. ASCB, CA, 1904, 3, 4, 2185, estratto del verbale della Giunta; and 766, letter by Pozzali to the mayor, 17 January 1904 and annotations by the *giunta* of 3 February 1904 and 10 February 1904.

259. ACC, 23 December 1903, 5 May 1904, 16 May 1905.

260. ACC, 16 May 1904.

261. Levi 1987: 33.

262. ACC, 16 May 1905, consigliere Moretti.

263. ACC, 29 August 1903, consigliere Negri. In the following years the price for tickets was discussed with certain regularity: ACC, 30 December 1910.

264. ACC, 30 December 1911, consigliere Zanardi.

265. ASCB, CA, 1904, Tit. X, 3, 4, 4437, letter Consorzio dei Palchettisti to the mayor, 7 April 1904.

266. ASCB, CA, 1913, Tit. X, 3, 4, 5023, letter by the Lega Navale Italiana to the mayor, 17 March 1913. The association's motto, which figured on the letter, was short and meaningful: "*Mare Nostrum.*"

267. ACC, 29 August 1903, sindaco Golinelli. See a similar dispute within the governing coalition 24 November 1903 and 28 December 1903.

268. ACC, 24 November 1903, consigliere Sandro.

269. ACC, 28 December 1903, consiglieri Tanari, Sarti.

270. ASCB, CA, 1904, Tit. X, 3, 4, 17914 and 17878, Nota del R.o Commissario.
271. ASCB, CA, 1904, Tit. X, 3, 4, 17850, 30 November 1904, Circolare del R.o Commissario.
272. ASCB, CA, 1904, Tit. X, 3, 4, 18126, letter by the R.o Commissario to the Direttore dell'Ufficio Regionale per la conservazione dei monumenti, 9 November 1904. ACC, 13 December 1904, 13 November 1905, 13 December 1907, 15 November 1911. ASCB, CA, 1912, Tit. X, 3, 1, 2146.
273. ACC, 30 December 1911, consigliere Muggia, consigliere Bianconi and sindaco Tanari.
274. Francfort 2005: 271. Socrate 2004: 41. Wilson, A. 2007: 18. Massenet was himself profoundly influenced by Wagner: Huebner 1993. On Wagnerism in France also Huebner 1999: 76–77. For an excellent analysis of the complexities of the debate in France see Strasser 2001; also Ther 2006: 266. On "nationalisation" Ther 2006: 18, 121 sq. Tusa 2006. Buyens 2006.
275. ASCB, CA, 1907, Tit. X, 3, 4, 15335, Estratto del verbale della Giunta, 30 August 1907 and 1908, Tit. X, 3, 4, 8550 Letter by the subscription committee to the mayor, 25 May 1908; deliberation of the *giunta*, 19 April 1908; reply by the mayor, 22 May 1908. The old tablet was given to the hotel where Wagner had stayed during his visit.
276. ASCB, CA, 1907, Tit. X, 3, 4, 14537, Progetto dell'impresario Ercole Casali, 16 October 1907, estratto del verbale della Giunta, 20 August 1907.
277. *La Traviata, Rigoletto, Aida, Don Carlos, I Lombardi.* Twice *Lohengrin, Meistersinger, Siegfried, Rheingold,* twice *Tristan, Walküre, Götterdämmerung, Tannhäuser, Parsifal.*
278. Other European cities used the category in a similar way. In Prague, for instance, Smetana was regarded as Wagnerian: Ther 2006: 311.
279. Quoted Jung 1974: 48.
280. Perlmutter 1952: 104–6. Somkin 1985: 195.
281. Macedo 1998: 101. Ther 2006: 339.
282. ASCB, CA, 1913, Tit. X, 3, 4, 2391 and alleagti, Deputazione dei pubblici spettacoli to the mayor, 17 January 1913; 9567, 9904, 10640, Lavori diversi. Costruzione del Golfo mistico: Corrado Ricci, director general for antiquities and fine art, Ministry of Education, to the mayor, 7 June 1913; 2391, Nota dell'Ufficio V Edilità ed Arte, 2 January 1913; Rapporto della Commissione, 15 June 1913; verbale della Giunta, 25 April 1913.
283. See Filippo Tommaso Marinetti, "Down with the Tango and Parsifal. Futurist letter circulated among cosmopolitan women friends who give tango-teas and Parsifalize themselves," 11 January 1914, in: Marinetti 1972: 69–72. Also Miller, M. 1984: 194–95. On Papini also Adamson 1993.
284. ACC, 29 September 1913, consigliere Rivari.
285. Giosuè Carducci, "Dello Svolgimento della Letteratura Nazionale. Discorsi tenuti nella Università di Bologna MDCCCLXVIII–MDCCCLXXI" (Discorso Primo: "Dei tre elementi formatori della letteratura italiana: l'elemento ecclesiastico, il cavalleresco, il nazionale"), in: Carducci 1913a: 45. Wagner himself was rather unhappy with parts of the original staging and Joukowsky's sketches, which remained unchanged until 1951. See Mayer 1978: 42–43.
286. De Man 1993: 151.
287. On references to the Easter myth see Mosse, G. 1975: 104–5.
288. ASCB, CA; 1914, Tit. X, 3, 4, 33, Economato to the mayor, 31 December 1913. For the production of this souvenir postcard Siegfried Wagner offered an original photograph of his father. Jung 1974: 29. Calore 1982: 100. Sani 1922: 160. Rosselli 1991: 116. The fact that also unfortunate characters such as Rigoletto were chosen as given names suggests that even people largely unfamiliar with the world of opera identified with what was going on in the theatre.

289. ACC, 23 May 1913.
290. See in particular Busoni 1935: 3–4 (5 and 7 December 1895). Kannonier 1987: 41. Pfitzner responded to Busoni's new aesthetic with a polemical pamphlet: Pfitzner 1917. Although Pfitzner's association of Busoni with *Futurismus* is questionable, as a neo-classicist composer he was not nostalgically looking backwards, but followed a formalist approach to new means of aesthetic expression. See also Stuckenschmidt 1954. Henke 2005: 241–42. Beaumont 1985: 136. I am grateful to Sebastian Prüfer and David Brown for their help regarding my work on Busoni in Berlin.
291. *Twenty-Four Preludes for Piano*, BV 181; *Three Pieces in the Old Style for Piano*, BV 159; *Racconti Fantastici: Three Character Pieces for Piano*, BV 100; *Il sabato del villaggio*, BV 192. Roberge 1991: 16, 21, 23–24. Vatiello 1921: 43. Silvestri 1966: 23.
292. On the concept of avant-garde see Kannonier 1992: 118 sq. Not unproblematic: Calinescu 1987: 95 sq. For a critique of the concept in Italy see Somigli and Moroni (eds) 2004: 9, and more generally Dahlhaus 1978a: 40–41.
293. Busoni 1954: 33–38, 41–42. On his harmonic language and his relationship to Rilke see Beaumont 1985: 27–28, 33, 91.
294. On Busoni's role in Berlin Henke 2005: 239–40.
295. The work of 1923 was based on his opera *Die Brautwahl*. This seems to contradict the fact that he worked closely with other Jewish composers, for instance Zemlinsky, who conducted his Turandot-Suite in Prague. Beaumont 1985: 136. Beaumont 2000: 190, 220. For the reference to Eliot: Blair 1999: 160. Also Boito presents in this respect a problematic legacy: Pompeati 1950.
296. Dent 1974: 212. Dent knew Busoni from Cambridge: Busoni 1935: 71.
297. ACC, 18 July 1913. This meant in the first place an increase in salaries for the teaching staff, but it also was a question of great prestige for its students and the city.
298. Busoni 1935: 293–94 (25 September 1913). Dent 1974: 2089, 218.
299. Balilla Pratella 1915. See in particular Castronuovo and Medri 2003.
300. Busoni 1935: 299, 305, 314 (3 and 11 October 1913, 21 June 1914). Dent 1974: 205, 208–9.
301. See in this context Deathridge and Dahlhaus 1984: 104.

NOTES TO CHAPTER 10

1. For a historical approach to futurism see Berghaus 1996 and for the relevant sources Apollonio (ed.) 1973.
2. Pfitzner 1917. Henke 2005: 241. Pfitzner might however have misunderstood Busoni. See Williamson 1992: 25.
3. See for instance the debates analysed in Roccatagliati 1993, but also the discussions about Wagner in the previous chapter. Furthermore Deathridge and Dahlhaus 1984: 92 sq.
4. Deathridge and Dahlhaus 1984: 99.
5. Bartlett 1995: 224.
6. Deathridge and Dahlhaus 1984: 114. It should be noted that Italian as well as Russian commentators applied the label *Zukunftsmusik* to any of Wagner's music.
7. Berghaus 1996: 58.
8. In addition to the bibliography cited in the previous chapter see in particular Lacombe 2001. Huebner 1999. Strasser 2001: 237–38. Large and Weber (eds) 1984.

9. Paret 1988: 60–91. Paret 1980. With regard to Italian modernism see on this issue also the introduction in Ben-Ghiat 2001.
10. Gentile 2003: 47–48. See also Pécout 1997: 274–75.
11. Af Malmborg 2002: 53. On the exchange of ideas between Italy and the rest of Europe during the Risorgimento see also Grew 2000: 207–8. Isabella 2003. Isabella 2006.
12. Meriggi 2001: 16.
13. Hoch 2001. Adamson 1993: 35–36. Braun 2002: 197. Jelavich 1985.
14. See for instance the Viennese *NFP*, 16 and 20 February 1907. (I am grateful to Chris Hailey for this reference.)
15. Some commentators speak of "*il primato di Bologna sulla cultura italiana,*" linking it to Carducci. See for instance Pasini 1980: 997–98. Carducci's neo-classicism influenced the Scapigliati as well as D'Annunzio, and also his own embrace of Wagnerian symbolism played a role in this. After his death, Florence became the key centre.
16. Bossi was Busoni's predecessor as director of the Liceo Musicale. The concert was the Phiharmonic Society's last evening. In addition to the works mentioned Mahler conducted Mendelssohn's Italian symphony and Leone Sinigalia's Ouverture *Le barouffe Chiozzotte.* See Roman 1989: 456. In 1910 Mahler conducted Busoni's *Turandot Suite:* Beaumont 1985: 145. Martucci had died in 1909, but in one of his last concerts, in October 1908, he conducted his second symphony in Frankfurt—from its musical idiom probably his most modern work, stretching the limits of tonality and breaking through internal structures.
17. *RB*, 3, 1869 (2), 295. Somigli Moroni (eds) 2004: 13. For the general context see Bellamy 2002.
18. He was equally at home in the study of early modern Spain, which was crucial for his understanding of the Kingdom of the Two Sicilies, as in the philo-sophical and literary developments of England, France and Germany from the Middle Ages to the modern day. His work on Shakespeare, Goethe and Dante influenced generations of Italian scholars, even if it was Giambattista Vico who remained "the guide and inspiration of all his intellectual life." Momigliano 1992a: 532–33. On Croce's Vico reception see Edler 2001: 38ff.
19. While Croce understood Fascism as the antithesis of liberal Italy, for Gramsci it was the natural consequence of the social conflicts it had generated. If Croce depicted Fascism as a parenthesis in the history of Italy it was primarily to reject the Fascists' own claims of a logical continuity between the Risorgimento and Fascism. On the critique of the "parenthesis" argument see Corner 1986: 12 and Bosworth 1998: 45–46. For Gramsci's critique of Croce see Davis 1979: 13. For the context of this historiographical debate see also the critique of Luigi Einaudi: Roberto Vivarelli, "Libralismo, protezionismo, fas-cismo. Per la storia e il significato di un trascurato giudizio di Luigi Einaudi sulle origini del fascismo," in: Vivarelli 1981: 162–344, in particular 170.
20. Roberts 1987: 6. Agazzi 1980. In particular Momigliano 1992a. Momi-gliano had been designated as the founding director of Croce's institute in Naples. On the Croce-Momigliano relationship see Dionisotti 1988. On the European dimension of Croce's work, rejecting the idea that he isolated Italy from the rest of Europe, see also Coli 1983, in particular 61 sq., 93. Eugenio Garin, "La casa editrice Laterza e mezzo secolo di cultura italiana," in: Garin 1962: 155–74. It should be noted that at least certain currents of Ital-ian Fascism tried to preserve this cosmopolitan ambition: Ben-Ghiat 2001: 35–36, 51. Also Stone 1998.
21. Coli 1983: 69ff., 82–90. Bobbio 1990b. Vivarelli 1991: vol. 2, 115–16. Rob-erts 1987: 4 for the concept of "absolute historicism." The wide European range of Croce's thought also resonates in Gramsci's writings: Körner 1999.

On this basis I disagree with Michael Mann's insistance on the narrow national boundaries of early twentieth-century sociology: Mann, M. 2004: 81.

22. Lyttelton 1973: 375–76. Gerschenkron 1962: 86. Gentile understood Fascism as heir of the Risorgimento in the spirit of Mazzini. On the assimilation of European thought in Italian Marxism Drake 2003. Zangheri 1997a: vol. 2, 337 sq.

23. Janik and Toulmin 1973: 239 sq. On the general discourse of decline in Europe since the *fin de siècle:* Pick 1989.

24. Gentile 2003: 1, 41–42. Thayer 1964: 376 sq. Adamson 2001. Roberts 1987: 11. Clark, M. 1977: 48. On the European dimension in Gramsci's thought also Tranfaglia 1995: 220.

25. Cammelli 1995: 28. For this historiographical context see Lyttelton 1973: 2–3. Salvemini 1973: 64–65. Trevelyan's otherwise sympathetic view of Italy nurtured these patterns, reaching well beyond academic circles: Cannadine 1992: xii, 61. For the general historiographical context: Berger 2005: 645. Davis 1994: 291ff.

26. Adamson 1993: 7.

27. De Man 1993: 147.

28. See on this concept Bauman 1991: Introduction.

29. George Kubler, quoted in Clark, T. 1999: 15.

30. Clark, T. 1999: 18.

31. Baudelaire 1992. Simmel 1908. Tönnies 1972. Walter Benjamin, "Franz Kafka" and "Max Brod's book on Kafka," in: Benjamin 1970: 111–48. Williams 1989: 31 sq. See also Harris 2006.

32. For the general debate see Von Schiller 1982. Koselleck 1989. Koselleck 2002: chpt. 10. Habermas 1987. Berman 1982. Bradbury and McFarlane (eds) 1991: chpt. 1. Calinescu 1987. Wagner, P. 1994: chpt. 1.

33. Here in particular Corner 1986: 11 and Griffin 2007.

34. Akcan 2006: 9.

35. Bloch 1985. Barta (ed.) 2000 argues that post-Petrine Russia was westernized in a metamorphic fashion, retaining to a significant degree the characteristics of the original entity, a fact reflected in the country's literary modernism. For Jenkins 2003 political resistance to democratisation coincided with a modern opening of public culture. Regarding the concepts of multiple and/or alternative modernities see Ben-Ghiat 2001. Griffin 2007: 2, 6. Miller, N. 2007. Hart and Miller (eds) 2007. For the hybridity of nationally defined cultures see also Said 1993: 15.

36. For a more cautious evaluation of Giolitti's success, with the focus on Bologna see Dunnage 1995.

37. Thayer 1964: ix, 308–9.

38. Lyttelton 1973: 1. For the general theoretical context of this debate see Bloch 1985. Horkheimer and Adorno 2001. Williams 1989. Herf 1984. See also Rieger 2005. Mann, M. 2004: 80. Blair 1999: 157. Specifically for Italy Asor Rosa 1975. On the connexion between aesthetic innovation and revolutionary politics Seigel 1986: 369 sq. See also the example of the Bavarian Soviet Republic of 1919: Jelavich 1985: 298ff. In cities like Turin, Pavia and Parma the Extreme Left experimented until the early 1920s with futurism: Berghaus 1996: 72, 197. Peter Paret's work on the Berliner Secession shows that the ideological context of modernism could differ according to national cases: Paret 1980: 4–5.

39. For the general context see Ben-Ghiat 2001 and Griffin 2007. Braun 2002. For an overview of aesthetic responses Perfetti 2001. For a municipal focus on Fascist modernism: Vannelli 1981. Fraticelli 1982. Etlin 1991. Adamson 1993. Stone 1998.

40. Masulli 1980: 73ff., 133. Zamagni 1986: 248 sq. Zamagni 1997: 131. On the food processing industry see in particular Finzi 1997.

41. Romanelli 1979: 279.
42. Zamagni 1986: 251. Cardoza 1982: 46. Also in other regions the situation of peasants deteriorated, with the *mezzadria* system in Tuscany collapsing under the impact of commercialisation: Snowden 1979.
43. Dunnage 1995: 389, 395.
44. Cardoza 1982: 7, 70–73.
45. Masulli 1980: 79. Zangheri 1997a: vol. 2, 69–70, 132–33. Dunnage 1995: 385 sq. Serra, F. 1951. Caracciolo 1952. On public works see Masulli 1980: 77–78. See for the debate among the mayors of the province *RdC*, 31 August 1890 and 14 September 1890. Numerous streets and bridges in the province were included in the project and there was competition between the various municipalities concerning the priorities: *RdC*, 18 September 1890. The committee also tried to persuade private business to undertake building works in order to resolve the crisis: 1 November 1890.
46. Arbizzani 1962: 333 sq. D'Attore 1986: 80. Zangheri (ed.) 1960: xxx, 6. Finzi and Tassinari 1986: 217.
47. Körner 2005.
48. Ragionieri 1976: 1939.
49. *Almanach Illustrée de la Libre Pensée Internationale*, 1908. For this information I am grateful to Daniel Laqua.
50. Malatesta, M. 1978.
51. Atkinson 2005: 17.
52. Quoted in Drake 1980: 93.
53. ACC, 15 November 1911, sindaco Nadalini.
54. ACC, 9 May 1910 and 15 November 1911, consigliere Sassoli De Bianchi.
55. ACC, 15 November 1911, consigliere Sacchetti.
56. ACC, 9 December 1911; 3 May 1912.
57. ACC, 2 March 1912, sindaco Nadalini.
58. ACC, 9 December 1914. Bologna named a school and a street after Pascoli: ACC, 5 December 1915; 15 November 1911. On the immediate effects of Italian rule see Abdullatif Ahmida 2005: 59–71.
59. Ragionieri 1976: 1827.
60. Salvadori 2001: 3–13.
61. Zangheri (ed.) 1960: xxx, 6. Finzi and Tassinari 1986: 217.
62. Cardoza 1982: 90ff.
63. Lotti 1980: 305.
64. Cardoza 1982: 98, 110.
65. Masulli 1980: 195, 293–96.
66. Degl'Innocenti 1999: 193.
67. ACC, 27 August 1914.
68. Quoted in Cavazza, G. 1984: 389.
69. Rugge 1986: 56, 64.
70. Furlan 1988. ACC, 31 December 1916, consigliere Grossi.
71. ACC, 31 December 1916, consigliere Ghigi.
72. Cavazza, S. 1998: 83.
73. Thorpe 2001.
74. ACC, 27 August 1914, assessore Longhena. On this asociation see Grange, 2005. ACC, 26 November 1914, consiglieri Venezian and Daddi. On the Socialist reaction to the German invasion of Belgium see Tranfaglia 1995: 31; De Felice 1965: 228ff. At the end of the war the same spirit led the Socialist administration to support the "children of the Viennese proletariat," "a conscious act of international fraternity": ACC, 17 January 1920, presidente Scota.
75. ACC, 30 December 1914, sindaco Zanardi.

76. Lyttelton 1973: 42–43. On the political implications of the Socialists' anti-interventionist position see Roberto Vivarelli's critique of Renzo de Felice in Vivarelli 1981; 82–83.
77. ACC, 27 February 1915.
78. Winter 1985: 75. Ragionieri, 2058. Mack Smith 1969: 313.
79. Clark, M. 1977: 13–14.
80. Clark, M. 1977: 21ff.
81. ACC, 31 December 1916, sindaco Zanardi. On the same occasion consigliere Ghigi spoke of 20,000 people. See also ASCB, CA, 1915, Tit. X, 3, 4, 2837, 11 December 1915.
82. ACC, 5 July 1919.
83. ACC, 29 September 1913, sindaco Nadalini.
84. ASCB, CA, 1914, Tit. X, 3, 4, 295, proposal of the committee, 4 January 1914, and letter by Pini, 6 January 1914; allegato, letter to the Commissario Regio al Comune di Bologna Conte Roascio, 14 January 1914.
85. ASCB, CA, 1914, Tit. X, 3, 4, 30586, committee Bonora to the mayor, 6 December 1914; letter by the committee Bonora to the mayor, 6 December 1914.
86. ASCB, CA, 1916, Tit. X, 3, 4, 25861, Progetto del 6 November 1916; verbale della Giunta, 8 November 1916.
87. ASCB, CA, 1916, Tit. X, 3, 4, 2170, 26907, 25901. Wilson 2007: 173.
88. Followed by *Tristan* in 1921, *Tannhäuser* in 1922, *Walküre* in 1923, *Rheingold* in 1924, *Siegfried* in 1925, *Lohengrin* and *Tristan* in 1926. Throughout the inter-war period and during World War II, Wagner appeared on average about once every year.
89. ASCB, 1920, Tit. X, 3, 4, 29381, allegato al 1914, Tit. X; 3, 4, 295, letter by the committee to the capo ufficio, 28 October 1920. ASCB, 1920, Tit. X, 3, 4, 29381, Estratto del verbale della Giunta, 8 November 1920.
90. ACC, 31 December 1914, consigliere Tonolla. See also the commemoration for Tonolla: ACC, 6 February 1916.
91. ACC, 18 June 1913, consigliere Zanardi.
92. ASCB, CA, 1914, Tit. X, 3, 4, 9584, 6 May 1914; idem, 30848, 9 December 1914.
93. ACC, 31 December 1914, consigliere Tonolla; 3 September 1914; 26 February 1916.
94. ASCB, CA, 1916, Tit. X, 3, 1, 7090 and 26689, correspondence between Dallolio and the mayor, 20 April 1916 and 15 November 1916.
95. ASCB, CA, 1915, Tit. X, 3, 4, 18336, circular by the prefect, 20 August 1915. ASCB, CA, Tit. X, 4, 3, 18336, prefect to the mayor, 23 August 1915. For example, the minister promised to arrange special train fares to allow visitors to attend theatre performances. Nevertheless, he was chiefly concerned to ensure that the municipalities kept the theatre open: free social services for artists and musicians; reduced fees paid by those running the theatres; a reduction in ticket prices.
96. ASCB, CA, 1918, Tit. X, 3, 4, 2143, trattazione del conte Pepoli per la vendita, 5 February 1918 and verbale della Giunta, 11 February 1918.
97. ACC, 5 July 1919.
98. ACC, 20 July 1920. For Walter Benjamin the telephone bell generated a sound which "disturbed the world-historical epoch"; following from there, the *théâtrophone* became for Marcel Proust the greatest asset to his later years. See Walter Benjamin, "Berliner Kindheit," in: Benjamin 1955: vol. 1, 589. Emil Berliner's live transmission of performances via telephone started in Paris in the 1870s. From the 1880s cheap installations

by Siemens, Böttcher and Bell allowed even provincial theatres to use the new technology.

99. ACC, 11 July 1920, assessore Scota.
100. ACC, 5 December 1915.
101. ACC, 31 May 1919.
102. ACC, 5 December 1915.
103. ACC, 26 August 1917. Due to overcrowding, some furniture was broken, enough for the Comunale's box owners to bring the case to court: ASCB, CA, 1917, Tit. X, 3, 4, 21693, 1 September 1917. (The document is located in a file of the year 1936, n.p.35798.)
104. "Le biblioteche popolari," in: *Vit. Citt.*, October 1918, 272–74.
105. ACC, 7 May 1915, consigliere Perozzi.
106. ACC, 26 November 1914, consigliere Perozzi.
107. ACC, 26 November 1914, sindaco Zanardi.
108. Tranfaglia 1995: 129. Vivarelli 1991: vol. 2, 14–15, 34ff., 220–21.
109. Vivarelli 1991: vol. 2, 160–65. Morgan 2004: 32–37.
110. De Felice 1965: 289–90.
111. Benito Mussolini, "Trenchocracy," in: Griffin (ed.) 1995: 28–29.
112. Lyttelton 1973: 56ff. The former anarchist Arpinati integrated a whole new social milieu into the movement. Of the 39,000 veterans, 22,000 had a rural background: D'Attore 1986: 126, 136. Wohl 1979: 173–74. Mann, M. 2004: 79, 96–97, 100 sq. The political positions of shopkeepers were rather more complex: Morris 2002. For a critique of the generational argument see Thayer 1964: 375.
113. Tranfaglia 1995: 197.
114. Lyttelton 1973: 364.
115. Reichardt 2002: 276–303.
116. Lyttelton 1973: 52.
117. Banti 1990: 91. Concerning the link between the introduction of agrarian capitalism and Fascism see Forgacs 1986a: 4; Corner 1979.
118. Antonio Gramsci, "Cos'è la reazione?" (*L'Ordine Nuovo*, 24 November 1920), in: Gramsci 1987, 765ff.
119. On the question as to whether Mussolini's was a counter-revolutionary movement or if he acted primarily against the Socialist party, as De Felice argues, see Roberto Vivarelli, "Rivoluzione e reazione in Italia negli anni 1918–1922," in: Vivarelli 1981: 129 sq. Also Vivarelli 1991: vol. 2, 883 sq. Tranfaglia 1995: 154, 189, 245 sq. On the factory councils Clark, M. 1977. Gaetano Salvemini was the first to dismiss the idea that Fascism was a reaction to a Bolshevik threat with the aim of saving the economy. He held the failures of Italian Liberalism, the Church, the Nationalistic plots and the army's backing of Mussolini responsible for the political crisis which brought Fascism to power and allowed Mussolini to establish a dictatorship. For an outline of Salvemini's evaluation see Vivarelli 1973: vii–xiii.
120. Zangheri (ed.) 1960: 403–4.
121. Ragionieri 1976: 2100–2101. (Here also the quote from Tasca).
122. On the events in particular Onofri 1980. Casali (ed.) 1982. For an evaluation of the Bologna events in a national context see Salvemini 1973: 287ff. Tranfaglia 1995: 245–50.
123. Ragionieri 1976: 2110, 2108. For Roberto Vivarelli the agrarian strikes in the Bolognese became the turning point in which the climate changed from revolution to reaction: Vivarelli 1991: vol. 2, 883. Vivarelli 1981: 146. The development of the conflict in the Ferrarese had a crucial impact: Corner

1974. Barrington Moore had little to say about Italy, but emphasises the ruralisation of Fascism: Moore 1966: 451–52.
124. Benito Mussolini, quoted in Pancaldi 1986: 376.
125. Pasquale Sfameni, quoted in Pancaldi 1986: 377.
126. Sombart 1893: 227. For a critique of Sombart's "reactionary modernism" see Herf 1984: 130 sq.

Bibliography

PRIMARY SOURCES

Archives:

Archivio Storico Comunale di Bologna:

Atti del Consiglio Comunale 1860–1920
Scritture private, 1863 (1, 2), 1867, 1871
Deputazione dei Pubblici Spettacoli, Miscellanea, 1860 II, 1861
Carteggio Amministrativo 1803–1862: Tit. XVI Spettacoli e Divertimenti Pubblici, 1860–1861
Carteggio Amministrativo 1863–1897: Tit.V Economato, Rubrica 3 Manutenzione delle proprietà comunali; Tit. X Polizia Municipale, Rubrica 3 Spettacoli e Divertimenti; Tit. XIV Istruzione, Rubrica 2 Musei; Rubrica 4 Liceo Musicale; Rubrica 5 Arti Belle
Carteggio Amministrativo 1898–1910: Tit.V Economato, Rubrica 3 Manutenzione delle proprietà comunali; Tit. X Polizia Municipale, Rubrica 3 Feste, Spettacoli, Divertimenti; Tit. XIV Istruzione, Rubrica 1 Università e corpi scientifici, Rubrica 2 Belle Arti; Rubrica 6 Musei e medaglieri; Rubrica 7 Liceo Musicale; Rubrica 8 Bande Musicali; Rubrica 9 Esposizioni e Congressi
Carteggio Amministrativo 1911–1920: Tit. V Economato, Rubrica 3 Proprietà comunali; Tit. X Polizia municipale, Rubrica 3 Feste, spettacoli, divertimenti, Sezione 1 Disposizioni particolari; Sezione 3 Feste Civili; Sezione 4 Teatri

Archivio di Stato di Bologna:

4506 Esposizione Emiliana: 1 Comitato Provisorio poi generale. Verbali delle Adunanze del Comitato Esecutivo; 3 Comitato Esecutivo. Verbali delle Adunanze; 9 Comitato Esecutivo. Atti Generali; 19–21 Comitato Esecutivo. Stampe; 22 Comitato Esecutivo. Atti particolari; 35–36 Commissione Festeggiamenti; 39–40 Commissione Stampa e Pubblicita'; 55–67 Commissioni ordinatrici: Musica, Belle Arti ed Arte Antica, Risorgimento, Operaia, Etrusca-Universitaria; 68 Giunte locali: Bologna; 111 Carte speciali delle Commissioni ordinatrici: Risorgimento; 112–14 Carte speciali delle Commissioni ordinatrici: Belle Arti ed Arte Antica; 118 Carte speciali delle Commissioni ordinatrici: Musica, Protocollo; 119 Carte speciali delle Commissioni ordinatrici: Comitato promotore dell'Esposizione di Musica nel 1879; 120–21 Carte speciali delle Commissioni ordinatrici, Musica, Atti Generali; 130 Carte speciali delle Commissioni ordinatrici: Musica, Giunte speciali: Amsterdam-Londra; 132 Carte speciali delle Commissioni ordinatrici: Musica, Atti speciali.

Biblioteca dell'Archiginnasio:

17. Biografie ed Elogi.
17. Sezione Autica

Newspapers and Periodicals:

Atti e Memorie della Deputazione di Storia Patria per le Province di Romagna;
Corriere dell'Emilia; Cronaca Wagneriana; Critica Sociale; Gazzetta delle
Romagne; Gazzetta dell'Emilia; Il Monitore di Bologna; Il Resto del Carlino;
Illustrazione Italiana; L'Arpa; La Vita Cittadina. Rivista mensile di cronaca
amministrativa e di statistica del Comune di Bologna; La Vita Civica; Neue
Freie Presse; Nuova Antologia di lettere, arti e scienze; Rivista Bolognese

PRINTED AND PUBLISHED PRIMARY SOURCES:

Apollonio, Umbro (ed.) 1973. *Futurist Manifestos*. London: Thames and Hudson.
Bacchelli, Giuseppe 1910. "'Giù le mani!' dai nostri monumenti antichi" (1910). In
Solmi and Dezzi Bardeschi (eds) 1981: 616–23.
Balilla Pratella, Francesco 1915. *Musica Italiana. Per una cultura della sensibilità*
musicale italiana. Bologna: Bongiovanni.
Baudelaire, Charles 1992. *Selected Writings on Art and Literature*. Translated and
with an introduction by P. E. Charvet. London: Penguin.
Bertolini, Francesco 1860. *Storia primitiva di Roma compilata dietro le opere dei*
critici moderni. Milan and Turin: Paravia.
———. 1876. *La battaglia di Legnano*. Naples: Morano.
———. 1880. *Storia d'Italia dal 1814 al 1878*. 2 vols. Milan: Vallardi.
———. 1882. *Garibaldi e la nuova Italia*. Naples: Detken.
———. 1887. *Bologna nella storia del Risorgimento Italiano. Discorso per la solenne*
inaugurazione degli studi nella R.Università di Bologna nell'anno academico
1887-1888. Bologna: Monti.
———. 1892. *Compendio di Storia scritta ad uso delle scuole econdarie inferiori*.
Bologna: Zanichelli.
———. 1895. *Letture Popolari di Storia del Risorgimento Italiano*. Milan: Hoepli.
Bignami, Luigi 1880. *Cronologia di tutti spettacoli rappresentati nel gran Teatro*
Comunale di Bologna dalla solenne sua apertura 14 maggio 1763 a tutto
l'Autunno del 1880. Bologna: Agenzia Commerciale.
Boito, Arrigo 1932. *Lettere di Arrigo Boito*. Ed. Raffaello De Rensis. Rome:
Novissima.
———. 1942. *Tutti gli scritti*. Ed. Piero Nardi. Milan: Mondadori.
Bologna e le sue Esposizioni 1888. *Pubblicazione straordinaria della Illustrazione*
Italiana. Milan: Treves.
Bordeux Vahdeh, J. 1926. *Margherita of Savoia*. London: Hutchinson.
Bottrigari, Enrico 1960–1963. *Cronaca di Bologna 1845-1871*. 4 vols. Ed. Aldo
Berselli. Bologna: Zanichelli.
Brizio, Edoardo 1885. *La Provenienza degli Etruschi*. Modena: Vincenzi.
Busmanti, Silvio 1876. *Cenni intorno al maestro Angelo Mariani*. Bologna: Tip.
Calderini.
Busoni, Ferruccio 1935. *Briefe an seine Frau*. Ed. Friedrich Schnapp. Zürich /
Leipzig: Rotapfel.
———. 1954. *Entwurf einer neuen Ästhetik der Tonkunst*. (Neue Ausgabe). Wies-
baden: Insel.

Cantoni, Fulvio 1916. "Il Museo Civico del Risorgimento nell'unidicennio 1904–1915." *Vita Civ.* 2:1–2, 17–32.

Capellini, Giovanni 1914. *Ricordi*. 2 vols. Bologna: Zanichelli.

———. et al. (eds) 1892. *Catalogo del Museo dell'ottavio centenario dello Studio Bolognese inaugurato il 14 giugno 1888 e aperto il 14 marzo 1892*. Bologna: R. Tipografia.

Carducci, Giosuè 1888. *Lo studio bolognese*. Repr. 1988. Bologna: Clueb.

———. 1913a. *Discorsi letterari e storici*. Bologna: Zanichelli.

———. 1913b. *Ceneri e Faville*. Bologna: Zanichelli.

———. 1921. *Confessioni e battaglie II*. Bologna: Zanichelli.

———. 1935–1968. *Edizione nazionale delle Opere di Giosuè Carducci*. Bologna: Zanichelli.

———. 1994a. *Selected Verse*. Trans. David H. Higgins. Warminster: Aris & Phillips.

———. 1994b. *Poesie* (1979). Ed. Guido Davico Bonino. Milan: Rizzoli.

Casarini, Camillo 1872. *Ai nostri Concittadini. Risposta dell'Ex-Sindaco Commend. Camillo Casarini e dei suoi colleghi di Giunta*. Bologna.

Causa, Cesare 1879. *Giovanni Passanante condannato a morte per avere attentato alla vita di S.M.Umberto I Re d'Italia*. Florence: Adriano Salani.

Chiarini, Giuseppe 1901. *Giosuè Carducci. Impressioni e ricordi*. Bologna: Zanichelli.

Congrès international d'anthropologie préhistorique 1873. *Compte rendu de la cinquième session de 1871*. Bologne: Fava & Garagnani.

D'Annunzio, Gabriele 1914. *La musica di Wagner e la genesi del "Parsifal."* Florence: Quattrini.

Darwin, Charles 1994. *A Darwin Selection*. Ed. Mark Ridley. London: Fontana.

De-Amicis, Fernanda 1900. *Il Re Buono e Generoso*. Milan: Aliprandi.

Del Vecchio, Giorgio 1917. "Gabriele D'Annunzio e la questione delle torri di Bologna." *Arch.* 7: 47–52.

Dempster, Thomas 1723. *De Etruria Regali libri septem*. Florence.

Dumoulin, Michel (ed.) 1979. *La Correspondance entre Emile de Laveleye et Marco Minghetti (1877–1886)*. Brussels: Institut Historique Belge de Rome.

Filopanti, Quirico 1858. *Miranda. A Book divided into three parts, entitled Souls, Numbers, Stars, on the Neo-Christian Religion with Confirmations of the old and new doctrines of Christ . . .* London: Morgan.

———. 1882–1883. *Sintesi di Storia Universale*. 4 vols. Bologna: Azzoguidi.

Foratti, Aldo 1940. "Commemorazione di Enrico Panzacchi. Parole dette nel centenario della sua nascità. Panzacchi oratore." *AMDSPR*, ser. 1, 5: 1–5.

Giorgio Giorgi, 1875 [?]. *I Goti e Gobatti giudicati dalla coscienza pubblica*. Bologna [?]: Pirloncino.

Gozzadini, Giuseppe. 1862. "Note per studi sull'architettura di Bologna al secolo XIII al XVI." *AMDSPR* 1.

———. 1864. "Del restauro di due chiese monumentali nella basilica stefaniana di Bologna." *AMDSPR* 3.

———. 1865. *Un' antica necropoli a Marzabotto nel Bolognese*. Bologna: Fava & Garagnani.

———. 1871. *Discours d'ouverture*. Bologna: Fava & Garagnani.

———. 1878. *Del ristauro di due chiese monumentali nella basilica stefaniana di Bologna*. (Estratto dagli Atti e Memorie delle Deputazioni di storia patria dell'Emilia. N. S., III.) Modena: Vincenzi.

———. 1881. *Nella solenne inaugurazione del Museo Civico di Bologna*. Bologna: Fava & Garagnani.

Grenier, Albert 1912. *Bologne Villanovienne et Étrusque VIIIe–IVe siècles avant notre ère*. Bibliothèque des Écoles Françaises d'Athènes et de Rome. Paris: Fontemoing.

Illustrazione Italiana 1888. *Bononia docet. Per l'VIII Centenario dello Studio Bolognese. Pubblicazione speciale dell'Illustrazione Italiana.* Milan: Treves.

Istituto Centrale di Statistica 1976. *Sommario di Statistiche Storiche dell'Italia, 1861–1975.* Rome.

Istituto di Studi Verdiani 1978. *Carteggio Verdi-Boito.* Ed. Mario Medici and Marcello Conati. Parma.

L'Esposizione illustrata delle provincie dell'Emilia in Bologna 1888. Bologna: succ.Monti.

Maccaferri, Alessandro 1881. *Camillo Casarini e il Comune di Bologna. Ricordi.* Bologna: Azzoguidi.

Malatesta, Errico 1936. *Pensiero e volonta. Scritti.* 4 vols. Repr. 1975. Ginevra: Risveglio.

Malvezzi, Nerio 1905. *Commemorazione di Enrico Panzacchi.* (Discorso tenuto nella R. Accademia di Belli Arti in Bologna il 21 maggio 1905). Bologna: Zanichelli.

Mariani, Angelo 1985. *Autobiografia e documenti, 1821–1873.* Ed. Amedeo Potito. Rimini: Bruno Ghigi.

Marinetti, Filippo Tommaso 1972. *Selected Writings.* Ed. R. W. Flint. London: Seder & Warburg.

Masi, Ernesto 1875. *Camillo Casarini. Riccordi contemporanei,* Bologna.

Masini, Cesare 1867. *Del Movimento Artistico in Bologna dal 1855 al 1866 in occasione della Esposizione universale di Parigi nel 1867.* Bologna: Regia Tipografia.

Mazzini, Giuseppe 1836. *Filosofia della musica* (1977). Ed. Marcello de Angelis. Rimini: Guaraldi.

———. 2004. *Giuseppe Mazzini's "Philosophy of Music."* Ed. Franco Sciannameo. Lewitson: Edwin Mellen.

Michelet, Jules 1843. *Histoire Romaine* (République), 7th ed. Bruxelles: Panthéon Classique.

Milani, Luciano 1887. *Nel primo anniversario della morte di Marco Minghetti, Discorso.* Bologna: Azzoguidi.

Miller, William 1879. *Wintering in the Riviera, with notes of travelling in Italy and France.* London: Longmans.

Minghetti, Marco 1865. *Marco Minghetti ai suoi Elettori.* Bologna: Monti.

———. 1879. *Discorso del Cav. Marco Minghetti al Banchetto ad onore del Cavaliere Marco Minghetti datosi nella gran Sala dell'Hôtel Brun a Bologna la sera del 9 febbraio 1879.* Bologna: Fava & Garagnani.

——— 1886. *Commemorazione del Conte Camillo di Cavour,* 3rd ed. Bologna: Zanichelli.

———. 1888–90. *Miei ricordi.* 3 vols. Turin: L. Roux.

———. 1896. *Scritti vari, raccolti e pubblicati da Alberto Dallolio.* Bologna: Zanichelli.

———. 1947. *Lettere fra la Regina Margherita e Marco Minghetti. 1882–1886.* Ed. Lilla Lipparini. Milan: Longanesi.

———. 1955. *Il Diario di Marco Minghetti, 1860–61.* Ed. Aldo Berselli. *ASI* 113, 406 (2): 283–305 and 13, 407 (3): 357–87, part 1.

———. 1988. *Discorsi parlamentari di Marco Minghetti, raccolti e pubblicati per deliberazione della Camera dei Deputati.* Rome: Tipografia della Camera dei Deputati.

Mommsen, Theodor 1976. *Tagebuch einer französisch-italienischen Reise 1844–1845.* Bern: Lang.

Mosconi, Ferruccio 1896. "Perché la borghesia abbandona il teatro e frequenta il Caffè-Concerto," *Critica Sociale. Quindicinale del Socialismo Scientifico* 6, 10 (16 May 1896).

Museo Civico di Bologna 1871. *Museo Civico di Bologna. Inaugurazione fatta il 2 Ottobre 1871.* Bologna: Regia Tipografia.

Neumann, Angelo 1907. *Erinnerungen an Richard Wagner.* Leipzig: Staackmann.

Nicolucci, Giustiniano 1866. *Il cranio di Dante Alighieri. Lettera del . . . all'ill. Antropologo F. Pruner-Bey.* Naples [?]: Fibreno.

Nietzsche, Friedrich 1983. *Untimely Meditations.* Trans. R. J. Hollingdale. Cambridge: Cambridge University Press.

Panizzardi, Mario 1914. *Wagner in Italia.* Genova: Palagi.

Panzacchi, Enrico 1872. *A Proposito del Tannhaeuser rappresentato a Bologna nell'autunno 1872.* Bologna: Nicola Zanichelli.

———. 1882. *A Giuseppe Garibaldi. Parole dette alla Associazione Progressista Costituzionale delle Romagne nell'adunanza dell'11 Giugno 1882.* Bologna: Tipografia Militare.

———. 1883. *Riccardo Wagner. Ricordi e studi.* Bologna: Zanichelli.

———. 1888. "L'ottavo centenario dello Studio bolognese," *NA* 99: 297–403.

———. 1895. *Nel Mondo della musica.* Florence: Sansoni.

———. 1900. *Parole di sdegno per il regicidio di Umberto I.* Florence.

———. 1901. *Commemorazione e pellegrinaggio nazionale alla tomba di SM Umberto I.* Rome.

———. 1908. *Conferenze e discorsi.* Milan: Cogliati.

———. 1910. *Poesie,* 2nd ed. Bologna: Zanichelli.

Pascoli, Giovanni 1910. "Prefazione," Panzacchi 1910: iii–xi.

Pepoli, Carlo 1862. *Il Vangelo di S.Matteo, volgarizzato in dialetto Bolognese dal Conte Carlo Pepoli.* London: Bonaparte.

———. 1871. *Del dramma musicale.* Bologna: Società tipografica dei compositori.

———. 1875. *Ricordanze Biografiche. Discorsi Accademici.* Bologna: Tipografica dei Compositori.

———. 1880. *Ricordanze Municipali. Discorsi di Carlo Pepoli.* Bologna: Tipografia Fava & Garagnani.

Pepoli, Gioacchino 1864. *Sulla politica di Napoleone III verso l'Italia. Memoria.* Milan: Alberti.

———. 1880. *Re e Popolo. Discorsi, lettere, scritti.* 2 vols. Bologna: Azzoguidi.

Pfitzner, Hans 1917. *Futuristengefahr. Bei Gelegenheit von Busoni's* [sic] *Ästhetik.* Leipzig and Munich: Süddeutsche Monatshefte.

R. D. 11 novembre 1885, n.3191. *Regolamento generale per la ricossione e pel conteggio della tassa d'ingresso nei Musei, nelle Gallerie, negli Scavi e nei Monumenti nazionali.*

Ricci, Corrado 1886. *Il Monumento a Vittorio Emanuele e La Piazza di Bologna.* Bologna: Fava & Garagnani.

———. 1888. *I Teatri di Bologna nei secoli XVII e XVIII. Storia aneddotica,* (repr. 1965). Bologna: Forni.

———. 1889. *Bologna e i Bolognesi.* Bologna: Monti.

———. 1924. *Riccordi Bolognesi* Bologna: Zanichelli.

Rilke, Rainer Maria 1929. *Briefe an einen jungen Dichter* (1998). Frankfurt / Main: Insel.

Romani, Felice 1888. "Alcuni cenni storici sull'arte musicale e della danza." In Bignami 1880: 5–12.

Rosmini, Enrico 1872. *La legislazione e la giurisprudenza dei teatri. Trattato dei diritti e delle obbligazioni degli impresari, artisti, autori, delle direzioni, del pubblico, degli agenti teatrali, ecc.* Milan: Manini.

Rousseau, Jean-Jacques 1993. *Essai sur l'origine des langues.* Ed. Catherine Kintzler. Paris: Flammarion.

Roux, Onorato 1901. *La Prima Regina d'Italia. Nella vita privata, nella vita del paese, nelle lettere e nelle arti.* Milan: Aliprandi.

Rubbiani, Alfonso 1981a. "Di Bologna riabbellita." In Solmi and Dezzi Bardeschi (eds) 1981: 603–15.

———. 1981b. "Prima relazione presentata al Comitato per Bologna Storica e Artistica per il restauro del complesso Palazzo Re Enzo—Podesta" (1908). In Solmi and Dezzi Bardeschi (eds) 1981: 251.

Saffi, Aurelio 1901. *Ricordi e Scritti pubblicati per cura del Municipio di Forlì.* Florence: Barbèra.

Sani, Sebastiano 1922. *Bologna di Ieri* 1983. Bologna: Arnaldo Forni.

Schünemann, Georg 1913. *Geschichte des Dirigierens.* Leipzig: Breitkopf und Härtel.

Segretariato Generale della Camera dei Deputati 1971. *La Politica Estera dell'Italia negli atti, documenti e discussioni parlamentari dal 1861 al 1914.* Ed. Giacomo Perticone. Rome: Grafica Editrice Romana.

Stendhal 1973. *Chroniques italiennes.* Paris: Gallimard.

Strang, John 1863. *Travelling notes in France, Italy, and Switzerland of an Invalid in search of health.* Glasgow: Robertson.

Torchi, Luigi 1890. *Riccardo Wagner.* Bologna: Zanichelli.

Trebbi, Oreste 1918. "Il Mefistofele di Arrigo Boito," *Vit.Citt.* 4, 9 (September): 231–42.

Tubertini, Ottavio 1871. "Cenni storici sul Museo Civico di Bologna." In Museo Civico di Bologna 1871.

Vatielli, Francesco 1921. *Cinquanta anni di vita musicale a Bologna (1850–1900).* Bologna: Cooperativa Tipografica Azzoguidi.

———. 1928. *Arte e Vita Musicale a Bologna.* New ed. 1976. 2 vols. Bologna: Arnaldo.

Veroli, Pietro s.a. *Cenni biografici del marchese Gioacchino Napoleone Pepoli.* (Archiginnasio 17. Biografie ed Elogi, Pepoli Gioacchino Napoleone, n.6, s.a.)

Vico, Giambattista 1953. *Opere.* Ed. Fausto Nicolini. Milan / Naples: Riciardi.

———. 1988. *On the Most Ancient Wisdom of the Italians.* Ithaca: Cornell University Press.

Wagner, Cosima 1976. *Die Tagebücher.* Munich: Piper.

Wagner, Richard 1873. *The Music of the Future.* Trans. E. Dannreuther. London: Schott.

———. 1887–88. *Gesammelte Schriften und Dichtungen.* 10 vols. Leipzig: Fritzsch.

Zanichelli, Domenico 1896. "Studio su Marco Minghetti." In Minghetti 1896: i–lxxix.

Zannoni, Antonio 1871. "Sugli Scavi della Certosa." In Museo Civico di Bologna.

SECONDARY SOURCES:

Abdullatif Ahmida, Ali 2005. "State and Class Formation and Collaboration in Colonial Libya." Ben-Ghiat and Fuller (eds) 2005: 59–71.

Accademia Filarmonica di Bologna 1966. *L'Accademia Filarmonica di Bologna 1660–1966.* Bologna.

Acerboni, Giovanni 2001. "Milano e il teatro, ovvero l'ambizione di essere esemplari." In Bigazzi and Meriggi (eds) 2001: 385–429.

Ackermann, Volker 2000. "Die Funerale Signatur." In Behrenbeck and Nützenadel (eds) 2000: 87–112.

Adamson, John (ed.) 1999. *The Princely Courts of Europe. Ritual, Politics and Culture under the Ancien Regime 1500–1750,* London: Weidenfeld & Nicholson.

Adamson, Walter L. 1993. *Avant-Garde Florence: From Modernism to Fascism.* Cambridge, MA: Harvard University Press.

———. 2001. "Avant-garde modernism and Italian Fascism: cultural politics in the era of Mussolini," *JMIS* 6 (2): 230–48.

Adani, Giuseppe and Bentini, Jadranka (eds) 1996. *Atlante dei Beni culturali dell'Emilia Romagna.* Milan: Silvana.

Adorno, Salvatore 1998. "Famiglie Commerciali e Notabili delle Professioni: Una Borghesia Locale." In Adorno (ed.) 1998: 129–56.

———. (ed.) 1998. *Siracusa. Identità e storia 1861–1915.* Palermo: Lombardi.

———. and Sorba, Carlotta (eds) 1991. *Municipalità e borghesie padane tra Ottocento e Novecento.* Milan: Angeli.

Af Malmborg, Mikael 2002. "The Dual Appeal of 'Europe' in Italy." In Af Malmborg and Stråth (eds) 2002: 51–75.

———. and Stråth, Bo (eds) 2002. *The Meaning of Europe. Variety and Contention within and among Nations.* Oxford: Berg.

Agazzi, Emilio 1980. "Benedetto Croce. Dalla revisione del marxismo al rilancio dell'idealismo." In Agazzi et al. 1980: 279–330.

———. et al. 1980. *Storia della società italiana.* Part 5, vol. 19: *La crisi di fine secolo.* Milan: Teti.

Agnelli, Arduino 1994. "L'idea di nazione all'inizio e nei momenti di crisi del secolo XX." In Spadolini (ed.) 1994: 15–36.

Agostiniani, Luciano 1993. "La conoscenzza dell'etrusco e delle lingue italiche negli studiosi italiani dell'ottocento." In Polverini (ed.) 1993: 31–77.

Agulhon, Maurice 1978. "'La statuomanie' et l'histoire," *EF* 8 (1): 143–72.

———. (ed.) 1998. *Histoire de la France Urbaine.* Vol. 4: *La ville de l'âge industriel* (1983). Paris: Seuil.

Aimo, Piero 1997. *Stato e poteri locali in Italia, 1848–1995.* Rome: La Nuova Italia Scientifica.

Akcan, Esra 2006. "Towards a Cosmopolitan Ethics in Architecture: Bruno Taut's Translation out of Germany," *NGC*, 99: 7–39.

Alaimo, Aurelio 1988. "Prima delle municipalizzazioni: Gas e Acqua a Bologna nella seconda metà dell'Ottocento (1846–1875)." In Berselli, Della Peruta and Varni (eds) 1988: 266–95.

———. 1990a. *L'organizzazione della città. Amministrazione e politica urbana a Bologna dopo l'Unità (1859–1889),* Bologna: Il Mulino.

———. 1990b. "Bologna." In ISAP 1990: 3–80.

———. 1992a. "La città assediata. Amministrazione comunale e finanze locali a Ferrara all'inizio del secolo (1900–1915)." In Mozzarelli (ed.) 1992: 23–76.

———. 1992b. "Società agraria e associazioni professionali a Bologna nell'Ottocento: Una proposta di ricerca." In Finzi (ed) 1992: 307–30.

Alatri, Paolo 1995. "Carducci e il Risorgimento," *Ris.* 47, 1/2: 102–9.

Albertazzi, Alessandro 1985. "Carducci *politico:* lo sviluppo della città." In Fasoli and Saccenti (ed.) 1985: 227–35.

———. 1986. "I sindaci di Bologna. Alberto Dallolio," *SSB,* 36: 11–22.

———. 1987. "I professori dell'Università di Bologna nella vita pubblica cittadina (1859–1889)," *SSB* 37: 27–60.

———. 1990. "I Sindaci di Bologna: Gioacchino Napoleone Pepoli," *SSB,* 40: 19–27.

Alberti, Carmelo 2002. "Teatro, musica e stagione teatrale." In Isnenghi and Woolf (eds) 2002: vol. 2, 1019–50.

Alliegro, Enzo Vinico 2003. "Il Flautista Magico. I Musicanti di Strada tra Identità debole e rappresentatzioni contraddittorie," *MEFRIM,* 115–1: 145–82.

Alonge, Roberto 1988. *Teatro e spettacolo nel secondo ottocento.* Rome and Bari: Laterza.

——. and Bonino, Guido Davico (eds) 2000. *Storia del teatro moderno e contemporaneo*. Vol. 2. Turin: Einaudi.

Alpers, Svetlana 1991. "The Museum as a way of seeing." In Karp and Lavine (eds) 1991: 25–32.

Anderson, Benedict 1991. *Imagined Communities: Reflections on the Origin and Spread of Nationalism*. Rev. ed. 1983. London: Verso.

Angelini, Franca 1988. *Teatro e spettacolo nel primo novecento*. Rome and Bari: Laterza.

Antolini, Bianca Maria 1994. "Rappresentazioni Rossiniane e dibattito critico in Italia nel decennio 1860–1870." In *La recezione di Rossini ieri e oggi*. 1994: 121–137.

Applegate, Celia 1990. *A Nation of Provincials: The German Idea of Heimat*. Berkeley: University of California Press.

——. 1999. "A Europe of Regions: Reflections on the Historiography of Sub-National Places in Modern Times," *AHR* 104, 4 (October): 1157–82.

——. 2005. *Bach in Berlin. Nation and Culture in Mendelssohn's Revival of the St Matthew Passion*. Ithaca / London: Cornell University Press.

Arbizzani, Luigi 1962. "La Camera del Lavoro di Bologna. Origini e primi anni di vita (1889–1900)," *MOS*, 8: 295–358.

Arendt, Hannah 1963. *On Revolution*. New York: Viking Press.

Arenhövel, Willmuth and Schreiber, Christa (eds) 1979. *Berlin und die Antike. Architektur, Kunstgewerbe, Malerei, Skulptur, Theater und Wissenschaft vom 16. Jahrhundert bis heute*. Berlin: Deutsches Archäologisches Institut.

Arrigoni, Giampiera 1988. "Autobiografia, religione e politica in Johann Jakob Bachofen." In Christ and Momigliano (eds) 1988: 119–44.

Artigas, Mariano; Glick, Thomas F.; Martínez, Rafael A. 2006. *Negotiating Darwin: The Vatican Confronts Evolution, 1877–1902*. Baltimore: Johns Hopkins University Press.

Ash, Mitchell G. 2002. "Wissenschaftspopularisierung und Bürgerliche Kultur im 19. Jahrhundert," *GG*, 28: 322–34.

Ashbrook, William 1988. "Boito and the 1868 Mefistofele. Libretto as a Reform Text." In Groos and Parker (eds) 1988: 268–87.

——. 1996. "The Nineteenth Century: Italy." In Parker (ed.) 1996: 114–37.

——. 2007. "Franco Faccio." In *Grove Music Online*. Ed. L. Macy, accessed 12 January 2007, http://www.grovemusic.com.

Asor Rosa, Alberto 1975. *La cultura*. (*Storia d'Italia*, vol. 4, tom. 2.) Turin: Einaudi.

Assmann, Jan 2000. *Das kulturelle Gedächtnis. Schrift, Erinnerung und politische Identität in frühen Hochkulturen*. Munich: Beck.

Atkinson, David 2005. "Constructing Italian Africa: Geography and Geopolitics." In Ben-Ghiat and Fuller (eds) 2005: 15–26.

Auerbach, Jeffrey A. 1999. *The Great Exhibition of 1851. A Nation on Display*. New Haven / London: Yale University Press.

Avellini, Luisa 1997. "Cultura e societa' in Emilia-Romagna." In Finzi (ed.) 1997: 649–99.

Bach Jensen, Richard 2004. "Daggers, Rifles and Dynamite: Anarchist Terrorism in Nineteenth-Century Europe." *TPV* 16, 1: 116–53.

Bagolini, Bernardino and Vitale, Daniele 1988. "La preistoria del territorio bolognese." In Morigi Govi and Vitali (eds) 1988: 81–109.

Baioni, Massimo 1994. *La 'Religione della Patria.' Musei e istituti del culto risorgimentale (1884–1918)*. Treviso: Pagus.

Bakhtin, Mikhail 1984. *Rabelais and His World*. (Trans. Hélène Iswolsky, 1968). Bloomington: Indiana University Press.

Ballini, Pier Luigi 1988. *Le elezioni nella storia d'Italia dall'Unità al fascismo. Profilo storico-statistico*. Bologna: il Mulino.

Balzani, Roberto 1987. "Politica e Gioco D'Azzardo: I circoli privati forlivesi del secondo ottocento." *BMR*, 32–33: 55–82.

———. 1997a. "Le tradizioni amministrative locali." In Finzi (ed.) 1997: 597–646.

———. 1997b. "'Filopanti all'ospedale lasciò Costa successor.' Mito del Risorgimento e politicizzazione della memoria: La 'fortuna' postuma di Quirico Filopanti." In Preti (ed.) 1997: 299–322.

Banti, Alberto M. 1989. *Terra e denaro. Una borghesia padana dell'Ottocento.* Venice: Marsilio.

———. 1990. "I proprietari terrieri nell'Italia centro-settentrionale." In Bevilacqua (ed.) 1990: 45–103.

———. 1994. "Note sulle nobiltà dell'Ottocento". *MRSS*, 19 (January): 13–27.

———. 1995. "Italian Professionals: Markets, Incomes, Estates and Identities." In Malatesta (ed.) 1995: 223–54.

———. 1996a. *Storia della borghesia italiana. L'età liberale.* Rome: Donzelli.

———. 1996b. "Redditi, patrimoni, identità." In Malatesta (ed.) 1996: 489–520.

———. 2000. *La nazione del Risorgimento. Parentela, santità e onore alle origini dell'Italia unita.* Turin: Einaudi.

———. 2002. "Le invasione barbariche e le origini delle nazioni." In Banti and Bizzocchi (eds) 2002: 21–44.

———. 2005. *Onore della nazione. Identità sessuale e violenza nel nazionalismo europeo.* Turin: Einaudi.

———. and Bizzocchi, Roberto (eds) 2002. *Immagini della nazione nell'Italia del Risorgimento.* Rome: Carocci editore.

———. and Ginsborg, Paul (eds) 2007. *Storia d'Italia.* Annali 22: *Il Risorgimento.* Turin: Einaudi.

———. and Meriggi, Marco 1991. "Premessa. Elites e associazioni nell' Italia dell'Ottocento." *QS* 26, 77, 2 (August): 357–62.

Barbanera, Marcello 2001. "Il sorgere dell'archeologia in Italia nella seconda metà dell'ottocento." *MEFRIM*, 113: 493–505.

Barblan, Guglielmo and Basso, Alberto (eds) 1977. *Storia dell'Opera.* Vol. 3, 1: *Aspetti e problemi dell'Opera.* Turin: UTET.

Barfield, Lawrence 1971. *Northern Italy before Rome.* London: Thames and Hudson.

Baroja, Julio Caro 1989. *Il carnevale.* Genova: Melangolo.

Barta, Peter I. (ed.) 2000. *Metamorphoses in Russian Modernism.* Budapest and New York: CEU Press.

Bartlett, Rosamund 1995. *Wagner and Russia.* Cambridge: Cambridge University Press.

Basini, Laura 2001. "Cults of sacred memory: Parma and the Verdi centennial celebrations of 1913." *COJ* 13, 2: 141–61.

Basso, Alberto 1976. *Storia del Teatro Regio di Torino.* Vol. 2. Turin: Cassa di risparmio.

———. 2001. "La musica." In Levra (ed.) 2001: 989–1006.

Battistini, Andrea 1986. "La cultura umanistica a Bologna." In Zangheri (ed.) 1986: 317–54.

———. 1997. "Lezioni all'area aperta. Claustofobia intellettuale e insegnante popolare." In Preti (ed.) 1997: 65–91.

Bauman, Zygmunt 1991. *Modernity and Ambivalence.* Oxford: Polity.

Baycroft, Timothy and Hewitson, Mark (eds) 2003. *What is a Nation? Europe 1789–1914.* Oxford: Oxford University Press.

Bazin, Germain 1967. *The Museum Age.* Brussels: Desoer.

Beard, Geoffrey 1978. *The Work of Robert Adam.* Edinburgh and London: John Bartholomew.

Beard, Mary; North, John; Price, Simon 1998. *Religions of Rome*. 2 vols. Cambridge: Cambridge University Press.

Beaumont, Antony 1985. *Busoni the composer*. London: Faber & Faber.

———. 2000. *Zemlinsky*. London: Faber & Faber.

Becker, Heinz and Gudrun 1989. *Giacomo Meyerbeer: A Life in Letters*. London: Helm.

Behrenbeck, Sabine and Nützenadel, Alexander (eds) 2000. *Inszenierungen des Nationalstaats. Politische Feiern in Italien und Deutschland seit 1860/71*. Cologne: SH-Verlag.

Bell, Duncan S. A. 2003. "Mythscapes: memory, mythology, and national identity." *BJS* 54, 1 (March): 63–82.

Bellamy, Richard 2002. "Social and political thought, 1890–1945." In Lyttelton (ed.) 2002: 233–48.

Bellocchi, Ugo 1977. "Il fenomeno giornalistico." In Berselli (ed.) 1976–1980: vol. 2, 339–59.

Benda, Julien 1927. *La trahison des clercs*. Paris: Grasset.

Ben-Ghiat, Ruth 2001. *Fascist Modernities. Italy, 1922–1945*. Berkeley: University of California Press.

———. and Fuller, Mia (eds) 2005. *Italian Colonialism*. New York: Palgrave Macmillan.

Benjamin, Walter 1955. *Schriften*. Frankfurt / Main: Suhrkamp.

———. 1970. *Illuminations*. Ed. H. Arendt, trans. H. Zorn. London: Cape.

Bennett, Tony 1988. "Museums and 'the people'." In Lumley (ed.) 1988: 63–86.

Berding, Helmut (ed.) 1994. *Nationales Bewußtsein und kollektive Identität. Studien zur Entwicklung des kollektiven Bewußtseins in der Neuzeit*. Frankfurt / Main: Suhrkamp.

Berger, Stefan 2005. "A Return to the National Paradigm? National History Writing in Germany, Italy, France, and Britain from 1945 to the Present," *JMH*, 77: 629–78.

Bergeron, Katherine 2002. "Verdi's Egyptian spectacle: On the colonial subject of *Aida*," *COJ*, 14: 1–2, 149–59.

Berghaus, Günter 1996. *Futurism and Politics. Between Anarchist Rebellion and Fascist Reaction, 1909–1944*. Providence: Berghahn.

Bergonzini, Luciano 1966. "L'Analfabetismo nell'Emilia-Romagna nel primo secolo dell'Unità," *Statistica* 26 (April-June): 279–393.

Berman, Marshall 1982. *All That is Solid Melts into Air*. London: Verso.

Bermond Montanari, Giovanna 1984. "La direzione dei Musei e degli Scavi e l'organizzazione degli uffici peiferici." In Morigi Govi and Sassatelli (eds) 1984: 55–59.

Bernabei, Giancarlo; Gresleri, Giuliano; Zagnomi, Stefano 1977. *Bologna moderna. 1860–1980*. Bologna: Pàtron.

Bernardini, Carla (ed.) 2004. *Pelagio Palagi alle collezioni comunali d'arte*. Ferrara: Edisai.

Bernardini, Paolo 1996. "The Jews in nineteenth-century Italy: towards a reappraisal," *JMIS* 1 (2): 292–310.

Berselli, Aldo 1963. *La Destra Storica dopo l'Unità. L'idea liberale e la Chiesa Cattolica*. Bologna: il Mulino.

———. 1980. "Primi decenni dopo l'Unità." In Berselli (ed.) 1976–1980: vol. 3, 257–304.

———. 1981. "Alfonso Rubbiani nella storia del movimento cattolico italiano," *SSB* 31: 27–46.

———. 2001. "Minghetti e la destra storica." In Marco Minghetti e le sue opere. Atti del convegno di Società Libera, Bologna 11 Novembre 2000. Bologna: Società Libera: 2001, 17–35.

———. (ed.) 1976–80. *Storia della Emilia Romagna.* 3 vols. Imola: Santerno.

Berselli, Aldo; Della Peruta, Franco; Varni, Angelo (eds) 1988. *La municipalizzazione nell'area padana.* Milan: Angeli.

Berti, Giampiero 2003. *Errico Malatesta e il movimento anarchico italiano e internazionale, 1872–1932.* Milan: Angeli.

Bertozzi, Elisabetta 1997. "L'edilizia civile medievale a Bologna. L'operato di Alfonso Rubbiani ed i suoi contemporanei nella Bologna del XIX secolo," *SSB* 48: 59–89.

———. 2000. "Sintesi sugli spazi pubblici e privati in Bologna dall'origine alla fine dell'Ottocento per una migliore lettura della città contemporanea," *SSB* 50: 93–133.

Bevilacqua, Piero (ed.) 1990. *Storia dell'Agricoltura italiana in età contemporanea.* Venezia: Marsilio.

Bhabha, Homi K. 1990. "Introduction: narrating the nation." In Bhabha (ed.) 1990: 1–7.

———. (ed.) 1990. *Nation and Narration.* London and New York: Routledge.

Biagi Ravenni, Gabriella 1992. "The French occupation of Lucca and its effects on music." In Boyd (ed.) 1992: 279–301.

Biagini, Mario 1961. *Il poeta della terza Italia. Vita di Giosuè Carducci.* Milano: Mursia.

Bianconi, Lorenzo and Pestelli, Giorgio 1987. *Storia dell'opera italiana.* Vol. 4: *Il sistema produttivo e le sue competenze.* Turin: EDT.

Bigaran, Mariapia 1986. "Introduzione." In Bigaran (ed.) 1986: 9–25.

———. (ed.) 1986. *Istituzioni e borghesie locali nell'Italia liberale.* Milan: Angeli.

Bigazzi, Duccio and Meriggi, Marco (eds) 2001. *La Lombardia. Storia d'Italia. Le regioni dall'Unità a oggi.* Turin: Einaudi.

Bignami, Paola 2002a. "L'edificio teatrale: acustica e funzionalità." In Alonge and Bonino (eds) 2000: 957–75.

———. 2002b. "L'edificio teatrale: estetica e razionalità." In Alonge and Bonino (eds) 2000: 977–96.

Bignardi, Agostino 1963. "Rubbiani Politico," *SSB* 13: 41–47.

Blair, Sara 1999. "Modernism and the politics of culture." In Levenson (ed.) 1999: 157–73.

Bloch, Ernst 1985. *Erbschaft dieser Zeit* (1935). (*Werkausgabe,* vol. 9.) Frankfurt / Main: Suhrkamp.

Blom, Ida; Hagemann, Karen; Hall, Catherine (eds) 2000. *Gendered Nations. Nationalisms and Gendered Order in the Long Nineteenth Century.* Oxford: Berg.

Blumenberg, Hans 1966. *Die Legitimität der Neuzeit.* Frankfurt / Main: Suhrkamp.

———. 1979. *Arbeit am Mythos.* Frankfurt / Main: Suhrkamp.

Bobbio, Noberto 1990a. "Teoria delle élites." In Bobbio et al. (eds) 1990: 350–56.

———. 1990b. *Profilo ideologico del '900.* Milan: Garzanti.

———. et al. (eds) 1990. *Dizionario di Politica.* Turin: Utet.

Bocquet, Denis 2001. "L'Archéologie à Rome après 1870," *MEFRIM,* 113, 2: 759–73.

———. 2004. "Moderniser la ville éternelle. Luttes politiques, rivalités institutionnelles et contrôle du territoire: Rome 1870–1900", *HU,* 9 (April): 97–104.

———. and De Pieri, Filippo 2002. "Public works and municipal government in two Italian capital cities: comparing technical bureaucracies in Turin and Rome, 1848–88," *MI*, 7: 143–52.

Bologna 1960. *Bologna e la cultura dopo l'Unità d'Italia*. Bologna: Zanichelli.

Borbein, Adolf Heinrich 1979. "Klassische Archäologie in Berlin vom 18. bis zum 20. Jahrhundert." In Arenhövel and Schreiber (eds) 1979: 99–150.

Bordone, Renato 1993. *Lo Specchio di Shalott. L'invenzione del Medioevo nella cultura dell'Ottocento*. Naples: Liguori.

Bosworth, Richard J. B. 1998. *The Italian Dictatorship: Problems and Perspectives in the Interpretation of Mussolini and Fascism*. London: Arnold.

Bourdieu, Pierre 1979. *La distinction. Critique sociale du jugement*. Paris: Les Editions de Minuit.

Boutry, Philippe 1988. "Società urbana e sociabilità delle élites nella Roma della Restaurazione: prime considerazioni," *Cheiron*, 9/10: 59–85.

Boyd, Malcolm (ed.) 1992. *Music and the French Revolution*. Cambridge: Cambridge University Press.

Braccesi, Lorenzo 1984. "Carducci e l'Etruria Padana." In Morigi Govi and Sassatelli (eds) 1984: 47–53.

Bracco, Giuseppe 2001. "La finanza comunale." In Levra (ed.) 2001: 527–45.

Bradbury, Malcolm and McFarlane, James (eds) 1991. *Modernism: A Guide to European Literature 1890–1930* (1976). London: Penguin.

Braun, Emily 2002. "The visual arts: modernism and Fascism." In Lyttelton (ed.) 2002: 196–215.

Brewer, John 1979. *The Pleasures of the Imagination: English Culture in the Eighteenth Century*. London: Harper Collins.

Brezzi, Paolo 1982. "Gli alleati italiani di Federico Barbarossa (feudatari e città')." In Manselli and Riedmann (eds) 1982: 157–97.

Brice, Cathérine 2001. "Antiquités, Archéologie et Construction nationale en Italie: quelques pistes de recherche," *MEFRIM*, 113, 2: 475–92.

———. 2002a. "*The King was pale:* Italy's National-Popular Monarchy and the Construction of Disasters 1882–1885." In Dickie, Foot, Snowden (eds) 2002: 61–79.

———. 2002b. "La Rome des Savoie après l'unité." In Charle and Roche (eds) 2002: 133–48.

———. 2005. *La monarchie italienne et la construction de l'identité nationale (1861–1911)*. Thèse de doctorat d'Etat, Institut d'Etudes Politiques de Paris, 2005, 3 vols.

Briquel, Dominique 1984. *Les Pélasges en Italie. Recherches sur l'histoire de la légende*. Rome: Ecole Française de Rome.

———. 1999. *La civilisation étrusque*. Paris: Fayard.

Brizzolara, Anna Maria 1984a. "Il Museo Universitario." In Morigi Govi and Sassatelli (eds) 1984: 159–66.

———. 1984b. "La gipsoteca e l'insegnamento dell'arheologia." In Morigi Govi and Sassatelli (eds) 1984: 465–74.

Brötel, Dieter 2002. "Die europäische und die asiatische Seidenindustrie 1860–1930. Modernisierung und Weltmarkteinbindung der Rohseideproduzenten China und Japan im Vergleich," *GG*, 28: 109–44.

Brunello, Piero 1998. "Pontida." Isenghi (ed.) 1998: 15–28.

Bruni, Silvia 2001. "Rapporti tra Stato e Municipio di Roma (1870–1911)," *MEFRIM*, 113, 2: 775–87.

Brunner, Otto; Conze, Werner; and Koselleck, Reinhart (eds) 1972–1997. *Geschichtliche Grundbegriffe: Historisches Lexikon zur politisch-sozialen Sprache in Deutschland*. 8 vols. Stuttgart: Klett-Cotta.

Buck, August 1989. "Der Beginn der modernen Renaissanceforschung im 19. Jahrhundert: Georg Voigt und Jacob Burckhardt." In Buck and Vasoli (eds) 1989: 23–36.
————. and Vasoli, Cesare (eds) 1989. *Il Rinascimento nell'Ottocento in Italia e Germania*. (Annali dell'Istituto storico italo-germanico in Trento, Contributi, 3). Bologna: il Mulino.
Budden, Julian 1981. *The Operas of Verdi*. Oxford and New York: Oxford University Press.
Burgio, Alberto (ed.) 1999. *Nel nome della razza. Il razzismo nella storia d'Italia. 1870–1945*. Bologna: il Mulino.
Burke, Peter 1978. *Popular Culture in Early Modern Europe*. London: Temple Smith.
Busch, Hans (ed.) 1978. *Verdi's Aida. The History of an Opera in letters and documents*. Minneapolis: University of Minnesota Press.
Buyens, Koen 2006. "Muziek en natievorming in België: het muziekleven te Brussel, 1830–1850," *BeM*, 121, 3: 393–417.
Cagli, Bruno 2001. "Stefano Gobatti." In Sadie (ed.) 2001: 65.
Calaresu, Melissa 1997. "Images of Ancient Rome in Late Eighteenth-Century Neapolitan Historiography," *JHI*, 641–61.
Calder III, William M. and Schlesier, Renate (eds) 1998. *Zwischen Rationalismus und Romantik. Karl Otfried Müller und die antike Kultur*. Hildesheim: Weidmann.
Calinescu, Matei 1987. *Five Faces of Modernity*. Durham: Duke University Press.
Calore, Marina 1981a. "Il fascino di un prestigio secolare: Alfonso Rubbiani segretario dell'Accademia Filarmonica di Bologna," *SSB*, 31: 91–111.
————. 1981b. "La musica a Bologna e Alfonso Rubbiani appendicista." In Solmi and Dezzi Bardeschi (eds) 1981: 579–85.
————. 1982. *Bologna a Teatro: l'Ottocento*. Bologna: Giudicini e Rosa.
————. 1988. "L'informazione teatrale. Pubblico e spettacolo nella stampa periodica tra Settecento e Ottocento," *SSB*, 38: 85–108.
————. 1998. "Dalle premesse giacobine alla rivoluzione del 1848." In Gavelli and Tarozzi (eds) 1998: 87–94.
Cammarano, Fulvio 1993. "Nazionalizzazione della politica e politicizzazione della nazione. I dilemmi della classe dirigente nell'Italia liberale." In Merggi and Schiera (eds) 1993: 139–63.
————. 1995a. "La costruzione dello stato e la classe dirigente." In Sabbatucci and Vidotto (eds) 1994–95: 3–111.
————. 1995b. "The Professions in Parliament." In Malatesta (ed.) 1995: 276–312.
————. 2002. "Le notable à l'époque libérale," *MEFRIM*, 114, 673–78.
————. 2004. *Storia politica dell'Italia liberale*. Rome and Bari: Laterza.
————. and Piretti, Maria Serena 1996. "I professionisti in Parlamento (1861–1958)." In Malatesta (ed.) 1996: 521–53.
Cammelli, Andrea 1995. "Universities and Professions." In Malatesta (ed.) 1995: 27–79.
————. and di Francia, Angelo 1996. "Studenti, università, professioni: 1861–1993." In Malatesta (ed.) 1996: 5–77.
Canfora, Luciano 1998. "La ricezione di K.O.Müller in Italia." In Calder III and Schlesier (eds) 1998: 151–85.
Cannadine, David 1983. "The Context, Performance and Meaning of Ritual: The British Monarchy and the 'Invention of Tradition,' c. 1820–1970." In Ranger and Hobsbawm (eds) 1983: 101–64.
————. 1992. *G.M.Trevelyan. A Life in History*. New York / London: Norton.
Capozza, Maria (ed.) 2002. *Garibaldi e l'antichità. Testi e dizionario storico*. (Da Roma alla Terza Roma. Documenti e Studi). Rome: La Sapienza.

372   *Bibliography*

Caracciolo, Alberto 1952. "Il movimento contadino nelle pagine della Critica Sociale," *Emilia*, 97–100.
———. 1973. *L'inchiesta agraria Jacini*. Turin: Einaudi.
———. 1976. "Crescita e potere della burocrazia dopo l'unificazione." In Cassese (ed.) 1976: 53–63.
———. 1977. *Stato e società civile. Problemi dell'unificazione italiana* (1960). Turin: Einaudi.
Caracciolo, Alberto; Cervelli, Innocenzo; Fohlen, Claude; Woolf, Stuart 1983. "L'Ombra dell'Ancien régime," *PeP*, 4: 11–33.
Caranti Martignago, Stefania 1995. *Un aspetto della archeologia ottocentsca: Pelagio Palagi e Eduard Gerhard*. Imola: Bologna University Press.
Cardoza, Anthony L. 1982. *Agrarian Elites and Italian Fascism: The Province of Bologna, 1901–1926*. Princeton, N J: Princeton University Press.
———. 1991. "Tra Casta e classe. Clubs maschili dell'élite torinese, 1840–1914," *QS*, 77: 363–88.
———. 1997. *Aristocrats in Bourgeois Italy: The Piemontese Nobility, 1861–1930*. Cambridge: Cambridge University Press.
Carpi, Umberto 1981. "Egemonia moderata e intellettuali nel Risorgimento." In Vivanti (ed.) 1981: 431–71.
Casalegno, Carlo 2001. *La regina Margherita*. Bologna: il Mulino.
Casali, Luciano (ed.) 1982. *Bologna 1920. Le origini del fascismo*. Bologna: Cappelli.
Casini, Paolo 1998. *L'antica sapienza italica. Cronistoria di un mito*. Bologna: il Mulino.
Cassese, Sabino (ed.) 1976. *L'amministrazione pubblica in Italia* (1974), Bologna, il Mulino.
Castelnuovo, Enrico and Sergi, Giuseppe (eds) 2004. *Arti e Storia nel Medioevo*. Vol. 4: *Il Medioevo al passato e al presente*. Turin: Einaudi.
Castelvecchi, Stefano 2006. "Was Verdi a 'Revolutionary'?," *JIH*, 36, 4: 615–20.
Castronuovo, Antonio and Medri, Sante (eds) 2003. *Il futurismo a Lugo*. Imola: La Mandragora.
Castronovo, Valerio (ed.) 1977. *Il Piemonte. Storia delle regioni italiane dall'Unità a oggi*. Turin: Einaudi.
Cattini, Marco 1997. "Le Emilie agricole al momento dell'Unità." In Finzi (ed.) 1997: 7–21.
Caullery, Maurice and Leroy, Jean F. 1965. "Theories of Evolution." In Taton (ed.) 1965: 472–79.
Cavaliero, Roderick 2005. *Italia Romantica: English Romantics and Italian Freedom*. London and New York: Tauris.
Cavazza, Giulio 1984. "Bologna dall'età napoleonica al primo Novecento (1796–1918)." In Ferri and Roversi (eds) 1984: 283–391.
———. 1997. "Il 'Rappresentante del popolo' nella Repubblica Romana." In Preti (ed.) 1997: 187–217.
———. and Bertondini, Alfeo 1976. *Luigi Tanari nella storia risorgimentale dell'Emilia-Romagna*. Bologna: Istituto per la storia di Bologna.
Cavazza, Stefano 1998. "Il regionalismo in una transizione di regime: 'La Pie' e l'identità culturale romagnola," *MeR*, 2: 77–99.
Cavazzana Romanelli, Francesca and Rossi Minutelli, Stefania 2002. "Archivi e biblioteche." In Isnenghi and Woolf (eds) 2002: vol. 2, 1081–122.
Cavina, Marco 2005. *Il sangue dell'onore. Storia del duello*. Rome and Bari: Laterza.
Cazzola, Franco 1997. "La richezza della terra. L'Agricoltura emiliana fra tradizione e innovazione." In Finzi (ed.) 1997: 51–112.

Cencetti, Giorgio 1962. "Giosuè Carducci nella Deputazione di Storia patria," *AMDSPR*, N. S., 9: 3–18.

Cesari, Carlo and Gresleri, Giuliano 1976. *Residenza operaia e città neo-conservatrice. Bologna caso esemplare.* Rome: Officina Ed.

Cerasi, Laura 2000. *Gli Ateniesi d'Italia. Associazioni di cultura a Firenze nel primo Novecento.* Milan: Angeli.

Cestaro, Gary P. (ed.) 2004. *Queer Italia: Same-Sex Desire in Italian Literature and Film.* New York: Palgrave Macmillan.

Chabod, Federico. 1951. *Storia della politica estera italiana, 1870–1896.* Bari: Laterza.

———. 1969. *Lezioni di metodo storico.* Rome and Bari: Laterza.

Chadwick, Owen 1998. *A History of the Popes, 1830–1914.* Oxford: Oxford University Press.

Chapman, Hugo; Henry, Tom; Plazzotta, Carol (eds) 2004. *Raphael from Urbino to Rome.* London: National Gallery.

Charle, Christophe 1990. *Naissance des "intellectuels" 1880–1900.* Paris: Les Editions de Minuit.

———. 1991. *Histoire sociale de la France au XIXe siècle.* Paris: Seuil.

———. 1994. *La République des Universitaires. 1870–1940.* Paris: Seuil.

———. 1996. *Les intellectuels en Europe au XIX siècle. Essai d'histoire comparée.* Paris: Seuil.

———. 2002. "Les théâtres et leurs publics. Paris, Berlin et Vienne. 1860–1914." In Charle and Roche (eds) 2002: 403–20.

———. and Roche, Daniel (eds) 2002. *Capitales culturelles Capitales symboliques. Paris et les expériences européennes.* Paris: Sorbonne.

Chiappini, Simonetta 2007. "La voce del martire. Dagli *evirati cantori* all'eroina romantica." In Banti and Ginsborg (eds) 2007: 289–328.

Choay, Françoise 1998. "Pensées sur la ville, arts de la ville." In Agulhon (ed.) 1998: 169–284.

Chorley, Patrick 1965. *Oil, Silk and Enlightenment. Economic Problems in XVIIIth Century Naples.* Naples: Istituto Italiano per gli Studi Storici.

Christ, Karl 1976. "Barthold Georg Niebuhr." In Wehler (ed.) 1971–82: vol. 6, 23–36.

———. and Momigliano, Arnaldo (eds) 1988. *L'Antichità nell'Ottocento in Italia e Germania.* (Annali dell'Istituto storico italo-germanico in Trento, Contributi 2.) Bologna: il Mulino.

Ciccarelli, Andrea 2001. "Dante and the Culture of Risorgimento: Literary, Political or Ideological Icon?" In Von Henneberg and Russell Ascoli (eds) 2001: 77–102.

Ciliberto, Michele 1989. "Interpretazioni del Rinascimento: Balbo e Romagnosi." In Buck and Vasoli (eds) 1989: 65–91.

Cioli, Monica 1993. "Ceti politici e modelli organizzativi alla ricerca di un nuovo equilibrio. Le associazioni costituzionali all'indomani della 'rivoluzione parlamentare' del 18 marzo 1876," *AFLET* 27: 427–60.

Clark, Martin 1977. *Antonio Gramsci and the Revolution that Failed.* London and New Haven: Yale University Press.

Clark, Timothy J. 1999. *Farewell to an Idea: Episodes from a History of Modernism.* London and New Haven: Yale University Press.

Clemens, Gabriele B. 2004. *Sanctus Amor Patriae. Eine vergleichende Studie zu deutschen und italienischen Geschichtsvereinen im 19. Jahrhundert.* Tübingen: Niemeyer.

Cole, Laurence (ed.) 2007. *Different Paths to the Nation: Regional and National Identities in Central Europe and Italy, 1830–70.* Basingstoke: Palgrave.

Coli, Daniela 1983. *Croce, Laterza e la cultura europea.* Bologna: il Mulino.

374   *Bibliography*

Colley, Linda 1992. *Britons. Forging the Nation 1707–1837.* New Haven and London: Yale University Press.

Collingwood, Robin G. 1999. *The Principles of History.* Ed. W. H. Dray and W. J. van der Dussen. Oxford: Oxford University Press.

Colliva, Paolo 1977. "Bologna dal XIV al XVIII secolo: 'governo misto' o signoria senatoria?" In Berselli (ed.) 1976–80: vol. 2, 13–35.

Colombo, Elisabetta 2005. *Come si governava Milano. Politiche publiche nel secondo Ottocento.* Milano: Franco Angeli.

Colombo, Paolo 1999. *Il Re d'Italia. Prerogative costituzionali e potere politico della Corona (1848–1922).* Milan: Angeli.

Confino, Alon 1997. *The Nation as a Local Metaphor: Württemberg, Imperial Germany, and National Identity, 1871–1918.* Chapel Hill: University of North Carolina Press.

———. 2001. "On Localness and Nationhood," *GHILB* 23, 2 (November): 7–27.

Connerton, Paul 1995. *How Societies Remember* (1989). Cambridge: Cambridge University Press.

Conti, Fulvio 1994. *I notabili e la macchina della politica. Politicizzazione e trasformismo fra Toscana e Romagna nell'età liberale.* Mandria, Bari and Rome: Lacaita.

———. 2000. *L'Italia dei democratici. Sinistra risorgimentale, massoneria e associazionismo fra Otto e Novecento.* Milan: Angeli.

———. 2003. "Massoneria e radicalismo in Europa dall'età dei Lumi alla Grande Guerra," *AFGF,* 39: 33–56.

Conze, Werner and Kocka, Jürgen 1985. "Einleitung." In Conze and Kocka (eds) 1985: 9–26.

———. (eds) 1985. *Bildungsbürgertum im 19. Jahrhundert.* Vol. 1: *Bildungssystem und Professionalisierung in internationalen Vergleichen.* Stuttgart: Klett.

Corbin, Alain (ed.) 1996. *L'invenzione del tempo libero (1850–1960).* Rome and Bari: Laterza.

Cornell, Timothy J. 1995a. *The beginnings of Rome: Italy and Rome from the Bronze Age to the Punic Wars (c. 1000–264 BC).* London: Routledge.

———. 1995b. "Ancient History and the Antiquarian Revisited: Some Thoughts on Reading Momigliano's *Classical Foundations.*" In Crawford and Ligota (eds) 1995: 1–14.

Corner, Paul 1974. *Il Fascismo a Ferrara.* Rome and Bari: Laterza.

———. 1979. "Fascist Agrarian Policy and the Italian Economy in the Inter-War Years." In Davis (ed.) 1979: 239–74.

———. 1986. "Liberalism, Pre-Fascism, Fascism." In: 11–20.

Cotta, Maurizio 1979. *Classe politica e parlamento in Italia.* Bologna: il Mulino.

Couvreur, Manuel (ed.) 1998. *La Monnaie wagnérienne.* Brussels: Gram-ULB.

Crane, Susan A. 2000. *Collecting and Historical Consciousness in Early Nineteenth-Century Germany.* Ithaca and London: Cornell University Press.

Crawford, Michael 1992. *The Roman Republic.* London: Fontana.

———. and Ligota, Carlotta R. (eds) 1995. *Ancient History and the Antiquarian: Essays in Memory of Arnaldo Momigliano.* London: Warburg Institute.

Crispolti, Enrico (ed.) 2001. *Futurismo 1909–1944. Arte, architettura, spettacolo, grafica, letteratura.* Milan: Mazzotta.

Cristofani, Mauro 1983. *La scoperta degli Etruschi. Archeologia e antiquaria nel '700.* Roma: CNR.

Cristofori, Franco 1985. "Giornali e giornalismo." In Fasoli and Saccenti (ed.) 1985: 219–26.

Croce, Benedetto 1891. *I teatri di Napoli. Secolo XV–XVIII.* Napoli: Pierro.

———. 1914. *La Letteratura della nuova Italia.* 2 vols. Bari: Laterza.

———. 1926. *Storia della storiografia italiana nel secolo decimono.* Bari: Laterza.

———. 1928. *Storia d'Italia*. Rome and Bari: Laterza.

———. 1953. *Giosuè Carducci, Studio Critico* (1910). Bari: Laterza.

———. 2001. *Teoria e storia della storiografia* (1915). Milano: Adelphi.

Crook, J. Mordaunt 1978. "Introduction." In Eastlake (ed.) 1978: 13–57.

Cuaz, Marco 1998. "L'identità ambigua: L'idea di 'nazione' tra storiografia e politica," *RSI* 101, 2: 573–641.

Cucchiella, Luisa 1993. "Bologna e i suoi prefetti dal 1882 al 1889." In Serio (ed.) 1993: 133–51.

Cuccoli, Maria Pia 1974–1975. "L'associazione costituzionale delle Romagne," *DSPR*, N. S., 25/26: 265–333.

Dahlhaus, Carl 1978a. *Schönberg und andere. Gesammelte Aufsätze zur Neuen Musik*. Mainz: Schott.

———. 1978b. "Oper." In Honegger and Massenkeil (eds) 1978: 105–19.

———. 1980. *Die Musik des 19. Jahrhunderts*. (*Neues Handbuch der Musikwissenschaft*, vol. 6.) Wiesbaden: Athenaion.

———. 1987. *Die Idee der absoluten Musik*. Kassel: Bärenreiter.

———. and Krummacher, Friedhelm 1996. "Historismus." In Fischer (ed.) 1998: vol. 4, 335–51.

Dahms, Sibylle 1998. "Ballet." In Fischer (ed.) 1998: vol. 9, 295–318.

Dalla Casa, Brunella 1987. "Associazionismo borghese ed emancipazione femminile a Bologna: Il comitato di propaganda per il miglioramento delle condizioni della donna (1890–1893)," *BMR*, 32/33: 145–65.

D'Angiolini, Piero and Pavone, Claudio 1973. "Gli Archivi." In *Storia d'Italia* 1973–76: vol. 5: 1 documenti, 2, 1661–94.

D'Attore, Pier Paolo 1986. "La Politica." In Zangheri (ed.) 1986: 63–188.

———. 1991. "Per un profilo delle classi dirigenti bolognesi." In Adorno and Sorba (eds) 1991: 87–113.

———. 1992. "La società agraria di Bologna nel novecento." In Finzi (ed) 1992: 235–72.

Daumard, Adeline 1987. *Les Bourgeois et la Bourgeoisie en France depuis 1815*. Paris: Aubier.

Davidoff, Leonore and Hall, Catherine 2002. *Family Fortunes: Men and Women of the English Middle Class 1780–1850* (1987). London: Routledge.

Davis, John A. 1979. "Introduction." In Davis (ed.) 1979: 11–30.

———. 1988. *Conflict and Control: Law and Order in Nineteenth-Century Italy*. London: Macmillan.

———. 1994. "Remapping Italy's Path to the Twentieth Century," *JMH* 66 (June): 291–320.

———. 2000. "Cultures of Interdiction: The Politics of Censorship in Italy from Napoleon to the Restoration." In Laven and Riall (eds) 2000: 237–56.

———. 2006a. *Naples and Napoleon: Southern Italy and the European Revolutions 1780–1860*. Oxford: Oxford University Press.

———. 2006b. "Opera and Absolutism in Restoration Italy, 1815–1860," *JIH* 36, 4 (Spring): 569–94.

———. (ed.) 1979. *Gramsci and Italy's Passive Revolution*. London: Croom Helm.

———. (ed.) 2000. *Italy in the Nineteenth Century*. Oxford: Oxford University Press.

———. and Ginsborg, Paul (eds) 1991. *Society and Politics in the Age of the Risorgimento. Essays in Honour of Denis Mack Smith*. Cambridge: Cambridge University Press.

D'Avray, David 1994. *Death and the Prince: Memorial Preaching before 1350*. Oxford: Clarendon Press.

Dean, Trevor 1995. "The Courts." In Kirshner (ed.) 1995: 136–51.

De Angelis, Marcello 1977. *Giuseppe Mazzini. Filosofia della musica.* Rimini: Guaraldi.
———. 1982. *Le carte dell'impresario: melodrama e costume teatrale nell'ottocento.* Firenze: Sassoni.
Deathridge, John 1992. "Wagner and the post-modern," *COJ,* 4, 2: 143–61.
———. and Dahlhaus, Carl 1984. *The New Grove Wagner.* London and Basingstoke: Macmillan.
Deathridge, John; Geck, Martin; Voss, Egon 1986. *Wagner Werk-Verzeichnis.* Mainz and London: Schott.
De Felice, Renzo 1965. *Mussolini il rivoluzionario, 1883–1920.* Turin: Einaudi.
De Giorgio, Michela 1992. *Le Italiane dall'Unità a Oggi. Modelli culturali e comportamenti sociali.* Rome and Bari: Laterza.
Degl'Innocenti, Maurizio 1999. "Socialismo e classe operaia." In Sabbatucci and Vidotto (eds) 1994–99: vol. 3, 135–98.
De Grand, Alexander J. 1978. *The Italian Nationalist Association and the Rise of Fascism in Italy.* Lincoln and London: University of Nebraska Press.
Della Peruta, Franco 1992a. *Momenti di Storia d'Italia fra '800 e '900.* Florence: Le Monnier.
———. 1992b. "Il Ducato di Parma nell'età di Maria Luigia." In Della Peruta 1992a: 44–85.
———. 1995. "Il mito del Risorgimento e l'estrema sinistra," *Ris.* 47, 1, 2: 32–70.
Della Seta, Fabrizio, 1993. *Italia e Francia nell'Ottocento. (Storia della Musica,* vol. 9.) Turin: EDT.
Delpino, Filippo 2001. "Paradigmi museali agli albori dell'Italia unita. Museo etrusco 'centrale,' museo italico, museo di Villa Giulia," *MEFRIM,* 113, 2: 623–39.
de Man, Paul 1984. *The Rhetoric of Romanticism.* New York: Columbia University Press.
———. 1993. *Romanticism and Contemporary Criticism.* Baltimore and London: Johns Hopkins University Press.
Dent, Edward J. 1974. *Ferruccio Busoni: A Biography.* London: Eulenburg.
De Pieri, Filippo 2005. *Il controllo improbabile. Progetti urbani, burocrazie, decisioni in una città capitale dell'Ottocento.* Milano: Franco Angeli.
Deputazione di Storia Patria per le Province di Bologna 1989. *La Deputazione di Storia Patria per le Province di Bologna: 125 anni dalla fondazione* (Documenti e Studi, 21). Bologna: Deputazione di Storia Patria.
Der Neue Pauly 1999–2003. *Rezeptions- und Wissenschaftsgeschichte.* Ed. Manfred Landfester. Stuttgart and Weimar: Metzler.
Derrida, Jacques 1995. *Mal d'Archive. Une impression freudienne.* Paris: Galilée.
Derrida, Jacques; Habermas, Jürgen; Borradori, Giovanna 2004. "Qu'est-ce que le terrorisme?," *MD* (February): 16–17.
Desittere, Marcel 1984. "Contributo alla storia della paletnologia italiana." In Morigi Govi and Sassatelli (eds) 1984: 61–85.
Détienne, Marcel 2005. "Histoire, mythologie, identité nationale. Un exercice comparatiste," *QdS* 31, 61 (Jan.–June): 5–24.
Dezzi Bardeschi, Marco 1979. "Introduzione." In Mazzei 1979: 3–16.
———. 1981. "Alfonso Rubbiani 'restauratore': quasi un'autoanalisi." In Solmi and Dezzi Bardeschi (eds) 1981: 33–48.
Díaz-Andreu, Margarita and Champion, Timothy (eds) 1996. *Nationalism and Archaeology in Europe.* London: UCL Press.
Dickie, John 1999. *Darkest Italy: The Nation and Stereotypes of the Mezzogiorno, 1860–1900.* Basingstoke: Macmillan.

———. 2002. "The Smell of Disaster: Scenes of Social Collapse in the Aftermath of the Messina-Reggio Calabria Earthquake, 1908." In Dickie, Foot, Snowden (eds) 2002: 235–55.

———. and Foot, John 2002. "Introduction." In Dickie, Foot, Snowden (eds) 2002: 3–56.

Dickie, John; Foot, John; Snowden, Frank M. (eds) 2002. *Disastro! Disasters in Italy since 1860: Culture, Politics, Society.* Basingstoke: Palgrave.

Dionisotti, Carlo 1988. "Arnaldo Momigliano e Croce," *Belfagor,* 43: 617–42.

———. 1989. "Rinascimento e Risorgimento: la questione morale." In Buck and Vasoli (eds) 1989: 157–69.

Dixon, Roger and Muthesius, Stefan 1985. *Victorian Architecture.* London: Thames and Hudson.

Douglas, Mary 1992. *Risk and Blame: Essays in Cultural Theory.* London: Routledge.

———. (ed.) 1982. *Essays in the Sociology of Perception.* London: Routledge.

Drake, Richard 1980. *Byzantium for Rome: The Politics of Nostalgia in Umbertian Italy, 1878–1900.* Chapell Hill: University of North Carolina Press.

———. 2003. *Apostles and Agitators: Italy's Marxist Revolutionary Tradition.* Cambridge, MA: Harvard University Press.

Dufour, Liliane 1998. "Problemi di Pianificazione Urbanistica a Siracusa tra 1880 e 1917." In Adorno (ed.) 1998: 231–48.

Duggan, Christopher 1997. "Francesco Crispi, 'political education' and the problem of Italian national consciousness, 1860–1896," *JMIS,* 2 (2): 141–66.

———. 2002. *Francesco Crispi: From Nation to Nationalism.* Oxford: Oxford University Press.

Dumézil, Georges 1970. *Archaic Roman Religion.* Chicago and London: University of Chicago Press.

Dunnage, Jonathan 1995. "Law and Order in Giolittian Italy: A Case Study of the Province of Bologna," *EHQ,* 25: 381–408.

Eastlake, Charles L. (ed.) 1978. *A History of the Gothic Revival.* Leicester: Leicester University Press.

Eco, Umberto 1984. "The frames of the comic 'freedom'." In Sebeok (ed.) 1984: 1–10.

Eder, Klaus 1997. "Institutionen." In Wulf (ed.) 1997: 159–68.

Edler, Markus 2001. *Der spektakuläre Sprachursprung. Zur hermeneutischen Archäologie der Sprache bei Vico, Condillac und Rousseau.* Munich: Fink.

Eggebrecht, Hans Heinrich 1991. *Musik im Abendland. Prozesse und Stationen vom Mittelater bis zur Gegenwart.* Munich: Piper.

Elias, Norbert 1999. *Über den Prozeß der Zivilisation. Soziogenetische und psychogenetische Untersuchungen.* (1969) Frankfurt / Main: Suhrkamp.

Elze, Reinhard and Schiera, Pierangelo (eds) 1988. *Italia e Germania. Immagini, modelli, miti fra due popoli nell'Ottocento.* Bologna: il Mulino.

Emiliani, Andrea 1973. "Musei e Museologia." In *Storia d'Italia* 1973–76: vol. 5: 1 documenti, 2: 1615–60.

Engels, Friedrich 1962. *Der Ursprung der Familie, des Privateigentums und des Staats.* MEW, vol. 21. Berlin: Dietz.

Etlin, Richard A. 1991. *Modernism in Italian Architecture, 1890–1940.* Cambridge, MA: MIT.

Everist, Mark 2005. *Giacomo Meyerbeer and Music Drama in Nineteenth-Century Paris.* Aldershot: Ashgate.

Fanti, Mario 1976. "Il concorso per la facciata di San Petronio nel 1933–1935," *Car.,* 2: 159–76.

———. 1981. "Alfonso Rubbiani: il restauro, la politica e la poesia," *SSB,* 31: 113–31.

Fasoli, Gina 1976. "Profilo storico dall'VIII al XV secolo." In Berselli, Aldo (ed.) 1976–80: vol. 1, 365–404.

———. 1982. "Aspirazioni cittadine e volontà imperiale." In Manselli and Riedmann (eds) 1982: 131–52.

———. 1984. "Gli archeologi nella Deputazione di Storia Patria per le provincie di Romagna." In Morigi Govi and Sassatelli (eds) 1984: 33–35.

———. 1989. "Premessa." In Deputazione di Storia Patria per le Province di Bologna 1989: 3–10.

———. and Saccenti, Mario (ed.) 1985. *Carducci e Bologna*. Bologna: Cassa di Risparmio.

Faucci, Riccardo 1976. "L'Osmosi tra politica e amministrazione nel primo trentennio unitario." In Cassese (ed.) 1976: 65–70.

Fedele, Francesco and Baldi, Alberto (eds) 1988. *Alle origini dell'antropologia italiana. Giustiniano Nicolucci e il suo tempo.* Naples: Guida.

Fehrenbach, Elisabeth 1971. "Über die Bedeutung der Politischen Symbole im Nationalstaat," *HZ*, 213 (2): 296–357.

Fellerer, Karl Gustav 1984. *Studien zur Musik des 19. Jahrhunderts.* Regensburg: Gustav Bosse.

Fernàndez, Henry Dietrich 1999. "The Patrimony of St. Peter: The Papal Court at Rome c. 1450–1700." In Adamson (ed.) 1999: 141–63.

Ferraboschi, Alberto 2003. *Borghesia e Potere Civico a Reggio Emilia nella seconda metà dell'ottocento.* Soveria Mannelli: Rubbettino.

Ferri, Antonio and Roversi, Giancarlo (eds) 1984. *Storia di Bologna* (1978). Bologna: Alfa.

Fincardi, Marco 1995. "La seccolarizzazione della festa urbana nel XIX secolo. L'immaginario del progresso dei Carnevali italiani e d'oltralpe," *MeR* 3, 5 (July): 11–27.

———. 2004. "Zwei Landpfarreien im Umbruch: Agrarmodernisierung in der Po-Ebene im Zeichen von politischer Konfrontation und Mentalitätswandel," *JMEH*, 2: 208–31.

Finelli, Pietro and Fruci, Gian Luca 2000. "L'Organizzazione della Politica nell'Italia Liberale: Due casi di studio," *SeS*, 88: 217–20.

Finley, Moses 1972. *Aspects of Antiquity: Discoveries and Controversies.* Harmondsworth: Penguin.

Finzi, Roberto 1990. "Lavoratori dell'incolto: i raccoglitori di canna in Val Padana." In Bevilacqua (ed.) 1990: 735–50.

———. 1997. "L'industria prima dell'industria." In Finzi (ed.) 1997: 23–50.

———. (ed.) 1992. *Fra studio, politica ed economia: La Società Agraria dalle origine all'età giolittiana. Atti del VI convegno.* Bologna: Istituto per la Storia di Bologna.

———. (ed.) 1997. *Storia d'Italia. Le regioni dall'Unità a oggi. L'Emilia-Romagna.* Turin: Einaudi.

———. and Tassinari, Franco 1986. "La società." In Zangheri (ed.) 1986: 191–244.

Firnkes, Manfred 1983. "Die Staufer in Geschichtsschreibung und Dichtung." In Pleticha (ed.) 1983: 337–46.

Fischer, Ludwig (ed.) 1998. *Die Musik in Geschichte und Gegenwart.* 2nd ed. Kassel: Bärenreiter.

Flasch, Kurt 1988. *Das philosophische Denken im Mittelalter. Von Augustin zu Machiavelli.* Stuttgart: Reclam.

Flora, Francesco 1960. "Il risorgimento e l'età Carducciana." In Bologna 1960: 41–123.

Fogu, Claudio 2003. *The Historic Imaginary: Politics of History in Fascist Italy.* Toronto: University of Toronto Press.

Foratti, Aldo 1940. "Commemorazione di Enrico Panzacchi. Parole dette nel centenario della sua nascità. Panzacchi oratore." *AMDSPR*, ser. 1, vol. 5, 1–5.

Forgacs, David. 1986a. "Why rethinking Italian Fascism?." In Forgacs (ed.) 1986: 1–10.

———. 1986b. "The Left and Fascism: Problems of Definition and Strategy." In Forgacs (ed.) 1986: 21–51.

———. (ed.) 1986. *Rethinking Italian Fascism: Capitalism, Populism and Culture*. London: Lawrence and Wishart.

Foschi, Paola 1997. "Il Complesso di Santo Stefano nella storia di Bologna." In Foschi et al. 1997: 7–26.

———. et al. 1997. *La Basilica di Santo Stefano a Bologna. Storia, arte e cultura*. Bologna: Gli Inchiostri Associati: 97–114.

Foucault, Michel 1966. *Les Mots et les Choses. Une archéologie des sciences humaines*. Paris: Gallimard.

Francfort, Didier 1988. "Nobili e borghesi al caffè: considerazioni sulla clientela dei caffè di Udine a metà del XIX secolo," *Cheiron*, 9/10: 133–47.

———. 2005. "Le crepuscule des Héros." Opéra et Nation après Verdi," *MEFRIM*, 117, 1: 269-93.

François, Etienne; Siegrist, Hannes; Vogel, Jacob (eds) 1995. *Nation und Emotion*. Göttingen: V&R.

Frandsen, Steen Bo 1998. "Le città italiane fra tradizione municipalistica e gerarchia nazionale durante il Risorgimento," *Meridiana*, 33 (November): 83–106.

Franzoni Gamberini, Lucetta 1961. "La morte del conte di Cavour in una corrispondenza fra Camillo Casarini e Ferdinando Pinelli," *SSB*, 9: 225–41.

Fraticelli, Vanna 1982. *Roma, 1914–1929: la città e gli architetti tra la guerra e il fascismo*. Rome: Officina.

Freitag, Sabine (ed.) 2003. *Exiles from European Revolutions. Refugees in Mid-Victorian England*. New York and Oxford: Berhahn.

Frevert, Ute 1993. "Il salotto." In Haupt (ed.) 1993: 127–37.

———. and Haupt, Heinz-Gerhard (eds) 1999. *Der Mensch des 20. Jahrhunderts*. Frankfurt / Main: Campus.

Fried, Robert C. 1963. *The Italian Prefects: A Study in Administrative Politics*. New Haven: Yale University Press.

Frisch, Walter 2005. *German Modernism: Music and the Arts*. Berkeley: University of California Press.

Fubini, Riccardo 1995. "The Italian League and the Policy of the Balance of Power at the Accession of Lorenzo de' Medici." In Kirshner (ed.) 1995: 166–99.

Furlan, Paola 1988. "Il servizio di nettezza pubblica a Bologna tra pubblico e privato (1890–1923)." In Berselli, Della Peruta, Varni (eds) 1988: 339–56.

Furon, Raymond 1965. "Geology." In Taton (ed.) 1965: 327–47.

Gabetti, Roberto 2001. "Architetture dell'eclettismo." In Levra (ed.) 2001: 319–40.

Gadamer, Hans Georg 1990. *Wahrheit und Methode. Grundzüge einer philosophischen Hermeneutik* (1960). Tübingen: Mohr.

Gaehtgens, Thomas W. 2002. "L'île des Musées à Berlin, symbole de la capitale de l'Empire allemand." In Charle and Roche (eds) 2002: 239–47.

Gal, Susan 2004. "A Semiotics of the Public/Private Distinction." In Scott and Keates (eds) 2004: 261–77.

Gall, Lothar 1990. "Stadt und Bürgertum im 19. Jahrhundert. Ein Problemaufriss." *HZ*, Beihefte (Neue Folge), vol. 12: 1–18.

Galli della Loggia, Ernesto 1998. *L'identità italiana*. Bologna: il Mulino.

Galzerano, Giuseppe 1988. *Gaetano Bresci. La vita, l'attentato, il processo e la morte del regicida anarchico*. Salerno: Galzerano editore.

Garin, Eugenio 1962. *La cultura italiana tra '800 e '900*. Bari: Laterza.

380   *Bibliography*

Garratt, James 2002. *Palestrina and the German Romantic Imagination: Interpreting Historicism in Nineteenth-Century Music.* Cambridge: Cambridge University Press.

Gavelli, Mirtide and Tarozzi, Fiorenza 1987. "*Anche sotto l'ombra dei cipressi*: La Società di cremazione a Bologna (1884–1914)". *BMR*, 32/33: 107–43.

———. and Tarozzi, Fiorenza (eds) 1998. *Risorgimento e Teatro a Bologna, 1800–1849.* Bologna: Pàtron.

Geertz, Clifford 1993a. *The Interpretation of Cultures* (1973). London: Fontana.

———. 1993b. *Local Knowledge: Further Essays in Interpretative Anthropology* (1983). London: Fontana.

Gellner, Ernest 1998. *Nations and Nationalism* (1983). Oxford: Blackwell.

Gentile, Emilio 1997. *La Grande Italia. Ascesa e declino del mito della nazione nel ventesimo secolo.* Milan: Mondadori.

———. 2003. *The Struggle for Modernity: Nationalism, Futurism, and Fascism.* Westport and London: Praeger.

———. 2006. *Politics as Religion.* Princeton, NJ and Oxford: Princeton University Press.

Gerbel, Christian et al. (eds) 1996. *Urbane Eliten und kultureller Wandel,* Vienna: Verlag für Gesellschaftskritik.

Gerhard, Anselm 2000. "*Kanon* in der Musikgeschichtsschreibung. Nationalistische Gewohnheiten nach dem Ende der nationalistischen Epoche." *AfM*, 57/1: 18–30.

Gerschenkron, Alexander 1962. *Economic Backwardness in Historical Perspective: A Book of Essays.* Camridge, MA: Harvard University Press.

Ghirelli, Antonio 1973. *Storia di Napoli.* Turin: Einaudi.

Ghisalberti, Carlo 1997. "Stato unitario e federalismo in Italia." In Janz, Schiera, Sigrist (eds) 1997: 93–105.

Gianni, Emilio 2006. *Liberali e democratici alle origini del movimento operaio italiano. I congressi delle società operaie italiane (1853–1893).* Milan: Pantarei.

Giannini, Massimo Severo 1976. "Caratteristiche degli enti locali." In Cassese (ed.) 1976: 493–95.

Giger, Andreas 1999. "Social control and the censorship of Giuseppe Verdi's operas in Rome (1844–1859)." *COJ*, 11, 3: 233–66.

Gigliozzi, Giovanni 1997. *Le regine d'Italia. La bella Rosina regina senza corona, Margherita l'ammaliatrice, Elena casalinga, Maria José la regina di maggio.* Rome: Newton & Compton.

Goldmann, Lucien 1959. *Le Dieu caché. Étude sur la vision tragique dans les Pensées de Pascal et dans le théâtre de Racine.* Paris: Gallimard.

Gombrich, Ernst 1986. *Aby Warburg: An Intellectual Biography* (1970). Oxford: Phaidon.

Goschler, Constantin 2004. "'Wahrheit' zwischen Seziersaal und Parlament. Rudolf Virchow und der kulturelle Deutungsanspruch der Naturwissenschaften." *GG*, 30: 219–49.

Gossett, Philip 1990. "Becoming a citizen: The Chorus in Risorgimento Opera." *COJ*, 2/1: 41–61.

Gottarelli, Elena 1976. "Ascesa e caduta di Alfonso Rubbiani, il 'cavalliere papista'." *Car.*, 2: 191–202.

———. 1977. "L'amara storia di Giuseppe Ceri, il censore dell'edilizia bolognese." *Il Carobbio* 3: 205–20.

———. 1985. "La salvaguardia dei monumenti medievali." In Fasoli and Saccenti (eds) 1985: 177–93.

Gramsci, Antonio 1971. *Selections from the Prison Notebooks of Antonio Gramsci*. Ed. Quentin Hoare and Geoffrey Nowell Smith. London: Lawrence and Wishart.
———. 1975. *Quaderni del Carcere*. 4 vols. *Edizione critica dell'Istituto Gramsci*. Ed. Valentino Gerratana. Turin: Giulio Einaudi.
———. 1987. *L'Ordine Nuovo, 1919–1920*. Ed. Valentino Gerratana and Antonio A. Santucci. Turin: Einaudi.
Gran-Aymerich, Eve 1998. *Naissance de l'archéologie moderne, 1789–1945*. Paris: CNRS.
———. 2001. *Dictionnaire biographique d'archéologie, 1789–1945*. Paris: CNRS.
Grange, Daniel J. 2005. "La Société Dante Aligheri et la défense de l'Haliamidà," *MEFRIM*, 117, 1, 261–67.
Grew, Raymond 2000. "Culture and Society, 1796–1896." In Davis (ed.) 2000: 206–34.
Griffin, Roger 2007. *Modernism and Fascism: The Sense of a Beginning under Mussolini and Hitler*. Basingstoke: Palgrave.
———. (ed.) 1995. *Fascism*. Oxford: Oxford University Press.
Groos, Arthur and Parker, Roger (eds) 1988. *Reading Opera*. Princeton, NJ: Princeton University Press.
Gualandi, Giorgio 1976. "La seconda età del ferro." In Berselli (ed.) 1976–80: vol. 1, 83–102.
Guarnieri Corazzol, Adriana 1988. *Tristano, mio Tristano: gli scrittori e il caso Wagner*. Bologna: il Mulino.
Gubin, Eliane and Van der Hoeven, Roland 1998. "Les premières manifestations wagnériennes à Bruxelles." In Couvreur (ed.) 1998: 1–24.
Guidi, Alessandro 1996. "Nationalism without Nation: the Italian case." In Díaz-Andreu and Champion (eds) 1996: 108–18.
Habermas, Jürgen 1987. *The Philosophical Discourse of Modernity: Twelve Lectures* (1985). Cambridge: Polity.
———. 1990. *Strukturwandel der Öffentlichkeit* (1961). Frankfurt / Main: Suhrkamp.
Hailey, Christopher 1986. "Die Vierte Galerie. Voraussetzungen für die Wiener Avantgarde um 1910." In Stephan and Wiesmann (eds) 1986: 242–47.
Halbwachs, Maurice 1968. *La Mémoire Collective*. Paris: PUF.
Hale Bellot, Hugh 1929. *University College London 1826–1926*. London: University of London Press.
Hall, Stuart 1996. "Introduction: Who needs Identity?." In Hall and Du Gay (eds) 1996: 1–17.
———. and Du Gay (eds) 1996. *Questions of Cultural Identity*. London: Sage.
Handelman, Don 1982. "Reflexivity in festival and other cultural events." In Douglas (ed.) 1982: 162–90.
Hardtwig, Wolfgang 1990. "Bürgertum, Staatssymbolik und Staatsbewußsein im Deutschen Kaiserreich 1871–1914." *GG*, 16, 3: 269–95.
Harris, Stefanie 2006. "Exposures: Rilke, Photography, and the City." *NGC*, 99, 3: 121–49.
Hart, Stephen and Miller, Nicola (eds) 2007. *When was Latin America Modern?* New York and London: Palgrave.
Haskell, Francis 1993. *History and its Images: Art and the Interpretation of the Past*. New Haven and London: Yale University Press.
Haupt, Heinz-Gerhard 1989. *Sozialgeschichte Frankreichs seit 1789*. Frankfurt / Main: Suhrkamp.
———. (ed.) 1993. *Luoghi quotidiani nella storia d'Europa*. Rome: Laterza.

Haupt, Heinz-Gerhard; Müller, Michael G.; Woolf, Stuart 1998. "Introduction." In Haupt, Müller, Woolf (eds) 1998: 1–21.

———. (eds) 1998. *Regional and National Identities in Europe in the Nineteenth and Twentieth Centuries*. The Hague: Kluwer.

Hay, Denys 1966. *Europe in the Fourteenth and Fifteenth Centuries*. London: Longman.

Hearder, Harry 1983. *Italy in the Age of the Risorgimento, 1790–1870*. London and New York: Longman.

Helbling, Hanno 1995. *Arrigo Boito. Ein Musikdichter der italienischen Romantik*. Munich: Piper / Schott.

Henke, Matthias 2005. "Bewegtheit und Bewegung." In Mauser and Schmidt (eds) 2005: 227–53.

Henningsen, Bernd and Beindorf, Claudia (eds) 1999. *Gemeinschaft. Eine zivile Imagination*. Baden-Baden: Nomos.

Herf, Jeffrey 1984. *Reactionary Modernism: Technology, Culture, and Politics in Weimar and the Third Reich*. New York: Cambridge University Press.

Hillebrecht, Frauke 1997. *Skandinavien—die Heimat der Goten? Der Götizismus als Gerüst eines nordisch-schwedischen Identitätsbewußtseins*. (Arbeitspapiere "Gemeinschaften.") Berlin: Humboldt-Universität.

Himmelfarb, Gertrude 1952. *Lord Acton: A Study in Conscience and Politics*. London: Routledge & Kegan Paul.

Hobsbawm, Eric 1989. *The Age of Revolution, 1789–1848* (1962). London: Abacus.

———. and Ranger, Terence (eds) 1983. *The Invention of Tradition*. Cambridge: Cambridge University Press.

Hoch, Christoph 2001. "Scrabrrrrraang! Sul programma e l'estetica letteraria del futurismo nel contesto europeo." In Crispolti (ed.) 2001: 75–88.

Hohendahl, Peter Uwe and Lützeler, Paul Michael (eds) 1979. *Legitimationskrisen des deutschen Adels 1200–1900*. Stuttgart: Metzler.

Honegger, Marc and Massenkeil, Günther (eds) 1978. *Das große Lexikon der Musik*. Freiburg: Herder.

Honigsheim, Paul 1973. *Music and Society*. New York: Wiley.

Horkheimer, Max and Adorno, Theodor W. 2001. *Dialectic of enlightenment* (1942). New York: Continuum.

Hornblower, Simon and Spawforth, Antony (eds) 2003. *The Oxford Classical Dictionary*. 3rd. ed. Oxford: Oxford University Press.

Hosking, Geoffrey 2001. *Russia and the Russians: A History*. London: Penguin.

Hübinger, Gangolf 1993. "Die Intellektuellen im wilhelminischen Deutschland." In Hübinger and Mommsen (eds) 1993: 198–210.

———. and Mommsen, Wolfgang J. (eds) 1993. *Intellektuelle im Deutschen Kaiserreich*. Frankfurt / Main: Fischer.

Hudson, Kenneth 1975. *A Social History of the Museum: What the Visitors Thought*. London and Basingstoke: Macmillan.

Huebner, Steven 1993. "Massenet and Wagner: Bridling the influence." *COJ*, 5/3: 223–38.

———. 1999. *French Opera at the Fin de Siècle: Wagnerism, Nationalism, and Style*. Oxford: Oxford University Press.

Hughes, Steven C. 1994. *Crime, Disorder and the Risorgimento: The Politics of Policing in Bologna*. Cambridge: Cambridge University Press.

Huizinga, Johan 1995. *De taak der cultuurgeschiedenis*. Ed. W. E. Krul. Groningen: Historische Uitgeverij.

Humphreys, Sally 2004. *The Strangeness of Gods: Historical Perspectives on the Interpretation of Athenian Religion*. Oxford: Oxford University Press.

Infelise, Mario 2002. "Venezia e il suo passato. Storie miti 'fole.'" In Isnenghi and Woolf (eds) 2002: vol. 2, 967–88.
Isabella, Maurizio 2003. "Italian exiles and British politics before and after 1848." In Freitag (ed.) 2003: 59–87.
———. 2006. "Exile and nationalism: The case of the *Risorgimento*," *EHQ*, 36/4: 493–520.
ISAP 1990. *Le riforme crispine*. Vol. 3, *Amministrazione locale*. Milan: Giuffrè.
Isler-Kerényi, Cornelia 1998. "K.O.Müllers Etrusker." In Calder III and Schlesier (eds) 1998: 239–81.
Isnenghi, Mario 1997. "La grande guerra." In Isnenghi (ed.) 1997a: 273–309.
———. 2004. *L'Italia in piazza. I luoghi della vita pubblica dal 1848 ai giorni nostri* (1994). Bologna: il Mulino.
———. 2005. *Le guerre degli italiani. Parole, immagini, ricordi 1848–1945*. Bologna: il Mulino.
———. (ed.) 1997a. *I luoghi della memoria. Strutture ed eventi dell'Italia unita*. Rome and Bari: Laterza.
———. (ed.) 1997b. *I luoghi della memoria. Personaggi e date dell'Italia unita*. Rome and Bari: Laterza.
———. (ed.) 1998. *I luoghi della memoria. Simboli e miti dell'Italia unita*. Rome and Bari: Laterza.
———. and Woolf, Stuart (eds) 2002. *Storia di Venezia. L'Ottocento e il novecento*. Rome: Istituto della Enciclopedia Italiana.
Istituto per la storia del Risorgimento 1968. *Clero e partiti a Bologna dopo l'Unitá*. Bologna: Istituto per la storia del Risorgimento.
Izenberg, Gerald N. 1979. "Die Aristokratisierung der bürgerlichen Kultur im 19. Jahrhundert." In Hohendahl and Lützeler (eds) 1979: 233–44.
Janik, Alan and Toulmin, Stephen 1973. *Wittgenstein's Vienna*. New York: Dee.
Janz, Oliver; Schiera, Pierangelo; Siegrist, Hannes (eds) 1997. *Centralismo e federalismo tra Ottocento e Novecento. Italia e Germania a confronto*. Bologna: il Mulino.
Jardin, André and Tudesq, André-Jean 1973. *La France des notables*. Paris: Seuil.
Jauss, Hans Robert 1970. "Literary History as a Challenge to Literary Theory." *New Literary History* 2, 1: 7–37.
———. 1989. *Studien zum Epochenwandel der ästhetischen Moderne*. Frankfurt / Main: Suhrkamp.
Jelavich, Peter 1985. *Munich and Theatrical Modernism. Politics, Playwriting, and Performance 1890–1914*. Cambridge, MA: Harvard University Press.
Jemolo, Arturo Carlo 1965. *Chiesa e Stato in Italia. Dalla Unificazione a Giovanni XIII*. Turin: Einaudi.
Jenkins, Jennifer 2003. *Provincial Modernity: Local Culture & Liberal Politics in Fin-de-Siècle Hamburg*. Ithaca: Cornell University Press.
Jocteau, Gian Carlo 1997. *Nobili e nobiltá nell'Italia unita*. Rome and Bari: Laterza.
Jones, Philip 1997. *The Italian City-State: From Commune to Signoria*. Oxford: Clarendon Press.
Jung, Ute 1974. *Die Rezeption der Kunst Richard Wagners in Italien*. Regensburg: Bosse.
Kaeser, Marc-Antoine 2002. "On the international roots of prehistory." *Antiquity*, 76: 170–77.
Kannonier, Reinhard 1984. *Zeitwenden und Stilwenden: Sozial- und geistesgeschichtliche Anmerkungen zur Entwicklungen der europäischen Kunstmusik*. Vienna: Böhlau.
———. 1987. *Bruchlinien in der Geschichte der modernen Kunstmusik*. Vienna: Böhlau.

384   Bibliography

———. 1992. "Gesellschaftliche Moderne und künstlerische Avantgarde." *Soc. Int.* (Beiheft 1: *Gesellschaft und Musik. Wege zur Musiksoziologie*), 115–30.
———. and Konrad, Helmut 1995. "Einleitung." In Kannonier and Konrad (eds) 1995: 7–16.
———. 1996. "Eliten, Konflikte und Symbole." In Gerbel et al. (eds) 1996: 7–16.
———. (eds) 1995. *Urbane Leitkulturen. Bologna, Leipzig, Linz, Lubljana 1890–1914.* Vienna: Verlag für Gesellschaftskritik.
Karbusicky, Vladimir 1995. *Wie Deutsch ist das Abendland? Geschichtliches Sendungsbewußtsein im Spiegel der Musik.* Hamburg: Von Bockel.
Karp, Ivan 1992. "Introduction: Museums and Communities: The Politics of Public Culture." In Karp, Mullen Kreamer, Lavine (eds) 1992: 1–18.
———. and Lavine, Steven D. (eds) 1991. *Exhibiting Cultures: The Poetics and Politics of Museum Display.* Washington: Smithsonian Institute.
Karp, Ivan; Mullen Kreamer, Christine; Lavine, Steven D. (eds) 1992. *Museums and Communities: The Politics of Public Culture.* Washington: Smithsonian Institute.
Kelikian, Alice 1996. "Science, gender and moral ascendancy in liberal Italy." *JMIS* I (3): 377–89.
Kernig, C. D. (ed.) 1968. *Sowjetsystem und Demokratische Gesellschaft. Eine vergleichende Enzyklopädie.* Freiburg: Herder.
Kertzer, David 1988. *Ritual, Politics, and Power.* New Haven and London: Yale University Press.
Kimbell, David 1991. *Italian Opera.* Cambridge: Cambridge University Press.
Kirk, Terry 2005. *The Architecture of Modern Italy. Vol. 1: The Challenge of Tradition, 1750–1900.* New York: Princeton Architecture Press.
Kirshner, Julius (ed.) 1995. *The Origins of the State in Italy, 1300–1600.* Chicago and London: University of Chicago Press.
Kneif, Tibor 1971. *Musiksoziologie.* Cologne: Gerig.
Knight, David M. 1998. *Science in the Romantic Era.* Aldershot: Ashgate.
Kocka, Jürgen 1988. "Bürgertum und bürgerliche Gesellschaft im 19.Jahrhundert. Europäische Entwicklungen und deutsche Eigenarten." In Kocka (ed.) 1988: vol. 1, 11–76.
———. 1989. "Bildungsbürgertum—Gesellschaftliche Formation oder Historikerkonstrukt?" In Kocka (ed.) 1989: 9–21.
———. 1995. "The Middle Classes in Europe." *JMH* 67 (December): 783–806.
———. (ed.) 1988. *Bürgertum im 19. Jahrhundert. Deutschland im europäischen Vergleich.* 3 vols. Munich: dtv.
———. (ed.) 1989. *Bildungsbürgertum im 19. Jahrhundert. Vol. 4: Politischer Einfluß und gesellschaftliche Formation.* Stuttgart: Klett.
——— and Macry, Paolo; Romanelli, Raffaele; Salvati, Mariuccia 1990. "Borghesie, ceti medi, professioni," *PeP* 9: 21–51.
König, Christoph and Lämmert, Eberhard (eds) 1999. *Konkurrenten in der Fakultät. Kultur, Wissen und Universität um 1900.* Munich: Fischer.
Köpping, Klaus-Peter 1997. "Fest." In Wulf (ed.) 1997: 1048–65.
Körner, Axel 1996a. "Bürgerliche Öffentlichkeit in Bologna. Soziale und politische Bedingungen urbaner Leitkulturen nach der italienischen Einigung." In Gerbel et al. (eds) 1996: 17–83.
———. 1996b. "Vom Campanilismo zur Europäischen Avantgarde. Bolognas Leitkulturen und das Teatro Comunale." In Gerbel et al. (eds) 1996: 85–120.
———. 1997. *Das Lied von einer anderen Welt. Kulturelle Praxis im französischen und deutschen Arbeitermilieu, 1840–1890.* Frankfurt / Main: Campus.
———. 1999. "Gemeinschaft durch kulturelle Hegemonie. Konzeptionen sozialer Wirklichkeit bei Tönnies und Gramsci." In Henningsen and Beindorf (eds) 1999: 63–82.

———. 2003. "The Theater of Social Change. Opera and Society in Bologna after Italian Unification." *JMIS*, 8, 3, 341–369.

———. 2005. "Local Government and the Meanings of Political Representation: A Case Study of Bologna between 1860 and 1915." *MI*, 10, 2 (November): 137–62.

———. 2007. "Per una svolta culturale e transnazionale." *Contemporanea* 10, 2 (April): 308–12.

———. (ed.) 2000. *1848: A European Revolution? International Ideas and National Memories of 1848*. Basingstoke: Macmillan.

Koselleck, Reinhart 1984. "Revolution." In Brunner et al. (eds) 1972–92: vol. 5, 653–788.

———. 1989. *Vergangene Zukunft. Zur Semantik geschichtlicher Zeiten*. Frankfurt / Main: Suhrkamp.

———. 1992. *Kritik und Krise. Zur Pathogenese der bürgerlichen Welt* (1959). Frankfurt / Main: Suhrkamp.

———. 2002. *The Practice of Conceptual History*. Stanford, CA: Stanford University Press.

———. 2006. "Crisis." *JHI*, 67, (April): 357–400.

———. (ed.) 1990. *Bildungsbürgertum im 19. Jahrhundert*. Vol. 2, Stuttgart: Klett.

———. and Jeismann, Michael (eds) 1994. *Der politische Totenkult. Kriegerdenkmäler in der Moderne*. Munich: Fink.

Koshar, Rudy 1986. *Social Life, Local Politics, and Nazism. Marburg, 1880–1935*. Chapel Hill and London: University of North Carolina Press.

Kretschmer, Winfried 1999. *Geschichte der Weltausstellungen*. Frankfurt / Main: Campus.

Kroll, Thomas 2005. *La Rivolta del Patriziato. Il liberalismo della nobilità nella Toscana del Risorgimento*. Florenz: Olschki.

Kuhn, Thomas S. 1970. *The Structure of Scientific Revolutions*. 2nd ed. Chicago: University of Chicago Press.

Lacombe, Hervé 2001. *The Keys to French Opera in the Nineteenth Century*. Berkeley and Los Angeles: University of California Press.

La reccezione di Rossini ieri e oggi 1994. Atti dei Convegni Lincei, 110. Rome: Accademia Nazionale dei Lincei.

Large, David C. and Weber, William (eds) 1984. *Wagnerism in European Culture and Politics*. Ithaca and London: Cornell University Press.

Laven, David 2003. "Italy: The Idea of the Nation in the Risorgomento and Liberal Eras." In Baycroft and Hewitson (eds) 2003: 255–71.

———. and Riall, Lucy (eds) 2000. *Napoleon's Legacy: Problems of Government in Restoration Europe*. Oxford: Berg.

Lenzi, Deanna 1977. "Il luogo teatrale." In Berselli (ed.) 1976–80: vol. 2, 731–51.

Léon, Pierre (ed.) 1978. *Histoire économique et sociale du monde*. Vol. 4. Paris: Armand Colin.

Lepsius, Rainer M. 1973. "Parteiensystem und Sozialstruktur: zum Problem der Demokratisierung der deutschen Gesellschaft" (1966). In Ritter (ed.) 1973: 56–80.

Lequin, Yves 1978. "Les hiérarchies de la richesse et du pouvoir." In Léon 1978: 299–354.

———. 1998. "Les citadins, les classes et les luttes sociales." In Agulhon (ed.) 1998: 491–590.

Lescure, Jean-Claude 1993. "Les enjeux du souvenir: le monument national à Giuseppe Mazzini." *RHMC*, 40 (2): 177–201.

Levenson, Michael (ed.) 1999. *The Cambridge Companion to Modernism*. Cambridge: Cambridge University Press.

386 Bibliography

Levi, Lionello 1987. "Due secoli di vita musicale." In Trezzini (ed.) 1987: vol. 1, 1–44.

Levine, Philippa 1986. *The Amateur and the Professional: Antiquarians, Historians and Archaeologists in Victorian England, 1838–1886*. Cambridge: Cambridge University Press.

Levra, Umberto 1992. *Fare gli Italiani. Memoria e celebrazione del Risorgimento*. Turin: Comitato di Torino dell'Istituto per la storia del Risorgimento italiano.

———. 1997. "Vittorio Emanuele II." In Isnenghi (ed.) 1997b: 47–64.

———. (ed.) 2001. *Storia di Torino*. Vol. 7. Turin: Einaudi.

Levy, Carl 1998. "Charisma and social movements: Errico Malatesta and Italian anarchism." *MI*, 3 (2), 205–17.

———. 2001. "The people and the professors: socialism and the educated middle class in Italy, 1870–1915." *JMIS* 6 (2): 195–208.

———. 2004. "Anarchism, Internationalism and Nationalism in Europe, 1860–1939." *AJPH*, 50, 3: 330–42.

———. (ed.) 1996. *Italian Regionalism: History, Identity and Politics*. Oxford: Berg.

Liakos, Antonis 1995. *L'Unificazione Italiana e La Grande Idea. Ideologia e azione dei movimenti nazionali in Italia e Grecia, 1859–1871*. Florence: Aletheia.

Lidtke, Vernon 1985. *The Alternative Culture: Socialist Labor in Imperial Germany*. New York: Oxford University Press.

Lill, Rudolf and Matteucci, Nicola (eds) 1980. *Il liberalismo in Italia e in Germania dalla rivoluzione del '48 alla prima guerra mondiale*. (Annali dell'Istituto storico italo-germanico. Quaderno 5.) Bologna: il Mulino.

Lindon, John 1998. "Del Conte Carlo Pepoli," *Raccordo*, 5, 18–22.

Lipparini, Lilla 1942. *Minghetti*. 2 vols. Bologna: Zanichelli.

Liva, Alberto 1992. "Amministrazione e società a Pavia nell'età giolittiana: dalla Giunta 'popolare' di Pietro Pavesi a quella del 'buon governo' di Emilio Franchi Maggi." In Mozzarelli (ed.) 1992: 139–218.

Lodolini, Elio 2001. *Storia dell'archivistica italiana. Dal mondo antico alla metà del secolo XX*. Milan: Angeli.

Lotti, Luigi 1980. "La vita politica tra Ottocento e Novecento," In Berselli (ed.) 1976–80: vol. 3, 305–28.

Löwith, Karl 1986. *Mein Leben in Deutschland vor und nach 1933. Ein Bericht* (1940). Stuttgart: Metzlersche Verlagsbuchhandlung.

Lucchese, Vincenzo 1996. *Vasi. Idee da Pelagio Palagi*. Trento: Temi.

Luciani, Francesco 1997. "La 'Monarchia popolare.' Immagine del re e nazionalizzazione delle masse negli anni della sinistra a potere (1876–91)." *Cheiron*, 19, 141–88.

Lumley, Robert (ed.) 1988. *The Museum Time-Machine: Putting Cultures on Display*. London: Routledge.

———. and Morris, Jonathan (eds) 1997. *The New History of the Italian South: The Mezzogiorno Revisited*. Devon: Exeter University Press.

Lützeler, Paul Michael 1988. "Bürgerkriegs-Literatur. Der historische Roman im Europa der Restaurationszeit (1815–1830)." In Kocka (ed.) 1988: vol. 3, 232–56.

Luzzatto, Sergio 1998. *Il corpo del duce*. Turin: Einaudi.

Lyttelton, Adrian 1973. *The Seizure of Power: Fascism in Italy 1919–1929*. London: Weidenfeld and Nicholson.

———. 1991. "The middle classes in liberal Italy." In Davis and Ginsborg (eds) 1991: 217–50.

———. 1996. "Shifting Identities: Nation, Region and the City." In Levy (ed.) 1996: 33–52.

———. 2001. "Creating a National Past: History, Myth and Image in the Risorgimento." In Russell Ascoli and Von Henneberg (eds) 2001: 27–74.

―――. (ed.) 2002. *Liberal and Fascist Italy. 1900–1945.* Oxford: Oxford University Press.

Macedo, Catharine 1998. "Between opera and reality: the Barcelona Parsifal." *COJ*, 10, 1: 97–109.

Mack Smith, Denis 1957. *Garibaldi.* London: Hutchinson.

―――. 1969. *Italy: A Modern History.* New ed. Ann Arbor: University of Michigan Press.

―――. 1989. *Italy and its Monarchy.* New Haven: Yale University Press.

―――. 1994. *Mazzini.* New Haven: Yale University Press.

Macry, Paolo 1984. "Borghesie, città e stato. Appunti e impressioni su Napoli. 1860–1880." *QS*, 56: 339–83.

―――. 1990. "Borghesie, ceti medi, professioni." *PeP* 9, 22: 23–35.

―――. 2002a. *Ottocento. Famiglia, élites e patrimoni a Napoli* (1988). Bologna: il Mulino.

―――. 2002b. *I Giochi dell'incertezza. Napoli nell'ottocento.* Naples: l'Ancora.

Maehder, Jürgen 2007. "Franchetti, Baron Alberto" and "Asrael." In *Grove Music Online.* Ed. L. Macy, accessed 5 April 2007: http://www.grovemusic.com.

Maestri, Gian Matteo 1984. "Bologna tra clericalismo e radicalismo: una politica di 'notabili'." In Pombeni (ed.) 1984: 181–208.

Mainardi, Matteo 2004. "Il Catalogo Generale delle edizioni G.Ricordi & C. Una prima analisi del gusto musicale di fine Ottocento." In Sorba (ed.) 2004: 221–42.

Malatesta, Maria 1978. *Il Resto del Carlino. Potere politico ed economico a Bologna dal 1885 al 1922.* Milan: Guanda.

―――. 1989. *I signori della terra. L'organizzazione degli interessi agrari padani (1860–1914).* Milan: Angeli.

―――. 1997. "Il Caffè e l'Osteria." In Isnenghi (ed.) 1997a: 53–66.

―――. 1999. *Le aristocrazie terriere nell'Europa contemporanea.* Rome and Bari: Laterza.

―――. 2006a. *Professionisti e gentiluomini. Storia delle professioni nell'Europa contemporanea.* Turin: Einaudi.

―――. 2006b. "Le professioni e la città. Bologna 1860–1914." *SeS*, 111: 51–111.

―――. (ed.) 1995. *Society and the Professions in Italy, 1860–1914.* Cambridge: Cambridge University Press.

―――. (ed.) 1996. *Storia d'Italia.* Annali 10: *I professionisti.* Turin: Einaudi.

Malraux, André 1951. *Les voix du silence.* Paris: La Pleiade.

Manacorda, Daniele 1982. "Per un'indagine sull'archeologia italiana durante il ventennio fascista." *AM*, 9, 443–70.

Mandrioli Bizzarri, Anna Rita and Meconcelli Notarianni, Gioia 1984. "L'attività e la vita del Museo attraverso le carte d'archivio." In Morigi Govi and Sassatelli (eds) 1984: 407–28.

Manera, Giogio and Pugliese, Giuseppe (eds) 1982. *Wagner in Italia.* Venice: Marsilio.

Mann, Michael 2004. *Fascists.* Cambridge: Cambridge University Press.

Mann, Thomas 1979. *Tagebücher 1918–1921.* Ed. Peter de Mendelssohn. Frankfurt / Main: Fischer.

Manselli, Raoul and Riedman, Josef (eds) 1982. *Federico Barbarossa nel dibattito storiografico in Italia e Germania.* Bologna: il Mulino.

Mansuelli, Guido A. 1979. "The Etruscan City." In Ridgway, D. and F. (eds) 1979: 353–71.

―――. 1984. "L'archeologia Etrusco-italica a Bologna." In Morigi Govi and Sassatelli (eds) 1984: 41–45.

Marabini Moevs, Maria Teresa 1971. *Fra marmo patrio e archeologia. L'antichità nella vita e nell'opera di Giosuè Carducci.* Bologna: Cappelli.

388   Bibliography

Marcelli, Umberto 1989. "La Deputazione di Storia Patria per le province di Romagna nel centoventicinquesimo anno: studi sull'età moderna." In Deputazione di Storia Patria per le province di Romagna 1989: 45–53.

Marchetti, Gaetano 1981. "Il Comitato per Bologna Storica e Artistica." In Solmi and Dezzi Bardeschi (eds) 1981: 567–69.

Martin, George 1979. "Verdi and the Risorgimento." In Weaver and Chusid (eds) 1979: 13–41.

Martin-Fugier, Anne 2003. Les salons de la IIIe République. Art, littérature, politique. Paris: Perrin.

Marx, Karl and Engels, Friedrich 1962. Die deutsche Ideologie. MEW, vol. 3. Berlin: Dietz.

Mascilli Migliorini, Luigi 1988. "Municipalizzazione e decentramento nel dibattito dell'Italia pregiolittiana." In Berselli, Della Peruta, Varni (eds) 1988: 43–57.

Masetti, Maria Luisa and Branchetta, Fulvia 1981. "Due profili: Azzolini e Collamarini." In Solmi and Dezzi Bardeschi (eds) 1981: 245–47.

Masini, Pier Carlo 1981. Storia degli anarchici italiani nell'epoca degli attentati. Milan: Rizzoli.

Masulli, Ignazio 1980. Crisi e trasformazione: strutture economiche, rapporti sociali e lotte politiche nel bolognese (1880–1914). Bologna: Istituto per la storia di Bologna.

Mauser, Siegfried and Schmidt, Mathias (eds) 2005. Geschichte der Musik im 20. Jahrhundert: 1900–1925. Laaber: Laaber.

Mayer, Arno 1981. The Persistence of the Old Régime: Europe to the Great War. London: Croom Helm.

Mayer, Hans 1978. Richard Wagner in Bayreuth, 1876–1976. Frankfurt / Main: Suhrkamp.

Mazzei, Otello 1979. Alfonso Rubbiani—La Maschera e il volto della città. Bologna 1879–1913. Bologna: Cappelli.

Mazzonis, Filippo 2001. "Uomini e gruppi politici a Palazzo di Città." In Levra (ed.) 2001: 433–526.

———. 2003. La Monarchia e il Risorgimento. Bologna: il Mulino.

McClellan, Andrew 1994. Inventing the Louvre: Arts, Politics, and the Origins of the Modern Museum in Eighteenth-Century Paris. Cambridge: Cambridge University Press.

Meinecke, Friedrich 1969. Weltbürgertum und Nationalstaat (1907). Ed. Hans Herzfeld. Munich: Oldenbourg.

Melis, Guido 1996. Storia dell'amministrazione italiana. Bologna: il Mulino.

Mengozzi, Dino 1999. "Obseques laiques et mouvement ouvrier en Italie." In Unfried (ed.) 1999: 231–48.

Meriggi, Marco 1988. "Italienisches und deutsches Bürgertum im Vergleich." In Kocka (ed.) 1988: vol. 1, 141-59.

———. 1992. Milano Borghese. Circoli ed élites nell'Ottocento. Venice: Marsilio.

———. 1994. "Societa,' istituzioni e ceti dirigenti." In Sabbatucci and Vidotto (eds) 1994–99: vol. 1, 119–228.

———. 1997. "Centralismo e federalismo in Italia. Le aspettative preunitarie." In Janz, Schiera and Siegrist (eds) 1997: 49–63.

———. 2000a. "State and Society in Post-Napoleonic Italy." In Laven and Riall (eds) 2000: 49–63.

———. 2000b. "Soziale Klassen, Institutionen und Nationalisierung im liberalen Italien." GG, 26: 201–18.

———. 2001. "Lo 'Stato di Milano' nell'Italia unità: miti e strategie politiche di una società civile (1860–1945)." In Bigazzi and Meriggi (eds) 2001: 5–49.

―――. and Schiera, Pierangelo (eds) 1993. *Dalla città alla nazione. Borghesie ottocentesche in Italia e in Germania*. Bologna: il Mulino.

Mesini, Candido 1979. "L'inaugurazione del monumento a Luigi Galvani in Bologna, 9 novembre 1879." *SSB*, 29: 243–60.

Mila, Massimo 1979. *Letture delle Nozze di Figaro. Mozart e la ricerca della felicità*. Turin: Einaudi.

Miller, Marion S. 1984. "Wagnerism, Wagnerians and Italian Identity." In Large and Weber (eds) 1984: 167–97.

Miller, Nicola 2007. *Reinventing Modernity in Latin America: Intellectuals Imagine the Future*. New York and London: Palgrave.

Momigliano, Arnaldo 1966a. *Terzo Contributo alla storia degli studi classici e del mondo antico*. Rome: Ed. di Storia e Letteratura.

―――. 1966b. "Roman 'Bestioni' and Roman 'Eroi' in Vico's Scienza Nuova." In Momigliano 1966a: 153–77.

―――. 1966c. "Tesi per una discussione sugli studi classici in Italia e i loro problemi metodici." In Momigliano 1966a: 803–05.

―――. 1966d. *Studies in Historiography*. London: Weidenfeld & Nicolson.

―――. 1966e. "Ancient History and the Antiquarian" (1950). In Momigliano 1966c: 1–39.

―――. 1972. "Tradition and the Classical Historian." *HaT*, 11, 3: 279–93.

―――. 1979. *Contributo alla storia degli studi classici* (1955). Roma: Storia e Letteratura.

―――. 1984. *Settimo Contributo alla Storia degli studi classici e del mondo antico*. Rome: Ed. di Storia e Letteratura.

―――. 1988a. "Introduzione." In Christ and Momigliano (eds) 1988: 9–20.

―――. 1988b. "Bachofen tra misticismo e antropologia." In Christ and Momigliano (eds) 1988: 99–118.

―――. 1992a. "Benedetto Croce" (1950). In Momigliano 1992b: 531–41.

―――. 1992b. *Nono Contributo alla Storia degli Studi Classici e del Mondo Antico*. Ed. di Riccardo di Donato. Rome: Ed. di Storia e Letteratura.

Montroni, Giovanni 1996. "Un rapporto difficile: nobiltà e professioni." In Malatesta (ed.) 1996: 411–35.

Moore, Barrington 1966. *Social Origins of Dictatorship and Democracy: Lord and Peasant in the Making of the Modern World*. Boston: Beacon Press.

Morabito, Pierfrancesco 1988. "Divertimento e élites sociali a Bologna nella prima metà dell'Ottocento: la Società del Casino." *Cheiron*, 9/10, 169–91.

Morelli, Giovanni 1998. "L'Opera." In Isnenghi (ed.) 1998: 43–113.

Morgan, Philip 2004. *Italian Fascism, 1915–1945*. Basingstoke: Palgrave.

Mori, Giorgio 1986. "Dall'unità alla guerra: aggregazione e disgregazione di un'area regionale." In Mori (ed.) 1986: 1–342.

―――. (ed.) 1986. *La Toscana. Storia d'Italia. Le regioni dall'Unità a oggi*. Turin: Einaudi.

Morigi Govi, Cristina 1976. "La prima età del ferro." In Berselli 1976–80: vol. 1, 63–81.

―――. 1984a. "Antonio Zannoni: dagli scavi della Certosa alle 'arcaiche abitazioni'." In Morigi Govi and Sassatelli (eds) 1984: 243–54.

―――. 1984b. "Il Museo Civico del 1871." In Morigi Govi and Sassatelli (eds) 1984: 259–67.

―――. 1984c. "Il Museo Civico del 1881." In Morigi Govi and Sassatelli (eds) 1984: 347–58.

―――. 1988. "La Storia del Museo." In Morigi Govi and Vitali (eds) 1988: 1–12.

―――. (ed.) 1996. *Il sepolcro villanoviano Benacci. Storia di una ricerca archeologica*. Bologna: Museo Civico Archeologico.

390   Bibliography

———. and Sassatelli, Giuseppe (eds) 1984. *Dalla Stanza delle Antichità al Museo Civico. Storia della formazione del Museo Civico Archeologico di Bologna.* Bologna: Grafis.

———. and Vitali, Daniele (eds) 1988. *Il museo civico archeologico di Bologna.* Bologna: University Press.

Morris, Jonathan 2002. "Traders, taxpayers, citizens: the lower middle classes from Liberalism to Fascism." *MI*, 7, 2: 153–69.

Mosca, Gaetano 1974. *Gaetano Mosca e la teoria della classe politica.* Ed. Ettore A. Albertoni. Florence: Sansoni.

Mosse, George L. 1975. *The Nationalization of the Masses: Political Symbolism and Mass Movements in Germany from the Napoleonic Wars through the Third Reich.* New York: Fertig.

———. 1985. *Nationalism and Sexuality.* New York: Fertig.

Mosse, Werner 1988. "Adel und Bürgertum im Europa des 19.Jahrhunderts. Eine vergleichende Betrachtung." In Kocka (ed.) 1988: vol. 2, 276–314.

Mozzarelli, Cesare (ed.) 1992. *Il governo della città nell'Italia giolittiana. Proposte di storia dell'amministrazione locale.* Trento: Reverdito.

Münster, Robert 2007. "Frank, Ernst." In *Grove Music Online.* Ed. L. Macy, accessed 12 January 2007: http://www.grovemusic.com.

Musella, Luigi 1995. "Professionals in Politics: Clientelism and Networks." In Malatesta (ed.) 1995: 313–36.

———. 2003. *Il trasformismo.* Bologna: il Mulino.

Museo Civico di Bologna 1976. *Pelagio Palagi, artista e collezionista.* Bologna: Grafis.

Musil, Robert 1990. *Der Mann ohne Eigenschaften* (1930). Hamburg: Rowohlt.

Musso, Stefano (ed.) 1999. *Tra fabbrica e società. Mondi operai nell'Italia del Novecento.* (Annali Feltrinelli, 33). Milan: Feltrinelli.

Nasto, Luciano 1994. *Le Feste Civili a Roma nell'Ottocento.* (Istituto per la Storia del Risorgimento Italiano: Risorgimento. Idee e Realtà. N.S., 19.) Rome: Gruppo Editoriale Internazionale.

Nesselrath, Arnold 2004. "Raphael and Pope Julius II." In Chapman, Henry, Plazzotta (eds) 2004: 280–93.

Neumann, Jens 2004. "Der Adel im 19. Jahrhundert in Deutschland und England im Vergleich." *GG*, 30: 155–82.

Niccolai, Nadi 1995. "'Contro il numero ignorante e proletario.' Proporzionalismo e riforma elettorale in Italia (1870–1882)." *PeP* 13: 79–99.

Nicolaisen, Jay 1980. *Italian opera in transition, 1871–1893.* Ann Arbor: UMI Research Press.

Nippel, Wilfried 1990. "Methodendiskussion und Zeitbezüge im althistorischen Werk Max Webers." *GG*, 16, 3: 355–74.

Nipperdey, Thomas 1995. *Deutsche Geschichte 1866–1918.* 2 vols. Munich: Beck.

O'Connor, Maura 1998. *The Romance of Italy and the English Imagination.* Basingstoke and London: Macmillan.

Oexle, Otto Gerhard 1985. "Alteuropäische Voraussetzungen des Bildungsbürgertums—Universitäten, Gelehrte und Studierte." In Conze and Kocka (eds) 1985: vol. 1, 29–78.

Olender, Maurice 1989. *Les langues du Paradis. Aryens et Sémites: un couple providential.* Paris: Gallimard.

Onofri, Nazario Sauro 1980. *La strage di Palazzo D'Accursio. Origine e nascita del fascismo bolognese 1919–1920.* Milan: Feltrinelli.

————. 1988. "Il dibattito sui servizi publici al consiglio comunale di Bologna negli ultimi decenni del secolo scorso." In Berselli, Della Peruta, Varni (eds) 1988: 492–523.

Orata, Niobe Alvisi 1968. "I partiti politici a Bologna dopo l'avvento della sinistra al potere (1876–1882)." In Istituto per la storia del Risorgimento 1968: 65–111.

Oteri, Annunziata Maria 2005. "Memorie e trasformazioni nel processo di ricostruzione di Messina dopo il terremoto del 1908." *SU*, 106/107: 13–64.

Ozouf, Mona 1976. *La fête révolutionnare 1789–1799*. Paris: Seuil.

Palazzolo, Maria Iolanda 1984. *I Salotti di Cultura nell'Italia dell'Ottocento*. Rome: La Goliardica.

Pallottino, Massimo 1957. "Scienza e poesia alla scoperta dell'Etruria." *Quaderni ACI*, 24: 5–22.

————. 1975. *The Etruscans*. Rev. ed. Bloomington & London: Indiana University Press.

Pancaldi, Giuliano 1986. "Gli scienziati, i filosofi, la città." In Zangheri (ed.) 1986: 355–87.

Paret, Peter 1980. *The Berlin Secession: Modernism and its Enemies in Imperial Germany*. Cambridge, MA: Harvard University Press.

————. 1988. *Art as History: Episodes in the Culture and Politics of Nineteenth-Century Germany*. Princeton, NJ : Princeton University Press.

Paris, Robert 1973. "L'Italia fuori d'Italia." In *Storia d'Italia* 1973–76: vol. 1, 509–818.

Parker, Roger 1988. "On Reading Nineteenth-Century Opera: Verdi through the Looking Glass." In Groos and Parker (eds) 1988: 288–305.

————. 1989. *Studies in Early Verdi, 1832–1844. New Information and Perspectives on the Milanese Musical Milieu and the Operas from Oberto to Ernani*. New York and London: Garland.

————. 1997a. *'Arpa d'or dei fatidici vati.' The Verdian patriotic chorus in the 1840s*. Parma: Istituto Nazionale di Studi Verdiani.

————. 1997b. *Leonora's Last Act: Essays in Verdian Discourse*. Princeton, NJ: Princeton University Press.

————. (ed.) 1996. *The Oxford History of Opera*. Oxford: Oxford University Press.

————. and Smart, Mary Ann (ed.) 2001. *Reading Critics Reading: Opera and Ballet Criticism in France from the Revolution to 1848*. Oxford: Oxford University Press.

Parmentola, Carlo 1977. "L'Opera come fatto di costume." In Barblan and Basso (eds) 1977: 439–520.

Partner, Peter 1972. *The Lands of St Peter: The Papal State in the Middle Ages and the Early Renaissance*. London: Eyre Methuen.

Pasini, Gian Franco 1980. "La letteratura dalla scuola carducciana a Longanesi." In Berselli (ed.) 1976–80: vol. 3, 991–1009.

Pasolini, Pier Paolo 2005. "Il romanzo delle stragi" (1974). In *Album Pasolini*. Milan: Mondadori: 116–30.

Passerini, Luisa 1991. *Mussolini immaginario*. Rome and Bari: Laterza.

Patriarca, Silvana 1996. *Numbers and Nationhood: Writing Statistics in Nineteenth-Century Italy*. Cambridge: Cambridge University Press.

Pécout, Gilles 1990. "Les sociétés de tir dans l'Italie unifiée de la seconde moitié du XIX siècle." *MEFRIM*, 102, 2: 533–676.

————. 1995. "Feste unitarie e integrazione nazionale nelle campagne toscane (1859–1864)." *MeR* 3, 5 (July): 65–81.

————. 1997. *Naissance de l'Italie contemporaine (1770–1922)*. Paris: Nathan.

Penny, Glenn 1995. "The Museum für Deutsche Geschichte and German National Identity." *CEH*, 28 (3): 343–72.

———. 1998. "Municipal Displays. Civic self-promotion and the development of German ethnographic museums, 1870–1914." *SocAnth*, 6, 2: 157–68.

———. 1999. "Fashioning Local Identities in an Age of Nation-Building: Museums, Cosmopolitan Visions and Intra-German Competition." *GH*, 17, 4: 489–505.

Perazzo, Giorgio 1983. "Wagner e il Wagnerismo a Bologna." *SSB*, 33: 191–207.

Peretti, Burton W. 1989. "Democratic Leitmotivs in the American Reception of Wagner." *NCM*, 13, 1: 28–38.

Perfetti, Francesco 2001. "Futurismo e fascismo, una lunga storia." In Crispolti (ed.) 2001: 33–51.

Perkin, Harrold 1989. *The Rise of Professional Society—England since 1880*. London and New York: Routledge.

Perlmutter, Sholem 1952. *Yiddishe Dramaturgen un Teater-Compositors*. New York: Yiddisher Kultur Farband.

Pernicone, Nunzio 1993. *Italian Anarchism, 1864–1892*. Princeton, NJ: Princeton University Press.

Perrino, Folco 1992–96. *Giuseppe Martucci*. 3 vols. Novara: Centro Studi Martucciani.

Petersen, Jens 1990. "Der italienische Adel von 1861 bis 1946." In Wehler (ed.) 1990: 243–59.

Petri, Rolf 2003a. "Die 'kleinen Räume der Nation." *QFIAB*, 83: 288–307.

———. 2003b. "The Meanings of *Heimat*." In Robin and Stråth (eds) 2003: 307–32.

Petronio, Giuseppe 1970. *L'attività letteraria in Italia. Storia della letteratura*. Milan: Palumbo.

Piazzoni, Irene 2004. "Il governo e la politica per il teatro: tra promozione e censura (1882–1900)." In Sorba (ed.) 2004: 61–100.

Pick, Daniel 1989. *Faces of Degeneration: A European Disorder, c. 1848–c. 1918*. Cambridge: Cambridge University Press.

Pietrow-Ennker, Bianka 2005. "Wirtschaftsbürger und Bürgerlichkeit im Königreich Polen: das Beispiel von Lodz, dem 'Manchester des Ostens'." *GG* 31: 169–202.

Piretti, Maria Serena and Guidi, Giovanni (eds) 1992. *L'Emilia Romagna in Parlamento, 1861–1919*. 2 vols. Bologna: Centro Ricerche di storia politica.

Piromalli, Antonio 1988. *Introduzione a Carducci*. Rome and Bari: Laterza.

Pivato, Stefano 1987. "Associazionismo sportivo e associazionismo politico nella Romagna d'inizio Novecento." *BMR*, 32, 33: 167–93.

Plato 1952. *Laws*. Vol. 1. (The Loeb Classical Library.) Cambridge, MA and London: Heinemann.

Pleticha, Heinrich (ed.) 1983. *Deutsche Geschichte*, II, 3: *Die Staufische Zeit 1152–1254*. Gütersloh: Bertelsmann.

Poirrier, Philippe 1990. "Politique Culturelle et Municipalité: Un discourse explicite? L'exemple de Dijon (1919–1989)." *Cahiers de l'Institut d'Histoire du Temps Present*. (Les Politiques Culturelles Municipales. Eléments pour une approche historique.) 16 (September): 11–40.

Pollard, John F. 2005. *Money and the Rise of the Modern Papacy: Financing the Vatican, 1850–1950*. Cambridge: Cambridge University Press.

Polsi, Alessandro 1984. "Possidenti e nuovi ceti urbani: l'élite politica di Pisa nel ventennio post-unitario." *QS*, 56: 493–516.

———. 1986. "Comuni e controlli: Il ruolo e la funzione delle deputazioni provinciali dalla legge comunale del 1865 alla Riforma Crispina." In Bigaran (ed.) 1986: 112–24.

Polverini, Leandro (ed.) 1993. *Lo studio storico del mondo antico nella cultura italiana dell'ottocento.* Naples: Edizioni Scientifiche Italiane.

Pombeni, Paolo 1984. "All'origine della 'forma partito' moderna. La vicenda delle organizzazioni politiche in Emilia-Romagna (1876–1892)." In Pombeni (ed.) 1984: 9–34.

———. 1993. *Autorità sociale e potere politico nell'Italia contemporanea.* Venezia: Marsilio.

———. 1995. "La rappresentanza politica." In Romanelli (ed.) 1995: 73–124.

———. (ed.) 1984. *All'origine della "forma partito" contemporanea. Emilia Romagna 1876–1892: un caso di studio.* Bologna: il Mulino.

Pomian, Krzysztof 1990. *Collectors and Curiosities: Paris and Venice, 1500–1800.* Oxford: Polity.

———. 1997. "Histoire culturelle, histoire des sémiophores." In Rioux and Sirinelli (eds) 1997: 73–100.

———. 1999. *Sur l'histoire.* Paris: Le Seuil.

Pompeati, Arturo 1950. "Rapporti con Gobineau." In Varjo (ed.) 1950: 47–53.

Ponziani, L. (ed.) 2000. *Le Italie dei notabili: il punto della situazione.* Naples: Edizioni Scientifiche Italiane.

Poppi, Claudio (ed.) 1996. *Pelagio Palagi pittore: dipinti dalle raccolte del Comune di Bologna.* Milano: Electa.

———. (ed.) 1998. *L'Ombra di Core. Disegni dal fondo Palagi della Biblioteca dell'Archiginnasio.* Bologna: Grafis.

Porciani, Ilaria 1981. "Sociabilità culturale ed erudizione storica in Toscana tra Otto e Novecento." *AISIG,* 7: 105–42.

———. 1988. "Il medioevo nella costruzione dell'Italia unita: la proposta di un mito." In Elze and Schiera (eds) 1988: 163–91.

———. 1993. "Stato, Statue, Simboli: I Monumenti Nazionali a Garibaldi e a Minghetti del 1895." *SAC. Annali ISAP,* 1: 211–42.

———. 1995. "Lo Statuto e il Corpus Domini. La festa nazionale dell'Italia liberale." *Ris.* 47, 1/2: 149–73.

———. 1996. "L'effimero di Stato." In Varni (ed.) 1996: vol. 2, 337–60.

———. 1997a. *La festa della nazione. Rappresentazione dello Stato e spazi sociali nell'Italia unita.* Bologna: il Mulino.

———. 1997b. "Identità locale—identità nazionale: la costruzione di una doppia appartenenza." In Janz, Schiera, Siegrist (eds) 1997: 141–84.

———. 2000. "Kirchlicher Segen für den Staat. Das Verfassungsfest in Italien von 1851 bis zum ersten Weltkrieg." In Behrenbeck and Nützenadel (eds) 2000: 45–65.

———. 2002. "Fêtes et célébrations dans les trois capitales italiennes." In Charle and Roche (eds) 2002: 45–60.

Porisini, Giorgio 1978. *Bonifiche e agricoltura nella bassa valle padana (1860–1915).* Studi e Ricerche di Storia Economica Italiana nell'età del Risorgimento. Milan: Banca Commerciale Italiana.

Pöschl, Wolfgang 1939. *Arrigo Boito, ein Vertreter der italienischen Spätromantik.* Berlin: Ebering.

Prayon, Friedhelm 1999a. "Etruskerrezeption." In *DNP* 1999–2003: vol. 13, 1050–53.

———. 1999b. "Etruskologie." In *DNP* 1999–2003: vol. 13, 1054–57.

———. 2001. *Die Etrusker.* Munich: Beck.

Preti, Alberto 1992. "La società agraria nella seconda metà dell'ottocento e il dibattito sull'industria e sul credito." In Finzi (ed.) 1992: 273–306.

———. 1997. "Filopanti politico." In Preti (ed.) 1997: 11–49.

———. (ed.) 1997. *Un democratico del Risorgimento: Quirico Filopanti.* Bologna: il Mulino.

———. and Tarozzi, Fiorenza 1988. *Democratici e progressisti a Bologna negli anni di Depretis*. Firenze: Olschki.

Preti, Luigi 1955. *Le lotte agrarie nella valle padana*. Turin: Einaudi.

Prior, Nick 2002. *Museums and Modernity: Art Galleries and the Making of Modern Culture*. Oxford: Berg.

Prodi, Paolo 1987. *The Papal Prince, One Body and Two Souls: The Papal Monarchy in Early Modern Europe*. Cambridge: Cambridge University Press.

Quine, Maria Sophia 2002. *Italy's Social Revolution: Charity and Welfare from Liberalism to Fascism*. Basingstoke: Palgrave.

Rabb, Theodore K. 2006. "Opera, Musicology, and History." *JIH*, 36, 3: 321–30.

Raccagni, Susanna 1988. "Il Touring Club Italiano e il governo del tempo libero." *Cheiron*, 9/10: 233–56.

Raffaelli, Sergio 1998. "I nomi delle vie." In Isnenghi (ed.) 1998: 215–42.

Ragionieri, Ernesto 1976. "La storia politica e sociale." In *Storia d'Italia* 1973–76: vol. 4, 1668–2391.

———. 1979a. *Politica e amministrazione nella storia dell'Italia unita*. Roma: Editori Riuniti.

———. 1979b. "Politica e amministrazione nello Stato unitario," In Ragionieri 1979a: 81–137.

———. 1979c. "Rileggendo la Storia d'Italia di Benedetto Croce" (1966). In Ragionieri 1979a: 265–92.

Ramella, Franco 1999. "Reti sociali e mercato del lavoro in un caso di emigrazione. Gli operai italiani e gli altri a Paterson, New Jersey." In Musso (ed.) 1999: 741–75.

Randeraad, Nico 1997. *Autorità in cerca di autonomia. I prefetti nell'Italia liberale*. Roma: Ministero per i beni culturali.

Raspanti, Mauro 1999. "Il mito ariano nella cultura italiana fra otto e novecento." In Burgio (ed.) 1999: 75–85.

Re, Lucia 2001. "Passion and Sexual Difference: The Risorgimento and the Gendering of Writing in Nineteenth-Century Italian Culture." In Von Henneberg and Russell Ascoli (eds) 2001: 155–200.

Reichardt, Sven 2002. *Faschistische Kampfbünde. Gewalt und Gemeinschaft im italienischen Squadrismus und in der deutschen SA*. Cologne: Böhlau.

Reulecke, Jürgen 1989. "Bildunsbürgertum und Kommunalpolitik im 19. Jahrhundert." In Kocka (ed.) 1989: 122–45.

Riall, Lucy 1994. *The Italian Risorgimento: State, Society, National Unification*. London: Routledge.

———. 1998a. *Sicily and the Unification of Italy: Liberal Policy and Local Power, 1859–1866*. Oxford: Clarendon.

———. 1998b. "Hero, saint or revolutionary? Nineteenth-century politics and the cult of Garibaldi." *MI* 3, 2: 191–204.

———. 2004. "Which Italy? Italian Culture and the Problem of Politics." *JCH*, 39, 3: 437–46.

———. 2007a. *Garibaldi: Invention of a Hero*. New Haven: Yale University Press.

———. 2007b. "Eroi maschili, virilità e forme della guerra." In Banti and Ginsborg (eds) 2007: 253–88.

Ricci, Giovanni 1989. *Bologna. Le città nella storia d'Italia*. Rome and Bari: Laterza.

Ridgway, David W. Robertson. 1996. "Etruscans." In Hornblower and Spawforth (eds) 2003: 510–11.

——— and Francesca R. (eds) 1979. *Italy before the Romans: The Iron Age, Orientalizing and Etruscan Periods*. London: Academic Press.

Ridolfi, Maurizio 1987. "Associazionismo e forme di sociabilità nella società italiana fra '800 e '900: Alcune premesse di ricerca." *BMR*, 32, 33: 7–53.

———. 1989. *Il partito della Repubblica. I repubblicani in Romagna e le origini del Pri nell'Italia liberale (1872–1895).* Milan: Angeli.

———. 1990. *Il circolo virtuoso. Sociabilità democratica, associazionismo e rappresentanza politica nell'ottocento.* Florence: Cet.

———. 1992. *Il Psi e la nascità del partito di massa, 1892–1922.* Rome and Bari: Laterza.

———. 1995. "Feste civili e religione politiche nel 'laboratorio' della nazione italiana (1860–1859)." *MeR* 3 (July): 83–108.

———. 1997a. "La terra delle associazioni. Identità sociali, organizzazione degl'interessi e tradizioni civiche." In Finzi (ed.) 1997: 275–371.

———. 1997b. "Mazzini." In Isnenghi (ed.) 1997b: 3–23.

———. 2003. *Le feste nazionali.* Bologna: il Mulino.

———. and Tarozzi, Fiorenza (eds) 1987–88. *Associazionismo e forme di sociabilità in Emilia Romagna fra '800 e '900.* (*Bolletino del Museo del Risorgimento,* 32–33.) Bologna: Museo del Risorgimento.

Rieger, Bernhard 2005. *Technology and the Culture of Modernity in Britain and Germany, 1890–1945.* Cambridge: Cambridge University Press.

Rioux, Jean-Pierre and Sirinelli, Jean-François (eds) 1997. *Pour une histoire culturelle.* Paris: Seuil.

Ritter, Gerhard A. (ed.) 1973. *Die deutschen Parteien vor 1918.* Köln: Kiepenheuer & Witsch.

———. (ed.) 1979. *Arbeiterkultur.* Königstein / Taunus: Athenäum.

Roberge, Marc-André 1991. *Ferruccio Busoni. A Bio-Bibliography.* Westport, CT: Greenwood Press.

Roberts, David D. 1987. *Benedetto Croce and the Uses of Historicism.* Berkeley and Los Angeles: University of California Press.

Robin, Ron and Stråth, Bo (eds) 2003. *Homelands: Poetic Power and the Politics of Space.* Brussels: Peter Lang.

Robinson, Paul 1993. "Is *Aida* an orientalist Opera?" *COJ,* 5, 2: 133–40.

Roccatagliati, Alessandro 1993. "Opera, Opera-Ballo e 'Grand Opéra': Commistioni stilistiche e recezione critica nell'Italia Teatrale di Secondo Ottocento (1860–1870)." *Studi di Musica Veneta. Opera & Libretto,* 2: 283–349.

Roman, Zoltan 1989. *Gustav Mahler's American Years 1907 1911: A Documentary History.* Stuyvesant: Pendragon.

Romanelli, Raffaele 1979. *L'Italia liberale. 1861–1900.* (*Storia d'Italia dall'Unità alla Repubblica,* vol. 2.) Bologna: il Mulino.

———. 1982. "Arno Mayer e la persistenza dell'antico regime." *QS,* 51: 1095–102.

———. 1986. "Il problema del potere locale dopo il 1865: autogoverno, finanze comunali, borghesie." Bigaran (ed.) 1986: 75–111.

———. 1988. "Le Regole del Gioco. Note sull'impianto del sistema elettorale in Italia (1848–1895)." *QS,* 69, 3: 685–725.

———. 1989. *Sulle carte interminate: Un ceto di impiegati tra private e pubblico: I segretari comunali in Italia, 1860–1915.* Bologna: il Mulino.

———. 1991. "Political Debate, Social History, and the Italian Borghesia: Changing Perspectives in Historical Research." *JMH* 63 (December): 717–39.

———. 1995a. "Urban patricians and 'bourgeois' society: a study of wealthy elites in Florence, 1862–1904." *JMIS* 1, 1: 3–21.

———. 1995b. *Il Comando impossibile. Stato e società nell'Italia liberale* (1988). Bologna: il Mulino.

———. 1995c. "Centralismo e autonomie." Romanelli (ed.) 1995: 125–86.

———. (ed.) 1995. *Storia dello Stato italiano dall'Unità a oggi.* Rome: Donizelli.

Romeo, Rosario 1959. *Risorgimento e capitalismo.* Rome and Bari: Laterza.

———. 1990. *Vita di Cavour.* Rome and Bari: Laterza.

Roncalli, Francesco 1993. "Gli etruschi nella cultura italiana dell'ottocento." In Polverini (ed.) 1993: 359–68.

Rosselli, John 1987. *The Opera Industry in Italy from Cimarosa to Verdi: The Role of the Impresario.* Cambridge: Cambridge Paperback Library.

——. 1991. *Music and Musicians in 19th-Century Italy.* London: Batsford.

——. 1996. "Opera as a Social Occasion." In Parker (ed.) 1996: 304–21.

——. 2000. *The Life of Verdi.* New York: Cambridge University Press.

Rostirolla, Giancarlo 1982. *Wagner in Italia.* Turin: ERI.

Rugge, Fabio 1986. "*La città che sale:* Il problema del governo municipale di inizio secolo." In Bigaran (ed.) 1986: 54–71.

——. 1993. "Le nozioni di città e cittadino nel lungo Ottocento. Tra 'pariforme sistema' e nuovo particolarismo." In Meriggi and Schiera (eds) 1993: 47–64.

Russell Ascoli, Albert and Von Henneberg, Krystyna (eds) 2001. *Making and Remaking Italy: The Cultivation of National Identity around the Risorgimento.* Oxford: Berg.

Russo, Salvatore 1998. "Siracusa dal 1860 al 1865: Il problema del Capoluogo." In Adorno (ed.) 1998: 13–33.

Rydell, Robert W. 1984. *All the World's a Fair: Visions of Empire at American International Exhibitions, 1876–1916.* Chicago and London: University of Chicago Press.

Sabbatucci, Giovanni 2003. *Il trasformismo come sistema. Saggio sulla storia politica dell'Italia unitaria.* Rome and Bari: Laterza.

——. and Vidotto, Vittorio (eds) 1994–99. *Storia d'Italia.* 6 vols. Rome and Bari: Laterza.

Sadie, Stanley (ed.) 1980. *The New Grove Dictionary of Music and Musicians.* London: Macmillan.

Said, Edward 1993. *Culture and Imperialism.* London: Chatto & Windus.

Salmeri, Giovanni 1993. "L'antiquaria italiana dell'ottocento." In Polverini (ed.) 1993: 265–98.

Salvadori, Massimo L. 2001. *La sinistra nella storia italiana* (1999). Rome and Bari: Laterza.

Salvarani, Marco 2002. "L'Orchestra del Teatro di Senigallia." *SV,* 16: 137–56.

Salvati, Mariuccia 1998. "Il Salotto." In Isnenghi (ed.) 1998: 173–95.

Salvemini, Gaetano 1973. *The Origins of Fascism in Italy.* New York: Harper Torchbooks.

——. 1976. "L'elefantiasi burocratica degli inizi del secolo." In Cassese (ed.) 1976: 71–74.

Santini, Claudio and Trezzini, Lamberto 1987. "La questione wagneriana." In Trezzini (ed.) 1987: vol. 1, 101–58.

Santoro, Marco 2004. "Imprenditoria culturale nella Milano di Fine Ottocento." In Sorba (ed.) 2004: 101–46.

Sassatelli, Giuseppe 1984a. "I dubbi e le intuizioni di Gherardo Ghirardini." In Morigi Govi and Sassatelli (eds) 1984: 445–62.

——. 1984b. "Il Carnevale del 1874: Balanzoneide ovvero gli Etruschi a Bologna." In Morigi Govi and Sassatelli (eds) 1984: 327–46.

——. 1984c. "Edoardo Brizio e la prima sistemazione storica dell'archeologia bolognese." In Morigi Govi and Sassatelli (eds) 1984: 381–400.

——. 1984d. "La 'Galleria della pittura etrusca' nel salone X." In Morigi Govi and Sassatelli (eds) 1984: 365–74.

——. 1988. "Bologna etrusca." In Morigi Govi and Vitali (eds) 1988: 269–311.

Saunier, Pierre-Yves 1998. "La ville comme antidote? Ou à la rencontre du troisième type (d'identité régionale)." In Haupt, Müller, Woolf (eds) 1998: 125–61.

Scalise, Gregorio 1981. "Rubbiani e il fantasma del Carducci." In Solmi and Dezzi Bardeschi (eds) 1981: 495–506.

Schiavina, Enrico 1982. "Il Teatro Comunale. Il recente restauro." *SSB* 32: 395–418.

Schieder, Theodor 1980. *Einsichten in die Geschichte*. Frankfurt / Main: Propyläen.

Schiera, Pierangelo 1997. "Centralismo e federalismo nell'unificazione statal-nazionale italiana e tedesca." In Janz, Schiera, Siegrist (eds) 1997: 21–46.

Schlesier, Renate 1994. *Kulte, Mythen und Gelehrte. Anthropologie der Antike seit 1800*. Frankfurt / Main: Fischer.

———. 1997. "Mythos." In Wulf (ed.) 1997: 1079–86.

———. 1999. "Anthropologie und Kulturwissenschaft in Deutschland vor dem ersten Weltkrieg." In König and Lämmert (eds) 1999: 219–31.

———. 2003. "Der letzte der Humanisten. Salomon Reinach und die europäische Kulturanthropologie." In *Nachrichten der Akademie der Wissenschaften zu Göttingen*. I. *Philolgisch-Historische Klasse*, 3: 117–33.

Schmitt, Carl 1954. *Gespräch über die Macht und den Zugang zum Machthaber*. Pfullingen: Neske.

Schnapp, Alain 1993. *La conquête du passé. Aux origines de l'archéologie*. Paris: Carré.

———. 1996. "French archaeology: between national identity and cultural identity." In Díaz-Andreu and Champion (eds) 1996: 48–67.

———. 2001. "France et Allemagne. L'archéologie, enjeu de la construction nationale." *MEFRIM*, 113, 2: 803–15.

———. 2002. "Between antiquarians and archaeologists—continuities and ruptures." *Antiquity*, 76: 134–40.

Schnapper, Dominique 1971. *L'Italie rouge et noire. Les modèles culturels de la vie quotidienne à Bologne*. Paris: Gallimard.

Schnitzler, Franco 1954. *Mondo teatrale dell'ottocento. Episodi, testimonianze, musiche e lettere inedite*. Naples: Fiorentino.

Schoffman, Nachum 1993. "D'Annunzio and Mann: Antithetical Wagnerisms." *JoM*, 11, 4: 499–524.

Schorske, Carl E. 2006. "Operatic Modernism." *JIH* 36, 4 (Spring): 675–81.

Schramm, Percy Ernst 1956. *Herrschaftszeichen und Staatssymbolik. Beiträge zu ihrer Geschichte vom dritten bis zum sechsten Jahrhundert*. 3 vols. Stuttgart: MGH.

Schwartz, Frederic J. 2005. *Blind Spots: Critical Theory and the History of Art in Twentieth-Century Germany*. New Haven: Yale University Press.

Sciannameo, Franco 2004. *Giuseppe Mazzini's Philosophy of Music: Envisioning a Social Opera*. Lewitson: Edwin Mellen.

Scott, Joan W. and Keates, Debra (eds) 2004. *Going Public: Feminism and the Shifting Boundaries of the Private Sphere*. Urbana and Champaign: University of Illinois Press.

Sebald, Winfried Georg 2003. *Logis in einem Landhaus* (1998). Frankfurt / Main: Fischer.

Sebeok, Thomas A. (ed.) 1984. *Carnival!* Berlin and New York: Mouton.

Seigel, Jerrold 1986. *Bohemian Paris: Culture, Politics, and the Boundaries of Bourgeois Life, 1830–1930*. New York: Viking.

Sennett, Richard 1977. *The Fall of Public Man*. New York: Knopf.

Serio, Mario (ed.) 1993. *L'Archivio centrale dello stato 1954–1993*. (Pubblicazzioni degli Archivi di Stato, Saggi 27.) Rome: Ministero per i beni culturali e ambientali.

Serra, Fleano 1951. "Scioperi in Emilia dal 1886 al 1891." *Emilia*: 275–77.

Serra, Rosanna Maggio 2001. "La cultura artistica nella seconda metà dell'Ottocento." In Levra (ed.) 2001: 575–615.

398   Bibliography

Serra Ridgway, F. R. 1996. "Tarquinia." In Thomson De Grummond (ed.) 1996: 1072–73.

Settis, Salvatore 1993. "Da centro a periferia: L'archeologia degli italiani nel secolo XIX." In Polverini (ed.) 1993: 299–334.

Shaw, Christine 1993. *Julius II: The Warrior Pope*. Oxford: Blackwell.

Sheehan, James J. 2000. *Museums in the German Art World: From the End of the Old Regime to the Rise of Modernism*. Oxford: Oxford University Press.

Sherman, Daniel J. 1989. *Worthy Monuments: Art Museums and the Politics of Culture in Nineteenth-Century France*. Cambridge, MA and London: Harvard University Press.

Sherratt, Andrew 2002. "Darwin among the archaeologists: the John Evans nexus and the Borneo Caves." *Antiquity*, 76: 151–57.

Siegrist, Hannes 1988. "Die Rechtsanwälte und das Bürgertum. Deutschland, die Schweitz und Italien im 19.Jahrhundert." In Kocka (ed.) 1988: vol. 2, 92–123.

———. 1992. "Gli avvocati nell'Italia del XIX secolo. Provenienza e matrimoni, titoli e prestigio." *Meridiana*, 14: 145–81.

———. 1994. "Profilo degli avvocati italiani dal 1870 al 1930. Omogeneità istituzionalizzata et eterogeneità reale di una professione classica." *Polis* 8, 2 (August): 223–43.

Silvestri, Luciano 1966. *Luigi Mancinelli. Direttore e Compositore*. Milan: Gastaldi.

Simmel, Georg 1908. *Untersuchungen über die Formen der Vergesellschaftung*. Berlin: Duncker & Humblodt.

Simoni, Luigi 1947. *Storia della Università di Bologna*. 2 vols. Bologna: Zanichelli.

Skinner, Quentin 1978. *The Foundation of Modern Political Thought*. Vol. 1. Cambridge: Cambridge University Press.

Smart, Mary Ann 2001. "Liberty On (and Off) the Barricades: Verdi's Risorgimento Fantasies." In Von Henneberg and Russell Ascoli (eds) 2001: 103–18.

———. 2006. "A Stroll in the Piazza and a Night at the Opera." *JIH*, 36, 4: 621–27.

Smith, Anthony D. 1998. *Nationalism and Modernism: A Critical Survey of Recent Theories of Nations and Nationalism*. London and New York: Routledge.

Smith, Bonnie G. 1998. *The Gender of History: Men, Women, and Historical Practice*. Cambridge, MA: Harvard University Press.

Snowden, Frank 1979. "From Sharecropper to Proletarian: The Background to Fascism in Rural Tuscany, 1880–1920." In Davis (ed.) 1979: 136–71.

———. 1995. *Naples in the Time of Cholera, 1884–1911*. Cambridge: Cambridge University Press.

Sobrero, Paola 1995. "Romagna in festa nell'ottocento: i riti religiosi, civili e politici." *MeR*, 5, (July): 109–37.

Socrate, Francesca 2004. "Commedia borghese e crisi di fine secolo." In Sorba (ed.) 2004: 21–60.

Soldani, Simonetta (ed.) 1989. *L'Educazione delle donne: Scuole e modelli feminili nell'Italia dell'ottocento*. Milan: Angeli.

———. 1993. "Nascità della maestra elementare." In Soldani and Turi (eds) 1993: vol. 1, 67–129.

———. 2000. "From Divided Memory to Silence: The 1848 Celebrations in Italy." In Körner (ed.) 2000: 143–63.

———. 2004. "Il Medioevo del Risorgimento nello specchio della nazione." In Castelnuovo and Sergi (eds) 2004: 149–86.

———. and Turi, Gabriele (eds) 1993. *Fare gli italiani. Scuola e cultura nell'Italia contemporanea*. Bologna: il Mulino.

Solmi, Franco and Dezzi Bardeschi, Marco (eds) 1981. *Alfonso Rubbiani, i veri e i falsi storici. Catalogo della mostra*, Bologna.

Sombart, Werner 1893. "Studien zur Entwicklungsgeschichte des italienischen Proletariats," *Archiv für Soziale Gesetzgebung und Statistik. Vierteljahresschrift zur Erforschung der Gesellschaftlichen Zustände aller Länder*, 6, 2: 177–258.

Somigli, Luca and Moroni, Mario (eds) 2004. *Italian Modernism: Italian Culture between Decadentism and Avant-Garde*. Toronto and London: University of Toronto Press.

Somkin, Fred 1985. "Zion's Harp by the East River: Jewish-American Popular Songs in Columbus's Golden Land, 1890–1914." *PAH* (N. S.), 2: 183–220.

Sorba, Carlotta 1993. *L'eredità delle mura. Un caso di municipalismo democratico (Parma 1889–1914)*. Venezia: Marsilio.

———. 1997. "Amministrazione periferica e locale." *SAC—ISAP*, 5: 153–85.

———. 2001. *Teatri. L'Italia del Melodramma nell'eta' del Risorgimento*. Bologna: il Mulino.

———. 2002. "Il Risorgimento in musica: l'opera lirica nei teatri del 1848." In Banti and Bizzocchi (eds) 2002: 133–56.

———. 2006a. "To Please the Public: Composers and Audiences in Nineteenth-Century Italy." *JIH*, 36, 4: 595–614.

———. 2006b. "The origins of the entertainment industry: the operetta in late nineteenth-century Italy." *JMIS*, 11, 3: 282–302.

———. (ed.) 2004. *Scene di fine Ottocento. L'Italia fin de siècle a teatro*. Rome: Carocci.

Spadolini, Giovanni 1960. "Un secolo di storia italiana." In Bologna 1960: 1–39.

———. 1993. *Gli Uomini che fecero l'Italia*. Milan: Longanesi.

———. (ed.) 1994. *Nazione e Nazionalità in Italia. Dall'alba del secolo ai nostri giorni*. Bari and Rome: Laterza.

Spini, Giorgio 1956. *Risorgimento e Protestanti*. Naples: ESI.

Staffieri, Gloria 2002. "Firenze, Teatro della Pergola. Materiali per una storia dell'orchestra." *SV*, 16: 97–136.

Steinhauser, Monika 1988. "'Sprechende Architektur.' Das französische und deutsche Theater als Institution und *monument public* (1760–1840)." In Kocka (ed.) 1988: vol. 3, 287–333.

Stephan, Rudolf and Wiesmann, Sigrid (eds) 1986. *Die Wiener Schule in der Musikgeschichte des 20. Jahrhunderts*. Vienna: Lafite.

Stichweh, Rudolf 1999. "Der Wissenschaftler." In Frevert and Haupt (eds) 1999: 162–96.

Stoczkowski, Wiktor 2002. *Explaining Human Origins: Myth, Imagination and Conjecture*. Cambridge: Cambridge University Press.

Stone, Marla Susan 1998. *The Patron State: Culture and Politics in Fascist Italy*. Princeton, NJ: Princeton University Press.

Storia d'Italia 1973–76. *Dall'Unità a oggi*. 3 vols. Turin: Einaudi.

Strasser, Michael 2001. "The Société Nationale and Its Adversaries: The Musical Politics of *L'Invasion germanique* in the 1870s." *NCM*, 24, 3: 225–51.

Straziota, Giovanni 1968. "I Partiti politici a Bologna nell'età del trasformismo (1883–87)." In Istituto per la Storia del Risorgimento 1968: 113–44.

Strong, Roy 2005. *Coronation: A History of Kingship and the British Monarchy*. London: Harper Collins.

Stuckenschmidt, Hans Heinz 1954. "Nachwort." In Busoni 1954: 52–55.

Surian, Elvido 1980. "Bologna." In Sadie (ed.) 1980: vol. 3, 1–9.

Susini, Giancarlo 1984. "Il Museo Civico Archeologico e la Facoltà letteraria bolognese." In Morigi Govi and Sassatelli (eds) 1984: 37–40.

———. 1987. "Tra Gozzadini e Brizio il tempo del centenario." *SSB* 37: 375–82.

Swales, Martin 2000. "Events and Non-Events . . . Cultural Reflections of and on 1848." In Körner (ed.) 2000: 50–63.

Tacke, Charlotte 1995. *Denkmal im sozialen Raum: nationale Symbole in Deutschland und Frankreich im 19. Jahrhundert.* Göttingen: Vandenhoeck & Ruprecht.

Tarozzi, Fiorenza 1997. "Filopanti Professore Universitario e Insegnante Popolare." In Preti (ed.) 1997: 93–119.

Taton, René (ed.) 1965. *Science in the Nineteenth Century.* London: Thames and Hudson.

Tedeschi, Rubens 1973. "L'Opera italiana." In *Storia d'Italia* 1973–76: vol. 5, 1 documenti, 2, 1141–80.

Tega, Walter (ed.) 1987. *Lo studio e la città. Bologna 1888–1988.* Bologna: Nuova Alfa.

Thayer, John A. 1964. *Italy and the Great War: Politics and Culture, 1870–1915.* Madison and Milwaukee: University of Wisconsin Press.

Ther, Philipp 2006. *In der Mitte der Gesellschaft. Operntheater in Zentraleuropa 1815–1914.* Munich: Oldenbourg.

Thomson de Grummond, Nancy 1996. "Etruscheria." In Thomson de Grummond (ed.) 1996: vol. 1, 410.

———. (ed.) 1996. *An Encyclopedia of the History of Classical Archaeology.* Westport, CT: Greenwood Press.

Thorpe, Wayne 2001. "The European Syndicalists and War, 1914–1918," *CEH*, 10, 1–24.

Tobia, Bruno 1993. "Associazionismo e patriotismo: il caso del pellegrinaggio nazionale a Roma del 1884." In Meriggi and Schiera (eds) 1993: 227–48.

———. 1998. *Una patria per gli Italiani. Spazi, itinerari, monumenti nell'Italia unita (1870–1900).* Rome and Bari: Laterza.

———. 2000. "Die Toten der Nation. Gedenkfeiern, Staatsbegräbnisse und Gefallenenkult im liberalen Italien (1870–1921)." In Behrenbeck and Nützenadel (eds) 2000: 67–86.

Toda, Misato 1988. *Errico Malatesta da Mazzini a Bakunin. La sua formazione giovanile nell'ambiente napoletano (1868–1873).* Napoli: Guida.

Tomasi di Lampedusa, Giuseppe 1974. *Il Gattopardo.* Milan: Feltrinelli.

Tomlinson, Gary 1986. "Italian Romanticism and Italian Opera: An Essay in Their Affinities." *NCM*, 10, 1, 43–60.

Tönnies, Ferdinand 1972. *Gemeinschaft und Gesellschaft. Grundbegriffe der reinen Soziologie.* Darmstadt: Wissenschaftliche Buchgesellschaft.

Tovoli, Silvana 1984a. "La collezione di Pelagio Palagi." In Morigi Govi and Sassatelli (eds) 1984: 191–99.

———. 1984b. "Il Museo Archeologico Communitativo e il progetto di unificazione delle collezioni comunali e universitarie (1860–1871)." In Morigi Govi and Sassatelli (eds) 1984: 211–15.

———. 1984c. "L'organizzazione nazionale degli 'Scavi di antichità' e la situazione bolognese." In Morigi Govi and Sassatelli (eds) 1984: 299–306.

———. and Sassatelli, Giuseppe 1988a. "La collezione etrusco-italica." In Morigi Govi and Vitali (eds) 1988: 191–202.

———. 1988b. "Bologna villanovana." In Morigi Govi and Vitali (eds) 1988: 221–62.

Tranfaglia, Nicola 1995. *La Prima Guerra mondiale e il fascismo. Storia d'Italia.* Vol. 22. Ed. Giuseppe Galasso. Turin: UTET.

Trezzini, Lamberto 2000. "Società e legislazione." In Alonge and Bonino (eds) 2000: vol. 2, 1023–46.

————. (ed.) 1987. *Due secoli di vita musicale. Storia del Teatro Comunale di Bologna* (1966). 3 vols. Bologna: Nuova Alfa.

Trigger, Bruce G. 1989. *A History of Archaeological Thought*. Cambridge: Cambridge University Press.

Trigilia, Lucia 1998. "Architettura e nuovi scenari urbani a Siracusa dopo l'Unità d'Italia." In Adorno (ed.) 1998: 217–29.

Troilo, Simona 2005. *La patria e la memoria. Tutela e patrimonio culturale nell'Italia unita*. Milano: Electa.

Turnaturi, Gabriella 1996. "Divertimenti italiani dall'Unita' al fascismo." In Corbin (ed.) 1996: 183–212.

Tusa, Michael C. 2006. "Comopolitanism and the National Opera: Weber's *Der Freischütz*." *JIH*, 36, 3: 483–506.

Ullrich, Hartmut 1978. "Die italienischen Liberalen und die Probleme der Demokratisierung 1876–1915." *GG* 4: 49–76.

————. 1980. "L'organizzazione politica dei liberali italiani nel Parlamento e nel Paese (1870–1914)." In Lill and Matteucci (eds) 1980: 403–50.

Umbach, Maiken 2005. "A Tale of Second Cities: Autonomy, Culture and the Law in Hamburg and Barcelona in the Long Nineteenth Century." *AHR*, 110, 3 (June): 659–92.

————. and Hüppauf, Bernd (ed.) 2005. *Vernacular Modernism: Heimat, Globalization, and the Built Environment*. Stanford: Stanford University Press.

Unfried, Berthold (ed.) 1999. *Riten, Mythen und Symbole—Die Arbeiterbewegung zwischen 'Zivilreligion' und Volkskultur*. Vienna: Akademische Verlagsanstalt.

Urbinati, Nadia 1996. "'A common Law of Nations': Giuseppe Mazzini's democratic nationality." *JMIS* 1, 2: 197–222.

Vallauri, Carlo 1971. *Lineamenti di storia dei partiti italiani*. Rome: Bulzoni.

Van Dijk, Henk 1988. "Bürger und Stadt. Bemerkungen zum langfristigen Wandel an westeuropäischen und deutschen Beispielen." In Kocka (ed.) 1988: vol. 3, 447–65.

Vannelli, Walter 1981. *Economia dell'architettura in Roma fascista: il centro urbano*. Rome: Kappa.

Varjo, Massimiliano (ed.) 1950. *Arrigo Boito nel trentennio della morte MCMX-VIII–MCMXLVIII*. Naples.

Varni, Angelo 1997. "I caratteri originali della tradizione democratica." Finzi (ed.) 1997: 551–75.

————. (ed.) 1996. *I Giacobini nelle legazioni. Gli anni napoleonici a Bologna e Ravenna*. 3 vols. Bologna: Costa Editore.

Vasina, Augusto 1976. "Il mondo emiliano-romagnolo nel periodo delle Signorie (secoli XIII-XVI)." In Berselli 1976–80: vol. 1, 675–748.

Vecchi, Giuseppe 1966. *L'Accademia filarmonica di Bologna 1666–1966: notizie storiche, manifestazioni*, Bologna.

————. 1976. "Musica e teatro, festa e spettacolo." In Berselli (ed.) 1976–80: vol. 2, 415–42.

Venturi, Giampaolo 1977. "Le Accademie." In Berselli (ed.) 1976–80: vol. 2, 463–78.

Verdi, Luigi (ed.) 2001. *Le opere di Giuseppe Verdi a Bologna (1843–1901)*. Lucca: Libreria Musicale Italiana.

Vianelli, Athos 1965. "Note su tre monumenti bolognesi della fine dell'800." *SSB*, 15: 269–81.

————. 1997. "Tradizioni, simboli e curiosità nel complesso delle Sette Chiese di Santo Stefano." In Foschi et al. 1997: 97–114.

Vigo, Giovanni 1993. "Gli italiani alla conquista dell'alfabeto." In Soldani and Turi (eds) 1993: vol. 1, 37–66.

Vinciguerra, Mario 1957. *Carducci uomo politico*. Pisa: Nistri-Lischi.

Vitali, Daniele 1984a. "La scoperta di Villanova e il Conte Giovanni Gozzadini." In Morigi Govi and Sassatelli (eds) 1984: 223–37.

———. 1984b. "Giovanni Capellini e i primi congressi di Antropologia e Archeologia Preistoriche." In Morigi Govi and Sassatelli (eds) 1984: 269–76.

———. 1984c. "Il V Congresso di Antropologia e Acheologia Preistoriche a Bologna." In Morigi Govi and Sassatelli (eds) 1984: 277–94.

———. 1988. "Confronti preistorici." In Morigi Govi and Vitali (eds) 1988: 110–22.

———. and Meconcelli Notarianni, Gioia 1984. "Le nuove acquisizioni del Museo: la sala dei confronti pristorici e le lapidi romane del muro del Reno." In Morigi Govi and Sassatelli (eds) 1984: 435–44.

Vivanti, Corrado (ed.) 1981. Storia d'Italia. Annali 4: Intellettuali e potere. Turin: Einaudi.

Vivarelli, Roberto 1973. "Introduction." In Salvemini 1973: vii–xiii.

———. 1981. Il fallimento del liberalismo. Studi sulle origini del fascismo. Bologna: il Mulino.

Vivarelli, Roberto 1991. Storia delle origini del fascismo. L'Italia dalla grande guerra alla marcia su Roma. 2 vols. Bologna: il Mulino.

———. 1995. "L'eredità del liberalismo risorgimentale dopo l'unità." Ris. 47, 1/2: 13–31.

Vogel, Jacob 1995. "Militärfeiern in Deutschland und Frankreich als Rituale der Nation (1871–1914)." In François, Siegrist, Vogel (eds) 1995: 199–214.

Volpi, Roberto 1983. Le regioni introvabili. Centralizzazione e regionalizzazione dello Stato pontificio. Bologna: il Mulino.

Von Beyme, Klaus 1968. "Elite." In Keinig (ed.) 1968: vol. 2, 110–12.

———. 1993. Die politische Klasse im Parteienstaat. Frankfurt / Main: Suhrkamp.

Von Krosigk, Rüdiger 1999. Die Rolle des Präfekten bei der Kontrolle der Kommunalverwaltung im 'liberalen Italien' (1861–1900). Magisterarbeit Universität Konstanz, Fachgruppe Geschichte.

Von Schiller, Friedrich 1982. On the Aesthetic Education of Man: In a Series of Letters. Trans. E. M. Wilkinson and L. A. Willoughby. Oxford: Clarendon.

Voza, Giuseppe 1998. "La città antica e la città moderna." In Adorno (ed.) 1998: 249–60.

Wagner, Peter 1994. A Sociology of Modernity. London and New York: Routledge.

Waley, Daniel 1988. The Italian City-Republics. London and New York: Longman.

Walker, Frank 1982. The Man Verdi. Chicago: University of Chicago Press.

Walsh, Kevin 1992. The Representation of the Past: Museums and Heritage in the Post-Modern World. London: Routledge.

Weaver, William and Chusid, Martin (eds) 1979. The Verdi Companion. New York: Norton.

Weber, Max 1980. Wirtschaft und Gesellschaft: Grundriß der verstehenden Soziologie. Tübingen: Mohr.

———. 1982. Politik als Beruf. Berlin: Duncker & Humblot.

———. 1988a. "Wissenschaft als Beruf" (1919). In Weber 1988c: 582–613.

———. 1988b. "Die 'Objektivität' sozialwissenschaftlicher und sozialpolitischer Erkenntnis" (1904). In Weber 1988c: 146–214.

———. 1988c. Aufsätze zur Wissenschaftslehre. Tübingen: Mohr.

Weber, William 1975. Music and the Middle Class: The Social Structure of Concert Life in London, Paris, and Vienna. New York: Holmes & Meier.

———. 1977. "Mass culture and the reshaping of European musical taste, 1770–1870," IRASM, 3, 1: 5–22.

———. 1979. "Die Handwerker in Londoner und Pariser Konzertleben." In Ritter (ed.) 1979: 109–21.

———. 1984. "Wagner, Wagnerism, and Musical Idealism." In Large and Weber (eds) 1984: 28–71.
Wehler, Hans-Ulrich 1995. *Deutsche Gesellschaftsgeschichte.* Vol. 3. *Von der 'Deutschen Doppelrevolution' bis zum Beginn des Ersten Weltkrieges 1849–1914.* Munich: Beck.
———. (ed.) 1971–82. *Deutsche Historiker.* 9 vols. Göttingen: V&R.
———. (ed.) 1990. *Europäischer Adel 1750–1950.* (*GG*-Sonderheft 13). Göttingen: V&R.
Weinstock, Herbert 1968. *Rossini: A Biography.* New York: Knopf.
Wenk, Silke 2000. "Gendered Representations of the Nation's Past and Future." In Blom, Hagemann, Hall (eds) 2000: 63–77.
White, Hayden 1975. "Historicism, History, and the Figurative Imagination." *HaT*, Beiheft 14: 48–67.
White, Morton and Lucia 1977. *The Intellectual Versus the City: From Thomas Jefferson to Frank Lloyd Wright.* Oxford: Oxford University Press.
Williams, Raymond 1976. *Culture and Society. 1870–1950* (1958). Harmonsworth: Penguin.
———. 1989. *The Politics of Modernism: Against the New Conformists.* London: Verso.
Williamson, John 1992. *The Music of Hans Pfitzner.* Oxford: Clarendon.
Wilson, Alexandra 2007. *The Puccini Problem: Opera, Nationalism and Modernity.* Cambridge: Cambridge University Press.
Wilson, Michael 1991. "Consuming History: The Nation, the Past and the Commodity at L'Exposition Universelle de 1900." *AJS* 8, 4: 131–54.
Winter, Jay 1985. *The Great War and the British People.* Basingstoke: Macmillan.
Wittmann, Michael 1993. "Meyerbeer and Mercadante? The reception of Meyerbeer in Italy." *COJ* 5, 2: 115–32.
Wohl, Robert 1979. *The Generation of 1914.* Cambridge, MA: Harvard University Press.
Wolfzettel, Friedrich and Ihring, Peter 1994. "Der föderale Traum: Nationale Ursprungsmythen in Italien zwischen Aufklärung und Romantik." In Berding (ed.) 1994: vol. 2, 443–83.
Woolf, Stuart J. 1981. *Il risorgimento italiano.* 2 vols. Turin: Einaudi.
———. 2004. "Nazione, nazioni e potere in Italia, 1700–1915." *I Quaderni del Cardello. Annuale di studi romagnoli della Fondazione 'Casa di Oriani'— Ravenna,* 13: 11–30.
Wulf, Christoph (ed.) 1997. *Vom Menschen. Handbuch Historische Anthropologie.* Weinheim and Basel: Beltz.
Zaghini, Tommaso; Ferri, Corrado; Verdi, Luigi (eds) 2002. *Stefano Gobatti. Cronache dai teatri dell'Ottocento. Un caso clamoroso nella storia della musica.* Bologna: Pàtron.
Zamagni, Vera 1986. "L'Economia." In Zangheri (ed.) 1986: 245–314.
Zangheri, Renato 1986. "L'unificazione." In Zangheri (ed.) 1986: 3–61.
———. 1997a. *Storia del Socialismo Italiano.* 2 vols. Turin: Einaudi.
———. 1997b. "Una vocazione industriale diffusa." In Finzi (ed.) 1997: 127–61.
———. (ed.) 1960. *Lotte agrarie in Italia. La Federazione nazionale dei lavoratori della terra 1901–1926.* Milan: Feltrinelli.
———. (ed.) 1986. *Bologna. Storia delle città italiane.* Rome and Bari: Laterza.
Zemon Davis, Nathalie 1975. *Society and Culture in Early Modern France.* Stanford: Stanford University Press.
Zoppelli, Luca 1996. "The twilight of the true gods: *Cristoforo Colombo, I Medici* and the construction of Italian history." *COJ,* 8, 3: 251–69.

Index

A

Acquaderni (family), 110
Acton, Laura di Camporeale, 30
Adam, Robert, 129
Adamson, Walter L., 268
Administration, municipal, 2, 10–13,
    16–18, 22, 24, 28–29, 31,
    34–36, 42, 51, 57–65, 66–83,
    92–102, 131, 141, 146–147,
    149–151, 154–155, 157, 160,
    164, 167, 168, 172, 175,
    185–186, 190, 196, 219–220,
    222–223, 233, 237, 240–242,
    247–250, 256–257, 259–260,
    271, 275–280, 282–283, 286n
Adowa, 127, 273
Adria, 7
Aemilia Ars, 41, 110, 113, 259
Aesthetics, 2, 3, 6, 7, 12, 13, 14,
    15, 17, 22, 44, 88, 96, 107,
    111–112–114, 125, 221–223,
    228, 230, 237, 239–240, 246,
    250–251, 254–256, 260–266,
    268–269, 287n
Aesthetics of reception. See Aesthetics
Af Malmborg, Mikael, 125, 131
Africa, 127, 273, 279
Agriculture, 1, 8, 18, 26, 27, 30–34,
    39–44, 83, 271–274
Agulhon, Maurice, 170, 180
Aimo, Piero, 22
Akcan, Esra, 269
Alaimo, Aurelio, 66, 286n
Alba, 24
Albert von Sachsen-Coburg-Gotha, 204
Albicini, Cesare, 222, 314n
Aldrovandi, Ulisse, 149
Alexander II, Russian Tsar, 178
Alexander III, Pope, 123

Alexander VI, Pope, 117
Alfieri, Vittorio, 186, 265
Alps, 134, 138, 168, 320n
Amba Alagi, 273
Amedeo of Savoy, 205, 213
Anarchism, 2, 178–179, 192, 207–208,
    215–217, 237, 239, 264, 274,
    292n, 331n
Ancien régime, 11, 16, 21, 23, 68, 166,
    189, 224
Ancient history. See Antiquity
Ancona, 69, 168, 191, 275
Ancora, L', 109, 153, 242
Anderson, Benedict, 7, 135–136
Animal shows, 55, 173
Anthropology, 133, 136, 144, 149–150,
    153–154, 160, 326n
Anti-clericalism, 104, 108–111, 114,
    116–117, 136, 147, 182,
    237–238, 255, 280, 290n
Anti-Fascism, 267, 357n
Anti-modernism, 1, 103, 263, 285n
Antiquarians, 16, 129, 140, 149, 160,
    316n, 317n
Antiquity / Antiquities, 16, 33, 78, 93,
    95, 96, 104, 108, 120, 128–160
Anti-Semitism, 235, 260–261, 285n
Antwerp, 251
Apennines, 7, 134–135, 137, 167
Applegate, Celia, 164
Arbesser, Rosa, 202
Archaeology. See Excavations, archaeo-
    logical
Architecture, 5, 12, 13, 22, 43, 73, 88–
    89, 91–94, 107–127, 129, 181,
    233, 259, 287n, 313n, 317n
Archives, 8, 16, 33, 91, 97–100, 104,
    167
Arezzo, 181

Aria, Giuseppe, 150
Aria, Pompeo, 144
Ariosto, Ludovico, 265
Aristocracy. *See* Nobility
Aristocracy, black. *See* Nobility
Arpa, L', 222, 228, 233–234, 236, 238
Art, 12–13, 22, 25, 33, 43, 48, 69, 73,
    135, 139, 149, 199, 263–264,
    269, 280, 314n
Artisans, 171, 224
Artusi, Giovanni Maria, 254
Aryans, 139
Assassinations, political, 178, 203,
    207–208, 215–217
Associations, Voluntary, 150, 169–176,
    184, 211–212, 256, 295n
Associazione Costituzionale delle
    Romagne, 31, 110, 288n
Associazione Nazionalista Bolognese,
    272
Assyria, 295n
Auber, Daniel, 246
Audinot, Rodolfo, 171
Augustus, 138
Austria, 2, 4, 9, 10, 45, 90, 95, 120,
    131, 157, 170–171, 176, 178,
    182, 186, 189, 191, 202, 205,
    214, 221, 228, 248, 259–260,
    267, 275, 349n
Autonomy, municipal, 66, 68, 107,
    111, 115, 122, 124–125, 131,
    164, 166–167
Avant-garde, 9, 10, 125, 221, 238, 248,
    255, 260–262, 265, 268, 281
Avanti, L', 216, 275
Avvenire, L, 276

B
Bacchelli, Riccardo, 12
Bach, Johann Sebastian, 229, 255
Bachelli, Giuseppe, 112–113
Bachofen, Johann Jakob, 321n, 322n
Backwardness, 6, 7, 8, 14, 17, 40, 166,
    210, 279
Badini, Giuseppe, 55
Badoglio, Pietro, 281
Bagnara, Pietro, 254
Bakhtin, Mikhail, 145–146
Bakunin, Michael, 2, 178–179,
    237–238
Balbo, Cesare, 106
Balilla Pratella, Francesco, 221, 261
Ballet, 49, 55, 57–65, 223, 229, 231,
    303n

Balls, 49, 53–54, 56, 298n
Balzani, Roberto, 180
Banca Nazionale, 44
Banca Pontificia delle Quattro
    Legazioni, 41
Banca Popolare, 29
Bands, municipal, 1, 56, 68–70, 155,
    173, 175, 223, 230, 250, 305n
Banti, Alberto M., 14, 27, 32, 35, 105,
    130, 136, 174
Barbarians, 134, 203
Barcelona, 178, 246, 259
Bardesono di Rigras, Cesare, 27
Baroque, 107–108, 112, 115–116
Barrett, Elizabeth, 210
Bartòk, Bela, 260
Bassani, Giorgio, 319n
Bassi, Ugo, 182, 186–187
Baths, public, 73, 219–220
Baudelaire, Charles, 235, 238–240,
    245–246, 263, 269
Baumann, Zygmunt, 268
Bayreuth, 243, 258–259, 296n
Bebel, August, 280
Beccaria, Cesare, 181, 265
Beethoven, Ludwig van, 221, 226,
    229, 240, 249, 252–254; *Fide-*
    lio, 226
Bel canto, 9, 52, 186, 223, 226, 228,
    231, 253
Belgium, 188–189, 264, 276, 345n
Belinzaghi, Giulio, 25
Bellini, Giovanni, 9, 25, 221, 224, 226,
    230, 236, 240, 242, 263, 341n; *I*
    Puritani, 25, 253, 289n; *Norma*,
    224
Beltramelli, Antonio, 12
Benacci (family), 150, 158
Benda, Julien, 287n
Benedict XIV, Pope, 117, 149
Benelli, Ignazio, 42
Ben-Ghiat, Ruth, 126
Benjamin, Walter, 269, 286n, 356n
Benni, Alfredo, 42
Bentham, Jeremy, 39
Bentivoglio (family), 9, 41, 48, 105–
    106, 314n
Bentivoglio, Giovanni, 47, 296n
Bentivoglio, Giovanni II, 105, 115
Bentivoglio, Paolo, 296n
Béranger, Pierre-Jean de, 195
Berchet, Giovanni, 128, 130, 224, 264
Beretta, Antonio, 25
Bergson, Henri, 265

Berlin, 46, 65, 129, 133, 155, 214, 226, 229, 255, 260–261, 266, 323n, 357n
Berlin Philharmonic Orchestra, 255–256
Berlin Secession, 264
Berlioz, Hector, 221, 226, 231, 246; *La Damnation de Faust*, 258
Bernhardt, Sarah, 9, 54, 251
Berni Degli Antoni (family), 45
Berselli, Aldo, 111
Berti (family), 29
Berti Pichat, Carlo, 31, 40
Berti, local councillor, 124
Bertolini, Francesco, 90, 123, 133, 138–139, 160, 308n
Bevilacqua (family), 9, 26, 29, 41, 44, 52, 60, 61, 70
Bevilacqua, Carlo, 41, 44
Bhabha, Homi K., 135
Bianconcini, Countess, 46
Bianconi, Giuseppe, 153
Bibiena, Antonio Galli, 9, 49, 65, 72, 73, 79, 259, 296n
Bigaran, Mariapia, 15
Bingham, Lady, 46
Bismarck, Otto von, 13, 155, 237
Bissolati, Leonida, 238
Bizet, Georges, 252
Bloch, Ernst, 270
Blume, Bianca, 241
Blumenberg, Hans, 126, 151
Boccherini, Luigi, 221, 253
Böcklin, Arnold, 265
Bocquet, Denis, 94
Boeckh, August, 323n
Boito, Arrigo, 9, 101–102, 245–248, 251, 254–255, 258, 261, 349n, 352n; *Mefistofele*, 9, 223, 225, 245–247, 250–251, 258; *Nerone*, 246
Boito, Camillo, 179
Bologna: Academy of Fine Arts, 50–51, 110, 123, 159, 187, 254; Accademia filarmonica, 7, 56, 110, 222, 230, 243, 247, 253–254, 349n; Archiginnasio, 8, 78, 98, 150, 154–155, 157, 176, 185, 187; Archives, 97–100; Caffè dei Cacciatori, 176; Caffè dell'Arena, 176; Caffè della Fenice, 176; Camera di Commercio, 41; Cappella di San Petronio, 249, 254–255, 280;

Casino dei Nobili, 45, 170, 172; Cassa di Risparmio, 29, 41–44; Centenary of Richard Wagner, 1–2, 7, 278; Certosa, 78, 92–93, 101, 131–132, 134–135, 139, 141–142, 154, 180–181, 185, 187; City Walls, 118–120, 241; Comitato per Bologna storica ed artisitica, 110, 120, 312n; Consiglio Comunale, 10, 13, 35, 37, 47, 52, 55, 57, 59, 60–83, 92, 100–102, 108, 110–114, 150, 156, 174–175, 177, 181–183, 185, 194–195, 212, 215, 217–220, 230, 233, 236, 240–243, 249–250, 259, 273, 275–280; Deputazione dei pubblici spettacoli, 51–52, 61, 70, 79, 173, 191, 230, 233, 250, 257, 279, 298n; Deputazione di Storia Patria, 13, 88–95, 98, 107, 110, 117, 118, 133, 138, 140, 142, 150, 154, 165, 254, 324n; *Duttòur Balanzòn. See* Carnival. Exhibition of 1888, 9, 13, 82, 101, 107, 147–148, 166, 169, 212, 245, 247–248, 253–254, 338n; Geological Museum, 158, 212; Giardini Margherita, 158, 212–213; Istituto delle Scienze, 149; Istituzione Rossiniana, 52, 56, 62, 64, 70, 72, 224, 230, 300n; Liceo Musicale, 8, 9, 46, 56, 68–70, 81, 185–186, 226, 230, 234, 243, 249–250, 253–256, 260–261, 279, 353n; Loggia dei Agricoltori, 41; Montagnola, 120, 145, 179–180, 192, 214; Monte di Pietà, 29; Museo Civico, 10, 16, 27, 78, 88, 91, 95–97, 140, 144, 148–159, 212; Neptune Fountain, 113, 188; Ospedale della Morte, 150; Palazzo Comunale, 111, 114–115, 280, 282; Palazzo del Podestà, 112–113; Palazzo del Re Enzo, 113, 123–124; Palazzo di Giustizia, 77; Palazzo Galvani, 157; Piazza Cavour, 183, 187; Piazza del Re Enzo, 124–125; Piazza Maggiore, 17, 43, 115, 117, 120, 123–124, 145, 155, 188, 194, 219, 286n; Piazza Minghetti, 42, 214; Piazza

Rossini, 212; Pinacoteca, 95, 100, 314n; Politeama D'Azeglio, 245; Porta di Galliera, 120; Porta Saragozza, 112; *Portici*, 77, 108, 118–120, 223; Bologna, Province of, 21, 29, 31, 34, 80–83, 118, 169, 304n, 307n; Risorgimento Museum, 212–213, 338n; San Domenico, 101, 108–109; San Francesco, 112, 132, 139, 158; San Michele in Bosco, 123, 214; San Petronio, 115, 117, 183, 254; Santo Stefano, 92, 116–118, 142, 145; Santuario della Madonna di San Luca, 245; Scuola Superiore di Agraria, 43; Società Agraria, 28, 29, 33, 40–41, 44, 170, 295n; Società per il risveglio della vita cittadina, 256; Società per pubblici divertimenti, 256; Società Protettrice, 172; Teatro Brunetti, 46, 54, 64, 217, 249; Teatro Comunale, 2, 9, 11, 14, 16, 17, 46–65, 69–74, 79, 94–95, 147, 159, 182, 186, 221–223, 225–262, 269, 278–280, 296n, 298n, 342n, 351n; Teatro Dal Verme, 229; Teatro dei Piccoli, 279; Teatro del Corso, 55, 64–65, 159; Teatro Duse. *See* Bologna, Teatro Brunetti; Teatro Marsigli, 238; Teatro Popolare, 279; Torre degli Asinelli, 115, 118; Torre della Garisenda, 118, 314n; Towers, 116, 118–120, 142; University, 8, 10, 16, 31–35, 37, 42–43, 45, 52, 68, 78, 90–91, 95–96, 98, 101, 107, 121, 133, 138, 140, 145, 149–158, 169, 175, 178, 181, 184, 188, 205, 212, 254, 272, 283; Via Farini, 43, 77, 108; Via Indipendenza, 120, 195; Via Rizzoli, 43; Workingmen's Society, 26, 123, 174, 182, 211–212, 218, 296n
Bombicci, Luigi, 153
Bonaini, Francesco, 98
Bonaparte (family), 27
Bonaveri, Ippolito, 123
Bonci, Alessandro, 256
Bonetti, Argentina, 175
Bonn, 133
Bononia (Roman Bologna), 131, 134
Bonora, Antonio, 42

Bordeaux, 157
Borders, 7, 165
Borghesia. *See* Middle Class
Borghesia terriera. *See* Landowners
Borghi-Mamo, Erminia, 246, 342n
Borgia (family), 105
Bossi, Marco Enrico, 261, 266, 353n
Boston, 246
Botta, Carlo, 28
Botticelli, Sandro, 135
Bottrigari, Enrico, 44, 72, 92, 227–228
Bourdieu, Pierre, 13, 14, 15, 32, 35
Bourgeoisie. *See* Middle Classes
Bozen / Bolzano, 182
Brabant, 247
Brahms, Johannes, 253
Bramante, Donato di Angeli di Pascuccio, 48
Brass bands. *See* Bands, municipal
Brazil, 188
Bresci, Gaetano, 215–217
Brice, Cathérine, 216
Brigands, 171, 177
British Library, 291n
Brizio, Edoardo, 94–95, 133, 139–140, 143, 148, 154–155, 158–159, 206, 321n
Brown, David, 352n
Browning, Robert, 210
Bruni, Leonardo, 186
Bruno, Giordano, 182, 265
Brussels, 53, 89, 188, 247, 344n
Budrio, 27, 34, 181, 288n
Buenos Aires, 250
Buggio, assessore, 72
Buildings, public, 44
Bülow (family), 30
Bülow, Hans von, 231, 235, 238
Buonarroti, Filippo, 170, 316n
Burckhardt, Jacob, 135
Bureaucratisation, 15, 35, 101
Busi, Alessandro, 254
Busi, Giuseppe, 243, 254
Busi, Luigi, 144, 158–159
Busoni, Ferruccio, 9, 255, 260–263, 266, 352n, 353n; *Die Brautwahl*, 260; *The Ballad of Lippold the Jew-coiner*, 261
Busseto, 226, 231
Byzantium, 75

C
Cadorna, Raffaele, 120
Café-Concert, 252

Cafiero, Carlo, 178
Cagliari, 227, 249
Caimi (family), 46
Cairo, 225
Cairoli (family), 211
Cairoli, Adelaide, 211
Cairoli, Benedetto, 207, 211, 337n
Calore, Marina, 58
Calvi, Pier Fortunato, 181
Camberwell, 210
Camerino, 8, 168
Cammarano, Fulvio, 215
Campania, 8, 42
Campanilismo, 17, 53, 79, 152, 168,
    180, 188, 221, 225
Campeggi (family), 59, 296n
Camporeale, Maria di, 30
Cannadine, David, 197
Canova, Antonio, 178
Capellini, Giovanni, 45, 150–154, 156,
    159, 205
Capitale, La, 203
Capitelli, Guglielmo, 27
Capua, 249
Cardoza, Anthony, 23, 38, 271
Carducci, Giosuè, 9, 10, 15, 16, 33–34,
    45, 75, 88–95, 98–100, 102,
    104, 106, 107, 111–113, 115–
    116, 118, 121–123, 127, 130,
    133–136, 138, 148, 152, 165,
    167, 175–176, 179, 181–182,
    184, 198–199, 205–207, 211,
    218, 237, 243, 246, 248, 251,
    260, 265, 273, 280, 319n, 353n
Carli, Carlo, 36, 293n
Carlo Alberto, King of Piedmont-Sar-
    dinia, 3, 91, 129, 149, 189, 192,
    197
Carnival, 49, 53, 56–57, 143–148, 172,
    241, 323n
Carnot, Sadi, 178–179
Caro Baroja, Julio, 145–146
Carpi, Leone, 39, 167, 292n
Carrara, 217
Carulli, Ferdinando, 223
Caruso, Enrico, 247, 256, 278
Casarini, Camillo, 24, 26, 36, 52,
    61–65, 70, 74–83, 92, 95, 100–
    102, 118, 150–152, 155–157,
    183, 186, 223, 230, 233–237,
    240–241, 243, 247–248, 256,
    259, 264, 288n, 297n, 306n
Caserio, Sante, 178, 179
Cassirer, Ernst, 200

Castel San Pietro, 288n
Castellina, 137
Castelmaggiore, 288n
Castrati, 253
Catalani, Alfredo, 226, 247–248;
    Loreley, 278
Catania, 304n
Catholicism, political, 6, 10, 28–29,
    36–37, 60, 90, 109–110, 113,
    115–116, 120, 124, 167, 175,
    219, 254, 257, 270–276, 281,
    293n
Cattaneo, Carlo, 163
Cattani, Giuseppina, 175
Causa, Cesare, 208
Cavallotti, Felice, 179, 219, 279
Cavazza Bianconi, Lina, 41
Cavazza, Francesco, 41
Cavour, Count Camillo Benso di, 3, 10,
    24, 26, 33–34, 44, 67, 75, 107,
    109, 167, 171, 183–184, 187,
    189, 191, 193, 202, 205, 272,
    292n
Celts, 134, 139
Ceneri, Giuseppe, 34, 108, 152, 182,
    279
Censorship, 53–54, 64, 170, 289n
Cento, 187
Centralisation, 28, 103, 107, 148,
    166–168, 189
Ceri, Giuseppe, 109, 113, 115–116,
    174
Certani, Annibale, 27
Certeau, Michel de, 13
Cerveteri, 159
Chabod, Federico, 14, 136, 165
Chamber of Commerce, 215
Chamber of Labour, 257, 275–276, 282
Charisma, 201, 336n
Charity, 144, 146, 172, 175, 213, 273,
    302n
Charle, Christophe, 15
Charlemagne, 227
Charles the Fat, 116
Charles V, Holy Roman Emperor, 8,
    109, 122
Chateaubriand, 195
Cherubini, Luigi, 186, 221, 226, 253
China, 40
Chiusi, 159
Church, Catholic, 6, 18, 28, 47–48,
    67, 90, 104–106, 108–109, 111,
    116–117, 124, 147, 152–153,
    170, 172–176, 182, 192–194,

201, 209, 213, 227, 237, 242, 247, 272, 285n, 290n
Ciccarelli, Andrea, 104
Cicero, 130
Cilea, Francesco, 256
Cipolla, Antonio, 44
Cities, Competition between, 6, 8, 9, 13, 17, 100, 152, 181, 185–189, 333n
Cities, Second, 5, 100
Citizenship, sense of, 7, 10, 110
Civil Society. *See* Culture, civic
Civilisations, pre-Roman, 10, 13, 16, 70, 87, 127–160, 169
Civiltà Cattolica, 227
Clark, Timothy J., 269
Class conflict, 71, 257, 275, 277–278
Class, political. *See Classe dirigente*
Classe dirigente, 29, 31, 33–34, 37, 73, 204, 294n
Classicism, 44, 89, 103, 132, 135, 147, 173, 209, 251, 317n
Clementi, Muzio, 253
Coccia, Carlo, 253
Cocteau, Jean, 267
Codronchi (family), 26, 29
Codronchi, Giovanni, 23, 27, 34, 148
Coffeehouses, 49, 176, 223, 273
Cole, Laurence, 331n
Collapse of liberal democracy. *See* Crisis, Liberalism
Collingwood, Robin, 88
Colombarini, Arturo, 43
Colonialism, 97, 126, 257, 272–274
Colonna, Michele Angelo, 280
Comitato liberale permanente, 31
Commemorations, 12, 17, 34, 68, 89–90, 108–109, 121, 123, 180, 183–184–186, 189–196, 211–212, 217–220, 230, 248, 258, 278–279, 335n
Communism, 238
Como, 188, 227
Concert life, 45–46, 52, 54, 70, 223–224, 228, 234, 239, 245, 249, 252–256, 279
Concerti Popolari. See Concert life
Conductors, role of, 9, 52, 230–233
Conestabile, Giancarlo, 139, 320n
Conferences, 54, 70, 78
Confino, Alon, 164
Congress of Geology, Second International, 158

Congress of Pre-Historic Sciences, Fifth, 78, 138–142, 144–145, 150–156, 205, 212, 234
Connerton, Paul, 87, 189
Conscription, 21
Conservation. *See* Architecture
Conservatism, political, 110, 215, 219, 257, 267, 272–273, 281
Constance of Sicily, 124
Constance, Treaty of, 103
Constantine the Great, 105
Constantinople, 231
Constitution. *See Statuto*
Contavalli, Antonio, 54
Copenhagen, 231
Cordero di Montezemolo, Massimo, 27–28
Coronaro, Gaetano, 222
Coronation, 214
Corriere dell'Emilia, 23, 26, 222
Cortona, 129
Cosmopolitanism, 2–3, 5, 14–15, 17, 53, 79, 156, 221–222, 230, 237, 241, 246, 261–262, 264–267
Cospi, Ferdinando, 149
Costa, Andrea, 175–176, 276, 279
Costa, Lorenzo, 280
Counterreformation, 48
Cremona, 282
Crisis of Liberalism, 3, 5, 11, 17–18, 266, 270–271, 281–283, 287n
Crisis, *fine secolo* , 79, 125–126, 179, 215, 249–252, 268, 274
Crispi, Francesco, 8, 37, 176, 178, 197, 200–201, 210–211, 273–274
Critica Sociale, 252
Croce, Benedetto, 15, 22, 23, 27, 87, 89, 130, 134, 169, 199, 201–202, 266–268, 319n, 353n
Cronaca Wagneriana, 238, 249
Crusades, 116
Cuccoli (family), 286n
Culture, civic, 12, 14–18, 28, 35, 38, 55, 79, 90, 100–102, 111, 146, 156, 169, 211–212, 220
Culture, material, 16
Culture, political, 2, 14
Culture, popular, 12, 143–148, 190, 286n
Cuneiform, 136
Cuoco, Vincenzo, 128
Curtatone, 181
Cusanus, Nicolaus, 128

D

D'Annunzio, Gabriele, 1, 9, 118, 216, 238–239, 246, 248, 265, 281, 346n, 353n
D'Arcais, Francesco, 246, 252, 344n
D'Attore, Pier Paolo, 44
D'Avray, David, 332n
D'Azeglio, Massimo, 199
D'Orléans, Antonio, 41
Da Bologna, Cristoforo, 314n
Da Silva, G., 156
Dahlhaus, Carl, 255, 264
Dall'Alpi, Violetta, 175
Dall'Argine, Constantino, 230
Dall'Olio, Cesare, 247
Dallolio, Alberto, 24, 30–31, 37, 52, 55, 100, 120, 169, 174, 249
Dallolio, Alfredo, 31
Dallolio, Cesare, 31
Dante Alighieri, 104, 118, 124, 133, 181–182, 265, 353n
Darío, Rubén, 239
Darwin, Charles, 32, 147, 150, 153, 160, 324n
David, Louis, 269
Davis, John, 10, 14
De Amici, Fernanda, 216
De Amicis, Edmondo, 229, 238, 279
De Flagney, Cosima, 231
De Lamennais, Félicité, 170
De Laveley, Emile, 290n
De Luca (family), 150
De Man, Paul, 135, 260, 319n
De Martino, 257
De Meis, Angelo Camillo, 198
De Pieri, Filippo, 286n
De Sanctis, Francesco, 104, 111, 157, 173, 264, 266, 312n, 319n
De Simonis, local councillor, 247
Debussy, Claude, 256
Decentralisation. *See* Centralisation
Deforestation. *See* Agriculture
Del Sarto, Andrea, 48
Delius, Frederick, 260
Della Quercia, Jacopo, 280
Democrats, 3, 6, 10, 14–17, 22–24, 32–37, 52, 61, 65, 70–83, 89, 92, 95, 97–98, 100–102, 108, 111, 118, 150, 152, 160, 167, 174, 176, 178, 186, 194, 197, 219, 223, 230, 233, 237–238, 240–241, 247, 250, 259, 264, 275, 280, 290n, 306n

Dempster, Thomas, 129
Dennis, George, 137
Denomination of Streets, 175, 179, 183–185, 216, 279–280
Dent, Edward, 261
Depretis, Agostino, 36–37
Derrida, Jacques, 97, 99, 179
Destra Storica, 3, 10, 23–25, 29, 30, 32, 35, 39, 67, 69, 75–77, 81, 94, 151, 164–165, 185, 250
Development, economic, 8, 11, 13, 26, 30, 34, 39–42
Dialect, use of, 25, 55, 145, 163, 166, 177, 276
Dickie, John, 177
Dionysius of Halicarnassus, 138, 320n
Diplmacy, 205
Disasters, natural, 177–178, 201, 203, 330n
Disraeli, Benjamin, 214
Division of labour, 39–40
Dönhoff (family), 30
Donizetti, Gaetano, 9, 70, 185, 221, 224, 226, 230, 236, 240, 242, 253, 263, 278, 342n
Donizetti, Gaetano, *La Favorita*, 248
Dostoyevsky, Fyodor, 265
Douglas, Mary, 201, 210
Drama. *See* Literature
Dresden, 2, 169, 247
Dreyfus Affaire, 251
Dukas, Paul, 257
Durkheim, Emile, 180, 267
Duse, Eleonora, 9, 54, 246

E

Eco, Umberto, 147, 323n
Education, 8, 14–15, 29, 31–33, 35–36, 55, 68, 77, 81, 88, 90, 95–97, 104, 106, 110–111, 117, 134, 138, 156–157, 164, 167, 175–176, 194, 202, 204, 209, 211–213, 240, 245, 252, 261, 268, 272, 280–281, 286n, 318n
Egypt, 78, 96, 130, 133, 136, 138–139, 142–143, 149, 158, 225, 321n, 322n
Einaudi, Luigi, 67, 353n
Elections, 22, 23, 28–29, 33, 35–36, 38, 274–275, 281; local, 17, 24, 26, 33, 35, 80, 275, 282
Electricity, 8, 303n
Elena of Montenegro, 213, 218

412 *Index*

Elgar, Edward, 256
Elias, Norbert, 48
Eliot, Thomas Stearns, 261
Elisabeth of Austria, 178, 216
Elites, 9, 11, 13–18, 21–40, 43–65,
    102, 105, 126, 149, 176,
    179–180, 182, 205, 230, 247,
    281, 286n, 287n, 294n, 340n
Emilia, 144, 165, 167, 282
Emilia Romagna, 7–9, 42, 73, 122,
    148, 165–167, 170, 211, 271,
    274, 281
Empire, Holy Roman, 3, 7, 8, 118, 121,
    123–127, 166, 182
Employees, 33, 35, 37, 59, 68, 80, 92,
    96
Engels, Friedrich, 87
England. *See* Great Britain
Enlightenment, 128, 266–267, 270,
    341n
Enslavement, papal, 16, 47, 90, 103,
    106, 111, 121, 127
Enzo, King of Sardinia, 123–124
Epidemics, 201–203, 277, 286n
Ercolani, Giambattista, 29, 32, 70, 96,
    163
Ercolani, Giovanni, 159
Ercolano, 91
Eschenbach, Wolfgang von, 260
Este (family), 48, 296n
Ethiopia, 273–274
Ethnicity, 14, 16, 130, 134, 136–142,
    147, 150, 160, 165, 182, 226,
    317n, 326n
Etruria. *See* Etruscans
Etruscans, 13, 16, 17, 25, 78, 92,
    128–160, 317n, 320n
Etruscology. *See* Etruscans
Etruscomania. See Etruscans
Europe, 1–3, 5–10, 14, 17, 21, 30, 32,
    39–40, 45, 47–48, 64, 66, 97,
    105–106, 115, 119, 124, 128,
    131, 136, 143, 149–151, 154,
    156–159, 166, 168–170, 174,
    179, 189, 203, 214, 216, 221,
    225–226, 228–229, 237–239,
    249, 252–253, 259–262,
    264–269, 273, 277, 293n
Evolution, Theory of, 145, 147,
    150–151, 153, 160, 267
Excavations, archaeological, 12, 78,
    88–96, 129, 131–160, 316n
Exhibitions, 2, 12, 68, 89, 101–102,
    123–124, 136, 139–140, 152,

169, 172, 196, 218, 221, 251,
    254, 323n, 338n
Exile, 25–26, 34, 158, 194, 210, 223,
    237–238, 253
Exoticism, 130, 132
Experience of modernity. *See* Moder-
    nity
Experts, 11, 14, 15, 22, 35, 64, 73,
    77–83, 100–102, 287n

F
Fabbri, Luigi, 110
Fabretti, Ariodante, 95, 133, 154
Faccio, Franco, 9, 52, 228, 245–246,
    248–249, 252, 256
Faccioli, Raffaele, 91
Faenza, 37, 227, 231
Fagnoli, local councillor, 66
Fanfulla, 246
Farfalla, La, 227
Farini, Luigi Carlo, 31, 44, 91, 97, 150
Farnese, 48, 285n
Fasci di combattimento, 281–282
Fascism, 1, 2, 3, 5, 6, 7, 9, 11, 17–18,
    95, 148, 175, 203–204, 221,
    266–268, 270–271, 278,
    281–283, 287n, 346n, 353n
Fasoli, Gina, 122
Federalism, 28
*Federazione italiana sindacati agri-
    coltori*, 281
Federconsorzi, 42, 274
Felsina (Etruscan Bologna), 25, 132,
    134–135, 137, 142, 145
Fergus of Kirkaldy, Elizabeth, 25
Ferrara, 8, 39, 144, 166, 249, 280, 282,
    296n, 357n
Festa dello Statuto. See Statuto Albertino
Fétis, François-Joseph, 230
Fiat, 277
Figaro, 239
Filippi, Filippo, 228–229, 242
Film, 1, 169, 217
Filopanti, Quirico, 34, 90, 106, 108,
    130–131, 137–138, 147, 152,
    154, 158, 163, 172, 179, 181,
    186–187, 205, 219, 250
Finance, municipal, 16, 29, 42, 49–83,
    95–97, 101–102, 149–151, 173–
    175, 177–178, 181–182, 195,
    223, 230, 233–234, 240–242,
    247, 249–250, 256–257, 273,
    276, 280–281, 304n, 305n,
    306n, 307n, 335n

Fine secolo, 3, 13, 16, 47, 127, 203, 210, 215, 221, 223, 237, 265
Fiori, Gaetano, 222
Florence, 8–12, 17, 27, 43–44, 46–47, 66, 69, 90, 94, 100, 105, 115, 122, 130, 133, 152, 166–169, 180–182, 186, 189, 194, 207, 228–229, 234–235, 261, 265, 268, 282, 291n, 316n, 333n; Accademia della Crusca, 94; Archaeological Museum, 152, 154; Mercato di San Lorenzo, 43; Santa Croce, 181, 186; Teatro della Pergola, 56, 71, 228, 231, 243; Teatro Pagliano (Teatro Verdi), 235
Fontana, Ferdinando, 247
Foot, John, 177
Forgacs, David, 287n
Forlì, 40, 166, 185
Foscolo, Ugo, 28, 128, 130, 186
Fossalta, Battle of, 124
Foucault, Michel, 99, 138, 140
France, 8, 9, 13, 25–26, 28, 35, 38, 62, 79, 109, 123, 135, 151, 154, 156–158, 166–168, 170, 173, 178–180, 184, 189, 194–195, 197, 200, 202, 205, 207, 221, 223, 225–226, 230, 235, 237, 240, 245, 248, 251–253, 258, 260, 263–264, 269, 276, 279, 288n, 293n, 304n
Francesco II, 290n
Franchetti, Alberto, 247; *Asrael*, 247; *Cristofero Colombo*, 247; *Germania*, 247
Franchetti, Leopoldo, 67–68
Frandsen, Steen Bo, 168
Frank, Ernst, 234
Frankfurt / M., 353n
Franz Joseph, Emperor, 178, 214
Frati, Luigi, 62, 94, 150, 154
Frederick Barbarossa, Holy Roman Emperor, 103, 123
Frederick II, Holy Roman Emperor, 123–124, 168
Freemasons, 34, 170, 292n, 306n
Freethinkers, 272
Fréret, Nicolas, 320n
Frescobaldi, Girolamo, 254
Freud, Sigmund, 267
Frizzi, Arturo, 238
Funeral Monuments and Rites, Ancient, 137, 138–140, 148, 154,

158–159; Modern, 168–169, 174–175, 179, 181–183, 186–187, 198–199, 203, 213, 216–218, 231–232, 269
Future, Music of the, 2, 9, 17, 53, 234–235, 239, 258, 263–265, 352n
Futurism, 125, 221, 239, 259, 261, 263–264, 268, 270, 352n, 354n

G
Gadamer, Hans Georg, 88
Gaibi, Cesare, 59, 222
Galileo Galilei, 108, 170, 186
Galletti, Stefano, 43
Galvani, Luigi, 8, 78, 157, 183–184, 187–188, 306n
Gandino, Giambattista, 130
Gardens, public, 67, 73; *See also* Bologna, Giardini Margherita;
Gardini, Carlo, 222
Gargiolli, Dafne, 248
Garibaldi, Anita, 211
Garibaldi, Giuseppe, 3, 4, 26, 34, 75, 89–90, 109, 130, 135, 169, 191, 193, 195, 200, 210–211, 218–220, 224, 245, 252, 273, 276, 280–281, 306n, 308n, 338n
Garnier, Charles, 109
Gaspari, Gaetano, 254, 350n
Gazzetta d'Italia, 246
Gazzetta del Popolo, 258
Gazzetta dell'Emilia, 39, 77, 92, 156, 163, 199, 209, 214, 222, 236, 239
Gazzetta Musicale, 67, 243
Gellner, Ernst, 126
Gender, 17, 35–36, 45, 91, 145, 175–176, 199, 202–204, 208–211, 315n
Gennarelli, Achille, 133
Genoa, 9, 185, 231, 243, 247, 270, 282
Genoa, Teatro Carlo Felice, 247
Gentile, Emilio, 179, 237
Gentile, Giovanni, 267
Gentiloni, Ottorino, 272
George IV, 214
George, Stefan, 265
Gerhard, Eduard, 149, 323n
Germany, 2, 8, 13, 25, 30, 35, 98, 103, 105, 124, 131, 136, 138, 140, 149, 151, 154, 157–158, 164–165, 170, 173, 180, 181, 186–189, 194, 197, 202, 205,

209, 214, 221, 226, 228–230,
   234–243, 247–248, 251,
   253–255, 258–260, 263–264,
   269, 276, 278, 280, 292n
Gerschenkron, Alexander, 286n
Ghelli, Raffaele, 182
Ghibellines, 90, 105, 121–127, 314n,
   315n
Ghirardini, Gherardo, 91, 95, 134,
   148, 159
Ghislanzoni, Antonio, 245
Giacobbi, Giramolo, 296n
Giambologna, 113, 188
Gide, André, 265, 267
Gilda di San Francesco, 111, 113
Gioberti, Vincenzo, 3, 128, 320n
Giolitti, Giovanni, 2, 73, 200, 267,
   270–272, 275
Giordani, local councillor, 282
Giordano, Umberto, 221, 226
Giornale Agrario Italiano, 40
Giovine Scuola, 225, 239
Giunta. See Administration, municipal
Gladstone, William, 30, 291n
Gluck, Christoph Willibald, 49, 63,
   235, 295n; *Trionfo di Clelia*, 49,
   296n
Gnecchi, Vittorio, 257
Gnudi, Ennio, 282
Gobatti, Stefano, 243–246; *Cordelia*,
   244–245; *I Goti*, 243–245;
   Luce, 243–244; *Massias*, 245
Goethe, Johann Wolfgang von, 353n
Goldberg, Fanny, 308n
Goldmann, Lucien, 159
Goldmark, Karl, 251, 349n
Golinelli, Enrico, 36, 52, 188, 243,
   256–257
Gombrich, Ernst, 135
Gounod, Charles, 9, 236, 240, 246;
   Faust, 9, 223, 229, 241, 258
Government, Italian, 23, 26, 28–35,
   39, 44, 68–83, 92, 95–96,
   98–99, 117, 152, 156–157,
   164, 166, 178–179, 188, 190,
   192–193, 198, 204–205, 215,
   220, 250, 257
Government, local. *See* Administration,
   municipal
Gozzadini Zucchini (family), 159
Gozzadini, Giovanni, 45, 88, 91–94,
   106, 107, 117–118, 131, 133,
   137–144, 148–155, 159–160
Gozzadini, Teresa, 45, 91

Grabinski (family), 26, 37, 41, 218
Grabinski, Giuseppe, 115
Gramsci, Antonio, 5, 6, 10, 14, 15, 21,
   126, 182, 223, 238, 268, 281,
   285n, 287n
Grand Opéra, 9, 52, 57, 79, 223, 229,
   247–248
Gravina, Luigi, 27
Great Britain, 13, 23, 35, 39, 55,
   103–105, 116, 129, 137, 153,
   158, 170, 173, 189, 194, 197,
   200, 202–204, 208, 210–211,
   214, 253, 264, 277, 291n
Greece, Ancient, 128–129, 133,
   136–139, 149, 158, 296n, 320n;
   Modern, 140, 257
Gregor XIII, Pope, 280
Gregorovious, Ferdinand, 209
Grenier, Albert, 135, 139
Gressoney, 207
Grinzane, 24
Grosseto, 8
Grossi, local councillor, 219
Guadagnini, Anacleto, 144, 151
Guardia Nazionale, 25, 67, 70, 193,
   211, 235
Guarnacci, Mario, 129
Guelphs, 90, 105, 121–128, 314n,
   315n
Guerrazzi, Domenico, 184, 199
Guerrini, Olindo, 12, 182
Guy, Constantin, 239, 263
Gyrowetz, Adalbert, 226

H
Habsburg, Rudolf of, 105
Halbwachs, Maurice, 89
Halévy, Fromental, 230; *La Juive*, 230
Hall, Stuart, 159
Hamburg, 247, 260, 270
Händel, Georg Friedrich, 229, 240
Haydn, Joseph, 226, 240, 295n
Hayez, Francesco, 106
Hegel, Georg Wilhelm Friedrich, 136,
   160, 240, 266–267
Hegemony, 10, 16, 22, 33, 37, 126–
   127, 160, 171, 238
Heimat, 164, 327n
Heine, 265
Hellenisation of Italy, 137, 140
Helsinki, 260
Hercolani (family), 26, 52, 57, 61, 226,
   256, 295n
Herodotus, 138, 140, 143

Hérold, Louis Ferdinand, 230
Historic Right. *See Destra Storica*
Historicism, 44, 89, 264, 267
Historicism, musical, 252–256
Historiography, 3, 6, 11–16, 22–24, 34, 38–39, 75, 87–91, 97–102, 105, 118, 121–123, 125–160, 165, 175, 203–204, 209, 266–268, 314n, 315n, 317n, 320n, 321n, 340n, 353n, 357n
History. *See* Historiography
Hobsbawm, Eric, 87, 230
Hohenzollern-Sigmaringen, Friederika, 25
Holidays, public, 192–195
Homoeroticism, 336n
Honoratioren, 37–38
Hudson, Kenneth, 96
Hugo, Victor, 182, 184, 238, 265
Huizinga, Johan, 87–88
Humanism, 103, 129
Humperdinck, Engelbert, 257–258
Humphreys, Sally, 87
Hungary, 214
Huxley, Aldous , 267

I

Ibsen, Henrik, 265
Iconoclasm, 109–110, 114–115, 118, 280, 313n
Idealism, 251, 264, 266–267
Identities, collective, 2, 5, 10, 11, 12, 14, 16, 17, 18, 75, 88, 94, 98–99, 102, 104–105, 107, 110–111, 121, 126, 146–147, 152, 156–157, 159–160, 163–167, 177, 179–180, 183, 189, 194–200, 215, 221, 252, 265, 282–283, 289n, 327n
Ideology, 14, 15, 126, 257, 268, 281
Illica, Luigi, 247
Imola, 37
Imperialism, 220
Impresari, 49–65, 70–72, 221–223, 234, 241–243, 247, 250, 301n
India, 136, 158, 214
Industrialisation, 39–43, 271–272, 277
Infrastructure, cultural, 6, 7, 11, 15, 39, 66–83, 223, 279; development of, 68, 74–75, 78, 100, 120, 155, 167
Innocent III, Pope, 105
Institutions, cultural. *See* Infrastructure, cultural

Intellectuals, 11–16, 32–35, 91, 100, 155, 205, 209, 215, 237–238, 240, 255, 265–267, 272, 281, 287n, 292n
International League of Socialist Communes, 124
Internationalists. *See* Socialists
Ireland, 216, 253
Iron Age, 133, 137, 139, 142, 320n
Irredentism, 182, 189–190, 272–273
Ischia, 201, 203
Isnenghi, Mario, 217
Isolani (family), 26, 41
Isolani, Francesco, 29
Istituto Nazionale di Statistica, 285n
Italia delle cento città, 5, 18, 83, 103, 167, 181, 283

J

Jacobins, 130, 287n, 308n
Janik, Alan, 15, 287n
Japan, 40
Jaurès, Jean, 238, 280
Jauss, Hans Robert, 128
Jerusalem, 116
Jesuits, 227
Jolanda Margherita of Savoy, 213
Joukowsky, Paul von, 259
Journalists. *See* Press
Judaism, 32, 57, 90, 174, 194, 226, 308n, 319n, 352n
Judea, 136
Julius II, Pope, 8, 47, 105–106, 117, 122

K

Kafka, Franz, 269
Kandinsky, Wassily, 265
Kant, Immanuel, 159
Karbusicky, Vladimír, 240
Kertzer, David, 197
Kneif, Tibor, 12
Kocka, Jürgen, 14
Komissarzhevsky, Fyodor, 264
Konrad IV, German King, 123
Koselleck, Reinhart, 13, 88, 179, 263
Kubler, George, 269
Kuhn, Thomas, 160
Kuliscioff, Anna, 175

L

L'Arpa, 26
La Fontaine, Henri, 345n
La Marmora, Alfonso, 167

Labour conflict, 11, 18, 34, 42, 77, 215, 257, 271–272, 274–275, 277

Labour movement, 3, 34, 77, 90, 92, 106, 171, 173–174, 207, 211–212, 215–216, 238, 267, 271–272, 274, 280, 282, 289n

Labour organisations. *See* Labour movement

Labriola, Arturo, 216, 267

Laibach / Ljubljana, 157

Lambertini, Leopoldo, 229

Lanari, Alessandro, 55, 222

Lancet, The, 201

Landowners, 22–45, 62, 73, 76, 80, 171, 174, 233, 271, 273, 281, 290n, 292n, 294n

Landscape, urban. *See* Space, urban

Laqua, Daniel, 345n

Lassalle, Ferdinand, 238

Laterza, publisher, 267

Latin-America, 106, 239, 270

Latium. *See* Lazio

Law, Roman, 7

Lawyers, 31–34, 36, 37, 69, 175, 291n, 293n

Lazio, 7, 137, 142, 152, 159

Left, Extreme, 71, 175, 179, 250, 272, 274–275, 354n

Legitimism, 28–29, 60, 88, 90, 94, 109–110, 116, 166, 192, 200, 207, 290n

Legnano, Battle of, 89, 123

Leipzig, 46, 157, 248, 252

Leisure, 7, 12, 95, 170–174

Leitkultur, 248

Lemnos, 138, 320n

Lenin, Vladimir Ilyich, 238

Leonardo, 265

Leoncavallo, Ruggero, 221

Leopardi, Giacomo, 170, 225

Leopold II, King of the Belgians, 188

Lequin, Yves, 38, 293n

Lessona, Michele, 265

Liberali. *See* Liberalism

Liberalism, 6, 14, 27, 29–31, 35, 38, 45, 66–83, 103, 109, 112–114, 117, 123, 167, 180, 193, 271–272, 274–275, 278, 280, 289n

Libraries, 33, 45, 62–65, 68, 78, 97, 170, 254

Lignana, Giacomo, 133

Liguria, 91

Lisbon, 246, 296n

Liszt, Franz, 226, 231, 249

Literacy, 8, 36, 268, 286n

Literature, 10, 25, 54–58, 88, 62–63, 105, 121, 124, 129–130, 133–136, 148, 160, 202, 207, 245–247, 251, 257, 260, 265–267, 273, 276, 289n, 311n, 336n

Livorno, 282

Lombards, 134

Lombardy, 6–8, 28, 123

London, 25, 34, 89, 129, 158, 210, 223, 226, 231, 238, 245–246, 252, 258; British Museum, 158; Covent Garden, 229, 250; Philharmonic Society, 252; University College, 25, 34, 210

Loreto, 168

Louis-Philippe, King of the French, 44

Lovatelli (family), 45

Lovejoy, Arthur, 268

Löwith, Karl, 308n

Lucca, 109, 303n

Lucca, Giovannina, 234, 243

Luccheni, Luigi, 216

Lugli, Cesare, 29, 36, 187

Lugo, 178, 186–187, 226, 261

Lukács, Georg, 265

Luzzatto, Sergio, 204

Lydia, 138

Lyon, 40

Lyttelton, Adrian, 103, 126–127, 270, 281

M

Macerata, 8, 168, 231

Machiavelli, Niccolò, 186

Mack Smith, Dennis, 24

Macry, Paolo, 28, 43, 176

Madrid, 247

Maeterlinck, Maurice, 257

Mahler, Gustav, 231, 266, 353n

Malalbergo, 29

Malatesta, Errico, 178, 215–216

Malibran, Maria, 55

Mallarmé, Stéphane, 238

Malraux, André, 88

Malta, 210

Malvezzi (family), 9, 26, 29, 35, 41, 45, 48, 60–61, 144, 177, 226

Malvezzi Medici, Giovanni, 24, 80, 172, 187

Malvezzi Trotti (family), 46

Malvezzi, Nerio, 23
Mameli, Goffredo, 105
Manaresi, local councillor, 175
Mancinelli, Luigi, 46, 52, 245, 247–
251, 253, 255, 258, 260; *Isora
di Provenza*, 249; *Paolo e Franc-
esca*, 249, 258
Mancinelli, Marino, 52, 248–249
Mann, Heinrich, 267
Mann, Klaus, 267
Mann, Thomas, 103, 265
Mannheim, 296n
Mantova, 282, 296n
Manzoni, Alessandro, 28, 105,
128, 130, 184; *Promessi
Sposi*, 28
Marcello, Benedetto, 302n
March on Rome, 5, 18, 271
Marches, 144, 168
Marchetti, Filippo, 248; *Ruy Blas*, 57
Marescalchi (family), 29
Marescotti, Galeazzo, 314n
Margherita, 208
Margherita of Savoy, Queen, 17,
32, 171, 194, 198, 202–209,
211–218, 248–249
Maria Adeleide of Savoy, Queen, 202
Mariani, Angelo, 9, 50, 52, 64, 71,
182, 186, 223, 230–236,
248–249, 264, 343n
Marie-Louise of Habsburg Lorraine,
285n
Mariette, Auguste, 322n
Marinetti, Filippo Tommaso, 203, 259,
263–264
Mario, Alberto, 207, 210
Marseille, 25, 157
Marsigli, Luigi Ferdinando, 149
Marsili (family), 37
Marsili, Carlo, 24, 41
Martini della Torre, Maria, 210
Martini, Giovanni Battista, 253
Martucci, Giuseppe, 9, 46, 221, 246,
248–249, 253, 255–256, 261,
264, 266, 353n
Martuzzi (family), 46
Marx, Karl, 216, 238, 267, 279–280
Marxism, 39, 266–267, 340n
Marzabotto, 131–133, 144, 150, 152,
321n
Marzocco, Il, 265
Mascagni, Pietro, 221, 225; *Cavalleria
Rusticana*, 250
Masci, Filippo, 266

Masi, Ernesto, 156, 183
Masini, Cesare, 51, 123, 187
Massei (family), 35
Massei, Francesco, 42
Massei, Giovanni, 24, 32
Massenet, Jules, 222, 251, 258, 297n
Mastiani Brunacci, 37
Mattei, Stanislao, 226, 253
May Day, 219–220, 280
Mayer, Arno, 16, 21–22, 38, 287n
Mayr, Carlo, 45
Mayr, Johann Simon, 226
Mazzacorati (family), 29, 31, 35
Mazzacorati, Giuseppe, 254
Mazzini, Giuseppe, 2, 3, 25, 33–34,
36, 75, 105–106, 133, 154,
173, 181, 195–196, 210–211,
218–220, 223–224, 226, 229,
238–239, 251, 274, 280, 335,
338n
Mazzoldi, Angelo, 128
Medici (family), 47, 137
Medici, Cosimo di, 128
Medici, Cosimo II di, 129
Medievalism. *See* Revival, medieval
Mediterranean, 27, 201, 210
Meinecke, Friedrich, 345n
Meister, The, 238
Memory, collective, 121, 135, 189
Mendelssohn Bartholdy, Felix, 221,
226, 255, 353n
Menganti, Alessandro, 280
Mengoni, Giuseppe, 43
Mentana, 26, 75, 219
Mercadante, Saverio, 224, 234, 253;
Giuramenti, 230
Meriggi, Marco, 32, 35, 265
Mesolithicum, 136
Messina, 177, 282, 330n
Metastasio, Pietro, 49
Meyerbeer, Giacomo, 17, 57, 59,
226, 229–230, 236, 240–241,
247, 342n, 343n; *Il Crociato
in Egitto*, 229; *Dinorah*, 233,
251; *Gli Ugonotti*, 229; *Il
Profeta*, 230; *L'Africaine*, 9,
223, 229–230, 278; *Le Pardon
de Ploërmel*, 230; *Margherita
d'Anjou*, 229; *Roberto il Dia-
volo*, 229; *Semiramide*, 229
Mezzadria, 274, 294n
Michelangelo Buonarroti, 43, 48, 152,
186
Michelet, Jules, 139, 317n

Middle Ages, 3, 16, 24, 43–44, 78, 90, 94, 97–98, 103–128, 130, 146, 149, 219, 259, 296n, 333n
Middle class, educated, 14, 15, 21–22, 26, 32–37, 43–44, 57, 74–77, 80, 91, 171–172, 174–176, 275–276, 286n, 290n, 291n, 292n
Middle class, professional. *See* Middle class, educated
Middle classes, 10–17, 22–24, 30–39, 41–46, 52, 57, 62, 64, 73, 87–97, 100, 102, 169, 171–176, 180, 187, 194, 198, 203, 230, 237, 251–252, 257, 272, 275–276, 292n, 293n
Milan, 7–9, 11–12, 17, 25, 28, 33, 49, 69, 102, 105, 107, 108, 122, 163, 166, 169, 179–181, 184, 214–215, 221, 228, 231, 238, 242–243, 245–246, 254, 256, 261, 265, 270, 272, 275, 277, 281–282, 291n, 293n; Teatro alla Scala, 9, 55, 64–65, 71, 221–223, 241, 243, 243, 247, 249, 258, 303n, 304n, 346n; Teatro Dal Verme, 245; Vittorio Emanuele Arcades, 43
Milani, Luciani, 203
Mill, John Stuart, 25, 289n
Minghetti, Marco, 9, 28–33, 36, 39–41, 44–45, 61, 70–76, 82–83, 106, 107, 121, 124, 130, 137, 151–152, 156, 158, 164, 166, 168, 170–171, 178, 182–183, 190, 199, 203, 209, 214, 234, 272, 291n
Mobility, social, 30–32, 43
Modena, 8, 12, 17, 22, 25, 37, 69, 71, 151–152, 155, 166–167, 249, 282; Palazzo Ducale, 44
Moderati, 3, 6, 9–11, 14–16, 22–31, 33–38, 41, 44–45, 49, 52, 54, 59–83, 92, 95, 98, 100–102, 106, 107, 118, 152, 157, 164, 167, 173–174, 176, 181–182, 187, 190, 192, 194, 212, 233, 237, 241–242, 247–248, 257, 259, 271, 293n, 295n
Modernisation, 13, 14, 15, 27, 39–42, 44, 64, 103, 107, 109, 120, 127, 163–164, 169, 268, 271, 274, 277, 295n

Modernism, 3, 13, 17, 103, 107, 113, 125–127, 230, 240–241, 251, 255–256, 259–266, 268–271, 354n
Modernity, 2–6, 10, 12–14, 17–18, 43, 45, 60, 64, 80, 87, 99, 103, 106, 108, 148, 179, 239, 259–269, 283
Modica, 167
Moeller van den Bruck, Arthur, 135
Momigliano, Arnaldo, 129, 131, 316n, 321n, 353n
Mommsen, Theodor, 130–131, 140, 317n
Monarchists, 6, 90, 281, 325n
Monarchy, 17, 23, 33, 125, 168, 197–220, 280
Mondo Artistico, 228
Mondo Illustrato, Il, 227
Monitore di Bologna, Il, 44, 59, 74, 77, 92, 98, 132, 142, 147, 153, 170, 200, 202, 204, 222, 226–227, 229–230, 233–235, 246
Monmasson, Rosalia, 210
Montalc, 155
Montanara, 181
Montanari, Antonio, 91
Montanelli, Giuseppe, 199
Montenegro, 213
Monteverde, Giulio, 214
Monteverdi, Claudio, 235, 254, 296n
Monti, Coriolano, 43, 116
Monuments, 1, 17, 35, 66–68, 89, 120, 179–188, 212, 217–218, 265–266; for Cavour, 183–184, 218; for Dante, 181–182; for Galvani, 187–188, 265; for Garibaldi, 218–220; for Rossini, 70; for Monuments, Verdi, 1; for Vittorio Emanuele II, 8, 169, 179, 212–213, 218, 338n
Monza, 215–217
Mosca, Gaetano, 38
Mosse, George, 180, 202
Mozart, Wolfgang Amadeus, 7, 221, 226, 236, 240, 253; *Don Giovanni*, 55
Müller, Karl Otfried, 130–131, 319n, 323n
Munich, 234, 237, 241, 247, 265, 317n
Murat, Antonietta, 25
Murat, Gioacchino, 195
Murat, Letizia, 25

Murri, Romolo, 272
Museums, 12, 33, 35, 43, 68, 81,
    88–89, 92–97, 99, 148–160,
    207, 309n, 3223n
Music, Sacred, 249, 253–256
Music, Symphonic. *See* Concert Life
Music-theatre. *See* opera
Musil, Robert, 214
Musorgsky, Modest, 257
Mussolini, Benito, 31, 41, 203–204,
    275, 281–283, 357n
Myths, 2, 3, 13, 16, 107, 121–124,
    126, 128, 130, 133–135, 138,
    143, 167, 179, 202, 247

N

Nabab, 246, 273
Naples, 8, 9, 27, 28, 36, 43–44, 49, 69,
    71, 128, 169, 176–177, 189,
    191, 195, 201–203, 207–208,
    228, 234, 236, 242, 249, 253,
    256, 261, 266, 282, 285n, 291n,
    292n, 294n, 304n ; Teatro San
    Carlo, 49, 55, 64, 69, 71, 222,
    249, 285n
Napoleon, 3, 8, 30, 45, 55, 63, 106,
    128, 168, 192, 194–195, 207,
    223, 247, 285n, 289n
Napoleon III, 25–26, 109, 178, 195,
    202, 209
Nation, concept of, 27–28, 132, 136–
    137, 139, 156, 160, 163–165,
    168, 179, 189, 197–199, 202,
    221, 233, 250, 258, 264, 280,
    283
National Socialism, 133, 264
Nationalism, 1, 2, 3, 10, 12, 14, 99,
    103, 121, 123, 126–129, 136,
    139, 163–165, 237
Nationalists, Italian, 124–125, 182,
    238–239, 257, 272–274,
    281–282, 315n
Nationality. *See* Nation, concept of
Nazione, La, 286n
Negri, Gaetano, 25
Neolithicum, 136, 153
Netherlands, The, 156
Neumann, Angelo, 248
New York, 216, 234, 246, 250, 258,
    266, 345n
Newspapers. *See* Press
Nicolò dall'Arca, 114
Nicolucci, Giustiniano, 153
Niebuhr, Barthold Georg, 140, 317n

Nietzsche, Friedrich, 125, 239,
    245–246
Nikisch, Arthur, 231
Nitti, Francesco Saverio, 33, 292n
Noale, 181
Nobel Prize, 9, 265
Nobility, 9–11, 16, 21–38, 41–65, 91,
    94, 98, 100, 106, 115, 118, 122,
    133, 142, 154, 159, 169–174,
    195, 209, 223, 229–230, 233,
    237–238, 247, 254, 257, 271,
    276, 279–280, 288n, 291n,
    293n, 295n, 300n
Norsa Guerrieri, Elisa, 175–176
Nostalgia, 103–104, 106, 111, 128,
    255
Notabili, 21–22, 37–39, 43–46, 160,
    169–170, 194, 286n, 293n
Notables. See Notabili
Noto, 167
Novara, 67
Nuova Antologia, 67, 121, 304n
Nuova Italia, La, 272
Nuovo Alfiere, Il, 229
Nürnberg, 169

O

O'Connor, Maura, 210
Oberdan, Guglielmo, 178, 182
Offenbach, Jacques, 251
Oldofredi Tadini, Ercole, 27
Opera, 1–3, 5, 9, 11, 17, 22, 32, 43,
    46–65, 69–72, 79, 127, 221–
    264, 269, 278
Opera buffa, 49, 54, 57, 223, 297n
Opera seria, 49, 55, 57, 59, 63, 297n
Operetta, 54
Opinione, L', 246
Orchestras. *See* Bologna, Istituzione
    Rossiniana
Ordone of Savoy, 213
Oriani, Alfredo, 273
Orsini, Cesare, 41
Orsini, Felice, 178
Orvieto, 159
Osima, local councillor,
Oxford, 131
Ozouf, Mona, 190, 194
Ozzano, 29

P

Pacchioni, Giuseppe, 43
Pace, La, 109
Padova, 95, 282

Padri Barnabiti, 29
Paër, Ferdinando, *Sofonisba*, 55
Palagi, Pelagio, 27, 106, 129, 149–150, 154
Paleolithicum, 136
Palermo, 36, 65, 91, 124, 261, 282
Palestrina, Giovanni Pierluigi, 254, 350n
Palladio, Andrea, 116
Pallottino, Massimo, 160
Palmerstone, Henry Temple Viscount of, 203
Panizzi, Antonio, 25
Panzacchi, Enrico, 9, 15, 36, 62, 77, 90, 100, 102, 114–116, 176, 186, 188, 203, 222, 226, 234–235, 242–243, 246, 248, 252, 260, 264, 273, 280, 346n
Panzini, Alfredo, 12
Papacy, 3, 21, 28, 47–49, 90, 105, 106, 121–124, 126–127, 129,136, 152, 273
Papal Legations, 3, 5, 7, 11, 21–22, 25–29, 36, 38, 53, 56, 64, 68, 75, 94, 97–98, 106, 130, 150, 163, 166, 171, 192, 195, 199, 207, 213, 227, 259
Papal regime. *See* Papal States
Papal States, 3–11, 16, 21, 24–25, 28–29, 37, 40, 44–45, 47–51, 56, 65–66, 68–72, 89–90, 94, 97–98, 104–106, 108–110, 114–116, 119, 121–123, 126–127, 135–136, 149, 152, 156, 163–166, 170–172, 189, 191, 210, 221, 226 227, 231, 280, 285n.
Papini, Giovanni, 259, 265
Paravicini (family), 61
Paris, 8, 26, 44, 57, 71, 109, 124, 216, 225–226, 229–231, 233, 235–236, 238–240, 246–247, 252–253, 257, 265, 302n, 357n
Parliament, Italian, 10, 22–23, 26, 29, 31, 33, 36, 75, 79, 92, 167, 175, 179, 186, 191, 198, 204–205, 240, 250, 270, 279, 281, 288n, 290n, 291n
Parma, 1, 2, 8, 37, 69, 71, 142, 152, 166–167, 188, 243, 261, 282, 285n, 289n, 293n, 303n, 354n; Teatro Regio, 56, 258
Parmeggiani, Carlo, 219
Parties, political, organisation of, 294n

Partito Socialista Italiano. *See* Socialists
Party of Action, 237, 245
Party of Order, 37
Pascal, Blaise, 159
Pascoli, Giovanni, 10, 176, 182, 216, 273, 335n
Pasha, Ismail, 322n
Pasolini, Pier Paolo, 15
Passanante, Giovanni, 207–208, 215
Passatore, 171
Passerini, Luisa, 203
Pasternak, Boris, 267
Paterson, New Jersey, 216
Patria, concept of, 27–28, 79, 83, 105, 111, 120–121, 126, 129–130, 170, 179–180, 185–186, 189–199, 202–204, 209, 211, 225, 264–265, 278
Patria, La, 222
Patrimony, 70, 73, 88, 92–94, 98, 100, 116, 120, 124, 181, 188
Patriotism. *See Patria*, concept of
Patronage, 48, 52
Patti, Adelina, 297n
Pavia, 69, 282, 296n, 354n
Pécout, Gilles, 170, 285n
Pelasgians, 129, 137, 139, 320n
Pelissier, Olimpia, 186
Pelloux, Luigi, 126, 215
Pepoli (family), 9, 25, 44, 60, 105
Pepoli, Carlo, 24, 25–26, 45, 57, 90, 158, 165, 253
Pepoli, Gioacchino Napoleone, 21, 23, 25–26, 67, 75, 82–83, 172, 184, 195, 204
Pepoli, Guido Taddeo, 25, 314n
Pepoli, Taddeo, 25
Pergolesi, Giovanni Battista, 302n
Perozzi, local councillor, 124–125, 280
Persistence of the *Ancien régime*. *See Ancien régime*
Perugia, 8, 29
Pesaro, 29, 70, 166, 186, 254
Pessimism, cultural, 3
Petite Bourgeoisie, 171, 224, 272, 281, 292n, 341n
Petra di Vastogirardi e di Caccavone, Nicola, 27
Petrarch, Francesco, 104, 121, 128, 181–182
Petri, Rolf, 327n
Pfitzner, Hans, 263, 352n
Philosophy of History, 240, 267
Philosophy of Praxis, 267

Photography, 143, 154, 260
Piacenza, 71, 142, 167, 227, 249, 292n
Pianora, 31
Piazza, Pietro, 34
Piccini, Niccolò, 235
Pico della Mirandola, Giovanni, 128
Piedmont, 3–8, 21–24, 27, 39–40, 51,
    53, 91, 97, 100, 106–107, 153,
    164, 166–168, 189, 191, 193,
    196–200, 209, 247, 288n, 290n
Pigorini, Luigi, 142
Pinelli, Ferdinando, 183
Pini, Enrico, 31, 42, 52, 278
Pippin, Frankish king, 105
Pisa, 29, 37, 69, 74, 95, 118, 189,
    304n; Teatro Nuovo, 74
Pius IX, Pope, 51, 109, 115, 123, 170,
    213, 227
Pius X, Pope, 272
Pizzardi (family), 29, 31, 41, 44
Pizzardi, Camillo, 46
Pizzardi, Luigi, 24, 41, 72, 168, 187
Planning, urban, 5, 12, 14, 22, 43,
    66–67, 73, 77–78, 82, 100–102,
    107, 116, 120
Plato, 47, 128, 316n
Plautus, 143
Pliny, 138
Po, 166, 193, 201
Poirrier, Philippe, 285n
Poland, 246
Polesine, 201
Police, 51, 57, 68, 170–171, 220, 229
Policy, cultural, 2, 5–18, 21–22, 52–53,
    55, 61–65, 67–83, 88–89,
    92–96, 100–102, 125, 147, 149,
    151–152, 157, 160, 175, 180,
    221–262, 278–280, 283, 285n,
    287n
Politics of Culture. *See* Policy, cultural
Politics, local, *See* Administration,
    municipal
Pomian, Krzysztof, 13, 88, 148
Ponatowski, 226
Ponchielli, Amilcare, 221, 252; *La
    Gioconda*, 225, 250
Pontida, 123
Poor relieve, 68
Popolani, 44
Popular University, 133
Porciani, Ilaria, 164, 192
Portugal, 156
Positivism, 234, 236, 251, 266–267
Poverty, 172–173, 271–272, 277, 292n

Practice, cultural, 6, 13
Praga, Emilio, 245
Prague, 259, 352n
Predieri, Paolo, 40
Prefects, 22, 26–29, 36, 44, 54, 67, 69,
    92, 107, 171, 176, 182, 271
Pre-history. *See* Civilisations, pre-
    Roman
Pre-Raphaelites, 105
Press, 10, 13, 17, 26–29, 33, 37, 45–46,
    52, 54, 60–61, 78, 90–91,
    102, 132–133, 136, 143, 147,
    151, 153–156, 170, 176, 184,
    197, 200–201, 203, 210, 213,
    222–223, 227, 234, 236, 239,
    242, 246, 249, 259, 276, 278,
    289n, 292n, 295n, 325n,340n
Preti (family), 185
Prezzolini, Giuseppe, 265
Professionalisation, 11, 14–15, 22–23,
    32–34, 36, 38, 73, 76–83, 92,
    94, 100–102, 142, 160, 249,
    286n, 287n, 293n, 306n
Professions, liberal. *See* Middle class,
    educated
Progress, 239–240, 267, 283
Propaganda, 15, 34
Prostitution, 143, 147
Protestantism, 105, 106, 255
Proudhon, Pierre Joseph, 179, 238,
    331n
Proust, Marcel, 356n
Prüfer, Sebastian, 352n
Prussia, 8, 23, 35, 155, 288n, 327n
Publishers of music, 50, 222–223, 234
Puccini, Giacomo, 65, 133, 221,
    225–226, 245, 247, 251, 278;
    La Bohème, 278; *La Rondine*,
    278; *Le villi*, 247, 251; *Madama
    Butterfly*, 257–258; *Tosca*, 250,
    258, 278
Pugin, Augustus Welby Northmore, 89,
    105
Pullé, local councillor, 137
Pythagoras, 128

Q
Question, social, 18, 272

R
Rabelais, François, 145–147, 265
Race, concept of, 131, 135, 139, 153,
    165, 216, 226, 276, 319n, 326n
Racine, Jean, 159, 264

Radicali, 34–36, 52, 75, 156, 215, 237, 272, 274–275, 281, 293n
Ragionieri, Ernesto, 15
Railways, 8, 41–42, 75, 77, 120, 151, 166, 233, 248, 275
Rambaldi, Gaetano, 55
Ramponi, Agostino, 42
Randeraad, Nico, 304n
Ranuzzi (family), 37, 60
Ranuzzi, Ferdinando, 254
Raphael Sanzio, 43, 48
Rassegna settimanale, 66
Rathenau, Walter, 267
Rattazzi, Urbano, 24, 26, 31
Ravenna, 37, 151–152, 166, 181–182, 185, 231
Razza Latina, 179, 239, 273
Realism, 64
Recanati, 168
Reception theory, 225
Reform, electoral. See Suffrage
Reggio Calabria, 177
Reggio Emilia, 22, 32, 45, 57, 110, 131, 167, 228, 247, 282
Region, 2, 4, 6, 16, 28, 32–34, 39, 69, 88, 99, 148, 152, 156, 160, 163–167, 271, 326n
Regnoli, local councillor, 106
Religion, 5, 25, 34, 54, 111, 116–117, 128, 130, 142–143, 145–146, 192, 268
Religion, political, 6, 179–180, 185, 195–196, 211, 218–220. 260
Renaissance, 27, 47–48, 55, 90, 128, 135, 254
Renan, Ernest, 164, 182, 321n
Reno, 34, 159, 166, 174
Repertoire, 221–262
Representation, cultural. See Policy, cultural
Republic, Cisalpine, 54, 167, 224
Republic, Cispadanian, 8, 10
Republic, Roman, 34, 131, 185, 219–220, 224
Republicanism. See Republicans
Republicans, 2–3, 6, 9–10, 34–38, 75, 90, 106, 113, 128, 156, 163, 171, 173–174, 176, 178, 187, 198, 201, 207, 215, 224, 237–238, 256–257, 274–275, 280–281, 293n
Respighi, Ottorino, 124, 261
Resto del Carlino, Il, 110, 174, 176, 195, 222, 250–251, 273

Restoration, 164, 170, 195
Reuchlin, Johann, 128
Revival, medieval, 2, 13, 16, 44, 87, 89, 103–127, 247, 254, 259
Revolution of 1830/1831, 8, 9, 25, 28, 53, 186
Revolution of 1848 / 1849, 2, 8, 25–26, 28, 45, 75, 120, 127, 131, 170–171, 180–181, 186, 189–192, 197, 214, 219, 227–228, 230, 237–238, 333n
Revolution of 1876, Parliamentary, 10, 22, 35, 250
Revolution of 1917, 264
Revolution, French, 65, 190, 269, 285n, 303n, 333n
Revue Wagnérienne, 238
Rhine, 134
Ricci, Corrado, 106, 112, 229, 248, 314n, 351n
Ricci, Matteo, 94
Richter, Hans, 231, 256
Ricordi, publisher, 59, 222, 243
Rieti, 186
Rifle Clubs, 169–170
Riforma, La, 197, 201
Rilke, Rainer Maria, 135, 260, 265, 269, 352n
Rimsky-Korsakov, Nicolai, 261
Rinnovamento Cattolico, 153
Rinnovamento, Il, 246
Rio de Janeiro, 249–250
Risorgimento, 3, 6–10, 17, 22, 27, 31, 45, 72, 79, 88–90, 99, 104–106, 108, 110, 120–121, 124, 128, 130–131, 133, 135–136, 138, 163, 167–168, 176, 179–180, 182, 189, 193, 198, 204, 210, 212, 218, 224–225, 228, 237, 245, 252, 259, 264, 272–273, 279, 285n, 319n
Rivari, local councillor, 113, 259
Rivista Bolognese, 39, 123, 198, 240, 266
Rivista Musicale, 228
Rivista Musicale Italiana, 254
Rocchi, Francesco, 133, 148
Rolland, Romain, 267
Romagna, 6, 8, 12, 26, 28, 31, 38–39, 41, 94, 98, 105, 165–166, 171, 178, 192, 205, 207, 237, 243, 261, 265, 274–275, 279
Romanelli, Raffaele, 27, 39, 167, 287n, 304n

Romanticism, 103–104, 113, 127, 255, 261, 268, 311n
Rome, 7–8, 13, 25, 29, 31, 45, 48, 56, 69, 75, 88–89, 91, 94, 100, 105, 115, 120, 129, 133, 135, 140, 152, 163, 166, 169–171, 179, 182, 189, 194, 198, 207–209, 217, 219, 227, 243, 246, 248, 253, 258, 265, 272, 304n, 323n; Liberation of, 28–29, 120, 148, 152, 170, 190, 225; Museo Gregoriano, 145, 152, 158; Pantheon, 168, 179, 217; Quirinale, 209, 218; Teatro Apollo, 56, 71, 243
Rome, Ancient, 16, 17, 44, 47, 78, 89, 94, 105, 117, 118–119, 127, 129–160, 165, 167, 203, 251, 273, 296n, 317n; Ronzani, Bianca, 202
Rosmini, Enrico, 54
Rosselli, John, 224, 231
Rossi, Lauro, 243
Rossi, Pellegrino, 322n
Rossini, Gioacchino, 8, 9, 17, 55, 70, 79, 115, 176, 185–186, 221, 223–227, 230–232, 234, 236, 240, 242, 246, 253, 263, 278, 342n, 344n; *Mosè*, 224, 242; *Barbiere di Siviglia*, 54; *Guillaume Tell*, 57, 178, 224–225; *L'Assedio di Corinto*, 224; *L'equivoco stravagante*, 55; *Stabat Mater*, 185
Rota, Giuseppe, *La Capanna di Tom (Bianchi e Neri)*, 58; *La Silfide del Pekino*, 58
Rouen, 157
Rousseau, Jean-Jacques, 62–63, 135, 140, 194, 302n
Rovigo, 282
Rubbiani, Alfonso, 28, 47, 90, 106, 109–114, 120, 124, 127, 137, 182, 255, 259, 260
Rubinstein, Anton, 243, 249, 260
Rugge, Fabio, 276
Ruiz, Gustavo, 248
Russia, 2, 9, 10, 178, 197, 237–238, 264, 270, 280, 354n

S

Sacchetti, Gualtiero, 62, 80, 116
Saffi, Aurelio, 9, 131, 163, 172, 176, 182, 185, 207, 210, 280

Said, Edward, 322n, 343n
Saint-Simon, Claude Henri de Rouvroy de, 238
Salandra, Alessandro, 73, 304n
Salina Armorini (family), 45, 60, 149
Salina di Donnafugata, Fabrizio, 32, 228
Salina, Agostino, 24, 29, 52, 152, 159, 187, 233, 243, 247, 254
Salotti, 170–171, 209
Salvemini, Gaetano, 17–18, 357n
Samoggia, Luigi, 43, 233
San Giorgio, 21
Sandoni, local councillor, 120
Sangiorgi, Gustavo, 61, 222, 228, 233, 236, 238
Sant'Agata, 232
Sardinia, 123
Sarti, local councillor, 257
Sassoli Tomba (family), 37
Sassoli Tomba, Achille, 24, 110
Saunier, Pierre-Yves, 180
Scalaberni, Luigi, 186, 222, 228, 230, 242, 248, 348n
Scapigliati, 238, 245–246, 353n
Scarabelli, Luciano, 181
Scarlatti, Domenico, 221
Schalk, Franz, 231
Schiller, Friedrich von, 225, 228, 264, 340n
Schillerfeiern, 181
Schliemann, Heinrich, 45, 154
Schmitt, Carl, 15
Schönberg, Arnold, 260–261
Schorske, Carl, 126
Schramm, Percy Ernst, 198
Schumann, Robert, 221, 249, 253
Schwartz, Maria Espérance von, 210
Scotland. *See* Great Britain
Sebald, Winfried Georg Maximilian, 140
Secchi, Angelo, 152
Segretario comunale, 34, 292n
Seidl, Anton, 248
Self-government, 167
Sella, Quintino, 67, 94, 130, 152, 212
Semiophores, 13, 88–89
Senate (upper house), 22, 23, 29, 31, 52, 151, 187, 205, 278, 288n
Senigallia, 308n
Serafini, Daniele, 332n
Serao, Matilde, 216
Settimana Rossa, 275
Sezanne, Giovanni Battista, 314n

Sfameni, Pasquale, 283
Sforza, Ginevra, 105
Shakespeare, William, 246, 264, 353n
Sheehan, James, 21, 95
Sibelius, Jean, 256, 260
Sicilies, Kingdom of the Two. *See* Sicily
Sicily, 7, 8, 27, 37, 42, 74, 105, 167,
    215, 228, 353n
Siena, 259
Signoria, 25, 47–48, 115, 122, 296n
Simmel, Georg, 87, 267, 269
Simonetta-Fava (family), 46
Simonetti (family), 57
Sinigalia, Leone, 353n
Sinistra Storica, 3, 23, 33–34, 36–37
Sirani, Elisabetta, 25, 280
Sismondi, Jean Charles Léonard Sis-
    monde de, 106, 122
Smart, Mary Ann, 225
Smith, Adam, 39
Sociability, 1, 28–29, 33, 38–39, 41–46,
    54, 56–57, 91, 146, 169–174,
    295n
Socialismo municipale, 11, 18, 124–
    125, 220, 275–276, 279–283,
    287n
Socialists, 3, 10, 11, 17, 23, 36–38,
    52, 90, 96–97, 113, 123–125,
    147, 171–173, 175–176, 178,
    194–196, 201, 207, 215–216,
    219–220, 238–239, 245,
    256–257, 267–283, 293n
Società Dante Alighieri, 182, 276
Società di Quartetto, 46, 170, 249, 253,
    256
Società Geografica Italiana,
Società Geologica Italiana, 158
Società Nazionale, 75, 241, 288n
Societies, Secret, 45, 171, 333n
Soffici, Ardengo, 265
Solera, Temistocle, 199
Sombart, Nicolaus, 209
Sombart, Werner, 283
Sommaruga, publisher, 246
Sonderweg, 38
Sonnino, Sidney, 67, 215
Sorba, Carlotta, 163
South, Italian, 8, 11, 33, 167, 177–178,
    190, 192, 201, 208, 211, 215,
    273, 285n, 292n, 311n
Space, urban, 43–46, 88, 92, 94,
    100, 107, 113–116, 119, 155,
    179–180
Spada (family), 57

Spadolini, Giovanni, 25
Spain, 108, 178, 224, 253, 259, 264,
    353n
Spaventa, Bertrando, 266
Spon, Jacob, 129
Spontini, Gaspare, 226
Sport, 173–174, 197
St. Petersburg, 26, 225, 227, 246
State ritual, 197–198, 200, 208, 211,
    214
Status, social, representation of, 27,
    31–32, 35, 38, 43–46, 56–65,
    67–68, 74, 152, 172, 291n, 295n
Statutes, municipal, 62, 73
Statuto Albertino, 22, 70, 184,
    189–197, 211, 214
Stendhal, 195, 311n
Stephen II, Pope, 105
Stockholm, 265
Stolz, Teresa, 228, 231–232, 241
Stone Age, 153
Stradella, 231
Strauss, Richard, 65, 256; *Salome*, 258
Stravinsky, Igor, 259
Strepponi, Giuseppina, 55, 232
Strikes. *See* Labour conflict
Students. *See* Education
Sturani, Giovanni Enrico, 41, 274
Subsidies, 49–65, 67, 69, 71–83
Suez Canal, 225
Suffrage, 22, 23, 33, 35–36, 39, 281,
    290n, 293n
Sweden, 260, 316n
Switzerland, 170, 189, 237–238, 261
Symbolism, 2, 6, 168, 236, 245, 260,
    269, 353n
Syndicalism, 264, 276
Syracuse, 37, 74, 167

T

Tableaux vivants, 55, 190, 299n
Tacconi (family), 26
Tacconi, Gaetano, 24, 35, 37, 64, 80,
    163, 188, 248, 250
Tanari (family), 41
Tanari, Giuseppe, 25, 41, 65, 219, 274
Tanari, Luigi, 24, 29
Tarquinia, 137, 152, 159
Tasca, Angelo, 282
Taxation, 21, 26, 29, 31, 35–36, 39,
    57, 67–83, 122, 276, 299n,
    304n
Tchaikovsky, Piotr Ilitch, 258
Teatri Arti e Letteratura, 222, 227

Tell, Wilhelm, 216
Terrorism, 178–179, 207–208,
    282–283
Terzo Partito, 288n
Textile Industry, 39–40
Theatre, 9, 10, 12, 47–74, 176, 218,
    221–230, 239–242, 246–250,
    296n, 297n, 301n, 310n
Theatre boxes, 57–65, 71–74, 95, 223,
    229–230, 243, 279, 300n, 301n
Theatre, commercial, 12, 53–56,
    64–65, 298n
Théâtrophone, 279
Theocracy, 136
Thessaly, 138
Thiers, Adolphe, 207
Thomas, Ambroise, 251
Time, Concept of, 163, 263, 268
Times, The, 201
Tinti, Ercole, 222, 297n
Tobia, Bruno, 169
Tolstoi, Leo, 216
Tomasi di Lampedusa, Giuseppe, 32,
    228
Tönnies, Ferdinand, 87, 269
Tonolla, Francesco, 279
Toponymy, 184–185
Torchi, Luigi, 248, 254
Torelli, Luigi, 150
Torelli-Viollier, music critic, 236
Torlonia, Carlo, 30
Toscanini, Arturo, 9, 52, 231, 246–248,
    255–257, 259, 266, 303n
Toulmin, Stephen, 15, 287n
Tourism, 55–56, 78, 119, 144, 151,
    157, 174, 223, 233, 310n
Traditions, 2, 11, 59, 72, 87, 90, 125,
    164–165, 167, 251, 255, 262
Transition, political, 34, 51, 53–54,
    56–57, 92, 299n
Trasformismo, 10, 36–37, 293n, 337n
Trento, 182, 331n, 343n
Trevelyan, George Macaulay, 268,
    338n, 354n
Treviso, 186, 249; Teatro Sociale, 247
Tribuna, La, 239
Trieste, 178, 182, 248, 260
Triple Alliance, 205, 275
Trotzky, Leo, 238
Troy, 138
Tubertini, Giuseppe, 173
Tubertini, Ottavio, 34
Tudesq, Jean, 38
Turati, Filippo, 238

Turin, 8, 37, 43, 46, 67, 69, 72, 89, 95,
    100, 107, 129, 133, 149, 152,
    154, 169, 190, 192, 196–198,
    200, 213, 218, 221, 243, 246–
    248, 254, 270, 277, 282, 289n,
    305n, 345n, 354n; Palazzo
    Cavour, 43; Teatro Regio, 59
Tuscany, 6, 7, 67, 91, 94, 98, 109, 128,
    133, 137, 142, 159, 165–167,
    181, 216, 235, 260, 282

U
Umberto I, 126, 156, 166, 178, 196,
    198–209, 211–217, 227, 248
Umbria, 26, 282
Umbrians, 134–135, 139–142, 153
Unemployment, 39, 43
Unification, Italian, 3–11, 14–16, 21,
    24–29, 33, 36–37, 43–44, 56,
    66–71, 75, 79, 82–83, 88–91,
    94, 100, 105–108, 116, 118–
    121, 125, 130–131, 150, 153,
    158–160, 163–171, 177–178,
    180, 182–184, 189–196, 198,
    221–222, 225–227, 238, 245,
    257, 262–263, 271, 281, 283,
    288n
Unione elettorale cattolica italiana, 272
Unione Monarchico Liberale, 31
Unione, L', 153
United States of America, 45, 154,
    158–159, 216, 240, 251, 256,
    260–261, 345n
Urbino, 8, 168

V
Vaudevilles, 55, 223, 276, 286n
Veio, 159
Velletri, 186
Venetia. *See* Venice
Venice, 6–7, 28, 45, 49, 69, 105, 107,
    116, 122, 169, 181, 189, 194,
    227, 230, 242, 246–248, 253,
    282, 328n
Venice, Ateneo Veneto, 91
Venice, Teatro La Fenice, 55, 65, 71,
    222
Ventura, Lionello, 230
Venturi, Vittorio, 42
Verardi, Carlo, 253
Vercellana, Rosina, 202
Verdi, Giuseppe, 1, 2, 7, 9, 17, 52,
    55, 59, 64, 79, 105, 130, 176,
    199, 221, 226–234, 236, 240,

243, 245–246, 253, 256, 258,
263, 265, 278, 342n, 347n;
Aida, 1, 59, 225, 227, 229,
232, 248–250, 258, 260, 278,
322n; *Alzira*, 227; *Aroldo*, 227;
Attila, 130, 224; *Don Carlos*,
9, 222–223, 225, 228–229,
231, 233; *Ernani*, 224, 227,
231; *Falstaff*, 225, 250; *I due
Foscari*, 227–228; *I Lombardi alla prima crociata*, 224,
227; *I Vespri Siciliani*, 228;
Il Corsaro, 227; *Il Trovatore*,
225; *Inno delle Nazioni*, 245;
Jérusalem, 227; *La Battaglia
di Legnano*, 123, 224–225,
227; *La Forza del Destino*,
225, 227–228, 233, 241; *La
Traviata*, 225, 228, 242, 251,
278; *Luisa Miller*, 228–229;
Macbeth, 224, 228, 233, 241;
Nabucco, 1, 130, 224, 226–
227; *Oberto*, 227; *Otello*, 64,
225, 250; *Quattro pezzi sacri*,
245; *Rigoletto*, 225, 227–228,
278, 351n; *Simon Boccanegra*,
227; *Stiffelio*, 227; *Un Ballo in
Maschera*, 227–229; *Un giorno
di regno*, 227
Verga, Giovanni, 251
Verismo, 251
Verona, 77–78, 282, 296n
Vicenza, 282
Vico, Giambattista, 128, 138, 316n,
321n, 353n
Victoria, Queen, 200, 204, 214
Vienna, 15, 26, 46, 214, 247, 251–254,
261, 296n, 355n
Villanova, 17, 133–134, 137, 139–140,
142, 149–150, 158–159, 320n,
322n
Villari, Pasquale, 67
Vincenza, 231
Viollet-le-Duc, Eugène, 109
Viotti, Giovanni Battista, 253
Virchow, Rudolf von, 154–155, 160,
325n
Visconti (family), 105
Visconti, Luchino, 228
Vitali, Raffele, 222
Vittorio Emanuele II, 3, 21, 26, 31, 33,
109, 123, 163, 168–169, 179,
191, 193, 195–196, 198–200,
202–205, 216, 218, 227

Vittorio Emanuele III, 1, 207, 213–214,
217–218, 270
Vivaldi, Antonio, 302n
Vivarelli, Roberto, 287n, 357n
Voce, La, 265
Vogelweide, Walter von der, 182
Volpe, Gioacchino, 267
Volta, Alessandro, 188
Volterra, 129
Volunteers, 4, 193, 200, 210, 245, 276

W

Wagner, Richard, 1–2, 7, 17, 52, 59,
64–65, 79, 125, 156, 176, 186,
221, 223, 226, 231, 234–243,
245–251, 253, 255–256,
258–264, 266, 278, 353n,
356n; *Der Fliegende Hol-
länder*, 243, 248, 346n; *Der
Ring des Nibelungen*, 9, 243,
248, 261, 346n; *Die Walküre*,
248, 345n; *Götterdämmerung*,
248; *Kaisermarsch*, 13; *Lohengrin*, 2, 9, 13, 223, 232–237,
239–243, 247–249, 258–261,
264–265, 269, 278, 344n,
346n; *Meistersinger*, 248, 256,
346n; *Parsifal*, 2, 9, 103, 245,
258–260, 278, 285n, 345n,
346n; *Rienzi*, 9, 238, 242–243,
248, 261; *Siegfried*, 2, 237,
257; *Tannhäuser*, 9, 234–235,
238, 242–243, 246, 248, 261,
301n, 346n; *Tristan und Isolde*,
9, 64, 101, 234, 242–243, 248,
252, 258, 261, 346n
Wagnerism, 2, 9, 234–245, 248–249,
251, 254–255, 258–262,
264–266, 278, 345n, 346n
Walsh, Kevin, 148
War, Abyssinian, 273
War, Franco-German, 78, 151, 154,
194
War, Libyan, 273, 279
Warburg, Aby, 128, 135, 322n
Warfare, 31, 34, 54, 106, 123, 134,
160, 190–191, 194, 199–200,
205, 273, 276–279, 286n,
291n, 305n
Wars of Liberation, Italian, 26, 67, 110,
120, 191, 198–200, 210–211,
219, 245, 274
Warsaw, 246
Washington, George, 308n

Weber, Carl Maria von, 226, 229; *Der Freischütz*, 228
Weber, Max, 38, 122, 267, 285n, 287n
Weber, William, 252
Weigl, Joseph, 226
Weingartner, Felix, 231
Werfel, Franz, 300n
White Mario, Jessie, 210, 337n
White, Hayden, 99
Wilde, Oscar, 238, 265
Williams, Raymond, 12, 103
Winckelmann, Johann Joachim, 130
Windelband, Wilhelm, 267
Winter, Peter von, 226
Women, 3, 6, 8, 17, 25, 36, 39, 46, 132, 143, 147, 170–171, 174–176, 194, 199, 208, 210–212, 277, 322n, 330n
Workers, rural, 171, 215, 271–272, 274, 281, 282
Working class, 45, 171, 215, 217, 220, 257, 271–272, 275, 277, 281, 287n
World Fairs. *See* Exhibitions
World War I, 1, 3, 9, 11, 15–16, 31, 36, 42, 65, 96, 124–125, 204, 218, 220, 228, 258–259,

266–267, 270, 273, 275–279, 281; Intervention in, 11, 124, 267–268, 270, 275–276, 281

Y
Yiddish, 258, 345n

Z
Zamagni, Vera, 41
Zanardi, Francesco, 36, 52, 256, 275, 280
Zanichelli, Domenico, 38
Zanichelli, publishing house, 9, 33, 153, 176, 346n
Zannoni, Antonio, 15, 92–93, 131, 135, 139–143, 148, 150, 154–155, 157, 159, 322n
Zemlinsky, Alexander von, 352n
Zola, Emile, 238, 251
Zoppi, prefect of Novara, 67
Zucchini (family), 26, 35, 41, 44, 46, 60, 174
Zucchini, Cesare, 41
Zucchini, Gaetano, 41, 254
Zucchini-Solimei Cagnola, Carmelita, 41, 46
Zweig, Stefan, 267